NOVELS
for Students

Advisors

Jayne M. Burton is a teacher of English, a member of the Delta Kappa Gamma International Society for Key Women Educators, and currently a master's degree candidate in the Interdisciplinary Study of Curriculum and Instruction and English at Angelo State University.

Mary Beth Maggio teaches seventh grade language arts in Schaumburg, Illinois.

Tom Shilts is the youth librarian at the Okemos branch of Capital Area District Library in Okemos, Michigan. He holds an MSLS degree from Clarion University of Pennsylvania and an MA in U.S. History from the University of North Dakota.

Amy Spade Silverman has taught at independent schools in California, Texas, Michigan, and New York. She holds a bachelor of arts degree from the University of Michigan and a master of fine arts degree from the University of Houston. She is a member of the National Council of Teachers of English and Teachers and Writers. She is an exam reader for Advanced Placement Literature and Composition. She is also a poet, published in *North American Review, Nimrod,* and *Michigan Quarterly Review,* among others.

Mary Turner holds a BS in Secondary Education from East Texas State University and a Master of Education from Western Kentucky University. She teaches English 7 and AP English 12 literature and composition at SBEC in Southaven, Mississippi.

Brian Woerner teaches English at Troy High School in Troy, Ohio. He is also a Program Associate of the Ohio Writing Project at Miami University.

NOVELS
for Students

**Presenting Analysis, Context, and Criticism
on Commonly Studied Novels**

VOLUME 43

Sara Constantakis, Project Editor

Foreword by Anne Devereaux Jordan

GALE
CENGAGE Learning·

Detroit • New York • San Francisco • New Haven, Conn • Waterville, Maine • London

130.00

GALE
CENGAGE Learning

Novels for Students, Volume 43

Project Editor: Sara Constantakis

Rights Acquisition and Management:
Robyn Young

Composition: Evi Abou-El-Seoud

Manufacturing: Rhonda Dover

Imaging: John Watkins

Product Design: Pamela A. E. Galbreath,
Jennifer Wahi

Digital Content Production: Allie Semperger

Product Manager: Meggin Condino

For product information and technology assistance, contact us at
Gale Customer Support, 1-800-877-4253.
For permission to use material from this text or product,
submit all requests online at **www.cengage.com/permissions**.
Further permissions questions can be emailed to
permissionrequest@cengage.com

Gale
27500 Drake Rd.
Farmington Hills, MI, 48331-3535

ISBN-13: 978-1-4144-9486-9
ISBN-10: 1-4144-9486-6

ISSN 1094-3552

This title is also available as an e-book.
ISBN-13: 978-1-4144-9272-8
ISBN-10: 1-4144-9272-3
Contact your Gale, a part of Cengage Learning sales representative for ordering information.

Printed in Mexico
1 2 3 4 5 6 7 17 16 15 14 13

Table of Contents

The Informed Dialogue: Interacting with Literature

When we pick up a book, we usually do so with the anticipation of pleasure. We hope that by entering the time and place of the novel and sharing the thoughts and actions of the characters, we will find enjoyment. Unfortunately, this is often not the case; we are disappointed. But we should ask, has the author failed us, or have we failed the author?

We establish a dialogue with the author, the book, and with ourselves when we read. Consciously and unconsciously, we ask questions: "Why did the author write this book?" "Why did the author choose that time, place, or character?" "How did the author achieve that effect?" "Why did the character act that way?" "Would I act in the same way?" The answers we receive depend upon how much information about literature in general and about that book specifically we ourselves bring to our reading.

Young children have limited life and literary experiences. Being young, children frequently do not know how to go about exploring a book, nor sometimes, even know the questions to ask of a book. The books they read help them answer questions, the author often coming right out and *telling* young readers the things they are learning or are expected to learn. The perennial classic, *The Little Engine That Could, tells* its readers that, among other things, it is good to help others and brings happiness:

"Hurray, hurray," cried the funny little clown and all the dolls and toys. "The good little boys and girls in the city will be happy because you helped us, kind, Little Blue Engine."

In picture books, messages are often blatant and simple, the dialogue between the author and reader one-sided. Young children are concerned with the end result of a book—the enjoyment gained, the lesson learned—rather than with how that result was obtained. As we grow older and read further, however, we question more. We come to expect that the world within the book will closely mirror the concerns of our world, and that the author will *show* these through the events, descriptions, and conversations within the story, rather than *telling* of them. We are now expected to do the interpreting, carry on our share of the dialogue with the book and author, and glean not only the author's message, but comprehend how that message and the overall affect of the book were achieved. Sometimes, however, we need help to do these things. *Novels for Students* provides that help.

A novel is made up of many parts interacting to create a coherent whole. In reading a novel, the more obvious features can be easily spotted—theme, characters, plot—but we may overlook the more subtle elements that greatly influence how the novel is perceived by the reader: viewpoint, mood and tone, symbolism, or the use of humor. By focusing on both the obvious and more subtle literary elements within a novel, *Novels for Students* aids readers in both analyzing for message and in determining how and why that message is communicated. In the discussion on Harper Lee's *To Kill a Mockingbird* (Vol. 2), for example, the mockingbird as a symbol of innocence is dealt with, among other things, as is the importance of Lee's use of humor which "enlivens a serious plot, adds depth to the characterization, and creates a sense of familiarity and universality." The reader comes to understand the internal elements of each novel discussed—as well as the external influences that help shape it.

"The desire to write greatly," Harold Bloom of Yale University says, "is the desire to be elsewhere, in a time and place of one's own, in an originality that must compound with inheritance, with an anxiety of influence." A writer seeks to create a unique world within a story, but although it is unique, it is not disconnected from our own world. It speaks to us *because* of what the writer brings to the writing from our world: how he or she was raised and educated; his or her likes and dislikes; the events occurring in the real world at the time of the writing, and while the author was growing up. When we know what an author has brought to his or her work, we gain a greater insight into both the "originality" (the world of the book), and the things that "compound" it. This insight enables us to question that created world and find answers more readily. By informing ourselves, we are able to establish a more effective dialogue with both book and author.

Novels for Students, in addition to providing a plot summary and descriptive list of characters—to remind readers of what they have read—also explores the external influences that shaped each book. Each entry includes a discussion of the author's background, and the historical context in which the novel was written. It is vital to know, for instance, that when Ray Bradbury was writing *Fahrenheit 451* (Vol. 1), the threat of Nazi domination had recently ended in Europe, and the McCarthy hearings were taking place in Washington, D.C. This information goes far in answering the question, "Why did he write a story of oppressive government control and book burning?" Similarly, it is important to know that Harper Lee, author

of *To Kill a Mockingbird,* was born and raised in Monroeville, Alabama, and that her father was a lawyer. Readers can now see why she chose the south as a setting for her novel—it is the place with which she was most familiar—and start to comprehend her characters and their actions.

Novels for Students helps readers find the answers they seek when they establish a dialogue with a particular novel. It also aids in the posing of questions by providing the opinions and interpretations of various critics and reviewers, broadening that dialogue. Some reviewers of *To Kill A Mockingbird,* for example, "faulted the novel's climax as melodramatic." This statement leads readers to ask, "Is it, indeed, melodramatic?" "If not, why did some reviewers see it as such?" "If it is, why did Lee choose to make it melodramatic?" "Is melodrama ever justified?" By being spurred to ask these questions, readers not only learn more about the book and its writer, but about the nature of writing itself.

The literature included for discussion in *Novels for Students* has been chosen because it has something vital to say to us. *Of Mice and Men, Catch-22, The Joy Luck Club, My Antonia, A Separate Peace* and the other novels here speak of life and modern sensibility. In addition to their individual, specific messages of prejudice, power, love or hate, living and dying, however, they and all great literature also share a common intent. They force us to *think*—about life, literature, and about others, not just about ourselves. They pry us from the narrow confines of our minds and thrust us outward to confront the world of books and the larger, real world we all share. *Novels for Students* helps us in this confrontation by providing the means of enriching our conversation with literature and the world, by creating an *informed* dialogue, one that brings true pleasure to the personal act of reading.

Sources

Harold Bloom, *The Western Canon, The Books and School of the Ages,* Riverhead Books, 1994.

Watty Piper, *The Little Engine That Could,* Platt & Munk, 1930.

Anne Devereaux Jordan
Senior Editor, TALL (Teaching and Learning Literature)

Introduction

Purpose of the Book

The purpose of *Novels for Students* (*NfS*) is to provide readers with a guide to understanding, enjoying, and studying novels by giving them easy access to information about the work. Part of Gale's "For Students" Literature line, *NfS* is specifically designed to meet the curricular needs of high school and undergraduate college students and their teachers, as well as the interests of general readers and researchers considering specific novels. While each volume contains entries on "classic" novels frequently studied in classrooms, there are also entries containing hard-to-find information on contemporary novels, including works by multicultural, international, and women novelists. Entries profiling film versions of novels not only diversify the study of novels but support alternate learning styles, media literacy, and film studies curricula as well.

The information covered in each entry includes an introduction to the novel and the novel's author; a plot summary, to help readers unravel and understand the events in a novel; descriptions of important characters, including explanation of a given character's role in the novel as well as discussion about that character's relationship to other characters in the novel; analysis of important themes in the novel; and an explanation of important literary techniques and movements as they are demonstrated in the novel.

In addition to this material, which helps the readers analyze the novel itself, students are also provided with important information on the literary and historical background informing each work. This includes a historical context essay, a box comparing the time or place the novel was written to modern Western culture, a critical essay, and excerpts from critical essays on the novel. A unique feature of *NfS* is a specially commissioned critical essay on each novel, targeted toward the student reader.

The "literature to film" entries on novels vary slightly in form, providing background on film technique and comparison to the original, literary version of the work. These entries open with an introduction to the film, which leads directly into the plot summary. The summary highlights plot changes from the novel, key cinematic moments, and/or examples of key film techniques. As in standard entries, there are character profiles (noting omissions or additions, and identifying the actors), analysis of themes and how they are illustrated in the film, and an explanation of the cinematic style and structure of the film. A cultural context section notes any time period or setting differences from that of the original work, as well as cultural differences between the time in which the original work was written and the time in which the film adaptation was made. A film entry concludes with a critical overview and critical essays on the film.

To further help today's student in studying and enjoying each novel or film, information on media adaptations is provided (if available), as well as suggestions for works of fiction, nonfiction, or film on similar themes and topics. Classroom aids include ideas for research papers and lists of critical and reference sources that provide additional material on the novel. Film entries also highlight signature film techniques demonstrated, and suggest media literacy activities and prompts to use during or after viewing a film.

Selection Criteria

The titles for each volume of *NfS* are selected by surveying numerous sources on notable literary works and analyzing course curricula for various schools, school districts, and states. Some of the sources surveyed include: high school and undergraduate literature anthologies and textbooks; lists of award-winners, and recommended titles, including the Young Adult Library Services Association (YALSA) list of best books for young adults. Films are selected both for the literary importance of the original work and the merits of the adaptation (including official awards and widespread public recognition).

Input solicited from our expert advisory board—consisting of educators and librarians—guides us to maintain a mix of "classic" and contemporary literary works, a mix of challenging and engaging works (including genre titles that are commonly studied) appropriate for different age levels, and a mix of international, multicultural and women authors. These advisors also consult on each volume's entry list, advising on which titles are most studied, most appropriate, and meet the broadest interests across secondary (grades 7–12) curricula and undergraduate literature studies.

How Each Entry Is Organized

Each entry, or chapter, in *NfS* focuses on one novel. Each entry heading lists the full name of the novel, the author's name, and the date of the novel's publication. The following elements are contained in each entry:

Introduction: a brief overview of the novel which provides information about its first appearance, its literary standing, any controversies surrounding the work, and major conflicts or themes within the work. Film entries identify the original novel and provide

understanding of the film's reception and reputation, along with that of the director.

Author Biography: in novel entries, this section includes basic facts about the author's life, and focuses on events and times in the author's life that inspired the novel in question.

Plot Summary: a factual description of the major events in the novel. Lengthy summaries are broken down with subheads. Plot summaries of films are used to uncover plot differences from the original novel, and to note the use of certain film angles or other techniques.

Characters: an alphabetical listing of major characters in the novel. Each character name is followed by a brief to an extensive description of the character's role in the novel, as well as discussion of the character's actions, relationships, and possible motivation. In film entries, omissions or changes to the cast of characters of the film adaptation are mentioned here, and the actors' names—and any awards they may have received—are also included.

Characters are listed alphabetically by last name. If a character is unnamed—for instance, the narrator in *Invisible Man*—the character is listed as "The Narrator" and alphabetized as "Narrator." If a character's first name is the only one given, the name will appear alphabetically by that name.

Variant names are also included for each character. Thus, the full name "Jean Louise Finch" would head the listing for the narrator of *To Kill a Mockingbird*, but listed in a separate cross-reference would be the nickname "Scout Finch."

Themes: a thorough overview of how the major topics, themes, and issues are addressed within the novel. Each theme discussed appears in a separate subhead. While the key themes often remain the same or similar when a novel is adapted into a film, film entries demonstrate how the themes are conveyed cinematically, along with any changes in the portrayal of the themes.

Style: this section addresses important style elements of the novel, such as setting, point of view, and narration; important literary devices used, such as imagery, foreshadowing, symbolism; and, if applicable, genres to which the work might have belonged, such as Gothicism or Romanticism. Literary terms are explained within the entry but can also be found in the Glossary. Film entries cover how the director conveyed the meaning, message, and mood of the work using film in comparison to the author's use of language, literary device, etc., in the original work.

Historical Context: in novel entries, this section outlines the social, political, and cultural climate in which the author lived and the novel was created. This section may include descriptions of related historical events, pertinent aspects of daily life in the culture, and the artistic and literary sensibilities of the time in which the work was written. If the novel is a historical work, information regarding the time in which the novel is set is also included. Each section is broken down with helpful subheads. Film entries contain a similar Cultural Context section because the film adaptation might explore an entirely different time period or culture than the original work, and may also be influenced by the traditions and views of a time period much different than that of the original author.

Critical Overview: this section provides background on the critical reputation of the novel or film, including bannings or any other public controversies surrounding the work. For older works, this section includes a history of how the novel or film was first received and how perceptions of it may have changed over the years; for more recent novels, direct quotes from early reviews may also be included.

Criticism: an essay commissioned by *NfS* which specifically deals with the novel or film and is written specifically for the student audience, as well as excerpts from previously published criticism on the work (if available).

Sources: an alphabetical list of critical material used in compiling the entry, with full bibliographical information.

Further Reading: an alphabetical list of other critical sources which may prove useful for the student. It includes full bibliographical information and a brief annotation.

Suggested Search Terms: a list of search terms and phrases to jumpstart students' further information seeking. Terms include not just titles and author names but also terms and topics related to the historical and literary context of the works.

In addition, each novel entry contains the following highlighted sections, set apart from the main text as sidebars:

Media Adaptations: if available, a list of audiobooks and important film and television adaptations of the novel, including source information. The list also includes stage adaptations, musical adaptations, etc.

Topics for Further Study: a list of potential study questions or research topics dealing with the novel. This section includes questions related to other disciplines the student may be studying, such as American history, world history, science, math, government, business, geography, economics, psychology, etc.

Compare and Contrast: an "at-a-glance" comparison of the cultural and historical differences between the author's time and culture and late twentieth century or early twenty-first century Western culture. This box includes pertinent parallels between the major scientific, political, and cultural movements of the time or place the novel was written, the time or place the novel was set (if a historical work), and modern Western culture. Works written after the mid-1970s may not have this box.

What Do I Read Next?: a list of works that might give a reader points of entry into a classic work (e.g., YA or multicultural titles) and/or complement the featured novel or serve as a contrast to it. This includes works by the same author and others, works from various genres, YA works, and works from various cultures and eras.

The film entries provide sidebars more targeted to the study of film, including:

Film Technique: a listing and explanation of four to six key techniques used in the film, including shot styles, use of transitions, lighting, sound or music, etc.

Read, Watch, Write: media literacy prompts and/or suggestions for viewing log prompts.

What Do I See Next?: a list of films based on the same or similar works or of films similar in directing style, technique, etc.

Other Features

NfS includes "The Informed Dialogue: Interacting with Literature," a foreword by Anne Devereaux Jordan, Senior Editor for *Teaching and Learning Literature* (*TALL*), and a founder of the Children's Literature Association. This essay provides an enlightening look at how readers interact with literature and how *Novels for Students* can help teachers show students how to enrich their own reading experiences.

A Cumulative Author/Title Index lists the authors and titles covered in each volume of the *NfS* series.

A Cumulative Nationality/Ethnicity Index breaks down the authors and titles covered in each volume of the *NfS* series by nationality and ethnicity.

A Subject/Theme Index, specific to each volume, provides easy reference for users who may be studying a particular subject or theme rather than a single work. Significant subjects, from events to broad themes, are included.

Each entry may include illustrations, including photo of the author, stills from film adaptations, maps, and/or photos of key historical events, if available.

Citing Novels for Students

When writing papers, students who quote directly from any volume of *NfS* may use the following general forms. These examples are based on MLA style; teachers may request that students adhere to a different style, so the following examples may be adapted as needed.

When citing text from *NfS* that is not attributed to a particular author (i.e., the Themes, Style, Historical Context sections, etc.), the following format should be used in the bibliography section:

> "*The Monkey Wrench Gang.*" *Novels for Students.* Ed. Sara Constantakis. Vol. 43. Detroit: Gale, Cengage Learning, 2013. 157–193. Print.

When quoting the specially commissioned essay from *NfS* (usually the first piece under the "Criticism" subhead), the following format should be used:

> Holmes, Michael Allen. Critical Essay on "*The Monkey Wrench Gang.*" *Novels for Students.* Ed. Sara Constantakis. Vol. 43. Detroit: Gale, Cengage Learning, 2013. 173–78. Print.

When quoting a journal or newspaper essay that is reprinted in a volume of *NfS,* the following form may be used:

> Bryant, Paul T. "Edward Abbey and Environmental Quixoticism." *Western American Literature* 24.1 (1989): 37–43. Rpt. in *Novels for Students.* Vol. 43. Ed. Sara Constantakis. Detroit: Gale, Cengage Learning, 2013. 189–92. Print.

When quoting material reprinted from a book that appears in a volume of *NfS,* the following form may be used:

> Norwick, Steve. "Nietzschean Themes in the Works of Edward Abbey." *Coyote in the Maze: Tracking Edward Abbey in a World of Words.* Ed. Peter Quigley. Salt Lake City; University of Utah Press, 1998. 184–205. Rpt. in *Novels for Students.* Vol. 43. Ed. Sara Constantakis. Detroit: Gale, Cengage Learning, 2013. 183–85. Print.

We Welcome Your Suggestions

The editorial staff of *Novels for Students* welcomes your comments and ideas. Readers who wish to suggest novels to appear in future volumes, or who have other suggestions, are cordially invited to contact the editor. You may contact the editor via e-mail at: **ForStudentsEditors@cengage.com.** Or write to the editor at:

Editor, *Novels for Students*

Gale

27500 Drake Road

Farmington Hills, MI 48331-3535

Literary Chronology

1819: Herman Melville is born on August 1 in New York, New York.

1837: William Dean Howells is born on March 1 in Martins Ferry, Ohio.

1851: Herman Melville's *Moby Dick* is published.

1856: Lyman Frank Baum is born on May 15 in Chittenango, New York.

1885: William Dean Howells's *The Rise of Silas Lapham* is published.

1890: Conrad Richter is born on October 13 in Pine Grove, Schuylkill County, Pennsylvania.

1891: Herman Melville dies of cardiac dilation on September 28 in New York, New York.

1900: Lyman Frank Baum's *The Wonderful Wizard of Oz* is published.

1919: Lyman Frank Baum dies of a stroke on May 6 in Hollywood, California.

1920: William Dean Howells dies of pneumonia on May 11 in New York, New York.

1925: Yukio Mishima is born on January 14 in Tokyo, Japan.

1927: Edward Abbey is born on January 29 in Indiana, Pennsylvania.

1934: Mary Ann Shaffer is born December 13 in Martinsburg, West Virginia.

1939: Director Victor Fleming's film of *The Wizard of Oz* is released.

1940: Victor Fleming's *The Wizard of Oz* is awarded the Academy Award for Best Song and Best Original Music Score (awarded to E. Y. Harburg and Harold Arlen) and Best Performance by a Juvenile (awarded to Judy Garland).

1941: Nancy Farmer is born on July 7 in Phoenix, Arizona.

1943: Sindiwe Magona is born on August 27 in Gungululu, in South Africa.

1948: Charles Johnson is born on April 23 in Evanston, Illinois.

1951: Conrad Richter is awarded the Pulitzer Prize for Fiction for *The Town*.

1952: Rohinton Mistry is born on July 3 in Bombay, India.

1953: Conrad Richter's *The Light in the Forest* is published.

1954: Yukio Mishima's *The Sound of Waves* is published in Japan in Japanese as *Shiosai*. It is published in English in the United States in 1956 as *The Sound of Waves*.

1956: Director David Lean's film of *Great Expectations* is released.

1957: Gail Tsukiyama was born on September 13 in San Francisco, California.

1958: Nancy Rawles is born.

1961: Nora Raleigh Baskin is born on May 18 in Brooklyn, New York.

1962: Annie Barrows is born in San Diego, California.

1968: Conrad Richter dies of paroxysmal atrial fibrillations on October 30 in Pottsville, Pennsylvania.

1970: Yukio Mishima dies of suicide on November 25 in Tokyo, Japan.

1975: Edward Abbey's *The Monkey Wrench Gang* is published.

1989: Edward Abbey dies of esophageal varices on March 14 in Tucson, Arizona.

1990: Charles Johnson's *Middle Passage* is published.

1995: Rohinton Mistry's A Fine Balance is published.

1995: Gail Tsukiyama' *The Samurai's Garden* is published.

1998: Sindiwe Magona's *Mother to Mother* is published in South Africa. It is published in the United States in 1999.

2002: Nancy Farmer's *The House of the Scorpion* is published.

2005: Nancy Rawles's *My Jim* is published.

2008: Mary Ann Shaffer dies on February 16 of abdominal cancer.

2008: Marry Ann Shaffer and Annie Barrows's *The Guernsey Literary and Potato Peel Pie Society* is published.

2009: Nora Raleigh Baskin's *Anything But Typical* is published.

Acknowledgements

The editors wish to thank the copyright holders of the excerpted criticism included in this volume and the permissions managers of many book and magazine publishing companies for assisting us in securing reproduction rights. We are also grateful to the staffs of the Detroit Public Library, the Library of Congress, the University of Detroit Mercy Library, Wayne State University Purdy/ Kresge Library Complex, and the University of Michigan Libraries for making their resources available to us. Following is a list of the copyright holders who have granted us permission to reproduce material in this volume of PfS. Every effort has been made to trace copyright, but if omissions have been made, please let us know.

COPYRIGHTED EXCERPTS IN NfS, VOLUME 43, WERE REPRODUCED FROM THE FOLLOWING SOURCES:

Andover Review 4.23, November 1885.—*Atenea* 25.2, December 2005. Copyright © 2005 by *Atenea*. Reproduced by permission of the publisher.—*Atlantic Monthly* 56.336, October 1885.—*Booklist* 101.6, November 15, 2004. Copyright © 2004 by *Booklist*. Reproduced by permission of the publisher.—*Booklist* 104.21, July 1, 2008. Copyright © 2008 by *Booklist*. Reproduced by permission of the publisher.—*Booklist* 105.11, February 1, 2009. Copyright © 2009 by American Library Association. Reproduced by permission of the publisher.—*Booklist* 91.13, March 1, 1995. Copyright © 1995 by *Booklist*. Reproduced by permission of the publisher.—*Booklist* 96.2, September 15, 1999. Copyright © 1999 by *Booklist*. Reproduced by permission of the publisher.—*Booklist* 99.2, September 15, 2002. Copyright © 2002 by *Booklist*. Reproduced by permission of the publisher.—*Bookseller* 15, November 2002. Copyright © 2002 by *Bookseller*. Reproduced by permission of the publisher.—*Catholic World* 42.248, November 1885.—*CEA Critic* 55.3, Spring/Summer 1993. Copyright © 1993 by *CEA Critic*. Reproduced by permission of the publisher.—*Coyote in the Maze: Tracking Edward Abbey in a World of Words*, edited by Peter Quigley. University of Utah Press, 1998. Copyright © 1998 by University of Utah Press. Reproduced by permission of the publisher.—*Durham University Journal*, July1991. Copyright © 1991 by *Durham University Journal*. Reproduced by permission of the publisher.—*English in Africa* 29.1, May 2002. Copyright © 2002 by *English in Africa*. Reproduced by permission of the publisher.—*Film & History* 15.2, May 1985. Copyright © 1985 by *Film & History*. Reproduced by permission of the publisher.—*Horn Book Magazine* 78.6, November/December 2002. Copyright © 2002 by *Horn Book Magazine*. Reproduced by permission of the publisher.—*Horn Book* 85.3, May/June 2009. Copyright © 2009 by *The Horn Book* (magazine). Reproduced by permission of the publisher.—***Journal for the Study of Religions &***

Ideologies 9.25, April 2010. Copyright © 2010 by *Journal for the Study of Religions & Ideologies.* Reproduced by permission of the publisher.— *Journal of Adolescent & Adult Literary* 47.4, December 2003. Copyright © 2003 by *Journal of Adolescent & Adult Literary.* Reproduced by permission of the publisher.—*Journal of Popular Film and Television* 23.4, Winter 1996. Copyright © 1996 by *Journal of Popular Film and Television.* Reproduced by permission of the publisher.— *Journal of Scholarly Publishing* 40.3, April 2009. Copyright © 2009 by *Journal of Scholarly Publishing.* Reproduced by permission of the publisher.—*Kliatt* 38.4, July 2004. Copyright © 2004 by *Kliatt.* Reproduced by permission of the publisher.—*Library Journal* 124.7, October 15, 1999. Copyright © 1999 by *Library Journal.* Reproduced by permission of the publisher.— *Library Journal* 129.20, December 1, 2004. Copyright © 2004 by *Library Journal.* Reproduced by permission of the publisher.— *Library Journal* 133.12, July 1, 2008. Copyright © 2008 by *Library Journal.* Reproduced by permission of the publisher.—*Literature Film Quarterly* 32.3, 2004. Copyright © 2004 by *Literature Film Quarterly.* Reproduced by permission of the publisher.—*Los Angeles Times Book Review*, June 24, 1990. Copyright © 1990 by *Los Angeles Times Book Review.* Reproduced by permission of the publisher.—*Postcolonizing the Commonwealth: Studies in Literature and Culture*, edited by Rowland Smith, Wilfred Laurier University Press, 2000. Copyright © 2000, Wilfred Laurier University Press. Reproduced by permission of the publisher.— *Publishers Weekly* 242.5, January 30, 1995. Copyright © 1995 by *Publishers Weekly.* Reproduced by permission of the publisher.— *Publishers Weekly* 246.37, September 13, 1999. Copyright © 1999 by *Publishers Weekly.* Reproduced by permission of the publisher.— *Publishers Weekly* 248.26, June 25 2001. Copyright © 2001 by *Publishers Weekly.*

Reproduced by permission of the publisher.— *Publishers Weekly* 249.26, July 1, 2002. Copyright © 2002 by *Publishers Weekly.* Reproduced by permission of the publisher.— *Publishers Weekly* 249.29, July 22, 2002. Copyright © 2002 by *Publishers Weekly.* Reproduced by permission of the publisher.— *Publishers Weekly*, 251.48, November 29, 2004. Copyright © 2004 by *Publishers Weekly.* Reproduced by permission of the publisher.— *Publishers Weekly* 255.16, April 21, 2008. Copyright © 2008 by *Publishers Weekly.* Reproduced by permission of the publisher.— *Publishers Weekly* 256.6, May/June 2009. Copyright © 2009 by PWXYZ, LLC. Reproduced by permission of the publisher.— *San Francisco Chronicle*, March 13, 1998. Copyright © 1998 by *San Francisco Chronicle.* Reproduced by permission of the publisher.— *School Library Journal* 49.2, February 2003. Copyright © 2003 by *School Library Journal.* Reproduced by permission of the publisher.— *School Library Journal* 51.5, May 2005. Copyright © 2005 by *School Library Journal.* Reproduced by permission of the publisher.— *School Library Journal* 55.3, March 2009. Copyright © 2009 by *School Library Journal.* Reproduced by permission of the publisher.— *School Library Journal* 55.8, August 2009. Copyright © 2009 by *School Library Journal.* Reproduced by permission of the publisher.— *Western American Literature* 24.1, May 1989. Copyright © 1989 by *Western American Literature.* Reproduced by permission of the publisher.—*Wordsworth Circle* 33.1, Winter 2002. Copyright © 2002 by *Wordsworth Circle.* Reproduced by permission of the publisher.— *World Literature Today* 76.1, Winter 2002. Copyright © 2002 by *World Literature Today.* Reproduced by permission of the publisher.— *Writer* 120.7, July 2007, for "How I Write" by Gail Tsukiyama. Copyright © *Writer* 2007. Reproduced by permission of the author.

Contributors

Susan Andersen: Andersen has a PhD in English. Entry on *A Fine Balance*. Original essay on *A Fine Balance*.

Cynthia A. Bily: Bily is an English professor at Macomb Community College in Michigan. Entry on *The House of the Scorpion*. Original essay on *The House of the Scorpion*.

Kristy Blackmon: Blackmon is a writer, editor, and critic from Dallas, Texas. Entry on *Anything but Typical*. Original essay on *Anything but Typical*.

Rita M. Brown: Brown is an English professor. Entry on *Moby Dick*. Original essay on *Moby Dick*.

Catherine Dominic: Dominic is a novelist and a freelance writer and editor. Entry on *The Rise of Silas Lapham*. Original essay on *The Rise of Silas Lapham*.

Kristen Sarlin Greenberg: Greenberg is a freelance writer and editor with a background in literature and philosophy. Entry on *The Samurai's Garden*. Original essay on *The Samurai's Garden*.

Michael Allen Holmes: Holmes is a writer with existential interests. Entries on *The Light in the Forest* and *The Monkey Wrench Gang*. Original essays on *The Light in the Forest* and *The Monkey Wrench Gang*.

Sheri Karmiol: Karmiol teaches literature and drama at the University of New Mexico, where she is an adjunct professor in the University Honors Program. Entry on *The Guernsey Literary and Potato Peel Pie Society*. Original essay on *The Guernsey Literary and Potato Peel Pie Society*.

David Kelly: Kelly is a professor of creative writing and literature. Entry on *My Jim*. Original essay on *My Jim*.

Amy Lynn Miller: Miller is a graduate of the University of Cincinnati and currently resides in New Orleans, Louisiana. Entry on *The Sound of Waves*. Original essay on *The Sound of Waves*.

Michael J. O'Neal: O'Neal holds a PhD in English. Entry on *Middle Passage*. Original essay on *Middle Passage*.

April Paris: Paris is a freelance writer with an extensive background writing literary and educational materials. Entry on *Mother to Mother*. Original essay on *Mother to Mother*.

Bradley A. Skeen: Skeen is a classicist. Entry on *The Wizard of Oz*. Original essay on *The Wizard of Oz*.

Anything but Typical

Nora Raleigh Baskin's sixth novel, *Anything but Typical*, published in 2009, is narrated by Jason Blake, a twelve-year-old boy with autism spectrum disorder, or ASD. The narrative takes the reader inside Jason's mind as he tries to explain what life is like for him in a language that "neurotypicals"—that is, people without autism—can understand. The stream-of-consciousness style conveys the way Jason's thought processes work, allowing the average reader to relate to his experiences on some levels. Meanwhile, Jason's obsession with writing fictional short stories for an online writing community gives him an outlet to work through some of his conflicts and provides parallels for his own experiences. In the growing field of disability studies and among the recent surge in young-adult disability fiction, *Anything but Typical* shines.

NORA RALEIGH BASKIN

2009

AUTHOR BIOGRAPHY

Baskin was born in Brooklyn, New York, on May 18, 1961, and spent her childhood in rural upstate New York. Her mother, Arlene Mayerson, died when she was three and a half years old. Her father, Henry P. Raleigh Jr., is an artist and painter, as was his father, the well-known illustrator Henry P. Raleigh Sr. Baskin wrote her first poem in the fifth grade, and by the sixth grade she knew she wanted to be a writer.

Baskin graduated from the State University of New York at Purchase with a degree in literature in 1983. She worked as a waitress, teacher, and homemaker before her first book, *What Every Girl (Except Me) Knows*, was published in 2001. Like much of Baskin's work, it draws inspiration from her own life story. "Most everything I write," Baskin says on her web page, "whether it is a novel or an essay or a short story is very much a part of my life." The book is based on Baskin's experiences growing up without a mother, and it resulted in Baskin's being chosen as a *Publishers Weekly* Flying Start winner. Baskin started out writing short stories for adult readers, but many of her characters were children. She wrote her first children's story for her son's second-grade class, and it was such a success that she decided to focus on fiction for younger readers. In the early 2010s, she was living in Weston, Connecticut, with her husband and two sons, Ben and Sam, who are also writers.

Anything but Typical won, in the middle-school category, the 2010 Schneider Family Book Award, which honors "an author or illustrator for a book that embodies an artistic expression of the disability experience for child and adolescent audiences," according to the American Library Association website.

PLOT SUMMARY

Anything but Typical is told from the first-person point of view of twelve-year-old Jason Blake, who has been diagnosed with autism spectrum disorder, or ASD. In the opening pages of the book, Jason explains that he is using the language of "neurotypicals"—people without ASD—to tell his story so that they can more easily relate to it.

In the first chapter, Jason relates an incident in which art class has been canceled, and instead the students are sent to the library. Jason is excited to log on to Storyboard, an online forum for amateur writers to post stories. However, there is another student at the computer he considers his, and he begins to panic. Eventually, a fellow student who is friendly to Jason, Aaron Miller, persuades the other student to move.

Jason's sportscaster father, Carl, and stay-at-home mom, Liz, have a younger son named Jeremy. He is neurotypical, meaning he does not have autism. However, Jason explains that there

MEDIA ADAPTATIONS

- Baskin discusses *Anything but Typical* at http://videos.simonandschuster.com/Author-Nora-Raleigh-Baskin-shares-insight-into/73431317001 in a discussion hosted by Simon & Schuster.

- Brilliance Audio published an audiobook version of *Anything but Typical* in 2009, read by Tom Parks.

are far more similarities between him and his brother than might be apparent at first. Some of Jeremy's "normal" neuroses—such as not wanting the foods on his plate to touch—are attributed to Jason's influence, but Jason knows that it is easier to blame him than try to explain normal human behavior.

Jason logs back on to Storyboard when he gets home from school to find a comment from another user with the handle PhoenixBird, who compliments the story and mentions having to go to cheerleading practice. From this clue, Jason deduces that PhoenixBird is a girl. Jason relates the reasons why he understands that he might never find a girl who would like him, so the comment from PhoenixBird is made more meaningful because it is something he never expected would happen to him.

Jason reveals more about how he came to be diagnosed and how his parents each dealt with his condition in their own way. He was a very good speller at a very young age, though in most other ways he was developmentally challenged. His mother focused on his "genius" at spelling as a way of distracting from all the ways in which he was already different from other children. His father, however, seemed more accepting and certainly more able to understand.

The next day at school, Jason has to attend art class, which he hates because it is so noisy and unstructured. His art teacher, Mrs. Hawthorne, chastises Jason for not drawing as the other students do, and he covers his ears and gets under his desk to keep from hearing her "sandy voice," which results in his being sent home. Usually he is extremely upset when he is sent home, but all he can think of is that PhoenixBird might have written to him again.

Jason, his parents, and his brother go to visit his Uncle Bobby for his birthday. Bobby and his wife, Carol, have two sons: Seth and Little Bobby. The adults make Seth take Jason into his room to show him his new computer, but Seth just ignores Jason. Jeremy comes in to ask if Jason will help him and Little Bobby get something down off of a high shelf, and Seth insults both Jason and Jeremy. Jason kicks Seth, and the family leaves. At home, Jason feels bad—not about Seth, but that he cannot be normal for his parents.

Jason writes a new story to post on Storyboard about a dwarf named Bennu, which is the Egyptian name for "phoenix." Bennu's family are all normal in size, and Jason describes both the physical and emotional frustrations that come from Bennu's experience trying to live in a world that is not easy for him to navigate. A doctor comes to Bennu and tells him that he can cure his dwarfism. Jason ends the first part of the story there and sends it to PhoenixBird with a note that tells her his real name. She writes him back and tells him her name is Rebecca.

Jason does better in school, and as a reward his parents tell him that he can go to the Storyboard convention in Dallas, Texas, where writers of all ages convene to talk about their stories and writing in general. Jason is overwhelmed with happiness, and he shows it by putting his head on his father's shoulder and putting his hand on his mother's leg in silent gratitude. From Jason, it is a huge expression of emotion.

Jason has to decide whether to go to the convention with his mother or his father because only one of them can afford to go. When Jason chooses his father, his mother tries not to show it, but he knows that he has hurt her. Jason wants to comfort his mother, to express his love for her as much for her benefit as for his own, but he does not know how.

Jason logs on to Storyboard to tell Rebecca that he will be going to the convention, but there is a message waiting for him. It is from Rebecca telling him that she is actually going to the convention. Jason is petrified because he does not want Rebecca to see him and know that he has ASD, that he is different. His parents think that his anxiety is caused by the prospect of flying in

an airplane, so the family sets chairs up in the living room to resemble an airplane, and they practice the ritual of flying. He cannot figure out how to explain that he does not want to go to the convention because he is afraid of Rebecca's reaction to him, but he feels stuck.

Jason continues writing his story about Bennu the dwarf. One day, Aaron gets Jason to sit with him at lunch, and Jason talks through his story about Bennu, trying to figure out whether or not he will have the operation to cure his dwarfism. Aaron wonders out loud if it would be strange to wake up one morning to find yourself so completely different, and the world around you so completely altered.

Jason's father has an emergency at work, and he will not be able to go to the convention. Jason is elated because he thinks that means he can stay home, too, but his father tells him that the airline agreed to switch his ticket so that his mother could go instead.

On the trip to Dallas, Jason wonders if Rebecca is just as nervous about meeting him as he is about meeting her. He remembers the trip to New Haven, Connecticut, where his mother took him to see a doctor at Yale and he was diagnosed with autism. He had thought then that she was crying because she was angry with him for being unable to behave, but in the years since he has come to realize that she is not angry or disappointed; she is sad for him. In the hotel, Jason notices how his mother is different without his father around, and he helps her in little ways, like telling her how much to tip the porter because he always watches his father do it.

At the convention, Jason meets Rebecca. Although she is polite, she is not friendly. It is obvious that his ASD has unnerved her, and he knows that he has lost a friend. He can also tell that his mother is hurting for him. On their way out of the restaurant after breakfast, Rebecca sees them and turns in another direction to avoid them. His mother notices and whimpers in the pain she feels for Jason. Out of love for her, he attends the convention nonetheless.

Jason thinks more about Bennu. He decides that Bennu has the operation, and it is successful. His feet touch the ground when he gets out of bed, and his arms are long enough to knock the clock off the nightstand. He runs to the mirror to look, and all he can see is his face, which has not changed. He thinks the operation has failed because he is "the same" as he was before the operation. Jason goes to the first convention workshop even though he does not want to be there. But when the instructor comes into the room, Jason is shocked to see that he is a little person, a dwarf, just like Bennu.

Jason is reenergized by this, and he participates actively in the rest of the conference. He even goes to the party that night, where he meets Rebecca again. This time, she does not walk away, but comes up and says hello. She is impersonal, but at least she is friendly. Jason and his mother return home understanding that she needs him just as much as he needs her. As soon as he gets home, Jason revises the end of Bennu's story. Bennu wakes up the morning of the scheduled surgery and decides that he is who he is: "This is me."

CHARACTERS

Uncle Bobby

Liz Blake's brother, Bobby, and his "perfect" family make her feel conspicuous and uncomfortable because of Jason's condition. Bobby cannot communicate with Jason, preferring instead to address Liz and Carl, even when asking things like what Jason wants to drink. Bobby brags about his own sons, Seth and Little Bobby, so much and so pointedly that it makes Liz feel as though he is always comparing them to Jason and finding Jason lacking.

Carl Blake

Jason's father, Carl, is a sportscaster. Although he struggles with his inability to make things easier for his son, he is able to accept that Jason has his own reality which, even though no one else can see it, is just as valid as his or anyone else's. Jason consistently portrays his father as accepting and understanding of the way Jason experiences the world physically. He takes care not to hold Jason too tightly or crowd him too much. He listens with Jason more than he talks.

Aunt Carol

Carol is Bobby's wife and Seth's mother. She constantly boasts about Seth and Little Bobby, which puts Liz on the defensive.

Jason Blake

Jason is the autistic twelve-year-old narrator of *Anything but Typical*, not as capable of perceiving or expressing emotion as most people. When Jason was in third grade, his mother took him to see a specialist who diagnosed him with ASD, and ever since, he and his parents have been trying to figure out how to navigate a world that was not made for him to be comfortable in. He develops his own means of expression that include body language, such as flapping his hands when he is agitated. He does not know how to express emotions such as gratitude and love, but he does feel them. He is trying to figure out where he fits in with the world of people without ASD, and he possesses very accurate insight about the nature of people and communication. This is why writing stories is such a cathartic and vital experience for Jason. Creating his own realities allows him to belong. To Jason, it seems clear why people act the way they do, and he cannot understand how other people do not see it, too. At the same time, he is aware that he perceives the world differently from others. He knows that most people are able to look others in the eye, make conversation, and express how they feel. He also knows that if he were able to do these things, or even successfully act as if he were doing these things, it would make life much easier for everyone. He is aware of the effect his disorder has on his ability to make friends, too, which is why his online friendship with Rebecca is such a revelation but also why it leaves him with such anxiety. However, Jason seems to understand that wishing he were different will not make him different, and by the end of the book he gives a sense that he has begun to accept himself in new ways.

Jeremy Blake

Jeremy is Jason's neurotypical younger brother. Jeremy both looks up to and protects his older brother, and Jason, in turn, takes great comfort from Jeremy. Jeremy is annoying to Jason, as most younger siblings are to older ones, but he knows how to make Jason feel more important. He gives his brother a sense of power and strength that Jason will never get from his protective parents. Jeremy can also understand Jason's unique way of communicating in a combination of body language, sounds, and brief, sometimes vague sentences.

Liz Blake

Liz, Jason's mother, seems to be in a perpetual state of simultaneous heartbreak for her son and denial of his condition. She wants Jason to fit in and constantly works to make him blend in better. Highly sensitive, she takes the traits of Jason's disorder personally, not realizing that the fact that Jason cannot say "I love you" does not mean that he does not feel love. When her oversensitivity is balanced by Carl's easy acceptance, it is manageable. However, when she and Jason travel to Dallas without his father, she is forced to face both that she is incapable of completely shielding Jason from pain and that he is stronger than she ever gave him credit for.

Mrs. Hawthorne

Jason's portrayal of his art teacher, Mrs. Hawthorne, is a prime example of what Jason himself suggests to the reader is the product of an *unreliable narrator*. Jason tells the reader that she is his least favorite teacher, but after the day he is sent home because of an anxiety attack during her class, Jason cannot quite recall whether she sent him home for the day or he chose to go himself. In Jason's world, in his reality, she is not a nice person. However, this might not be the case with the other students.

Little Bobby

Little Bobby is Bobby and Carol's youngest son. He is Jeremy's age.

Aaron Miller

Aaron is a classmate who is often very kind to Jason. He makes sure that Jason has someone to sit with at lunch, stands up for him among the other kids, and seems genuinely interested in the things Jason talks about. Jason considers him a friend, and Aaron is one of the things in life that Jason can count on. He will never be cruel to Jason, and his presence puts Jason more at ease.

PhoenixBird

See Rebecca

Rebecca

Rebecca, also known by her Storyboard handle, PhoenixBird, is a Storyboard writer whom Jason befriends on the site. She is Jason's age and a cheerleader at her middle school in Dallas, Texas. Although they begin to build a friendship communicating online, once Rebecca meets Jason in person, she has difficulty seeing him as a friend because of his autism. However, at the farewell party, she makes sure to say goodbye to Jason in person, saying she hopes to hear from him again. Although their relationship does not turn out the way Jason fantasized it would, by the end of the novel she makes an effort to help him feel more comfortable, and her parting leaves the door open for further communication in the future.

Seth

Seth is Jason's cousin, and his character is a foil for Jason. That is, Seth embodies everything that Jason is not. He is, according to his parents, highly accomplished, but he is not kind and shows no understanding of anyone other than himself.

THEMES

Language

Jason explains that he is using the language of "neurotypicals"—people without ASD—to tell his story so that they can more easily relate to it. This is an important point that the reader should keep in mind throughout the rest of the book. Jason is not writing in what he considers his language. Because he sees the world differently and experiences it differently from neurotypicals, the text is almost a translation of his own making as he relates his story in language others will understand. He wants neurotypicals to understand his story and his message: "I will try—To tell my story in their language, in your language." However, since Jason is not a neurotypical, he is not communicating in his "native" language, so to speak. Instead he is relating experiences that are unique to him in a language he thinks will be understood, because "more than *talking* in their own language, people like to hear things in a way they are most comfortable."

In the first chapter, Jason describes his symptoms both as they appear to outsiders and as they are experienced by him. In this way, Baskin develops a unique mode of expression for Jason that allows the reader to empathize with his struggles and conflicts while at the same time being informed about how it might feel to be a person with ASD living in a world designed for neurotypicals. There are certain phrases he has learned to say in order to make neurotypicals feel more at ease, such as "I am okay just as I am." However, he says these things without really knowing what they mean. He just knows that people want to hear them. In other cases, such as when it is appropriate to say "thank you," he is unaware that he is expected to give these words, to speak this language. Similarly, he often does not understand the words that other people say. He does not

TOPICS FOR FURTHER STUDY

- In chapter 2, Jason outlines the seven major plot structures evident in fiction. All of them involve man (or woman), that is, the main character, versus seven elements: nature, man, environment, machine, the supernatural, self, and religion. The conflict between the protagonist of a story and one or more of these elements drives the narrative action forward. Which of these conflicts is or are central to *Anything but Typical*? Pull examples from the work to support your choice. As a class, vote on which elements are most evident and discuss how these conflicts are central to the novel. Finally, which of these conflicts are most evident in your own life, and how so? Discuss as a class, or write an essay on the topic.

- Think of the character traits that are portrayed as symptoms of Jason's ASD, such as high anxiety, fear of crowds and loud noises, or the inability to communicate. In some ways, as Jason points out when he talks about Jeremy's fear of sandals and bananas as a young child, everyone has characteristics that others may deem "abnormal." Do you have any phobias or anxieties that most of your friends do not share? Why are these neuroses normal in some people but abnormal in Jason? Does recognizing these things about yourself make you more able to relate to Jason? Why or why not? What do you think would happen if everyone was honest about their compulsions, anxieties, or phobias? Would society's definition of what is "normal" behavior and what is "abnormal" behavior change? Write an essay explaining your stance.

- Certain kinds of media do place disability issues at the front of the narrative. There are television shows and movies that feature physically or mentally disabled characters. Sometimes these "disabilities" even result in superpowers, creating heroes like Spiderman. Choose a character from a television program or movie who is disabled. Using the Internet, search for video clips of that character in situations where their disability provides some sort of conflict or challenge. Create a blog and post several of these videos along with a brief summary of the conflict, any resolution, and the emotional state of the character in regard to his or her disability. Invite other students to comment on your blog.

- Jason finds an escape from the constant reminders of his disability by writing fiction and posting it on Storyboard, an online writing community. Each of his stories relates to his life in some way. Write a short story of your own in which the characters or central conflict parallel experiences from your own life. Choose an online writing community such as Writing. Com (http://www.writing.com/), WritersCafé (http://www.writerscafe.org), or AuthorNation (http://www.authornation.com) and post your story. Make sure to tell your teacher how to find your story on the site, and see if you get any comments on it.

- Autism spectrum disorder comes in many different forms, from severe cases to those in which the autistic person is relatively high-functioning, like Jason. Read the young-adult novel *Rules* (2006), by Cynthia Lord. How is David, the autistic younger brother of the main character, like Jason, and how is he different? Research ASD on the topic pages of sites such as those of the National Institute of Child Health and Human Development (http://www.nichd.nih.gov/health/topics/asd.cfm), the Centers for Disease Control and Prevention (http://www.cdc.gov/ncbddd/kids/autism.html), and Kids Health (http://kidshealth.org/teen/diseases_conditions/learning/autism.html#cat20167) to get an idea of the different forms autism can take. Write an essay and explain where you would place Jason and David on the spectrum. Give examples from your research to support your conclusion.

understand teasing or sarcasm or flirting. Whenever someone says something that has a literal meaning that is different from their words, Jason is confused. He also knows that a person's saying something does not make it true. "People don't mean everything they say," his mother tells him. But no one has ever given him a good reason for why they say things they do not mean.

Though Jason has problems with the spoken language of neurotypicals, written language makes much more sense to him. Without all of the other stimuli that a person has to deal with when engaged in a conversation, like body language and facial expressions, when Jason writes, he can focus on exactly what he wants to say. Jason's e-mails to Rebecca give no indication that he has ASD. He is able to intelligently discuss her stories and share personal information about himself because he knows that she cannot see him and the written medium allows him the freedom to take his time choosing his words.

Appearance versus Reality
Jason knows that in many cases his appearance matters more to people than reality. He is told over and over by his aides, therapists, and parents things to say and do that will make him appear more normal. In chapter 3, Jason describes what it is like to look at himself in the mirror and see a regular boy: "If I didn't talk and I didn't move, if I held my hands at my sides and stood very straight, I'd look like any other twelve-year-old boy." Perhaps people are more shocked by Jason's behavior because unlike people with more obvious disabilities, such as being in a wheelchair, Jason appears at first glance to be just another preteen boy. Everyone from his mother to his teachers expects him to try to blend in and act more like other people. His mother is always telling him to loosen his belt, even though the feel of the fabric of his clothing rubbing on his skin bothers him greatly, so that he will not stand out as much. Jason understands this. He says, "I think my mother wants to fix me." The main disconnect between appearance and reality that Jason addresses is that of emotion. He notes that many people assume that just because he does not speak or express much emotion, he does not feel. However, Jason does feel. Further, he understands the pain and confusion that his lack of expression results in. He knows, for example, that his mother wishes he would hug her as Jeremy does or tell her he loves her, and it hurts him that he cannot make himself give her what she wants. Jason's obsession with

Storyboard is a reflection of his need to reconcile his reality with the reality of neurotypicals. In his stories, he creates both appearance and reality. When he writes, Jason is in control, and he can create whatever sort of world he wants.

Sibling Relations
Jason knows how love feels, he tells the reader: it is how he feels when he is with his mother, safe and warm. He knows that love is something that has to grow. For Jason, it is completely understandable that he did not automatically love his younger brother, Jeremy, when he was born. He was just a smelly baby who took his mother's attention and cried all the time. But as Jeremy grew up, they developed their own special friendship and relationship. Now nine years old, Jeremy, because he has been exposed to Jason since his birth, has learned to speak Jason's special language. "The best thing about Jeremy," Jason says, "is that I don't ever have to answer him, not with words anyway." Jeremy understands what Jason is trying to communicate when he flaps his hands or rocks back and forth. Jeremy looks up to Jason, but he also watches out for him. He takes extra care to make Jason feel important. Jason tells the reader that Jeremy is always asking Jason to help him with things. The reader knows that Jeremy, at nine years old, is probably capable of zipping his own jacket and does not need anyone to push him on the swings, but he asks Jason to help with things like this anyway. It is Jeremy's way of giving happiness to Jason.

In turn, Jason is protective of Jeremy, in his own way. He could probably have handled Seth's being mean to him, for example. But when Seth is also mean to Jeremy, Jason gets very angry. He kicks Seth, and for a moment it seems as though he will have one of his anxiety attacks. But Jeremy pulls him out of the room and jokes with him, and instead of getting upset, he feels relief. This scene is a particularly touching example of the relationship between Jeremy and Jason. Jeremy makes Jason feel needed at the same time that he takes care of him. In many ways, Jeremy understands Jason as no one else in the book does. The inverse is also true, for Jason teaches Jeremy life lessons through his example. When their mother tells Jeremy he can no longer use the plates he has always used, which have dividers so that his food does not touch, Jeremy gets upset, but Jason realizes that this is just one in a very long line of things that Jeremy will have to learn to deal with as he grows up. He tells Jeremy that "sometime your food is going to have to touch,"

Jason Blake is a preteen autistic boy. *(© Synchronista / Shutterstock.com)*

but what he really means is that there are times in life when people do not get what they want. Not every desire can be or will be accommodated. Jason has always known this, but Jeremy is just learning. In this way, Jason is wiser than Jeremy, and this scene shows that he still has things to teach his younger brother. Eventually Jason feels he has outgrown going to his mother when the world seems like a frightening place. When he was younger, he would rub his mother's hair between his fingers, and it would make him feel safe. Now Jeremy provides this same form of love for Jason. He is always there, and they each know that the other loves him just as he is.

STYLE

Metafiction

Metafiction is a device in literature that references the craft of fiction within the work of fiction itself, drawing attention to the elements that are used to shape a work of literature in order to

highlight the question of fiction versus reality. Baskin uses metafiction in *Anything but Typical* to make the reader question the narrative that Jason provides and think about the relative nature of "reality." Jason's own writing and the techniques of fiction writing that he chooses to explain to the reader offer parallels for the way that his entire life—in a way, anyone's life—is a juxtaposition of reality as he experiences it and reality as others may see it. Baskin never lets the reader forget that Jason is using the language of neurotypicals to tell his story in a way he thinks others will understand; therefore it cannot help but be at least a little bit fictitious. Meanwhile, Jason's stories parallel his own experiences, allowing the reader to better identify conflicts and themes in the larger novel because they are evident in his short stories.

For example, the first story Jason writes is about a man with a giant tumor in his throat that prevents him from speaking, so everyone in his town thinks that he is stupid. He lives in isolation carving figures out of wood. Eventually, he carves a little boy to have as a friend, like Pinoc-chio. This story is representative of how Jason feels. Just because he cannot communicate like other people, they assume that he is stupid or that he has no feelings. His second story, about the dwarf named Bennu, is even more of a paral-lel to the action in the novel. Bennu's central conflict is similar to Jason's. Conflict, Jason explains, is the most important part of a story. Bennu's conflict is that he is coming to terms with the fact that he is a dwarf and that inside it does not matter whether or not he is normal-sized. He is the same on the inside, and he can never be any different. This is the conclusion that Jason comes to as well at the end of the novel. Bennu learns to appreciate the advantages of his short height. Because everyone talks over his head, he "has learned to listen better" than other people.

Throughout the novel, Jason gives the reader small insights into the craft of writing fiction, which are always related to what is going on in the novel. For example, in chapter 7 he details the formula for writing a romance: "Boy gets girl. Boy loses girl. Boy gets girl again." As his friendship with Rebecca progresses, Jason points out to us the moment when he first "gets" her as well as when he "loses" her. It is poignant and notable that he never completes this formula in the novel. It turns from a story in the genre of romance to what Jason explains is a literary story, meaning that it does not necessarily follow any formula or have a resolved ending. *Anything but Typical*, like the stories Jason writes, is a literary story.

He explains story arcs, defines the concept of irony, and explains different plotlines, and all of these concepts become evident in the book about the same time that he introduces the reader to them. For example, he writes, "Irony is also when the true meaning of a character's actions or words are clear to the reader but, *ironically*, not to the character himself." This is often the case in *Anything but Typical*, when the reader under-stands the motives behind the actions of certain characters but the characters do not. Often, this is the case with Jason's mother, whose fierce denial that anything is wrong with her son in the face of obvious evidence to the contrary is an example of heartbreaking irony. She uses certain symptoms of his ASD—such as his ability to spell at a very young age—as evidence that he is perfectly healthy. Her dependence on Jason at the conven-tion for things like working the GPS and

knowing how much to tip the porter is also ironic, because in her eyes she is supposed to be the one protecting him.

Similarly, Jason exemplifies an unreliable nar-rator, a narrator that the reader cannot completely trust to give an objective or accurate view of the truth. Jason explains to the reader the literary concept of an unreliable narrator, who "can be telling the truth or just the truth as they see it," when he is detailing the incident in art class during which he breaks the potter's wheel. He reasserts that he did not do anything that would have caused Mrs. Hawthorne to send him home, but especially since he has just talked about unreliable narrators, the reader cannot quite trust that his account of what happened is completely accurate. It is not that Jason is deliberately lying to the reader but that he does not remember things the way other people do. Details get lost or exagger-ated, and it is clear what a confusing place Jason's world must be to live in.

Stream of Consciousness

Stream of consciousness is a mode of narration that relates the flow of thoughts in a narrator's mind as they happen, without refining them into clearly defined concepts. It is a type of interior monologue that can sometimes be difficult for the reader to follow, just as it would be difficult for one person to understand the leaps of logic and mental associations that occur in another person's mind.

Because so much of Jason's world is com-posed of stimuli such as sights and sounds that he receives but cannot process, and because the way his mind works is so different from how other people's minds work, Baskin portrays his thoughts much of the time in stream of consciousness. An example can be taken from chapter 22, when Jason and Aaron are in the cafeteria:

> Chairs scraping across the floor.
> Paper bags crumpled.
> Angry voices.
> Happy voices.
> Laughing.
> Whispering.
> *Nobody wants to eat alone.*

It is difficult for Jason to distinguish back-ground noise from the things he should be paying attention to, like people talking to him. He has to make an effort to focus in order to concentrate on communication, both given and received. His thought processes operate differently from most people's, and sometimes it can be hard to follow his thoughts as they move between concepts and conclusions. The difference between Jason's stream-of-consciousness narration and other examples of stream of consciousness is that this is not just the way his mind works internally but also the way he communicates with others. For instance, it probably makes no sense to Mr. Shupack when Jason says the name of a minor baseball player and then says that he is meaning to reference his father, but because the reader is able to see Jason's mind at work, one can understand the thought process that led Jason from "Vizcaino" to "my father."

HISTORICAL CONTEXT

Disability Studies in the Twenty-First Century

The field of disability studies grew out of the civil rights movement, first emerging as a direction in literary criticism in the 1960s. However, it was not until the 1990s that it received much attention, and only in the beginning of the twenty-first century has disability studies made much headway in the academic mainstream. In his article "Disability Studies 2.0," the prominent scholar Leonard Cassuto points out that, like gender and ethnicity studies, disability studies is part of the larger field of cultural studies. It treats disability as a factor in the formation of both social and personal identity and an indicator of minority status, since it compares the experience of disabled people to "abled," or able-bodied, people. Disability studies explores what the term *disabled* means and how "abled" society has marginalized and oppressed those who fall into that minority.

In the field of disability studies, critics challenge what is meant by "disabled," maintaining that it is a label given to those whose bodies do not match society's irrationally high physical ideals, rather than the reality of existence. Considering how many conditions "disabled" defines, they further allege that there is no such thing as a purely "abled" body at all, since at some point, whether owing to age or accident, every human becomes "disabled." Studying disability is, therefore, very much like studying other minority categories. However, it is unique in that any person can become disabled, while other identity factors are immutable. For instance, a white person cannot suddenly become black or a man become a woman (when

that transition is unwanted). This is not the case with disability. In fact, Cassuto invites abled people to see that every "abled" person is simply "temporarily able-bodied." Whether due to accident, disease, or old age, all able-bodied persons will become disabled if they live long enough. If physical and mental limitations will happen to all able-bodied people, then it can be argued that it is actually more natural to be disabled than abled. Therefore, disability scholars and activists for disabled rights view disability not as a failure of the body but as a failure of society to open itself to people with different identities and modes of living.

Disability studies involves looking at the construction not only of physical disability but of mental disability as well. Scholars examine scientific texts, legal documents, works of fiction, and nonfictional accounts to show how the concepts of madness and sanity have been constructed by societies through different historical periods. Prior to the scientific revolution of the eighteenth century, the human mental state was seen as binary: that is, one was either mad or not. However, modern views of mental illness, explained by Cassuto as "a set of behaviors that could be variously shared by large numbers of people," are much more flexible. In other words, the idea of "insanity," a category with clear boundaries created to be the opposite of "sanity," was gradually replaced by the idea of "mental illness," which is not so easily defined. Like physical disability, mental illness is a minority label that in many cases can be gained or lost over the course of a lifetime, such as in cases of amnesia or temporary depression. This makes it much more difficult to simply label someone as either "sane" or "insane."

Critics argue that all of this research and theory has a political purpose: to remove the stigma that has historically been associated with disability by showing that disability is not a personal flaw that makes the disabled individual less than a person or a problem to be solved but is part of a person's identity and experience. Critics and activists attempt to use these arguments to eliminate discrimination against the disabled, a fight that has resulted in the passage of laws such as the Americans with Disabilities Act of 1990, which guarantees equal employment and access to disabled persons. Ending discrimination in this case means not only treating the disabled as fully human but also changing societal standards to include the disabled as a group worthy of accommodation rather than expecting them to try to fit

Jason could be himself while writing on a blog site. (© Dmitriy Shironosov | Shutterstock.com)

into a world that often will not adapt to them. In other words, disability studies aims to show that disabled people are no different from any other minority group. Just as modern society has evolved to accommodate people of different races and the changing roles of women, it can and should change to accommodate the disabled and to allow all people the full extent of their rights as human beings.

CRITICAL OVERVIEW

Anything but Typical won a 2010 Schneider Family Book Award for the way that Jason, the twelve-year-old autistic protagonist, "sees and responds to the world, rendering what could be perplexing reactions understandable," as described by Deborah Stevenson in the *Bulletin of the Center for Children's Books*. "While other spectrum-disorder kids may see themselves in Jason, the book is particularly skilled at translating his reality for those who may not otherwise understand it," notes Stevenson. As many critics emphasize, it is Baskin's ability to make the world as perceived

through the lens of autism understandable to those that Jason calls "neurotypicals" that make this narrative shine so brightly. Susan Dove Lempke, writing for *Horn Book*, praises how Baskin details Jason's "perceptions of and reactions to people that might help readers better understand their autistic peers." Her depiction of Jason as fully aware of the limitations he experiences is said to be powerful. According to a 2009 *Kirkus Reviews* writer, Baskin's portrayal of the world as experienced by an autistic boy is "brilliant," showing readers that Jason "understands how his parents feel about him, frets about fitting in and yearns to find at least one friend in the world."

Many critics praise Baskin's delicate portrayal of Jason's relationship with his family. Wendy Smith-D'Arezzo, writing for *School Library Journal*, says that Baskin skillfully shows Jason's "parents and younger brother as real people with real problems, bravely traversing their lives with a differently abled child without a road map, but with a great deal of love." The individual ways in which each family member understands and copes with Jason's disability are said to amount to as powerful a theme as the way he uses his fiction to reconcile his own reality with that of the rest of the world. Mark Letcher, in his article "Autism in Young Adult Literature," writes that "the relationship that is established between Jason and his parents will at turns break and warm readers' hearts, as Baskin shows how parents can misread situations as much as someone with an ASD can." And Stevenson is particularly struck by Jason's "closeness with Jeremy, his younger brother, who matter-of-factly reads and accepts Jason's behaviors and looks up to his big bro."

Jason's own short stories are a vehicle for his own understanding of himself. The *Kirkus Reviews* contributor notes that readers are even provided with tips about writing fictional stories "as they observe Jason composing his way to self-acceptance." The stories not only show how Jason views himself but also function as a cathartic process in his struggle to come to terms with his disability. "Through his stories and thinly veiled fictional characters, Baskin reveals not only the obstacles that Jason faces, but also his fierce determination to be himself at all costs," writes Smith-D'Arezzo. Stevenson remarks that "his writing offers an additional window into his psyche."

It may be this "window into his psyche" that constitutes the book's most significant gift, as readers begin to not only understand Jason but also empathize with him. "The book's greater strength," writes Lempke, "is communicating to readers how some of the same things that bother Jason might also bother them—whether it is bright lights, noisy rooms, or foods that touch—and establishing common ground." Jason expresses his feelings differently, but that does not necessarily mean that he feels differently. As Letcher puts it, "The tremendous voice that Baskin creates for Jason allows readers to see that people with ASDs do indeed feel emotions, but those emotions are expressed in different ways from 'neuro-typical' standards." It is the ability of readers to relate to Jason that makes his voice unique and the story so noteworthy. As Smith-D'Arezzo says, "Jason is a believable and empathetic character in spite of his idiosyncrasies"—or even, perhaps, because of them.

CRITICISM

Kristy Blackmon

Blackmon is a writer, editor, and critic from Dallas, Texas. In the following essay, she examines the use of psychoanalytical defense mechanisms displayed by the secondary characters in Anything but Typical.

Creating realities is anything but atypical. Everyone filters reality through one's personal point of view, and therefore we all create our own realities in some sense. In cases where individuals experience great emotional stress, reality can become even more subjective. Psychoanalytic theory states that a natural and instinctual need for self-preservation can trigger subconscious strategies called *self-defense mechanisms* that manipulate truths, filtering them through processes that allow the mind to perceive reality in a way that results in a lessening of emotional distress. These processes are normal and a natural way to give a person the calm needed to handle anxiety. However, the longer these feelings last, the higher the likelihood that the subconscious strategies we employ to protect ourselves will instead develop into chronic behaviors that are ultimately self-detrimental. Jason learns certain self-defense mechanisms to help him navigate mainstream culture. He deliberately utilizes repression, a classic defense mechanism, to manage his compulsions by pushing them to his subconscious. He also, subconsciously, engages in projection, in which he attributes his own feelings to another person. This is apparent in his interactions with his art teacher, Mrs. Hawthorne, who he claims does not like him, though it is more likely that Jason does not like Mrs. Hawthorne. Most evident in the novel, Jason consciously utilizes the defense mechanism of sublimation. In sublimation, a person displaces negative emotions such as anxiety, confusion, and fear into a constructive activity. For Jason, this is his writing. It is healthy for him because it enables him to work through his anxieties using his characters as an emotional shield. Almost every character in *Anything but Typical* utilizes one or more self-defense mechanisms when Jason's condition becomes too stressful for them to consciously confront, and the individual ways in which his family members understand and cope with his disability constitute as powerful a theme as the way he uses his fiction to reconcile his own reality with that of the rest of the world.

Jason's mother and brother most obviously employ defense mechanisms of different sorts to deal with the anxiety associated with Jason's ASD in a subconscious effort to create a reality in which they are not emotionally overwhelmed.

WHAT DO I READ NEXT?

- Rachel Anderson's 1995 book *The Bus People* is a collection of stories each told from the perspective of one of the seven students who regularly rides a bus for the disabled. Some of the students are physically handicapped, while others are mentally ill, and they all have their own stories to tell.

- Mark Haddon's novel *The Curious Incident of the Dog in the Night-Time*, published in 2004, tells the story of Christopher, a fifteen-year-old autistic boy who finds his neighbor's dog dead on the front lawn. Determined to find out who is responsible and encouraged by his school social worker, Christopher decides to write a book about his investigation. The result is a story told the way only Christopher could tell it, complete with illustrations.

- *Freak the Mighty*, by Rodman Philbrick, is a 1993 novel that tells of the unlikely friendship between Max, who is big and strong but struggles with school, and Kevin, his brilliant but physically disabled friend. Though the other students make fun of them, together their combined strengths allow them to stand against life's obstacles.

- In Terry Spencer Hesser's debut 1998 novel *Kissing Doorknobs*, fourteen-year-old Tara Sullivan recounts her development of obsessive-compulsive disorder starting at the age of eleven. Based on the author's personal experiences with OCD, the novel is a touching and accurate portrayal of the confusion that accompanies the development of mental disorders in teens.

- Bebe Moore Campbell's 2006 novel *72 Hour Hold* examines one African American family's experience with mental illness. Keri's eighteen-year-old daughter suffers from bipolar disorder, and Keri must learn how to deal with not only her daughter's condition but the stigma of mental illness in the African American community as well.

- Nora Raleigh Baskin's 2001 debut novel, *What Every Girl (Except Me) Knows*, is based on her own experience of losing her mother at the age of three. Gabby Weiss is twelve years old and decides she needs a mother figure to help her navigate the confusion of puberty. Along the way, Gabby becomes curious about her mother's death and is determined to uncover the mystery behind it.

- Temple Grandin is an accomplished animal scientist who is autistic. In 1996, she published *Thinking in Pictures: And Other Reports from My Life with Autism*. The book tells how she overcame the restrictions of her disability to not only function but, indeed, excel in mainstream society.

Jason's younger brother, Jeremy, is nine years old, and he is best able to understand Jason's special "language"—that is, his method of communication—because he has been exposed to it since birth. Cognitively, they are more or less evenly matched during the time frame of the novel. Jeremy is still young enough to look up to Jason, but he is also approaching an age where he is beginning to understand the discrimination toward Jason and to feel protective of him. To Jeremy, Jason is just his older brother whom he loves; to society, however, Jason is different and disruptive. The defense mechanism Jeremy employs most to avoid the confusion and anxiety of these two warring influences is called *identification*, a process that results in Jeremy's taking on certain traits or characteristics that he has learned from Jason. Jason explains this in chapter 4 when he talks about how aspects of Jeremy's personality are based on Jason's example: "Some of the weird things he does my mother says are 'modeled behavior,' which is just another way of saying he learned them from me." For example, Jason freely admits that Jeremy's temper is modeled on his own.

> JASON'S MOTHER AND BROTHER MOST
> OBVIOUSLY EMPLOY DEFENSE MECHANISMS OF
> DIFFERENT SORTS TO DEAL WITH THE ANXIETY
> ASSOCIATED WITH JASON'S ASD IN A SUBCONSCIOUS
> EFFORT TO CREATE A REALITY IN WHICH THEY
> ARE NOT EMOTIONALLY OVERWHELMED."

Yet Jeremy also develops neuroses of his own; though his parents attribute them to Jason, they are entirely of his own construct. Through the process of identification, Jeremy is partially transformed; parts of his personality are modeled not on Jason's exact actions but on the attributes that Jason displays. Jeremy's aversion to having the food on his plate touch is a compulsion that he did not learn directly from Jason. Rather, he assimilated the concept of his brother's compulsive behavior and developed his own habits modeled on that concept. In an attempt to avoid the unpleasantness that can accompany a full recognition of Jason's disability, he has identified with Jason.

At the same time, Jeremy has developed a protective instinct toward Jason such as that which parents feel for their children. It is not unusual for older siblings to feel protective of younger ones, especially in the case of absent or neglectful parents. However, Jeremy and Jason have attentive and loving parents, and Jeremy is three years younger than Jason. At the age of nine, Jeremy does not know the hardships that Jason will have to face as well as his parents do, but he knows that Jason needs special care and that he is vulnerable. Perhaps because he understands Jason so well, Jeremy can sense Jason's frustration with himself and his own limitations. To watch a loved one in emotional distress is often an extremely painful experience, and Jeremy tries in his own way to mitigate Jason's hurt and raise his sense of self-worth. He asks for Jason's help even when he does not need it, such as when zipping his jacket, a task most nine-year-olds can manage easily. He compliments Jason's stories, and he even has Jason taste new foods before he will so that his brother can tell him if he will like them or not. By giving Jason these small satisfactions, Jeremy works to protect himself from the

anxiety of witnessing Jason's disappointment with his limitations.

More than any other character in the book, Jason's mother, Liz, employs a variety of self-defense mechanisms in an attempt to handle her anxiety about Jason. Like Jeremy, Liz finds it difficult to watch Jason in pain. "When you hurt, I hurt," she tells Jason. Her intense natural desire for her son to have the happiest life possible is constantly at war with her acute awareness of what being autistic means in a social sense. When Jason was younger, Liz utilized the common strategy of rationalization to manage her anxiety about her son. When a person rationalizes something, they explain upsetting conditions through a personal form of logic, which is often twisted. Oddities that would normally be cause for anxiety are turned around and used as evidence that nothing upsetting has happened. Sometimes, these oddities are even held up as examples of superiority. For instance, despite his inability to communicate, Liz would often point to Jason's savant talent for spelling as evidence for his normal intelligence; when he was around four, she went so far as to call it "genius." Though he ascribed no meaning to the words he spelled and displayed evidence of developmental abnormalities, she refused to admit even the possibility that something might be wrong, rationalizing the fear away. She blamed other children for Jason's lack of social skills, citing exaggerated cases of meanness or bullying. When Jason's kindergarten teacher suggested that Liz take Jason to Yale to undergo testing, Liz called her "ridiculous" and refused to acknowledge any kernel of truth in the teacher's concern. In doing so, she displayed another self-defense tactic, denial. Denial occurs when the conscious mind is confronted with something that is too painful to accept and the subconscious rejects it as untrue. Factual evidence does not sway a person in denial toward admitting the truth of a situation.

After Jason's diagnosis, Liz still struggled with the societal judgments of her son, which has led to her constant concern for appearances. She wants him to look as normal as possible to attract as little attention as possible, even if that means making him unhappy for a little while. She corrects his posture and is always adjusting his clothing to create the appearance of normalcy. She is motivated by the threat of two anxieties, for herself and for Jason. She is almost desperate to prove his worth to the rest of the

PhoenixBird turned out to be Rebecca and Jason worries that she will not accept his autism. *(© StockLite / Shutterstock.com)*

family, especially to her mother and her brother. She tries to create a reality where Jason does not appear to be disabled, mostly because she wants to protect Jason. She is so busy denying the truth of his condition that she does not allow herself to see him or their relationship accurately. It is not until they are alone at the convention in Dallas that Liz begins to see not only that it is impossible for her to protect Jason from all of life's hurts but also that Jason does not need her protection nearly as much as she thinks he does. In fact, she has come to rely on him in her own way.

Both Jeremy and Liz utilize subconscious methods to protect themselves and Jason from the anxiety and fear that accompanies his disability, but these behaviors cannot go on forever. Jeremy is already surpassing Jason in many ways, and as he ages, he will, in all likelihood, stop identifying with Jason in large part. In any case, he has already reached the age where he can no longer model his behavior on Jason's. Liz has lived in some degree of rationalization and denial for nearly a decade, but she shows signs at the end of the novel of finally being able to

face the truth of the situation without becoming overwhelmed by the pain of it. As they grow to understand and accept the necessity of reconciling Jason's condition with societal expectations, they are able to decrease their dependence on these thought processes.

Source: Kristy Blackmon, Critical Essay on *Anything but Typical*, in *Novels for Students*, Gale, Cengage Learning, 2013.

Suzanne Crowley

In the following review, Crowley compares books revolving around autism, including Anything but Typical.

Recently while perusing the site Library-Thing, I saw someone had tagged my novel *The Very Ordered Existence of Merilee Marvelous* (Greenwillow, 2007) as the "current cool disability." My book, loosely based on a loved one and set in my beloved Texas, took more than five years to write and publish. At the time I started it, Mark Haddon's *The Curious Incident of the Dog in the Night-Time* (Doubleday, 2003), written from the viewpoint of an autistic character, had not been

" TO SIMPLY DISMISS ADOLESCENT
LITERATURE WITH AUTISM AS THE CURRENT
HOT THING GREATLY MISSES THE MARK."

published, and I was sure I was entering new ground with my manuscript. I certainly had not jumped on a literary bandwagon and I suspect no other authors had, either. I stayed away from reading other books during the writing and publishing process of VOE, but after finding the LibraryThing tag, I became curious and set out to read some recent and upcoming novels with autistic characters. What I found were some richly textured works with highly unusual voices, individuals trying to cope and navigate their worlds in unusual ways, and, most surprisingly, characters who possessed sharp insights into human nature and who had much to teach us. And their authors had heartfelt and personal reasons for sharing their stories.

Cynthia Lord's heartwarming and humorous *Rules* (Scholastic, 2006), told from the viewpoint of 12-year-old Catherine, is the story of a sister coming to terms with her autistic brother, David, and the "rules" she sets for him, like "no toys in the fish tank" and "keep your pants on in public." A Newbery Honor Book and winner of the Schneider Family Book Award, as well as many state awards, *Rules* is loosely based on Lord's now 19-year-old daughter and her 17-year-old son, who is on the autism spectrum. "It was the sibling's story that I most wanted to tell. I've watched my daughter grow up straddling two different worlds. In one world, she navigated the challenges and joys of having a brother with autism and in another, she just wanted to be her own person. It was my daughter's experiences that drew me to the story," says Lord. "It's a big honor to be trusted with a child's true feelings. Some of the most heartfelt, beautiful letters I receive are from siblings of children with disabilities. They often read the book and then asked their parents to read it, too, so they can talk about it. One mom told me her child handed *Rules* to her and said, 'Because I want you to know how I feel.'" In a time of more awareness of autism in the population, Lord hopes that by reading *Rules* and getting to know David, "readers will feel less fearful and more

understanding of people with autism. One great thing about book characters is that we can talk freely about them. With real people, we worry so much about their feelings and ourselves being judged. Those worries keep us silent sometimes, instead of talking; we writers write about the things that matter to us—and having a person with autism in your life matters greatly."

In Nora Raleigh Baskin's *Anything but Typical* (S & S, 2009), readers meet Jason Blake, who, on the first page, tells them in halting, spare sentences, "Most people like to talk in their own language. I will try to tell my story in their language, in your language." Jason, a boy with autistic spectrum disorder (ASD), is unable to communicate freely with people, but finds his true voice in writing stories on the computer on a Web site called Storyboard. "When I write, I can be heard. And known. But nobody has to look at me. Nobody has to see me at all," Jason says. Baskin explains, "I knew before I started writing this book that autism is NOT a lack of emotion, but rather a difficulty in giving and receiving emotion/connectiveness that in no way diminishes intensity but may, in fact, increase it so much that it becomes unbearable. I have real-lived experience and incredible compassion for this concept." After meeting a girl named Phoenixbird on Storyboard, Jason begins to write a story about Bennu, a dwarf who ultimately must decide between being "cured" or staying as he is, a story that echoes the struggles Jason has in accepting his disability and navigating his world. "As Bennu finds acceptance for his 'handicap,' so does Jason," continues Baskin. "When I was in middle school I wrote stories all the time, which only upon re-reading as an adult do I realize were truly fictionalized autobiography. I was using 'story' as a way of making sense, or expressing confusion and pain in my 'real' life. And it worked. Writing is an empowerment. There is no question about that."

"The term 'cognitive disorder' implies that there is something wrong with the way I think or with the way I perceive reality. I perceive reality just fine. Sometimes I perceive more of a reality than others," Marcelo Sandoval explains to readers, near the beginning of Francisco X. Stork's *Marcelo in The Real World* (Scholastic, 2009). "Marcelo has a childlike sensitivity, a capacity for awe and for questioning, that we probably all had as children but lost as we grew up," Stork, who worked with kids on the autism spectrum in college, explains. "There is a kind of purity and 'egolessness' about Marcelo that I wanted to capture.

Marcelo is also a keen observer, more of a witness than a doer. He lacks a distance between him and the outside world." The teen, who has Asperger's Syndrome, attends Patterson, a school for kids with special needs, where he tends to ponies. "Patterson is where Marcelo belongs," he tells readers in his quiet, authentic, straightforward voice. In his alone time he hides in his tree house, makes lists of the day's events, and "remembers," uses a special form of internal music or IM, and thinks about his "holy books" and scriptures of which he is so fond. He goes to work at his father's law firm during the summer to become more connected to the "real world" and ultimately must move from being a quiet observer to one who takes action.

"My daughter was diagnosed with Asperger's in second grade," explains Kathryn Erskine, author of the upcoming *Mockingbird* (Philomel, April 2010) a nuanced and poignant story about Caitlin Ann Smith, who, like Erskine's daughter, has Asperger's. "Since then, with a lot of work, she has become more socially adjusted but still often sees things differently. I'd like readers to see that there's always an ability to change and grow no matter who you are, but MUCH more importantly, I want readers to see that just being different doesn't mean 'weird' or 'bad.' It's just different and, in fact, can be positive. I think people in Caitlin's world benefit from her and find that they themselves are changing and growing because of her."

Caitlin, who has much difficulty navigating her world, must also cope with the loss of her brother Devon, who was tragically killed in a school shooting. Her few comforts are sucking on her sleeve, her dictionary and TV, her computer, and gummy worms that she gives names to. Rarely is she able to relate to people around her, who she describes as the "puffy blue-marshmallow wall" person or her brother's Cub Scout friends—those kids in "green pants."

In trying to find the true meaning of "closure," one of the words she has found in her beloved dictionary, Caitlin researches the human heart, literally and figuratively, in order to understand how her brother died, and along the way she reaches out to Michael, a younger boy who lost his mother in the same school shooting. By coming out of her "hidey holes," both real (under her brother's bed) and imagined, to find her closure, Caitlin shows us what true determination is.

In his brilliant memoir, *Episodes: My Life as I See It* (Roaring Brook, 2009), 21-year-old Blaze Ginsberg, who is a high-functioning autistic, presents his world to readers in a highly unusual format inspired by the movie-based Web site IMDb.com, including lists of casts, trivia ("the Powerade was blue"), goofs ("on the way to lunch the red light stayed red for five minutes"), notes ("I really wanted a girlfriend in this episode"), and soundtracks and summaries of what went on any given day at his special private school in southern California. Among the exhaustive minutiae of his life are poignant, telling details of his heartaches, crushes (Hilary Duff), obsessions (buses, recycling trucks, and PBS Kids programs), and meltdowns, but most importantly, Ginsberg give readers a unique glimpse into an adolescent mind that is simply wired differently. He says, "At times being autistic is not easy; it is known for getting in the way of things. Sometimes it stops you from doing things like everyone else because you don't understand something or it's difficult to figure out what people mean. Also you think about things differently from other people and that can be difficult."

To simply dismiss adolescent literature with autism as the current hot thing greatly misses the mark. There is much in these works that will resonate with all readers, whether they have a disability or not. The trials and triumphs of the human heart are the same for all. Blaze Ginsberg says, "I try to connect with the world like everyone else, through people, my family and friends." Adds Cynthia Lord, "I keep one email from a 10-year-old sibling on the wall next to my desk. It says simply, 'I was so scared I was the only person who felt this way.' Sometimes books say the things we can't."

Source: Suzanne Crowley, "The Voices of Autism," in *School Library Journal*, Vol. 55, No. 8, August 2009, pp. 18–19.

Wendy Smith-D'Arezzo

In the following review, Smith-D'Arezzo examines the voice of the protagonist in the novel.

Baskin writes in the voice of a high-functioning boy who identifies himself as having numerous disorders, most with labels that appear as alphabet soup. In the third grade, after yet another battery of tests, Jason receives the diagnosis of autism. Now in sixth grade, he relates how he does not fit in, even though he tries to follow the instructions of his therapists and helpers. He labels the rest of his classmates and teachers as neurotypicals, or NTs for short. While humor resonates throughout the book, the pathos of Jason's situation is never far from readers' consciousness. If only he could act on what he knows he needs to do, his life would be so much easier. Jason also shows himself to be a deep thinker and an excellent writer. Through his stories and thinly veiled fictional characters, Baskin reveals not only the obstacles that Jason faces, but also his fierce determination to be himself at all costs. Jason is a believable and empathetic character in spite of his idiosyncrasies. Baskin also does a superb job of developing his parents and younger brother as real people with real problems, bravely traversing their lives with a differently abled child without a road map, but with a great deal of love.

Source: Wendy Smith-D'Arezzo, Review of *Anything But Typical*, in *School Library Journal*, Vol. 55, No. 3, March 2009, p. 141.

Publishers Weekly

In the following review, a contributor points out the "powerful and perceptive viewpoint" of the protagonist.

Baskin (*All We Know of Love*) steps into the mind of an autistic boy who, while struggling to deal with the "neurotypical" world, finds his voice through his writing ability. Though Jason initially seemed a prodigy, by third grade he had fallen behind academically, and his parents reluctantly had him tested ("A year later the only letters anybody cared about were ASD, NLD, and maybe ADD or ADHD, which I think my mum would have liked better. BLNT. Better luck next time"). Now in sixth grade, Jason still has behavioral difficulties, but is passionate about his writing and actively posts stories in an online forum. There he strikes up a friendship with (and develops a crush on) a fellow writer, though he becomes distraught when he discovers they will both be attending the same writing conference. The first-person narration gives dramatic voice to Jason's inner thoughts about his family and his own insecurities, even as he withholds details (usually about incidents at school) from readers. Jason's powerful and perceptive viewpoint should readily captivate readers and open eyes.

Source: Review of *Anything but Typical*, in *Publishers Weekly*, Vol. 256, No. 6, February 9, 2009, pp. 49–50.

Susan Dove Lempke

In the following review, Lempke notes that communication is the great strength of the novel.

Baskin sets herself a difficult challenge by making her narrator both an aspiring writer and autistic, seemingly more severely so than, for instance, Ted in Siobhan Dowd's *London Eye Mystery*. Sixth-grader Jason is being mainstreamed this year (forgoing his one-on-one classroom aide), and sometimes the noises, smells, and interpersonal demands overwhelm him. One of his greatest comforts is the website Storyboard, where he posts a story about a dwarf considering a treatment that would make him normal-sized. When Jason's story attracts positive online comments from a girl, he begins to feel that he has a friend—even a girlfriend—but is panic-stricken when he learns they are both planning to attend the Storyboard conference. He's also distressed that his mother, not his father, ends up accompanying him to the conference, but both Jason and his "neurotypical" mom come to realize that in some ways he is more competent than she is. Baskin writes with striking honesty, especially about Jason's relationship with his parents, and incorporates many details about Jason's perceptions of and reactions to people that might help readers better understand their autistic peers. The book's greater strength, though, is communicating to readers how some of the same things that bother Jason might also bother them—whether it is bright lights, noisy rooms, or foods that touch—and establishing common ground.

Source: Susan Dove Lempke, "Nora Raleigh Baskin: Anything but Typical," in *Horn Book*, Vol. 85, No. 3, May/June 2009, p. 289.

Ian Chipman

In the following review, Chipman exclaims that Baskin makes a difficult subject universal without being overly sentimental or dramatic.

Baskin tells this luminous story entirely from the point of view of Jason, an autistic boy who is a creative-writing whiz and deft explainer of literary devices, but markedly at a loss in social interactions with "neurotypicals" both at school and at home. He is most comfortable in an online writing forum called Storyboard, where his stories kindle an e-mail-based friendship with a girl. His excitement over having a real friend (and maybe even girlfriend) turns to terror when he learns that his parents want to take him on a trip to the Storyboard conference, where he'll no doubt have to meet her in person. With stunning economy, Baskin describes Jason's attempts to interpret body language and social expectations, revealing the extreme disconnect created by his internalization of the world around him. Despite his handicap, Jason moves through his failures and triumphs with the same depth of courage and confusion of any boy his age. His story, while neither particularly heartbreaking nor heartwarming, shows that the distinction between "normal" and "not normal" is whisper-thin but easily amplified to create the chasm between "different" and "defective." This is an enormously difficult subject, but Baskin, without dramatics or sentimentality, makes it universal. As Jason explains, there's really only one kind of plot: "Stuff happens. That's it."

Source: Ian Chipman, Review of *Anything but Typical*, in *Booklist*, Vol. 105, No. 11, February 1, 2009, p. 40.

Linda Brill Comerford

In the following excerpt, Comerford discusses Baskin's beginnings as a writer.

. . . Nora Raleigh Baskin has been writing about the same character, "a sad, motherless little girl," since she was in the sixth grade, but it took the 40-year-old author almost three decades to find the right "story" for her heroine, who, she admits, is a younger version of herself.

It wasn't until 1999, after many unsuccessful writing attempts, that Baskin began transforming her sometimes humorous, often painful childhood memories into the novel *What Every Girl (Except Me) Knows* (Little, Brown, Apr.), which traces sixth-grader Gabby's quest to discover the "special knowledge" about being a woman that girls with mothers seem to have. Like her protagonist Gabby, Baskin (now married and the mother of two boys) grew up in New Paltz, N.Y., with a father and older brother, and like Gabby, she sorely missed having a mother to guide her through her adolescence.

Acutely aware of past mistakes she'd previously made in autobiographical writing, Baskin approached her new manuscript with a fresh attitude. "This time, I was going to write what I wanted to write instead of trying to please an audience," she says, explaining that in a former (unpublished) chapter book, she made her characters too "generic" and avoided addressing any "real issues" because she was trying too hard to reach all children.

"I realized I could use my life but I didn't have to be tied to it. This was a huge breakthrough for me," she says, noting how, nearly 20 years ago, when she was a student at SUNY Purchase, her writing teacher told her she could "choose and edit" what she wrote and she "didn't necessarily have to tell the truth." Not able to fully appreciate his words, she "burst into tears" at the time, but now she was ready to apply his advice to her writing.

"When creating *What Every Girl (Except Me) Knows*, I was able to alter my life, make it turn out the way I would have liked it to be," Baskin states. "It allowed me to let go of a burden [her mother's death] I'd been carrying all my life. I gave Gabby knowledge it took me years to learn—that all people suffer insecurities." One of the more touching moments in her novel is when Gabby, struggling to come to terms with her mother's suicide, discovers she is not the only one feeling isolated and vulnerable among her friends, two of whom also carry sad family secrets.

Since Baskin was already well acquainted with her protagonist (variations of whom had already appeared in her college creative-writing thesis and previous chapter book), she was able to complete her novel in only five months' time. While she wrote, she kept a copy of Ruth White's *Belle Prater's Boy* by her side for inspiration, hoping to mirror White's ability to "write about a tragic incident with insight, humor and hope."

When she finished, Baskin showed the story to her good friend and staunch supporter, novelist Elinor Lipman, who, Baskin says appreciatively, "really stuck her neck out for me." Baskin considers what happened next to have been an "act of serendipity." Lipman found the name of an editor, Maria Modugno, whom she contacted by phone. Coincidentally, Modugno had just read one of Lipman's books and was therefore well acquainted with the author, and more than willing to read her friend's manuscript. She asked that it be sent to her through overnight mail. The only problem was that the book did not yet have a title. Lipman offered a list of suggestions; from that list Baskin chose *What Every Girl (Except Me) Knows*.

"The first clue that the title was going to be a hit came at the little post office in my town [of Weston, Conn.]," Baskin says wryly. "As the postmistress packed the book up to mail, she glanced at it and said, 'What a great title!'"

As it turned out, Modugno and her colleagues at Little, Brown were as enthusiastic about the novel as Lipman had been, and agreed to accept it for publication. Baskin and Modugno worked on the manuscript together for the next year and a half. "I trusted her [Modugno's] opinions and she allowed me to be the one to make final decisions in revisions," Baskin states. "You expect editors to be hard-nosed, but Maria was always kind and generous."

Having people actually read her book after its publication was the "icing on the cake" for Baskin. She's had a chance to talk to some of her readers at book signings and local schools, and has also heard from many fans through e-mail. The positive response she has received makes her even more grateful that Modugno "took a chance" with her. Mulling over the positive aspects of her writing and publishing experience, Baskin concludes, "It's magical how writing about a tragedy in my life has allowed my greatest dream to come true." ...

Source: Linda Brill Comerford, "Flying Starts," in *Publishers Weekly*, Vol. 248, No. 26, June 25, 2001, pp. 23–26.

SOURCES

Baldick, Chris, *The Oxford Dictionary of Literary Terms*, 3rd ed., Oxford University Press, 2008, pp. 203, 318.

Baskin, Nora Raleigh, "A Little More . . . or Less," Nora Raleigh Baskin website, http://norabaskin.com/a_little_more....html (accessed August 20, 2012).

———, *Anything but Typical*, Simon & Schuster, 2009.

Cassuto, Leonard, "Disability Studies 2.0," in *American Literary History*, Vol. 22, No. 1, 2009, pp. 218–20, 225, 230.

"Defense Mechanisms," in *The Gale Encyclopedia of Psychology*, 2nd ed., edited by Bonnie Strickland, The Gale Group, 2001, pp. 168–70.

Lempke, Susan Dove, Review of *Anything but Typical*, in *Horn Book*, Vol. 85, No. 3, May/June 2009, p. 289.

Letcher, Mark, "Autism in Young Adult Literature," in *English Journal*, Vol. 100, No. 2, 2010, p. 115.

Linton, Simi, "What Is Disability Studies?," in *PMLA*, Vol. 120, No. 2, March 2005, pp. 518, 521.

Review of *Anything but Typical*, in *Kirkus Reviews*, Vol. 77, No. 3, February 1, 2009, p. 169.

"Schneider Family Book Award," American Library Association website, http://www.ala.org/news/media presscenter/presskits/youthmediaawards/schneiderfamily bookaward (accessed August 20, 2012).

Smith-D'Arezzo, Wendy, Review of *Anything but Typical*, in *School Library Journal*, Vol. 55, No. 3, March 2009, p. 141.

Stevenson, Deborah, Review of *Anything but Typical*, in *Bulletin of the Center for Children's Books*, Vol. 62, No. 8, April 2009, p. 313.

FURTHER READING

Choldenko, Gennifer, *Al Capone Does My Shirts*, Putnam Juvenile, 2004.

In this novel, Moose Flanagan and his family move to Alcatraz in 1935 so that his autistic sister, Natalie, can attend a special school. In order for Natalie to get permission to enter the school, however, Moose and his father must ask the help of Al Capone, the most famous inmate of Alcatraz. The relationship between Moose and Natalie is especially touching.

Davidson, Michael, *Concerto for the Left Hand: Disability and the Defamiliar Body*, University of Michigan Press, 2008.

Davidson is a prominent scholar in the field of disabilities studies, and this book examines the relationship between disability and aesthetics across a wide range of artistic expression. From film noir to deaf poetry, Davidson explores the ways in which the experience of being disabled can shape art and provide a new and vital way for all people to study artistic culture.

Davis, Lennard J., *Obsession: A History*, University of Chicago Press, 2008.

Modern America is obsessed with obsession. Americans are workaholics, devoted to favorite celebrities or television shows, and passionate about interests. Further, Americans admire obsession in others. However, obsession goes beyond culture to include genuine psychological disorders, making it a unique blend of disability and desired trait. Davidson traces the history of obsession from its roots in religious and social life to its definition as a psychiatric and medical problem.

Garland-Thomson, Rosemarie, ed., *Freakery: Cultural Spectacles of the Extraordinary Body*, New York University Press, 1996.

This collection of essays examines the cultural phenomenon of the freak show from antiquity to today. It is divided into four sections: the historical exploitations of "freaks" in circuses and other arenas for money, the role of the "freak" in literature, the ways in which contemporary society identifies modern-day "freaks," and theoretical studies of the culture of "freaks." *Freakery* is a groundbreaking work that openly examines Western culture's fascination with human "oddities".

———, *Staring: How We Look*, Oxford University Press, 2009.

This unique book by respected disabilities studies scholar Garland-Thomson examines the human compulsion to stare: what motivates people to stare, the kinds of things people stare at, and the effects that staring can have. It is a study that overlaps psychology and the humanities as the author draws on art, media, history, and memoir to illustrate the reasons why people stare.

Mitchell, David T., and Sharon L. Snyder, eds., *The Body and Physical Difference: Discourses of Disability*, University of Michigan Press, 1997.

Mitchell and Snyder argue that many writers use disabled characters to represent the disruption in the normal flow of society that they hope their books will effect; that is, they wish to challenge existing social norms through the exploration of disability. The disabled characters become the vehicle for their social message, but since these characters are typically defined only by one type of disability, it hampers the ability of the writers who use them to fully address the issue of disability in society.

SUGGESTED SEARCH TERMS

Anything but Typical

Nora Raleigh Baskin

disability studies

autism AND disability studies

Nora Raleigh Baskin AND Anything but Typical

Nora Raleigh Baskin AND young-adult fiction

young-adult fiction

Jason Blake AND Anything but Typical

defense mechanisms

A Fine Balance

ROHINTON MISTRY

1995

Rohinton Mistry is an Indian Parsi writer now living in Canada. His second novel, *A Fine Balance* (1995), is set primarily in Bombay (Mumbai), India, and covers the state of emergency (1975–1977) declared by Indira Gandhi, through which she became a virtual dictator. Depicting the lives of four main characters who help each other survive the hardship experienced during this time, Mistry shows a broad spectrum of Indian society in fine realistic detail, from the city to a small village to a mountain hill station.

Dina Dalal is a Parsi widow living in a run-down Bombay flat. She must take in a student border, Maneck, and two tailors from the Untouchable caste, Om and Ishvar, to work in her home business. With the help of young Maneck, Dina learns to overcome her prejudice against the lower-caste men, sympathizing with their terrible history. Mistry is not a sensationalist, but he does not withhold the tragic facts and details about the atrocities against the Untouchables and the terrorism of Gandhi's government.

Mistry's fiction is realistic, set in historical periods or dealing with the postcolonial condition of Indians at home and abroad, having to cope with losing their traditions in modern society. Most of Mistry's plots occur in his native Parsi community in Bombay, focusing on individuals struggling to make sense of a world fragmenting around them. Mistry is known for his humanistic plea for tolerance and human solidarity. He is

Rohinton Mistry (© *John Li* / *Getty Images Entertainment* / *Getty Images*)

now recognized as a major migrant author of Canada, and his works have been translated into many world languages.

AUTHOR BIOGRAPHY

Mistry was born in Mumbai, India, on July 3, 1952, to Parsi parents, Behram Mistry, who worked for an advertising agency, and Freny Mistry. He has two brothers and a sister. The younger brother, Cyrus, is also a writer. Mistry was inspired by Indian art but was more in love with English literature, theater, and movies and American music. He played the guitar and harmonica as a member of a folk-rock band that played the songs of Leonard Cohen, Bob Dylan, and Simon and Garfunkel. Mistry is fluent in Hindi, Gujarati, and English.

Mistry earned a degree in mathematics and economics from Bombay (Mumbai) University in 1973. In 1975, he migrated to Canada to join his fiancée, Freny Elavia, in Toronto, where they married the same year. He worked in a Toronto bank before returning to school at the University of Toronto to study English and philosophy. There he won two Hart House literary prizes. He published a collection of short stories, *Tales from Firozsha Baag*, in 1987. His three subsequent novels, *Such a Long Journey* (1991), *A Fine Balance* (1995), and *Family Matters* (2002), were all short-listed for the prestigious Man Booker Prize. *Such a Long Journey* was made into a 1998 film. Mistry published *The Scream*, a collection of short fiction, in 2006. He is noted for his realistic portraits of India and of Parsi life in both India and Canada.

In 2002, Mistry cancelled a US book tour when he and his wife were racially profiled at airports. The recipient of numerous literary awards, he is now considered one of Canada's best-known writers.

PLOT SUMMARY

Prologue

A Fine Balance opens in the year 1975, in Bombay, India, although the city is not named. When the train arrives with Parsi student Maneck Kohlah, he is jostled in the sudden stop by two Hindu men, forty-six-year-old Ishvar Darji and his teenaged nephew, Omprakash Darji. The Darjis are tailors from a small village seeking work in the city. The train has stopped because another body has been found on the tracks. A passenger says that perhaps the apparent suicide is connected to the state of emergency that the prime minister has declared. The country is in trouble.

Maneck asks the tailors for directions to the address he has, and they find they have the same address. All three seek the home of Parsi widow Dina Dalal. Maneck will board with her, and the tailors seek her for employment. Maneck tells them of his home in the northern mountains, and the tailors speak of their village by a river. The widow answers the door to her shabby and small flat. She is still beautiful and tells the tailors they will sew dresses for an order she has arranged with an export firm. Now she will not have to ask her brother for financial help.

Chapter I: City by the Sea

This chapter tells of Dina Dalal's background as she grew up in Bombay (Mumbai) before Indian independence from Britain. She was the daughter

MEDIA ADAPTATIONS

- An abridged audiobook of *A Fine Balance*, read by Madhur Jaffrey, was released by Random House Audio in 2002 (six hours on four cassettes). Jaffrey is an Indian actress whose voice is raspy, but she reads Dina's part well. This version omits some of the worst violence.

- An unabridged version of *A Fine Balance*, parts 1 and 2, is read by John Lee on Books on Tape, 2002 (part 1, fifteen hours on ten cassettes; part 2, ten and a half hours on seven cassettes). John Lee's dignified delivery and character dialects make listening to this version, with its complete texture, an epic experience.

- In 2006, *A Fine Balance* was adapted as a play by Kristine Landon-Smith and Sudha Buchar and directed by Kristine Landon-Smith for the Tamasha Theatre Company in association with Hampstead Theatre in London. The life and feeling of the novel are preserved but liberated from the page in a series of scenes going back and forth from Dina's apartment, a central refuge from the gigantic backdrop of Indira Gandhi's India.

of Dr. Shroff, who died of a cobra bite he received while treating the poor in the surrounding villages. Nusswan, Dina's older brother, renounced his father's profession for business. The idealistic doctor dies when Dina is twelve, after which Mrs. Shroff declines and withdraws, leaving Dina under the care of her tyrannical brother. He makes her do all the housework and intimidates her through their Parsi religion, but she is rebellious and defies him. Nusswan tries to make Dina marry the Parsi man of his choice, but she finds her own husband, Rustom Dalal, at a library concert. They spend three happy years together before he dies on their third anniversary.

Nusswan tries to make Dina remarry, but she stays in her flat and supports herself through

sewing. When her eyes go bad, she becomes a contractor for Mrs. Gupta's Au Revoir Exports, hiring her own tailors to produce dresses on consignment. The Darjis arrive with their sewing machines as Maneck arrives to rent her bedroom.

Chapter II: For Dreams to Grow

The action returns to the present in 1975. Mrs. Gupta praises Prime Minister Indira Gandhi for declaring the "Internal Emergency," which throws parliamentary members and thousands of dissidents into prison. Dina gives the patterns she receives to the Darjis, who sew secretly in her back room because it is illegal for Dina to have a business in her flat. Dina is disgusted by the smells and habits of the low-caste tailors and gives them separate dishes. The Darjis do not discuss their extreme poverty and suffering with Dina, a higher-class Parsi lady. The Muslim rent collector, Ibrahim, has had a hard life and is forced to earn his money by threatening Dina and other tenants for the landlord. She hides the tailors, locking them in when she delivers the dresses so they will not spy on her source of business.

Chapter III: In a Village by the River

Chapter III recounts the tailors' story. Their family belongs to the Chamaar caste of tanners and leatherworkers, one of the groups of Untouchables, called that because they are a caste that does the dirty work of society. Dukhi Mochi has two sons, Narayan and Ishvar. He decides to give them a better life by apprenticing them to a Muslim tailor in a nearby town so they can raise their caste status. This has never been done, for the village operates as it has for millennia, by the arbitrary rule of the Brahmins (priests) and landowners. The Chamaars are essentially slaves, beaten and punished for any real or imaginary crossing over caste lines. Mahatma Gandhi has preached against the idea of Untouchability, but it is still a force in the villages, even after independence.

Ishvar and Narayan become tailors under the guidance of the Muslim, Ashraf. Because they are literate and earn money, they become leaders in the village. When Narayan tries to vote in an election, the landowner tortures and kills him and burns his whole family alive in their house. Ishvar and Narayan's son, Omprakash, escape because they work for Ashraf and are not at home. Ashraf gives them a reference so they can move to the city.

Chapter IV: Small Obstacles

The tailors rent a place in a slum of tin huts where they share a single outside faucet with hundreds of others and use the railroad tracks for a latrine. Rajaram the hair collector becomes their friend and guide. They meet Monkey-man, who does a circus act with monkeys on the street. The Darjis can get a food ration card only if they agree to have a vasectomy (an operation that makes a man unable to father children), a new government policy. They refuse because Om wants to get married. Om is depressed because of the loss of his family and the terrible conditions of the city. He is very thin and suffers from hunger, worms, and lice.

Chapter V: Mountains

Maneck thinks Dina's flat is shabby; worms crawl out of the shower drain. He is homesick for the mountains where he grew up happy with his family. His Parsi father owns a general store, and in the basement he makes his own soda, Kohlah's Cola, from a secret recipe. Maneck wants to help his father in the store and get his approval, but he makes Maneck feel rejected. The countryside becomes commercially developed, and large corporations move in with soft drinks that drive Kohlah's Cola off the market. Maneck is sent to the city to learn refrigeration and air conditioning but falls into a lifelong depression because of being separated from his family and beloved mountains.

On the train, Maneck meets Vasantrao Valmik, a proofreader who gives Maneck his philosophy of success: "You have to maintain a fine balance between hope and despair." Maneck is shocked by the violent and dirty life in the city and in the student hostel. His neighbor, Avinash, a student from a low-class mill family, becomes his friend and teaches him chess. Avinash is a student leader and tries to get Maneck interested in politics. Maneck leaves the filthy hostel for Dina's flat.

Chapter VI: Day at the Circus, Night in the Slum

The police arrive and force the slum dwellers into buses for a meeting with the prime minister. They are promised a free snack for attending the political rally. In a field on the outskirts of the city, thousands of poor people wait for Indira Gandhi, who comes by helicopter to tell them about the twenty-point emergency program that will eliminate slums and provide birth control.

When the people are returned to their neighborhood, Monkey-man's hungry dog has killed and partially eaten his monkeys. Monkey-man is hysterical and tries to kill the dog. An old woman predicts that the murder of the dog is not the worst crime Monkey-man will commit.

Maneck is upset to learn that Avinash has disappeared, hiding out until political pressure is off. Dina shows Maneck the quilt she has started from scraps. She lectures him not to mingle with the lower-caste tailors. The next day, however, Maneck has lunch with the tailors, who are becoming his friends. They introduce him to the legless beggar Shankar. In the slum, Monkey-man finally kills his dog and then replaces the monkeys in his act with his sister's two children.

Chapter VII: On the Move

Dina and Maneck argue over caste distinctions, and Maneck tells her that he was brought up by his parents to be liberal. Ishvar and Om's slum hut has been destroyed by bulldozers in the city beautification plan. They ask Dina if they can sleep on her verandah, but she refuses, to the disgust of Maneck, who thinks she is prejudiced. The tailors bribe a night watchman to let them sleep in a shop doorway, joining many other people living on the streets. The next night, Maneck goes with them to see where they are sleeping. Rajaram the hair collector visits them to borrow money. He has become a "Motivator for Family Planning," trying to talk men into getting vasectomies.

Chapter VIII: Beautification

All the pavement dwellers, including Om and Ishvar, are gathered up in the night and transported by truck to a work camp. The homeless are sold to a developer to dig ditches or carry gravel for new roads. They get room, board, and clothes but are no more than slaves. The tailors become very ill. Om and Ishvar befriend Shankar, the legless beggar, who cannot work but who tends to the sick, moving around on his cart. Maneck finds out from the night watchman what happened and berates Dina for not taking care of her workers. Now a consignment is due, and Dina's business will fail. Maneck takes off from school and helps her finish the dresses. Then he tells her the story of how the tailors' family was murdered in their village for trying to get out of the Untouchable caste. Her faith in God is shaken at such injustice.

Chapter IX: What Law There Is

Dina searches for new tailors but has no luck. Ibrahim the rent collector dislikes his job but has to keep threatening Dina. She is forced into borrowing money from her brother, Nusswan.

There are fights in the labor camp between the beggars and the paid workers. The management brings in entertainment in the evening. Monkey-man arrives with his new act using his niece and nephew in dangerous balancing stunts on a pole. Finally, Shankar's owner, Beggarmaster, comes to fetch his favorite beggar. He offers to buy all the injured street people to use in his begging syndicate. Shankar talks Beggarmaster into bringing the tailors. He agrees on the condition that they will pay him a monthly fee. Monkey-man is comatose from an injury, so Beggarmaster takes the two children.

Chapter X: Sailing under One Flag

Beggarmaster delivers the tailors to Dina's house and becomes their protector because they pay him. Dina finally offers to let the tailors live with her. They are excellent cooks and make the flat into a home. They become a family, working together on Dina's quilt. Rajaram visits again, asking for money. In the tailors' trunk, he stores the hair he collects to sell.

Chapter XI: The Bright Future Clouded

Maneck and Om become close and spend their vacation time together. Ibrahim gives Dina a final notice to vacate. When she threatens a lawsuit, the landlord's goondas, or thugs, trash the flat. Ibrahim breaks down watching this violence and sobs, asking forgiveness. Dina says she will stay and fight.

Chapter XII: Trace of Destiny

Beggarmaster offers protection to Dina because his clients live there. His goondas attack the landlord's goondas, and the landlord is forced to give Dina money to cover her damages. She is able to continue her business. Beggarmaster informs them of the bizarre murder of two of his beggars. Their long hair was removed. Om and Ishvar immediately suspect Rajaram.

On another visit, Beggarmaster tells the story of one of his beggars with her nose cut off. As she lay dying, she admitted that Beggarmaster's father was also the father of Shankar, making the two of them brothers. Beggarmaster does not know whether to tell Shankar this news,

because he is the one who mutilated him to make him into a beggar.

Chapter XIII: Weddings, Worms, and Sanyas

Ishvar begins to pressure Om that it is time for them to return to their village so he can get married. Dina tries to dissuade them, but it is a religious duty that Ishvar takes seriously as Om's uncle. He writes to Ashraf, who arranges a meeting with four interested families in their village. Dina prepares the verandah for the newlyweds. Rajaram comes to ask for money and admits to Om and Ishvar that he killed the two murdered beggars for their hair. The tailors give him money so he can escape.

Chapter XIV: Return of Solitude

Maneck prepares to leave after graduation, and the tailors prepare to leave for their village. They all work on the quilt together. Meanwhile, Beggarmaster tries to make up for Shankar's hard life by spoiling him. He hires a barber named Rajaram to give him a shave. Shankar starts screaming when Rajaram wants to cut his long hair. Shankar produces two long plaits given to him by the tailors from Rajaram's collection. People assume Shankar is the killer of the beggars, and as Rajaram quietly slips away, they chase Shankar on his cart until he loses control, sails out into traffic, and is killed.

Maneck goes to his old student hostel to give back Avinash's chess set but instead finds his grieving parents, who tell him that Avinash is dead. He was taken by the police and tortured for his political activities. Maneck is shaken. As he studies for his final exam, Beggarmaster comes to tell of the death of Shankar. Maneck and Dina agree to go to the cremation. The funeral procession is like a freak show of beggars.

Chapter XV: Family Planning

Ishvar and Om stay with Ashraf as they prepare for Om's wedding. They find out Thakur Dharamsi, the landowner who killed their family, is in charge of the new family planning center. He makes money on all the sterilizations performed in the villages. On market day in the town, Dharamsi's men and the police begin to abduct people at random for sterilization. In the panic, Ashraf is hit on the head by the police and dies. Ishvar and Om are taken to the camp, where they are forced to have vasectomies on the eve of Om's wedding. Ishvar is sobbing, for it means the end of their family line and the end of all their hopes. Dharamsi does not stop at this, however. He orders a full castration to be done on Om. Ishvar takes care of Om as he recovers, but he himself suffers from blood poisoning because the surgeon used unclean tools. Eventually his legs have to be amputated. Om pulls Ishvar around on a cart. They return to the city as beggars.

Chapter XVI: The Circle Is Completed

Dina waits in vain for the bride and groom. She has completed the quilt for a wedding present. A letter comes from Maneck saying he will not be coming back to the city because he has a job in Dubai in refrigeration. Monkey-man comes to ask where Beggarmaster lives, and Dina tells him.

Ibrahim visits and says he is no longer the rent collector; he has been fired and has become a beggar. Dina gives him food and money. He has heard that Beggarmaster was killed by Monkey-man in revenge for taking his niece and nephew and making maimed beggars of them. Ibrahim tells her this means she no longer has protection. He advises her to go to court to get an injunction against the landlord. Dina finds a lawyer at the courthouse who turns out to be Vasantrao Valmik. In the end, she has to give up her flat and move back with her brother, becoming his housekeeper.

Epilogue: 1984

Maneck returns to India for his father's funeral after eight years in Dubai. The taxi driver is a disguised Sikh, terrified of the killing spree against Sikhs after the assassination of Indira Gandhi by her Sikh bodyguards. When Maneck reaches his home in the mountains, he decides he can no longer live there. He returns to the city to visit Dina and the tailors. He meets Rajaram again, now transformed into the fake holy man Bal Baba, who tells fortunes by touching peoples' hair. When he finds her at her brother's house, she tells the story of Ishvar and Om. They have become beggars, but they come once a day to the house when her brother is gone, and she cooks them a meal. Maneck is so shocked he leaves the house and pretends not to recognize the altered Om and Ishvar as they pass him in the street. At the train station, he throws himself under a train in despair. In the house, Dina and the tailors laugh and chat about old times.

CHARACTERS

Ashraf

Ashraf is Dukhi's Muslim friend, a tailor to whom the Untouchable Dukhi apprentices his sons, Narayan and Ishvar, so they can escape their caste. Ashraf becomes a second father to Narayan and Ishvar, who save him and his family during Partition. Ashraf gives Om and Ishvar a reference so they can escape to the city after their family is killed. He himself is killed during a market raid.

Avinash

Avinash is Maneck's friend at college who teaches him chess and then mysteriously disappears during the state of emergency because he is a student activist. Avinash is from a poor mill family and is supposed to be studying to get a better job so he can provide dowries for his three sisters.

Beggarmaster

Beggarmaster is the half brother of Shankar and also the boss of a network of beggars. He gives protection to Dina and the tailors from their landlord. Beggarmaster is a powerful underworld criminal yet has tender feelings about his beggars. He is killed by Monkey-man in revenge for stealing his niece and nephew and mutilating them for his beggar network.

Dina Dalal

Dina (Shroff) Dalal is one of the four main characters, a Parsi widow in her forties who tries to maintain her independence by sewing dresses for an export company. She takes in the other three main characters (Maneck, Ishvar, and Om) as tenants in her city flat. Constantly short of money and harassed by the landlord for having a business, she challenges every curb to her freedom. Dina has a sharp mind but was denied an education by her brother, Nusswan, who wants to make her into a subservient Parsi wife, married to a man he chooses. Instead Dina rebels against her brother, chooses her own husband, maintains herself, and does not give in until she has nothing left. Even as a servant in her brother's house, she secretly cooks for her beggar friends and lets them in when he is gone. Dina is stiff and fearful until Maneck and the tailors loosen her up. She is basically good and generous, even turning around and giving charity to the rent collector who has hassled her.

Rustom Dalal

Rustom Dalal is Dina's late husband. Her brother tried to arrange her marriage, but she chose Rustom herself. They were happy together until he died on their third wedding anniversary.

Thakur Dharamsi

Thakur Dharamsi is a brutal landowner who kills Om's family and is later in charge of the village family planning and its enforced castrations. He singles out the Darjis for punishment for daring to cross caste lines.

Ishvar Darji

Ishvar Darji, the forty-six-year-old son of Dukhi Mochi, is a tailor from a village who lodges with Dina in the city and works for her. He is one of the main characters, a patient and kindly man who has tried to raise himself from the Untouchable caste. His strong sense of family and religious duty make him risk everything to take his nephew, Om, back to the village to get married. That proves his undoing. He is sterilized and loses his legs from gangrene after the operation. He ends as a beggar. Generous to a fault, Ishvar befriends beggars and even a killer (Rajaram), loaning him money he cannot afford. Ishvar is a restraining influence on Om's youthful energy.

Narayan Darji

Narayan Darji is the older brother of Ishvar and the father of Om, who became a tailor and returned to the village as a literate man. He leads other Untouchables in demanding their right to vote and is killed by the landowner, Thakur Dharamsi.

Omprakash Darji

Omprakash "Om" Darji is one of the main characters and Ishvar's seventeen-year-old nephew. He is a tailor working for Dina. He is angry and rebellious because of the persecution and deaths of his family members. Om is always looking at pretty women. He feels he cannot marry because of his poverty and misfortune, but Ishvar works hard to provide for his future, even arranging for four families in the village as prospective in-laws. Om is tragically singled out by Thakur Dharamsi not only for sterilization but also for castration. This ends Om's chances for a normal life and for continuing the family line.

Mrs. Gupta

Mrs. Gupta is the owner of Au Revoir Exports. She hires Dina to sew pattern dresses for export. She is conservative and defends Indira Gandhi's policies during the state of emergency.

Ibrahim

Ibrahim is the old Muslim rent collector, who cannot make enough money to hold his family together. He tries to have Dina thrown out for having a business and extra lodgers in her apartment. He is miserable in his job and finally can no longer do it when he sees the thugs destroy Dina's apartment. After he is fired and begging on the street, Dina gives him some money and sympathy.

Aban Kohlah

Aban Kohlah is Maneck's mother.

Farokh Kohlah

Farokh Kohlah is Maneck's father.

Maneck Kohlah

Maneck Kohlah is one of the main characters. He is a young Parsi from the mountains who comes to the city for college and lodges with Dina. Maneck is a sensitive and good young man, treating the tailors as equal and befriending Om and Avinash, both poor boys. Maneck teaches Dina not to have caste prejudice and to open her heart. Maneck's own father misunderstands his son's need to help him in the store; he feels threatened. Although he loves Maneck, he sends him away to school and to Dubai for a job. Maneck feels rejected and depressed most of his life. He cannot find the family he needs and is forced to live away from his beloved mountains. Losing faith, he commits suicide after he sees what happens to all his friends.

Madam

Madam refers to the prime minister, Mrs. Indira Gandhi. Mrs. Gandhi declared the country to be in a state of internal emergency from 1975 to 1977 so she could suspend all civil rights and rule as a dictator. The novel ends with her assassination in 1984 by her Sikh bodyguards.

Dukhi Mochi

Dukhi Mochi is an Untouchable leatherworker who apprentices his sons, Ishvar and Narayan, to become tailors so they can move into a higher caste. Dukhi and most of his family are murdered by the landowner when Narayan tries to vote in an election.

Monkey-man

Monkey-man is one of the slum neighbors of Om and Ishvar. He makes a living with his monkey act on the street. When his dog kills the monkeys, he substitutes his young niece and nephew in his act. He kills Beggarmaster for crippling the children to use as beggars.

Rajaram

Rajaram is a sinister character, a hair collector who sells the hair he finds and becomes a friend to Om and Ishvar when they move to the slum. Afterward he becomes Bal Baba, a phony holy man. He murders two of Beggarmaster's beggars for their long hair and gets money from Om and Ishvar to change his appearance and identity.

Shankar

Shankar is a crippled beggar, also known as Worm, a friend of Ishvar's and Om's. Shankar has a generous heart, despite his lack of legs and hands. He takes care of the sick in the labor camp by taking them food on his cart. Beggarmaster never gets a chance to tell him that they are brothers. Shankar is chased by a crowd and killed in traffic.

Dr. Shroff

Dr. Shroff is Dina's father. He died of a snake bite when Dina was twelve years old.

Mrs. Shroff

Mrs. Shroff is Dina's mother. After her husband's death, she suffered a rapid decline and left Dina to the care of her unkind brother.

Nusswan Shroff

Nusswan Shroff is Dina's bullying brother, a bigoted businessman who raised her after their parents died. By the end of the novel, she has to move in with him, becoming his servant or housekeeper.

Vasantrao Valmik

Vasantrao Valmik is the old proofreader and lawyer who gives advice about life to Maneck on the train as he travels to the city. He is also Dina's legal adviser. Eventually he is a staff member for the sham guru, Bal Baba.

Worm

See Shankar

THEMES

Loss

Vasantrao Valmik tells Dina Dalal his philosophy about the current state of affairs in India: "I'm inspired by the poet Yeats. I find his words especially relevant during this shameful Emergency. You know—things falling apart, centre not holding." Dina replies with Maneck's favorite saying, "And everything ends badly." In terms of the country and in terms of the main characters, loss is the main principle of life. They start life with promise, and that hope is steadily eroded, as though life is all downhill.

Dina is a bright and spirited girl, denied an education. As a widow, she fights for independence, but inch by inch she loses every gain, until she ends up as a dependent servant in her brother's house. Maneck has a happy childhood in the mountains, but his father, embittered by the loss of the mountains as developers destroy them, sends Maneck away to school to prepare him for the modern world. Maneck is deprived of home and parental love but also loses his hope in the city as he sees his friends Avinash, Dina, Om, and Ishvar destroyed by poverty and injustice. He throws away his own life, unable to bear the constant loss around him. The loss suffered by Ishvar and Om is never-ending because of their caste status as Untouchables. Ibrahim loses his entire family, his faith, and then his job. Even the minor characters—Avinash and his family, Beggarmaster, Shankar, Monkey-man, and Ashraf—all lose their lives, freedom, or loved ones.

Decay

Mistry is well known for his theme of decay. Moral decay is illustrated by physical decay. He dwells on gruesome sights and smells, such as the way the poor live in the slum, going to the toilet on the railroad tracks, the way the worms come up in Dina's shower drain, or how she gets rid of Om's worms and lice. The narrative focuses on Ishvar's facial scar, his legs turning black and needing amputation, and how the urine of the tailors smells to Dina.

Mutilation is a subcategory under decay. Many characters undergo some kind of mutilation. The tailors suffer vasectomies and castration. We hear of the punishments imposed on Untouchables in the village, such as hands being cut off. Beggars have noses and limbs cut off. Many bodies are found on the railroad tracks.

TOPICS FOR FURTHER STUDY

- Watch the movie *Slumdog Millionaire* (2008) and compare the scenes with those presented in the novel *A Fine Balance*. Are the modern scenes of slums and poverty similar to those in the novel, or has Bombay (Mumbai) changed since the Emergency in 1975? Do slum dwellers have more chance to rise in class status? Using film clips and excerpts from the novel, explain your conclusions to a group. Students should note that this film is rated R for violence and language.

- Do a group presentation using PowerPoint or slides on the religions of India, including the four mentioned in the book: Hindu, Muslim, Parsi (Zoroastrianism), and Sikh. Use the Internet for your research. How do these religions differ? What are their beliefs?

- Find relevant websites showing how Mahatma Gandhi was able to unify the diversity of Indian cultures around the issue of independence from Britain. Use a social bookmarking service such as Delicious.com to share your results. On a large screen, share sample websites and your conclusions with the class.

- Although Parsi writers like Mistry have been influenced by British literature, the English were equally fascinated by Persian literature. Victorian author Edward Fitzgerald did a famous translation of the *Rubaiyat* of the medieval Persian philosopher and poet Omar Khayyam. Write a report on the *Rubaiyat* and read aloud your favorite verses, explaining the philosopher's view of life.

- Read *The Absolutely True Diary of a Part-Time Indian* (2007), by Sherman Alexie, a young-adult book dealing with racism, poverty, and tradition, which won the National Book Award. Just as the Darjis leave their village for the city, so does the young hero of Alexie's novel leave his reservation to make a life in the wider world. In a group discussion, compare and contrast how Alexie makes his points against prejudice with satiric humor while Mistry makes his points using tragedy, giving specific examples of each. In your opinion, which mode, tragic or comic, is most effective for expanding the reader's awareness about the negative effects of class and race prejudice?

- Make an online wiki explaining the parallels between the tyranny of Indira Gandhi's Emergency in India in 1975 and the takeover of Chile by General Augusto Pinochet in 1971. How were the tactics similar? What were the fates of dissidents, artists, intellectuals, and students? Did these dictators permanently scar their countries, or were India and Chile able to recover and move to more democratic forms of government? Gather web pages, references to books, photos, interviews, and cultural background about each country that will make these historical periods vivid.

Dina's husband's body is crushed in a bicycle accident, and Shankar is killed by his cart rolling into traffic. The government bulldozes the slum homes of the poor.

Valmik tells Dina, "Our society is decaying from the top downwards." Corruption in the government is matched by corruption of human bodies. In the last scene, Maneck sees the once beautiful Dina old and haggard, Om as a fat and bloated eunuch, and the legless Ishvar pulled around on a cart. It is a tragic tale with life coming apart at the seams.

Hope

Throughout the novel, there are moments of hope, and most of them are centered on human fellowship. Avinash, the poor mill boy, takes Maneck under his wing and teaches him chess. The upperclass Dina relents and lets the Untouchables live with her. Ishvar and Om turn out to be excellent

Dina tries to distance herself from the government and political issues but finds herself reflecting on her position. (© MartiniDry | Shutterstock.com)

cooks and delight Dina and Maneck with their company. Dina's heart expands; she lets in a cat from the alley to have its kittens. Dina makes a quilt from the scraps of her dressmaking work. Soon Maneck, Om, and Ishvar, all living as a family, help her piece it together, representing the harmony of disparate lives.

India is made up of many castes and religions. Despite the politics of division in the country, it is suggested that society is actually held together with human sympathy and cooperation. The Muslim tailor Ashraf helps the Hindu outcastes Narayan and Ishvar to become tailors. In return, they risk their lives to save their Muslim friend and benefactor during Partition. Shankar has no hands or legs, but he cares for the sick in the work camp. Human love and kindness are shown to be the only antidote to the arbitrary cruelty of Indira Gandhi's government and the forces of decay at work in the country, providing hope in a story that includes much tragedy.

STYLE

Realistic Social Novel

The portrait of the chaotic city during the Emergency in *A Fine Balance* has been compared to the writing of Anton Chekhov and Charles Dickens in terms of irony, satire, and grotesque underworld characters. Mistry claims *A Fine Balance* is a faithful record of Mrs. Gandhi's Emergency. Realism purports to represent the social and personal stories of people with historical accuracy. Mistry gives details of modern Indian life mixed with its traditional customs and phrases. The novel has an omniscient narrator who quickly and deftly switches to the points of view of various characters and back and forth to other time periods such as independence and the Partition.

Realism is thought by many Indian writers to be a politically conservative style, the favored technique of the British colonial authors. Mistry, however, is able to show a complex and diverse society full of contradictions, striving to remain coherent through human sympathy. Mistry's prose is polished and economical. The injustice he portrays is all the more shocking because the narrator presents incidents in an objective, unemotional tone. Mistry has been likened to Dickens and Leo Tolstoy in being able to produce individual portraits against large social canvases. He has been accused, however, of being unable to draw female characters. In *A Fine Balance*, he has answered that charge with his portrait of Dina Dalal.

Modern Indian Novel in English

Since India gained its independence in 1947, its writers have used the novel as an artistic vehicle to express the contemporary condition of their country. There are many native languages in India, but English, the language of their former oppressor, Great Britain, has the advantage of being a common second language for India's millions. Through the novel in English, writers from diverse backgrounds and languages have been able to share their visions and memories of India.

When Salman Rushdie published *Midnight's Children* in 1981, for which he won the Booker Prize, he produced a new art form, the modern Indian novel. The name of his novel refers to the children born after Indian independence into a different world than traditional India and has stuck as a name for a whole generation. This type of novel has been used by many famous writers in the last twenty-five years and includes such works as Arundhati Roy's *The God of Small Things* (1996) and Anita Desai's *Fasting, Feasting* (1999). These novels are all in English, and although they use traditional references, they are secular in emphasis (without a particular religious bias), speaking of colonial or postcolonial (after independence in 1947) events. They probe the political, psychological, and historical confusion of a people who are both traditional and modern at the same time. Because they write in English, these novelists have a world audience.

Rohinton Mistry is inevitably compared in style to Salman Rushdie, who, like Mistry, settled in the West and wrote about Bombay during the Emergency. Rushdie's *Midnight's Children* (1981) depicts Bombay in a postmodern fantastic style. Rushdie's style became the standard for modern Indian fiction, and so Mistry is seen as out of tune with contemporary Indian fiction writers. Much of today's Indian fiction uses magical realism (unexplained magical elements in everyday life) and mythic symbolism derived from traditional Indian forms of storytelling. Like Rushdie, these authors write about history from an Indian perspective. Mistry makes references to the Indian legacy, but these references are embedded in realistic storytelling and do not inform the style itself. He thus reinforces the charge that the Parsis are the group most tied to the British Raj, even to the point of imitating British writing.

Postcolonial Fiction

Postcolonial literature deals with issues of decolonization after European colonial rule. Racial inequality, modernization, and cultural domination are frequent themes. Postcolonial fiction chronicles the history of cultural stereotypes, the history of colonization, the loss of culture, and the suffering of minorities. Mistry's *Tales of Firozsha Baag*, for instance, looks at Parsis, both in India and Canada, who face a transition to the modern world. Other postcolonial novels include Columbian Gabriel Garcia Marquez's *One Hundred Years of Solitude* (1967), Indian V. S. Naipaul's *A Bend in the River* (1989), and Chilean Isabel Allende's *The House of Spirits* (1982).

In addition, Mistry is one of the many postcolonial writers classified as part of a cultural diaspora, or dispersal. Twice displaced, his ancestors came from the Persian diaspora to India; then he became one of the Indian writers who

emigrated to Canada. Migrant literature explores the difficulties of cultural adjustment or the history of the homeland.

Postcolonial authors usually favor a postmodern style. Postmodernism emphasizes fragmentation, discontinuity, pastiche, irony, magical realism, hybridity (a mixture of styles), and self-conscious narration. Mistry's realism is thus seen as old-fashioned by postcolonial critics. In his defense, however, Mistry does undercut realism by ironically showing the devastation of colonial history on India. He shows the hybrid or mixed cultural nature of the postcolonial condition. He experiments with Indianized English. Words from several Indian languages (Hindi, Gujarati, Parsi, and Marathi) are sprinkled throughout the narrative without translation.

HISTORICAL CONTEXT

Persian Migration to India

The Parsis, represented by the characters of Dina Dalal and Maneck Kohlah, are a religious group mostly in and around Bombay (Mumbai), India. They are descended from Zoroastrians who emigrated from Iran after the Muslim conquest between the eighth and ninth centuries CE. The Parsis were allowed to settle in Gujarat as farmers and traders. Their religion was founded by the prophet Zoroaster, or Zarathustra, five or six centuries before Christ. The religion is monotheistic, calling God "Ahura Mazda," the light that fights the darkness of the devil, Angra Mainyu (or Ahriman). Ordinary people are called on to choose the good to assist the struggle of good against evil.

Colonial India

The British East India Company was given permission by a Mughal emperor in 1617 to trade in India. In protecting its trading interests, Britain used more and more military force, until it took over large areas of India and its administration, with the cooperation of local rulers. In 1857, after the rebellious Indian Mutiny, the English Crown took over the whole country, adding India to its empire. The upper Hindu and Muslim classes of India lost their traditional power, and in order to gain advancement in the new system of the British Raj, Indians had to have an English education and training to get positions. In this situation, the Parsis rose to the top of the social ladder because of their lighter skin

COMPARE
&
CONTRAST

- **1970s:** Bombay, the setting of the story, is a large modern city with suburbs and a population of millions. It is the financial capital of India and the capital of India's film industry, Bollywood.

  Today: Bombay is renamed Mumbai in 1996 and is the largest city in the world and the fourth-largest urban agglomeration. It gets world attention through the film *Slumdog Millionaire* and terrorist attacks on the city.

- **1970s:** Women like Dina Dalal are struggling to break away from traditional roles to have careers and more independent lives.

  Today: Middle-class Indian women are expected to have higher degrees and be in the workforce, like their Western counterparts.

- **1970s:** The atrocities committed against Untouchables, or Dalits, as depicted in *A Fine Balance*, are commonplace, despite the fact that untouchability was outlawed in the 1950 Indian constitution.

  Today: Atrocities against the Untouchables are still common and go unpunished, even though they are widely reported in newspapers and banned by the Prevention of Atrocities Act of 1989. Now, however, there is a Dalit human rights movement fighting back, and the international Human Rights Watch reports such crimes.

- **1970s:** The Parsi Zoroastrians of India, once powerful because of their alliance with the British colonial government, are declining in numbers, influence, and wealth after the British leave.

  Today: The decline of Parsi numbers continues; in addition, there is a crisis of faith caused by the strict Parsi ban against intermarriage and the traditional method of burial of the dead in the Towers of Silence (where bodies are devoured by vultures). Many Parsis emigrate to the West.

---

and identification with Western ways. They became wealthy bankers, businessmen, professionals, and philanthropists, responsible for the establishment of many cultural and charitable institutions in Bombay.

India's Independence

From the 1920s, leaders such as Mohandas Gandhi sought to break the colonial bondage. Gandhi taught the people to boycott English products and used the principle of nonviolence to protest the presence of the British. He preached against caste discrimination, and he was able to unify all the religious factions of India, particularly the Hindus and Muslims. Independence was granted in 1947, with the traumatic Partition of the country into Muslim Pakistan and Hindu India, referred to in the novel when the Darji brothers save their Muslim friend, Ashraf. India today is a secular multicultural democracy, including the Hindu, Muslim, Jain, Sikh, Parsi, and Buddhist religions.

Although Parsis loyally took part in the independence movement, once the British left, they lost their status and were looked down on as British collaborators by the Hindus and Muslims.

Indira Gandhi and the Emergency

Mistry paints an unsympathetic portrait of Indira Gandhi, the daughter of the first Indian president, Jawaharlal Nehru. She became the Indian prime minister in 1966. In 1975, she was found guilty of electoral corruption and was asked to step down. She responded by declaring a national state of emergency, claiming the country was in danger. She took control of the government, threw all opposition leaders in jail, suspended civil liberties, and enforced her own policies for two years until she allowed elections in 1977 and was defeated. She again became prime minister in 1980 but was assassinated in 1984 (the year of the novel's epilogue) by her own Sikh bodyguards after attacking their Golden Temple in search of terrorists.

The group of male characters in the novel are from diverse backgrounds but are brought together by the economic crisis called "the emergency." *(© Calvin Chan | Shutterstock.com)*

The scenes of caste violence in *A Fine Balance* are based on conditions in the villages at this time, where landowners like Thakur Dharamsi were still acting as feudal lords toward the lower castes. The four traditional Hindu castes—Brahmins (priests), Kshatriyas (warriors, administrators), Vaisyas (merchants), and Sudras (servants)—are social boundaries still operating in Indian daily life, although the constitution outlaws caste-based discrimination. The Untouchables or Harijans (self-named the Dalits) are the workers who do the dirty work of collecting garbage, attending the dead, and, in the case of Ishvar's family, tanning the hides of dead animals. Their touch is thought to be polluting.

Postcolonial India

The postcolonial nations such as India often exhibit symptoms of displacement, shock, and schizophrenic values, amounting to a modern identity crisis. They cannot go back to the way things were, yet they cannot forget their past. They try democracy without having a history of it. People have to move to the cities where jobs exist; the old extended families and customs break down, as seen in the stories of the Kohlahs in the mountain hill station and the Darjis from the villages. Large corporations displace local economies represented by Kohlah's General Store and local brand of cola and Ashraf's tailor shop. Maneck wants to take over his father's store but must study refrigeration and move to Dubai for a job. The tragic cost and trauma of rapid modernization is pictured in great detail.

CRITICAL OVERVIEW

A Fine Balance, Mistry's second novel, was published in 1995 and won the Commonwealth Writers Prize, Canada's Giller Prize, and the Los Angeles Times Book Prize in Fiction. It was also shortlisted, as was his first novel, for Britain's Man Booker Prize. In addition, Oprah Winfrey selected the book for her television book club and an on-air discussion of the book with the author in 2001.

Although critics continue to debate whether Mistry's style is a sell-out to old-fashioned realism, the reviewers are impressed. The book reviews of 1996 note Mistry's move from his previous fine miniature portraits of India to the epic scope of *A Fine Balance*, reminiscent of nineteenth-century European masters. Brad Hooper for *Booklist* predicts that readers will be gripped by the story, because "for all its length, [the book] does not sprawl." Pico Iyer pronounces the novel "monumental" in a review for *Time*. He calls Mistry "a rigorous humanitarian" who "gives faces and voices to the suffering and takes us into the lives and huts of dirt-poor souls," showing both the positive and negative sides of India. In a *Commonweal* review, David Lodge remarks that the book reminds him of the work of acclaimed French writer Émile Zola in "its harrowing account of life among the poor" and in "touching but unsentimental examples of redeeming human kindness." Aamer Hussein for *New Statesman & Society* gives a Pakistani's response to the novel as "a parable of India's unwieldy pluralism and the chaos it can create." Hussein appreciates the complexity of *A Fine Balance*, pointing out that "in Mistry's universe, nothing is utterly good or bad."

Later reviews, such as W. H. New's in *Journal of Modern Literature* (2000), focus on the tragic elements: "A wrenching tale—one that the reader resists finishing" because it is "inevitable that the characters are doomed." A 2003 *Kliatt* review for young-adult readers calls the book "heart-wrenching, but a revelation of the lives of the world community." Emma Harrow, in the *Bookseller* (2010), finds the book "authentic" but warns that the reader is also forced to walk "a tightrope between hope and despair." *Native Intelligence: Aesthetics, Politics, and Postcolonial Literature* (2003), by Deepika Bahri, is an example of the critical tide turning in Mistry's favor, showing that his realism subverts colonial writing rather than imitating it. Although different from the accepted fantastic fictional model established by Salman Rushdie, Mistry is included in the list of masters of postcolonial fiction.

CRITICISM

Susan Andersen

Andersen has a PhD in English. In the following essay, she explores Rohinton Mistry's moral universe in A Fine Balance.

> IN THE END, ONLY HUMAN KINDNESS AND THE TELLING OF STORIES CAN CREATE A FINE BALANCE IN POSTCOLONIAL INDIA."

Some readers feel that Rohinton Mistry is manipulative with the plot of *A Fine Balance* by ending with Maneck's suicide, but that is not the hardest point of the plot to swallow. The novel ends with a string of deaths and mutilations and defeats as if to prove the truth of the saying so often repeated by Maneck: "Everything ends badly." The headnote Mistry chooses from Honoré de Balzac's *Le Père Goriot*—"But rest assured: this tragedy is not a fiction. All is true"—seems designed to forestall any doubts that the picture painted of Gandhi's Emergency is not exaggerated. The novel's title, *A Fine Balance*, indicates the theme of the story for the main characters. How can one stay balanced in the face of suffering and injustice?

Dina, Ishvar, and Om experience the most extreme setbacks, and yet, at the end, they are still together, helping each other to bear the worst through their love and humor. Maneck, who has had an easier life, is the one who finds it hardest to stay balanced. He discusses this problem with Vasantrao Valmik, the old proofreader he meets on the train. Valmik tells Maneck that in order to survive one cannot give way to anger about the way things are. Maneck's revulsion at the gratuitous suffering of the masses, and particularly of his friends Ishvar, Om, and Avinash, causes him to question God and finally to commit suicide. All the characters are looking for answers, and all give their bits of philosophy. Mistry makes a many-colored quilt of their wisdom, patched from their troubled lives. In the end, only human kindness and the telling of stories can create a fine balance in postcolonial India. The old institutions of religion, family, and politics no longer provide solutions. India is a land of ancient religions, for instance, passionately held and fought over. In the novel, none of them seems adequate to address the suffering of the people. Even Mistry's birth religion, Parsi Zoroastrianism, is criticized in the story as hypocritical: Dina is pinched and

WHAT DO I READ NEXT?

- The young-adult novel *Hullabaloo in the Guava Orchard* (1998), by Indian author Kiran Desai, is a humorous look at the discrepancies of postcolonial life in a small town in India, where a young man who wants to run away from modern confusion, lives in a tree with monkeys and is mistaken for a holy man.

- Sheila Gordon's young-adult novel *Waiting for the Rain* (1996) tells a story of overcoming racial and class prejudice. Tengo, son of black workers on a Dutch colonial farm in the Transvaal in South Africa, befriends the white nephew of the farm's owner. The two grow up together innocently, until they find out as adults they are on opposite sides of the apartheid question.

- *India: A History*, by John Keay (2000), tells of Indian civilization from the ancient cities of the Indus Valley around 2000 BCE to today's computer culture and megacities.

- Pico Iyer's article for *Time International*, "The New Arrival: Rohinton Mistry" (Vol. 160, No. 25, 2002, p. 47), details Mistry's status as one of Canada's most important and best-loved authors.

- *Dr. Ambedkar and Untouchability: Fighting the Indian Caste System*, by Christophe Jaffrelot (2004), is the history of an Untouchable, Dr. Bhimrao Ramji Ambedkar (1891–1956), who rose to become a scholar, activist, journalist, and educator, helping to draft the Indian constitution as law minister in Nehru's first cabinet.

- Mistry's *Swimming Lessons and Other Stories from Firozsha Baag* (1987) is a collection of short stories, including the much anthologized "Swimming Lessons," illustrating the double lives of Indian Parsi immigrants in Toronto.

- Salman Rushdie and Elizabeth West, editors of the important anthology *Mirrorwork: 50 Years of Indian Writing 1947–1997* (1997), present an overview and excerpts of the significant writers in English since Indian independence, including Parsi writers Bapsi Sidhwa and Rohinton Mistry. Rushdie's introduction is a defense of Indian writers using English instead of Indian languages.

- In her novel, *Cracking India* (1991), Pakistani Parsi writer Bapsi Sidhwa tells of the partition of India in 1947 through the eyes of an eight-year-old girl, Lenny Sethi, who lives in Lahore. The book was originally published as *Ice Candy Man* in 1988 (which became the 1998 film *Earth*, directed by Deepa Mehta).

---

fondled by the priest in the Fire Temple, and Nusswan uses the forms of Parsi faith to keep his sister in line. When the Untouchable Dukhi goes to the Hindu Brahmin in the village to complain about his sons being beaten for wanting to go to school, the fat and bloated Brahmin invokes the sacredness of the caste system and claims that the boys have defiled the school with their presence. The Muslim rent collector Ibrahim has become embittered by his miserable life and concludes, "There no longer seemed any point in going to the masjid." He, like Maneck, blames God for imbalances: "Did the Master of the Universe take no interest in levelling the scales—was there no such thing as a fair measure?"

Ibrahim also comments on the danger of wearing the wrong headgear at the wrong time. A fez, white cap, and turban (traditionally worn by Muslim, Hindu, and Sikh, respectively) could mean losing one's head. This is proved in the epilogue when the Sikh cabdriver tries to escape the Sikh slaughter after Indira Gandhi's assassination by shaving and removing his turban to save his life. He warns that the religious war will go on and that one day Maneck may be persecuted for his Parsi belief.

One legacy of the Western lifestyle is that families are falling apart. Maneck wants an old-fashioned life with his family but is sent to the city to work. The Darjis try to continue their family line in the village of their ancestors despite persecution but are forced back to the city to beg. Politics is also not the way to justice and balance. The chapter titled "Day at the Circus, Night in the Slum" points out the gross deception of Gandhi's government, seeming to woo the poor in a political rally, only to enact unjust laws aimed not to alleviate poverty but to wipe out the slums and the poor by bulldozing their shacks, moving them to labor camps, and forcing sterilization. The young idealist Avinash believes that he can organize the students to get better conditions in the hostel. He disappears like thousands of other dissidents, abducted by the police, tortured, and killed. Valmik tells Dina, "The country's leaders have exchanged wisdom and good governance for cowardice and self-aggrandizement." Avinash admits to Maneck that all he does is play chess, because politics has become a dangerous game of chance and power.

The only characters who prosper are Mrs. Gupta and Nusswan Shroff, westernized business people who support Gandhi's economic policies to get rid of the poor by force. There are also some who maintain balance by being shifty opportunists. Rajaram, the hair collector and family planning motivator, literally gets away with murder and becomes the false guru, Bal Baba. In reality, it is Vasantrao Valmik, the former lawyer, proofreader, and political slogan writer, who secretly answers the spiritual questions of Bal Baba's devotees with his glib pen. Valmik and Rajaram know how to move with the times and stay on their feet. Mistry satirically shows this to be a false moral balance.

In *Rohinton Mistry*, Peter Morey points out a paradox in Parsi Zoroastrian belief that shows up in Mistry's work. Zoroastrians are concerned with maintaining the purity of the body, yet in *A Fine Balance* the body is constantly under attack, with dirt, hunger, and, in particular, violent assaults like accidents and mutilations. An even higher ethical ideal for Parsis is to engage with the world rather than to withdraw to protect oneself. Maneck leads Dina out of her protective shell to discover the common humanity of the tailors and the others around her, even if it means sharing their wounds and suffering. Maneck is open to the best in others and never thinks of Om and Ishvar's social status as Untouchables. In this way, Maneck is being a "good Parsi" by following his religion's ethic to be part of the battle against evil.

Zoroastrians conceive the world to be a struggle between the light and dark, good and evil. God (Ahura Mazda) needs the help of every human to fight the evil Satan figure, Ahriman. In *The Good Parsi: The Fate of a Colonial Elite in a Postcolonial Society*, T. M. Luhrmann points out that in the Zoroastrian faith of the Parsis, "*Asha*, cognate with and similar in meaning to *dharma*, is perhaps the most important word in the religion. It evokes a seamless fabric of truth, purity, and goodness." Mistry's Parsi characters, like Maneck, are bewildered in the modern world because these ethics are almost impossible to achieve. Maneck and Dina, like good Parsis and decent people everywhere, engage in benevolent acts and charity to others. Om and Ishvar are also generous despite their tragic lives, threading their way through the city's slum and underworld making friends of beggars (Shankar), criminals (Beggarmaster), and even a killer (Rajaram). Mistry's humanistic plea for tolerance among all groups is a theme in every one of his novels.

Mistry likes to speak of his craft by making the power of language and storytelling into a theme. Stories can be shared to ease suffering and create bonds, or else stories can be imposed on others. At the political rally, propaganda leaflets are dropped from the sky on the poor people, outlining the government's version of what is going on; this only makes the people cynical. On the other hand, when Om and Ishvar share their family's story about the persecution of the Untouchables, class prejudice begins to melt in Dina's heart.

Maneck complains to Dina that God made the giant quilt of life; it is so big it has lost its design, and God has abandoned it. Valmik agrees about the lack of order, saying that, on the one hand, "our lives are but a series of accidents . . . one big calamity" yet "to share the story redeems everything." Dina sees the words of Valmik's narrative like her own patchwork quilt made of the random pieces of life. She and her friends work on their quilt together, tell their stories, and find solace. She believes that "the very act of telling created a natural design" and that this is a human talent for survival.

And what of the design of Mistry's storytelling? In *Rohinton Mistry: An Introduction*, Nandini Bhautoo-Dewnarain defends him as a forward-looking postcolonial author who pushes realism in a new direction. The European realistic novel concerned cultural hierarchies and reinforced class distinctions, but Mistry overturns these hierarchies and focuses on the working class and poor: "Mistry's novels prove to us that realism is not outdated."

Although Mistry does not mine cultural myths the way fantastic storytellers do, he refers to the great Indian and Persian epics in the background, in a sense, rewriting the cultural memory to reflect its tragic demise in the modern world; many postcolonial authors do just this, as explained by Justin Edwards in *Postcolonial Literature: A Reader's Guide to Essential Criticism*. Frequently, Mistry makes indirect references to the tenth-century Persian epic poem *Shah Nameh*, especially in terms of father-son conflicts. In the epic, the hero Rustum ignorantly kills his own son, Sohrab, in battle. In *Such a Long Journey*, Mistry evokes this theme in the fight between Gustad and his son, who is also named Sohrab. In *A Fine Balance*, the stiff and insensitive Farokh Kohlah sends his own child, Maneck, into an exile that will end in his death. Persian, or Parsi, mythology concerns a dualistic battle of good versus evil, and this notion permeates the book. Every time Dina or the tailors make headway, there is an opposing force to bring them down.

The character Valmik brings up the topic of storytelling, explaining to Maneck that he must tell his story to know who he is. Valmiki is the name of the author of the Hindu epic *Ramayana*, which is about the incarnation of Vishnu as the virtuous King Rama. The *Ramayana* ends with Ram Raj, the just rule of King Rama. Valmik sarcastically mentions that present-day India is saddled with "Goonda Raj," the rule of *goondas*, or thugs. Another great Hindu epic, *Mahabharata*, is referred to ironically in the story of the tailors. The *Mahabharata* concerns the great war between two branches of the same royal family that was such a holocaust of destruction it brought about Kaliyuga, the Age of Darkness. The tailors are not epic warriors, but their small everyday battles, and the destruction of their family, are referred to by the cook at the Vishram Hotel as a modern *Mahabharata*.

Finally, *A Fine Balance* can be seen as a postcolonial story because Mistry embraces what Bill

Mumbai, India, like the characters in A Fine Balance, *is diverse.* (© *Nickolay Stanev | Shutterstock.com*)

Ashcroft, Gareth Griffiths, and Helen Tiffin describe in *The Empire Writes Back* as "marginality"—"the fabric of social experience." It is Indira Gandhi who makes a cameo appearance, while the pages of the book chronicle the lives of the people she affects but who do not count: the Untouchables, the beggars and homeless, a widow, a rent collector, a depressed student, a boy from a poor mill family, and criminals like Beggarmaster and Rajaram. Amin Malak, however, makes the ironic point in "From Margin to Main: Minority Discourse and 'Third World' Fiction Writers in Canada" that Mistry, as a migrant minority storyteller in Canada, has moved from the margin to an exalted place of recognition in the mainstream: "The immigrant has arrived!" The success of such postcolonial authors as Mistry demonstrates the power of story to create balance and human fellowship in society.

Source: Susan Andersen, Critical Essay on *A Fine Balance*, in *Novels for Students*, Gale, Cengage Learning, 2013.

"AS WITH THE SOCIAL REALISTS, AT POINTS
MISTRY CAN BE ACCUSED OF BEING OVERLY
ROMANTIC IN HIS PORTRAIT OF POVERTY."

Laura Moss

In the following essay, Moss explores Mistry's realist style, comparing it with the magic realism increasingly evident in South American novels.

On the back cover of the American paperback edition of Rohinton Mistry's recent novel *A Fine Balance*, there is an excerpt from the *New York Times*: "Those who continue to harp on the decline of the novel ought to . . . consider Rohinton Mistry. He needs no infusion of magic realism to vivify the real. The real, through his eyes, is magical." The celebration of Mistry's choice of "a compassionate" realism (and the implicit denigration of magic realism) is but one critic's perception of Mistry's prose, yet it is also a comment on contemporary attitudes to the form of realism. The back cover, written to appeal to an "average" American consumer, depoliticizes Mistry's novel as it is placed in the company of "masters from Balzac to Dickens." In this light it can appear as if Mistry's use of the form rescues the (European) novel from the uncomfortable possibility of being overtaken—threatened, even—by magic realism, a form that has been most often associated with Latin American writing and therefore recognized as fundamentally non-European. Furthermore, the use of realism by a writer of what has recently been called the "far rim" (whether that be India or Canada) is taken to resuscitate the humanist traditions of the realist novel. Mistry's novel is accepted as having a sweeping appeal by the back-cover critic precisely because it does not resemble what has come to be viewed as a postcolonial novel of resistance—whether that be to caste in India or racism in Canada. The reason for this is simple: Mistry's novel is unequivocally realist and the prevalent view—both popular and academic—is that, for whatever reason, realism and resistance do not converge.

While Mistry's novel *resists* on every page, his resistance comes in the form of realism and is therefore often ignored as a focus of the text.

The problematic nature of critical assumptions about postcolonial examples of realism stems, at least partially, from the privileging of the notion of resistance in postcolonial discourse. The concept of "resistance" has been fetishized to the point where it is even often presented without an object. At the same time, there has been a critical elevation of writing perceived to be experimental or writing that plays with non-realistic form. Within postcolonial criticism, these simultaneous developments have converged in the production of a profusion of studies linking, and sometimes suggesting the interdependence of, political or social resistance and non-realist fiction. If a text does not fit the profile of postcolonial resistance, as realist texts seldom do, it is generally considered incapable of subversion.

David Carter, in his article "Tasteless Subjects," notes that postcolonial critics tend to present realism as a monolithic whole that is "complicit with the process of imperialism" and therefore with "universalism, essentialism, positivism, individualism, modernity, historicism, and so on" (1992:296). In spite of many examples of recent politically charged realist texts, the critical expectations about the form often hold that it is a reinforcement of conservative, specifically imperialist, ideology. On one hand, this assumption has led to the co-option of literary realism by conservative critics. On the other, it has led to the virtual dismissal of the realist novel by those critics looking for an apparently radical form to hold disruptive content. As part of the larger body of critics in the Academy, postcolonial critics are prominent in establishing such expectations. Non-realist writing is frequently privileged by the critics because of the assumption that its various forms are inherently conducive to political subversion because of their capacity for presenting multiplicity. I challenge the idea, as it has been developed or assumed by many postcolonial critics, that realism is almost necessarily conservative, and non-realist forms are inherently somehow *more* postcolonial—and therefore subversive. What is at issue in this paper, then, is the limited function of criticism when critics place too tight an ideological hold on realism and are not inclined to recognize the varieties of its possibilities or its capacity for multiplicity. I challenge this critical hegemony, arguing that realism is a viable, perhaps even indispensable, form for political and social engagement in postcolonial contexts. As such, the study is a reaction to the positioning of realism as a foil for other more "accepted" forms of insurgence regardless of whether such positioning is driven from the left or the right.

Realism, for example, is repeatedly set in opposition to magic realism. Because of its Latin American literary origins, magic realism has become privileged as a suitable form for the inclusion of politicized commentary in what Jeanne Delbaere has called the "energy of the margins" and Stephen Slemon has now notoriously labeled "postcolonial discourse." Wendy Faris and Lois Parkinson Zamora argue that in magic realist texts "ontological disruption serves the purpose of political and cultural disruption: magic is often given as a cultural corrective, requiring readers to scrutinize accepted realistic conventions" (1995:3). In this formulation, realism has "accepted conventions" to which the politically active magic realist text can react. Magic realism opens up a space for the political to enter the text precisely because it is not realism here, while realism without magic is taken to be less capable of opposition. While I quarrel with the *New York Times* reviewer's depiction of magic realism as infused with a dose of magical rhetoric by an invisible but lurking trickster of the "far rim," it does seem that the increasingly popular form has either been characterized as a catch-all of political action or is emptied of its politics.

Realism has a history of political activity in India, but it does not have the international recognition that magic realism has as a form capable of carrying resistance. Rohinton Mistry's *A Fine Balance* traces the day-to-day lives of fictional characters through non-fictional incidents in the 1975 State-of-Emergency. The primary function of the "ordinary" characters in *A Fine Balance* is not to be synecdochic of the "Indian citizen" in the Emergency but rather to represent possible examples of what might happen in such a state. Mistry's characters populate a novel that is critical of the resilience of the caste system, the pervasive nature of corruption, the hiring of political crowds, forced labour camps, sexism, "Family Planning" and Indira Gandhi herself.

The four main characters converge in Dina's apartment. As refugees from constricting caste, gender or social roles, they each inhabit a marginal position in the context of India: Dina as a woman and a Parsi; Maneck as a rural Parsi; and Ishvar and Omprakash as leather workers transgressively transformed into tailors. The apartment is a setting at the interstices of culture, or "the overlap and displacement of difference," to use Homi Bhabha's phrase (1997:3). The four characters resist the social positions to which they are relegated by the community and try to foreground their own individuality. If the apartment is viewed as the secular site of convergence of individuals in a disruptive society, then the collapse of the community in the apartment is inevitable in the Emergency—a fact which the more conservative critics tend to ignore. The point is crucial: the individual can not be extricated from the community in this narrative. Bhabha writes that "political empowerment comes from posing questions of solidarity from the interstitial perspective" (1997:3). However, Mistry disempowers his characters after placing them in the putatively interstitial space of Dina's apartment.

The focus on the individual within the community evokes Bhabha's idea of the proximate, the "minority position," the moderate subject, or the "first-in-third" (Bhabha 1997:434). For Bhabha, this position depends on the interstitial space of identification, on the ambivalent position of being at once one in a community (third person) and an individual in society (first person). The moderate subject is articulated in a movement between third and first persons. It is constituted "as an effect of the ambivalent condition of their borderline proximity—the first-in-the-third/one-in-the-other" (Bhabha 1997:434). However, in the Emergency context of *A Fine Balance*, there is no movement allowed between the first and the third. In this realist example the moderate position cannot exist. Conversely, magic realism *relies* on the possibility of the moderate position: the in-betweenness or the "all-at-onceness" which "encourages resistance to monologic political and cultural substructures" (Parkinson Zamora and Faris 1995:3). In Mistry's novel the point of resistance lies precisely in its representation of the impossibility of the moderate position. Mistry's realist novel concludes with the collapse of the apartment community which, in turn, leads to Dina's loss of independence, Ishvar's loss of his legs, Om's loss of his "manhood" and Manek's loss of life.

Some critics have argued about the applicability of the term realism to Mistry's mode of representation. The argument runs like this: it is degrading to see Mistry's writing as derivative of a European form, where the Indian writer has now "caught up," in the literary evolutionary scheme of things, to the point where British writers were in the nineteenth century. While such criticism can fairly be aimed at those critics who call Mistry "worthy of the nineteenth-century masters," such a view is not necessarily the impetus for all those who label the text realist. A focus on the limitations of social structures is by no means exclusively a feature of Victorian realism, although such fiction was an integral part of the education system in India. A concentration on the undistinguished lives of the lower classes clearly does not suggest that the text's precursor is necessarily Victorian realism. One only has to turn to such disparate classics of "social realism" in India in English as Mulk Raj Anand's *Untouchable*, Raja Rao's *Kanthapura* or Bhabhani Bhattacharya's *So Many Hungers* to think of critical depictions of a diversity of castes. Still, I agree with John Ball's comment that the realist novel is a precursor to Mistry's text, but I add that works of Indian social realism are also likely to be prominent precursors (1996:87).

As with the social realists, at points Mistry can be accused of being overly romantic in his portrait of poverty. The following tableau of workers trying to unblock an overflowing drain illustrates Mistry's propensity to present a lyrical view of poverty.

> then a boy emerged out of the earth, clinging to the end of a rope. He was covered in the slippery sewer sludge, and when he stood up, he shone and shimmered in the sun with a terrible beauty. His hair, stiffened by muck, flared from his head like a crown of black flames. Behind him, the slum smoke curled towards the sky, and the hellishness of the place was complete. (1997:67)

The "interminable serpents of smoke" of Dickens's description of Coketown in *Hard Times* surface here in the slimy serpentine "s's" where the slippery sewer sludge stood up, shone and shimmered in the sun near the slum where fires smouldered, with smoke smudging the air (1990:28). Such alliteration adds to the self-consciously lyrical and somewhat melodramatic qualities of this depiction of the "underworld" (Mistry's word); yet, sewers *do* have black sewer sludge spilling from drains in a state of civic unrest and governmental corruption. This is a romanticized portrait of poverty and filth, but even such a portrait carries pointed commentary

within it. It is important to note that Dina views this scene because her train is blocked by "demonstrations against the government" (1996:67). So the sewer scene for Dina—on the top level of a double-decker bus—is juxtaposed with a view of "banners and slogans [that] accused the Prime Minister of misrule and corruption, calling on her to resign in keeping with the court judgments finding her guilty of election malpractice" (1997:67). Mistry's explication of the Emergency context is not simply to provide a setting for a lyrical alliterative passage. There is an irrefutable link between slime and corruption.

In her review of Mistry's first novel *Such a Long Journey*, Arun Mukherjee argues with the comparison to a Victorian realist novel because such a comparison does not consider how the characters' lives are "negotiated in the context of a social environment" (1992:83). Mistry's narrative form, according to Mukherjee, is not realism but rather a representation of the real, as it "attempts to make sense of actual historical events by narrativising them" (1992:83). The necessity for cultural and historical specificity in realist novels is not fully taken into account in this comment. In Mukherjee's configuration of realism, the form simply provides a background for the action of the novel. The use of realism as background is sharply criticized by Chinua Achebe in his essay on Joseph Conrad's use of Africa in *Heart of Darkness*:

> Africa as setting and backdrop...eliminates the African as human factor. Africa as a metaphysical battlefield devoid of all recognizable humanity, into which the wandering European enters at his peril. Can nobody see the preposterous and perverse arrogance in thus reducing Africa to the role of props for the break-up of one petty European mind? (1988:257)

While I agree with Achebe's analysis of *Heart of Darkness*, I do not think that such a criticism should be launched against all examples of realism, as Mukherjee seems to. Mistry's realist novel is a case in point. Like Achebe, Mistry works against the notion of using context as a background for development of the individual in the novel. Mistry's recent novel relies closely and clearly on an understanding of its Indian context set in a specific time and place. *A Fine Balance* is emphatically not a World text in Franco Moretti's terms, where the "geographical frame of reference is no longer the nation-state, but a broader entity—a continent, or the world-system as a whole" (1996:50); nor is it a postnational text with sites as interchangeable as postcards, to use Frank Davey's formulation of postnational settings, nor are the political issues constructed in purely globalized terms. *A Fine Balance*, although we follow the quotidian lives of fictional characters through non-fictional incidents in Indian history, "History is emphatically not the backdrop. Indeed, Dina is proven wrong when she dismisses the Emergency as background. Early in the narrative she explains the Emergency as "Government problems—games played by people in power. It doesn't affect ordinary people like us" (Mistry 1997:75). However, the remainder of the novel slowly details just how it does affect the "ordinary" character in the destruction of the apartment community.

This is clearly a tragic novel; yet many reviewers seem to rely heavily on the assumed conservative nature of its realist form and focus on the universally applicable elements of the apartment community (the optimism evoked in such a communal gathering), rather than the clear disruption of those elements in the conclusion (the pessimism that leads to the inevitable disruption of the community). This is particularly well illustrated in the comments that adorn the novel paratextually: "*A Fine Balance* creates an enduring panorama of the human spirit in an inhuman state"; and "The four strangers start sharing their stories, then meals, then living space, until over the divides of caste, class, and religion, the ties of human kinship prevail"; and even "in this one shabby little apartment, at least, the human family becomes more than a phrase, more than a metaphor, a piety" (Mojtabai 1996:29). Such responses to the novel are undeniably humanist. My response is repeatedly: yes, but—yes, but the fundamental point of Mistry's text is that the "ties of human kinship" do not prevail in his 1970s India. Things have fallen apart; the universalist paradigm can not hold.

Perhaps the finest example of a conservative—even neoimperialist—co-option of Mistry's realism is presented on the flyleaf of the novel. From the *Literary Review of London*, it reads: "A Work of genius . . . *A Fine Balance* is the India novel, the novel readers have been waiting for since E. M. Forster." This comment not only exposes the vision of realism as an orientalist technique; it addresses itself specifically to the readers who would consider realism as such. The thinking behind this comment seems to be that, because *A Fine Balance* is not written in the quick syntax of Raja Rao, or the innovative styles of G. V. Desani,

Amitav Ghosh or Salman Rushdie, it must be exemplary of the English tradition and therefore more valuable, more marketable, and ultimately more easily canonized in the Great Tradition. To equate Mistry's novel with *A Passage to India* (and to ignore the products of the intervening seventy-one years) thoroughly negates the context of both novels. I can only think that this is done because the reviewer, like many other critics, blindly accepts the notion of an ideologically conservative realism which is by definition an imperial product. The publicists of the American edition of *A Fine Balance* foreground the universal humanist elements of the novel in the comments found on the physical body of the text in order to decontextualize, dehistoricize and ultimately depoliticize the realism in the novel and thus ostensibly make it more palatable for a general American public. Although I do not particularly believe that the novel needed rescuing, I do think that realism does.

Source: Laura Moss, "Can Rohinton Mistry's Realism Rescue the Novel?," in *Postcolonizing the Commonwealth: Studies in Literature and Culture*, edited by Rowland Smith, Wilfred Laurier University Press, 2000, pp. 157–65.

SOURCES

Ashcroft, Bill, Gareth Griffiths, and Helen Tiffin, *The Empire Writes Back: Theory and Practice in Post-Colonial Literatures*, Routledge, 1989, p. 104.

Bahri, Deepika, *Native Intelligence: Aesthetics, Politics, and Postcolonial Literature*, University of Minnesota Press, 2003, pp. 121, 131, 161, 173.

Bhautoo-Dewnarain, Nandini, *Rohinton Mistry: An Introduction*, Foundation Books, 2007, p. 42.

Boehmer, Ellike, *Colonial and Postcolonial Literature: Migrant Metaphors*, 2nd ed., Oxford University Press, 2005, pp. 225–36.

Brass, Paul R., *The Politics of India Since Independence*, 2nd ed., Cambridge University Press, 1994, pp. 72–73, 338–42, 344–45, 348–50.

Edwards, Justin D., *Postcolonial Literature: A Reader's Guide to Essential Criticism*, Palgrave Macmillan, 2008, pp. 129–38.

Harrow, Emma, "Reading for Pleasure: Simon & Schuster's Publicity Manager on Rohinton Mistry's Modern Classic," in *Bookseller*, No. 5433, 2010, p. 20.

Hooper, Brad, Review of *A Fine Balance*, in *Booklist*, Vol. 92, No. 14, 1996, p. 1241.

Hussein, Aamer, Review of *A Fine Balance*, in *New Statesman & Society*, Vol. 9, No. 394, 1996, p. 36.

Iyer, Pico, Review of *A Fine Balance*, in *Time*, Vol. 147, No. 17, 1996, p. 90.

Lodge, David, "Critics' Choices for Christmas," in *Commonweal*, Vol. 123, No. 21, 1996, p. 20.

Luhrmann, T. M., *The Good Parsi: The Fate of a Colonial Elite in a Postcolonial Society*, Harvard University Press, 1996, p. 100.

Malak, Amin, "From Margin to Main: Minority Discourse and 'Third World' Fiction Writers in Canada," in *From Commonwealth to Post-Colonial*, edited by Anna Rutherford, Dangaroo Press, 1992, p. 51.

Mistry, Rohinton, *A Fine Balance*, Vintage, 1997.

Morey, Peter, *Rohinton Mistry*, Manchester University Press, 2004, p. 101.

New, W. H., Review of *A Fine Balance*, in *Journal of Modern Literature*, Summer 2000, p. 565.

Review of *A Fine Balance*, in *Kliatt*, Vol. 37., No. 4, 2003, p. 3.

FURTHER READING

Clark, Peter, *Zoroastrianism: An Introduction to an Ancient Faith*, Sussex Academic Press, 1998.
> An overview of the basic beliefs of the Zoroastrians summarizes what it is to be human, the nature of good and evil, and the human relationship to the natural world.

Dodiya, Jaydipsinh, ed., *The Fiction of Rohinton Mistry: Critical Studies*, Sangam, 1998.
> Indian critics speak on general topics concerning Indian literature in English and examine each of Mistry's works.

Frank, Katherine, *Indira: The Life of Indira Nehru Gandhi*, Houghton Mifflin Harcourt, 2002.
> Stressing Gandhi's human side, the biography describes her sad childhood, her feeling of duty to her father's vision of India, and her later years of tyrannical rule during the Emergency, which contradicted her father's beliefs.

Mantel, Hilary, "States of Emergency," in *India: A Mosaic*, New York Review Books, 2000, pp. 181–93.
> *A Fine Balance* is a strongly political novel critical of the political forces in India, but some of the portraits of the poor seem to be stereotypes.

In "States of Emergency," Mantel provides a factual, historical depiction of India's people, including the plight of the poor so prominently featured in *A Fine Balance*.

Mistry, Rohinton, *Such a Long Journey*, Vintage, 1991.
> Short-listed for the Booker Prize, this portrait of the corruption of Indira Gandhi's regime begins earlier than the Emergency, during the 1971 Indo-Pakistani War, focusing on the story of a Parsi bank clerk who is drawn into political intrigue.

Naipaul, V. S., *India: A Wounded Civilization*, Vintage, 2003.
> Nobel laureate Naipaul visited India during the state of emergency in 1975, describing in this famous and controversial book the paradoxical images of Indian life, such as the feudal villages and the space program.

Samantrai, Ranu, "States of Belonging: Pluralism, Migrancy, Literature," in *Essays on Canadian Writing*, Vol. 57, Winter 1995, pp. 33–50.
> Samantrai discusses the problem of classifying Rohinton Mistry as a Canadian author because of his overlapping identities as Parsi, Indian, and Canadian.

Tokaryk, Tyler, "Keynes, Storytelling, and Realism: Literary and Economic Discourse in Rohinton Mistry's *A Fine Balance*," in *Studies in Canadian Literature/Études en Littérature Canadienne*, Vol. 30, No. 2, 2005, pp. 1–31.
> Tokaryk argues that *A Fine Balance* represents a postmodern understanding of realism by comparing Mistry's theory of language with the ideas of economist John Maynard Keynes.

SUGGESTED SEARCH TERMS

Rohinton Mistry

A Fine Balance

Indira Gandhi AND Emergency

Untouchable caste

Parsi

Zoroastrianism

Postcolonial novel

Realism AND novel

Indian novel in English

The Guernsey Literary and Potato Peel Society

MARY ANN SHAFFER
ANNIE BARROWS

2008

The Guernsey Literary and Potato Peel Pie Society is an epistolary novel that takes place on Guernsey, an island off the English coast in the English Channel, between England and France. The events in the novel occur during the first nine months of 1946, just after the end of World War II and after the German occupation of the Channel Islands ended. While the central protagonist lives in London, her correspondents live on Guernsey.

Mary Ann Shaffer and Annie Barrows's novel shows the courage and fortitude of the people who lived on Guernsey during the five long years of German occupation. The islanders' humanity is revealed through their bravery in protecting one another from the ever-present threat of arrest and deportation. There is also a gentle humor in *The Guernsey Literary and Potato Peel Pie Society* that is evident in the creative character studies of some of the islanders' more eccentric and quirky characters. The islanders bond over a mutual love of books that they did not even know existed before the creation of the Guernsey Literary Society. Through their reading, the islanders are transported to worlds they might never have visited, or ever experienced.

The Guernsey Literary and Potato Peel Pie Society is Shaffer's first novel. She became ill and was unable to finish the final edits and rewrites that the publisher required. Shaffer's niece Annie Barrows completed the novel, which was published in 2008, after Shaffer's death.

Amelia hosted the impromptu dinner party that started the society. (© jannoon028 | Shutterstock.com)

AUTHOR BIOGRAPHY

The writing of *The Guernsey Literary and Potato Peel Pie Society* was a joint effort. Shaffer was the principal author, but when she became ill during the final stage of writing the novel, she asked her niece Annie Barrows to complete the novel for her.

Shaffer, whose maiden name was Fiery, was born on December 13, 1934, in Martinsburg, West Virginia. She graduated from Martinsburg High School in 1952 and attended Miami University of Ohio for two years but left without completing a degree. She married Dick Shaffer in 1958, and in 1962 the couple moved to Greenbrae, California. The couple had two daughters. Shaffer worked as an editor and in libraries and in bookstores for many years, but she always dreamed of writing a novel. Several times during her adult life, Shaffer would begin writing a mystery novel but never finished any of them. She loved telling stories but found it difficult to make the transition from telling a story to writing a story. She began writing *The Guernsey*

Literary and Potato Peel Pie Society only after members of her writing group pushed her to start writing as a serious endeavor.

The genesis for *The Guernsey Literary and Potato Peel Pie Society* was a 1980 visit to England, when Shaffer decided to fly to Guernsey. Fog kept Shaffer stranded in the airport on Guernsey for seventy-two hours. She spent her time reading books from the airport gift shop, where almost all of the books told the story of the German occupation of Guernsey during World War II. Shaffer found the occupation of the Channel Islands fascinating history and bought nearly every book she could find.

Although she found the history of Guernsey compelling, it still took Shaffer more than twenty years to begin writing her novel and then only after encouragement from friends. Shaffer began writing the novel in 2003 and chose the epistolary format because it was one she enjoyed reading and that she thought would be easy to duplicate. By the time *The Guernsey Literary and Potato Peel Pie Society* was accepted for publication, Shaffer was ill with cancer and could not complete the revisions and additional writing the publisher required. She asked Barrows to help finish the book. Shaffer died of cancer February 16, 2008, before the novel's publication.

Barrows, the daughter of Shaffer's sister, Cynthia Fiery Barrows, was born in San Diego in 1962. She was raised in Northern California and graduated from the University of California, Berkeley, with a bachelor's degree in medieval history. Barrows also earned a master of fine arts from Mills College. Barrows lives in California with her husband and two daughters. After working as a book editor for several years, Barrows began writing books. Her first books–nonfiction for adults–were published under the name Ann Fiery. Barrows' first nonfiction book was *The Book of Divination* (1999). This first book was soon followed by two additional works of nonfiction: *The Completely and Totally True Book of Urban Legends* (2001) and *At the Opera: Tales of the Great Operas* (2003).

In 2006, Barrows published the first of the *Ivy and Bean* children's book series. Nine children's books in this series were published between 2006 and 2012. The *Ivy and Bean* books have received numerous accolades, including being named one of the New York Public Library's 100 Titles for Reading and Sharing (2006), *Book Links* Best New Books for the Classroom (2006), *Kirkus Reviews* Best Children's Book (2006), *Booklist*'s Best Books of 2007, and ALA Notable Children's Book (2007). The books were also nominated for the Kentucky Bluegrass Award (2008), North Dakota Flicker Tale Children's Book Award (2010–2011), and the Bluestem Award (2011). The *Ivy and Bean* books were not individually selected for these awards; instead, the series has been celebrated for excellence as a whole. In 2008, Barrows published a children's chapter book, *The Magic Half*, which was also nominated for several awards, including the Kentucky Bluegrass Award, the Mark Twain Award, the Virginia Readers' Choice, the Massachusetts Children's Book Award, the Maud Hart Lovelace Award, and the Sunshine State Young Readers' Award, all in 2011.

In 2007, Shaffer asked Barrows to help complete the required editing and rewrites for *The Guernsey Literary and Potato Peel Pie Society*. Barrows, who had grown up listening to her aunt's stories and knew her storytelling style well, began working to finish the novel, which was published in the summer of 2008,

MEDIA ADAPTATIONS

- An audiobook of *The Guernsey Literary and Potato Peel Pie Society*, with multiple unnamed readers, was released by Random House Audio in 2008.

- As of 2012, a film of *The Guernsey Literary and Potato Peel Pie Society* is under way, to be directed by Kenneth Branagh. The book is adapted by Don Roos, and filming is to begin in 2013 and will star Kate Winslet as Juliet Ashton.

after Shaffer had died. *The Guernsey Literary and Potato Peel Pie Society* is Barrows's first adult fiction book.

PLOT SUMMARY

Part One

JANUARY 1946

The first few letters that open *The Guernsey Literary and Potato Peel Pie* Society are an exchange between Juliet Ashton and her publisher and friend, Sidney Stark. They are largely filled with idle chitchat about how dissatisfied Juliet is with her current activity, which consists of a book tour to promote and sell *Izzy Bickerstaff Goes to War*, a collection of the columns that Juliet wrote during the war. In response, Sidney offers vague encouragement about writing another book. Juliet also writes to her childhood friend Sophie Strachan about the destruction that Juliet sees during her book tour of postwar England.

While on the book tour, Juliet is accosted by a reporter, who badgers her about a broken engagement that occurred four years earlier. The near groom was killed in action only three months later, and obviously Juliet is sensitive about these events, since she throws a teapot at the offending journalist. The reason for the broken engagement is soon revealed. The day before the wedding, Juliet's fiancé packed up all her books and was in the midst of storing them in the basement, when she arrived home to find all her bookshelves filled with his athletic trophies. After a huge fight over the displacement of her books and about how little the couple actually had in common, Juliet and her fiancé broke off their engagement. The irony is that when her London home was later bombed, her books might have been safe in the basement, had she left them there.

During her book tour, Juliet also receives many bouquets of flowers from Mark Reynolds, a wealthy American publisher who seems to be courting Juliet. His purpose is not clear, but readers learn that he is very handsome and that many ladies find him difficult to resist. Since Juliet has never met Mark, his pursuit of her is both intriguing and romantic to Juliet, who is bored and without any real direction in her life.

Juliet receives her first two letters from Guernsey, from Dawsey Adams, who has found Juliet's name and address inside a used book and who, in his first letter, asks that Juliet help him find copies of Charles Lamb's writings. Juliet does find the requested Lamb books and makes sure that Dawsey receives them. In their correspondence, Juliet reveals that her home was bombed during the war and that she has now rented a less attractive apartment in London. Both Juliet and Dawsey are great lovers of books and reading.

In his second letter, Dawsey tells Juliet the story of the founding of the Guernsey Literary and Potato Peel Pie Society, which was organized on the spur of the moment after several of the Guernsey residents were stopped by German soldiers and had to explain why they were out after curfew. Dawsey's letter relates details about the shortage of food during the German occupation of Guernsey and the lack of war news as well. The Germans did not allow any letters, newspapers, magazines, or other written items to be imported during the war years.

FEBRUARY 1946

The correspondence between Juliet and Dawsey continues with letters that reveal quite a lot about their respective lives. Juliet says that she was a writer during the war and that she wrote the Izzy Bickerstaff columns but that she is now going to write under her own name. Juliet also tells Dawsey that she has been asked to write a feature story for the *London Times* about the philosophical benefits of reading. Juliet asks

Dawsey for help from him and the Guernsey Literary and Potato Peel Pie Society. In response, Amelia Maugery writes to Juliet to ask for references before she begins to write anything about the society. Amelia is concerned that the islanders not become objects of derision in any article that Juliet writes.

The two letters of reference that Amelia receives focus on Juliet's honesty and her love of books, although the letters also make clear that she can be reckless at times. Readers also learn that Juliet was orphaned and sent to live with an elderly uncle, who in turn sent her to a boarding school. After she receives the letters of reference, Amelia writes to Juliet to tell her more about the founding of the Guernsey Literary Society, which had to be transformed from a fictional book club to a real book club. Amelia explains how she and Elizabeth McKenna bought every book they could find and began lending them out to their neighbors. The plan was to make the Guernsey Literary Society an actual book club, just in case the German forces decided to check on the members' alibi for breaking curfew. Isola Pribby writes and tells Juliet about her passion for the Brontë sisters and how she came to love their books. Isola also explains that Elizabeth was arrested and deported after she was caught hiding a Polish slave worker.

Eben Ramsey then writes to Juliet and tells her about the day the Germans invaded the island and the more than thirty men, women, and children they killed. Eben also tells Juliet about the deprivation and hunger that everyone suffered during the years that the Germans occupied the island. At first, the islanders' diets consisted of just potatoes and turnips, but eventually there were no more potatoes to eat. They also had no fuel for heating their homes or candles for light. Eben's seven-year-old grandson, Eli, was sent to England to safety and only returned five years later, after the Germans left.

Juliet finally meets Mark Reynolds and discovers that he is quite handsome and polished, is accustomed to ordering people around, and is used to having his own way. He has read Juliet's book and has set out to impress her. She goes out with Mark several times and describes evenings spent at the cinema and at dinner parties and nights out dancing. She also mentions that he is an American and seems to have put the war behind him, as the British have not yet done.

MARCH 1946

Juliet receives a letter from Adelaide Addison, who sits in judgment over her neighbors and considers most of them to be ill-bred, unintelligent, and scarcely capable of reading, much less actually belonging to, a true literary society. A letter from Clovis Fossey also arrives, in which he details how the Guernsey Literary and Potato Peel Pie Society and a book of poetry helped him win the love of a local widow.

Eben writes in a letter about the food rationing during the German occupation. He explains that the Germans kept track of every farm animal and every ounce of milk, all of the butter and eggs produced, and every fish caught. He tells Juliet that the island people learned tricks to fool the Germans, which is how they had a pig to eat the night they were almost caught and formed the Guernsey Literary and Potato Peel Pie Society.

Adelaide writes again and tells Juliet about Elizabeth's love for a German doctor and the child that she had after he left the island. Adelaide thinks Elizabeth's behavior was a disgrace. After Elizabeth was arrested and deported, the members of the Guernsey Literary Society decided to raise her baby, Kit, and everyone took turns caring for the child. Adelaide did not approve of any of these activities and pleads with Juliet not to use the people of Guernsey in the article she is writing.

John Booker also writes to Juliet and tells how he came to impersonate his employer, Lord Tobias, and how he chose to pretend to be a lord of the mansion. He had the help of Elizabeth and Amelia, who told him not to reveal his Jewish ancestry and to claim that he was a lord. Elizabeth and Amelia saved his life, as did reading the Roman philosopher Seneca, whose witty writings filled John's days.

In her last letter of March, Juliet writes to Sidney, who is in Australia visiting a friend and healing a broken leg. She tells him about the letters she has been exchanging with the people of Guernsey and that she wants to write a book about the people who spent the war years on the Channel Islands as prisoners of the Germans.

APRIL 1946

Dawsey writes to Juliet and explains why some islanders were friendly to the Germans and how the food that they received in return helped feed their families. Dawsey also details how his friendship with Christian Hellman, the man whom Elizabeth loved, started. Dawsey writes about how the German doctor helped him carry saltwater for cooking to the older islanders, who could not fetch the water themselves. He tells Juliet how Christian drowned when his ship was bombed and sank in the Channel.

A letter from Amelia tells Juliet about how Adolf Hitler sent sixteen thousand Todt slave laborers to the Channel Islands to build fortifications and bunkers on the islands. Todt was the name of a German construction firm that depended on laborers captured in the countries that the Nazis invaded and conquered. Amelia asks Juliet to come to Guernsey and write a book about the war there.

A letter from Eben tells Juliet that the islanders never thought Germany would bother with the small Channel Islands, because their focus was on the larger prize of England. When the invasion seemed inevitable, people had to decide whether to send their children to England for safekeeping, but the decision was very difficult for parents, and not all children were sent.

Even as she receives more letters from the islanders, Juliet begins researching the history of Guernsey. In response to a request from Isola, Juliet describes her appearance, how she got her start writing, and many of the small details surrounding her life. Juliet tells Isola that she began writing professionally after she won an essay contest and her essay was published. The resulting fan letters led the *Daily Mirror* newspaper to offer her a job writing feature stories. This job eventually led the *Spectator* to offer her a regular position writing a humorous war column, which was the start of the Izzy Bickerstaff columns.

The final letters of April tell Juliet how Elizabeth slapped Adelaide across the face after she scared a group of children waiting to be evacuated. Juliet's suitor, Mark, continues his pursuit of her. His letters make clear that he cares little for her opinions or desires. He is accustomed to getting things done his way.

MAY 1946

Juliet's first letter in May is to Mark, who is upset and jealous about the time she devotes to her friendship with Sidney and to the people of Guernsey. Mark has asked Juliet to marry him, and her reply that she needs time to think about it has angered him. Juliet writes to Sophie that when she did not immediately accept his proposal, Mark began shouting at her, reducing Juliet to tears. Juliet's letter to Sophie is a plea for advice concerning what to do about Mark. Should she drop her goals and marry Mark and be the ideal society wife he expects? Or should she stick to her career and not marry Mark? These are Juliet's questions as May begins. In her letter to Sidney, Juliet never mentions Mark but instead writes of how much she wants to go to Guernsey, meet the people who have been writing to her, and learn more about the German occupation.

The islanders are thrilled that Juliet plans to visit Guernsey and begin preparing for her visit. In their letters, they describe their efforts to find her housing and their plans for a welcome party. Even more people have been enticed to write to Juliet about their experiences during the occupation. An anonymous writer tells Juliet that the authorities in London ordered all feral dogs and cats, who had no owner, and all pets in excess of one per household to be destroyed. The reason for the order was that there was insufficient food on the island to feed so many dogs and cats. There was also insufficient food to feed either the islanders or the German soldiers. At one point near the end of the war, the German soldiers were so hungry they resorted to eating stray cats.

While the preparations for Juliet's arrival on Guernsey continue, Mark continues to implore her to forget her plans. His tone is increasingly condescending. Juliet is to stay in Elizabeth's cottage, which has been empty since she was arrested.

Part Two

MAY 1946

When Juliet arrives on Guernsey, she is greeted by many of the islander correspondents. She takes the time to describe each of them in a letter to Sidney. They are so warm and welcoming that Juliet's initial nervousness evaporates. The many letters that finish the month of May are written to Sidney and to his sister, Sophie. These letters are filled with Juliet's small observations of life on Guernsey and the lives of the people who live there. Juliet devotes her time to getting to know the island and the people, even as she continues to learn more about the German occupation of the Channel Islands. Juliet also bonds with four-year-old Kit, who spends much of her time with Juliet at Elizabeth's former cottage.

JUNE 1946

The Guernsey Literary and Potato Peel Pie Society receives a letter from Remy Giraud, who was friends with Elizabeth while both were imprisoned at Ravensbrück concentration camp. Remy writes to tell Elizabeth's friends of her death at the camp. She describes the camp and the way the women lived and tells how Elizabeth was killed for defending another prisoner, who was being beaten. When Amelia and Dawsey learn of Elizabeth's death, they travel to Louviers, France, to convince Remy that she must journey to Guernsey, just as she and Elizabeth had planned before her death. After everyone learns of Elizabeth's death, Kit is told. Because Amelia was in France and then feels unwell upon her return, Kit stays with Juliet in Elizabeth's former cottage.

JULY 1946

Sidney travels to Guernsey to meet all the people Juliet has been corresponding with and writing about for the previous six months. His observational skills are excellent, and it takes him no time at all to realize that Kit loves Juliet, that Juliet loves Kit, that Dawsey is very attracted to Juliet, and that Juliet is very attracted to Dawsey. When Isola wants to know whether Sidney and Juliet are in love and getting married, Sidney tells her that he is homosexual, which pleases Isola very much.

Sidney reads all of Juliet's interview notes and the letters she has received and tells her that Elizabeth needs to be at the center of her book about Guernsey. It is Elizabeth who was so instrumental in everyone's lives and is the focus of all the other islanders whose stories Juliet has been collecting.

Mark appears on the island at an inopportune moment, just as Juliet realizes that she wants Dawsey to kiss her and just as it appears he will. Mark is rude and condescending, and Juliet sends him packing back to London with a firm rejection of his marriage proposal. Unfortunately, Dawsey thinks Juliet is in love with Mark. Dawsey leaves for France without saying goodbye. His plan is to bring Remy to Guernsey to continue her recovery.

AUGUST 1946

Remy has arrived, and everyone works hard to be cheerful and to help her convalesce. Life on the island continues, as do meetings of the Guernsey Literary Society, where people still read and discuss books. The ending of the war is no reason to abandon the literary society that has come to mean so much to everyone. Isola brings forth a collection of letters that her granny once received, and it is determined that they were written by Oscar Wilde, a fact that elicits a great deal of attention on and off the island. Dawsey continues to ignore Juliet, never speaking and barely looking at her. Juliet is blind to the fact that his new behavior toward her is tied to the appearance of Mark and to the notion that Juliet is in love with either Mark or Sidney. Meanwhile, Juliet is worried about Remy and a possible romance with Dawsey and wishes that Remy would return to France to recover.

SEPTEMBER 1946

Juliet wants to adopt Kit and begins telling Amelia of her plans. Juliet knows that Kit loves and trusts her and also understands that both she and Kit need to remain on Guernsey. Juliet will not be returning to London when her book is completed.

Isola begins keeping a journal and writes that she is convinced that Dawsey loves Remy but is too shy to tell her. Remy is to leave for Paris, where she has plans to start her life over. Isola searches through Dawsey's home looking for evidence that he is in love with Remy so that he can declare himself before Remy leaves. All she finds is that he has been keeping photos and keepsakes that belong to Juliet. Isola still fails to understand, but when she tells Juliet what she found, Juliet does understand. She immediate goes to find Dawsey and asks him to marry her. He agrees. In her final letter, Juliet writes to Sidney to tell him that she is getting married right away and needs him to come to Guernsey on the following Saturday to give her away. Eben will be the best man, and Isola will be the maid of honor. Always one to take control, Juliet is marrying Dawsey immediately and is ready to start the next chapter of her life.

CHARACTERS

Dawsey Adams

Dawsey is a pig farmer who lives on Guernsey. He is the first inhabitant of the island with whom Juliet corresponds. Dawsey facilitates the connections between Juliet and the other island inhabitants. He is a good man but socially inexperienced and shy. However, he is also very generous and willing to help others. His father died when he was eleven, and his mother had no time for him. Dawsey used to stutter and, as a result, is unsure of himself around other people. He has been alone and lonely most of his life. Because of the Guernsey Literary and Potato Peel Pie Society, Dawsey makes friends for the first time and learns to communicate with people. He is attracted to Juliet when he finally meets her but is too shy to declare his feelings. The experiences that result from his membership in the Guernsey Literary Society and his friendships with the group members help Dawsey assume a new strength that had been hidden previously. He is stronger and braver and more willing to take chances. At the end of the novel, Dawsey finally realizes that Juliet loves him as much as he loves her.

Adelaide Addison

Adelaide is the island grump and a notable elitist who cares more about social conventions than about people. She finds fault with everyone, including Elizabeth. She is not a part of the Guernsey Literary and Potato Peel Pie Society and thinks it a waste of time. Her role is to reveal details about each person's life that she thinks casts aspersions on his or her character. In truth, her letters reveal the writer to be a petty and judgmental woman, filled with bitterness.

Juliet Ashton

Juliet is the protagonist in this novel. She is a writer and journalist, and, during World War II, she wrote a column for the *Spectator* using the pseudonym Izzy Bickerstaff. The column that she wrote was light and humorous, designed to take people's minds off the war. When the war ended, Juliet wanted to write something more serious. She is thirty-two when the novel begins, and in her first letters, she is quickly defined by her sense of humor and her unhappiness at being only a columnist. She yearns to be taken seriously as a writer. Through the letters that she writes, readers learn about Juliet's values and her efforts to create a life after her parents died in an automobile crash.

Juliet was orphaned at age twelve and attended boarding schools. She easily makes friends and is very loyal to them. She is used to being independent, which is why she is still unmarried when *The Guernsey Literary and Potato Peel Pie Society* begins. Juliet has a great deal of strength and resiliency and is capable of being good and loyal when called upon.

Juliet loves books, and thus her initial connection to Guernsey is established through a mutual love of books. The members of the Guernsey Literary and Potato Peel Pie Society are also great book lovers, and the initial exchange of letters focuses on the favorite books of each member. Juliet is determined to tell the story of the wonderful people of Guernsey and especially that of Elizabeth, whose love for her friends and neighbors and whose kindness toward everyone made her a focus for the islanders.

Throughout the novel, Juliet grows and changes, but her inner strength and compassion are always at the center of her humanity. She falls in love with the orphaned Kit and wants to adopt her. It takes Juliet a long time to become aware that she loves Dawsey, but once she understands that he loves her, she is willing to take control. She tells him that she loves him and asks him to marry her. Her independence is a big part of her strength.

Billee Bee

Billee is Sidney's secretary, who, unbeknownst to Sidney, conspires with a disgraced journalist to steal the Oscar Wilde letters that Isola inherited from her granny. Billee completely underestimates the intelligence of the islanders and is caught with the stolen letters before she can escape from the island.

John Booker

John is a former valet who assumed the identity of his employer, Lord Tobias, during the German occupation. When his wealthy employer left Guernsey just before the Germans invaded the island, John took over his employer's estate and pretended to be a man of wealth. He did so because his mother was Jewish. If he pretended to be a wealthy member of the British aristocracy, he could bluff his way out of revealing any kind of documentation that might require him to register as a Jew. Eventually, another islander turned him in, and John was shipped to a series of concentration camps, including Bergen-Belsen, in Germany. At the end of the war, John returned to Guernsey as soon as he was liberated from the concentration camp where he was imprisoned.

Clovis Fossey

Clovis is a local farmer, who has never been one to read books. When he learns that women like poetry, he gets his first book of poetry, discovers that he loves it and William Wordsworth, and then wins the hand of the widow he has been courting.

Remy Giraud

Remy was Elizabeth's friend at Ravensbrück concentration camp. Remy writes to the members of the Guernsey Literary and Potato Peel Pie Society after the war ends and tells Elizabeth's friends how she died. Once she is well enough, Remy visits Guernsey to recover. At the end of the novel, she leaves to return to Paris and continue her recovery.

Christian Hellman

Christian was the German doctor with whom Elizabeth fell in love. He has been dead several years before Juliet receives her first letter from Guernsey. He is Kit's father. Unlike many of the other German occupiers, Christian was kind to the people on Guernsey and tried to make their lives easier during the wartime occupation. He was also a friend to Dawsey and to several of the islanders. He genuinely loved Elizabeth and wanted to marry her and return to Guernsey after the war but was killed when his transport ship was sunk in the Channel.

Amelia Maugery

Amelia is everyone's mother figure on Guernsey; she is also sophisticated and wise. She is the first host of the Guernsey Literary and Potato Peel Pie Society and is highly regarded by her neighbors for her wise counsel. She befriends Juliet and is a sort of grandmother figure to Kit.

Elizabeth McKenna

Elizabeth is not one of Juliet's correspondents. Her story is told by the other inhabitants of the island. Elizabeth was deported to a concentration camp and, when the novel begins, has been missing for several years. She was arrested after the Germans caught her hiding and feeding a teenage Polish slave worker. Because Elizabeth was a good friend to many of the people who live on Guernsey, her absence is an important part of their correspondence with Juliet. Elizabeth was kind and caring toward others and was always willing to help people. When she fell in love with a German doctor, some of her neighbors disapproved of her choice, but they still liked her. It was Elizabeth who dreamed up the Guernsey Literary and Potato Peel Pie Society, and it is her memory, even after her deportation, that unites many of the islanders. The islanders learn that Elizabeth was killed at the Ravensbrück concentration camp. Elizabeth is at the center of all the stories that people tell about the German occupation, and it is Elizabeth's story that Juliet decides to tell in the book she plans to write about the German occupation of Guernsey.

Kit McKenna

Kit is Elizabeth's four-year-old daughter. Like her mother, Kit is loving and good. After Juliet visits Guernsey, Kit bonds with Juliet and begins to see Juliet as a mother figure. At the end of the novel, Juliet prepares to adopt Kit.

Isola Pribby

Isola is the village eccentric. Through her activities, she provides much of the humor in the book. She loves to read romances and is passionate about the novels of the Brontë sisters. She describes herself as unattractive, with a large nose that has been broken and with wild hair that cannot be controlled. She cooks up many strange potions, but when Sidney sends her a book on phrenology—the reading of bumps on people's heads—Isola begins to "read" people's heads. Her insights are remarkably accurate. Isola's description of her appearance initially suggests the image of a witch, but her personality is gentle and caring toward others.

Eben Ramsey

Eben is also a member of the Guernsey Literary and Potato Peel Pie Society. He describes himself as an elderly gentleman who has discovered that he loves to read Shakespeare. Eben is very observant and quite smart; as a result, he became a repository for small details about life on Guernsey during the German occupation. Eben is also the guardian of his twelve-year-old grandson, Eli, who was sent to England for safety when the island was initially occupied by the Germans. Like so many others on the island, Eben is a good friend to his neighbors and to Juliet.

Eli Ramsey

Eli is Eben's grandson. He was sent to England at age seven and did not return to Guernsey until he was twelve years old. Both of his parents died during the war. Eli's mother and her new baby died the day the Germans bombed Guernsey. His father died in 1942, while fighting in World War II. Eli's actual last name is uncertain. His mother, Jane, was Eben's daughter, but his father's name is never provided.

Mark Reynolds

Mark is an American publisher who courts Juliet. He is wealthy and handsome and offers Juliet a life of glamour and wealth. He is not a man who accepts no for an answer, and he is not pleased when Juliet tells him she needs time to think about his marital proposal. Mark wants Juliet as a sort of English trophy wife and cares little for her happiness. He has no interest in her writing and does not wish her to write or work. His idea of a marriage partner is someone devoted to him and his interests. Mark comes to Guernsey intending to storm the island and sweep Juliet off her feet and back to London. When Juliet declines his proposal and sends him back to London, Mark is very angry.

Susan Scott

Susan is a minor character who accompanies Juliet on the book tour that opens *The Guernsey Literary and Potato Peel Pie Society*. She represents the publisher of Juliet's book and is expected to keep an eye on her charge. She occasionally writes to Juliet when she is on Guernsey.

Sidney Stark

Sidney Stark is Juliet's publisher. He is also a childhood friend, although Sidney is ten years older than Juliet. The correspondence between Juliet and Sidney is central to much of the novel. Sidney is the clear voice of reason and the one friend Juliet can count on to be honest with her. His advice to Juliet is always focused on her well-being, which makes him a true friend. Like his sister, Sophie, Sidney functions as a sounding board for Juliet. He is capable of seeing what she does not see, which makes his advice especially valuable. Sidney does not like Mark and quickly understands that he would be a very bad match for Juliet. Sidney is homosexual and is not a romantic interest for Juliet. The letters that Juliet writes to Sidney are a primary source for readers to learn everything that Juliet is learning about the people and the island of Guernsey.

Sophie Strachan

Sophie is Juliet's childhood friend from boarding school and also Sidney's younger sister.

Juliet writes letters to Sophie but does not receive replies. As a result, readers do not really get to know Sophie's voice. Sophie functions as a sounding board for Juliet when she needs to work through something that is bothering her. The letters that Juliet writes to Sophie provide many of the details about Guernsey life, especially in the second half of the book, when Juliet is living on Guernsey.

Will Thisbee

Will is one of the members of the Guernsey Literary and Potato Peel Pie Society. He wanted food at the meetings and was responsible for the inclusion of the potato peel pie in the title. He is a terrible cook but means well and often brings food to people's homes.

THEMES

Courage

In *The Guernsey Literary and Potato Peel Pie Society*, there are many examples of courage in how people dealt with the days before the German occupation, the actual occupation, and the year following the end of the war. Before the German invasion of Guernsey, parents had to decide whether to send their children to safety in England. It took enormous courage to send children to an unknown future, where they would be unable to contact their parents.

In creating the Guernsey Literary and Potato Peel Pie Society, Elizabeth was extraordinarily brave. She did not cower when confronted by German soldiers after being out after curfew. Although there were guns aimed at her head, she instinctively created a story that would save herself and her companions. When another islander found a young Polish slave laborer near death, he and Elizabeth made the decision to help the boy. Elizabeth had her own infant child, but she did not hesitate to step forward to help care for this teenage boy, who would die without her intervention. As a prisoner at Ravensbrück, Elizabeth chose to be a friend to another woman who desperately needed a friend in the camp. Remy's own experience and survival are tied to Elizabeth's friendship and support. Then when Elizabeth saw the beating of another woman, she stopped the guard from beating the woman and even seized the weapon and began to beat the guard. Elizabeth was executed for her bravery. Her choice to face her enemies and to act out of humanity and not cowardice was one of her most important characteristics. It is Elizabeth's courage that unites the islanders and infuses them with the courage to survive the occupation of the island during war.

Elizabeth is not the only example of a courageous person whose actions helped the islanders survive the German occupation of Guernsey. The people who attended the Guernsey Literary Society initially did so to protect Elizabeth's story and as a way to fight the effects of German intimidation. People hid food and devised ways to fake a pig's death as a means to provide extra food. Everything that the islanders did during the five years of German occupation reveals their bravery in the face of real and significant danger.

Humanity

Although there is little doubt about the humanity of many of the islanders, which is aptly displayed by their loyalty to and care of one another in the face of danger, some of the German soldiers are revealed to possess humanity as well. Kit's father, Christian, helped Dawsey bring water to the islanders unable to carry their own cooking water. In addition, some of the German soldiers "accidentally" let potatoes and oranges fall from German transport trucks, so that the children chasing the trucks could gather up the extra food to eat. One German soldier delivered medicine to an islander whose child was sick. The examples of the German soldiers' humanity make clear that the enemy was not always a simple stereotype of evil. The more humane German soldiers are a reminder that even in war the enemy can have good and humane soldiers within their ranks.

Loyalty

The islanders are very loyal to one another. When Juliet first begins to consider writing about the German occupation of Guernsey, the islanders decide that she must prove that her intentions are good. She must be a person of character, and she must be trustworthy, since the islanders do not wish to be a topic of derision. Both Elizabeth, who arrived as a child, and Juliet, who arrives to write a book, are strangers who are taken into the islanders' lives and who become part of the community. The islanders are protective of one another and loyal to their island family.

TOPICS FOR FURTHER STUDY

- Research the women's prison at Ravensbrück. Search for photos, illustrations, and video taken of the camp and prepare a multimedia presentation in which you carefully integrate photos, video, and quotations from survivors' memoirs. Explain to your classmates what the experience at Ravensbrück was like for the prisoners who were sent there.

- Based on your readings of *The Guernsey Literary and Potato Peel Pie Society*, write an imaginary obituary for either Juliet or Dawsey in which you relate his or her history, as you know it from reading the novel, and your prediction of how either of their futures plays out over the fifty years following their marriage. Post the obituary on a blog and allow classmates to comment.

- Research the Channel Islands (primarily Jersey, Guernsey, Alderney, and Sark), which have a rich lifestyle based on both their British and French heritages. Prepare an oral presentation in which you discuss the French aspects and the British aspects of life on the islands and how the islanders have adapted to and incorporated two such distinct cultures into their lives.

- Research the German occupation of the Channel Islands during World War II and then pretend that you lived there as a teenager. Write your own short story about what the experience would have been like. Write your story as a series of eight to ten letters to a friend who lives elsewhere. Describe the island, the people you know, and the events that are happening around you. Your story has to be long enough to incorporate events and your personal history, including that of your family.

- *Island at War* is a British miniseries that aired in England in 2004 and was then shown on PBS's Masterpiece in 2005. This miniseries focuses on the German occupation of the Channel Islands. Watch the first episode, "Eve of the War," and write an essay in which you compare the information included in the episode with information from *The Guernsey Literary and Potato Peel Pie Society*. Note both the factual consistencies and inconsistencies.

- The novel *Code Talker: A Novel about the Navajo Marines of World War Two* (2005), by Joseph Bruchac, focuses on two Navajo teenagers whose experiences in the Pacific in the war against Japan were very different from those of the people of the Channel Islands. Read this novel and write an essay in which you compare the roles of the islanders on Guernsey with the activities of the Navajo code talkers. Each group was active in resisting the enemy and aiding the war effort. In your essay, consider which experiences are similar and which experiences are different.

- Potato peel pie, as it might have been cooked during World War II, contains potatoes, beets, and milk. Preheat an oven to 375 degrees. Wash and dry two or three potatoes. Peel the potatoes and line a nine-inch pie plate with the peelings. Peel and trim one beet. Boil the potatoes and the beet for about fifteen minutes (until they can be pierced with a fork); then drain and mash, adding two tablespoons of milk. Fill the pie pan with the mashed potato and beet mixture. Bake at 375 degrees for fifteen minutes or until browned (being careful not to waste your fuel ration). Report to your classmates how the pie tastes.

Elizabeth was especially loyal to the people of Guernsey. She created the Guernsey Literary and Potato Peel Pie Society to save her friends' lives, but she also made it a reality. She helped find the books for the literary society, made sure that all her friends chose one, and then organized

Will Thisbee created the first potato peel pie.
(© GekaSkr / Shutterstock.com)

the twice-a-month meetings. When Elizabeth was arrested, her friends stepped forward to care for and raise her daughter, Kit. They cared and continue to care for this child as if she were their own. Because Elizabeth formed the Guernsey Literary Society to protect her friends, Kit has a family to raise her in her mother's absence. It is Elizabeth who painted a portrait of John as Lord Tobias and who fabricated the story of John as the disguised lord to save his life, because John's mother was Jewish and John would himself have had to register as a Jew. While at Ravensbrück, Elizabeth accepted the punishment for a stolen potato, even though she did not steal the potato. Her loyalty was to her fellow prisoners.

Juliet has her own loyal friends, who constitute her family. Although Juliet's parents were killed when she was twelve years old, Sophie and Sidney took her into their lives and became family for her. Readers never see the letters from Sophie, but Juliet's letters to her friend make the closeness of their relationship obvious. When Juliet is unsure about the choices she is making and the nature of her feelings, she writes to Sophie for advice. The same is true of Juliet's relationship with Sidney. He offers her advice and guides her career. When she is going to be married, it is Sidney who will fly to Guernsey to give away the bride.

Epistolary Novel

The epistolary novel is one written entirely in letter form. The narrative of the novel is advanced through a series of letters written by one or more characters. The advantage of an epistolary novel is that the author is able to provide several points of view. The narration is not limited to one voice but can instead provide multiple voices and stories. In *The Guernsey Literary and Potato Peel Pie Society*, the reader learns the story of the German occupation of Guernsey during World War II. The story is told from many different perspectives, which also helps the reader grasp the complexity of the five-year occupation. For example, Juliet receives several letters describing the creation of the Guernsey Literary and Potato Peel Pie Society. Each letter adds slightly more information about the event, with each writer including a description as he or she remembers it.

Historical Fiction

Historical fiction tells a story that is set in a historical period different from the one in which the author lives. In historical fiction, the setting can be one of the most important elements in the story. The events and the characters' responses depend on the location and time in which the novel is set. In *The Guernsey Literary and Potato Peel Pie Society*, the time covers the years of World War II and the year immediately after the war ended. The events that occurred on the Channel Islands during the German occupation are the focus of the novel. The historical novel reconstructs a period in time so that readers are able understand the events. The persons depicted might be fictional, but the setting and events are basically accurate to the place and time. *The Guernsey Literary and Potato Peel Pie Society* reconstructs the invasion of Guernsey by the Germans and their occupation of the island. Although the actual islanders in the novel are fictional, the characters reveal the basic events surrounding the takeover, which are true.

The Channel Islands

The Channel Islands are located off the coast of Normandy, closer to France than to England. Still, the islanders have always considered

COMPARE & CONTRAST

- **1940s:** In 1939, as war seems increasingly certain, the British government evacuates 1.5 million children from London. There will be two more evacuations of children during the course of the war.

  Today: Children are no longer singled out for evacuations in Britain; instead, efforts are made to evacuate entire families, as in the case of flooding in Wales in 2012. Fears of terrorism can lead to mass evacuations, as was the case in July 2005, when twenty thousand people were evacuated from Birmingham, owing to a bomb scare.

- **1940s:** Food rationing begins in Britain. Meat, butter, bacon, cheese, milk, eggs, sugar, and several other foods are all rationed. People are urged to eat potatoes and carrots. Everyone is provided with ration books. Because every person suffers equally, there is little complaining about the rationing of food.

  Today: Food insecurity is a huge issue in many countries, where food shortages are a result of war and drought. Even today, food insecurity is not unheard of in Great Britain. In 2012, the price of food increased nearly 5 percent over the previous year. While this increase may not seem onerous, inflation coupled with the economic recession has made hunger a reality for many British citizens.

- **1940s:** In December 1941, British women are drafted into the armed forces. Unmarried women in their twenties serve in the military, police, and fire services throughout the war. Older women are drafted to work in factories.

  Today: Although many women have died and continue to die as a result of combat in the war in Afghanistan, official British policy is that women are not combat troops. The Ministry of Defense argued in 2010 that allowing women to be combat troops would be distracting to male combat troops.

---

themselves to be English, rather than French. Originally the Channel Islands were part of Normandy, when William of Normandy conquered England in 1066 and became the English King William I. When William's son, Henry I, seized the Duchy of Normandy in 1106, the Channel Islands became part of England. Although the Duchy of Normandy was subsequently lost from English possession in 1204, the Channel Islands have continued to be a part of England, as self-governing possessions. Eight inhabited islands belonging to the Channel Islands; according to size from largest to smallest, the five main islands are Jersey, Guernsey, Alderney, Herm, and Sark.

The Channel Islands are considered to be dependent territories of the Crown. The islands are self-governed, under the authority of two bailiwicks, one each for Guernsey and Jersey. All the main islands except Jersey are in the Bailiwick of Guernsey. The islands have their own legal, fiscal, and administrative systems. Although the islands are essentially self-governing, primary legislation is approved by the queen's privy council. Great Britain is responsible for defense and international relations. While the Channel Islands have adopted British laws and the residents consider themselves British subjects, their cuisine has traditionally been French, notwithstanding the potato peel pie described in *The Guernsey Literary and Potato Peel Pie Society*.

Many notable writers have visited the islands, including Sir Walter Raleigh, Anthony Trollope, and George Eliot. Victor Hugo spent sixteen years living in exile on Jersey and then on Guernsey, where he finished writing *Les Misérables*. Juliet's decision to write a book about Guernsey is in keeping with the Channel Islands' literary past.

Guernsey Island, in the English Channel between England and France (© DavidYoung | Shutterstock.com)

German Occupation of the Channel Islands

On June 15, 1940, officials in London decided that the Channel Islands had no strategic importance and that Great Britain would not defend the islands from a German invasion. Four days later, on June 19, parents were advised to send their children to Great Britain for safety. People were given only a few hours to decide whether they wanted to evacuate their children or keep them at home on the islands. Children, mothers of small children, and schoolteachers were the first to be evacuated. The first boat left Guernsey on June 20, 1940. On June 28, German forces began bombing Guernsey. During the bombing, thirty-four islanders were killed and another sixty-seven were injured. The first German troops landed on Guernsey on June 30, 1940. Nine people were killed on the island of Jersey, which was also bombed. The neighboring island of Alderney had already been almost entirely evacuated. By the time that German troops arrived ashore only twelve civilians remained there. Germans took advantage of the abandonment of Alderney and established four concentration camps on the island. The small island of Sark was similarly invaded, with a German contingent of only ten soldiers. Herm, the smallest of the main Channel Islands, received a German visit, but no soldiers were stationed there.

As was common in other occupied territories, the German command established a civilian governing council designed to maintain order. There were not many Jewish citizens remaining on the islands. Many had already evacuated, but twelve Jews on Jersey and four on Guernsey registered with the Nazi commander. By 1941, persecution of Jewish residents was under way, and the first Jewish citizens were deported to concentration camps in April 1942. Initially food and other supplies were delivered from France. In the first few years, food shortages were not especially severe. Adolf Hitler was convinced that the British would try to retake the Channel Islands and ordered that impregnable barriers be built. Todt slave laborers were imported to built the barricades, and it is estimated that four of every ten died. The occupation ended May 9, 1945, with the surrender of the German commandant to British forces. Liberation Day is still celebrated every May 9 on Guernsey.

CRITICAL OVERVIEW

The Guernsey Literary and Potato Peel Pie Society has received a great deal of attention from critics. Among the many critics who reviewed the book is Craig Wilson, who writes in *USA Today* that Shaffer has "produced . . . a charming book" of letters. Wilson notes that booksellers like the book and that the historical setting is interesting, as are the eccentric characters who populate the novel. Wendy Smith writes in the *Washington Post* that *The Guernsey Literary and Potato Peel Pie Society* is not quite perfect. There are a few improbabilities, such as a book club where all the members actually read good literature and not "trashy thrillers." Still, Smith points out that these minor problems can be ignored as readers relish a novel that "is a sweet, sentimental paean to books and those who love them."

Although the review in *People* magazine was brief, the critics responsible for reviewing books did choose *The Guernsey Literary and Potato Peel Pie Society* as a People Pick in August 2008. These three critics—Moira Bailey, Clarissa Cruz, and Oliver Jones—call *The Guernsey Literary and Potato Peel Pie Society* "a jewel." Later in the same review, they write that "the book combines quirky and delightful characters with fascinating history, bringing alive the five-year occupation of Guernsey." In the final sentence, the three critics call *The Guernsey Literary and Potato Peel Pie Society* a "poignant and keenly observed" novel with romance and love that is rich in "the immeasurable sustenance to be found in good books and good friends." Equally enthusiastic is Yvonne Zipp, critic for the *Christian Science Monitor*. After first writing that people who love books really love books about books, Zipp compliments the "enchanting" discussions about "authors from Catullus to Shakespeare." Zipp labels *The Guernsey Literary and Potato Peel Pie Society* a "labor of love" that "shows on almost every page."

As might be expected for a novel set in wartime Britain, the London newspapers were especially enthusiastic. In a notice printed in the *Guardian*, reviewer Stevie Davies focuses on the characters who populate this novel. Davies writes that the inhabitants of Guernsey are commemorated as "beautiful spirits who pass through our midst and hunker undercover through brutal times." According to Davies,

these characters emerge from history as eccentric and kind and are "a comic version of the state of grace." Although the people of Guernsey suffer during the German occupation of their island, the evil of their German oppressors never overpowers the innate decency of the islanders. As for Shaffer's writing, Davies calls it "delicately offbeat, self deprecating," and "exquisitely turned." Shaffer's recreation of history is, Davies writes, especially effective at recreating the period of the London Blitz.

Laura Thompson's review of *The Guernsey Literary and Potato Peel Pie Society* for the London newspaper *Telegraph* initially focuses on the novel's protagonist, calling Juliet's voice "original and delightful." Like Smith in her *Washington Post* review, Thompson does not think the book perfect. This reviewer suggests that the plotting in the second half of the book is not as strong as in the first half and that the epistolary format is less effective after Juliet arrives on Guernsey; however, these weaknesses are not sufficient to distract from the book's many other strengths. According to Thompson, *The Guernsey Literary and Potato Peel Pie Society* has "substance beneath the delicious froth." This novel, writes Thompson, "is funny" and "moving." Thompson joins many other reviewers who continue to find much to enjoy in Shaffer and Barrow's novel.

CRITICISM

Sheri Karmiol

Karmiol teaches literature and drama at the University of New Mexico, where she is an adjunct professor in the University Honors Program. In the following essay, she discusses an important premise of The Guernsey Literary and Potato Peel Pie Society: *that reading books expands the reader's world, enriches his or her life, and can even save a reader's life.*

The Guernsey Literary and Potato Peel Pie Society has as a central premise that reading books is an experience of great importance that is not simply about entertainment. Reading creates community, educates, and even saves lives. Shaffer and Barrows's novel supports that premise with many examples of the practical and philosophical ways in which reading can do far more than bring enjoyment to the reader. *The Guernsey Literary and Potato Peel Pie Society*

WHAT DO I READ NEXT?

- Annie Barrows's children's novel *The Magic Half* (2009) is a story about a non-twin in a family of twins who discovers that she really does have a twin who lived in 1935.

- *Jersey under the Jack-Boot* (1992), by R.C.G. Maugham, is a nonfiction, first-person account of life on one of the Channel Islands after the German invasion of 1940.

- *Life in Occupied Guernsey: The Diaries of Ruth Ozanne 1940–1945* (2012), edited by William Parker, provides an eyewitness account of the German occupation of Guernsey. These diaries capture both the happy times for islanders and the deprivation of wartime shortages of food and fuel.

- *84 Charing Cross Road* (1970) is a story told through a collection of letters exchanged between Helene Hanff, who lived in New York, and a London bookseller whose establishment was located at 84 Charing Cross Road. The correspondence covers twenty years, beginning in 1949. Filled with a love for books, the letters end in 1969, when the London correspondent, Frank Doel, dies. Unlike an epistolary novel, these letters are not fictional. *84 Charing Cross Road* is a wonderful complimentary pairing to *The Guernsey Literary and Potato Peel Pie Society*, with their joint focus on a love of books.

- Peter Lihou's novel *Rachel's Shoe* (2010) is a young-adult novel set on one of the Channel Islands during World War II. This novel traces the lives of two teenagers into the 1970s to solve a mystery that began during the German occupation of the island.

- Arnold Griese's novel *The Wind Is Not a River* (1997) is written for middle-school students. The book focuses on the lives of two Native American children hiding from the Japanese army, which has captured and occupied their Attu village on the largest of the Alaskan Aleutian Islands, then a US territory.

- *Shattered: Stories of Children and War* (2003), by Jennifer Armstrong, is a collection of twelve short stories about children trying to survive war. The stories cover a vast period of time and distance, beginning during the American Civil War and continuing up to the war in Afghanistan.

- Alice Walker's novel *The Color Purple* (1982) is another modern example of epistolary fiction. This book tells the story of a young black woman, Celie, who finds that her inner strength is what she needs to survive racism and physical abuse in the American South during the first forty years of the twentieth century.

---

does not just promote generic reading, although reading of all sorts is heavily promoted in the novel. Instead, much of the focus of the novel is on books of literary repute, books often embraced for their literary merit, including drama and poetry, the reading of which saves people's lives both literally and figuratively in the novel. In reading *The Guernsey Literary and Potato Peel Pie Society*, readers learn that a love of books enriches the reader's life, expands the reader's world, and provides comfort when disappointment and pain threaten to destroy our recognizable world.

Reading books can erase the present, recreate the past, and refashion the future. In her review of *The Guernsey Literary and Potato Peel Pie Society* for the *Telegraph*, Laura Thompson writes that, although the Guernsey Literary Society may have begun as fiction, the society soon becomes reality. Thompson notes that as the group members begin to read and discuss books, the literary society "becomes a refuge from their grimly ambiguous situation." As Thompson notes in her review, the real topic of Shaffer's novel is not the events of the occupation of Guernsey but instead "the power of

IN READING *THE GUERNSEY LITERARY AND POTATO PEEL PIE SOCIETY*, READERS LEARN THAT A LOVE OF BOOKS ENRICHES THE READER'S LIFE, EXPANDS THE READER'S WORLD, AND PROVIDES COMFORT WHEN DISAPPOINTMENT AND PAIN THREATEN TO DESTROY OUR RECOGNIZABLE WORLD."

literature," which transforms the islanders' lives. The books that the Guernsey Literary Society members read do not just help occupy their time as they wait for the end of war. The books fill the islanders' minds with ideas and with possibilities for life that help erase the chaos and fear of the known and unknown that have colored their daily existence through five years of German occupation.

A love of books lies at the center of *The Guernsey Literary and Potato Peel Pie Society*. The protagonist, Juliet, is so focused on the value of books that she calls off her engagement when she discovers that her fiancé not only fails to see the need for books in her life but also fails to find any value in them. Juliet loves books so much and sees so much potential for books that she chooses to make significant changes in her own life based solely on her belief in the power of books. In writing to Dawsey Adams, Juliet explains what it is about books and reading that is so important to her. She writes that "one tiny thing will interest you in a book, and that tiny thing will lead you onto another book, and another bit there will lead you onto a third book." Each book that she reads leads to another book, whose pages offer new opportunities. Reading helps Juliet transcend her own life and opens her life to fresh possibilities that expand her world. She even risks her life for books. The letter from Juliet's fire warden partner is filled with disapproval of Juliet's choice to sprint toward the flames that threatened to burn the Temple Hall Library, thereby diverting the firemen from their job of fighting the fire so that they might save Juliet. For Juliet, however, all she sees are books burning. The decision to rush into the fire may be foolish, but for Juliet the need to save books is more important than her own life.

Reading enriches Juliet's life, as is the case for everyone who belongs to the Guernsey Literary Society. Through her correspondence with the Guernsey islanders, Juliet discovers that she is not alone in her love of books. The literary society that is formed on Guernsey turns the introvert Dawsey into a new person, and thus reading enriches and transforms his life. Where before he was shy and unwilling to spend time with people, the community dinners and the discussion of books lead him to be more social; the literary society also encourages Dawsey to become involved in people's lives. In an early letter to Juliet, Amelia Maugery admits that she has known Dawsey for more than thirty years but has exchanged few words with him that did not involve farming or weather. That all changes after they both become part of the Guernsey Literary Society.

The Guernsey Literary Society was created to save lives. It provided an excuse to explain breaking curfew, which ordinarily would have resulted in arrest and, possibly, deportation off the island. The result, though, is a book club that turns a group of mostly strangers into a group of friends, who not only help one another in many small ways but also make the German occupation easier to bear. As important as the friendships that lend support is the intellectual stimulation that the Guernsey Literary Society offers to the members. At a time when no letters, newspapers, or magazines are permitted, intellectual activity is in short supply on Guernsey. People who remain isolated and alone need an outlet, and the books that are chosen present the opportunity to read and then argue about the merits of a particular book. In one of her letters to Juliet, Amelia writes that the members of the Guernsey Literary Society "read books, talked books, argued over books, and became dearer and dearer to one another." Thus books represented more that just reading material or even much-needed intellectual stimulation. They created a whole new community of good friends and a path to intellectual discussion that allowed each member to grow.

In her letter to Juliet, Isola writes about the Brontë sisters and what their novels mean to her. The books allow Isola to experience something that is missing in her life. She writes that she likes "stories of passionate encounters," because she has never experienced a passionate encounter. Reading takes readers to another world and to another time that is foreign to them. When Isola reads *Wuthering Heights*, the book transports her to Cathy and Heathcliff's world and to the kind of romance that changes their world. Books can do that for a reader, and a reader such as Isola, who lives alone, who admits that she is unattractive in appearance, and who has never been in love, can experience vicariously the emotions of characters who do feel passionate love, even if this kind of love is lacking in her own life.

The members of the Guernsey Literary Society read books they would never have read before the creation of the society forced their participation in reading serious literature. Although they might never have read such serious literature as Catullus, Seneca, Shakespeare, or Charles Lamb, the islanders find that the challenge of reading these books and arguing their merit helps them grow intellectually. When Eben writes to Juliet, he tells her that most of the members of the Guernsey Literary Society had not read a book since they were last forced to do so when they were in school. Eben discovers that Shakespeare's words have meaning in a world in which the German occupation has seemed to bring perpetual darkness to the lives of the islanders. When the Germans invaded Guernsey, Eben lacked the vocabulary to express how he felt, but after he begins reading Shakespeare, Eben finds the words that he lacked and that express his pain and grief. The words are from *Antony and Cleopatra*: "The bright day is done, and we are for the dark." Reading Shakespeare gives Eben the words he needs to express himself. That is one of the wonderful benefits of reading. Readers expand their vocabulary, just as Shakespeare's audiences did as they learned the new words that he coined. But readers like Eben also learn that there are other ways to express oneself beyond "*damn them, damn them*," which was all that Eben could think to say when the German invaders arrived.

Literature is universal. It reveals the breadth of human experience, both the good and the terrible. It eliminates the boundaries in our lives and permits readers to escape the misery of the world and imagine a better one. That is what literature did for John Booker, who writes to Juliet that he loved reading *The Letters of Seneca*, which were funny enough to take John's mind off the risk he was facing every day. John writes that Seneca and the Guernsey Literary Society are what kept him "from the direful life of a drunk."

John is the child of a Jewish mother. To avoid arrest and deportation to a concentration camp, he pretends to be Lord Tobias, a British aristocrat. For three years, John lives in fear of being caught. This was exceedingly stressful, but Seneca brightened John's days while his friends in the literary society conspired to help keep him safe. For John, reading and the literary society saved his life and kept him sane. Laughing at Seneca also helped him learn about a world he would never have visited if not for the literary society. John also sees connections between his own world of occupation and Seneca's world and is able to compare the German soldiers, with their desire for perfectly coiffed hair, to the soldiers of the Roman Praetorian Guard, who are also too much devoted to their hair. For John, who "came to love" the book club meetings, the literary society "helped to make the Occupation bearable."

The men and women of Guernsey discover what other readers have also discovered—that reading books has the power to transport readers to experience a life beyond their own world. In his essay "What is Literature For?" Tzvetan Todorov writes about his own narrowly defined existence under the Communist regime in Bulgaria, where he was told what to read and what to think. Todorov writes that, while he was still a student, he read books that provided him the opportunity to "satisfy my curiosity, live adventures, experience fright and happiness." These books opened a world beyond the world that was experienced by his classmates. The books that he read inspired Todorov to try writing his own poems, dramas, and stories. Many years later, and after a lifetime studying literature and reading vast amounts of fiction and nonfiction, Todorov writes about what he learned from his many years of reading. He writes that, although it is "denser than daily life but not radically different from it, literature expands our universe, prompts us to see other ways to conceive and organize it." Literature is like life but with infinitely more possibilities. In defending the value of literature as something more than just entertainment, Todorov claims that there are infinite possibilities to be found in reading, which make the world "more beautiful" and infuse it with meaning. As *The Guernsey Literary and Potato Peel Pie Society* makes clear, reading is not just for people of a certain class or education. As Todorov suggests, "literature lets each one of us fulfill our human potential."

Juliet begins a correspondence with Dawsey that eventually draws her to Guernsey. *(© Kudryashka / Shutterstock.com)*

In her acknowledgments for *The Guernsey Literary and Potato Peel Pie Society*, written before her death, Shaffer writes that she hopes "that my book will illuminate my belief that love of art—be it poetry, storytelling, painting, sculpture, or music—enables people to transcend any barrier man has yet devised." It is safe to say that Shaffer's own love of books, as well as the love of books revealed through her characters' lives—Juliet, Dawsey, Amelia, Eben, John, Isola, and others—shines through *The Guernsey Literary and Potato Peel Pie Society*. A book about the love for books cannot help but make all readers love books just a bit more.

Source: Sheri Metzger Karmiol, Critical Essay on *The Guernsey Literary and Potato Peel Society*, in *Novels for Students*, Gale, Cengage Learning, 2013.

Susan Clifford Braun

In the following review, Braun positively reviews the novel, calling it a "marvelous debut."

In January 1946, London is beginning to recover from World War II, and Juliet Ashton is looking for a subject for her next book. She spent the war years writing a column for the *Times* until her own dear flat became a victim of a German bomb. While sifting through the rubble and reconstructing her life, she receives a letter from a man on Guernsey, the British island occupied by the Germans. He'd found her name on the flyleaf of a book by Charles Lamb and was

writing to ask if she knew of any other books by the author. So begins a correspondence that draws Juliet into the community of Guernsey and the members of the Literary and Potato Peel Pie Society. Named to protect its members from arrest by the Germans, the society shares their unique love of literature and life with a newfound friend. Seeing this as the subject of her next book, Juliet sails to Guernsey—a voyage that will change her life. Reminiscent of Helene Hanff's *84 Charing Cross Road*, this is a warm, funny, tender, and thoroughly entertaining celebration of the power of the written word. This marvelous debut novel, sure to have book club appeal, is highly recommended for all collections.

Source: Susan Clifford Braun, Review of *The Guernsey Literary and Potato Peel Pie Society*, in *Library Journal*, Vol. 133, No. 12, July 1, 2008, pp. 67–68.

Publishers Weekly

In the following review, a contributor remarks that the novel is "charming."

The letters comprising this small charming novel begin in 1946, when single, 30-something author Juliet Ashton (nom de plume "Izzy Bickerstaff") writes to her publisher to say she is tired of covering the sunny side of war and its aftermath. When Guernsey farmer Dawsey Adams finds Juliet's name in a used book and invites articulate—and not-so-articulate—neighbors to write Juliet with their stories, the book's epistolary circle widens, putting Juliet back in the path of war stories. The occasionally contrived letters jump from incident to incident—including the formation of the *Guernsey Literary and Potato Peel Pie Society* while Guernsey was under German occupation—and person to person in a manner that feels disjointed. But Juliet's quips are so clever, the Guernsey inhabitants so enchanting and the small acts of heroism so vivid and moving that one forgives the authors (Shaffer died earlier this year) for not being able to settle on a single person or plot. Juliet finds in the letters not just inspiration for her next work, but also for her life—as will readers.

Source: Review of *The Guernsey Literary and Potato Peel Pie Society*, in *Publishers Weekly*, Vol. 255, No. 16, April 21, 2008, p. 30.

Mary Ellen Quinn

In the following review, Quinn describes the novel as a "literary soufflé."

Winding up her book tour promoting her collection of lighthearted wartime newspaper columns, Juliet Ashton casts about for a more serious project. Opportunity comes in the form of a letter she receives from Mr. Dawsey Adams, who happens to possess a book that Julia once owned. Adams is a member of the Guernsey Literary and Potato Peel Pie Society—no ordinary book club. Rather, it was formed as a ruse and became a way for people to get together without raising the suspicions of Guernsey's Nazi occupiers. Written in the form of letters (a lost art), this novel by an aunt-and-niece team has loads of charm, especially as long as Juliet is still in London corresponding with the society members. Some of the air goes out of the book when she gets to Guernsey; the humorous tone doesn't quite mesh with what the islanders suffered. But readers should enjoy this literary souffle for the most part, and curiosity about the German occupation of the British Channel Islands will be piqued.

Source: Mary Ellen Quinn, Review of *The Guernsey Literary and Potato Peel Pie Society*, in *Booklist*, Vol. 104, No. 21, July 1, 2008, pp. 34–35.

SOURCES

Amos, Deborah, "Tales of a Nazi-occupied British Isle in 'Guernsey,'" Interview with Annie Barrows, National Public Radio website, July 29, 2008, http://www.npr.org/templates/transcript/transcript.php?storyId=93018411 (accessed July 16, 2012).

Bailey, Moira, Clarissa Cruz, and Oliver Jones, "Picks and Pans Review: Letters from a Troubled Isle," in *People*, Vol. 70, No. 6, August 11, 2008, http://www.people.com/people/archive/article/0,,20221668,00.html (accessed July 16, 2012).

"British Police Order Evac of Central Birmingham District," in *USA Today*, July 9, 2005, http://usatoday30.usatoday.com/news/world/2005-07-09-birmingham-evac_x.htm (accessed September 30, 2012).

"The Channel Islands," *Island at War*, PBS website, http://www.pbs.org/wgbh/masterpiece/islandatwar/islands.html (accessed July 20, 2012).

Cohen, Frederick E., "The Jews in the Islands of Jersey, Guernsey and Sark during the German Occupation 1940–1945," in *Journal of Holocaust Education*, Vol. 6, No. 1, 1997, pp. 27–81.

Courtenay-Thompson, Fiona, and Kate Phelps, eds., *The 20th Century Year by Year*, Barnes & Noble, 1998, pp. 142, 147, 149, 151.

Cummings, Angela, "Martinsburg Native Authors Heralded Book," in *Martinsburg Journal*, August 17, 2008, http://www.journal-news.net/page/content.detail/id/509545/Martinsburg-native-authors-heralded-book.html (accessed July 16, 2012).

Davies, Stevie, Review of *The Guernsey Literary and Potato Peel Pie Society*, in *Guardian*, August 8, 2008, http://www.guardian.co.uk/books/2008/aug/09/fiction4 (accessed July 12, 2012).

"Genocides, Politicides, and Other Mass Murder Since 1945, with Stages in 2008," Genocide Watch website, http://www.genocidewatch.org/images/Genocidesand Politicidessince1945withstagesin2008.pdf (accessed July 20, 2012).

"German Occupation of the Channel Islands," BBC History website, http://www.bbc.co.uk/history/topics/occupation_channel_islands (accessed July 20, 2012).

Glennon, Lorraine, ed., *The 20th Century*, JG Press, 1999, pp. 298–301.

Grant, George, "Why Food Security Is Not Just a Problem for the Third World," in *Telegraph*, April 24, 2012, http://www.telegraph.co.uk/news/uknews/9224240/Why-food-security-is-not-just-a-problem-for-the-Third-World.html (accessed September 30, 2012).

Grossman, Lev, "Temptation Island," in *Time*, July 24, 2008, http://www.time.com/time/magazine/article/0,9171,1826283,00.html (accessed July 16, 2012).

Harmon, William, and Hugh Holman, *A Handbook to Literature*, 11th ed., Prentice Hall, 2009, pp. 95–96, 205–206, 270, 420–22, 508.

"Interview with Annie Barrows," LitLovers Online website, http://www.litlovers.com/reading-guides/13-fiction/406-guernsey-literary-and-potato-interview (accessed July 16, 2012).

Jennings, Peter, and Todd Brewster, "Over the Edge," in *The Century*, Doubleday, 1998, pp. 215–30.

"Jews of the Channel Islands," Holocaust Research Project website, http://www.holocaustresearchproject.org/nazioc cupation/channelislands.html (accessed July 20, 2012).

McAuliff, Michael, "Women Allowed in Combat under Senate Defense Bill," in *Huffington Post*, May 24, 2012, http://www.huffingtonpost.com/2012/05/24/women-combat-senate-defense-bill_n_1543763.html (accessed July 20, 2012).

Norton-Taylor, Richard, "Women Still Banned from Combat Roles after Ministry of Defence Review," in *Guardian*, November 29, 2010, http://www.guardian.co.uk/uk/2010/nov/29/women-combat-ban-remains (accessed September 30, 2012).

"The Occupation of the Channel Islands 1940–45," Heritage Guernsey website, http://www.heritageguernsey.com/historical-guernsey/ (accessed July 20, 2012).

Shaffer, Mary Ann, and Annie Barrows, *The Guernsey Literary and Potato Peel Pie Society*, Dial Press, 2008.

Smith, Wendy, "The Resistance," in *Washington Post*, August 3, 2008, http://www.washingtonpost.com/wp-dyn/content/article/2008/07/31/AR2008073102685.html (accessed July 12, 2012).

Thompson, Laura, Review of *The Guernsey Literary and Potato Peel Pie Society*, in *Telegraph*, August 30, 2008, http://www.telegraph.co.uk/culture/books/fictionreviews/3559411/Review-The-Guernsey-Literary-and-Potato-Peel-Pie-Society-by-Mary-Ann-Shaffer.html (accessed July 12, 2012).

Todorov, Tzvetan, "What Is Literature For?," in *New Literary History*, Vol. 38, No. 1, Winter 2007, pp. 13–32.

Wilson, Craig, "'Potato Peel Pie' Has Ingredients for Success," in *USA Today*, July 31, 2008, http://www.usatoday.com/life/books/news/2008-07-29-potato_N.htm (accessed July 16, 2012).

Zipp, Yvonne, Review of *The Guernsey Literary and Potato Peel Pie Society*, in *Christian Science Monitor*, July 28, 2008, http://www.csmonitor.com/Books/Book-Reviews/2008/0728/the-guernsey-literary-and-potato-peel-society (accessed July 12, 2012).

FURTHER READING

Baer, Elizabeth R., and Myrna Goldenberg, eds., *Experience and Expression: Women, the Nazis, and the Holocaust*, Wayne State University Press, 2003.

> This text contains a collection of essays that focus on the experiences of women during the Holocaust. Several of the essays examine the ways in which women nurtured one another and thus enabled one another to survive.

Baines, Valerie, *Guernsey Sketchbook*, Book Guild, 2001.

> This book is a collection of sketches and watercolor prints that cover the author's forty years of visits to Guernsey.

Batiste, Rob, *Guernsey's Coast*, Guernsey Books, 2010.

> This book is a collection of essays, with many accompanying photographs, that explore the coastline of Guernsey.

Bunting, Madeleine, *The Model Occupation: The Channel Islands under German Rule 1940–1945*, Random House, 2004.

> Bunting's book is a sociological study of how people react when living in an occupied territory. Bunting's portrait of the islanders is not always flattering. The focus on islanders as Nazi collaborators is not a popular view for the people of the Channel Islands.

De Gaulle Anthonioz, Geniviev, *The Dawn of Hope: A Memoir of Ravensbrück and Beyond*, Arcade, 1999.

> This memoir by a member of the French resistance recounts her life as a political prisoner at Ravensbrück, the women's concentration camp in Germany.

Dwork, Deborah, ed., *Voices and Views: A History of the Holocaust*, Jewish Foundation for the Righteous, 2002.

> This text provides an unusual historical account because it is formatted as a collection of personal essays that explore both the events of the Holocaust and the impact and meaning of this period of history.

Lang, Suzanne, *Displaced Donkeys: A Guernsey Family's War*, Pinknote Press, 2009.

> This memoir tells the story of one family's decision to send their children to England. Families were given just twenty-four hours to decide whether to send their children to safety and whether to send them alone or with their mothers; likewise they had to choose whether fathers should also evacuate to join the British armed forces to defend England against invasion.

Rittner, Carolm and John K. Roth, eds., *Different Voices: Women and the Holocaust*, Paragon House, 1993.

> This book is an anthology divided into three separate sections. The first section contains memoirs written by Jewish women who experienced the Holocaust. The second section provides a collection of essays that interpret the events of the period, from racism to resistance to moral choice. The final section contains essays that reflect on the events of the Holocaust.

Turner, Barry, *Outpost of Occupation: The Nazi Occupation of the Channel Islands, 1940–1945*, Aurum Press, 2010.

> This account of the German occupation of the Channel Islands is rich in first-person testimonies by the people who were present on the Channel Islands at the time. It is a serious but readable historical account of the German occupation of the Channel Islands during World War II.

SUGGESTED SEARCH TERMS

Mary Ann Shaffer AND The Guernsey Literary and Potato Peel Pie Society

Annie Barrows AND The Guernsey Literary and Potato Peel Pie Society

Mary Ann Shaffer AND Guernsey visit

Shaffer and Barrows AND epistolary novels

Channel Islands AND Jewish deportations

Channel Islands AND World War II

Guernsey AND German Occupation

Channel Islands AND Todt prisoners

The House of the Scorpion

NANCY FARMER

2002

The House of the Scorpion (2002) is a novel by
Nancy Farmer, a celebrated author of science fiction and fantasy for young adults. It is set about one
hundred years in the future, when Mexico (renamed
Aztlán in this future time) and the United States
have each turned over part of their border territory
to a group of drug lords, who produce drugs freely
in the land they call "Opium" while they keep people from crossing the borders illegally. The novel
interweaves a recognizable not-too-distant past, as
the residents of Opium live without computers, cell
phones, and other modern conveniences, and a
frightening future, when cloning and interfering
with people's brains to make them into compliant
workers are taken for granted. The protagonist is
Matt, a clone created from the tissue of El Patrón,
the wealthiest and most powerful of the drug lords.
As he ages to adolescence, Matt struggles to determine his identity and his worth, as a clone and as a
human, and tries to find friendship and family.

 The House of the Scorpion, Farmer's third
Newbery Honor Book, also won the National
Book Award. It has been translated into at least
seven languages, including Chinese, French, and
Slovenian.

AUTHOR BIOGRAPHY

Farmer was born on July 9, 1941, in Phoenix,
Arizona, the youngest of three children of Frank
and Sarah Coe. At the age of three, she caught

Nancy Farmer (© *AP Images* | *Mark Lennihan*)

was forty years old, Farmer enjoyed reading books to the couple's four-year-old son, Daniel, and decided to try writing. The quality of her work was quickly recognized, and her second novel, *The Ear, the Eye, and the Arm* (1989), first published in Zimbabwe, became a success in the United States as well when it was reissued in 1994; it was named a Newbery Honor Book, among other recognitions. In 1988, Farmer and her family returned to California, where she wrote and sometimes took work as a lab technician. By 1992, she was able to write full-time.

As 2012 drew to a close, Farmer had published ten novels for young adults in addition to four picture books, and her work had been published in twenty-six languages. Three of her novels, *The Ear, the Eye and the Arm*; another novel set in Africa, *A Girl Named Disaster* (1996); and *The House of the Scorpion* (2002), were named Newbery Honor Books; *The House of the Scorpion* also won the 2002 National Book Award for Young People's Literature. Between 2004 and 2009, she published the three novels in the Sea of Trolls series before beginning to draft a long-promised sequel to *The House of the Scorpion*. She and her husband lived in Menlo, California, near the Cargill Salt-works, which she used as the model for the shrimp-harvesting factory in *The House of the Scorpion*.

measles from her sister Mary; to make amends, Mary taught Farmer to read at a level far beyond her years. However, dyslexia kept Farmer from doing well in school. By the time she was nine, her father was running a hotel in Yuma, Arizona, near the United States–Mexico border. Farmer helped out at the front desk and made friends with cowboys, railroad men, and other travelers. Many days, she skipped school to explore the desert and the banks of the Colorado River, but she read all of the books and magazines left behind at the hotel and eventually found her way to the public library.

After graduating from Reed College in 1963, Farmer took a two-year Peace Corps assignment in India. For a few years after returning, she worked in a biology lab at the University of California, Berkeley. In 1972, she went to Africa, where she lived for seventeen years. First she lived in Mozambique, where she worked as a chemist and entomologist. Next she went to Zimbabwe to work on tsetse fly eradication; in 1976, she met literature professor Harold Farmer in Harare, Zimbabwe, and they married. When she

PLOT SUMMARY

Chapters 1–5: Youth: 0 to 6

The House of the Scorpion opens in a laboratory, where human embryos are being grown in petri dishes. Only one survives long enough to be gestated—in a cow's uterus—and "harvested." Ordinarily, the newborn would have its brain damaged intentionally to dull its intelligence, but because this one is "a Matteo Alacrán," it is spared. Five years later, that newborn is a boy named Matt, who lives with a woman named Celia in a small house surrounded by poppy fields. Celia is a cook in the Big House, and when she goes to work each day, she leaves Matt alone with the doors locked and the windows nailed shut. There is a clear bond of love between Matt and Celia, but she will not allow him to call her *Mamá*, explaining that he has only been loaned to her.

One day, two children see Matt through the window, but he is too afraid to speak to them.

MEDIA ADAPTATIONS

- *The House of the Scorpion*, recorded as an unabridged audiobook and read by Broadway performer Raul Esparza, was produced by Simon & Schuster Audio in 2004.

Celia identifies them as Steven Alacrán, a thirteen-year-old boy from the Big House, and his friend Emilia Mendoza, also thirteen, whose father is a US senator. The next day, Steven and Emilia return with Emilia's younger sister, María. Matt breaks through the window and jumps out, landing in his bare feet on the shattered glass.

Steven carries Matt, who is bleeding profusely and in great pain, to the Big House. As Rosa, the housekeeper, and the children try to remove the glass, they discover writing on the bottom of Matt's foot: "Property of the Alacrán Estate." Just then, Steven's father comes into the room and orders that Matt, whom he calls "this little beast," be taken from the house and the sheet he is lying on be burned. Rosa dumps Matt on the lawn, where he lies alone as darkness falls. The children watch from a distance, and Steven explains that Matt is a clone of El Patrón, who is so powerful that he can protect his clones' intelligence. Clearly all the children know about clones, whom they despise as less than human. Willum, the doctor, arrives, removes the last bit of glass, and turns Matt over to an unwilling Rosa to care for. Later that night, María sneaks into Matt's room with food and sleeps curled up by his side. When she is discovered, she is sent away, and Matt is imprisoned by Rosa in a small room filled with sawdust. He lives there for six months, visited only by insects, the doctor, and Steven's younger brother, Tom, who torments Matt through the window. Finally Matt withdraws into silence. Even when María and Celia find him and call to him through his window, he does not speak.

Chapters 6–14: Middle Age: 7 to 11

One morning, Rosa cleans Matt up and takes him to meet Matteo Alacrán, the old man known as El Patrón who visits this house only occasionally. Celia is also there, and she describes Matt's poor treatment. El Patrón is angry, and Rosa is taken away. Matt and the old man take an instant liking to each other. The old man shares a fine dinner with Matt and talks about his impoverished childhood in what used to be called Mexico but is now Aztlán. People from his town were called *alacránes*, or scorpions, and when the man became rich he changed his name to Matteo Alacrán to honor them. Matt, who has the same name, is happy to share something with his new friend. Matt is returned to Celia's care in a fine apartment in the mansion. The Alacrán family is instructed to treat Matt with respect, although they continue to despise him, and El Patrón appoints a bodyguard, Tam Lin, to protect Matt.

María remains his friend, although she also spends time with Tom, who is cruel to Matt and not very nice to María. Tom can look apologetic and sincere when he has done something bad, and most people fall for his innocent looks. He and Matt hate each other. Soon vacation is over, and María and the other children go back to school. Tam Lin finds a teacher for Matt: she is a slow-witted woman who repeats the same lesson over and over. Matt becomes so frustrated that he shouts at her—the first time he has spoken in months. Tam Lin gently sends her away and eventually explains that she is an "eejit," a person whose brain has been treated so that she can perform only one task. Now that Matt is speaking again, Tam Lin decides to begin Matt's real education.

Tam Lin and Matt get a horse and ride away for a picnic. As they pass the poppy fields, they see a farm worker lying dead. Tam Lin explains that this man is also an eejit, programmed to work in the fields without stopping; the man probably did not hear the command to drink water and kept working in the heat until he died. Past the Alacrán boundary, they climb a steep mountain to a secret oasis where they can speak privately. Tam Lin wants Matt to know what a clone is, how he was created from a bit of El Patrón's flesh, that most people hate clones, and that the old man wants his clone to be brought up well.

Tam Lin and Celia arrange for Matt to study through distance learning, and he does very well. María comes to visit on holidays, bringing her dog Furball, but when he is alone, Matt explores the house. He enjoys hiding behind the plants and listening to Felicia, the mother of Steven and Tom, play the piano. Once a concert pianist, she is now a sad, lonely alcoholic whose husband ignores her. Matt discovers a series of tunnels running through the house behind the closets with peepholes into most of the rooms. Spying on the family, he overhears a strange conversation. The doctor and Mr. Alacrán (Steven's father), are trying to persuade Mr. Alacrán's sick father, called El Viejo ("the old man"), to seek treatment or a transplant.

El Patrón returns to celebrate his one hundred and forty-third birthday. All of the children come back for the party, and Tom plays a mean trick on María, hiding Furball in the toilet with the lid closed. In addition to the Alacrán and Mendoza families, important business and government leaders from around the world attend the party, including Mr. MacGregor, who runs a large Farm near San Diego. El Patrón has received fetal brain implants to give him more vitality. He and MacGregor compare health treatments and make fun of El Viejo, El Patrón's grandson, because he refuses to extend his life beyond what he believes God has given him.

All of the guests pay homage to El Patrón, bringing him expensive presents and listening to his life story, which they have heard many times. Matt, resentful that María is being nice to Tom, switches the place cards so that María will sit next to him at dinner and Tom will be at the baby table. Tam Lin quietly scolds Matt, but El Patrón praises him for dealing in this way with an enemy. El Patrón's birthday is, in a way, also Matt's, and on this day Matt can ask for anything. Still angry with María, he orders her to give him a kiss. The crowd protests—the idea of a human's kissing a clone is repulsive to them—but El Patrón insists, and no one dares go against him. Too late, Matt realizes that he is humiliating his friend, not winning her back.

The next day, Tom tricks Matt and María into meeting him in the hospital wing and shows them a deranged, sick clone of MacGregor's strapped to a bed, howling. Matt and María are upset about the suffering clone. Matt worries that as he ages he will go mad as well. Celia explains that the clone's brain was damaged when he was born and that Matt was spared this damage. She also explains that while Felicia is Tom's mother, his father is not Mr. Alacrán but Mr. MacGregor, with whom Felicia once

ran off. El Patrón made her and Tom come back, but no one in the family loves or respects them. Matt still has questions: How can he gain María's forgiveness? Will his brain be damaged later? Why does MacGregor need a clone at all?

Matt decides to force María to listen to his apology by kidnapping Furball and holding him hostage until she agrees to meet with Matt. He steals a bottle of Felicia's laudanum, a sleeping drug made from opium, planning to give some to Furball to keep him quiet. When he kidnaps Furball, the dog stays quiet, so Matt does not give him the drug. The next day, Furball is found dead, killed with an overdose of laudanum from a bottle with Matt's fingerprints on it. No one, not even Tam Lin or Celia, believes that Matt did not kill the dog, and María's father, Senator Mendoza, takes the girl away. To make things even worse, Tam Lin tells Matt that El Patrón is leaving again and Tam Lin is going with him.

Chapters 15–22: Old Age: 12 to 14
Lonely with Tam Lin and María gone, Matt returns to the hidden oasis, getting a horse from Rosa, now an eejit who does not even recognize him. At the oasis, Matt finds blankets, pots, food, and books that Tam Lin has left for him with a note signed, "Yor frend." Feeling better, Matt returns to the mansion and learns that El Viejo has died. During the funeral, attended by family and friends, the priest orders that Matt be removed from the holy event. María defends Matt, and he knows he has been forgiven. Matt and María slip off to the tunnels to talk. From there, they overhear Tom and Felicia talking disrespectfully about El Viejo, and Felicia laughingly tells Tom that she killed Furball. María is shocked, but she does not have time to talk with Matt about it before Tam Lin comes to sneak her back to her father.

Matt is alone again, and returns to the oasis. He begins to read a book called *A History of Opium*, which claims that El Patrón is evil, a powerful man who became wealthy through the illegal drug trade. This is news to Matt. For his lifetime, drugs have been legal. The book explains that a hundred years before, when Mexico and the United States could not control either their borders or the drug trade, the dealers proposed that each country give up a strip of land in the middle and turn it over to the drug lords, who would guard the borders and promise not to sell drugs in Mexico or the United States.

The new country in the middle, called Opium, is run by the two biggest Farmers, El Patrón and MacGregor. Matt tosses the book away, refusing to believe its story.

Matt visits the water purification plant to learn how it works. He has reasoned that El Patrón must have given him a good education because he intends Matt to help run the Farm one day. Matt sees long rows of buildings with bars and small windows, where the eejit farmworkers live, and is nearly killed by the fumes from the chemical holding tanks nearby. He is rescued by two Farm Patrol guards, who become friendly when they learn who Matt is. They tell him that Tam Lin was once an activist fighting for Scottish nationalism and that, in attempting to bomb the British prime minister, he accidentally blew up a bus full of schoolchildren.

The next day, Matt is summoned to see El Patrón, who has had a heart attack. The old man receives a piggyback heart transplant, a small heart that will work in concert with his own. But it becomes clear that the small heart will not be enough. Tam Lin and Celia argue about how much Matt should know, and finally Matt realizes that he was created to provide spare parts for El Patrón. Overwhelmed by all his new knowledge, Matt returns to the oasis and uncovers one more secret: *The History of Opium* was written by Esperanza Mendoza, the mother María thought had died years ago.

El Patrón stabilizes, and again the house is busy, this time with the wedding of Steven and Emilia. MacGregor arrives looking young and healthy, and María arrives looking happy and beautiful. María reveals that she knows Matt's fate and that she is expected to marry Tom when they are old enough, and Matt tells María that her mother seems to be alive. Matt is not invited to the wedding, but he watches it from one of the peepholes. When El Patrón has another heart attack, everyone looks for Matt so they can use his heart for a transplant. María tries to help him escape, but he is caught and taken to the hospital.

Chapters 23–25: Age 14
Matt is brought to El Patrón, who wonders why Matt, like the clones before him, does not appreciate that he has been given fourteen years of life and education. But when it is time to prepare Matt for surgery, Celia announces that she has been giving him low doses of arsenic for months, making his organs unfit for transplant. El Patrón

dies. Tam Lin offers to "dispose of the clone" but instead takes Matt to the oasis and helps him pack up to escape to Aztlán, where he will be able to find María at school. Back at the mansion, Celia was to be turned into an eejit, but she is only pretending to be one. Tam Lin says goodbye to Matt for the last time. Matt hikes over the mountains, evades the Farm Patrol, and literally falls over the border into Aztlán.

Chapters 26–38: La Vida Nueva
Matt is picked up by two border guards, who take him to an orphanage. There, for the first time, he is surrounded by other children who treat him as an equal. The orphanage is staffed by Keepers who make the boys work endlessly and feed them nothing but plankton. They indoctrinate the boys to make them docile, having them recite the Five Principles of Good Citizenship and the Four Attitudes Leading to Right-Mindedness over and over. The orphans are from Aztlán, captured when they were trying to cross the border into Opium with their parents. Many boys believe that their parents have found better lives across the border, and Matt does not tell them that they were probably caught and turned into eejits. Matt becomes friends with the tough, cynical Chacho and Fidelito, a small, sickly boy. All three boys are transferred to a plankton-processing plant near San Luis, the city where María's convent is.

The Keepers at the plankton factory are cruel to the boys. In the evenings, the boys are supposed to confess transgressions, but Matt does not believe he has done anything wrong and stays quiet. A new friend is Ton-Ton, an older boy. He appears to be unintelligent, but Matt can see that Ton-Ton is just a slow, deliberate thinker. One night, Ton-Ton is punished for a small offense by being beaten with a cane until he is bloody. Matt is also hit a few times, and when he does not cry out, the other boys admire his bravery. But when he still does not seem to accept his position and the Keepers' teachings, they turn on Fidelito as a last attempt to break Matt's will. Jorge, a Keeper, tries to beat Fidelito with the cane. Matt knows the beating could kill the smaller boy, and he and Chacho attack Jorge and hold him down. The Keepers break up the fight, and Jorge taunts the boys by revealing that Matt is a clone, or *crot*, and calling Ton-Ton stupid.

That night, Jorge orders Matt's and Chacho's mouths, wrists, and ankles bound with tape and has them tossed into a massive pit filled with bones. The boys manage to escape, and they are picked up by Ton-Ton and Fidelito, who are driving a shrimp harvester. The boys have staged a mutiny, locked the Keepers in their rooms, and dosed them with enough laudanum to keep them asleep for a long time. After Ton-Ton drives the large machine to the fence and uses its claws to tear a hole in it, the boys escape into San Luis and make their way to the Convent of Santa Clara. Chacho has been seriously injured, and the sisters care for him in their hospital. Jorge and the other Keepers show up and try to take the four escapees back, but they are stopped by the strong, sharp-tongued woman in charge, Doña Esperanza—María's mother. María appears and greets Matt with an excited hug.

Esperanza has been trying for years to bring down the drug lords and free the eejits. Now she is especially concerned because Opium has been under a lockdown for months, with no one allowed in or out. Esperanza hopes that Matt, an exact copy of El Patrón. will be able to use his fingerprints and DNA code to get through Opium's elaborate security system. She asks him to try, although it could be dangerous, and tells him that according to international law Matt is now the only El Patrón, the head of the drug business and the owner of everything the old man owned. Matt sneaks into Opium and returns to the mansion. He reunites with Celia, who tells him a horrible story: at El Patrón's funeral, the guests went down to the vaults where the dead man kept his treasure and, according to his wishes, drank a toast with special wine he had saved. Nearly all of the guests, including Tam Lin, died. Matt rides to the oasis and begins to plan how he will repurpose his poppy fields for food crops and bring in doctors to reverse the damage to the eejits. He knows that he will succeed, with the help of Celia and María and his friends from Aztlán.

CHARACTERS

Felicia Alacrán

Felicia is the wife of Mr. Alacrán and the mother of Steven, Tom, and an older son named Benito. Before her marriage, she was a concert pianist, and she still plays beautifully. However, no one

listens to her play; she spends most of her time alone, ignored by her family. Felicia, like all of the Alacrán family, is under the thumb of El Patrón. Years before the novel begins, Felicia had an affair with Mr. MacGregor and went to live with him, bearing him a son, Tom. But El Patrón, who does not willingly give up anything—or anyone—made them come back, and now Felicia lives in a home where no one wants her. She drinks heavily and also takes laudanum, a drug that helps her sleep. Felicia feels powerless, but she is protective of Tom and resentful of the attention Matt gets. To get back at the family for their bad treatment of Tom at El Patrón's birthday party, she kills María's dog Furball and lets Matt take the blame. Months later, Matt and María overhear Felicia telling Tom that she killed the dog, and they also discover that she has been spying on the family with the cameras set up through the house.

Matteo Alacrán
See El Patrón

Mr. Alacrán
Mr. Alacrán is the father of Steven and another son, the son of El Viejo, and the great-grandson of El Patrón. When El Patrón is away, Mr. Alacrán is the master of the Big House, but El Patrón makes all the important decisions. His first action in the novel is to enter the room where five-year-old Matt has been brought because of his bleeding foot. Mr. Alacrán recognizes Matt as a clone and orders him out of the house. Like most people, he hates clones, and he is cordial to Matt only because El Patrón has ordered it. Mr. Alacrán was humiliated years ago when his wife, Felicia, ran off with Mr. MacGregor, and his humiliation was compounded when El Patrón ordered that Felicia and her illegitimate son, Tom, come back to the mansion to live. Mr. Alacrán completely ignores Felicia and sends Tom to boarding school. His only tenderness is for his father, El Viejo. He pleads with his father to extend his life with transplants from clones, but El Viejo refuses and Mr. Alacrán is genuinely saddened when his father dies.

Steven Alacrán
Steven is the son of Felicia and Mr. Alacrán, the grandson of El Viejo, and the great-great-grandson of El Patrón. He is thirteen years old when he and his friend Emilia discover five-year-old Matt living in a small house in the poppy fields. When Matt jumps out of the window and

cuts his foot, Steven carries him to the Big House, not yet realizing that Matt is a clone. When Matt's identity is revealed, Steven explains to the younger children what clones are and why Matt's brain was not damaged when he was born. Steven is away at school most of the year, and when he is home, he generally ignores Matt but does not actively try to hurt him. When he is old enough, it is arranged that he is to marry Emilia to solidify the bonds between the two important drug families; fortunately, the two like each other. It is during their wedding that El Patrón suffers his last heart attack. María tries to help Matt escape, but she is stopped by Steven and Emilia; Steven declares that Matt is the same as livestock and turns him over to the bodyguards.

Tom Alacrán

Red-haired Tom lives as the youngest son of the Alacrán family, but he is really the son of Felicia and Mr. MacGregor. El Patrón wants Tom in his house when the boy is not at school, but he speaks openly about how he does not like Tom. In fact, there is little to like. Tom is cruel to Matt, taunting him through the bars of his prison when Matt is under Rosa's care and relentlessly pointing out that Matt, as a clone, is not human and not worthy of the most basic respect. Tom is even unkind to María, playing little tricks on her, such as hiding Furball in the toilet with the lid closed and then pretending to help look for him. As Matt observes, Tom has mastered looking innocent and sincere when he is neither. Shortly after the birthday party, when Matt humiliates Tom by sending him to the baby table, Tom tricks Matt and María into going to the hospital wing of the mansion and shows them a howling, insane clone of Mr. MacGregor; he tells them that soon Matt will also become insane. The hospital and the clone were supposed to be a secret, so Tom is sent to a year-round boarding school as punishment. When the children come back for Emilia and Steven's wedding, María tells Matt that she is expected to marry Tom one day and that she does not mind; she believes that with love and patience she can change him, while Matt continues to believe that Tom is evil. But when Matt learns that Tom has died with the other funeral guests, he realizes that "Tom had been no more in charge of his fate than the dullest eejit."

Celia

Celia is a cook in the Big House and is the woman charged with raising Matt from babyhood. She and Matt live alone in a small house surrounded by poppies, and she loves and protects him, knowing that he is a clone and will live only until his organs are needed to save El Patrón's life. She forbids Matt to call her *Mamá;* she tells Matt that he has only been loaned to her but does not explain until he is much older what his fate is to be. After Matt is taken to the Big House at the age of five, he is taken from Celia's care for several months, but then she and Matt are given an apartment in the mansion and Celia and Tam Lin act as his surrogate parents. When Matt is fourteen and El Patrón has his first heart attack, Celia begins slowly poisoning Matt so his organs will not be fit for transplanting. Her trick is revealed, and she is sent to work in the stables; she is supposed to be turned into an eejit, but Tam Lin only marks her forehead to make it look as though her brain has been interfered with. Matt does not see her again until the novel's end, when he finds her in the mansion. As a mere servant, Celia was not with the family when they all died at El Patrón's funeral. Matt knows he can count on her love and wisdom to help him rebuild the land of Opium.

Chacho

Chacho is one of the boys Matt meets in the orphanage at the Aztlán border. He is tough, with big hands and dark hair. He is a skilled woodworker and is making himself a guitar from a scrap of wood until it is taken away from him because orphans are not allowed to have hobbies. Chacho is the only one of the orphans who dares to say out loud that he hates the Keepers, and he warns Matt from the beginning that life in the orphanage will be difficult. Chacho believes that his father is wealthy and living in the United States, waiting only until he owns a home before he sends for Chacho, but Matt is sure that Chacho's father, like all the others who have tried to get across the border, was caught and made an eejit. Chacho is sent to the plankton factory in San Luis with Fidelito and Matt, and he gradually comes to respect Matt and protect Fidelito, though he avoids showing any emotion. When Matt attacks Jorge to keep him from beating Fidelito, Chacho joins him, and the two are bound and thrown into the boneyard to die. Chacho is seriously injured, and when the boys manage to get him out, he is weak and in terrible pain. Once the boys make their way to San Luis, Chacho is taken to be cared for to the hospital at the Convent of Santa Clara.

The Doctor

The doctor, whose first name is Willum, is the personal physician to the Alacrán family, charged with keeping El Patrón alive and with keeping Matt healthy until his organs are needed for transplants.

El Patrón

El Patrón, whose title means "the boss" or "the landlord," is the head of the Alacrán family and the biggest drug lord and most powerful person in the land known as Opium. His overwhelming bitterness is traced to his childhood: he lived in extreme poverty and was the only one of nine siblings to live to adulthood. His legal name is Matteo Alacrán, but this is a name he gave himself when he started to become successful; *alacrán* is the Spanish word for "scorpion," and the poor common people of the small village where he grew up were called *alacránes* by others who looked down on them. El Patrón is ruthless and heartless. He has no affection for his family and friends, no consideration for others, and no regard for human life. People fear and obey him, and he controls his family even so far as dictating where they live and whom they marry. His poppy fields are tended by eejits, or people whose brains have been manipulated so they work tirelessly and make no demands.

When the novel opens, El Patrón is nearly one hundred and forty years old, having extended his life by having clones created and then harvesting their tissues and organs whenever one of his own parts begins to fail. Many wealthy people use clones this way, but El Patrón is unusual in insisting that his clones' intelligence be preserved when they are harvested. He wants them to have the comfort and education that he did not have as a child, and he does not understand why they are not grateful for their privileged lives when it is time for them to die.

For a time, Matt admires El Patrón and enjoys being under his protection. He can see that the older man is cruel but also that he is successful. When Matt is fourteen years old, El Patrón suffers a series of heart attacks, and Matt finally understands that his own heart is required for a transplant. However, Celia has been gradually poisoning Matt so his heart cannot be used, and El Patrón dies. Even at his funeral, held while Matt is escaping, everyone follows the orders El Patrón has left behind. They carry his jewel-encrusted coffin down into the catacombs where he has been stockpiling treasure for years, and they drink a toast with special wine that El Patrón has set aside for this day. The wine is poisoned, and nearly everyone in attendance— El Patrón's family, competitors, bodyguards, and colleagues—dies.

El Viejo

El Viejo is the father of Mr. Alacrán and the grandson of El Patrón. Everyone calls him "El Viejo," the old man, because he is old and sick. Unlike El Patrón and Mr. MacGregor, he refuses to be cloned and have treatments that will keep him young and healthy. Instead he insists that he is ready to accept only the years of life that God gives him. When El Viejo dies, many in the family mock him for not fighting death, but Mr. Alacrán grieves.

Fidelito

Fidelito, about eight years old, is a small, skinny orphan who misses his *abuelita*, or grandmother, and is desperate for approval. He looks up to Matt, and Matt takes him under his wing, helping him reach his work quota each day and making sure he gets enough food. With Matt and Chacho, Fidelito is transferred to the plankton factory in San Luis. When Jorge, one of the Keepers there, notices that Fidelito idolizes Matt, he begins tormenting Fidelito to punish Matt. Finally, Jorge attempts to beat Fidelito with his cane, and Matt and Chacho stop the beating by attacking Jorge. When they are thrown into the boneyard to die, Fidelito and Ton-Ton come to their rescue with a large shrimp-harvesting vehicle, and the four boys escape into San Luis.

Furball

Furball is María's little dog. María carries the dog everywhere, kisses it, and talks to it. Others do not treat Furball so nicely: Tom hides him in the toilet with the lid down, and Felicia kills the dog and allows Matt to take the blame.

Jorge

Jorge is one of the Keepers assigned to watch over the boys at the plankton factory outside San Luis. He is cruel to the boys under his charge, delighting in bringing them under his control. Unable to break Matt's spirit and get him to accept the wisdom of the Five Principles of Good Citizenship and the Four Attitudes Leading to Right-Mindfulness, Jorge tells the rest of the boys that Matt is an escaped *crot*, or a zombie from Opium. He starts picking on small, frail Fidelito as a way to bring Matt in line. When Jorge's taunts and threats are about to turn to physical violence, Matt attacks him to protect Fidelito. Jorge orders Matt and Chacho, who joined in the attack, to be bound with tape, tossed into the boneyard, and left to die. That night, while Matt and Chacho struggle, Ton-Ton gives Jorge and the other Keepers enough laudanum to knock them out and barricades their compound. Jorge shows up again later, at Chacho's bedside in the hospital at the Convent of Santa Clara, but instead of taking the boys back to the factory, Jorge is arrested on charges of dealing drugs.

Mr. MacGregor

Mr. MacGregor is an old friend and competitor of El Patrón's, the owner of the second-largest drug Farm in Opium. The two men share talk of business and swap stories about how they have extended their lives using transplants from clones. MacGregor is also the father of Felicia's son Tom; she ran off with him for a time but returned to the Alacrán home with Tom under orders from El Patrón. This transgression does not seem to have affected the relationship between Mr. MacGregor and El Patrón, but neither man shows any affection or respect for either Felicia or Tom.

Matt

Matt, the protagonist, is just an embryo when he is introduced and fourteen years old when the novel ends. He is a clone of the drug lord El Patrón, created in a laboratory and gestated in a cow. Unlike other clones, Matt does not have his brain damaged when he is harvested; El Patrón likes to have his clones' intelligence spared. What Matt does not understand until much later is that he was created to provide spare parts; whenever El Patrón requires replacement of a major organ, it will come from Matt. Until that time, Matt lives under the care of Celia. For his first five years, he and Celia live alone in a small house out in the poppy fields. When he comes to the mansion for the first time, Matt learns that he is a clone and that he has not had any companions because clones are despised by humans, who do not even want to touch fabric that he has touched.

Matt meets El Patrón when he is five. He is attracted to El Patrón, who seems to like him, too, but Matt does not understand their relationship. As he grows older, he sees that the rest of the Alacráns hate and fear the old man. Matt

befriends María Mendoza, and she, Celia, and the bodyguard Tam Lin are the only people who treat Matt with affection. When Matt is fourteen, El Patrón suffers a series of heart attacks, and Matt comes to understand what everyone else has always known: he will now be killed and his heart transplanted into the old man. Matt escapes to a secret oasis in the desert, where Tam Lin has left equipment and maps for him to sneak across the border into Aztlán.

When Matt gets away from the Farm, he lands in an orphanage with other boys, most of whom lost their parents while trying to get across the border, through Opium, and into the United States. Matt makes new friends—Chacho, Fidelito, and Ton-Ton—and helps them escape the cruel treatment of the orphanage. They make their way to San Luis, where Matt reunites with María. Soon he is sent back to the Farm and discovers that El Patrón and his colleagues and family members are dead. As the only surviving Matteo Alacrán—as the new El Patrón—Matt begins to plan a new future of peace and justice for the Farm.

Emilia Mendoza

Emilia, the older sister of María, is the first of the children to see Matt through the window of the little house he shares with Celia. She is thirteen years old at the time, with pretty dark hair and eyes, and Matt likes her right away. In the following years, after Matt's identity is revealed, she generally ignores him rather than outwardly showing any distaste, and Matt thinks of her as relatively kind. When she and Steven are about twenty-two, they are ordered to marry to solidify the bonds between the Alacrán and Mendoza families; fortunately, the two like each other and are happy to be wed. During the wedding, however, El Patrón suffers a serious heart attack, and in the ensuing hunt for Matt, Emilia shows her true nature by stopping Matt from escaping with María and turning him over to the bodyguards. She also reveals that, unlike María, she has known all along that their mother is alive and that she has no respect for either María or Esperanza, their mother, because they have too much sympathy for clones and eejits.

Esperanza Mendoza

Esperanza is the long-lost mother of María and Emilia. She left home when María was five years old, and the girl has always assumed that her mother was dead. Instead Esperanza left her family to escape the evil dealings of her husband, Senator Mendoza, who is a close ally of El Patrón, and she has been working from outside Opium to unseat the drug lords. Esperanza helped start a group called the Anti-Slavery Society of California, dedicated to freeing the eejits, and wrote the book *The History of Opium* that Tam Lin leaves for Matt. She also won the Nobel Peace Prize. When Matt gets to the Convent of Santa Clara to see Chacho, he finds Esperanza there, reunited with María. Esperanza explains to Matt that under international law he is now the only Matteo Alacrán, and she persuades him to return to Opium and undo the harm that El Patrón created.

María Mendoza

María, about the same age as Matt, is the younger sister of Emilia and the daughter of Senator Mendoza; as far as she knows through most of the novel, her mother, Esperanza, died when María was five. When María first sees Matt through the window, she invites him to play. She never believes the bad things the others say about clones, and she takes care of Matt and pets him the same way she treats her dog, Furball. María is Matt's only friend. The two are together whenever María visits the Alacrán house, but she also is friendly with Tom, who constantly teases her. Matt and Tom are rivals for María's affection. At El Patrón's birthday party, Matt orders María to kiss him in front of the guests. María obeys, but she is humiliated and angry. To win her forgiveness, Matt makes a plan to kidnap Furball and hold him hostage until María listens to his apology, but the plan goes horribly wrong and Furball is killed. No one will believe that Matt did not kill the dog, and the rift between the friends grows deeper.

María is sent to a convent school and returns ready to forgive. When El Viejo dies and Matt is ordered away from the funeral by the priest, María speaks out in Matt's defense. The two escape into the hidden tunnels to talk privately, and they overhear Felicia telling Tom that it was she who killed Furball, letting Matt take the blame. María and Matt next meet at the wedding of Steven and Emilia. El Patrón has a serious heart attack, the bodyguards look for Matt to use his heart for a transplant, and once again Matt and María hide in the tunnels. This time Matt tells María that Esperanza, her mother, is still alive, and María reveals that she has known for some time what Matt's fate was to be. She also indicates that she expects to marry Tom when they are old enough and that she does not mind.

She tries to sneak Matt to safety in her hovercraft, but they are stopped by Steven and Emilia, and Matt is taken away.

When Matt escapes from the Farm and then from the plankton factory, it is with the hope that he can reach the Convent of Santa Clara in San Luis and find María there. Eventually he does reach the convent and finds not only María but Esperanza as well. María greets Matt with an excited hug.

Senator Mendoza

Senator Mendoza is the father of Emilia and María, husband of Esperanza, and a close friend of El Patrón. He is also a US senator. Mendoza is a frequent visitor to the Alacrán mansion and sends his daughters there during school vacations. He does not like María to spend time with Matt and is particularly enraged when, during El Patrón's birthday party, Matt orders María to kiss him in front of the guests. He takes María away, vowing she will never see Matt again. After that, when María returns to the house for a funeral or a wedding, she and Matt have to meet in secret. Late in the novel, when Esperanza tells Matt that Opium has been under a lockdown for months, she chides María for worrying about her father, "an evil man." In fact, Senator Mendoza has died along with the other mourners at El Patrón's funeral.

Rosa

At the beginning of the novel, Rosa is the housekeeper in the Alacrán mansion. When Matt is handed over to her for safekeeping, she resents having to be near a clone and treats him cruelly. She gives him only enough food to keep him alive and makes him live in a room filled with sawdust so she will not have to clean up after him. When El Patrón learns how she has cared for Matt, he has her sent out of the house. She is turned into an eejit and given a job in the stables.

Tam Lin

Tam Lin is one of El Patrón's bodyguards, assigned to protect Matt. Tam Lin is loyal to El Patrón, but he becomes a father figure to Matt and tries to protect him. Tam Lin takes Matt to a hidden oasis in the desert where they will not be overheard, and there he talks to Matt about responsibility and honor and teaches him to climb mountains and survive in the desert. Tam Lin is Matt's moral guide: he tries to keep Matt from demanding a kiss from María at the birthday party and expresses his disappointment when Matt will not confess to killing Furball. Tam Lin leaves the mansion to accompany El Patrón, but he leaves survival gear and food for Matt in the oasis, as well as a book about El Patrón's ascendancy to power. When Celia begins to poison Matt to make his organs unfit for transplanting, Tam Lin tries to talk her out of it, but he stands by her and protects her when she is found out: he has her sent to work in the stables and marks her forehead so it looks as though she has had her brain damaged. When Matt finally escapes from the Farm, he does it with the training and the equipment Tam Lin has given him. But Tam Lin does not escape. Before working for El Patrón, he was a political activist in Scotland, where, trying to assassinate the prime minister, he accidentally killed twenty schoolchildren. Accepting that he deserves to be punished, Tam Lin knowingly drinks the poisoned wine with the others at El Patrón's funeral.

The Teacher

The teacher is a woman whose brain has been intentionally damaged—an eejit. She comes to the Big House to be Matt's tutor after El Patrón orders that Matt be educated, but she has been programmed to deliver only one very simple lesson over and over. Matt is so frustrated with her that he breaks his months-long silence to shout at her.

Ton-Ton

Ton-Ton is one of the boys at the plankton factory near San Luis. A bit older, he has the responsibility of driving the big shrimp harvester and of cleaning the Keepers' rooms. He is loyal to the Keepers even when he is beaten because they rescued him from the Farm Patrol. Ton-Ton is a slow thinker, but a deep thinker. When Jorge calls Ton-Ton stupid, Ton-Ton realizes that the Keepers have never respected or cared for him. And when Matt and Chacho are tossed into the boneyard, Ton-Ton drugs the Keepers with laudanum, and he and Fidelito take the shrimp-harvester to rescue the boys. As the four work their way toward the Convent of Santa Clara, Ton-Ton figures out how to break through the fence, knows how to treat Chacho's injuries, and gives Matt and Fidelito last-minute advice about how to get to get to town.

Willum

See The Doctor

THEMES

Identity

The central questions facing Matt throughout the novel are questions of identity: Who and what is he? Is he a *him* or an *it*? As a clone, harvested rather than born of a mother, is he truly less than human, incapable of the human decency that almost no one expects him to demonstrate? Does he have a right to live a full life— a basic human right—or must he willingly accept that when his time comes, he must sacrifice his own body to save El Patrón?

In the beginning, Matt does not know he is different, and when the Alacráns identify him as a clone and have him thrown out of the Big House, he does not understand why they think he is "a little beast" and "a bad animal." Gradually he learns what a clone is and accepts the view that he is like an animal; when María tries to get him to talk, he snaps at her, thinking, "Being a clone was bad no matter what you did, so why bother being good at all?" He observes that Tom is often punished for teasing María, while Matt is never punished. To Matt, this means that no one thinks him capable of learning right from wrong, that he and the dog, Furball, are "both animals and thus unimportant." Even when Matt's life is going relatively well, when he is doing well at his studies and enjoying playing music, he is dragged down emotionally by his status: "He understood he was only a photograph of a human, and that meant he wasn't really important."

Celia and Tam Lin, however, always treat Matt as though he is valuable and teachable. Celia cherishes him and vows to protect him, and she shields him as long as she can from the hurtful knowledge that he is a clone. Tam Lin teaches Matt the values and qualities that will make him a man of character. Matt has flashes of understanding that he is not simply a copy. For example, he is a talented musician, although El Patrón, as Felicia puts it, "doesn't have a...musical bone in his body." That talent, Matt senses, is his own, is Matt. Still, he horribly misunderstands his relationship with El Patrón, thinking he "could read and write, climb hills, play music, and do anything a real human might do—all because El Patrón loved him." He resolves that "if he wasn't human, he might become something even better."

Like many young men, Matt does not fully come into his own identity until he is separated

TOPICS FOR FURTHER STUDY

- Novelists have long been interested in exploring what happens to children when they are separated from their families and placed under harsh control. What qualities of Matt's character help him survive and build community in the orphanage and the plankton factory in *The House of the Scorpion*? Compare Matt's qualities with those that shape the fate of any of the young men in William Golding's *Lord of the Flies* or characters from other novels. With a few classmates, stage a panel discussion or create a blog, with each member taking on the role of a different character explaining how she or he thrived or the mistakes she or he made. Invite classmates to ask questions or make comments.

- Using information gleaned from the novel, as well as information from Farmer's "Author's Note" and any interviews you can find with the author, draw a map that includes the land of Opium, the oasis, the Farms of El Patrón and Mr. MacGregor, the Convent of San Luis, the boneyard, and other landmarks. With your classmates, trace Matt's journey of escape on your map.

- Read a few other stories that feature dragon hoards. You might consider *The Hobbit* by J. R. R. Tolkien, *The Dragon Hoard* by Tanith Lee, *Beowulf*, or any number of Scandinavian folk tales. Or you might turn to the "Dragon Hoard" board games, card games, online games, or video games. Write a paper in which you explore how Farmer retained some common qualities of dragon hoard stories while changing others when she set her own dragon hoard beneath a future Arizona desert.

- The eejits in *The House of the Scorpion* work in terrible conditions with no ability to ask for more. Learn what you can about the workers who harvest crops in the American Southwest today. Put together a presentation for your class, showing the working and living conditions of these workers.

- Consider the positions of El Viejo, the old man who refuses to accept extreme treatments to extend his life, and of Mr. Alacrán, who does not wish to see his father die. Write a short play or screenplay showing a debate between the two men. Incorporate dialogue from the novel if you like, but give the debate a fuller treatment to more completely articulate their beliefs.

- El Patrón's chief crop is opium poppies, used to make heroin. Research the production of heroin today and write a paper explaining what you learn. Where is most of the drug produced? How does it get into the United States? What efforts is the United States engaged in to combat heroin production and distribution?

from his home and family and is out on his own. Only when El Patrón reveals his real plans for Matt (plans that all the other characters—as well as the reader—have understood well before Matt does) and then dies, only when Matt has crossed the desert and faced emotional and physical dangers in Aztlán, only when he has relied on himself, can he know who he really is. And so he is ready to receive the truth when Esperanza Mendoza gives it to him: with El Patrón dead he *is* El Patrón. "You have his body and his identity," she says. When María asks whether Matt is human, Esperanza replies clearly, "He always was."

Family

Just as Matt tries to figure out what it means to be human, he has to learn what a family is. For the first five years of his life, he lives with Celia in what seems to be a normal, loving, single-parent

Matt is a clone of the 143-year-old drug dealer El Patrón. *(© Nomad_Soul | Shutterstock.com)*

family. However, Celia does not allow Matt to call her *Mamá*, a name he has heard on television, because he is not her child but only "loaned" to her. Of course, Matt learns later that does not have a mother and was not even gestated in a woman's body. As a clone, he feels that he has no family at all.

The families he observes, on the other hand, are nothing to envy. The Alacráns are bitter and fearful, ruled over by El Patrón, the great-great-grandfather of María who refuses to die, refuses to share power, refuses to let his descendants make their own decisions. El Patrón himself had an unhappy family life; none of his five brothers and three sisters lived long enough to start their own families. The only married couples who appear in the novel are Mr. Alacrán and Felicia, who hate each other, and the sons of Mr. Alacrán, who had their wives chosen for them by El Patrón to further his business interests. Senator and Esperanza Mendoza do not live together; in fact, Esperanza left the family when María was five years old, and she refers to the Senator as "an evil man." Felicia and Mr. MacGregor are Tom's parents, but MacGregor does not acknowledge Tom on the rare occasions he sees him. Tom spends most of his time away at boarding schools, or at the mansion with his sad, alcoholic mother. Tom is insufferably cruel and dull, but even Matt comes to see at

the end that "Tom had been no more in control of his fate than the dullest eejit." The orphans in Aztlán are all separated from their families, and though they dream of reuniting with them one day across the border, Matt knows that the parents are in truth dead or turned to eejits.

The only happy, loving family in the novel is the family of Matt, Celia, and Tam Lin. Scenes of the three of them together in their wing of the mansion, telling stories or celebrating Matt's birthday, seem like normal family moments, although they are bound not by blood but only by love. Celia and Tam Lin have no other family, either, but their love for each other and for Matt is clear. But because Matt does not recognize his own humanity, he does not recognize that he is living in a family. When he is escaping with the other boys, however, and he mentions Celia's name, he suddenly realizes that Celia is, in every important way, his mother. "No one else cared for him the way she did. No one protected him or loved him so much, except, perhaps, Tam Lin. And Tam Lin was like his father." Only when Matt is away from the poisonous atmosphere of El Patrón's mansion can he understand what a real family is. By the end of the novel, there are hints that he and María, who is now under the influence of her own mother, will be able to form a new family of their own as they create a new future for Opium.

STYLE

Third-person Point of View

The point of view of *The House of the Scorpion*, or the way in which the narrator looks at the action and "speaks" to the reader, is called "third person limited." It is third person because the narrative voice is not one of the characters, but uses *he* and *she* and *they* to refer to them. In other words, the narrator of the story is not part of the story but an observer. The point of view is limited because the narrator cannot see equally into the feelings and thoughts of all the characters but only into Matt's. This creates an interesting experience for the reader because, especially early on in the novel, when Matt is still quite young, the reader understands things about Matt's situation that Matt does not. For example, as a toddler, Matt does not realize that living alone with Celia out in the middle of poppy fields is strange; to him, it is normal, but the reader immediately senses that something is not right. When Matt and the reader overhear Celia and Tam Lin arguing about how much Matt should be told, the reader understands already that Matt is a clone destined for death, but Matt does not. And when Matt thinks to himself that he can "read and write, climb hills, play music, and do anything a real human might do—all because El Patrón loved him," the reader is already aware that El Patrón is incapable of love and certainly feels none for Matt. Because of the third-person limited point of view, the reader knows things that Matt does not, and this tension elevates the *pathos*—the deep feelings of pity and affection—that the reader feels for him.

Science Fiction

Science fiction is a label given to works of fiction that are on most levels completely believable but that accept as true certain scientific ideas or inventions that do not exist in the real world. These stories are often set in the future or on faraway planets, when and where these new rules of science are plausible. The characters behave as characters would in more realistic stories, so it can be easy for readers to forget that the world these characters inhabit is imaginary. *The House of the Scorpion* is a work of science fiction, set in a future world of new technology, and yet the feelings and actions of Matt, Celia, María, and the others make perfect sense because the rules established within the world of the novel are consistent and clear.

The House of the Scorpion takes place in the future, after Mexico and the United States have each given away territory to the new world of Opium and Mexico has changed its name to Aztlán. In many ways, Opium resembles the southwestern United States of the early twenty-first century, but there are important underlying differences. The ability to clone humans and gestate them in cows is highly advanced, and a scene of a technician nurturing the group of embryos that will produce Matt is the opening scene of the novel. These clones can be used to grow replacement organs for wealthy men, and the ability to alter the clones' brains at harvest is also well developed. It is also taken for granted—at least in Opium—that people and horses can be turned into docile worker drones called eejits by the manipulation of their brains. But aside from these differences, which do not have much effect on the daily life of a child in the Big House, and the fact that visitors come and go on hovercraft, Matt's world is similar to that of the readers. As a young child, he drinks lemon soda, watches Westerns on television, and reads stories about Peter Rabbit. When he is older, he plays the piano and the guitar, studies, and loads the dishwasher.

When he prepares to leave Opium, however, Matt learns that he has been living in a deliberately old-fashioned world. El Patrón, as Tam Lin hurriedly explains, "has kept Opium from one hundred years in the past." El Patrón never arrives in a hovercraft but instead rides in a big limousine—only because he is too frail to ride a horse. Celia cooks over a wood-burning stove when El Patrón visits, but "at other times she was allowed to use microwaves." The mansion is usually cooled by breezes and roof overhangs during most of the year, using air-conditioning in the desert heat only when there are important guests to impress. Even the TV shows Matt used to watch are hundred-year-old shows broadcast under El Patrón's control. And of course, as Tam Lin points out, "the fields are harvested by people, not machines. Even rockets aren't allowed to fly over." (Tellingly, Matt does not respond in surprise to the mention of rockets.) As Matt ventures off into Aztlán and then returns to Opium as the new El Patrón, he will have to learn to use the new technologies, but as in most works of science fiction, he will be surrounded by people who feel and behave in entirely human ways.

HISTORICAL CONTEXT

Illegal Immigration

According to *A History of Opium*, the history of El Patrón and his colleagues written by Esperanza Mendoza, the country of Opium was formed when the drug dealers "approached the leaders of the United States and Mexico. 'You have two problems,' [El Patrón] said. 'First, you cannot control your borders.'" Matt remembers hearing that, when Celia was young, when Aztlán was still called Mexico, "many thousands of Mexicans had flooded across the border in search of work." Because the two countries had failed to stop illegal immigration, they allowed the creation of Opium with the understanding that the drug lords would do it for them. In 2002, when *The House of the Scorpion* was published, illegal immigration—particularly from Mexico into the United States—was an important topic for politicians and policy makers, as it continued to be for at least a decade afterward.

Mark Krikorian of the Center for Immigration studies reports in a 2012 article appearing in *National Interest* that between 2000 and 2005 approximately 850,000 illegal immigrants entered the United States each year. The most common way they entered, he writes, was by crossing the border illegally, although many simply overstayed visas that had allowed them to enter legally. In the novel, people who are caught trying to cross the border into Opium and then on to the United States are rounded up and turned into eejits who will work in the poppy fields for the rest of their lives. According to Esperanza's book, the creation of eejits is a new phenomenon, developed after even El Patrón and the others found it difficult to control the illegals: "They slipped through his fingers. They helped one another escape. The flooded across Opium to the border of the United States until that government threatened to put El Patrón out of business." In the real world, Krikorian reports that more than one million people were arrested on the border between the United States and Mexico every year from the early 1980s to 2005. The Border Patrol prevented these people from entering the United States and sent many back to their hometowns.

After about 2005, the number of immigrants illegally crossing the border between the United States and Mexico began to decline, along with the number of arrests made by the Border Patrol.

In the summer of 2012, a study by Princeton University's Mexican Migration Project reported that with decreased illegal immigration, coupled with increased deportation of illegal immigrants and an increase in immigrants choosing to return home to Mexico, "the net immigration traffic had dropped to zero for the first time in 60 years," as reported in an article by Scott Zhuge in the *Harvard International Review*. However, immigration policy continued to be an important topic for debate, reaching even into the presidential campaigns of 2012.

Drug Traffic

The second problem addressed by the creation of Opium, according to Esperanza Mendoza's *A History of Opium*, was drug traffic. As El Patrón pointed out to the leaders of the United States and Mexico, "You have two problems.... First, you cannot control your borders, and second, you cannot control us." As part of the agreement that created the land of Opium, the drug lords were free to conduct their business as long as they promised "not to sell drugs to the citizens of the United States and Mexico. They would peddle their wares in Europe, Asia, and Africa instead." Thus El Patrón grows vast fields of opium poppies—the plant used to make heroin—and becomes rich and powerful. The drug lords themselves seem to live and work harmoniously, ruled by El Patrón and governed also by a council that "dealt with international problems and kept peace between the various Farms."

At the time *The House of the Scorpion* was published in 2002, there was an active drug trade that relied on a steady supply of drugs—particularly cocaine and marijuana—smuggled over the border between the United States and Mexico. International drug trafficking groups, sometimes called cartels, ran the trade from headquarters in Colombia, El Salvador, and Mexico, the drugs needed to cross the border to reach their customers in the United States. In a 2007 report to Congress, Colleen W. Cook stated that "Mexican drug cartels now dominate the wholesale illicit drug market in the United States." She reported that 90 percent of the cocaine entering the United States came across the border with Mexico and that a large portion of the heroin entering the United States also came from Mexico, although Mexico did not produce much of it. Mexico was also said to be "the main foreign supplier of marijuana and

El Patrón's workforce consists of illegal immigrants captured by his Farm Patrol. (© *Richard Thornton /
Shutterstock.com*)

a major supplier of methamphetamine to the United States." Many lives, and many millions of dollars, were lost each year to the drug trade. The governments of the United States and Mexico were indeed at a loss for how to control drug trafficking.

CRITICAL OVERVIEW

Considering that *The House of the Scorpion* earned so many awards when it was published—the National Book Award for Young People's Literature, Germany's prestigious Buxtehuder Bulle, the Bay Area Book Reviewers' Association Award for Children's Literature, the Arizona Young Readers' Teen Award, and the South Carolina Junior Readers' Award, as well as being named a Newbery Honor Book, a Michael L. Printz Award Book, an ALA Notable Children's Book, and an ALA Best Book for Young Adults—surprisingly little has been written about it. The novel was reviewed in 2002 when it

was published in hardcover, but no formal criticism of the novel appeared in the first decade after the book's publication.

Still, the critics' praise was nearly unanimous. *Kirkus Reviews* calls the novel a "must-read" for science fiction fans, citing Farmer's "talent for creating exciting tales in beautifully realized, unusual worlds." In a starred review, *Publishers Weekly* praises the book for raising questions that "will haunt readers long after the final page." However, the review in *Publishers Weekly* is not alone in quarrelling with the novel's ending, which it labels "rushed." Barbara Scotto, writing for *Horn Book*, praises Farmer's "great imagination in creating a unique and plausible view of the future" but finds that in the conclusion "all problems are resolved in an ending that seems too good to be true." Roger Sutton, writing for the *New York Times Book Review*, agrees that "while the question of Matt's humanity drives the novel, it gets answered and then dropped too easily"; he concludes that the novel is a "big ambitious tale" that raises "questions of literature."

CRITICISM

Cynthia A. Bily

Bily is an English professor at Macomb Community College in Michigan. In the following essay, she examines the roles of mothers in The House of the Scorpion.

During Matt's first day in the orphanage in Aztlán, he tells the other boys how he was captured by the Farm Patrol: "I saw a flash of light. Papá shouted for me to go back to the border. I saw Mamá fall down, and then a man grabbed my backpack. I slipped out of the straps and ran." Of course, Matt does not have a Papá or a Mamá; he was cloned using tissue from El Patrón and gestated in a brood cow. In many ways, Matt's harsh and sterile origins set him far apart from the other characters in *The House of the Scorpion*, and he feels this separation deeply through his childhood. But in one important way, he is no different from the other characters in the miserable world described in the novel. For there is something strange about Opium: there are no mothers there.

The novel introduces several characters without mothers. El Patrón, of course, has outlived his mother, who did not survive to attend her son's one hundred and forty-third birthday party. What he remembers about her is that she brought his two sisters to the parade and the feast, where they caught typhoid and died. Celia, when she was a girl, worked in a factory on the border, living in a dormitory with other girls. By the time she tried to escape, she explains, "I hadn't heard from my family in years. Maybe they were all dead. I didn't know." Tam Lin, born in Scotland, is thousands of miles from any family he might have left. And no mention is ever made of the women who bore El Patrón's children or his son Felipe's children or El Viejo's children. Benito, Felicia's oldest son, has been married for some years to Fani, who shows up at Steven's wedding "almost as loaded as Felicia," but they have no children.

In the orphanage, Matt learns the stories of the other boys. One, hearing Matt describe a "flash of light," instantly recognizes it and explains, "It's a kind of gun, and it kills you dead. *Mi mamá*—." Fidelito had already lost his parents when he came to the orphanage and was living with his *abuelita*, his grandmother. Chacho insists that he is not an orphan like the others; his father is "living in the United States. . . . and he's going to send for me as soon as he buys a house." Chacho does not mention a mother. Ton-Ton's mother crossed the border years earlier, followed by his father, and neither returned. But Ton-Ton has come to accept his status and has not even tried to find his surviving grandmother, because he hopes to be a Keeper one day and, as Jorge taught him, "Keepers don't have families, only one another, but . . . it's, uh, better because families only run off and abandon you."

In fact, Tom, Steven and Benito, the only characters in the novel who grow up with their mother, are each abandoned by her. Felicia got bored with life in the Big House and ran off with Mr. MacGregor, abandoning her two older sons years before the novel opens. Tom is the child of Felicia and MacGregor, but he has never shared a loving home with his parents. In fact, soon after he was born, El Patrón made Felicia come back to the mansion, leaving the baby behind. According to Celia, "Tom showed up about six months after she returned." Whatever this might have meant for early bonding between Tom and Felicia, she is not a loving or effective mother. She spends most afternoons alone, playing the piano and drinking, and the rest of her time sleeping off the alcohol and drugs she takes.

Most readers will feel sorry for Felicia, as Matt does—at first. She is desperately unhappy, lonely, and addicted, simply unable to be a good mother to Tom or his brothers. Her actions during El Patrón's birthday party are typical: she stares down at her plate, not eating, drinking constantly, looking to MacGregor, "although Matt couldn't guess what she could want from him. In any case, he ignored her—and so did her husband and everyone else for that matter." When Tom is humiliated at the birthday party, first by Matt and then by El Patrón, "Felicia balled up her napkin in her fist, but she didn't say anything."

With Tom away at boarding schools most of the time, there is little opportunity to see him and Felicia together. But the few moments they share

> THE WORLD EL PATRÓN HAS CREATED FOR HIMSELF SIMPLY HAS NO ROOM FOR MOTHERS."

WHAT DO I READ NEXT?

- On July 24, 2012, Farmer announced in the blog on her home page that she had finished writing and revising the sequel to *The House of the Scorpion*. The book, to be called *The Lord of Opium*, is expected to be published in the fall of 2013.

- Farmer's fifth novel, *A Girl Named Disaster* (1996), is set in Africa, where Farmer lived while she was writing the novel. It tells the story of twelve-year-old Nhamo, from a small village in Mozambique, who must travel alone down the river to her father's people in Zimbabwe. During her year-long journey, she struggles with hunger, animal attacks, and loneliness, relying mainly on her own intelligence and the guidance of spirits.

- In Margaret Peterson Haddix's *Double Identity* (2005), twelve-year-old Bethany is sent away from her parents to live with her aunt. There she learns that her parents had an older daughter, Elizabeth, who died in a car accident, and that Bethany is a clone created to replace her sister.

- *Holes* (1998), by Louis Sachar, won the National Book Award and the 1999 Newbery Medal. It tells the story of Stanley Yelnats, a thirteen-year-old boy, who ends up in a juvenile detention facility. Stanley must learn to deal with extreme physical demands, uncaring supervisors, and tough boys who are afraid to show emotion and become friends.

- M. T. Anderson's satirical novel *Feed* (2002) takes place in a world where almost everyone is directly connected to the Internet through chips implanted in their brains. The story revolves around Titus, a typical teenage boy, and Violet, a girl who has decided to resist the "feed."

- Sherman Alexie's *The Absolutely True Diary of a Part-Time Indian* (2007) tells the story of Arnold "Junior" Spirit, who does not fit in with his Native American peers because of his success at school and his dreams for the future and does not fit in at high school because he is disabled and not white. The controversial novel, which won the National Book Award, follows Junior through difficult times at home and at school, using humor to explore serious issues, including alcoholism and death.

- *After Dolly: The Uses and Misuses of Human Cloning* (2006), by Ian Wilmut and Roger Highfield, tells how scientists created Dolly the sheep, the first cloned mammal, in 1996. It also explores questions about how cloning might be used in medicine and draws a clear line between what the authors find to be ethical and unethical uses.

- *Cloning* (2006), edited by Louise I. Gerdes, is part of Greenhaven Press's Introducing Issues through Opposing Viewpoints series. It includes fourteen essays that debate the ethics of human cloning, stem cell research, and the cloning of pets and endangered species.

---

reveal that Felicia's love for her son has become twisted with her feelings of jealousy and powerlessness. Felicia and Tom work together to lure Matt and María to the bedside of MacGregor's insane clone—a coded warning that Matt and María should stay away from each other. The only extended scene in which Felicia and Tom speak to each other is in the computer room, where they have gone to spy on the rest of the family and to find Matt and María. Felicia reveals that she was the one who killed María's dog, Furball, and that in her own way it was a demonstration of motherly love. She tells Tom, "I was . . . so *angry* . . . at how they treated you at the birthday party. I wanted to *kill* that abomination El Patrón keeps at his heels."

María was also abandoned by her mother at a young age. As Celia explains, "One day María's mother...walked out of the house and never returned. No one knew where she'd gone, or if they did, they weren't talking about it....[María] woke up at night crying that she could hear her mother's voice, but of course she couldn't." In fact, Esperanza Mendoza must have left her family at about the time Matt and María first met at the little house in the poppy fields. María has always assumed that Esperanza is dead, somehow lost in the desert—a natural assumption for a young girl who does not want to believe that her mother has left of her own choosing. Emilia, older when her mother left, has always known the truth and does not seem to have missed her mother. She has no regrets about having deceived María: "What difference does it make? She didn't care about us. She thought taking care of losers was more important."

When María finds out that Esperanza is alive, she is devastated. She wonders why her mother never came back or even sent a letter. Matt points out that because she has worked against El Patrón and Senator Mendoza, Esperanza could not have returned if she wanted to. He thinks to himself but does not say aloud, "El Patrón was capable of ordering her death. It wouldn't have been the first time he'd gotten rid of an enemy." The world El Patrón has created for himself simply has no room for mothers, and his domination has effectively cut off the only mother-child relationships that might have flourished in his domain. In the poisoned atmosphere of Opium, motherhood cannot thrive. (And Farmer herself does not seem to hold romantic notions about motherhood. In the "Author's Note" appended to the novel she comments, "El Patrón has some resemblance to my mother.")

And then there is Matt. He spends his toddler years with Celia in a loving home, but Celia is not his mother and will not let him call her *Mamá*. Matt remembers, "Celia had told him long ago that she wasn't his real mother. The children on TV had *mamás*, though, and Matt had fallen into the habit of thinking of Celia that way." On the other hand, one of the stories Matt learns from Celia, and one that he shares with María, is the Mexican legend of La Llorona (the weeping woman), who "drowned her children because she was angry with her boyfriend. And then she was sorry and drowned herself." Rejected by both heaven and hell for the sin of killing her children, La Llorona walks alone through the night, moaning. Matt has never had a mother, but his sense of what they are like must be confusing for him. Rosa does not even try to be motherly when Matt is placed in her care and tells him, "I'm your master now, and if you make me angry—watch out!" When Rosa declines to be a mother, Matt shuts down the emotional side of himself; though he does not know exactly what a mother is, if he cannot have one, he will simply withdraw from the world.

Of course, Celia is Matt's mother in every way that really matters, even if she will not admit it. (Though when she finds him in Rosa's prison, the first words out of her mouth are, "*Mijo! Mi hijo!*...My child! My child!") An interesting juxtaposition highlights the difference between Felicia and Celia: Felicia uses poison to kill Furball and gain vengeance against Matt, while Celia uses poison to save Matt's life. Matt passes through some years of adolescent self-pity but finally comes back to realizing more deeply what he knew instinctively as a toddler: Celia is his mother. As he talks to the other boys, "All those years she'd told him not to think of her as his mother fell away. No one else cared for him the way she did. No one protected him or loved him so much, except, perhaps, for Tam Lin. And Tam Lin was like his father." Interestingly, Matt's realization of this is also a sign that he has grown past the point of being able to depend on a mother's guidance.

By the time Matt is finally rescued at the Convent of Santa Clara (by a group of Sisters, or nuns, whose vows will prevent them from becoming mothers), he has learned enough to embrace both his family and his independence. As a man, as the new El Patrón, he will need to rely on himself. Now that he has met her, Matt finds himself pulling away from María's long-lost mother. Tam Lin earlier described Esperanza as a velociraptor; Tam Lin said she was "a good person to have on your side." Now Matt sees her as "one of the guided missiles El Patrón used to get for his birthday" and guesses that she still cares "less for her daughters than her desire to destroy Opium." Esperanza is not going to be a new mother figure for Matt. And in Matt's last moment with Celia in the novel, he runs away from her in anger, heading for the oasis.

El Patrón's estate where Matt eventually lived *(© Horizon Aerials / Shutterstock.com)*

At the end of the novel, Matt sits alone at the oasis, planning the rebuilding of Opium. Again at the end, the reader is reminded that mothers are tricky figures in this novel: "He had Celia and Daft Donald to advise him and María to be everyone's conscience. He also had Esperanza, but he couldn't see a way out of that." What has growing up in the shadows of absent mothers and dubious mothers done to Matt and his understanding of adulthood? He hopes that María will want to live with him and take care of the eejits and three-legged cats, but while the reader might like to think that the two will marry, there is no real hint of it in Matt's thoughts. He knows only that he will have to start over. What he observed in the Alacrán mansion about business, about morality, and about justice will not serve him as he moves into the future. Neither will what he has seen of conventional family life serve him well as he creates a different kind of Opium.

Source: Cynthia A. Bily, Critical Essay on *The House of the Scorpion*, in *Novels for Students*, Gale, Cengage Learning, 2013.

Paula Rohrlick

In the following review, Rohrlick concludes that this novel will attract readers of both science fiction and adventure stories.

To quote the review of the hardcover in *KLIATT*, September 2002: In a future world where an evil empire called Opium is tucked in between the U.S. and Aztlan (formerly Mexico), a young clone named Matt comes of age. His foot is tattooed "Property of the Alacran Estate"; he is the clone of El Patron, the cruel 142-year-old ruler of Opium, a drug kingdom farmed by "eejits," brain-dead clones. Matt has not had his brain deadened; he is a favorite of El Patron, reminding him of his lost youth, though the man's nasty, conspiring family hates Matt, considering him "livestock." Matt's other champions are a cook and a bodyguard, who conspire to save him from a fate of being harvested for organs for El Patron. A girl named Maria comes to love Matt, too, and when El Patron dies and the remaining family try to kill Matt, all his friends work to help him escape from the Alacran estate. Matt runs off to Aztlan but is captured and taken to an awful orphanage, which is more of a Nazi-style work camp. There he makes friends, helps incite a rebellion, and is thrown into a bone pit and almost dies. He escapes, finds Maria, and returns at last to his inheritance, the Alacran estate, with plans to undo the evil of El Patron.

This is a long but engrossing SF adventure by the Newbery Honor-winning author of *A Girl*

I TOOK A TRIP TO ARIZONA AND SORT OF SOAKED UP THE SUNLIGHT AND THE AMBIENCE AND THEN SET ABOUT WRITING [THE HOUSE OF THE SCORPION]."

Named Disaster, The Ear, the Eye and the Arm, and other books for young readers. Farmer grew up in Yuma, Arizona and evokes the landscape of this Mexican border area beautifully. Matt is an appealing hero, despised by many for being a clone but noble and brave in the face of the many hardships he encounters. He learns to value himself, ignoring the opinion of others, and comes to understand that he has the power to make change for good. This will appeal to adventure story lovers as well as SF fans. (National Book Award winner, Newbery Honor Book, and an ALA Best Book for YAs.)

Source: Paula Rohrlick, Review of *The House of the Scorpion*, in *Kliatt*, Vol. 38, No. 4, July 2004, p. 28.

Kathleen T. Horning

In the following interview, Horning and Farmer converse on how Farmer became a children's writer, what inspires her writing, and plans for future novels.

Nancy Farmer's latest novel, *The House of the Scorpion* (S & S/Atheneum, 2002), tackles some of society's thorniest challenges—human cloning, the fate of the environment, and the rights of individuals. *Scorpion*, the winner of the 2002 National Book Award for Young People's Literature, is the story of a young clone named Matt, a replica of El Patrón, the rapacious drug lord and ruler of the nation of Opium. In Farmer's cautionary tale, clones are little more than a source of spare parts, enabling the rich and powerful to live virtually forever.

Although she grew up in Arizona, Farmer spent most of the 1970s and 1980s working in Zimbabwe and Mozambique as a scientist and later as a freelance writer. After she returned to the States in the early '90s, she continued writing, producing a short children's novel, *Do You Know Me?* (Orchard, 1993). Farmer's next book, *The Ear, the Eye and the Arm* (Orchard, 1994), a

seriocomic tour de force featuring a take-charge teenager and an unforgettable trio of gumshoes, won a 1995 Newbery Honor award and brought the author to the attention of American readers. Two years later, Farmer earned a second Newbery Honor for *A Girl Named Disaster* (Orchard, 1996), a novel that charts the terrifying journey of Nhamo, a contemporary Shona girl who flees her village rather than marry a violent man. We spoke to Farmer, who now lives in northern California, in early December, shortly after she received the National Book Award.

What did you do before you became a writer?

I did a lot of things. I was working in Mozambique on controlling waterweeds in Lake Cabora Bassa. I had a lab at the dam wall, and my job was to go around and check water purity in little villages around the lake, and to check on people's welfare. Quite a few of the events in *A Girl Named Disaster* actually happened to me. After I left Mozambique, I went to work on tsetse fly control in Zimbabwe. The second part of *A Girl Named Disaster* takes place in Zimbabwe. I described the camp, Ruckomechi, where I worked. Some of the characters in *A Girl Named Disaster* are real people I knew at that camp. That's what I did until I was eight and a half months pregnant. To get to the camp, we used to fly into the bush. It was during the civil war and it was very dangerous. There was a cleared part of the forest there that we had to buzz to scare the antelopes and warthogs off so that we could land. Then we had to watch out to make sure there weren't any people waiting for us with machine guns in the bushes before we got to the lab.

How did you begin writing for children?

When I was pregnant, it occurred to me that this wasn't an ideal place to go into labor. So I decided to take time off to have the baby. I had had no experience with babies; I had never even picked one up. I thought, well, the African women put their babies on their backs and go back to work in two weeks, and I will do the same. Unfortunately, I was a lot older than most African women are when they have their first [child]. Once I [had my son] Daniel [in my late 30s], all these instincts kicked in. You absolutely can't take [children] out where they're going to get chewed by tsetse flies and blasted with machine guns. So I had to quit the job. For about four years, I did nothing but be a housewife—and went quietly insane because I was used to a really active life. One day I was reading a book and suddenly I was moved by a description in [it] and thought, "I can do this." I sat down at a typewriter, and four hours later, I had a short story. It opened up a brand-new world to me. It was just so pleasurable to write, that from then on, I wrote every opportunity I got. I didn't become a full-time writer until later when we came to the United States.

After you returned to the States, did you get published right away?

No, I didn't. I sent stuff out and it was rejected. Actually, in Zimbabwe, I realized I wasn't a good writer, and I sat down and trained myself. I got John Braine's book on how to write a novel, and Joan Aiken's book on writing for children, and read instructions from Raymond Chandler on how he wrote books, and I followed their advice. I also read Stephen King. Those were the four sources for how to write a novel that I used. And I just practiced and practiced and practiced. Eventually I had a short book called *Do You Know Me?* I [sent] the first 40 pages to the National Endowment for the Arts and got a grant, which helped a huge amount toward making me a full-time writer. It gave me breathing space. When I finished that book, someone gave me a list of editors. I really didn't know how to market [my work], and I picked the editor who was closest to me, which was Dick Jackson [who is now with Simon & Schuster].

Closest geographically?

Yes. He was down the road. So I sent him the manuscript, and he said, thank you, and sent it back and said it needed some rewrites. I just put in some more commas and took out a few words and sent it back to him. Then he called me up and he said, "I meant a real rewrite." He gave me some instructions on what I should be doing. So I followed them, and he bought the book. It was really pretty simple. I've been with Dick Jackson ever since.

Do you think you'll ever write a sequel to any of your novels?

There came a point at which the situation in Zimbabwe deteriorated so much that it was just too depressing to write about it any more. I didn't want to write about Africa. I was going to do a sequel to *The Ear, the Eye and the Arm*— and I may yet do it—but I just didn't want to get into it. So I went back to a happier time, which was my childhood in Arizona. I took a trip to

Arizona and sort of soaked up the sunlight and the ambience and then set about writing [*The House of the Scorpion*].

Did you do a lot of reading about cloning before you began writing The House of the Scorpion?

Yes, I've thought about the implications of cloning for years. The original source for the idea was Aldous Huxley's *Brave New World*. Then [in 1932], of course, it was totally a fantasy. I read a lot about Dolly the sheep, and discovered that out of 256 tries, I believe, only one succeeded. Some of the fetuses didn't develop, and some were born deformed. The question is: What do you do with the 50 deformed babies in order to get one perfect one? That's when the problem of cloning became real to me. This is something [scientists] haven't worked out yet. You can't just kill a baby like you can a deformed sheep. It's a huge problem.

I'm not actually against cloning as long as it's pretty near to flawless, because it's just like creating a twin. But at the moment, I think it's a really bad thing to try. Plus, why do people do it? It's a kind of vanity; it's the will to live forever.

What was your inspiration for the nation of Opium, a haven for narcotics?

I grew up in Yuma on the Arizona-Mexico border. The place that I describe [in *Scorpion*] is sort of a never-never land somewhere on the border. What I was mostly describing was the Chiricahua Mountains. But I went back to Ajo [AZ] to look at it and make sure that I had been accurate about what I described. The inspiration is that area. Even when I was a child, there were problems with drug imports and illegals all along that border—and we're talking 50 years ago. This is an old problem, and I felt impelled to write about it.

Talk about the environmental issues in Scorpion. *You describe some very polluted landscapes.*

Some of it's based on real things. The pollution in the Colorado River is real. I read a book when I was doing research called *By the Lake of Sleeping Children* by Luis Alberto Urrea, about children who live in slums along the Mexican border—right around Tijuana and over toward San Luis. There are actually rivers that are so poisonous that they're dangerous to go into, and yet people trying to cross into the United States go into them.

*Based on the two novels you've set in the future—*The Ear, the Eye and the Arm *and, of course,* Scorpion—*would you say that your outlook for tomorrow is pretty gloomy?*

No. I think people are ultimately hopeful. I don't have a totally bleak view of the future, and I don't want to give that impression to children either. There are little pockets of happiness wherever you happen to live. In both of those books, although there are a lot of problems, there's the hope of ultimate happiness. I don't like writing a hopeless book, where it's all depressing. It's not really about showing a dystopia but about showing children who can work their way out of the dystopia and find a kind of fulfillment. The children in all three of [my] better-known books don't ever give up. They keep trying. It's all about the struggle and the will to survive and also to stay human and to be good to other people. It's ultimately a hopeful look at people, not a sad one.

Source: Kathleen T. Horning and Nancy Farmer, "The House of Farmer," in *School Library Journal*, Vol. 49, No. 2, February 2003, pp. 48–50.

Kathleen Harris

In the following review, Harris describes the novel as "elegantly written and fascinating."

Meet Matt Alacran. Little does he know that he's the fifth human clone of the Mexican drug lord El Patron, who just celebrated his 140th birthday. Matt has no reason to believe he is a clone. He lives in a small cottage on El Patron's estate with one of the cooks, Celia, who cares for him and loves him like a son. Matt reads books, plays games, and has thoughts and feelings like other boys his age. Yet when Celia leaves to go to work she locks him up inside the cottage and tells him to hide if anyone comes to the door. Matt does just that until, one day, children his age show up outside the cottage—children Matt decides to meet.

The children take Matt to El Patron's mansion where he is scorned and ushered to the stables like a barnyard animal. Even Celia can't help him because Matt is a clone, and like the other clones that work on El Patron's estate he is considered to be not much more than livestock. The difference between Matt and the other clones, or "eejits" is that Matt's memory and intelligence were not blunted at birth. Direct clones of El Patron are allowed to develop just like any other human—this is El Patron's "gift"

ONE GETS THE SENSE THAT HER LEAP FROM A SCIENTIFIC SENSE OF AN ORDER IN THE UNIVERSE TO THE POSSIBILITY OF A DIVINE SPIRIT PERHAPS BEGINS WITH AN ACCEPTANCE OF HER OWN MYSTERIOUS CREATIVE PROCESS."

to them. Yet this gift becomes a curse once Matt meets El Patron face to face and begins to realize the old man's intentions for him.

The House of the Scorpion is an elegantly written and fascinating book that explores the topic of human cloning and the ethics of organ harvesting. Nancy Farmer has created a frightening world in which human clones exist to serve a purpose—to either become slaves or organ donors for humans. Readers will be drawn to Matt's world and his fight for survival. Although *The House of the Scorpion* is over 300 pages long, it is a quick read and a captivating story. Even teenagers who don't consider themselves fans of science fiction will enjoy this novel.

Source: Kathleen Harris, Review of *The House of the Scorpion*, in *Journal of Adolescent & Adult Literacy*, Vol. 47, No. 4, December 2003, pp. 349–50.

Jennifer M. Brown

In the following interview, Brown and Farmer discuss Farmer's career and the themes of tolerance and acceptance as they apply to her life and work.

Yuma, Ariz., on the U.S.-Mexico border, 1950. Nine-year-old Nancy Farmer works at the desk of her family's hotel, surrounded by truck drivers, fruit packers, cowboys, railroad workers, even Grand Ole Opry singers. She stays up until 1 a.m. listening to their stories and learning to play cards. Little does she know that the seeds of a future novelist are being planted.

Fast forward to an unspecified year in the future, the setting of her forthcoming novel, *The House of the Scorpion* (Atheneum/Jackson, Oct.). What was once Yuma, Ariz., is now contained within the country of Opium, run by Matteo Alacran (aka El Patron). In a deal struck with the governments of America and Aztlan (formerly Mexico), Alacran produces drugs to sell abroad and catches illegal interlopers between the two border countries, transforming them into eejits (by implanting a computer chip in the brain) to tend his endless fields of poppies. This is the landscape in which Alacran's unwitting clone and Farmer's protagonist, young Matt, is growing up.

To look at her early career, one might never guess that Farmer would become a writer. After graduating from Reed College in Oregon, she served in the Peace Corps in India, worked as a chemist and entomologist in Mozambique, then as a freelance scientist in Zimbabwe. Not a typical path for an author. "It happened very suddenly," said Farmer in a telephone interview from her home in Menlo Park, Calif. "I was technically a scientist, an entomologist, working in a lab. When I married and had a child, I was at home, spinning my wheels and feeling bitter about it. One day when my son was four years old, I was reading a story by Margaret Forster [author of *Georgy Girl*] about people walking around a pond in London. Something about the description sparked something in me, I thought, I could do this."

Farmer remembers that it took her about four hours to write that first story, but she had no sense of time while she was writing: "It was as if I woke up out of a trance and it was finished." The story was about 15 pages long, and she never published it. She was 40 years old.

The Shona, the tribe in Zimbabwe among which Farmer and her husband were living at the time, described her sudden inspiration as the result of a shave (shah-vay) visitation. According to the Shona, these unsettled spirits search for a host—and a storyteller's spirit found one in Farmer. "That's sort of what I believe," Farmer says. "I don't know how it works, but suddenly I turned into a writer."

It was another four years before Farmer's first novel, *Lorelei*, a story about hippies, was published, by College Press in Zimbabwe. In the meantime, she published some school stories, also for College Press, for which she was paid per word. She met her editor while sunbathing in Zimbabwe. "They would ask me how many words were in the story and pay me for them— they didn't even count them. They would say, Write something about the romance of open pit copper mining or baking bread.' My job was to make it interesting."

All of her novels brim with details that immediately capture readers' imaginations. Three children sneak out of their father's (the general's) house in 2194 Harare, Zimbabwe, at the beginning of the Newbery Honor book *The Ear, the Eye and the Arm* (Orchard, 1994). Readers first meet Nhamo, the heroine of *A Girl Named Disaster* (Orchard, 1996), Farmer's second Newbery Honor book, as she hides out on a branch of a mukuyu tree in her Mozambique village. *The House of the Scorpion* begins with a scientist bringing to life one of 36 cells, taken from El Patron and frozen more than a century before with the intention of creating a clone.

In each case, the author plunges readers into an elaborately imagined world, exotic yet also grounded in the details of smells and tastes, temperature and sounds. Foreign though they may be, the settings soon seem completely familiar, as the characters make their way through intricately constructed ecologies, societies or cities.

In a starred review of *Scorpion* (Children's Forecasts, July 1), *PW* said, "Farmer's novel may be futuristic, but it hits close to home, raising questions of what it means to be human, what is the value of life, and what are the responsibilities of a society." The same could be said of nearly all of her novels, and always the underdog—the child—prevails.

Asked if this is a favorite theme, Farmer says, "I hadn't thought about it, but of course they are small people in a world of giants who are not too friendly. You can send a kid to a horrible boarding school, and they think it's normal. They adjust to it and they don't know it's not supposed to be that way." Matt in *Scorpion* provides just such an example when, at age six, he is shut up in a room, literally like farm stock, with sawdust so high he must wade through it.

Yet Farmer repeatedly sees to it that goodness triumphs. Those around Matt consider clones to be subhuman, but no matter how others mistreat him, his innate sense of what's right persists. "I think there is an order in the universe and a divine spirit that's directing things," Farmer says.

The two adults in *Scorpion* who are kind to Matt also teach him the ways of the world: Tam Lin, El Patron's bodyguard, and Celia, El Patron's cook who also raises Matt (until he is found out and imprisoned in the room filled with sawdust). Celia emphasizes faith, Tam Lin freewill. Tam Lin also plants clues to a way out of Opium for Matt. "There should be some elder around who will tell kids what should be done and how to behave so that they're not growing up like barnyard animals," Farmer says.

TOLERANCE AND ACCEPTANCE

Farmer's life and work have exposed her to a great many places, cultures and religions. She believes this exposure has "made me tolerant of all kinds of points of view. I've been around a lot of other religions, and I find them all valuable." She pauses for a moment, and adds, "I've just met a lot of people in a lot of parts of the world and found them to be good people."

With her direct manner and her low, powerful voice, Farmer speaks with the assurance of a scientist who has a wealth of research to draw upon. One gets the sense that her leap from a scientific sense of an order in the universe to the possibility of a divine spirit perhaps begins with an acceptance of her own mysterious creative process. When she sits down to begin a book, she says, "I don't know what I'm going to write about. I don't have an outline. It's like the whole novel is in my head on a subconscious level. I don't want to explore it too much, I just want it to come out naturally."

Mornings are Farmer's most productive time for writing. "If I get going in the morning, I can keep it up for hours," she says, "I write the whole book, go straight through, and I don't do any rewriting until I finish. Then I go back and make some changes. It's gotten to the point where my first draft is very close to my last draft."

She and her husband live in a small apartment near Stanford University. "We got [it] when we were very low on money and haven't had the energy to move on. It's rundown and there are no gardening possibilities. We aren't allowed to keep pets. When we first moved in, we weren't even supposed to be allowed to keep children, but that eroded," she says with a laugh.

She has her own room that also serves as her office. "When there's no one in the house, I go in and close the door and work. Once people are home, as much as I would prefer to stay in there and write, it's not really fair. You don't want to neglect your family for writing." Her husband of 25 years, Harold Farmer, teaches nearby at Foothill College. "When he's off in summer, I tend to disappear because I have to keep writing. It's the family income."

Farmer wrote her first book published in the U.S., *Do You Know Me* (Orchard, 1993), under what she calls "extremely trying conditions." The couple had moved to Humboldt County with the understanding that there were jobs available, but there were none. "We had a little apartment with no beds, no car, nothing. Whenever I wasn't looking for work, I was writing *Do You Know Me*. Then my husband got a scholarship to Stanford, and I had to go to work because his scholarship didn't cover much."

Farmer landed a job in a lab at Stanford and could write only for a few hours a week. Then she saw a notice for a contest sponsored by the National Endowment for the Arts and sent off a 40-page section of the manuscript as her entry. Soon after, she quit her job because her fingernails were falling off. "I was afraid I would lose the use of my hands if I stayed." But there was good news waiting for her that night. "Daniel [her son] was bouncing up and down. I had received $20,000 from the NEA, and with that money I was able to finish the book. I think it was the first time they'd ever awarded anything to a children's writer."

When it came time to publish the book, her process of finding the right publisher was nearly as natural as finding her African editor while sunbathing had been. "Someone gave me a list of editors, and I picked the one closest," she recalls. "Dick Jackson." Farmer has spent her entire U.S. career with Jackson. She says that with her first book, the editorial process was quite involved, but that Jackson has not had to be quite as hands-on with the novels that followed. "He's a delight to work with, obviously," Farmer reports. "Sometimes he works very closely with an author, and he knows when to leave it alone. Mostly what he asks me to do is to expand a scene or explain something that's murky. He's very willing to leave me to do what I wish to do."

When she wrote *The Ear, the Eye and the Arm* (1994) for an American audience, she says she did not refer to the original version, first published in Zimbabwe. "The African version was sort of clumsy, and it wasn't a very good plot. It didn't sound like an American book," she says. She credits that voice (in the original African version) to C.S. Lewis, whose Narnia books she had read: "Unfortunately, because he wrote in the 50s, my books sounded like they were written in the '50s." Other authors she admires are J.R.R. Tolkien, Roald Dahl and George

Orwell. "Orwell because of his extremely clear language and his uncompromising approach to things. He says exactly what he means. If he wants to criticize something, he does it. 'Lying is the most personal act of cowardice,' he said. He was my role model long before I became a writer."

"Uncompromising" could describe Farmer's work as well. Yet she presents the truth gently. She uses her characters' gradual awakening to introduce harder realities: Nhamo's coming-of-age during the course of her journey from her small village in Mozambique to Zimbabwe; Matt's growing awareness that El Patron considers him just another possession rather than a son.

Asked why she has moved on from the African backdrop of her earlier books, Farmer responds with a trace of sadness, "Zimbabwe became so very depressing that I just don't want to write about it now. So I switched to my childhood, which was very much nicer to write about."

Switching to her childhood meant returning to the desert area of the Ajo Mountains, the setting for *Scorpion*. Even when she was a girl, she says, the area was a treacherous place for Mexicans to cross into the U.S.: "The Ajo Mountains are covered with cactus. Alot of illegal immigrants come through because it's so easy to cross the border. On the other hand, it's so dry and dangerous that people die there all the time, of thirst."

When she visited the Sanguinetti House (now a museum), the model for El Patron's mansion, it was just as she remembered it. Her voice brightens, "Yuma is very dry and not a terrifically attractive town, although I loved it. The one green patch was this mansion, and I used to sneak in to watch the birds. It was just like a paradise to me."

With her latest novel, Farmer completes the circle: the nine-year-old girl who loved to listen to stories in Yuma is now a storyteller herself. And she is already in the throes of writing her next tale, *The Sea of Trolls*, "half based on Viking history, and partly legend," Farmer explains. In the book, a boy and his sister are kidnapped from the coast of England in 1790 and carried off to Ivar the Boneless. "He has a cloak made of the beards of his enemies," she says enthusiastically. "This one is in the past, but it's in another galaxy, far, far away."

When asked what she would like readers to take away from her books, Farmer replies, "My first aim is to entertain, to keep them riveted. Secondly, I want them to come away with the feeling that they can be strong, that they can do things—and that they mustn't give in."

Source: Jennifer M. Brown and Nancy Farmer, "Nancy Farmer: Voices of Experience," in *Publishers Weekly*, Vol. 249, No. 29, July 22, 2002, pp. 154–55.

Sally Estes

In the following review, Estes calls the novel a "remarkable coming-of-age story."

Young Matteo (Matt) Alacran is a clone of the original Matteo Alacran, known as El Patron, the 142-year-old absolute ruler of Opium, a country separating the U.S. and Aztlan, once known as Mexico. In Opium, mind-controlled slaves care for fields of poppies, and clones are universally despised. Matt, on El Patron's orders, is the only clone whose intelligence has not been blunted. While still quite young, Matt is taken from the loving care of El Patron's cook and placed into the abusive hands of a maid, who treats him like an animal. At 7, brought to El Patron's attention, he begins an indulged life, getting an education and musical training, though he is never allowed to forget that he is not considered human. Matt doesn't learn until he is 14 that El Patron has had other clones, who have provided hearts and other organs so El Patron can go on living. This is a powerful, ultimately hopeful, story that builds on today's sociopolitical, ethical, and scientific issues and prognosticates a compelling picture of what the future could bring. All of these serious issues are held together by a remarkable coming-of-age story, in which a boy's self-image and right to life are at stake.

Source: Sally Estes, Review of *The House of the Scorpion*, in *Booklist*, Vol. 99, No. 2, September 15, 2002, p. 232.

Barbara Scotto

In the following review, Scotto notes the credibility of the storyline despite its categorization as science fiction.

Between the United States and Aztlan lies a narrow strip of land called Opium, where eejits, controlled by computer chips implanted in their brains, tend endless fields of poppies. This area is ruled by iron-fisted El Patron, the patriarch of the Alacran family, who with the help of numerous transplants has lived over 140 years. Matt Alacran is the key to El Patron's future, and though he feels loved by the old man who truthfully calls him Mi Vida, he is treated with thorough distaste by almost everyone because he is a clone. Unlike most clones whose brains are destroyed at birth, Matt, as El Patron's clone, has been raised by a loving woman, and after a brief period of imprisonment, educated and allowed free run of the estate. Matt often wonders about his future, but when he finally grasps what lies ahead for him, he realizes he must make a desperate attempt to escape. Though certain portions of the book go on far too long, other parts of the story are riveting. Suspense and tension continue right up to the book's conclusion when Matt is asked to do something that could easily result in the loss of the life for which he has fought so fiercely. Then suddenly all problems are resolved in an ending that seems too good to be true. Still, Farmer has shown great imagination in creating a unique and plausible view of the future with enough connections to current issues to make her vision particularly disquieting. Throughout the story, she has raised questions about the meaning of life and death and about the nature of one's responsibility for others, and in so doing, has created a thought-provoking piece of science fiction.

Source: Barbara Scotto, Review of *The House of the Scorpion*, in *Horn Book Magazine*, Vol. 78, No. 6, November/December 2002, pp. 753–54.

Bookseller

In the following article, a contributor comments on the role of the novel in making Farmer an award-winning author.

The House of the Scorpion by Nancy Farmer, which has just been published in the UK by Simon & Schuster, has been shortlisted for the US literary prize the National Book Award, in the category of Young People's Literature.

Farmer, who lives in California, has already been awarded the American Newbery Honor for two of her titles for young adults, including *A Girl Named Disaster*, which was published in the UK by Orion. Like *The House of the Scorpion*, it focuses on a child's passage into adulthood. Farmer says: "Feeling alienated and unwanted is the natural condition of teenagers. Turning into an adult is a scary process for kids. That's why I write for them."

In *The House of the Scorpion*, a young boy called Matt grows up on a drug baron's estate. As a child, he finds out that he is a clone of the family's head, El Patron. What he does not realise until his teenage years is that in this world, clones are bred as "body parts" to lengthen the lives of their maker. The unremitting cruelty Matt faces from all but a handful of people is a bleak subject, but the novel is fast-paced, and Farmer acknowledges that his character could develop in either direction.

Farmer's focus on "the outsider" is, she says, a reflection of her own childhood years. "I grew up in a hotel on the Mexican border. The hotel patrons—retired railroad men, cowboys, circus performers and bank robbers on vacation—stayed up all night, gossiping and playing cards. They were so entertaining, I never got to bed before 3 a.m." Instead of school, she says, "I spent the days playing with the children of illegal aliens who lived on the mud flats of the Colorado River."

Farmer comments: "Growing up on the Mexican/US border and living under various oppressive regimes has taught me that good people are an endangered species. They need to be protected at all times. I have a bleak viewpoint of all governments and dislike borders of all kinds."

Farmer's adult life has included stints at teaching chemistry in India and working as an entomologist in Southern Africa, where she lived for 17 years after meeting her husband, Harold Farmer, an English teacher at the University of Zimbabwe. She wrote her first short story when she was 40—and has been a writer ever since. Penelope Webber, S&S UK children's marketing manager, says of *The House of the Scorpion*: "As a co-published title, it is also eligible for most prizes in the UK. We've already had a terrific response to the title over here, including a lot of support from libraries." NBA winners will be announced on 20th November.

Source: "Nancy Farmer Shortlisted for National Book Award," in *Bookseller*, November 15, 2002, p. 34.

Diane Roback, Jennifer M. Brown, Jason Britton, and Jeff Zaleski

In the following review, the authors determine that the novel poses questions with no answers but does so in a satisfying way.

Farmer's (*A Girl Named Disaster*; *The Ear, the Eye and the Arm*) novel may be futuristic, but it hits close to home, raising questions of what it means to be human, what is the value of life, and what are the responsibilities of a society. Readers will be hooked from the first page, in which a scientist brings to life one of 36 tiny cells, frozen more than 100 years ago. The result is the protagonist at the novel's center, Matt—a clone of El Patrón, a powerful drug lord, born Matteo Alacrán to a poor family in a small village in Mexico. El Patrón is ruler of Opium, a country that lies between the United States and Aztlán, formerly Mexico; its vast poppy fields are tended by eejits, human beings who attempted to flee Aztlán, programmed by a computer chip implanted in their brains. With smooth pacing that steadily gathers momentum, Farmer traces Matt's growing awareness of what being a clone of one of the most powerful and feared men on earth entails. Through the kindness of the only two adults who treat Matt like a human—Celia, the cook and Matt's guardian in early childhood, and Tam Lin, El Patrón's bodyguard—Matt experiences firsthand the evils at work in Opium, and the corruptive power of greed ("When he was young, he made a choice, like a tree does when it decides to grow one way or the other... most of his branches are twisted," Tam Lin tells Matt). The author strikes a masterful balance between Matt's idealism and his intelligence. The novel's close may be rushed, and Tam Lin's fate may be confusing to readers, but Farmer grippingly demonstrates that there are no easy answers. The questions she raises will haunt readers long after the final page.

Source: Diane Roback, Jennifer M. Brown, Jason Britton, and Jeff Zaleski, Review of *The House of the Scorpion*, in *Publishers Weekly*, Vol. 249, No. 26, July 1, 2002, pp. 80–81.

SOURCES

Cook, Colleen W., *Mexico's Drug Cartels*, Congressional Research Service Report for Congress, October 16, 2007, pp. i, 4.

Farmer, Nancy, Author's Note in *The House of the Scorpion*, Atheneum, 2002, pp. 383–88.

———, "Bio," Nancy Farmer's Official Home Page, http://www.nancyfarmerwebsite.com/bio.html (accessed August 10, 2012).

———, *The House of the Scorpion*, Atheneum, 2002.

———, "Karoshi," Nancy Farmer's Official Home Page, July 24, 2012, http://www.nancyfarmerwebsite.com/blog.html (accessed July 25, 2012).

Krikorian, Mark, "The Perpetual Border Battle," in *National Interest*, July/August 2012, pp. 44–52.

Marcus, Leonard S., ed. "Nancy Farmer," in *The Wand in the Word: Conversations with Writers of Fantasy*, Candlewick, 2006, pp. 48–61.

Review of *The House of the Scorpion*, in *Kirkus Reviews*, Vol. 70, No. 3, July 1, 2002, p. 954.

Review of *The House of the Scorpion*, in *Publishers Weekly*, Vol. 249, No. 26, July 1, 2002, pp. 80–81.

Scotto, Barbara, Review of *The House of the Scorpion*, in *Horn Book Magazine*, Vol. 78, No. 6, November/December 2002, pp. 753–54.

Sutton, Roger, "Disorder at the Border," in *New York Times Book Review*, November 17, 2002, p. 39.

Zhuge, Scott, "Going Home: Illegal Immigration Reverses Course," in *Harvard International Review*, Summer 2012, pp. 7–8.

FURTHER READING

Bould, Mark, *The Routledge Companion to Science Fiction*, Routledge, 2009.
    This reference book gives a solid overview of science fiction. Articles describe major authors and texts, trace subgenres and literary movements, and explain how scholars and readers have approached these works.

Datlow, Ellen, and Terri Windling, eds., *A Wolf at the Door and Other Retold Fairy Tales*, Aladdin, 2000.
    In this collection, thirteen award-winning fantasy and science fiction writers retell familiar fairy tales from new angles. Farmer's contribution is "Falada," a version of "The Goose Girl" narrated by Falada, the horse.

Grant, Richard, *God's Middle Finger: Into the Lawless Heart of the Sierra Madre*, Free Press, 2008.
    In this gritty and dark book, journalist Richard Grant describes the fifteen years he spent in the Sierra Madre mountains, near the border between Mexico and Arizona, and the healers, students, cowboys, and drug traffickers he encountered there.

Marcus, Leonard S., ed., *The Wand in the Word: Conversations with Writers of Fantasy*, Candlewick Press, 2006.
    As the subtitle suggests, this volume contains interviews with thirteen writers of fantasy fiction for young adults, including Farmer, Lloyd Alexander, Susan Cooper, Brian Jacques, and Philip Pullman. In Farmer's chapter, she discusses her childhood reading habits, her laboratory work, and her writing practice.

November, Sharyn, ed., *Firebirds: An Anthology of Original Fantasy and Science Fiction*, Penguin, 2003.

This volume is a collection of sixteen original stories by fantasy and science fiction writers of the twenty-first century, including Lloyd Alexander, Diana Wynne Jones, and Garth Nix. It includes Farmer's story "Remember Me."

Urrea, Luis Alberto, *The Devil's Highway: A True Story*, Little, Brown, 2004.

In 2001, twenty-six men tried to cross the border from Mexico into Arizona, moving through the landscape depicted in *The House of the Scorpion*. As this dramatic book tells, only twelve made it back alive through the rugged terrain.

SUGGESTED SEARCH TERMS

Nancy Farmer

House of the Scorpion

science fiction AND cloning

U.S.-Mexico border AND drugs

young-adult AND science fiction

scorpion AND science fiction

Nancy Farmer AND cloning

Nancy Farmer AND science fiction

Nancy Farmer AND scorpion

The Light in the Forest

CONRAD RICHTER

1953

The Light in the Forest is a faithfully wrought frontier novel with a stirring plot by mid-twentieth-century American fiction writer Conrad Richter. Although his name is often omitted from lists of the most accomplished novelists of his era, Richter earned critical admiration for the insightfulness and historical accuracy of his tales of life on the frontier in and around his home state of Pennsylvania, as well as in the Southwest. In 1951, he was awarded the Pulitzer Prize for *The Town*, the concluding volume—following *The Trees* and *The Fields*—of a trilogy on the advances of early American civilization in Ohio.

0.3pt?> Two years after winning the Pulitzer, Richter wrote what has become his most enduring novel, *The Light in the Forest*. The tale opens in the mid-eighteenth century with the impending return of True Son, a fifteen-year-old white boy who has been raised in the Ohio wilderness as a Delaware Indian, to the white family and society he feels no affiliation with—and is even repulsed by. As he draws toward his original home and the family he belongs to, the tale explores the comparative merits of Indian and white American civilization. As True Son—now called by his birth name, John Butler—clashes with his family, the book's meditations and action alike intensify. The novel does include secondhand, nongraphic reference to scalping and even more appalling violence. Although Richter wrote the novel for audiences of any age, the focus on the fifteen-year-old

Conrad Richter (The Library of Congress)

protagonist has led to *The Light in the Forest*'s being widely considered a young-adult classic.

AUTHOR BIOGRAPHY

Conrad Michael Richter was born in Pine Grove, Schuylkill County, Pennsylvania, on October 13, 1890, the eldest of three sons. Though generally quiet, he possessed a certain restlessness that manifested itself in a plan, enacted at the age of six along with his eight-year-old cousin Henry Irwin, to escape to life among the Indians in the Wild West. But Henry's sister, fearing that the Sioux would torture the boys, exposed and foiled their plan. Richter escaped instead into books, becoming so entranced by fictional worlds that he would finish one book only, dive into another by the same author. While his father went to college and became a minister, Richter attended Susquehanna Preparatory School in Selinsgrove and then high school in Tremont, graduating at age fifteen. Although his parents hoped that he, too, would join the ministry, the young Richter instead cycled through various jobs: teamster, machinist, farmer,

bank clerk, timberman, and periodical salesman. In 1910, inspired by an article series, "The American Newspaper," he resolved to become a journalist and immediately found a reporting job with the *Johnstown Journal*.

Richter proceeded to develop the craft of writing while subsequently working for the *Patton Courier*, *Pittsburgh Dispatch*, and *Johnstown Leader*. He published his first story in 1913 and gained national recognition for a 1914 story, "Brothers of No Kin," that was twice reprinted in widely circulating magazines. Editors began soliciting his efforts—but somehow their financial terms blocked his creativity, and he would not break out as a novelist until more than two decades later. Meanwhile, he married Harvena Achenbach in 1915 and had a daughter, also named Harvena, in 1917. Getting into the publishing business, he produced his own *Junior Magazine* for a year and later worked in Reading, Pennsylvania, and then Harrisburg. His first story collection, *Brothers of No Kin and Other Stories* (1924), was soon followed by a pair of philosophical treatises—including *Human Vibration: The Underlying Mechanics of Life and Mind* (1925)—that would inform his work but gain little recognition otherwise. When his wife became critically ill, Richter sold his farmhouse and moved the family to New Mexico in 1928.

The southwestern air would prove to be helpful for Richter's writing efforts. After another volume of short stories, he brought out his first novel, *The Sea of Grass*, to critical acclaim and popular success in 1937. He proceeded to write, among other works, his famed Ohio trilogy between 1940 and 1950—the year his family moved permanently back to Pine Grove, Pennsylvania—and won the Pulitzer Prize for *The Town* in 1951. *The Light in the Forest* (originally titled "My Enemy, My Son") was published in 1953, first as a serial in the *Saturday Evening Post* in March and April and then as a book. Richter published steadily through the later 1950s and 1960s. He died of a heart condition, marked by excessive fibrillations that ultimately stopped his heart, on October 30, 1968.

PLOT SUMMARY

Chapters 1–2
At fifteen years old, True Son, a white boy adopted at the age of four by the Lenni Lenape—known to whites as the Delaware Indians—learns that he

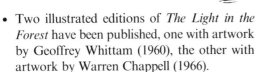

MEDIA ADAPTATIONS

- Two illustrated editions of *The Light in the Forest* have been published, one with artwork by Geoffrey Whittam (1960), the other with artwork by Warren Chappell (1966).

- As one of several of Richter's novels adapted to film, *The Light in the Forest* was made into a motion picture by Walt Disney Studios. Produced in 1958, the film stars James MacArthur as True Son, with Jessica Tandy appearing as Myra Butler.

- *The Light in the Forest* was recorded as an unabridged audiobook by Audio Bookshelf in 2000. Read by Terry Bregy, it has a running time of four hours.

must return to the white people. His father takes him to an encampment and, after waiting with him until sundown, leaves him there. A white guard, Del, laughs at the curious boy.

Del was pessimistic when his regiment was ordered to march from Fort Pitt straight into the heart of Indian territory. But they made it safely to the Forks of the Muskingum, in Ohio, where the Tuscarawas River and the White Woman's River meet. The Indians, fearing an all-out invasion, agreed to the demand that all white captives be returned, though many tears were shed. True Son, aggressively resisting, must be tied up; he scorns white people.

Chapters 3–5

As they march east to Pennsylvania, True Son plans to find a root of the May apple to eat, to commit suicide. But his cousin Half Arrow appears, walking in the woods alongside the regiment, boosting True Son's spirits. Also among the company, Little Crane is walking alongside his departing white wife. Half Arrow gives presents to True Son from his family, including True Son's beloved bearskin. At night, he retires to the forest.

The two cousins and Little Crane talk about how strange, inauthentic, and foolish white people are. A Mohawk man meets them that day but is killed during the night. When they reach a river crossing, Del forces Half Arrow to remain behind, though True Son attacks Del and must be restrained. Half Arrow gives True Son a last message from his father, urging him to do as told to avoid being killed.

The returned captives are marched first to Fort Pitt, then through and beyond a mountain range. At Carlisle, the captives are claimed, but True Son is left over—until a small man arrives late and says he is True Son's father. When True Son rejects the man, Del is ordered to remain with the family to interpret and offer security.

Chapters 6–7

Del was relieved to reach Fort Pitt. Now he and Mr. Butler take the boy across the Susquehanna River by ferry, but at the other side the boy escapes on horseback. Trailing him, Del finds him by the riverbank in the bushes. Arriving at the Butler home in Paxton, True Son, originally named John, is introduced to his birth family. His mother tries to teach him English, but he is indifferent.

At night, True Son remembers having heard about how the men of Paxton once slaughtered a village of Conestogo, including Christianized ones who sought sanctuary. He moves from the bed to the floor to sleep. The next day, he is forced to bathe and wear white people's clothes, as relatives will be visiting. Uncle Wilse is suspicious of True Son and tells a different version of the Conestogo story. Uncle George Owens defends their vigilante justice. When True Son asks about a possible relation to a murderous white man named David Owens, Wilse slaps him hard.

Chapters 8–9

New suits and boots are made for True Son. Aunt Kate confiscates his Indian clothes. Going with his young brother, Gordie, to the basket-maker, an elderly slave named Bejance, True Son learns of Corn Blade, an even older Indian said to live on Third Mountain. The winter months pass. In March, True Son sets out on horseback toward Third Mountain, allowing Gordie to come. But they are sighted by Cousin Alec, and before long Mr. Butler and Uncle Wilse catch up to them and force them to return.

True Son's mother, Myra, remembers the awful day when Indians attacked her husband and others in the field while they were doing farmwork; the Indians killed one man, wounded a woman, and abducted John. Parson Elder visits to counsel her, and Aunt Kate reports her suspicion that True Son has stolen a gun, food, and other things. True Son is summoned, and Parson Elder fails to persuade him to drink whiskey with them. They debate over white and Indian violence. Afterward, Elder is optimistic about John's development.

Chapters 10–11

True Son is bedridden with a mysterious illness. Elder's son arrives to warn Mr. Butler that two Indians have come to town. They were directed to Wilse Owens's cooper shop, where one of them had a few mugs of rum and reportedly began slandering whites; later, that Indian was shot and killed out in a pasture in an ambush. Mr. Butler, hoping to calm his nerves, makes an entry in his farm ledger and derives great relief from reckoning his accounts.

True Son misses Indian life. He does farm work, though the Delaware consider it to be women's work. Aunt Kate notices an Indian scouting the house. At night, True Son slips out and discovers his cousin, Half Arrow. Half Arrow reports the death of Little Crane, who had tried to tell "happy stories" about silly white people to Uncle Wilse. They go find and bury Little Crane, and then they go to see Uncle Wilse, who implies that he was behind the murder and then seizes True Son. Together the boys knock Uncle Wilse down and nearly scalp him—but others frighten them away. Going back to the Butlers' barn, they collect the supplies that True Son has stashed there and flee.

Chapters 12–13

After waking up on Kittaniny Mountain, the cousins hurry on with their journey. A day passes, and they cross a river and continue beyond Third Mountain, the white men in pursuit far behind. They find an Indian path and pass by a white colony, going through the mountains. At a river, the Alleghi Sipu, they find a trader's two canoes in the water. That night, True Son continues downstream alone, on foot. In the river, he meets Half Arrow, who has stolen the smaller canoe. The next night, as dawn approaches, they row past Fort Pitt and into the Ohio River.

Going through Indian country, the boys feel safe and welcome. At a creek, they row up a way and make camp. The next morning, they find that the area is perfect for fishing and a self-sufficient lifestyle. When it rains, they use the overturned canoes as shelter, and later they hunt. After a month or more, they row up the Tuscarawas to their village, to be greeted heartily by all.

Chapters 14–15

After a few celebratory days, Little Crane's family starts beating a drum and forming a war party. True Son and Half Arrow join up along with their fathers, Cuyloga and Black Fish, and, led by Thitpan, they leave in their war paint. At a fork, they split into two parties. Thitpan and Cuyloga find whites and kill them—including a young girl—for their scalps. True Son is disconcerted. When the war party reaches a river, Thitpan declares that True Son will be called upon to trick the next boat carrying white people past. That night, True Son dreams that his white family is going down a river toward a waterfall. After several days' waiting, True Son initially succeeds in luring a boatful of whites toward the shore to be attacked. But then he sees a boy in the group—reminding him of Gordie—and warns them away. The Indians shoot one man, but the boat escapes.

The Indians hold a trial to see whether True Son should be killed for his traitorous action. Many vote yes, but Cuyloga insists that they will have to fight both him and True Son. When the others defer, Cuyloga orders True Son to march out with him but to end their relationship when they reach a fork leading toward white country. After a turkey dinner, they reach a fork and part as enemies, with True Son crossing the river into the constraint and loneliness of the white world.

CHARACTERS

A'astonah

A'astonah, True Son's little sister among the Lenape, is very happy when he returns.

Bejance

Bejance, the basketmaker in town, is an old slave whose humble mode of living reminds True Son of the Indians. Bejance recognizes how all the whites, too, are slaves to their property; he points out that True Son has become harnessed when he sees the boy doing farmwork.

Black Fish

Called Sumakek in Lenape, Black Fish is Half Arrow's father and Quaquenga's brother. He joins the war party and follows the example set by Cuyloga.

Colonel Bouquet

The commander who orders Del's regiment to march into Indian country is Colonel Bouquet. He successfully prevents his troops from engaging in battle unnecessarily and persuades the Indians to peacefully give up their white prisoners. He later commands Del to remain with the Butler family until he is no longer needed.

Gordon "Gordie" Butler

True Son's biological little brother idolizes him and wants to be an Indian too.

Harry Butler

True Son's birth father strikes the boy as a pathetic imitation of a man, being meek, withdrawn, and deferential toward his wife. Butler's psychological distance from reality is evident in his affection for losing himself in his financial figures.

John Cameron Butler

See True Son

Myra Butler

Ever since her four-year-old son was abducted by Indians, Myra Butler has been a so-called invalid, remaining in her quarters, usually in bed with the curtains drawn. She tries to be forceful in urging Johnny to use English, but she proves ineffective and becomes distressed. With a mother's loyalty, she defends Johnny against Aunt Kate's accusations of theft.

Dr. Childsley

Dr. Childsley, the doctor who tends to True Son during his illness, keeps bleeding his feet, as bloodletting was commonly thought of as a general remedy in that era. The doctor has no clue what is wrong with the boy; he considers it one of the "mysterious forest miasmas" Indians were inexplicably liable to suffer.

The Conestogo

A story about a massacre of a group of Conestogo Indians, including women and children, is a point of contention. The Indians tell that peaceful, Christianized Conestogo had sought sanctuary in a white jail but were slaughtered there by a raiding party. The Paxton boys—the white militia group that is behind the massacre—tell that those Indians were only pretending to be converted and were actually fronting for warlike Indians.

Corn Blade

A hundred-year-old speaker of the Lenape said to live on Third Mountain, Corn Blade intrigues True Son. But when True Son tries to visit the old Indian, his father tells him that Corn Blade is dead.

Cuyloga

True Son's adoptive Indian father has instilled in his son a profound appreciation for the Indian way of life. He sympathetically—though with Indian reserve—remains with True Son through the early evening when he is handed over to the whites, and when True Son later returns, Cuyloga is quietly delighted. But after the Indians form a war party, Cuyloga participates in the murder of a child, and he condemns True Son for bringing dishonor to the party by warning the boat of whites away from a massacre. His fatherly feelings lead him to prevent True Son from being executed, but he disowns the boy and forces him into exile.

Disbeliever

Part of the Indian war party, Disbeliever scouts the river until a white boat comes through.

Parson Elder

The gray-haired local parson, Elder visits Myra for company and support. He finds a glass of whiskey in the afternoon to be a good spiritual elixir but cannot persuade True Son to join in. Elder is the leader of the murderous Paxton boys, holding the militia rank of colonel.

Elder's Son

The young Elder visits Mr. Butler to warn him that Indians are in the area; he reports the death of Little Crane.

Half Arrow

True Son's Indian cousin is his closest friend. Half Arrow tags along when True Son marches east with the regiment, bearing gifts from True Son's family and a duly recited message from Cuyloga. In the spring, Half Arrow visits the area with Little Crane, asking after True Son (and evidently declining to drink any alcohol, which perhaps saves his life). After Little Crane is killed, Half Arrow finds True Son, and they set out to get revenge; Half Arrow is excited to scalp Uncle Wilse, but they must flee. When True Son laments leaving his young brother, Gordie, behind, he asks Half Arrow to be his brother. After their pleasant month in the woods, the cousins return and soon join the war party. Again, Half Arrow is especially excited to take part in murderous activity, making a patchwork scalp from the pieces of the three taken by others. When True Son fails the group at the river, Half Arrow disdains him.

Del Hardy

Having been raised near a settlement of Lenni Lenape, Del Hardy knows the Delaware language (which perhaps earned him the nickname "Del" among his regiment), but he does not understand their ways. He resents True Son's aggressive resistance and is frustrated when he must stay with the Butlers after their reunion.

Kringas

While among the whites, True Son recalls wise words spoken by Half Arrow's great-uncle Kringas about Indians' relationship with the Great Spirit.

Little Crane

Being especially fond of his white wife, Little Crane is distraught when she must go and accompanies her as far as possible. When he and Half Arrow later return, Little Crane tells stories that seem joyful to him but which revolve around white people's ignorance and insult Uncle Wilse. Having had a few drinks, Little Crane is later ambushed and killed.

The Mehargues

Little Crane is found by the Mehargue family, dead in their pasture.

Mohawk

During the march east, a Mohawk happens upon the company but is murdered in the night; the cousins presume whites were responsible.

Neal

Neal is a farmer who works alongside Uncle Wilson.

Cousin Alec Owens

On his first day back with the Butlers, True Son borrows clothes from his slightly larger cousin Alec, Uncle Wilse's son. When True Son tries to go visit Corn Blade with Gordie in tow, Alec spots them leaving town and tells their parents.

David Owens

True Son tells his white uncles a story about a white man who had a family with an Indian woman but eventually killed his wife and daughters and fled back to the whites. His name was David Owens, but the uncles claim he is no relation.

Uncle George Owens

When True Son and Uncle Wilse spar verbally, Uncle George Owens vigorously defends the need for their brand of frontier justice. When Little Crane and Half Arrow, seeking True Son, are sent to his shop, Mr. Owens gives Little Crane a few drinks.

Uncle Wilson "Wilse" Owens

True Son's white uncle Wilse Owens has reached the conviction that all Indians are savage and untrustworthy; he extends his suspicions to True Son. He participated in what he considered the justified slaughter of the Conestogo. Uncle Wilse is a cooper (barrel maker). When Little Crane and Half Arrow, seeking True Son, are sent to his shop, Uncle Wilse gives Little Crane a few drinks. After Little Crane is killed—presumably by Wilse's hand—Half Arrow and True Son take revenge by nearly scalping Wilse.

Quaquenga

When True Son returns to the Indian village on the Tuscarawas River, his adoptive mother greets him silently, in deference to her husband.

Aunt Kate Stewart

An imposing presence, Aunt Kate's threat to bathe True Son herself persuades him to bathe and dress on his own. In her opinion, as she tells Parson Elder, True Son finds Indians flawless. After he gets sick, she returns his Indian clothing, which she has confiscated.

Thitpan

Little Crane's brother leads the war party that sets out to exact revenge. Angry at Half Arrow and True Son's failure to procure a scalp to avenge Little Crane, Thitpan's family scorns their family until they join his war party.

True Son

Though he was originally named John Cameron Butler, True Son (in Lenape, Lenni Quis) feels his Indian identity foremost, as the majority of his childhood, from age four to age fifteen—all he remembers—has been spent with the Lenni Lenape. He is appalled by white civilization, and even when he is returned to his birth family, he resists assimilation and plans his escape. He secretively procures and stashes the things he will need for the expected journey, including a knife, a gun, powder, lead, and Indian meal (that is, cornmeal, or maize flour). Meanwhile, he vigorously defends the Indians and seems not entirely aware of the extent to which they participate in the same atrocities as whites. He remains fully Indian at heart through his return home and the formation of the war party. But when Thitpan procures a young white girl's scalp, he is dismayed. And when he realizes that his successful tricking of a boat of white people will mean the death of a boy (who reminds him of Gordie), he warns them away, saving their lives. He is then rejected by the Lenape, and only his father's authority saves him from execution; instead he is exiled to the white civilization that he still finds repellent.

THEMES

Native American Culture

The main action of *The Light in the Forest*—True Son's return to white civilization—prompts the characters to reflect on the comparative merits of the cultures of American Indians, specifically the Lenni Lenape, or Delaware, and the white colonists. In addition, various facets of those cultures are evoked through the characters' attitudes and behavior. The overall picture of Lenape culture is one of resourcefulness, dignity, emotional restraint, and above all integration of society with nature. The reader learns a little about Lenape ways in the opening passage, in which True Son recalls such masculinizing rites as scalding his flesh with hot stones and sitting in an icy river; the ability to endure hardship is a prized characteristic among these people who brave the elements continually and are not unfamiliar with war. True Son soon leaves Indian culture behind, but it follows him eastward in the person of Half Arrow, his Lenape cousin. Half Arrow's self-assurance is evident in his boasting, a habit

often frowned upon as marking excessive pride in whites—but such self-assurance is founded not simply in egotism but in his proven ability to survive independently: to sleep in the forest at night unafraid of wild animals, hunt and cook his own food, and venture on a journey of many days from his home.

Lenape culture is praised directly by True Son, Half Arrow, and Little Crane as they march eastward. They assert their culture's inherent sense of goodness and justice, evident in their having no need to consult a "Good Book" (the Bible) to know how to behave. They speak of the Indians' superior awareness of their surroundings, evident in their acute senses of sight and hearing and in their knowing the advantages and drawbacks of different kinds of firewood, camping sites, and so forth. And they speak of and demonstrate Indians' ability to transcend base emotions, maintaining stoic attitudes about parting indefinitely, withstanding insults from whites, and successfully reuniting. The reader can easily see, then, why True Son remains so attracted to the Indian way of life: in matters of self-development, Indian existence is essentially elevated above white existence. Like monks, the Indians forgo creature comforts and sentimental indulgences that suggest psychological or spiritual weakness; like practical philosophers, they live by communal ethical codes that maintain the fabric of society; and like naturalists, they value the wilderness most in its original state, as the Great Spirit or God has presented it to them. True Son, in returning to white society, is essentially asked to compromise all of these aspects not only of Indian culture but also of his mature self.

American Culture

The perspectives offered in Richter's novel are especially valuable to twenty-first-century readers not only because the cultures he depicts—of both the forest-dwelling Indians and the pioneering whites—have largely faded away but also because he inverts the ordinary white point of view. Instead of starting in white culture and proceeding to encounter Indian culture, Richter opens the novel within Indian culture and proceeds to encounter white culture. This inverted approach to white American culture is unique to the circumstances of the novel: the perspective of a white captive with no memory of white culture who is unwillingly returned to that culture is unlike any other. And from this perspective, True Son is fairly appalled by what he sees.

TOPICS FOR FURTHER STUDY

- Write a personal-reflection essay that addresses the following questions in detail, exploring your own perspectives and emotional states. What aspects of the civilization in which you live are you grateful for and why? What aspects of that civilization trouble you or inspire resentment, and why? When and how often do you get a chance to immerse yourself in the wilderness to some extent? Include a lengthy recollection of what the experience of engaging with the wilderness feels like and means to you and also relate the experience of returning to civilization afterward. Do you think you are dependent on certain aspects of civilization? If you had a chance to temporarily or permanently transition to a simpler state of living, would you take it?

- Read *The Winter People* (2002), a novel by Abenaki author Joseph Bruchac written for middle-school and early-high-school students, set in 1759, and based on an actual event during the French and Indian War. Fourteen-year-old Saxso survives when English soldiers carry out a massacre raid on his village, but his mother and sisters are carried off as captives; he must try to rescue them. Write an essay comparing this book with *The Light in the Forest*, remarking on whatever aspects of the two works of fiction—plot, captivity theme, character development, dialogue, treatment of Native culture, and so forth—stand out to you.

- Consulting a variety of websites, write a research paper relating the history of the Lenni Lenape, or Delaware, people from the time period of Richter's novel to the present day. Include at least one graphic (such as a map), and cite all of your sources.

- Richter uses dozens of Lenape words in *The Light in the Forest*. Locate a Lenape-English dictionary and use it to gain a better understanding of pronunciation and syntax. Write a brief dialogue or speech—such as one that True Son might have given in an imagined situation—using Lenape words from the novel as well as other words and phrases. Either recite the speech or dialogue (with a friend) in front of your class or make a recording that can be turned in or posted online.

Going into white towns at the end of the eastward march, he especially bristles at white civilization's changes to the landscape. The Indians are careful to leave nature the way the Great Spirit has shaped it, and they ultimately conceive of nature as being available to all but belonging only to the Great Spirit. White American culture, on the other hand, is centered on the division of property into plots of land owned by individuals, as divided and signified by fences, roads, and such structures as houses and barns. From True Son's perspective, all of these facets of white civilization are veritably sacrilegious. The houses like "prisons" completely disconnect the person inside from the world the Great Spirit created, while the "glittering ostentation and falseness" of the painted surfaces accomplish a similar disconnection on the level of appearances.

The parallel description of Del Hardy's sentiments upon returning to white civilization offers a telling contrast to True Son's sentiments. Del, having been distressed by the wildness and uncertainty of Indian country, is deeply reassured upon their return by the sight of the houses especially, including the walls, roofs, and chimneys—signifying security from the rest of society, shelter from the elements, and the ability to produce and retain warmth. Few white people would question the value of the house as a structure that is essential to human existence, especially because the entire society depends upon what the house can provide. Capitalism is founded on the right to private property, which can be secured only if the doors and windows of the property can be locked up. In turn, crucial documents like deeds and receipts can be preserved only if they can be protected from damage inside a building. The central role of capitalism in American culture is signified through the character of Mr. Butler, whose deeply felt sense of ownership and financial security is illustrated in the relief he experiences upon reckoning his accounts. Interestingly, the description of the ledger itself—"the double pages with their solid lines . . . stable and reassuring"—calls to mind the sight of the geometrically precise houses and the stability that they, too, represent.

Good and Evil

Overall, white American culture's emphasis on, in Mr. Butler's formulation, "the satisfaction and benefits of honest work, the solace and support of ready cash, and the remuneration and accumulation of active property" quite directly puts it at odds with Delaware culture's belief in, as befits "an original people," maintaining an original relationship with the land, recognizing "how the Great Being made our country beautiful with trees for the forest, water for the river, and grass for the prairies," and, ideally, "abandoning themselves to the forest and the bounty of its wild beasts." In other words, white life is domesticated and enclosed, opposed to nature, while Indian life is wild and open, allied with nature. Each culture views itself as good and the other as evil. The Indians primarily see evil in white culture where their civilization involves the destruction of the natural world for the sake of a secure domestic existence. True Son witnesses with dismay "the sad, incredible region where the Indian forest had been cut down by the white destroyers and no place left for the Indian game to live"—a region he is led to characterize as "the barbarous homeland of his white enemies." The constrictive clothes given to him by his white family are seen as "symbols of all the lies, thefts, and murders by the white man." Indians prioritize nature even at their own expense—accepting that famines and times of hardship are part of the deity's plan—but True Son can see white civilization, which puts human interests ahead of nature, only as evil.

As for Lenape culture, it is not strictly wild; the people do cultivate crops, and there is a distinct order to their society, as seen in the hierarchy of sachems (chiefs) and the unwritten rules

True Son, a young boy kidnapped by Indians, is the story's protagonist. (© Shchipkova Elena / Shutterstock.com)

of honorable conduct. But where Indian life does seem wild—especially in the conduct of men on the warpath—the whites respond with fear and distrust. Life in the forest is conceived by Myra Butler as a life of "heathen darkness and ignorance," and Aunt Kate inaccurately imagines that True Son simply "believes it's right to lie and steal." The uncles think all Indians are irredeemable butchers and murderers, such that even the slaughter of Indian children is justified as preemptive punishment for future misdeeds. True Son, of course, rejects all the racist notions of his white kin, and upon escaping he basks in the ideal version of wild living—the "primitive deliciousness" in which he and Half Arrow "lived as happy animals." But soon, Indian wildness becomes overwhelming even to True Son. He knows about the savagery that whites are capable of, such as the Paxton mob's slaughter of the Conestogo, including children. But he is confronted firsthand with Indian savagery when

Thitpan takes pride in having procured the scalp of a white girl whose family was believed to have encroached on Indian lands. True Son is expected to contribute to the deaths of an entire party of whites, including a small boy, when they are met on the river. The Delaware are acting as if they are at war, just as the Paxton group did in slaughtering the Conestogo. But True Son himself cannot abide taking the lives of people who are clearly guilty only of being in the wrong place at the wrong time, even though Lenape culture expects it of him. With True Son's ethical stance leading to his being exiled from the Indians but still alienated from the whites, Richter's novel leaves the reader in a balanced, indefinite state of mind as to the various ways in which both white and Indian culture can be alternately seen as good and as evil.

STYLE

Objectivity

In both his own and others' estimation, Richter provides in *The Light in the Forest* an objective, unbiased accounting of the material at hand. His preface, noting how resistant many white captives of Indians were to being assimilated back into white society—as well as noting his own inclination to run off to Indian country as a lad—seems to suggest a favoring of Indian culture. But he then notes, "Not that the novel represents the novelist's particular beliefs or opinions. He can understand and sympathize with either side. His business is to be fair to them both." Maurice D. Schmaier, in his expansive essay "Conrad Richter's *The Light in the Forest*: An Ethnohistorical Approach to Fiction," affirms that the novel constitutes "an objective and sympathetic presentation of both White and Indian points of view." A surface examination of the themes of the novel supports these assertions, given the balanced presentation of each culture from both internal and external perspectives and given the portrayals of both positive and negative characters within each group.

In the end, the reader may think that the narration and the plot together suggest that the author has indeed reached certain conclusions about the cultures he explores. On the one hand, it would seem that Richter believes that the Indian way of life—at least in times of peace—is superior to the white way of life. As if

the precepts of white civilization have infected every last adult, the only unreservedly positive portrayal of a white person is that of the innocent young Gordie. Del Hardy is a good soldier but also decidedly and contentedly ignorant of "savage" Delaware culture. The novel's one clear-cut idealization of a mode of living comes with True Son and Half Arrow's interlude along the river, where they live for a month in the most natural way possible. And yet the narrator nonetheless at times shows a bias against Indian character. Relating the discussion among the two cousins and Little Crane during the march eastward, the narrator notes that the idea of killing their guards is a "pleasant subject"; the notion that the Indians found killing to be downright pleasant seems like a notion dreamed up and propagated by whites to emphasize the supposed savagery of the Indians. In the depictions of the Indians going out as a war party, the stoic demeanor previously attributed to them is cast aside, and they are depicted as not just preparing for but, indeed, reveling in the violence to come; Half Arrow now seems actually sadistic. Again, without reading Richter's sources, it is hard for the modern reader to know how historically accurate these depictions are. Richter surely leaves the reader condemning the Paxton boys for their atrocities, but those men represent an extreme within white society; the Indians, on the other hand, go so far as to collectively believe that True Son should be executed for failing to help slaughter defenseless people. In other words, as the plot is laid out, evil acts exist in white culture, but Indian culture *requires* evil acts. In the end, individual readers may have varying opinions as to how objective Richter's portrayals truly are.

Frontier Literature

The Light in the Forest can be classed broadly as historical fiction but more specifically as an example of the disappearing genre of frontier literature. Since the American frontier itself, of course, has disappeared, fewer and fewer authors are inclined to conceptually reach back in time to try to flesh out just what life was like in the time period when American Indians and colonizing whites confronted each other. Those times are well beyond living memory; no elders remain to relate firsthand their pioneering experiences and reflections. Writers like Richter have thus been obligated to read historical accounts in order to flesh out a vision of the early American frontier.

Richter acknowledges a pair of sources in his preface, books by the Reverends John Heckewelder and David Zeisberger that, as it happens, were also relied upon by America's most famous author of frontier literature, James Fenimore Cooper, whose "Leatherstocking Tales" hero, Natty Bumppo, was raised among the Delaware after the deaths of his parents and represents a merging of white and Indian traits.

In his essay, Schmaier puts Cooper and Richter in the context of a progression of approaches to fictionalizing frontier life and the nature of American Indians. The earliest frontier novels were "pseudo-historical" tales that were essentially exercises in vivid imagination. Later writings told of Puritan encounters with Indians in the interest of justifying military action against them. In the eighteenth and nineteenth centuries, the idealization of the "noble savage" appeared in works such as Henry Wadsworth Longfellow's epic poem *The Song of Hiawatha* (1855), while others took the opposite approach and portrayed Indians in strictly negative terms, even advocating their extermination. Cooper wrote a series of five novels, including *The Last of the Mohicans* (1826) and *The Pathfinder* (1840), that represented advances in the complexity of character treatment, presenting various Indians in dramatic circumstances that bring out a range of positive and negative qualities. Yet some consider his treatments melodramatic. Richter, as a writer with journalistic training in a much later generation, was even more inclined to objectivity, seeking to provide the reader with as realistic as possible an accounting of what life on the early American frontier was like.

HISTORICAL CONTEXT

The Lenni Lenape, the Paxton Mob, and Colonel Bouquet's March

Perhaps the finest aspect of Richter's novel is the loyalty with which it evokes the historical circumstances of frontier life in Pennsylvania and eastern Ohio in the mid-eighteenth century. The year is pinpointed with Mr. Butler's ledger entry for May 31, 1765, meaning the action occurs just over a decade before the American Revolution. Richter drew quite heavily from historical accounts, not only for essential plot points such as Colonel Bouquet's march and the exploits of

the "Paxton boys" but also for the perspectives of the Lenni Lenape.

Richter acknowledges in his preface that he owes a debt to a pair of historical volumes, though this is perhaps an understatement. The full titles of those volumes, both written by Moravian missionaries, are *An Account of the History, Manners, and Customs of the Indian Nations Who Once Inhabited Pennsylvania and the Neighbouring States* (1819), by the Reverend John Heckewelder (1743–1823), and *History of the North American Indians*, by the Reverend David Zeisberger (1721–1808). The former volume, especially, provides extensive discussion of the Lenape, who were given the name "Delaware" by the whites who first encountered them in the region of that future state. By the 1760s, the Lenape had been pushed as far west as the Pennsylvania-Ohio border, though not without strife and lingering resentment, especially where whites had encroached on acknowledged Indian lands. The Lenape were among the Indians who participated in the war effort, often called a rebellion or uprising, led by the Ottawa chief Pontiac. The Delaware besieged Fort Pitt in June 1763 and proceeded to attack many white settlements in the region, killing or capturing some two thousand people and displacing thousands of others. In his novel, Richter reports, through the character of George Owens, how the peaceable Quaker governance of Pennsylvania from the eastern region left the settlers on the state's western frontier to effectively defend themselves.

Colonel Henry Bouquet, of Swiss origin, was a field commander in Pennsylvania at the time, and with an army of some 460 men, he accomplished a crucial defeat of Indian forces at Bushy Run in August 1963 and then ended their siege of Fort Pitt. The majority of the Delaware thus settled back along the western banks of the Ohio rivers mentioned in Richter's novel—the Muskingum, Tuscarawas, and White Woman's Rivers. But some Indians remained in western Pennsylvania, and although the real-life Paxton pastor John Elder urged the governor to remove the Indians for their protection, some fifty-seven men, dubbed the Paxton boys, proceeded to invade Conestogo Town and kill the six Indians they found there; later, another Paxton mob slaughtered the remaining fourteen Conestogo who were sheltered at the Lancaster County jail. Much as *The Light in the Forest* relates, these Indians were all old men, women, and children, and the murders were horrendously carried out.

COMPARE & CONTRAST

- **1760s:** Although they had occupied a majority of Pennsylvania in the 1750s (having been pushed west from the coast), the Lenni Lenape, or Delaware Indians, are being pushed farther by purchases and treaties—some just, some unjust—to the western margins of the state and into Ohio.

  1950s: The Delaware no longer have a presence in Pennsylvania. The largest Delaware communities have become established in Oklahoma—originally founded as Indian Territory—and in Ontario, Canada.

  Today: One of the federally recognized Delaware groups in Oklahoma, the Delaware Nation, files a lawsuit in 2004 seeking to regain lands in Pennsylvania in the interest of building a casino, but the lawsuit is ultimately rejected by the Supreme Court in 2006.

- **1760s:** In the wake of the French and Indian War, in which the Delaware ally themselves with the French and which ends in 1763, Pontiac's War sees Indians who had allied with the British turn back against them. The Delaware join the Ottawa, Seneca, Shawnee, and others in this effort, but they are ultimately subdued, with peace obtained through the treaty negotiated by Colonel Bouquet at the Forks of the Muskingum.

  1950s: No more wars are fought between American Indians and other residents of the continent, but as members of the US military, about 10,000 Native Americans participate in the Korean War. Three are high-ranking officers, and three earn Medals of Honor.

  Today: As of 2010, more than 22,500 servicemen and some 1,300 officers are of Native American heritage—a total of 1.7 percent of the military population, while Native Americans account for just 1.4 percent of the total population. More than sixty American Indians have died in the recent wars in Iraq and Afghanistan.

- **1760s:** Accounts of American Indian life have been written only by whites and other outsiders, though some of these accounts draw on the experiences of people who lived among the Indians as captives.

  1950s: The majority of literature with Native American characters is still written by non-Natives, such that a novel like *The Light in the Forest* can be seen as providing excellent insight into American Indian culture.

  Today: A great number of American Indian authors have made their mark on American literature—including N. Scott Momaday, Leslie Marmon Silko, Louise Erdrich, and Sherman Alexie—and have demonstrated through the quality of their prose that only Native writers can provide truly authentic views of Native culture.

Even the detail of Parson Elder's deferring to the mob for fear of having his horse killed is derived from historical records.

The atrocities carried out by the Paxton boys were a primary motivating factor for the expedition led by Colonel Bouquet into Indian territory in Ohio to reclaim white captives. The hope was that doing so would suppress the violent impulses demonstrated by the Scots-Irish settlers of western Pennsylvania. The real-life march described by Richter's fictional character

Del Hardy left Fort Pitt on October 4, 1764, with some fifteen hundred troops, including many family members of white captives. By November, the army was able to return east with 206 reclaimed captives in tow—many unwillingly. As for the details of True Son's sentiments upon returning to white society, Richter had a variety of stories of white captivity to turn to, such as "Narrative of John Brickell's Captivity among the Delawares," published in *American Pioneer* in 1842.

The reader can see that the framework of Richter's novel is extremely faithful to historical circumstances, which may not come as a surprise. Furthermore, a majority of the ideas and even anecdotes of the story were derived from existing sources, especially Heckewelder's history. That book records many Lenape attitudes toward white culture, which are loyally reflected in the dialogue between True Son, Half Arrow, and Little Crane, as well as elsewhere in the novel. The anecdote about Cuyloga chastising a defeated bear is a compressed version of an anecdote also found in Heckewelder (as supplemented by information from a second anecdote), with almost no details changed, from the broken backbone to the panther's cry to the Delaware hunter's monologue. In Heckewelder's version, the hunter speaks as follows:

> Hark ye! bear; you are a coward, and no warrior as you pretend to be. Were you a warrior, you would shew it by your firmness and not cry and whimper like an old woman. You know, bear, that our tribes are at war with each other, and that yours was the aggressor.... Had you conquered me, I would have borne it with courage and died like a brave warrior; but you, bear, sit here and cry, and disgrace your tribe by your cowardly conduct.

If the reader compares this anecdote with Richter's version at the end of chapter 4, it is clear that he borrowed—or perhaps lifted—virtually ll of his phrasing, sometimes word for word. Likewise, the story told by Little Crane about the white missionary who tried to keep Indians from letting their horses eat his grass is derived from a personal experience of Heckewelder's. Focusing on Richter's dependence on sources for *The Light in the Forest* in his essay in *Ethnohistory*, Schmaier presents two points of view: historically speaking, he praises "the care with which Richter has utilized authentic source material," but fictionally speaking, he points out that, "for example, Richter's version of Heckewelder's whimpering bear anecdotes is so condensed and reworded that most of their original flavor is lost." As admirable as Richter's effort to re-create the frontier past is, the reader may still get a sense for how Richter's profound distance from that past must have made it difficult for him to infuse details from historical sources with the original workings of his imagination.

Much of the story takes place along the rivers of the mid-Atlantic region of the American colonies.
(© Andrew Williams | Shutterstock.com)

CRITICAL OVERVIEW

By virtue of his 1951 Pulitzer Prize, Richter was in high standing among critics upon the 1953 publication of *The Light in the Forest*, and contemporary reviews were favorable. Schmaier cites several reviews in his *Ethnohistory* essay: in *Library Journal*, M. D. Read called the book a "rich little story" appropriate "for all boys," while a reviewer for the *New Yorker* considered it a "fine short novel." Edwin W. Gaston, Jr., in *Conrad Richter*, also cites early reviewers, including Lewis Gannett, who in the *New York Herald Tribune Book Review* called the novel an "evocative parable"; a *Nation* writer who considered it a "touching idyll"; and Edward Weeks, who, writing in the *Atlantic Monthly*, found fault with the "moralizing at each end" but asserted that the novel "does succeed in probing closer than I can remember to the resentment which the Indians felt against the whites and to that inflammable mob spirit which the conquering American too often let loose."

Schmaier and Gaston themselves, writing with greater hindsight in the 1960s, had additional critical commentary. Schmaier duly notes that as a work of fiction, the novel "is relatively short and uninvolved." But giving consideration to historical value, he asserts that in *The Light in the Forest*, "Richter does more than any conventional scholar has done to bring mid-18th century Delaware-White relations into clear, three-dimensional focus." He notes that historical facts and circumstances are successfully "presented as an intrinsic part of a dramatic, continually unfolding story" in a way that "contributes to the novel's total effect." All in all, the novel is said to aptly produce

> a sensation that the reader is among the flesh-and-blood Indians, Indianized White men, and White settlers who composed mid-18th century Pennsylvania contact society, and that he is sharing each societal group's problems, hopes, and attitudes.

Gaston, considering the novel in the context of Richter's oeuvre, acknowledges that it should be considered not as one of his masterpieces but as one of his "interludes," or "decidedly minor works," which "seem to represent for the author a respite from the creative rigors of the more ambitious works."

Recent reviewers have sustained praise for the novel. In *Twentieth-Century Young Adult Writers* (1994), Charles R. Duke affirms that *The Light in the Forest*

> has attracted consistent attention in the public schools and has developed an acceptance among adolescent readers and teachers of adolescent literature. Because it is brief, challenging on several different levels of reading appreciation and because it addresses a timeless issue, the novel has continued to appear on many reading lists for adolescents.

Duke considers the book ideal for teachers "wishing to raise the awareness of their students about the original relationships between whites and Indians during the settling of America." The novel's continued relevance was further attested to by the production of an audiobook in 2000. Reviewing the audiobook in *Booklist*, Pat Austin called the original novel a "provocative story of culture and belonging," while a *Publishers Weekly* reviewer declared the book to be a "classic tale of a boy torn between families and cultures."

CRITICISM

Michael Allen Holmes

Holmes is a writer with existential interests. In the following essay, he reflects on what seems to be missing from The Light in the Forest.

Conrad Richter's short novel *The Light in the Forest* has been spoken of in largely favorable critical terms ever since it appeared in 1953. Richter was well established as a significant American fiction writer by this point in his career, especially after winning the Pulitzer Prize in 1951. Comments on this novel were generally positive, if not effusively so, with many taking note of the evident historical precision of Richter's re-creation of the pioneer days and Lenni Lenape, or Delaware, culture. The strain of praise has continued into the twenty-first century, with reviewers especially highlighting the novel's effectiveness in teaching adolescents about the era in question through vicarious experience (that is, living through someone else). The educational benefits of the novel are indeed apparent in the narrative's studied consideration of the two contrasting cultures. And yet, in the twenty-first century, with online venues creating a more democratic environment for readers to respond, one may be struck by the negative terms in which the novel is frequently discussed by adolescent readers. The word *boring*, especially, is liable to surface. Granted, the opinions of teenagers who are perhaps a bit too accustomed to the fast-paced action of modern thriller films should be taken with a grain of salt; still, even more-discerning readers may find the novel to be a bit of a disappointment, perhaps without knowing why. A closer look at not what the novel contains but what is lacking may shed light on this matter.

The possibility that *The Light in the Forest* is actually a substandard Richter novel has been raised before, notably by Edwin W. Gaston, Jr., in his mostly approving critical volume *Conrad Richter* (1965). Gaston classes the novel as one of the author's four "less ambitious...interludes" between the major literary achievements of his Ohio trilogy and other works. Gaston qualifies his comments by assuring readers that these interludes are not merely "light exercises to keep authorial techniques sharpened for bigger things," but he does concede that they are marked by "artistic lapses." Discussing *The Light in the Forest*, Gaston affirms that it is at

WHAT DO I READ NEXT?

- Readers wishing to find out where True Son's life leads after *The Light in the Forest* can turn to Richter's *A Country of Strangers* (1966), which focuses on a female white captive, Stone Girl, who is returned to white civilization. The story also features the reappearance of True Son.

- Richter received the National Book Award for his autobiographical novel *The Waters of Kronos* (1960), an allegorical fantasy in which an old man travels from the West back to his birthplace in Pennsylvania to find himself back in the era of his childhood.

- Though it was written last in James Fenimore Cooper's series of five "Leatherstocking Tales," *The Deerslayer* (1841) presents the earliest portrait of frontier hero Natty Bumppo, when he goes on his first warpath in his early twenties with his companion Chingachgook. The infallibly honest Bumppo has a great deal to say about Indian virtue, white character, and the interaction of the races. The book is profoundly evocative of life on the far side of the frontier in the 1740s, and some of the action is startlingly intense.

- N. Scott Momaday, who won the Pulitzer Prize for his breakthrough novel *House Made of Dawn* (1968), also wrote *The Way to Rainy Mountain* (1969), a short, engrossing postmodern story that blends a modern-day Kiowa's thoughts about the world with Kiowa myth, as well as a journey undertaken by his ancestors.

- *Do All Indians Live in Tipis?* (2007) is an introduction to Native American culture aimed at young adults, authored by the National Museum of the American Indian, answering the most common questions people have about the way Native Americans have lived throughout history.

- The collection *Taken by the Indians: True Tales of Captivity* (1976), edited by Alice Dickinson, draws heavily on diaries and letters to relate a number of true captivity stories, accessible to young adults.

- The Brazilian professor Eduardo Viveiros de Castro wrote *From the Enemy's Point of View: Humanity and Divinity in an Amazonian Society* (1992), which explores the Araweté, a culture that has successfully resisted European imperialism thanks to their societal practices.

---

least "superior to Richter's other" interludes, and, as it happens, he makes no mention of specific artistic lapses therein. But he perhaps had some in mind nonetheless.

By virtue of the tagline at the top of the Fawcett Juniper edition of the book—"The classic adventure story of a frontier boy raised by Indians"—many a modern-day reader will approach the book expecting a fair degree of action and excitement. A precedent for such frontier literature was set by, among others, James Fenimore Cooper, who included plenty of chase scenes, captivities, and life-or-death situations in novels like *The Deerslayer*. Cooper did, however, also include wide swaths of expository narration and contemplative dialogue that perhaps serve as obstacles for modern readers; even before people's attention spans began to shrink with exposure to films and television, critics such as, most famously, Mark Twain had plenty of cutting remarks about Cooper's slow pacing, overblown prose, and the impressive talkativeness of truth-telling frontiersman Natty Bumppo. As it happens, Richter, according to Marvin J. LaHood in an *English Journal* essay, was "not a great reader nor an admirer of Cooper's fiction." And indeed Richter's journalistic training is apparent in the concision and

FROM MOSTLY WALKING AND TALKING, THE PLOT EVOLVES TO INCLUDE A WIDER VARIETY OF DRAMATIC ACTION. YET NARRATIVE DISAPPOINTMENT PERSISTS."

objectivity with which he relates dramatic episodes. But if Cooper as narrator perhaps says too much, Richter perhaps says too little.

Examining the workings of the plot of *The Light in the Forest*, the reader finds a multiplicity of instances where the most heated action occurs either in the past or offstage or is related in text so concise that to describe it as "action" would be a bit misleading. The novel's relative inaction begins with the very first paragraph, where True Son hears news that leaves him standing "very straight and still." He is led to recall past instances of putting "a stone hot from the fire on his flesh" and sitting "in the icy river" until his Indian father allowed him to emerge. These are striking acts for True Son to have experienced, undoubtedly quite unfamiliar to modern readers, but it seems clear that they were also unfamiliar to Richter himself. He might have included a chapter preceding this one to present one or both of these episodes live, so to speak, but he did not. And the existing text gives the reader no vicarious sensation of what it was like to perform these acts—there is no description of what True Son actually thought or felt while enduring the trials. He is only said to have endured them. That is, it seems Richter did not even bother to imagine for himself what those experiences would have been like; he simply reports them. Related with similar disconnection is the incident where True Son hides in a hollow tree for some time to avoid being turned over to the whites. The narrator duly reports this episode; but what goes unsaid is what it felt like for True Son to escape to the tree and remain hidden there indefinitely—was it the span of a morning? A day? Did his muscles ache? Did he hear his father approaching? Did his father yank him out roughly or coax him out? The reader learns no such details about the episode.

A different sort of letdown may be caused by unfulfilled threats or narrative possibilities. At the end of the first chapter, chafing at Del Hardy's attitude, True Son boldly asserts to himself, "Once my hands are loose, I'll get his knife.... Then quickly I'll kill him." But True Son never makes any attempt on Del's life. This fits with the plot, since True Son's spirits improve considerably with the appearance of Half Arrow, and his father's message serves to calm his vengeful impulses. Still, the chapter-ending threat of murder builds an expectation or anxiety in the reader, and this feeling is never resolved by a future occurrence. True Son does attack Del when the soldier prods Half Arrow with his gun. But the action is brief: True Son "made a lunge at the guard. He knocked him down, tried to pull out first the guard's knife and then his hatchet. Over the ground they rolled, while...others came running to pull True Son off." The conflict ends there. The reader is told what True Son *tried* to do, but what *did* he do? Did Del seize one or both of his arms? Did he seize Del's arms in return, or did he put an elbow in Del's stomach or even get a hand on one of Del's weapons? In place of such details, the reader is told only that "over the ground they rolled." Richter might have been trying to avoid Cooper's supposed flaw of being melodramatic, but such a description of action is downright nondramatic, and it fails to enhance the reader's sympathy for the protagonist, which a more detailed description of action would accomplish. The reader is left not within but just outside True Son's individual consciousness.

The first example of action that occurs offstage is the death of the Mohawk in chapter 4. The Mohawk meets and communicates with the Lenape young men, but he is not directly quoted, and he is not given a name. The death of this character does not bear directly on the plot, but it is highly relevant to True Son's state of mind, since his bitterness over what is suspected to be murder by a white man soon boils over in the fight with Del. The reader is told of this bitterness, but the reader is not as surely struck with that bitterness as might have been the case if Richter had fleshed out the Mohawk character, with an individuated description of his appearance, lines actually spoken by him, and a demonstration of the relationship that these Indians of different tribes would have had with one another.

More action is glossed over in chapter 6, when True Son briefly escapes from Del and

Mr. Butler while crossing a river on a ferry. The reader may get a burst of adrenaline from the description of the horse bounding into the water and up the bank out of sight—a chase might liven up what has so far been mostly contemplation, dialogue, and a long march east. But this thread of action is another red herring: the reader is told of how Del calmly followed the trail revealing that True Son dismounted and continued on foot toward the riverbank, and "in a tangle of alders and sweetbrier he stopped and soon pulled out the kicking and biting boy." In this instance, pretty much the entire encounter, whatever it consisted of, is encapsulated in the one word "soon." This is disappointing enough, but considering further the reader may wonder why the boy acted as he did. Did he imagine Del would not be able to track him? Was he so exhausted from the marching (which seems unlikely) that he could not push himself any farther? Was he hoping to get the jump on Del? If so, why did he not? In this instance, Richter's failure to detail True Son's thought process or intentions seems to represent a failure to fully envision the situation at hand. Without understanding why True Son did as little as he did to avoid recapture, the reader may even find the action unconvincing; some may imagine that Richter has miswritten his own novel here—that given how he has developed the characters, the situation would not have played out as uneventfully as it does.

The reader is likely appreciative when the pace of the novel picks up in the second half. From mostly walking and talking, the plot evolves to include a wider variety of dramatic action. Yet narrative disappointment persists. In chapter 8, True Son gets a horse and sneaks away from home in a "stealthy way" toward Third Mountain in search of Corn Blade, agreeing to take Gordie along. Yet when Cousin Alec sights them and rushes off to inform Uncle Wilse, "True Son didn't care." But why has he abandoned the stealth with which he fled the house? They proceed without haste, and at one point True Son "stopped the horse for a long time," as if he indeed does not even care whether he gets where he is trying to go. The reader is not at all surprised when Mr. Butler and Uncle Wilse soon catch up and force them to return home—with not a hint of melodrama—and another thread of action proves to be a dead end. In chapter 10, Half Arrow and Little Crane arrive in town. Little Crane is murdered, but once

again this occurs offstage and is related second-hand, by Parson Elder's son (another character whose lack of a name signals a lack of investment by the author), and the reader gains no vicarious sense of the import of the action. The reader *learns* of this unjust murder but does not actually *experience* the injustice of it. In chapter 11, the fight between the two cousins and Uncle Wilse represents the most sustained action of the entire novel, but even this action makes up only a paragraph, padded by the boys' argument over what to do with their defeated foe. (The reader may be glad that the scalping is not accomplished—but it may also seem that if these two young men had really set about trying to scalp the man, "one cutting, one hacking," they would have succeeded in a matter of moments.) In chapter 12, the boys escape with the white men in pursuit, but that pursuit fades into the distance, and the tension of the chase quickly dissipates.

Through the closing chapters, the reader may be left still wondering just what is so adventurous about this novel. Half Arrow's theft of the canoe from the trader on the river occurs offstage, and a chance for the reader to gain a greater sympathetic attachment to Half Arrow is lost. Of course, Half Arrow as a character is ultimately cast aside anyway: despite the fact that Half Arrow is True Son's closest companion, in the final chapter the reader is told only that at various points he "turned away," "turned and stumbled off in the forest," and bore a "look of bitter emotion." Occurring offstage, again, is Thitpan and Cuyloga's assault on the three white people they scalp, though in this case, at least, it would have been crass and unnecessary for the action to have been detailed further; likewise, the reader is surely glad that no atrocities take place when the party of whites barely avoids falling into the Indians' trap. Still, the Indians have formed a war party, and through the depictions of the war dances and so forth, Richter's narrator has heightened the sense of their desire for revenge. Thus another plot thread is left unfulfilled when this war party engages in no battles at all. Where, meanwhile, are Mr. Butler and True Son's white uncles? Are they livid with rage? Did they abandon their search, to go back home and count their pennies? Might the reader not expect the novel to be working toward a final confrontation between the war party and the men of Paxton? Such an expectation, if the reader has it, is dashed when the novel ends instead with the Indian equivalent of a courtroom scene. It is

John Cameron Butler, the protagonist, is kidnapped from his frontier home at the age of four during an Indian raid. *(© Andrew F. Kazmierski / Shutterstock.com)*

quite appropriate, after all, for this novel patched together with long stretches of contemplative discussion on the merits of the whites and Indians of the region to end, in turn, with a contemplative discussion on the fate of this young man stranded between those two cultural worlds.

The Light in the Forest has earned high praise for its historical accuracy and the depth of its cultural and conceptual explorations. But the best novelists present cultural and conceptual explorations not merely through the voices of their characters but through the actions of their characters as well. As the reader is made to feel and sympathize with the characters' actions, to that same extent will the reader feel and sympathize with the novel's thematic import. With *The Light in the Forest*, arguably the reader is not made to sympathize with the characters through genuine action nearly enough, and one may be led to the uncharitable conclusion that Richter

has not so much written this novel as he has simply reported it.

Source: Michael Allen Holmes, Critical Essay on *The Light in the Forest*, in *Novels for Students*, Gale, Cengage Learning, 2013.

Marianne Cotugno

In the following excerpt, Cotugno examines the relationship between Conrad Richter and his agent, Paul Reynolds, Jr.

> Here we are again with Conrad [Richter]. Having nothing better to worry about, he has this time dug pretty deep into the past. I enclose a copy of his latest effusion and I confess quite frankly that I don't like its tone. No one should know better than Conrad that over the years I have pretty damn well broken my neck to give him every possible break and to deal with his strange eccentricities. So the answer to this letter, which I enclose but which I have not mailed, expresses pretty much the way I feel and, I might add, expresses the way Pete

> COMMENTS IN CORRESPONDENCE AND
> IN REYNOLDS' PUBLISHED WORK REFLECT
> THE RESPECT HE HAD FOR CONRAD RICHTER AS
> AN AUTHOR."

Lemay, who has also done his damnedest, far beyond the line of duty, for Conrad, feels too. It's really a great pity that Conrad seems constitutionally incapable of ever saying anything pleasant or gracious to any of us. As in the past, let me have your advice.

—Alfred A. Knopf to Paul Reynolds, Jr. (12 June 1962)

Pleas like this one, from the publisher to the agent for advice on how to handle the author, mark difficult moments in an otherwise productive relationship. Although the American author Conrad Richter and the publisher Alfred Knopf enjoyed a thirty-plus-year professional and personal collaboration, Richter's concerns—particularly the way he expressed them—sometimes caused a strain in this otherwise fond, successful partnership. In these instances, the well-known literary agent Paul Reynolds, Jr., often intervened with just the right approach to mitigate any conflict between author and publisher.

These disagreements threatened not only a personal relationship but a professional one as well. For an author who, despite critical success—including the Pulitzer Prize in 1951 for *The Town* and the National Book Award in 1961 for *The Waters of Kronos*—never quite had the commercial success he might have achieved, this professional relationship was significant. Richter may have needed Knopf more than Knopf needed Richter, and one wonders whether another publisher would have been such an enthusiastic supporter of this author.

Reynolds had a stake in the Richter-Knopf relationship too. Employed by Richter, the agent could be expected to be an advocate for the author, but for Reynolds, who worked with Knopf on behalf of other authors, helping Richter to maintain a good working relationship with Knopf was in the best interests of all whom he served.

Reynolds, as a second-generation literary agent, represented a new wave of men and women who no longer had to answer 'Why are you here?' but instead had to answer 'On whose side are you?' In response, it would be too simple to say merely that the agent functioned as an advocate for the client, because the agent's role required him or her to maintain strong ties not only with the author but also with the publisher, with whom the agent would hope to work again with this or another author.

Reynolds' efforts on behalf of Conrad Richter offer a case study for understanding the triangular author-agent-publisher relationship. In his capacity as agent, Reynolds functioned as editor, promoter, advocate, negotiator, and, perhaps most significantly, mediator. Fulfilling these roles in a manner that balanced the needs of both author and publisher was essential to Reynolds' professional success and coincided with a change in the way literary agents were perceived by publishers—moving from an adversarial relationship to a cooperative one. This cooperative relationship between Reynolds and Knopf can be described as a benevolent conspiracy.

Literary agents, who emerged in England in the mid-nineteenth century, initially faced opposition from publishers. This opposition resulted from the ways in which agents challenged the existing system, posing a threat to the power of publishers and editors. Yet even in the earliest days of literary agents, both authors and publishers were clients of the agent. For example, an agent might work for a publisher who had acquired the copyright in works by an author when that publisher was looking to profit from the copyright. One reason for A.P. Watt's success was that he served both authors and publishers, for whom he sold book rights that the publishers themselves were unable to sell. So this supposed antagonism between agent and publisher was not inherent to the agent-publisher relationship but, rather, resulted when the agent seemingly stepped between author and publisher. Ironically, publishers' worry about agents as intrusive middlemen ignores or forgets that publishers themselves had been recently considered middlemen who came between author and printer-bookseller.

An 1895 piece in the *New York Times*, reprinted from *The Nineteenth Century*, opens, 'The agent is an unpleasant excrescence on literature, and one who is doing it incalculable harm.' The essay contrasts the hardworking publisher, who has read many manuscripts and devoted many hours to searching for a potentially successful author, with the opportunistic and lazy agent, who acts as a vulture. The piece concludes by condemning agents for making authors into indentured servants by selling contracts for future stories: 'At the end of this business the author finds himself turned into a fiction mill with contracts staring him in the eyes for three or four novels a year for, say, the next five years.' From the 1890s until his death in 1920, the British publisher William Heinemann was the main spokesperson for his profession's view that agents got in the way of the relationship between author and publisher and also 'debased literature by emphasizing the commercial aspect.'

Yet signs appeared of literary agents' increasing acceptance. In 1898, another piece in the *New York Times* begins, 'Is the literary agent a benefit to authors, or is he not?' The writer notes that this debate has continued for several years and that if the agent did not benefit the author in some way, he would cease to exist. He comments on how the agent has done for authors what the trade union has done for the working man: 'The literary agent has made authorship a vastly more peaceful and profitable calling than it could have been without him.'

As the son of one of the first successful literary agents, Reynolds knew this history. Writing in the late 1950s, he asserts,

> Forty years ago there existed in the minds of many editors and publishers an antipathy toward the literary agent. He was often considered a person who interfered with the personal relationship and friendship of author and editor, or author and publisher. Also, the agent was thought to be something of a pirate, an individual who held up the buyer and forced him to pay an unreasonable price.

Reynolds' efforts on behalf of Richter illustrate the opposite: He helped to preserve the relationship between author and publisher and, while helping to negotiate reasonable contracts for his author, also worked on behalf of the publisher when the latter wished to offer the author less than he had been receiving when the price seemed justified by the author's previous sales.

In contrast to the view of the agent as interloper or vulture, Reynolds asserts the power of the agent as an instrument of fairness for the author:

> There is no question that the pressure of the agent has made many an erring editor pay the market price or has induced the publisher to draw a fairer contract than he would otherwise have prepared. The effect of the agent has been to equalize the bargaining power of the author with the editor and to increase competition; more than that the agent has been unable to do.

Agents used competition—the threat that a manuscript would be sold to another publisher—to acquire the best possible price for an author's work.

Reynolds' claim that 'more than that the agent has been unable to do' seems disingenuous. As Reynolds' experience with Richter shows, agents did more than 'equalize the bargaining power of the author' and 'increase competition' for manuscripts; Reynolds served as an editor, promoter, and mediator for his author.

Because agents served in these roles, publishers came to see them as allies, not adversaries. The very things for which publishers criticized agents became the things with which agents helped publishers—such as the relationship between author and publisher and contractual matters. As in the case of Knopf and Reynolds, publishers and agents entered into a benevolent conspiracy on behalf of authors. Agents had to establish a delicate balance between their responsibilities to the authors who were their clients and their responsibilities to the publishers with whom they worked on behalf of other authors. Reynolds' ability to do this facilitated his professional success.

Paul Revere Reynolds, Jr., was the son of Paul Revere Reynolds, who became the first successful literary agent in America. Reynolds, Sr., began his career as an intermediary between British and American publishing interests, and he came to acquire individual authors as clients in the late nineteenth century. The Paul R. Reynolds agency began in 1927 with Reynolds, Sr., and a partner, Harold Ober, who soon thereafter left to create his own successful agency. His son joined the firm in 1923 and became a well-respected agent in his own right.

Drawing on these experiences, Reynolds wrote several books about the literary marketplace, and his writings provide insight into his approach to his role as a literary agent. Often these books offered advice to authors and would-be authors, but they also reveal how Reynolds envisioned the roles of author, agent, and publisher.

As an agent, Reynolds could offer his most extensive remarks about the functions served by agents for both authors and publishers. He describes an agent as possessing 'the editorial ability of a good editor, good business judgment plus the qualities of a good salesman, infinite tact and patience, and a certain amount of charm.' Reynolds notes that the agent also has 'all kinds of piddling jobs' that often involve repeated phone calls to clarify royalty statements or extract overdue payments. Obtaining a contract for an author marks only the beginning of an agent's work; the agent also markets rights that the publisher does not acquire, such as motion picture rights and translation rights. Business concerns rather than aesthetic ones prompt the agent's editorial interest in the book, because a better book means a larger sale. The agent worries about the book's title and even about the book jacket and blurb. A thick skin is required, because the agent 'must be able to take the ill will of editors and publishers who think they have been charged too much, and the criticism of authors who think they have received too little.'

Challenging the perception that agents interfered with author-publisher relationships, Reynolds describes how the agent improves those relationships by dealing with topics, such as negotiating financial arrangements, that might cause unpleasantness between author and publisher. He continues,

> Furthermore, the editor and publisher have discovered advantages in dealing with an agent. Authors are at times temperamental, and it is pleasant for the editor not to have to soothe ruffled feelings but to leave that to the agent. Also, some authors through ignorance can be very unreasonable and at the same time quite naturally hesitate to accept as true what an editor or publisher tells them. An agent is a business person, he knows or should know what an editor can pay, how books and magazines are published, and what conditions are necessary. He is able to insist upon fairness and liberality to the author and yet restrain him from making unreasonable or impossible demands.

This passage describes a partnership between agent and publisher, who work to manage the author. In this account, authors seem somewhat childlike in their naïvety and volatility. The agent must soothe the 'ruffled feelings' of an author and convince him or her of the realities of the marketplace. Reynolds characterizes a fiduciary

relationship in which the agent clearly knows more than the author about the book business; the author must trust the agent in these matters.

Reynolds' depiction of the author suggests the need for a benevolent conspiracy between agent and publisher—a collaborative relationship that serves the interests of all. The image of author that emerges from the agent's writings is of one who needs to be handled carefully, lacks good business sense, and needs to recognize his place in the literary marketplace. Repeatedly Reynolds describes authors as sensitive, saying that they need a thick skin. He argues that authors should allow publishers to do their job and not meddle:

> In general an author should not try to interfere in decisions pertaining to the selling of his book. Sometimes authors desire to write the blurb for the jacket, have a say as to jacket design, and stipulate the book's retail price or the time of publication. A publisher who agrees to such requests or demands is doing so only to please the author and thus increase the likelihood of obtaining his next book. As the average author has neither the knowledge nor the experience to make this judgment of value in such matters, the result is apt to hurt the sale of the book and thus be injurious to both author and publisher.

Reynolds lacks faith in an author's business sense and instead sees the potential for harm if a publisher indulges an author's wish to have a say in marketing. His explanation as to why a publisher might allow the author input reflects his ranking of business concerns over aesthetic ones. The agent does not allow for the possibility that a publisher might respect an author's aesthetic sense, as in the case of a jacket design.

Reynolds notes that when a book does not sell, the author often blames the publisher for not advertising enough; 'only gradually does he come to realize that the factor which sells books is what is printed on the pages, that advertising, publicity, autograph parties, and all the rushing around that some authors do have only an infinitesimal effect on the actual sale.' Agents often help authors to recognize this fact.

Despite Reynolds' admiration for Richter, the very concerns that Reynolds expresses about authors were exemplified in his relations with the often difficult, frequently sensitive author, who did interject himself into the work of the publisher—something to which Knopf also objected—and also blamed his publisher for not promoting him enough. Luckily—for both author and publisher—Reynolds served effectively as an agent who mediated these conflicts between author and publisher.

Although the agent would serve the author for decades, Richter was unimpressed by Reynolds the first time they met. David Johnson writes that Reynolds

> turned out to be a tall, thin man, not as young as Richter expected (he was thirty-one), with a reddish mustache, a slightly pockmarked face, dark brown eyes, and a habit of averting his eyes when talking. Richter was not impressed with the younger Reynolds, whose manner seemed to him affected and not particularly welcoming.

Despite this initial awkward meeting, a bond—though never as strong as the one between Richter and Knopf—developed between the two. Comments in correspondence and in Reynolds' published work reflect the respect he had for Conrad Richter as an author. Richter's biographer notes that in the summer of 1934 Reynolds was one of the first to encourage Richter to write a novel. Of course it might be expected that Reynolds would offer encouraging words both to and about his client, but Reynolds also used Richter in his published works as an exemplar of qualities he admired in authors. To illustrate that authors write out of compulsion, he relates an anecdote shared with him by Harvena Richter about her husband. The Richters went to Florida on a vacation, and Richter left his typewriter at home. By the second day, however, he had rented a typewriter and was working away when his wife discovered him on awakening from a nap.

Reynolds' most extended comments about Richter appear when he writes about Hollywood. Richter exemplifies a writer who 'beat the Hollywood system.' Reynolds describes how Richter refused to work with a contract and would only agree to be paid for what Metro-Goldwyn, which bought the movie rights to *The Sea of Grass*, liked. He notes that Richter even declined the initial offer of $750 a week, which he felt was too generous, before agreeing to $600 a week. After working for several weeks for the studio and delivering a script that was approved, Richter left Hollywood. Eddie Knopf, studio executive and brother of the publisher, tried to locate Richter because he wanted the author to continue writing for Metro-Goldwyn—and even contemplated asking the police to track Richter down. Reynolds writes, 'Richter was not much of a letter-writer and for weeks I did not hear from him. One day he turned up at my office.' Richter

had driven from California back to Pine Grove, Pennsylvania, and started work on a novel. Although Richter said he had been well treated in Hollywood, the environment did not suit him, so he left. Reynolds notes that although Richter's behaviour seemed 'eccentric,' the author 'had retained his independence and dignity. I admired him very much.' Despite Richter's nearly constant worries about money, the free spending of Hollywood failed to tempt him for long.

Reynolds' views on publishers are helpful in understanding the nature of his collaboration with Knopf. Reynolds wrote broadly about the status of the publisher in the literary marketplace. A point of emphasis in his early work *The Writing Trade* is the business of the publisher. The book opens with a lengthy discussion of the costs of book publication and how publishers make a profit, which emphasize that it is the agent, not necessarily the author, who understands these dynamics.

Elsewhere, Reynolds writes about the importance of a publisher's having enthusiasm for an author, and how authors often doubt that support:

> Publishers react favorably to praise and most of them would privately maintain that authors seldom register anything but complaints.... Authors, being sensitive people, often think that their publishers are men of little faith, when actually the contrary is true.

Although enthusiasm is important, Reynolds believes a publisher should be judged by how good a bookseller he is. Reynolds concludes by stating that although authors believe publishers know what will sell, publishers 'are in the twilight zone of being amateurs,' and because each manuscript is affected by new known and unknown factors, publishers 'do not know what they are doing.' To Reynolds, publishing is a 'gambling business,' but these are gamblers 'who on the whole have a code of honor and are fun to deal with.' . . .

Source: Marianne Cotugno, "A Benevolent Conspiracy: Conrad Richter, Paul Reynolds, Jr., and Alfred A. Knopf," in *Journal of Scholarly Publishing*, Vol. 40, No. 3, April 2009, pp. 263–86.

SOURCES

Austin, Pat, Review of *The Light in the Forest* (audiobook), read by Terry Bregy, in *Booklist*, June 1, 2000, p. 1921.

"Delaware Nation Lawsuit Review Rejected," in *Casino City Times*, November 28, 2006, http://www.casinocity-times.com/news/article/delaware-nation-lawsuit-review-rejected-162754 (accessed September 17, 2012).

Duke, Charles R., *Twentieth-Century Young Adult Writers*, edited by Laura Standley Berger, St. James Press, 1994.

Gaston, Edwin W., Jr., *Conrad Richter*, Twayne Publishers, 1965, pp. 5–7, 26–32, 117, 125–31.

Heckewelder, John, *History, Manners, and Customs of the Indian Nations Who Once Inhabited Pennsylvania and the Neighbouring States*, rev. ed., Historical Society of Pennsylvania, 1876, p. 255.

Johnson, David R., *Conrad Richter: A Writer's Life*, Pennsylvania State University Press, 2001, pp. 277, 280, 340, 347, 351–65.

LaHood, Marvin J., "*The Light in the Forest*: History as Fiction," in *English Journal*, Vol. 55, March 1966, pp. 298–304.

LeMay, Konnie, "A Brief History of American Indian Military Service," Indian Country website, May 28, 2012, http://indiancountrytodaymedianetwork.com/2012/05/28/a-brief-history-of-american-indians-military-service-115318 (accessed September 17, 2012).

Marsico, Lynn, "Teaching *Light in the Forest* in Its Historical Context," 2006, http://www.chatham.edu/pti/curriculum/units/2006/Marsico.pdf (accessed September 18, 2012).

Mauser, Linda, "Delaware Indian History," Delaware Indian/Lenni Lenape website, http://www.delawareindians.com/ (accessed September 17, 2012).

Review of *The Light in the Forest* (audiobook), read by Terry Bregy, in *Publishers Weekly*, Vol. 246, No. 50, December 13, 1999, p. 31.

Richter, Conrad, *The Light in the Forest*, Fawcett Juniper, 1991.

Richter, Harvena, ed., *Writing to Survive: The Private Notebooks of Conrad Richter*, University of New Mexico Press, 1988, pp. 113–25.

Schmaier, Maurice D., "Conrad Richter's *The Light in the Forest*: An Ethnohistorical Approach to Fiction," in *Ethnohistory*, Vol. 7, No. 4, Fall 1960, pp. 327–98.

Wallace, Paul A. W., *Indians in Pennsylvania*, Pennsylvania Historical and Museum Commission, 1961, pp. 126–57.

FURTHER READING

Bierhorst, John, *The White Deer and Other Stories Told by the Lenape*, HarperCollins, 1995.

> This is a collection of twenty-five Lenape folktales, ranging from creation stories to trickster tales to children's stories.

Namias, June, *White Captives: Gender and Ethnicity on the American Frontier*, University of North Carolina Press, 1993.

> Taking a step back from the firsthand perspective provided in captivity narratives, Namias explores what those narratives reveal about pre- and postcolonial society in America with regard to gender roles and attitudes toward Native Americans.

Schutt, Amy, *Peoples of the River Valleys: The Odyssey of the Delaware Indians*, University of Pennsylvania Press, 2007.

> This volume provides a complete yet accessible history of the trials and travels of the Lenape, or Delaware Indians, between 1609 and 1783.

Silko, Leslie Marmon, *Yellow Woman and a Beauty of the Spirit*, Simon and Schuster, 1997.

> Best known for her novel *Ceremony* (1977), about the complicated return of a Native participant in World War II, Silko, a Laguna Pueblo, offers here a collection of essays on the state of American Indian life and society at the turn of the twentieth century.

SUGGESTED SEARCH TERMS

Conrad Richter AND The Light in the Forest

The Light in the Forest AND history

Delaware Indians AND history

Lenni Lenape AND history

Delaware Indians AND Pontiac's War

Delaware Indians AND Pennsylvania

Native American OR Indian AND captivity narratives

Delaware Indians AND James Fenimore Cooper

Conrad Richter AND interview

Middle Passage

CHARLES JOHNSON

1990

Middle Passage, published in 1990 and winner of the National Book Award for Fiction that year, is a historical novel by Charles Johnson. Its title refers to the middle leg of the triangular route sailed by slave ships in the Atlantic from the 1500s to the early 1800s. On the first leg, ships left Europe for Africa, carrying goods that were traded for captured and kidnapped Africans. During the Middle Passage, these Africans were transported across the Atlantic to the New World, where they were either sold or traded for raw materials. The ships then transported the materials back to Europe, completing the triangular voyage. The term *Middle Passage* has become synonymous not only with the journey across the Atlantic but also with the evils of the slave trade and the unimaginable hardships Africans faced on their forced journey to the New World, a journey that took weeks, sometimes months, under appalling and even horrific conditions that typically resulted in numerous deaths.

Johnson's novel is set in 1830. Although slavery was still legal in the United States, the slave *trade* no longer was; that is, slaves could be owned, bought, and sold, but they could no longer be imported. The novel tells the story of the final voyage of an illegal slave ship, the *Republic*. The novel's protagonist is Rutherford Calhoun, a free black who lives by his wits in New Orleans as a thief, con man, and womanizer. To escape debts and marriage to Isadora, a prim schoolteacher

from Boston, and to embark on a new adventure, he poses as a cook aboard a ship bound for Africa to pick up a cargo of slaves. Through his adventures, Calhoun acquires a new understanding of the evils of slavery. Some of the material in *Middle Passage* may not be suitable for younger readers. Calhoun comments briefly on some of his sexual experiences and describes a sexual encounter, and a cabin boy aboard the ship is molested by the ship's captain.

AUTHOR BIOGRAPHY

Charles Richard Johnson was born on April 23, 1948, in Evanston, Illinois. He achieved some prominence in the 1960s as a political cartoonist. He studied at Southern Illinois University, receiving a bachelor's degree in 1971 and a master's degree in 1973. In 1988, he earned a PhD in philosophy from the State University of New York at Stony Brook. Meanwhile, Johnson established himself as a leading African American scholar and writer. He joined the faculty at the University of Washington in Seattle, where he held an endowed chair in writing, the S. Wilson and Grace M. Pollock Professorship for Excellence in English. He also became director of the university's creative writing program, in which he taught fiction writing.

At the university, Johnson enjoyed a long and prolific career. He is the author of four novels, including *Middle Passage*. The others are *Faith and the Good Thing* (1974), *Oxherding Tale* (1982), and *Dreamer* (1998). He also has published three collections of short stories: *The Sorcerer's Apprentice: Tales and Conjurations* (1986), *Soulcatcher and Other Stories* (2001), and *Dr. King's Refrigerator and Other Bedtime Stories* (2005). *Being and Race: Black Writing since 1970* (1988) is a book about aesthetics. His two collections of comic art are *Black Humor* (1970) and *Half-Past Nation Time* (1972). He coedited a collection of essays and interviews titled *Black Men Speaking* (1997). Further, he is the author of *Africans in America: America's Journey through Slavery*, the companion book for a 1998 PBS series of the same title. He chronicled his conversion to Buddhism in *Turning the Wheel: Essays on Buddhism and Writing*, published in 2003. Among his later works is *Remembering Martin Luther King, Jr., 40 Years Later: His Life and Crusade in Pictures* (2008), and he wrote the text for *Mine Eyes Have Seen: Bearing Witness to the Struggle for Civil Rights* (2007). Also, he is the coauthor of *Philosophy: An Innovative Introduction; Fictive Narrative, Primary Texts, and Responsive Writing* (2010). Johnson has written numerous screenplays, among them *Booker*, which received the international Prix Jeunesse; dozens of reviews published in the *New York Times, Los Angeles Times, Wall Street Journal, Washington Post*, and other American and British newspapers; and numerous scholarly and critical essays. He attracted attention for criticizing Alice Walker's *The Color Purple*—the National Book Award winner in 1983—for its negative portrayal of African American men.

Throughout his career, Johnson won numerous awards. In addition to the National Book Award for Fiction for *Middle Passage* (1990), he was a MacArthur Fellow, and in 2002 he received an American Academy of Arts and Letters Award for Literature. *The Sorcerer's Apprentice* was one of five finalists for the 1987 PEN/Faulkner Award. His short fiction is included in *Prize Stories 1993: The O. Henry Awards, The Best American Short Stories 1992*, and *The Best American Short Stories of the Eighties* (1990).

PLOT SUMMARY

Middle Passage is presented as a series of dated journal entries written by Rutherford Calhoun during the summer of 1830. The entries were purportedly later recorded in the ship's log.

Entry, the first: June 14, 1830

Rutherford Calhoun, twenty-three years old, was a slave in Illinois, but after being recently freed, he moved to New Orleans. There, for a period of some months, he lived by his wits as a petty thief and con man, falling into debt and barely managing to stay out of trouble. He meets Isadora Bailey, a black schoolteacher from Boston, and although the two seem to be just friends, Isadora wants to marry him. Calhoun, though, believes that he is not the marrying kind and refuses. He is accosted by Santos, who runs the docks for Philippe "Papa" Zeringue, a gangster. Santos takes Calhoun to Papa, who informs Calhoun that he is the owner of Calhoun's debts, including money he owes to his landlady and to a moneylender. Papa tells Calhoun that Isadora has offered to pay off his debts if he

MEDIA ADAPTATIONS

- An abridged audiobook version of *Middle Passage* narrated by the author was produced in 1991 by Highbridge Audio on cassette.
- An unabridged *Middle Passage* audiobook was produced by Recorded Books in 2003, read by Dion Graham and with a running time of just over seven hours. This production is available on CDs or for download from Audible.com and AudioBookStore.

marries her—and the wedding is scheduled for the following day. Calhoun gets drunk and goes to Isadora to tell her that he will not marry her, despite her confession that she loves him. Later, Calhoun is in a tavern and meets Josiah Squibb, who has recently signed on as the cook for the *Republic*, an illegal slave ship bound for Guinea, on the western coast of Africa. As the two men talk and drink, Squibb passes out. Calhoun takes Squibb's rolled-up papers from his boot and boards the *Republic*, intending to escape marriage to Isadora by posing as the *Republic*'s cook.

Entry, the second: June 20, 1830

Just an hour out of port, the first mate, Peter Cringle, discovers Calhoun, who tries to pass himself off as Josiah Squibb until Cringle informs him that Squibb is aboard the ship. Cringle takes Calhoun to the cabin of the captain, Ebenezer Falcon. The captain, who Calhoun discovers is a dwarf, tells Calhoun about their mission, which is to pick up forty Allmuseri tribesmen at Bangalang, a trading post in Guinea. (Both the Allmuseri and Bangalang are fictional.) The captain tells Calhoun about an incident at sea when he and the crew engaged in cannibalism. He seems unconcerned that Calhoun has stowed away on the ship and instructs Cringle to take Calhoun below decks, where he will bunk. Calhoun describes the ship as filthy and diseased and notes that the Middle Passage is an occasion for the crew to become—and remain—drunk.

Calhoun also describes how the members of the crew, forty in all, try to assert their masculinity around one another. Cringle indicates to Calhoun that he does not feel good about the voyage, for the Allmuseri are sorcerers and wizards who cast spells and worship the devil.

Entry, the third: June 23, 1830

After a journey of forty-one days, the ship arrives at the trading post at Bangalang, which is under the control of Owen Bogha, described as a sensualist, a fop, and an Anglophile (lover of things English). Calhoun breaks into the captain's cabin to examine the captain's papers. This leads to an extensive examination of the captain's character, particularly his paranoia, his desire for plunder, his unreasoning quest for perfection, his loneliness, and his disdain for others. Calhoun is caught, but rather than punishing him, the captain gives him a pistol and, because he is black, asks him to serve as his spy after the slaves are brought aboard. The following day, the exchange of cargo is to take place. Squibb describes the actions the Arab slave trader Ahman-de-Bellah will have taken to make the slaves appear more valuable. Peter Cringle, who abhors what he sees, warns Calhoun about the captain, pointing out that the captain is mad and very likely wants to end his own life by losing the ship on the return voyage. Cringle also hints that he and a number of the crew plan a mutiny, and he wants to know whether Calhoun will join them. Calhoun describes the cargo the *Republic* picks up, including hides, gold, ivory, beeswax, and the forty slaves. Falcon also brings aboard a mysterious crate, which he hides. Tommy O'Toole, the cabin boy, investigates the crate on behalf of the crew, learning that it contains an equally mysterious, and frightening, creature. Tommy is so struck by what he sees that he goes half-mad.

Entry, the fourth: June 28, 1830

The ship departs Africa for North America. Nathaniel Meadows, originally described as a dangerous member of the crew, offers to wash Calhoun's shirt for him. One of the slaves, Ngonyama, is placed in charge of the others; he acts in a mysterious fashion and appears to be studying everything about him while trying to learn some English. Calhoun summarizes what he learns about the Allmuseri, including their language. One of the slave children, Baleka, forms an attachment to Calhoun after he is kind to her. A storm blows up, then passes away as quickly as it arose. Ngonyama issues a cryptic warning to Calhoun, urging him to lay low the next day. Calhoun is in the galley with Squibb when a group of men enter, led by Cringle and Matthew McGaffin, the boatswain (the petty officer in charge of hull maintenance and related work). The men are planning a mutiny, and they decide that rather than killing Falcon, they will maroon him. They persuade Calhoun to agree to break into the captain's cabin to launch the mutiny. Later, when Calhoun takes Falcon's dinner to him, the captain questions him; Calhoun breaks down and tells the captain about the men's plans.

Entry, the fifth: June 30, 1830

Falcon reveals to Calhoun that the mysterious crate contains the Allmuseri god. The captain then launches into a disquisition about the nature of the god and of creation. Afterward, Calhoun comes across Meadows, who is beating the ship's dogs and using the clothing he gathered from Calhoun and others to bait them. Calhoun concludes that Meadows is loyal to the captain and that his actions, as well as his ability to imitate Cringle, Calhoun, and others, are designed to train the dogs to attack the mutineers. Squibb informs Calhoun that Baleka seems to be falling ill. This prompts a conversation in which Calhoun talks about his life in Illinois under his master, Peleg Chandler, and about the circumstances surrounding his manumission and Chandler's death.

Entry, the sixth: July 3, 1830

Some of the slaves are brought on deck to dance to Tommy's flute, thereby getting some exercise. Calhoun is forced to help throw a dead slave overboard. The mutiny is supposed to begin, but Falcon has taken steps to quash it, including booby-trapping his cabin, where the ship's small arms are kept. Simultaneously, however, the slaves revolt, killing Meadows and overcoming other members of the crew. Just fifteen of the slaves survive the revolt. In the cook room, Ngonyama and three other slaves hold Cringle prisoner, but Ngonyama urges Calhoun to plead for the life of any crewman he believes should be saved. In the debate that ensues among the Allmuseri, they urge Calhoun to kill Cringle, but he refuses. He also pleads for the life of the captain (held captive in his cabin), telling the Allmuseri that they can make the captain their slave and that he and Cringle are needed to steer

the ship to a port where the Africans will be safe. The Africans sanctify the ship, then announce that they want to be taken to Senegambia (in the nineteenth century, a loose confederation of Senegal and the Gambia).

Entry, the seventh: Same Day

Calhoun goes to the captain's cabin to rescue him from the wreckage the Africans caused. The injured Falcon asks Calhoun to keep a log of what has happened on the voyage. After Calhoun leaves the cabin, Falcon commits suicide by shooting himself. For some two weeks, the ship sails about in the Atlantic, with Cringle, now acting as captain, unable to get a fix on the ship's position. Calhoun describes the horrible diseases some of the Africans and remaining crew contract, along with the amputations Squibb has to perform on infected limbs and fingers. Finally, none of the crew except Squibb and Cringle are alive. Calhoun goes down into the ship's hold to examine the contents of the mysterious crate the captain brought aboard. It bursts open, and a shape-shifting creature that looks like Calhoun's father, a runaway slave from Chandler's farm, appears.

Entry, the eighth: August 1, 1830

Calhoun describes the fantastic creature from the crate, prompting him to comment on his father's escape from the Chandler farm in 1811. Overcome by fear and the creature's stench, Calhoun lapses into unconsciousness for three days, awakening as Squibb is ministering to him. Squibb informs him that a ship is following them. When Calhoun asks whether Cringle hailed the ship, Squibb responds that Cringle persuaded him to stab Cringle to death and offer his body as food for the starving survivors on the *Republic*. Calhoun then falls ill with fever and pain. He is roused by Squibb, who tells him a storm is coming and that the survivors on board, now twelve in number, need to get lifeboats into the water. The ship, with Ngonyama at the wheel, collapses, falls apart, and sinks. Calhoun almost drowns, but he manages to save himself by hanging on to a hammock as he watches the Allmuseri go down with the ship.

Entry, the ninth: August 20, 1830

Calhoun finds himself pulled aboard the *Juno*, a pleasure ship commanded by Captain Cornelius Quackenbush. He learns that the ship was just southwest of Guadeloupe and that the *Juno* was on its way back from the West Indies. Also surviving are Squibb, Baleka, and two other Allmuseri children. Calhoun spends two weeks in a room writing down his journal entries, so he sees no one else on the ship. Finally, Baleka lures him out of his room, telling him that they are obligated to a rich man on the ship—who turns out to be Zeringue. The gangster is on the ship with Isadora, and the two are engaged to be married. Calhoun, now a different man, sees Isadora's beauty and asks her to marry him. She initially refuses, although she confesses that Zeringue frightens her. The gangster, as a part owner of the illegal *Republic*, tries to bribe Calhoun to say in any official reports that Zeringue invested in the ship believing that it was going to Africa only to pick up commodities, not slaves. In response, Calhoun promises not to implicate Zeringue in the slave trade if he breaks off his engagement with Isadora and contributes to the support of the three surviving Allmuseri children. Zeringue orders Santos to seize Calhoun's logbook, which contains evidence of his crime, but Santos refuses because he, as a black man, now feels betrayed by his boss and, he reveals, because his grandfather was a member of the Allmuseri tribe. Zeringue submits to Calhoun's blackmail, leaving Isadora free to agree to marry Calhoun. He considers returning to Illinois with Isadora and Baleka.

CHARACTERS

Ahman-de-Bellah
Ahman-de-Bellah is a cruel, violent Arab slave trader who herds the Allmuseri to the trading fort at Bangalang.

Isadora Bailey
Isadora is a prim Boston schoolmistress living in New Orleans. She wants to marry Calhoun and even offers to pay off his debts to Papa Zeringue if he marries her. Later, after the *Republic* sinks, when Calhoun is rescued and taken aboard the *Juno*, he discovers that Isadora and Zeringue are aboard and that, primarily out of fear, Isadora has agreed to marry him. Calhoun, though, has changed, so she agrees to marry him instead.

Baleka
Baleka is a young slave girl on the ship who forms an attachment to Calhoun after he is kind to her. She survives the destruction of the *Republic* and is rescued; Calhoun vows to take her with him (and Isadora) if and when he returns to Illinois.

Owen Bogha
Bogha is the overseer of the trading post at Bangalang. He is described as a fop, a sensualist, and an Anglophile, and he appears to be friends with Ebenezer Falcon.

Rutherford Calhoun
Calhoun is the protagonist and narrator of the novel. The pretense is that he has written a series of journal entries in the ship's log during the late spring and summer of 1830. These entries chronicle his experiences aboard the illegal slave ship *Republic* earlier that year. Calhoun is twenty-three years old and, until recently, was a slave in Illinois, where his master, Peleg Chandler, educated him. Accordingly, Calhoun is given to alluding to a wide range of writers and philosophers. After Chandler died and Calhoun was freed, he lived in New Orleans, where he got by as a petty thief and a con man. He then learns that a local gangster, "Papa" Zeringue, owns his debts; the gangster tells him that if he marries Isadora, she will pay off his debts. Calhoun has no interest in marriage, so after he meets Josiah Squibb, the *Republic*'s cook, and after Squibb passes out, Calhoun steals his papers and tries to pass himself off as Squibb on the ship. He is exposed, but the captain, rather than punishing him or throwing him overboard, enlists him as a spy. Calhoun agrees to join the planned mutiny, but he then informs on the mutineers to the captain. After the slaves rebel, Calhoun is saved because Ngonyama regards him as an ally, in large part because Calhoun has developed empathy for the slaves and sees himself in them. Because of this change in outlook, Calhoun is eager to marry Isadora after he is rescued and finds her aboard the *Juno*. He makes plans to return to Illinois with Isadora and Baleka.

Peleg Chandler
Chandler was Calhoun's slave master in Illinois. Chandler freed Calhoun and his brother and left Calhoun a small bequest on his death. Chandler provided the two slaves with an extensive education, largely because he felt guilty about owning slaves.

Peter Cringle

Cringle is the first mate of the *Republic*. Unlike the rest of the crewmen, he is educated and genteel, and Calhoun notes that he can remember everything he has ever read. Calhoun learns that Cringle signed on to the voyage as a way of appeasing his businessman father. Throughout, Cringle is horrified by the things that he sees with regard to the slave trade. He is one of the leaders of the planned shipboard mutiny, but when the slaves rebel, he seems to become as cruel as the other crewmen are, vowing revenge and refusing to help the slaves. In the end, as the ship is adrift in the Atlantic, he persuades Squibb to stab him to death and offers his body as food to the starving survivors.

Captain Ebenezer Falcon

Falcon, the captain of the illegal slave ship *Republic*, is regarded by many members of the crew as mad. He is of dwarfish size. He is paranoid, delusional, and determined to plunder the places he visits of their treasures, but he is also highly educated and of a philosophical outlook. Many of the crew members feel that under Falcon, the voyage is doomed. Calhoun, after he breaks into the captain's cabin and reads his journal, sums him up this way:

> The man who emerged in these journal entries possessed a few of the solitary virtues and the entire twisted will of Puritanism: a desire to achieve perfection; the loneliness, self-punishment, and bouts of suicide this brings; and a profound disdain for anyone who failed to meet his nearly superhuman standards.

In time, Calhoun concludes that Falcon is evil for the way he treats the slaves. After the slave rebellion, Falcon commits suicide by shooting himself.

Matthew McGaffin

McGaffin is the ship's boatswain and one of the leaders of the planned mutiny.

Nathaniel Meadows

Meadows is the ship's barber-surgeon—that is, he functions as a doctor. He is initially described as dangerous, but Calhoun is confused when Meadows offers to launder his shirt and the clothing of other members of the crew. It turns out, though, that he knows that some of the crew plan to mutiny and he remains loyal to the captain. He wants the clothing so that he can use its smell to train the dogs aboard the ship to act aggressively toward the mutineers.

Ngonyama

Ngonyama, one of the Allmuseri slaves, is placed in charge of the other slaves with the duty of keeping them in line. He begins to act very mysteriously, doing all he can to learn about the ship and to acquire snippets of English. Finally, he warns Calhoun to keep himself out of the way the following day, suggesting that the slaves are planning a rebellion. As one of the leaders of the rebellion, he regards Calhoun as an ally, and Calhoun comes to feel a strong sense of identification with him. He appears to perish when the *Republic* breaks apart and sinks.

Tommy O'Toole

Tommy is a cabin boy on the *Republic*. He is sexually abused by the captain. He can play the flute, and he is required to play for the slaves so that they can dance and thereby get some exercise. He is driven virtually insane after investigating the mysterious crate the captain brings aboard in Africa.

Cornelius Quackenbush

Quackenbush is the captain of the *Juno*, the pleasure craft that rescues Calhoun, Baleka, and Squibb at sea.

Santos

Santos, a henchman who runs the docks for Papa Zeringue, brings Calhoun to his boss, setting the events of the novel in motion. Later, after Calhoun is taken aboard the *Juno*, Santos is present with Zeringue. He reveals that his grandfather was from the Allmuseri tribe.

Josiah Squibb

Squibb is the cook for the *Republic*. When he first encounters Calhoun in a New Orleans tavern, he passes out from drink, prompting Calhoun to try to assume his identity by stealing his papers. Later, Calhoun's ruse is exposed when Squibb recovers and takes his place aboard the ship. Calhoun becomes his assistant. Calhoun is sympathetic when he learns that Squibb takes for himself food intended for the slave children. Squibb is one of the few survivors aboard the *Republic*, and he is persuaded by Cringle to stab him to death and serve his body as food.

Philippe "Papa" Zeringue

Papa is a gangster who controls much of the illegal activity in New Orleans. When he has his henchman Santos bring Calhoun to him, Isadora is present. After she leaves, Papa tells Calhoun that he now owns Calhoun's debts to his landlady and to a moneylender—but that Isadora has agreed to pay off the debts if Calhoun will marry her. At the end of the novel, he is on a pleasure cruise aboard the ship that rescues Calhoun, and he is engaged to Isadora, who then rejects him in favor of Calhoun. The reader learns that he was a part owner of the *Republic*, enabling Calhoun to blackmail him into giving up Isadora.

THEMES

Slavery

The central theme of *Middle Passage* concerns the evils of the slave trade. The emphasis is less on the institution of slavery itself than on the horrors experienced by Africans whose villages were invaded by slave traders, who were seized and forced overland to a slave trading post, and who then had to endure a journey of weeks or months under the worst possible conditions aboard a ship sailing across the Atlantic. In numerous passages, Johnson, through Calhoun, recreates the conditions aboard the ship. In "Entry, the sixth," Calhoun says that Falcon

> was, as they say, a 'tight-packer,' having learned ten years ago...that if you arranged the Africans in two parallel rows, their backs against the lining of the ship's belly, this left a free space at their rusty feet, and *that*, given the flexibility of bone and skin, could be squeezed with even more slaves if you made them squat at ninety-degree angles to one another.

Calhoun continues, "So when they came half-dead from the depths, these eyeless contortionists emerging from a shadowy Platonic cave, they were stiff and sore and stank of their own vomit and feces." These and numerous other passages detail the horrific conditions that Africans endured—or succumbed to—on the Middle Passage.

African Culture

Africa, it goes without saying, encompasses numerous cultures. In *Middle Passage*, Johnson chose to create a fictional tribe called the Allmuseri to represent the African tribes that slave traders plundered. Throughout the novel, Johnson, through his narrator Calhoun, suggests ways in which African cultures might differ from the Western cultures of Europe and America. For example, Calhoun describes the Allmuseri language in "Entry, the fourth":

> Not really a language at all, by my guess, as a melic [intended to be sung] way of breathing deep from the diaphragm that dovetailed articles into nouns, nouns into verbs.... Nouns or static substances hardly existed in their vocabulary at all. A "bed" was called a "resting," a "robe" a "warming." Furthermore, each verb was different depending on the nature of the object acted upon, whether it was vegetable, mineral, mammal, oblong or rotund.

Calhoun goes on to discuss Ngonyama's use of language with his tribesmen as functioning "as if the objects and others he referred to flowed together like water, taking different forms, as the sea could now be fluid, now solid ice, now steam swirling around the mizzenpole." The suggestion inherent in this description, as well as in that of the Allmuseri's written language, is that the people see the world in fundamentally different ways compared to Westerners. To them, the world is more organic, more fluid—not something fixed and static that can be analyzed, parsed, and divided into categories in a scientific way but rather something to be experienced.

The point is made later, in "Entry, the seventh," when Calhoun tries to rescue the captain. Calhoun makes the observation that the Allmuseri would be no more able to understand the captain's life than he would be to understand theirs. Calhoun further notes that the captain believes that a person has to conquer death through "some great deed or original discovery" and thus to "soar above contingency." The Western mind is able to "invent gadgets" but lacks the "genuine insight" of the Allmuseri. As a Westerner, the captain could exhibit brilliance, but he was "adrift from the laws and logic of the heart." Again, the implication is that the Western mind analyzes and breaks down; it is awash in information; it creates technologies to conquer death and the world; it tries to possess, to dominate. In contrast, the Allmuseri mind follows less rational laws that do not produce gadgets but that lead to a more organic sense of unity and oneness with the world.

Identity

Although the subject matter of *Middle Passage* is the illegal slave trade, the book, on one level, is

TOPICS FOR FURTHER STUDY

- Watch *Amistad*, a 1997 film directed by Steven Spielberg about a slave revolt aboard a ship off the northeastern coast of North America and the legal case that evolved from the revolt. Prepare a PowerPoint presentation that outlines the movie's similarities to and differences from *Middle Passage*. Students should be aware that *Amistad* is rated R for violence.

- Read "Aboard a Slave Ship, 1829," which can be found on the EyeWitness to History website (http://www.eyewitnesstohistory. com/slaveship.htm); this account was written by Robert Walsh and published in his *Notices of Brazil in 1828 and 1829* (1831). Compare this author's account with the conditions described in *Middle Passage*. Prepare a chart comparing the two works and the conditions they describe and share it with your classmates.

- Prepare a map that traces the journey of the *Republic* and that includes the other places mentioned in the story (e.g., New Orleans, Guinea, Senegambia, Guadeloupe, West Indies). Post the map on a social networking site and invite your classmates to comment on its accuracy.

- Locate on the Internet or in a book a copy of *Slave Ship*, an oil painting formally titled *Slavers Throwing Overboard the Dead and Dying—Typhoon Coming On*. This painting, done by British artist J. M. W. Turner, was first exhibited in 1840 and is now housed in the Museum of Fine Arts in Boston. The painting depicts a ship sailing through a churning sea and leaving human forms floating in its wake. Share a reproduction of the painting with your classmates using Flikr or a similar tool and invite them to comment on the emotions it elicits.

- Paula Fox's Newbery Medal–winning young-adult novel *The Slave Dancer* (1997) is about a thirteen-year-old boy kidnapped in New Orleans in 1840. He is forced to play music on a slave ship to help keep the slaves healthy by dancing (just as Tommy O'Toole does in *Middle Passage*). Read the novel and then write an essay comparing the experience of its protagonist, Jessie Bollier, with that of Rutherford Calhoun, emphasizing their growth as a result of their experiences.

- Robert Southey was an English romantic poet who wrote a group of poems under the title "Poems concerning the Slave Trade." Locate Sonnet IV, available on the PoemHunter.com website at http://www.poemhunter.com/ poem/poems-on-the-slave-trade-sonnet-iv/. Read the poem aloud to your classmates and invite them to speculate with you on how creative writers may have helped persuade the British, and later Americans, to outlaw the slave trade.

- At the Trans-Atlantic Slave Trade Database (http://www.slavevoyages.org/tast/assess ment/intro-maps.faces), you will find a number of maps pertaining to the transatlantic slave trade. Study the maps and then select three that you wish to present to your classmates. In a brief oral report, explain to your classmates the significance of what the maps show. For example, you might explain how Map 8 demonstrates that South America was a major market for African slaves.

- Herman Melville's *Benito Cereno* (1855), a novella about a slave rebellion aboard a Spanish ship in 1799, has long been a source of controversy: some readers see it as racist and pro-slavery, others as precisely the opposite. Some readers see the book as being fundamentally about race; others see it as not about race at all. Persuade a friend to read the novella with you and then stage a debate for your classmates on the controversy surrounding it.

The Republic *travels to Africa to pick up a new cargo of slaves.* (*The Library of Congress*)

really about the change that takes place in Rutherford Calhoun as a result of his experiences. When the reader first meets him, he is a rogue and a petty thief. He rambles about New Orleans, taking part in any sort of disreputable activity he can find, falling into debt along the way. He has the opportunity to marry a respectable woman who loves him, but he refuses, instead lighting out on an adventure.

His adventure changes him, and he begins to see the world and the people around him in a new way. In "Entry, the sixth," for example, he takes note of the effect contact with the mystical, magical, numinous Allmuseri has had on him: "Some part of me was a fatherless child again. Alone in an alien world. Wanting to belong somewhere and to someone" (which explains why he later changes his mind about marrying Isadora). The scene continues after some fifteen minutes of stillness pass: "Then, involuntarily, my hands clamped together in a bedside, precynical posture I'd not taken since boyhood, one of surrender and bone-felt frailty in the face of troubles.... My worldly wits were

gone." Later, in "Entry, the ninth," Calhoun is explicit about the change he has undergone:

> Looking back at the asceticism of the Middle Passage, I saw how the frame of mind I had adopted left me unattached, like the slaves who, not knowing what awaited them in the New World, put a high premium on living from moment to moment.... The voyage had irreversibly changed my seeing, made of me a cultural mongrel, and transformed the world into a fleeting shadow play I felt no need to possess or dominate, only appreciate in the ever extended present. Colors had been more vivid at sea, water *wetter*, ice *colder*.

The reader senses that, at the start of the novel, Calhoun would have been incapable of making these kinds of observations about himself and his relationship with others.

STYLE

First-person Point of View

The point of view of *Middle Passage* is in the first person. Thus the main character, Rutherford Calhoun, is also the narrator of the novel. Johnson might have chosen to have his novel told through the voice of a third-person omniscient narrator, but the first-person narration gives the story a greater sense of immediacy, for the reader shares with Calhoun his observations and growth. Further, throughout the book, the reader gets to know Calhoun through his unique voice and way of looking at the world, a combination of bookishness and street smarts. This enables Johnson to incorporate considerable humor into the book through observations from his narrator such as this one: "For my part, I wanted to live a little longer. I was only twenty-three years old. The Apocalypse would definitely put a crimp in my career plans." Johnson, then, can tackle the serious, weighty themes in the novel—slavery and the horrors of slave ships are not pleasant topics—while drawing his readers in with humor and wry observations.

Allusion

Middle Passage contains numerous allusions— that is, references to people, places, events, works of art and literature, and the like. Allusions establish a connection between the matter the author is discussing or describing and some element from history or another literary work. Allusions can enrich the reader's understanding by placing a text within a historical and artistic context or tradition. Thus, for example, if an author alludes to a character or incident from Homer's *Iliad*, the reader is being encouraged to think of the text in the context of heroic, mythic literature. In *Middle Passage*, it is made clear that Calhoun is highly intelligent and was thoroughly educated by his slave master. Thus, although he is a bit of a rogue, he is able to learn from his experiences aboard the slave ship and to undergo a kind of conversion to a new point of view by seeing events in the context of the flow of history. Meanwhile, his allusions come fast and furious: he makes reference to the ancient Greeks, the Neoplatonist and nominalist philosophies, the theologians Saint Thomas Aquinas and Jakob Böhme, the ancient philosopher Thales, the Hindu deity Krishna, Piltdown man (a supposed early hominid, which was in fact a paleontological hoax), Gothicism, Chaucer's "Wife of Bath's Tale" from the *Canterbury Tales*, and the Black Maria (likely a reference to the Black Madonna, depicted in medieval European paintings)—all just in the first chapter. Elsewhere, he quotes the ancient Greeks and Romans. Incidentally, the reference to the Piltdown man is an anachronism in *Middle Passage*, for the pseudo-discovery was not made until the early twentieth century.

Simile

Middle Passage is laced with similes—that is, explicit comparisons between otherwise unlike things, usually signaled by words such as *like*, *as*, or *than*. These similes serve at least two purposes. One is to enliven Calhoun's narration, allowing him to make use of his education and powers of observation to comment with intelligence and insight into the events around him. The other is to enable him to make some sort of sense out of unfamiliar people, places, and experiences by comparing them to the known quantities of his life. Nearly any page could provide examples of similes. In "Entry, the second," Calhoun describes Captain Ebenezer Falcon by saying that he has "eye sockets *like* anthracite furnaces, medieval lines *more complex than* tracery on his maps, a nose slightly to one side, and a great bulging forehead that looked *harder than* whalebone.... His hands, *like* roots" (italics added). Later, in "Entry, the third," Falcon's "emotions permeated the ship *like* the smell of rum and rotting wood."

Picaresque Novel

The plot of *Middle Passage* revolves around a sequence of events that could be described as episodic, as Calhoun abandons his life in New Orleans, stows away aboard a ship, travels to Africa and back, flashes back to his earlier life, is caught up in a slave rebellion aboard the ship, is shipwrecked, falls ill, survives on human flesh (although unknowingly), and is ultimately saved so that he can marry Isadora Bailey. Thus, the novel adopts some of the conventions of the picaresque novel, a form that originated in sixteenth-century Spain. At the heart of the picaresque novel is the *pícaro* (feminine form: *pícara*), a usually lowborn or roguish character who narrates his story as he moves about from place to place in an effort to survive in differing social circumstances. In the eighteenth century, the picaresque novel was declining in popularity as novelists were beginning to create more elaborate plots and emphasize character development, but some of the characteristics of this type of fiction survived into the twentieth century. Clearly, Calhoun is a picaro: as a former slave he is lowborn, as a petty thief and con man in New Orleans he is roguish, and he tells his own story as he takes part in a voyage that exposes him to people of various social classes and to varying social milieus, usually with great comic effect. These encounters allow the author to comment satirically on rogues and impostors as well as on the institution of slavery.

HISTORICAL CONTEXT

At the time of the American Revolution, opposition to the slave trade was growing throughout the United States, particularly in the North, with its mixed economy of manufacturing, small farms, and merchants for whom slave labor held little economic appeal. Much of the opposition to the slave trade resulted from the way in which it was conducted. Slave traders crowded Africans into ships so tightly that they could not turn over when they slept. The Middle Passage was a horrific ordeal, with high rates of illness, rampant malnutrition, no fresh air, filth, and numerous deaths. Some slaves hurled themselves overboard in the middle of the ocean rather than face the fate that awaited them. Humanitarians and philanthropists abhorred this system and did what they could to stop it, and in the years

COMPARE
&
CONTRAST

- **1830:** According to the 1830 federal census, free blacks own upwards of 10,000 slaves in Louisiana, Maryland, South Carolina, and Virginia; most live in Louisiana and plant sugarcane.

  1990: William Jefferson becomes the first African American to represent a Louisiana district since Reconstruction, after the Civil War.

  Today: The New Orleans African American Museum of Art, Culture and History, located in the city's oldest black neighborhood, preserves the history of the African American community in New Orleans.

- **1830:** New Orleans is the nation's fifth-largest city, with a population of about 46,000.

  1990: New Orleans is the nation's twenty-fourth-largest city, with a population of about 497,000.

  Today: Largely because of Hurricane Katrina in 2005, the population of New Orleans has shrunk to about 344,000.

- **1830:** Under the terms of a treaty Britain signed in 1826 with Portugal, March 13 is the date for the abolition of the Brazilian slave trade, although illegal trading in slaves in Brazil will continue until 1852.

  1990: Afro-Brazilian activists engage in ongoing efforts to influence the Brazilian people to recognize their African ancestry and to not deny their blackness.

  Today: About 49.6 percent of Brazil's population, a slight plurality, is black or mulatto, reflecting in large part the nation's heritage of slavery.

following the Revolution, many states began a process of ending slavery. Pennsylvania adopted a policy that would emancipate slaves born after 1780. Massachusetts banned slavery outright. North Carolina, Maryland, and New York banned the importation of new slaves. Slavery, however, remained entrenched in the South, and the demand for slave labor would later grow with the invention of the cotton gin and with other agricultural advances (as Calhoun himself notes in "Entry, the third").

When the Constitutional Congress met in 1787 to draft a new constitution for the fledgling nation, it adopted article 1, section 9, a compromise provision that kept open the transatlantic slave trade until 1808 and gave the South time to adapt. Abolitionist groups continued to exert pressure to end slavery. In March 1794, Congress passed a law making it illegal for Americans to transport slaves to a foreign country or to outfit a ship for the purpose of transporting slaves. Later, Senator Stephen Rowe Bradley of Vermont introduced legislation to ensure that the slave trade to

the United States would end in 1808. President Thomas Jefferson recommended passage of the bill, which he signed into law the day after it was passed on March 2, 1807. As of January 1, 1808, the importation of slaves to the United States was outlawed. Abolitionists were jubilant, but the victory was only a partial one. Slaves continued to be imported illegally, and trade in slaves within the United States continued. Meanwhile, the British navy continued to board American ships and press Americans into service, a practice that contributed to the War of 1812 (and which in part motivates Captain Ebenezer Falcon in *Middle Passage* to practice piracy at sea).

The issue of slavery remained on the front burner. In 1819, Congress passed legislation deeming intercontinental slave trading an act of piracy, punishable by death. In 1820, the Missouri Compromise formalized a divide between North and South, with the North consisting of free states and the South of slave states, and provision was made for the status of slavery in new states admitted to the Union. By 1830, the year in which *Middle*

The slaves on the Republic *teach Rutherford many lessons about humanity during the voyage.* *(© Library of Congress Prints and Photographs Division Washington, D.C. [LC-DIG-ppmsca-05933])*

Passage is set, thousands of people had joined the American Anti-Slavery Society, which mounted public relations campaigns and legal action to free as many slaves as possible. In the meantime, Illinois, the state where Rutherford Calhoun was granted his freedom, made slavery illegal in its 1818 constitution. Pro-slavery citizens of Illinois, though, wanted to call a constitutional convention to repeal that provision. The matter was put to a popular vote, but after months of furious campaigning, the proposal to call a convention was defeated in the election of 1824. The status of African Americans in Illinois remained a fractious issue. The state continued to exclude blacks from the polls, required them to register with county clerks, failed to emancipate slaves of long standing, and imposed other restrictions on blacks, prompting men like Calhoun to leave the state— ironically, often to head south to New Orleans, with its teeming, diverse population.

Slavery remained a problematic issue on the diplomatic front. The slave population in the South continued to grow; it is estimated that the number of illegal slaves brought into the country in the first half of the nineteenth century was as high as 1.2 million. The Caribbean slave trade continued to be a source of slaves. Although treaties with Spain and other countries outlawed the trade, Cuba, a Spanish colony, provided large numbers of illegal slaves, particularly since Cuba is located so close to the United States. It should be emphasized that slavery was not practiced exclusively in North America, particularly the United States. Slavery was a deeply entrenched institution in Central and South American in such nations as Brazil. With the nation becoming more deeply divided over the issue of slavery, the ban on the importation of slaves was hard to enforce and often simply ignored. The matter would not be resolved until the 1860s brought the Civil War.

CRITICAL OVERVIEW

Middle Passage was greeted with enthusiasm by critics and reviewers after it was published in 1990, and it won the National Book Award for that year. In a *New York Times* review of the novel, however, Thomas Keneally seems torn. On the one hand, he points out that the novel has problems. One is that it embodies "genre switches," meaning that it shifts, for example, from being a "bodice-ripper" of a romance to a "metaphysical drama." Another is that it contains numerous anachronisms. Keneally refers to "Rutherford's gift for hyperbole and bathos." In his view, the ending of the novel introduces an "artificial jollity," and he believes that Johnson does not resolve the matter of the god in the crate very effectively. The novel is also flawed by its "frequent straining for meaning." In sum, the critic writes that the author "manages to break with heretic abandon many of the cherished axioms of the writing academies." On the other hand, Keneally seems to see these flaws almost as a source of strength in this "engrossing" novel, which he says is written with "panache" and "just about transcends its faults." In the end, Keneally maintains that the novel "speaks of the legacies and griefs the peculiar institution has brought to the life of the American Republic." (The phrase *peculiar institution* was a historical euphemism often used to refer to slavery.)

Arend Flick, in a review in the *Los Angeles Times*, focuses his attention ore on the philosophical underpinnings of Johnson's prose. He states of the novel,

> Though never preachy, it's informed by a remarkably generous thesis: that racism generally, and the institution of slavery in particular, might best be seen as having arisen not from political or sociological or economic causes . . . but from a deep fissure that characterizes Western thought in general, our tendency to split the world into competing categories: matter and spirit, subject and object, good and evil, black and white.

Flick goes on to remark, "The Allmuseri become Rutherford's vehicle for self-knowledge, providing him with a passage beyond categories, beyond opposites, beyond desire and fear, and toward what we would want for him, and for ourselves."

Eugene B. Redmond, in a review published by Illinois Periodicals Online, focuses more on a description of the novel's genre—on trying to define for the reader what the novel *is*. He begins by noting that *Middle Passage* is

> a funny-gloomy novel that will dazzle and distress readers with its syntactical gymnastics, philosophical sparring matches, word wizardry, sudden flights of imagination, cultural cross-fertilizations and intimate incursions into the nether regions of human psyches— both contemporary and ancestral.

Later, Redmond wraps up his description in this way:

> *Middle Passage*. A horror story. A philosophical standoff. A treatise on the creolization of ethnicities and ideas. A meditation on Eurocentrism v Afrocentrism. A Romance. A text of defiance and rebel criminality. A joltingly brilliant ritual of revelation, cultural self-discovery and personal hunger/thirst.

Finally, in an article in *African American Review*, Daniel M. Scott III takes a somewhat more academic approach to the novel, developing this thesis:

> Staging an inquiry into the nature of origin, experience, and meaning, Charles Johnson's *Middle Passage* scrutinizes the structures of identity and the role writing plays in the reconfiguration of the self. *Middle Passage* confronts fundamental assumptions about human and literary identity and problematizes these assumptions by means of allusion and appropriation, which subvert—and, through subversion, re-vitalize—textual authority.

Later, Scott asserts that Johnson demonstrates how

> the intersection of consciousness and experience is identity. For Johnson and for *Middle Passage*'s protagonist, Rutherford Calhoun, that identity is the precarious "middle" experience of the African-American: offspring of the middle passage, refugee from an uncertain origin, subject to the marginalization of his experience, searcher for meaning.

CRITICISM

Michael J. O'Neal

O'Neal holds a PhD in English. In the following essay, he examines Middle Passage *as an extended metaphor for one version of the American experience.*

Johnson's selection of *Republic* as the name of his ship—and indeed, of *Middle Passage* as the name of his novel—is no accident, for both names serve to underline the metaphorical nature

WHAT DO I READ NEXT?

- Johnson's *Oxherding Tale* (2005) is a hilarious romp that tells the story of Andrew Hawkins, who was conceived and born after a slave owner in the pre–Civil War South and his African American butler became drunk and decided to trade places in each other's beds. The book examines racism, but with a comic touch.

- Robert Hayden is an African American poet and the author of "Middle Passage," a poem that can be found in his *Collected Poems* (1997). Johnson quotes from this poem on the epigraph page at the front of his book.

- Marcus Rediker's *The Slave Ship: A Human History* (2007) is a historical work based on the author's research in maritime archives. The book is a history of slave ships and of the human drama played out on them. Rediker examines the lives of captains, sailors, and enslaved Africans, including, for example, a young African kidnapped from his village and a would-be priest who is horrified by what he sees.

- Sharon M. Draper's *Copper Sun* (2006) is a young-adult novel that details the experiences of an African girl whose village is invaded and demolished by slave traders. Friends and family are brutally killed before her. She is then seized and taken on a forced march to a West African slave fort.

- *From Slave Ship to Harvard: Yarrow Mamout and the History of an African American Family* (2012) is a nonfiction work by James H. Johnston. It narrates the fortunes of an African American family over a period of six generations, starting with the arrival of Yarrow Mamout, a slave from Guinea who arrived in America on the slave ship *Elijah*.

- Ira Berlin's *Slaves without Masters: The Free Negro in the Antebellum South* (1974) is an award-winning book that has been reissued. It provides readers with a glimpse of the struggle for community and economic independence among the American South's free black population, numbering about a quarter million, in the years before the Civil War.

- Paul E. Lovejoy's *Transformations in Slavery: A History of Slavery in Africa* (2011) details the slave trade *within* Africa, including discussion of the medieval Islamic slave trade in North Africa.

---

of the novel's characters and incidents. This elaborate metaphor stands for nothing less than the nature of the American republic itself.

"Middle Passage," of course, is the literal name of the middle leg of the Europe–Africa–New World–Europe slave trade. But if the phrase is stripped of its capital letters, "middle passage" could stand for the position that Rutherford Calhoun—and perhaps by extension, all African Americans in 1830 and even today—occupied with reference to his nation. Calhoun, for example, straddles a middle position as he makes his passage from slavery in Illinois, where, under the tutelage of his master, he acquires an extensive Western education, to freedom in New Orleans,

where he gets by as a rogue and ne'er-do-well on his street smarts. Neither fish nor fowl, he is given a choice of remaining a petty thief and con man or marrying a respectable schoolteacher who loves him; instead of deciding, he runs off, boarding a ship on which he occupies a kind of middle position as a member of the crew (a cook's assistant) but not as a member of the crew (as a stowaway and a spy and as the only black American on the ship). On board the ship, his loyalties are divided, falling somewhere in the middle between loyalty to the Africans, with whom he begins to feel a strong identification, and loyalty to his white crewmates, who after all are Americans, just as he is. Calhoun's own middle passage eventually takes him

IN THE MEANTIME, THE *REPUBLIC* COLLAPSES AND SINKS. THE METAPHOR IS ALMOST TOO OBVIOUS—SO OBVIOUS THAT THE READER MIGHT ACTUALLY MISS IT. BUT IN A NUMBER OF WAYS, JOHNSON (ALWAYS THROUGH CALHOUN) MAKES CLEAR THAT THE SHIP, ITS VOYAGE, AND ITS CREW ARE EMBLEMATIC OF THE AMERICAN PSYCHE."

from southern Illinois—occupying its own position in the middle ground between outlawing slavery and yet imposing severe restrictions on African Americans—to New Orleans, across the ocean to Africa, and back, with the promise of returning as a freeman to Illinois. He comments then, "I felt precariously balanced between my old life in New Orleans and the first rung of another with Isadora."

In the meantime, the *Republic* collapses and sinks. The metaphor is almost too obvious—so obvious that the reader might actually miss it. But in a number of ways, Johnson (always through Calhoun) makes clear that the ship, its voyage, and its crew are emblematic of the American psyche. Calhoun, for example, sneaks aboard, posing as Squibb. Like most slaves, he "posed" as an American. His name is one that was undoubtedly imposed on him by his slave master, making him in a sense an impostor and a stowaway aboard the United States, a person of African descent bearing a northern European name, for both "Rutherford" and "Calhoun" are Scottish. That the *Republic*, like the American republic, is a microcosm is stressed. After the mysterious storm that the Allmuseri seem to conjure, Calhoun reflects:

> Without speaking, we all clapped our hands together as one company—thirty-two sopping-wet cutthroats black-toothed rakes traitors drunkards rapscallions thieves poltroons forgers clotpolls sots lobcocks sodomists prison escapees and debauchees simultaneously praying like choirboys, our heads tipped, begging forgiveness after this brush with death in Irish, Cockney, Spanish, and Hindi for a litany of collective sins so long I could not number them.

Earlier, Calhoun offers this reflection on the crew:

> We were forty of a company. And we'd all blundered, failed at bourgeois life in one way or another—we were, to tell the truth, all refugees from responsibility and, like social misfits ever pushing westward to escape citified life, took to the seas as the last frontier that welcomed miscreants, dreamers, and fools.

The comparison with the fundamental American impulse, with misfits pushing beyond the western horizon to a new life, is clear.

But the American experience, at least from the perspective of its slaves and black freemen, was one of plunder. In this regard, Captain Falcon, who commands the *Republic* and whom Calhoun calls an "imperialist," becomes in many ways a symbolic character. Here is Calhoun commenting on the captain:

> Falcon . . . knew seven African coastal dialects and, in fact, could learn any new tongue in two weeks' time. More, even, he'd proven it with Hottentot, and lived among their tribe for a month, plundering their most sacred religious shrines. . . . He'd translated the *Bardo Thodol* [the Tibetan *Book of the Dead*, a kind of scripture]—this, after stealing the only scroll from a remote temple in Tibet—and . . . he was a patriot whose burning passion was the manifest destiny of the United States to Americanize the entire planet.

(Recall that *manifest destiny* was a phrase used in the nineteenth century to refer to the inevitability of the nation's expansion to the Pacific Ocean.) Later, Calhoun learns this about the captain: "He had a standing order from his financiers, powerful families in New Orleans who underwrote the *Republic*, to stock Yankee museums and their homes with whatever of value was not nailed down in the nations he visited." And in case the reader has missed the point, Johnson/Calhoun is explicit: "[Falcon], like the fledgling republic itself, felt expansive, eager to push back frontiers, even to slide betimes into bullying others and taking, if need be, what was not offered." Thus, by calling his ship the *Republic*, Johnson can comment with only partial indirection on the republic of the United States, which, in the context of chattel slavery, plundered, bullied, sought empire, and tried to Americanize the world—not necessarily in 1830, at least in all respects, but perhaps, in Johnson's view, in the generations that followed.

The voyage of the *Republic*, though, is doomed. The first mate, Cringle, hints as much early in the voyage. The ship ultimately cracks apart, collapses, and sinks, and the reader suspects that the mystical Allmuseri are somehow responsible. Commenting on how he conceived and developed his fictional tribe, Johnson once had this to say:

> What I wanted was a whole tribe of Gandhis, Martin Luther Kings, and Mother Teresas, the most spiritual people on planet Earth, who also just happened to be the first tribe of humankind. They are mysterious, magical, and philosophically they represent the complete opposite of Capt. Ebenezer Falcon's conflict-based, Western vision of the world.

Johnson continued,

> True enough, there are fanciful things rumored about them by white sailors on The Republic, *i.e.*, that they have a second brain; and I did decide that they would have no fingerprints (their palms being blank like the Uncarved Block, a metaphor for the state of *wu wei* in Daoist thought).

Faced with the intensity of this spirituality, Falcon and his ship, embarked on a voyage of exploitation and plunder, are doomed. Falcon (perhaps a glancing allusion to the American eagle) can only commit suicide, and Cringle is left with no choice but to offer his flesh as sustenance for those who became victims of his actions.

In the end, Calhoun accepts his identity as an American:

> If this weird, upside-down caricature of a country called America, if this land of refugees and former indentured servants, religious heretics and half-breeds, whoresons and fugitives—this cauldron of mongrels from all points on the compass—was all I could rightly call *home*, then aye: I was of it....Do I sound like a patriot? Brother, I put it to you: What Negro, in his heart (if he's not a hypocrite), is not?

Neither Calhoun nor his creator rejects his identity as an American, as a member of a motley, mongrel brood. Both remain patriots, planted in the soil of the American experiment. But what both ask for is a change in perception, a sinking of the Republic of conflict and exploitation in favor of a more spiritual, more Taoist view of human experience, perhaps one expressed by the non-Western concept of *wu wei*, the paradox of nondual action, where past and future meet and where movement and fixity become one. Or perhaps the view is one in which peoples remain the Uncarved Block, before the imprint of a corrupting culture destroys their primordial simplicity.

Source: Michael J. O'Neal, Critical Essay on *Middle Passage*, in *Novels for Students*, Gale, Cengage Learning, 2013.

Arend Flick

In the following review, Flick compliments Johnson for skillfully combining beautiful language with a philosophical examination of the nature of racism.

Charles Johnson's first book, *Black Humor*, was published 20 years ago in Chicago, and that collection of drawings—political cartoons, really—startles now, when viewed through the lens of history, his and ours. The art is skillful, the captions trenchant. The theme is race relations, but the tone not what we might have expected from a young black college student living near one of the most racially polarized of American cities, in one of its worst times: Bobby Seale bound and gagged at the Chicago 8 trial; Fred Hampton dead in a police raid on his southside apartment.

Johnson remembers these cartoons as inspired by the black separatist philosophy of Amiri Baraka, whom he'd heard lecture at Southern Illinois University, taking no questions from whites. What strikes you about *Black Humor* now, though, is its gentleness, and its tentative exploration at times of territory beyond racial polarization. A raceless kangaroo whose pouch contains two joeys—one black, one white—reads a newspaper with the headline "New Open Housing Rules." A black rally speaker, having excoriated black integrationists as Uncle Toms, leaves through the stage door with a white woman who calls him "Tom." A black couple prepare to tell their white child what he apparently hasn't yet figured out.

Fast forward two decades, and Johnson—having done graduate work in philosophy and turned from visual art to fiction—is director of the Creative Writing Program at the University of Washington, with three published novels to his credit, as well as a collection of short stories

(*The Sorcerer's Apprentice*) nominated in 1986 for the PEN/Faulkner award and a recent book-length study of black writing since 1970.

In his highly readable though densely philosophical fiction, Johnson gives us characters forced to chart a middle passage between competing ways of ordering reality: sensual or ascetic, Marxist or Freudian, Christian or pagan. They quest for a unity of being beyond all polarities, for what the heroine of his first novel calls "the one thing all...things have in common. And happily for them and for us, they usually find it.

Johnson describes *Middle Passage* as an effort at "serious entertainment," a blurring, in other words, of another ancient pair of opposites, philosophy and art. He shares with his mentor, the late novelist and critic John Gardner, the Tolstoyan conviction that all true art is moral, not the promulgating of doctrine (which inevitably distorts morality) but the exploration and testing of values.

The formula fits *Middle Passage*. Though never preachy, it's informed by a remarkably generous thesis: that racism generally, and the institution of slavery in particular, might best be seen as having arisen not from political or sociological or economic causes, not (God help us) from pigment envy, but from a deep fissure that characterizes Western thought in general, our tendency to split the world into competing categories: matter and spirit, subject and object, good and evil, black and white. One of the novel's epigraphs, from the "Upanishads," grows increasingly rich in implication as we read *Middle Passage*: "Who sees variety and not the Unity wanders on from death to death."

Rutherford Calhoun, a newly freed 22-year-old slave from southern Illinois, drifts into New Orleans in 1829 and experiences a shock of recognition. For Rutherford, who narrates the story, the city is a place of sensory overload, an assault of smells, "if not a town devoted to an almost religious pursuit of Sin, then at least to steamy sexuality." The city suits his desire for adventure, experience, excess; it seems to be himself. His opposites are the Creoles downstream, who "sniffed down their long Continental noses at poor, purebred Negroes" like him. So he falls in among the thieves and gamblers upriver and becomes one of them.

Rutherford further defines himself in opposition to Woman. Isadora Bailey, whom he encounters one morning at the waterfront, is pretty "in a prim, dry, flat-breasted way," and everything

Rutherford isn't: "frugal, quiet, devoutly Christian." She is completely, in other words, out of place in New Orleans. Rutherford regards this daughter of a large Boston family free since the Revolutionary War as "positively ill with eastern culture." Naturally, she wants to reform him. Naturally, he resists reformation—to the point of stowing away on a slave clipper bound for Africa to escape marriage to her. (She has arranged the marriage with his creditor by paying off Rutherford's debts.)

By turns mimicking historical romance, slave narrative, picaresque tale, parable, and (finally) sea yarn, indebted (among many other writers) to Swift, Coleridge, Melville, and Conrad, *Middle Passage* invites but frustrates categorization. And that's exactly its point. The storytelling sounds historically credible at first (Johnson's research and command of language are impressive), but the counternaturalistic signals begin early, and they're intended. Idioms have sometimes a distinctly modern flavor: "down to earth" to describe Isadora's father, "hung over" to describe Rutherford. All the characters in *Middle Passage* in fact, sound as if they're double majors in classics and philosophy. "It seemed so Sisyphean," says Rutherford of a lovelorn fellow sailor, "this endless seeking of a single woman's love...in all others, because they would change, grow old, and he'd again be on a quixotic, Parmenidean quest for beauty beyond the reach of Becoming." His narrative comes to resemble an act of ventriloquism, a dreamlike projection of 20th-Century writer into the voice of roguish ex-slave, the writer winking behind the mask at time, blurring past and present. There's no clear line between Rutherford's world and our world, his journey and our journey. All polarities collapse by design here.

The opposition between Ebenezer Falcon and Peter Cringle, captain and first mate of the metaphorically named *Republic*, furthers Rutherford's process of self-definition on the passage to Africa. Cringle is Isadora in drag: a gentleman whose "whole air spoke of New England gentility."

Falcon, by contrast, is a carnival sideshow: a pederast, solipsist, and dwarf. He too seems to have taken a first in philosophy. Dualism is a permanent biological condition, he tells Rutherford: "Subject and object, perceiver and perceived, self and other—these ancient twins are built into the mind like the stem-piece of a merchantman. *think* without them, sir. And what, pray, kin such a thing mean? Only this, Mr. Calhoun, they are signs of a transcendental Fault, a deep crack in consciousness itself.... Slavery, if you think this through, forcing yourself not to flinch, is the social correlate of a deeper, ontic wound."

No wonder Cringle plans to set him adrift.

Between Cringle and Falcon, Rutherford can't choose, though both try to force him to. He can't find his loyalties, though he seems to take up and put down each of their perspectives at times. His unwillingness to choose makes sense, since Johnson blurs all ethical categories, showing the ministerial Cringle unable to "see himself, his own blighted history, in the slaves," the satanic Falcon ("known for his daring exploits and subjugation of the colored races" capable of generosity in the end. Not until *The Republic* takes on its cargo in Africa—40 Allmuseri tribesmen and their mysterious totem—does Rutherford finally begin to declare an allegiance.

Johnson creates the Allmuseri for pretty obvious thematic reasons. An ancient tribe of magicians, they are less a biological clan than one held together by shared values. For Rutherford, who feels "the presence of countless others in them," they are the "Ur-tribe of humanity itself." Without fingerprints, incapable of abstract thought, unable to distinguish the white crewmen as individuals, the Allmuseri envision Hell as the failure to experience "the unity of Being everywhere." And their god—which Falcon has plundered for the most Western of reasons, fame and fortune—is King Kong, Tolkien's ring and Spielberg's ark all rolled into one. Even Falcon recognizes it's beyond dualism: "The Allmuseri god," he tells Rutherford, "is everything, so that the very knowing situation we mortals rely on—a separation between knower and known—never rises in its experience."

The Allmuseri become Rutherford's vehicle for self-knowledge, providing him with a passage beyond categories, beyond opposites, beyond desire and fear, and toward what we would want for him, and for ourselves. *Middle Passage*, suffused with the quasi-Buddhist sensibility that seems increasingly common in Western writing today ends quietly, surprisingly.

What always saves the novel from the intellectual scheme that would otherwise kill it is the sheer beauty of its language. Here is Rutherford's vision of his father's death 20 years earlier: "I beheld his benighted history and misspent manhood turn toward the night he plotted his

escape to the Promised Land. It was New Year's Eve, *anno* 1811. For good luck he took with him a little of the fresh greens and peas Chandler's slaves cooked at year's end (greens for "greenbacks" and peas for "change"), then took himself to the stable, saddled one of the horses and, since he had never ventured more than ten miles from home, wherefore lost his way, was quickly captured by padderolls and quietly put to death, the bullet entering through his left eye, exiting through his right ear, leaving him eternally eight and twenty, an Eternal Object, pure essence rotting in a fetid stretch of Missouri swamp."

Philosophy and art are not simply joined here. They are one.

Source: Arend Flick, "Stowaway on a Slave Ship to Africa," in *Los Angeles Times Book Review*, June 24, 1990, pp. 1, 7.

SOURCES

"The African Slave Trade," National Archives and Records Administration, Southeast Region, Atlanta, website, http://www.archives.gov/southeast/finding-aids/african-slave-trade.pdf (accessed July 6, 2012).

"The African Slave Trade and the Middle Passage," PBS website, http://www.pbs.org/wgbh/aia/part1/1narr4.html (accessed July 4, 2012).

"Afro-Brazilians," World Directory of Minorities, Minority Rights Group International website, http://www.minorityrights.org/?lid = 5285&tmpl = printpage (accessed July 5, 2012).

"Arts and Letters Awards in Literature," American Academy of Arts and Letters website, http://www.artsandletters.org/awards2_popup.php?abbrev = Academy%20Literature (accessed July 4, 2012).

"Black Population Becomes the Majority in Brazil," MercoPress website, April 25, 2009, http://en.mercopress.com/2009/04/25/black-population-becomes-the-majority-in-brazil (accessed July 5, 2012).

"The Boldest Hoax," NOVA, PBS website, http://www.pbs.org/wgbh/nova/hoax/ (accessed July 10, 2012).

"Charles Johnson: Biography," *Oxherding Tale* website, http://www.oxherdingtale.com/index.htm (accessed July 4, 2012).

Flick, Arend, "Stowaway on a Slave Ship to Africa," in *Los Angeles Times*, June 24, 1990, http://articles.latimes.com/print/1990-06-24/books/bk-712_1_middle-passage (accessed July 11, 2012).

"Geographical Names: Bangala–Bangba," Geographic.org, http://www.geographic.org/geographic_names/b/ba_291.html (accessed July 6, 2012).

Holloway, Joseph E., "The Black Slave Owners," The Slave Rebellion website, http://slaverebellion.org/index.php?page = the-black-slave-owners (accessed July 5, 2012).

Hopkins, Desiree R., "Abolition of the Atlantic Slave Trade in the United States," Trade and Environment Database, http://www1.american.edu/ted/slave.htm (accessed July 6, 2012).

"Illinois, Indiana," Slavery in the North website, http://www.slavenorth.com/northwest.htm (accessed July 6, 2012).

Johnson, Charles, "All You Need to Know about the Allmuseri," E-Channel, April 17, 2011, http://ethelbert-miller.blogspot.com/2011/04/all-you-need-to-know-about-allmuseri.html (accessed July 12, 2012).

———, *Middle Passage: A Novel*, Atheneum, 1990.

Keneally, Thomas, "Misadventures in the Slave Trade," in *New York Times*, July 1, 1990, http://www.nytimes.com/1990/07/01/books/misadventures-in-the-slave-trade.html?pagewanted = print&src = pm (accessed July 11, 2012).

Krupa, Michelle, "New Orleans' Official 2010 Census Population is 343,829, Agency Reports," in *Times-Picayune*, February 3, 2011, http://www.nola.com/politics/index.ssf/2011/02/new_orleans_officials_2010_pop.html (accessed July 5, 2012).

Loy, David, "Wei-wu-wei: Nondual Action," in *Philosophy East and West*, Vol. 35, No. 1, January 1985, pp. 73–87, http://ccbs.ntu.edu.tw/FULLTEXT/JR-PHIL/loy3.htm (accessed July 12, 2012).

Redmond, Eugene B., "Inner and Outer Voyages," Illinois Periodicals Online, January 1992, http://www.lib.niu.edu/1992/ii920129.html (accessed July 11, 2012).

Scott, Daniel M., III, "Interrogating Identity: Appropriation and Transformation in *Middle Passage*," in *African American Review*, Vol. 29, No. 4, Winter 1995, pp. 645–55.

"Table 6. Population of the 90 [Largest] Urban Places: 1830," U.S. Bureau of the Census website, June 15, 1998, http://www.census.gov/population/www/documentation/twps0027/tab06.txt (accessed July 5, 2012).

"Table 22. Population of the 100 Largest Urban Places: 1990," U.S. Bureau of the Census website, June 15, 1998, http://www.census.gov/population/www/documentation/twps0027/tab22.txt (accessed July 5, 2012).

"William J. Jefferson: Representative, 1991–2009, Democrat from Louisiana," Black Americans in Congress website, http://baic.house.gov/member-profiles/profile.html?intID = 98 (accessed July 5, 2012).

FURTHER READING

Byrd, Rudolph P., ed., *I Call Myself an Artist: Writings by and about Charles Johnson*, Indiana University Press, 1999.
    This volume consists of two parts: One is a compilation of Johnson's writing, including essays, short stories, interviews, and speeches, along with some of his cartoons. The other is a collection of scholarly commentary on Johnson and his work by academic writers, providing readers with insight into his views and artistry.

Conrad, Robert Edgar, *Children of God's Fire: A Documentary History of Black Slavery in Brazil*, Pennsylvania State University Press, 1994.
    Americans tend to associate slavery entirely with the pre–Civil War United States, but many African slaves were taken to South and Central America. This volume presents a large number of primary sources about the Brazilian slave trade.

Lowther, Kevin G., *The African American Odyssey of John Kizell: The Life and Times of a South Carolina Slave Who Returned to Fight the Slave Trade in His African Homeland*, University of South Carolina Press, 2011.
    John Kizell was thirteen years old when he was brought to South Carolina as a slave on the eve of the American Revolution. He escaped to the British and then returned to Africa, where he helped establish a colony for freed slaves and fought the slave trade.

Thomas, Hugh, *The Slave Trade: The History of the Atlantic Slave Trade, 1440–1870*, Simon and Schuster, 1999.
    This volume is a comprehensive account of the slave trade, beginning with the first Portuguese slaving expeditions. Thomas shows that from 1492 to 1870 this immense commercial and maritime venture transported some 11 million slaves.

Yetman, Norman R., ed., *Voices from Slavery: 100 Authentic Slave Narratives*, Dover, 2000.
    This volume, as the title indicates, consists of one hundred first-person accounts of the lives of slaves in the pre–Civil War South. It includes descriptions of slave auctions and a number of photographs.

SUGGESTED SEARCH TERMS

abolition

Act to Prohibit the Importation of Slaves

Amistad

Charles R. Johnson

Charles R. Johnson AND Middle Passage

international slave trade

Middle Passage AND Atlantic slave trade

slave mutinies

slaving ships

US Constitution AND slavery

US slave trade

Moby Dick

1956   Herman Melville's 1851 *Moby-Dick* is today generally acknowledged as the greatest of all American novels. At the time of its publication, though, it was savagely attacked by critics and ended Melville's literary career. It ranges widely in style, from adventure story to biology textbook to high drama. John Huston's 1956 film *Moby Dick* (cowritten by Huston and science fiction author Ray Bradbury) had to keep the adventure story squarely in the foreground to meet the expectations of American audiences and Hollywood producers, but Huston manages to explore some of the novel's philosophical depths, even if no film could ever reproduce everything about the novel. Although the lavish production was a business failure during its initial release, the film has steadily gained in popularity as well as critical approval through the years.

PLOT SUMMARY

The film begins with the narrator walking to the whaling port of New Bedford. (This narrator, in the novel's famous first line, tells readers to call him Ishmael, suggesting that this might not be his actual name. In the film, the narrator gives his name in a voice-over, a technique that is used occasionally throughout the film.) He stays the first night at an inn, intending to sign up as a crew member on the first whaling ship he can find. He

FILM
TECHNIQUE

- During his research for the film, Huston consulted a large number of old books about whaling, most of which were illustrated with black-and-white engravings, others with hand-tinted images. Huston wanted to recreate the impression he received from these images in the film and so devised a unique technical process that indeed makes Moby Dick look like no other film. Each print is made from two superimposed negatives of the same film footage: one black and white and one in color.

- The whales in *Moby Dick* are created using a combination of different special effects. In some shots, they, and the ship's boats pursing them, are miniatures filmed in a water tank before a curved background painting that creates the illusion of depth. The film is then played back in slow motion to make the tiny waves seem to move at the same speed as the full-sized objects they simulate. But for the most part, Huston used a number of remote-controlled robot craft fashioned to resemble whales (similar to the robot shark famously used in *Jaws*). This effect was at the limit of available technology in the 1950s, and the production was plagued by the constant sinking of the robots. Other shots were filmed in a tank with actors and a mechanical copy of only parts of a whale's body, such as its head or fluke.

- *Moby Dick* was filmed in the widescreen format (1:2.75), that Hollywood had devised to compete with television. However, all video transfers of the film that have been released were cut down to fit the 4:3 proportions of older television screens. According to the critic Page Laws (in the article "King Adapter: Huston's Famous and Infamous Adaptations of Literary Classics"), widescreen prints of the film may no longer exist.

- Melville provides many striking visual images, and Huston capitalized on them in making the film. One result is the paintings of whales seen on the walls of the inn in New Bedford at the beginning of the film, all of which were commissioned for the film and show scenes described by Melville, such as a sperm whale leaping over a ship and impaling himself on the mast (which is also a foreshadowing of the fate of the *Pequod*).

---

is assigned a room where he must share a bed (an ordinary arrangement in the nineteenth century) and is surprised to find that Queequeg, the harpooner who is his roommate, is Polynesian; Ishmael refers to him as a cannibal.

The next day is Sunday, so Ishmael attends a church service. Father Mapple is a retired whaler; his pulpit is fashioned in the shape of a ship's prow, and he enters it by climbing a rope ladder. He preaches on the Book of Jonah. He interprets the great fish that swallows Jonah as a sperm whale and notes that when he is in the whale's belly, which might as well be hell, Jonah accepts God's will and God's judgment, even though they are contrary to his own and place a terrible punishment on him.

Queequeg befriends Ishmael, and the next day they sign on with the whaling ship *Pequod*. They learn that its captain, Ahab, was attacked by a whale on his last voyage and lost his leg, which has been replaced with a peg made of whale ivory. The ship's owner doubts whether he should hire a man who is not a Christian, but he is soon convinced when he sees how well Queequeg can throw a harpoon.

When Ishmael and Queequeg go to board the ship, they are stopped by a seemingly insane man who calls himself after the biblical prophet Elijah. He gets their attention by asking them about the contract they signed to join the crew of the *Pequod*: "Was there anything down about signing away your souls? Perhaps ye haven't

© *Photos 12 | Alamy*

got any?" He denounces Ahab as a cursed and evil man, saying, "Did they tell you how the whale marked him inside and out? Did they tell you about the mystic it worked on his soul?" But Ishmael dismisses him as someone who is trying to make himself seem important by pretending to have secret knowledge. Ishmael makes a seemingly impossible prophecy that includes foretelling that Ahab will go to his grave and rise again and that the whole crew of the *Pequod* will die except for a single man. Every detail of this prophecy comes true by the end.

The ship soon puts out to sea, although Ahab has not yet made an appearance to the crew. One of the more experienced sailors tells the first mate, Starbuck, and the other sailors about the history of the white whale called Moby Dick. He claims this whale has killed more than a thousand seamen over the years and has been spotted on the same day at the same hour in two places over a thousand miles apart. He also claims Moby Dick is immortal.

In narration, Ishmael introduces the ship's principal officers: Starbuck; Flask, the third mate; and Stubb, the second mate. When Ahab finally appears, he announces to the crew that they are hunting Moby Dick. He announces that the first man to spot the whale will be rewarded a Spanish gold coin, which he dramatically nails to the mast of the ship.

Some time later, an ordinary whale is spotted, and the *Pequod* sends out the ship's boats to hunt it down. The process of whale hunting is shown in loving detail by Huston (as, indeed, it was by Melville). When Starbuck reports on the action to Ahab, the captain explains that he has consulted the log books of hundreds of whaling voyages to establish the migration patterns of various species of whales. Starbuck has never heard of such a thing, and it seems like a kind of fortune-telling to him, but he immediately sees that this will simplify the process of finding whales and allow them to profit far beyond an ordinary whaling voyage. But Ahab has no interest in this; he wishes to use his new knowledge only to find Moby Dick.

The voyage continues into the Pacific Ocean, with more whale hunts along the way. Ahab does not interfere with Starbuck and the other ship's officers to prevent these, but he takes no interest in them either. Huston's editing suggests that while there is something majestic and exciting about the hunts, they also have a tragic edge when such a magnificent animal as a sperm whale is killed.

The *Pequod* has a rendezvous with the *Samuel Enderby* (a historical whaling ship), whose Captain Boomer brings news of the location of the white whale. This scene condenses many such encounters in the novel. Boomer wears an artificial arm, having lost his arm to Moby Dick. He mentions that he saw the whale only a month before. Now Ahab orders the crew to stop the hunt and even cut loose the whale carcass that was about to be rendered for oil in order to make all speed to search for the white whale, over the objections of all three officers. Starbuck now confides to the others that he considers the voyage doomed by Ahab's obsession. Starbuck points out to them that under the laws of the sea the crew can legally seize a ship from a captain who is not obeying the instructions of the ship's owners. But Stubb and Flask will have nothing to do with such a plan.

As they search for Moby Dick, Queequeg uses divination to try to find the outcome of their voyage. He throws a group of pig's knucklebones and reads the future in the pattern they make on the deck. The audience is supposed to believe this is pagan Polynesian magic, but (like voodoo dolls) this is an entirely Western practice that goes back to classical antiquity. Queequeg reads in the bones that he is going to die, and he pays the ship's carpenter to build him a coffin. Queequeg enters a trance, leaving him unresponsive to any of the ship's crew. One of the crewmen, noticing Queequeg's scarification (a form of body art in which patterns are formed of scars), starts to cut him. Ishmael fights the man to defend his friend, but he loses the fight. Queequeg comes back to consciousness to save Ishmael from being killed. At this moment, the lookout spots Moby Dick, and everyone's attention turns to the hunt.

Ahab orders the boats lowered to go after the white whale, although it is against standard practice to do so at night. Ahab rides out in Stubb's boat with Queequeg and Ishmael. Ahab figures out that Moby Dick is about to breach (that is, break the surface of the water) from the flight of a flock of seagulls. Foretelling the future from the behavior of birds is another ancient form of divination. Since the wind has died down, Ahab orders the ship's boats to be tied to the *Pequod* and rowed to pull it along after the whale. This lasts for several days until the wind picks up.

Ahab awards the gold coin nailed to mast to the lookout who first spotted Moby Dick, and he declares to the rest of the crew that once they have killed Moby Dick, his share of the voyage's profits will be distributed among them. They soon meet the *Rachel*, another whaling ship, and discover that it has gone after Moby Dick and met with disaster: the whale has destroyed one of the ship's boats, killing Captain Gardiner's son on it. Gardiner wants Ahab to help search for survivors from that wreck, but Ahab refuses, preferring to go after the whale.

Ahab now plans a bizarre ritual. He intends to take blood from himself and each of the crew members and have the ship's blacksmith reforge the harpoons and spears, quenching them in the blood. He tells the men this will bind them all together in a pact to carry out Ahab's vengeance against Moby Dick. This idea is described clearly but not shown in the film; it is not clear whether there is no time to do it before a storm strikes the ship or whether it is done off camera.

The storm drives them swiftly after Moby Dick, but only at the risk of sinking the ship. Ahab wants to raise more sails to pursue the whale as fast as possible, while Starbuck wants to lower the sails and even break down the mast in order to prevent the ship from overturning in the wind. The two men are about to come to blows over their dispute when suddenly the top masts are bathed in Saint Elmo's fire (a bright plasma that forms around the tips of the masts, whose shape concentrates the electrical field of the storm). The display transfixes everyone's attention. A plasma body forms around the tip of a harpoon Ahab is holding, and he takes it as an infusion of heavenly power, sent to help him. Although Starbuck considers him more insane than ever, Stubb and Queequeg interpret this as a miracle, justifying their faith in Ahab.

Sometime after the storm, Ahab favors Starbuck with a long speech. Since God is responsible for everything in the world, he says, from the course of the sun through the sky to the slightest human thought or movement, God is the one responsible for evil, but how can God be judged? The deeply religious Starbuck cannot tolerate this blasphemy and is on the point of shooting Ahab in the back, but he lowers the gun when he ponders that the divine judgment he believes in would condemn him for such a murder. He sees that he has no choice but to help Ahab accomplish his purpose, however insane and blasphemous he considers it. Ahab reassures him that since God is omnipotent and omniscient (that is, all-powerful and all-knowing), God must be behind everything they are doing and everything that has been done since the beginning of time. Therefore, Ahab says, Starbuck should not worry about taking responsibility for his own actions.

As the *Pequod* finally approaches Moby Dick, Ahab and the crew smell the scents of an island in the wind. Ahab says it is Moby Dick, who smells like land because "he is an island unto himself." Ishmael reveals Elijah's prophecy, that Ahab would die on a day when they smelled land but were not near land and then the rest of the crew except one would die. But Ahab has no patience for anything except the hunt, and the ship's boats are quickly lowered. Moby Dick is soon stuck with three harpoons (including one thrown by Ahab in Queequeg's place), but the whale is not killed and is able to pull the three boats along, even submerging one. Moby Dick turns on the boats and bites Ahab's in half. Ahab pulls himself onto the whale's back by the ropes that now encircle his body and stabs him with his spear, uttering the famous lines, "From hell's heart I stab at thee. For hate's sake I spit my last breath at thee." But Ahab is now entangled in the ropes and is pulled down when the whale submerges. When Moby Dick breaches again, Ahab has clearly been drowned, but the rocking motion of the whale's swimming causes his arm to flail, as if he were urging the men in the remaining boats on to attack the whale. Starbuck, who is now in command, seeing Ahab dead, is suddenly seized by his own desire for vengeance and orders the other boats on after Moby Dick. But the whale quickly destroys the remaining ship's boats, and he rams the *Pequod*, battering a hole in its side and sinking it also. The whole crew drowns except Ishmael. He is able to climb up onto the coffin that Queequeg had ordered to be made; since he had instructed it to be made watertight, it floats. Within a day, Ishmael is rescued by the *Rachel*.

CHARACTERS

Ahab
Ahab is played by Gregory Peck. Huston did not like him for the role but had to cast him to satisfy producers who wanted a well-known actor in the lead. Ahab is one of the most enigmatic

characters in literature. Ishmael, the narrator, says he cannot fathom him: "all this to explain would be to dive deeper than Ishmael can go." His body and his life have been essentially destroyed by his former encounter with Moby Dick, and the body and soul he has now were re-created by that event. But his new form is twisted and broken. As Ahab himself says, "Moby Dick . . . tore my soul and body until they bled into each other." His lost leg and its replacement with a piece of sperm whale ivory is only a symbol for his broken character.

The new Ahab has qualities that suggest the superhuman. During the search for Moby Dick, Ahab stays on deck continuously for seven days, eating nothing and dozing only briefly while he stands watch. Since ancient times, this kind of denial of sleep and food to the body has been a sign of a human being who is something more than an ordinary mortal. The Christian Gospels describe a forty-day fast in the wilderness undertaken by Jesus, and such feats have also been attributed to Christian saints, Hebrew prophets, and holy people from other cultures. It is not an accident that so many of Ahab's actions in the novel suggest parallels with the life of Jesus, though he is scarcely a Christ-like figure. Indeed, the new Ahab is filled with hate and vengeance instead of love and forgiveness. He has been formed in the likeness of Moby Dick, his creator.

Captain Boomer
The cheerful Boomer is the captain of the *Samuel Enderby*. Boomer brings Ahab news of Moby Dick's location. Boomer has a prosthetic arm made of ivory fitted with a hook. Injuries of this kind were quite common among nineteenth-century sailors, since amputation (rather than any kind of reconstructive surgery) was one of the few operations that could be performed by physicians of that era. Boomer lost his hand to Moby Dick, just as Ahab lost his leg, but the reactions of the two men could hardly be more different. Boomer's unfailing optimism makes his injury a point of pride that demonstrates his identity as a whaling captain. Boomer is played by James Robertson Justice, a well-known character actor of the 1940s and 1950s.

Elijah
Elijah, who stops Ishmael and Queequeg and tells them a prophecy about the destruction of the *Pequod*, seems to be a madman possessed by some kind of religious mania or by hatred for

Ahab. One of the great themes of Western philosophy is that the kind of inspiration that can give rise to prophecy is dangerously close to madness. Elijah's prophecy is far more explicit in the film than the book. Elijah is played by a character actor known by the stage name Royal Dano.

Flask

Flask, played by Seamus Kelly, is the third mate of the *Pequod*. "He bullies anyone bigger than himself," as if he is at war with the greater part of nature. The Greek philosopher Plato famously speculates in his *Republic* that human beings are composed of three elements: the body, which is the source of desires; the heart or spirit (*psyche*), which links together the physical and nonphysical parts of a person and is responsible for drives such as justice and ambition; and the mind, which Plato considers wholly nonmaterial and which is responsible for abstract thought. Plato further suggests that although everyone has these three parts, they find different balances in different individuals. People dominated by the body might become greedy and tyrannical or might become the fathers of large families; people dominated by the spirit might become soldiers or politicians, while those dominated by mind might become intellectuals. Many authors have based groups of three characters on Plato's theory, as Melville certainly did the three ship's mates in *Moby-Dick*. Flask is the bodily mate. However, this theme receives a comparatively superficial treatment in the film.

Captain Gardiner

Gardiner, played by Francis de Wolf, has only a small role in the film. It is significant, however, that he asks Ahab to help save his lost crewmen but Ahab refuses because of his thirst for vengeance against Moby Dick.

Ishmael

Ishmael, played by Richard Basheart, is the narrator of *Moby Dick*. His actual role, as one of the most junior members of the *Pequod's* crew, is quite small after the establishment of his friendship with Queequeg in the early scenes, but his role is greatly expanded by his voice-over narration. Huston has him speak some of the narration of the novel on screen as dialogue with his fellow crewmen. Huston does not allow the narration to foreshadow the final events of the film or meditate upon them, as he moves the story along

firmly in the present tense. Huston has to give up the sense of mystery and the sense of melancholy that pervades the narration of the novel.

Landlord

The landlord of the inn where Ishmael and Queequeg stay in New Bedford is a minor character, and the role is played by a local Irish villager rather than a professional actor. Perhaps because he considered the man's reading poorly acted or too heavily accented, Huston dubbed in his own voice reading the role. Huston also dubbed some of the dialogue from anonymous sailors later in the film.

Father Mapple

Mapple, played by the great Orson Welles, is the minister at the church service attended by Ishmael in New Bedford the Sunday before he signs on the *Pequod*. He is a former whaling captain, and his pulpit is built in the likeness of the prow of a whaling ship. He ascends it by climbing a rope ladder that he pulls up after him. This is often taken as a suggestion that the whaling ship is something cut off from and superior to the ordinary world, using the symbolism of Jacob's ladder from the Bible, which connects heaven and earth. Mapple's sermon is an important text in the film that helps to establish God as separated from the world.

Pip

Pip is the ship's cabin boy, meaning the personal servant of the officers. He is a black teenager. He is a focus of pity, especially in the novel, because of the unequal treatment he faces in the world. Although his part is small, it is Pip who explicitly identifies Moby Dick as God. The role is uncredited on screen, but Pip is played by Tamba Allenby, who had a brief career as a child actor on British television.

Queequeg

Queequeg is played by Friedrich von Ledebur. Von Ledebur was not a professional actor but a personal friend of Huston's, whom he knew from their common interest in the horse sport of dressage. Queequeg reminded Huston of von Ledebur and he searched for an actor who did also, but he finally asked his friend to take the role himself. Von Ledebur went on to have a successful film career in Hollywood and Europe. Queequeg is a Polynesian, who, much like Ishmael, first joined the crew of a whaler that put in at his home island to see more of the world. His body, including his face, is covered with decorative tattoos and scarifications, making him appear entirely alien to his American shipmates. He is looked down upon by many because he is not a Christian, and he is frequently called a cannibal. The charge is not so much related to his actually being a cannibal (which is unlikely) as to his following the traditional polytheist religion of his own culture. Despite the vast differences between himself and Ishmael, Queequeg quickly recognizes the kinship between them; he considers Ishmael a friend that is another self. The bond between the two men from alien cultures is symbol of the universal brotherhood of man. Queequeg cannot read or write, so he signs the ship's papers (the contract of employment) with his mark. In the novel, it is a sideways 8, the symbol for infinity. But Huston transforms it in the film, turning it into a sketch of a sperm whale, a figure evocative of the fish symbol used by the early Christians.

Starbuck

Starbuck is played by the British stage actor Leo Genn, whose film career was mostly in British productions and on British television. Starbuck is the first mate on the *Pequod*. He effectively runs the ship under Ahab's supervision. Starbuck's thinking is highly rational and legalistic. In the three-part scheme of human character that Melville illustrates with the three ship's mates, Starbuck is the intellectual, dominated by mind. He wants to do no more and no less than what is right under both human and divine law. He opposes Ahab's irrational desire for vengeance but does not feel he can oppose his captain's legal authority. When Ahab reveals his scientific discoveries about whale migration, Starbuck is interested only insofar as it will make whaling more efficient and profitable. His great moment of conflict comes when he must choose between, on the one hand, killing and replacing Ahab (which he feels is both his duty under maritime law and his contractual obligation to the *Pequod*'s owners) and, on the other hand, obeying God's commandment against murder. In the end, he follows divine law. When Starbuck sees his captain, the source of legal authority, killed, he is infected with Ahab's irrational desire for vengeance, and his actions doom the ship and crew as much as Ahab's did.

Stubb

Stubb, played by Harry Andrews, is the second mate of the *Pequod*. In Plato's scheme of three kinds of people, Stubbs is the man dominated by heart or spirit. When Ahab orders the whale hunt ended to go and search for Moby Dick, Stubb at first refuses, but he finally obeys and offers this excuse: "We've been killing so fast, our blood's so high, we wouldn't 've heard the last trump." He is able to surrender completely to his warlike passions.

THEMES

Nature

The British romantic poets of the early nineteenth century, such as William Wordsworth, regarded nature as purely good, pristine, and perfect and in every way superior to human culture. This view was taken up by the first generation of American romantics, such as Henry David Thoreau and Ralph Waldo Emerson. Their successors—Nathaniel Hawthorne, Edgar Allan Poe, and Melville—took just the opposite view, that nature was hostile to human culture and interests. Moby Dick himself is a symbol of nature's destructive effect on human life and aspirations. He is a wild animal and is said to encompass the whole of the living world in himself, but he maims or kills every human being he comes into contact with, not only Ahab but also Captain Boomer, the son of Captain Gardiner, and finally the whole crew of the *Pequod*. It is a symbolic destruction of all of human civilization (represented in miniature by the *Pequod*) by nature. As a brute animal, Moby Dick is unable to plot out or take sadistic pleasure in his hateful, destructive acts, but he does them automatically, simply because of the character of his existence. Melville is a making a statement about the innate hostility of the world to humanity.

Comradeship

At its beginning in Greece and the Near East, Western culture was highly xenophobic; that is, foreigners—and this could mean the people in the next village—were often considered hostile and inferior. This strain of thought, or more properly of feeling, has unfortunately not died out. But a different way of thinking arose eventually in ancient Greece. While the philosopher Aristotle observed that the natural state of a Greek city was to be at war with its neighbors, Diogenes the Cynic, who lived at around the same time, critically examined every aspect of Greek culture, including its division of humanity

READ, WATCH, WRITE

- Make a presentation to your class about the authenticity of the nautical terms and ideas in *Moby Dick*. As a point of comparison, refer to C. S. Forester's Horatio Hornblower novels, which have long been favorites of juvenile readers. Illustrate your talk with images from the Internet showing the various types of knots, rigging, and sails used on nineteenth-century sailing ships. If possible, demonstrate the tying of various kinds of knots in class and involve your classmates in tying some of the more complicated knots. Steven Spielberg has suggested that Huston's film was badly flawed in its treatment of these matters. Was he correct?

- Contact some of the clergy in your community and ask them what their religious tradition teaches about the problem of evil. You may find that many world religions (such as Islam, Sikhism, or Hinduism) have communities in your area, besides the various Christian denominations and Judaism. Write up your findings and compare them with the answers offered by *Moby Dick*.

- Cetology is the scientific study of whales. It was a passionate interest of Melville's, as he was himself a former whaler, and its exploration is a major theme of the novel (less so of the film). Write up a paper on the natural history of the sperm whale, addressing particularly the misconceptions of nineteenth-century whalers (for instance, about the nature of the spermaceti oil that the sperm whale was chiefly prized for) compared with modern knowledge on the subject.

- Research Melville's life, especially his career as a sailor. On a blog or a social media site, hold a discussion with your classmates about how scenes from the film *Moby Dick* might be based on Melville's own experiences. Discuss various scenes and explain your reasons.

into the superior Greeks and the inferior and wicked barbarians. Diogenes found the whole idea laughable and taught that people—Greek, Iranian, or anything else—were the same, neither good nor bad but all members of the same human family. This idea of the brotherhood of man was taken up by Stoic philosophy and from there made its way into the mainstream of philosophy in the Roman world and into Christianity. It was enthusiastically embraced by the romantic movement in the early nineteenth century and was expressed in such works as Friedrich Schiller's famous poem "Ode to Joy" (set to music in Ludwig van Beethoven's Ninth Symphony), which celebrates all men as brothers.

Melville worked at the very end of the romantic movement (which flourished a generation later in America than Europe) and produced in *Moby-Dick* one of the finest examples of the theme of the brotherhood of man. Moreover, Melville, unlike earlier romantics, had traveled extensively in non-Western cultures and knew foreign peoples first-hand from his days sailing on merchant ships and whalers. In *Moby-Dick*, Melville approaches the unity of humankind through the friendship of Ishmael, a Christian American, and Queequeg, a pagan South Seas islander. They recognize that the differences between them are irrelevant compared to their common humanity. Page Laws, in his article "King Adapter," asks, "What are Queequeg and Ishmael, if not a mismatched couple who rise above gender and race to form a marriage of true minds?" In the film, Queequeg expresses the idea directly. (He speaks in broken English, but language is not a barrier to brotherhood.) "Your boat, my boat. We eat same food. We sail on same water. We kill same whale. We friend. Same blood. Same head. All same." Ishmael leads the reader to look down on characters such as the agent of the *Pequod*'s owners, who superstitiously rejects Queequeg because he is different—in this case, not a Christian, leading to the contemptuous slur of calling him a cannibal. Even Ishmael has to make a mental effort to overcome his culture's prejudice. Even after Ishmael at first threatens to kill him when he finds him unexpectedly in his bed, Queequeg rationalizes to himself: "Better a sober cannibal than a drunken Christian."

The whalers, who represent for Melville a kind of ideal society (expressed in the film through the somewhat compressed expression "remote from all the cares of the people of the land"), do

© *United Archives GmbH | Alamy*

not pay much attention to differences such as nationality, religion, or race but care only about a man's excellence as a human being and a whaler. This is particularly true of the three harpooners on the *Pequod*, who are Polynesian, American Indian, and African. Huston, in adapting the long and complex novel for a two-hour film, was forced to carefully pick and choose which themes of Melville's to emphasize, or even mention. The movie develops the theme of the brotherhood of man quite fully. This theme held a special importance in the 1840s, when millions of blacks were held as slaves in the United States and when many Americans looked upon Native Americans as a group to be exterminated or at least forcibly removed from any land that white settlers might want. It was just as important in the 1950s, when African Americans were still struggling for basic civil rights and the equality that they were guaranteed as American citizens but that in practice was denied to them. Both the book and the film make powerful statements about racial justice without bringing the issue into the foreground

(which could well have invited censorship by publishers or studios unwilling to openly deal with such issues).

STYLE

Natural History

Several chapters early in *Moby-Dick* break away from the novelistic format of description of action relevant to the plot or dialogue between the characters. Instead they provide basic information about whales and the practice of whaling in a form modeled after contemporary natural history textbooks. This would be an extremely difficult form to convey directly on film. Huston paraphrases some of this material as ordinary dialogue between the characters, which loses the effect of the shift in genre and is not naturalistic either, since it calls for one character to point out to another something that would be obvious to him, even if not familiar to the audience. However,

Huston succeeded in finding a cinematic parallel in an ingenious manner. He filmed much of *Moby Dick* on the island of Madeira, where fishermen still hunted whales in a traditional manner, little changed since the nineteenth century. He filmed Madeira whalers on an actual whale hunt and used that material as stock footage for the whale hunts in the film. In doing so, Huston was imitating a common genre of the short films that often accompanied feature films in the first half of the twentieth century: the natural history subject or travelogue.

Drama

In several chapters late in *Moby-Dick*, Melville abandons the narrative convention of the novel in which the narrator describes the action from his point of view, and reports dialogue set off by stock phrases such as "he said". Instead, he gives the text in the form of a drama. He presents the bare dialogue following attribution to the character speaking, with occasional brief stage directions printed in italics, just like the published form of a play. This mixing of genres was such a startling innovation that it became one factor that led contemporary reviewers to suggest that Melville needed to check himself into a mental hospital. Huston made no effort to mimic this technique in the film. In one sense, it would hardly have been possible, since the entire novel had to be transposed into a shooting script, which inevitably takes the form of a play. But Huston might have achieved the same effect by the transposition of the idea to the realities of filmmaking. He might have suddenly emerged from behind the camera to give the actors their directions (and hardly any director would have been more capable of this than Huston, who was himself an accomplished actor) and shown the other camera crews filming the scene from other angles. But if he ever considered such measures, Huston must have suspected the result would have been too radical to find easy acceptance among the audience.

CULTURAL CONTEXT

Whaling

In the mid-nineteenth century, when *Moby-Dick* was written, whale hunting was probably sustainable. The relatively primitive technology used on a whaling ship like the *Pequod* could not threaten to exterminate entire populations of the animals. Whale oil was much in demand for use in lamps and as a mechanical lubricant, while more esoteric whale secretions, such as the spermaceti of the sperm whale, were used in manufacturing perfumes. As these markets declined in the late nineteenth century because of the use of petroleum, the chief market for whale products shifted to Japan and East Asia, where whale meat was much in demand as a delicacy. In the twentieth century, whale fishing fleets became mechanized and soon posed a serious threat to whale populations, so whaling became controlled and, for the most part, banned by the International Convention to Regulate Whaling, first established in 1946.

In theory, whaling is now limited to scientific research and to a few indigenous communities in places such as Alaska and the Faroe Islands, where whales are still hunted using traditional techniques and for which whaling was judged a cultural rather than a commercial enterprise. In practice, it is an open secret that countries such as Japan and Iceland take large numbers of animals for food under the cover of scientific whaling. In the United States, especially since the ecological movement of the 1960s, whaling has acquired an increasingly evil reputation, both because it is unsustainable and as consciousness of the unusual intelligence of whales among animals has been recognized. These concerns, barely recognized in 1955 when the film was being made, are completely ignored in *Moby Dick*. Huston was an enthusiastic big game hunter, and it probably never occurred to him that there could be an ethical objection to whaling. Some scenes of the film were shot during a traditional whale hunt by fishermen from the Island of Madeira (off Portugal) and actually show whales being killed, which would not be acceptable in an entertainment film today.

The Cold War

The Cold War (the political rivalry between the United States and the Soviet Union) might seem completely unrelated to a nineteenth-century novel like *Moby-Dick*, but many of the overwhelming social and historical factors of the 1950s had an impact on the film. Huston filmed the movie in Ireland (and at other locations in Europe), where he had been living for some years. He moved there because he wanted nothing to do with Hollywood. This was the time of the "Red scare," when rabble-rousing politicians like Edward J. Hart and Joseph

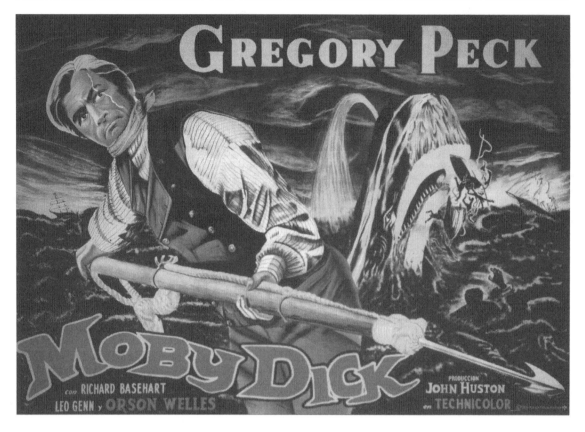

© Pictorial Press Ltd | Alamy

McCarthy whipped up their own popularity by pretending that they were fighting a Communist menace lurking in every corner of American society. In 1947, Hart's House Un-American Activities Committee grilled a number of Hollywood executives and directors over the supposed Communist sympathies of themselves or their employees. Hollywood executives responded by creating a secret blacklist of supposed Communist sympathizers who would no longer be allowed to work in the film industry. Huston was disgusted by this injustice and washed his hands of the whole Hollywood establishment. It was for this reason that Huston had moved to Ireland and shot *Moby Dick* entirely in Europe, as much as possible without the participation of the Hollywood studios (although Warner Brothers eventually had to bail out the badly over-budget production).

A more direct nod to Cold War concerns in the film occurs when Ahab describes his plan of hunting down Moby Dick by following the whale's migration pattern. He puts his finger on the map to show Starbuck where he expects to find the whale, a detail not in the book. Neither of them reads aloud the name of the island where Ahab is pointing, but it can be clearly read on the screen as the Bikini Atoll. Prior to 1954, hardly anyone in the audience would have heard of this remote South Seas location. But in 1954, it was the site of the first test of the hydrogen bomb and became world famous for its complete destruction in the resulting explosion. In this way, Huston was able to foreshadow the disaster at the end of the film.

CRITICAL OVERVIEW

At the time of its publication, the novel *Moby-Dick* was universally panned by critics, who completely failed to comprehend it. The rejection by the public, as well as critics, essentially ended Melville's writing career. In the 1920s, however, the novel was rediscovered and championed by intellectuals such as Eugene O'Neill as a masterpiece, establishing the place it still holds in the literary cannon. Huston's *Moby Dick* is an adaptation of one the very greatest novels. Lesley Brill, in *John Huston's Filmmaking*, points of that thirty-four of Huston's thirty-seven films were adapted works of literature (including the Bible, hardly a more ambitious undertaking than *Moby Dick*). Huston's obsession—his *idea*, as he called it—revolved around the translation of literature to the screen. But he was far from seeing himself as a passive agent in the process, as Laws points out in "King Adapter": "Huston's career can be 'read' as an attempt to 'master' or dominate various literary masters, by recreating their work in a wholly different medium." The French critic Robert Benayoun (translated and quoted by Laws) believes that "*Moby Dick* . . . is the total justification of Huston . . . the summit of his expression and his thoughts." Viewed in that way, *Moby Dick* is Huston's most important film, as his most ambitious adaptation, but in another sense it is a grand failure. If Huston desired to dominate the book in this case, he failed. Huston himself, writing his memoir, *An Open Book*, says, "Looking back now, I wonder if it is possible to do justice to *Moby Dick* on film." Vivian C. Sobchack, among many others, takes Huston to task for attempting the impossible: not only filming *Moby Dick* but trying to adapt any written work, which she considers a categorical error. According to Sobchack, Huston failed to interpret Melville in any insightful way, though Sobchack does concede that Huston created an independent work of art.

Laws's more positive assessment of the film offers a Freudian reading of Huston's artistic process, which, as he says, is only fair, since Huston himself was a Freudian; one of Huston's few films that was not a literary adaptation was a study of Freud's development of psychoanalysis (*Freud: The Secret Passion*). He sees Huston as purposefully misreading his source materials (the product of his artistic father surrogates), an act that simultaneously destroys them as it becomes an act of new creation when the film comes into being. In Freudian terms, this is like the son who figuratively destroys the father in order to carve out his own identity. And identity—the search for an identity and the legitimating of a truly masculine identity—is agreed as the main theme of Huston's work. In this sense, *Moby Dick* is a quest by Ahab to reestablish his sense of identity, which was destroyed when Moby Dick destroyed his ship and bit off his leg. Laws offers another metaphor for Huston's creativity: Huston and Melville enter into "an implied, almost mystical marriage

of author and . . . adapter." Richard T. Jameson, in his article "John Huston," observes that the reputation of the film has risen through the years: "It has become a mainstay of repertory programming."

CRITICISM

Rita M. Brown

Brown is an English professor. In the following essay, she discusses Melville's use of Gnostic symbolism in Moby Dick *and its realization in Huston's film.*

When *Moby Dick* was published in 1851, reviewers did not realize that it was primarily a philosophical and theological work. *Moby Dick* is many things at once, but its most important aspect is a meditation upon the nature of God. Huston was keenly aware of this. In his memoir, *An Open Book*, Huston summarizes his theological understanding of the film. He considers it utterly blasphemous. He recognizes that Moby Dick is a disguise for God (the phrase used by Melville, and retained in the film, is "pasteboard mask," meaning something made out of papier-mâché). Ahab tells Starbuck, "All visible objects are as pasteboard masks. . . . It is the thing behind the mask I chiefly hate; the malignant thing that has plagued and frightened man since time began." The least likely of characters, Pip the cabin boy, leaves no doubt about Moby Dick's identity when he cries out, "That ain't no whale. That a great white god." But Moby Dick is a destructive monster, something far removed from any traditional understanding of God in Melville's nineteenth-century American culture.

When Huston calls the film blasphemous, he is referring to Ahab's long speech to Starbuck immediately before the final hunt for the whale, in which Ahab holds God responsible for the damage to his body. Indeed, Ahab argues, who else could be responsible? Since God is all-powerful and all-knowing, he must be responsible for everything that happens: "Is Ahab Ahab? Is it I, God, or who, that lifts this arm? . . . Where do murderers go? . . . Who's to doom, when the judge himself is dragged to the bar?" Once Ahab has held God himself responsible for the evil that he has suffered, how can he judge God? How can he punish for sin the one who is responsible for punishing sinners? His solution is to treat God no differently than he would anyone else who

WHAT DO I SEE NEXT?

- Millard Webb made the first film adaptation of *Moby-Dick* in 1926 as *The Sea Beast*. Although this was in the period of the novel's rediscovery, Webb abandoned all but the most superficial elements of the book and filmed an adventure story complete with a romantic backstory and happy ending for Ahab. In 1930, Lloyd Bacon reshot *The Sea Beast* in a sound format as *Moby Dick*.

- *Moby-Dick* is deeply concerned with the ancient Christian heresy of Gnosticism as a way of understanding the universe. Usually this emphasis is lost in film versions, being reduced to occasionally powerful symbolic images. A film that takes the same rarefied interest in ancient religion and philosophy as Melville is the surrealist Luis Buñuel's 1969 *The Milky Way*. In this movie, two homeless men from modern-day Paris go on their own quest, a pilgrimage to the Cathedral of Santiago de Campostela in Spain. Along the way, they meet with representatives of heretical movements from every period of French and Spanish history in a completely unreal manner.

- Paul Stanley directed a version of *Moby Dick* in 1978 that attempts to recreate the psychological intensity of the story, merely showing the Shakespearean actor Jack Aranson reading excerpts on a bare stage for a little over an hour.

- Science fiction author Ray Bradbury shares credit with Huston for writing the screenplay of *Moby Dick*. In 1986, the television show *Ray Bradbury Theater* adapted Bradbury's short story "Banshee," which deals with his relationship with Huston while they were writing the script in Ireland. (A slightly different version of this story was later included as a chapter in Bradbury's 1992 novel, *Green Shadows, White Whale*.) Peter O'Toole plays the role of Huston.

- In 1998, Franc Roddam directed a television miniseries adaptation of *Moby Dick* that cast Gregory Peck as Father Mapple, in an homage to Huston's film (in which Peck plays Ahab). Much of the dialog is more faithful to the original than in other versions.

- In 2010, *Moby Dick* was again adapted into a miniseries, this time by Mike Barker. This version wanders far from the novel, supplying an extensive backstory concerning Ahab's wife. It was produced by Gate Filmproduktion and Tele München Fernseh Produktionsgesellschaft.

- Steven Spielberg's 1975 *Jaws* is, in many ways, intended as an homage to *Moby Dick*. The plot has certain similarities, and the character of Quinn, in particular, is based on the maniacal obsession of Ahab. It also uses a robot shark, as Huston's film used robot whales. Spielberg had originally intended to have his Captain Quinn watch Huston's film and laugh at its nautical inaccuracies, but he was unable to obtain the rights to show the film-within-a-film. The uncut version of the film is shown on television today with a TV-14 rating.

---

damages him. Ahab had told Starbuck earlier, "Speak not to me of blasphemy. I'd strike the sun if it insulted me." Ahab means to kill God as punishment for what God did to him.

Within a Christian context, Ahab's desire for revenge against God is insane. To start with, how can a powerless human being take revenge against an omnipotent God? And, indeed, Ahab cannot. Instead he brings the judgment of God down on himself and nearly his whole crew, resulting in their deaths. But more fundamentally, God is merciful and the source of all good; he cannot be held responsible for evil. How, then, can evil in the world be explained? A common Christian response is to refer it to human sin and to the devil, who rebelled against

> *MOBY DICK* IS MANY THINGS AT ONCE, BUT
> ITS MOST IMPORTANT ASPECT IS A MEDITATION
> UPON THE NATURE OF GOD."

God and brought sin into the world. But if God is omnipotent and omniscient, he did nothing to prevent the rebellion of Satan and the Fall of man; Got allows sin and the devil to operate. This contradiction is the crux of the novel and of the film. Melville has put his finger on what seems to be a logical contradiction within Christian theology, and *Moby Dick* is his attempt to work it out to a satisfactory conclusion.

When Melville set out to examine the paradox of evil in a world created by a good God, he was by no means the first to investigate the problem. Ancient Christians, who today are generally called Gnostics (from *gnosis*, the Greek word for "knowledge") had pondered the problem; they came up with answers very different from those of orthodox Christians. One has to imagine ancient Gnostics having existed as something like specialized reading groups within ancient Christian communities. They offered their members something more than the canonical books of the New Testament, while claiming to have a truer and fuller understanding of those texts. Each group throughout the Roman Empire shared certain basic ideas but adapted them to their own needs and concerns, so that probably hundreds of unique Gnostic systems must have existed. In Melville's day, these systems were known only through writings of orthodox Christian bishops, who condemned the Gnostic ideas as heresies. In 1948, a number of Gnostics books were discovered at Nag Hammadi in the Egyptian desert, so that today we know far more about Gnostic beliefs than Melville could have.

Gnostic writings seem bizarre. They are filled with elaborate mythological speculations, for example, about events before the first verse of Genesis, and are filled with elaborate genealogies of divine beings with incomprehensible names such as Ialdabaoth and Abraxas. But Melville was interested not in Gnostic mythology but in the Gnostic analysis of the origin of evil. Melville mentions the Gnostic sect of the

Ophites when he describes Ahab's obsession with Moby Dick, so it is probably their system that he had in mind. He would have known it from its refutation by Irenaeus, the bishop of Lyons in the late second century, in his book *Against Heresies* (1.30), although several books with similar ideas, such as the *Apocryphon of John*, were discovered at Hag Hamamdi.

If one looks at the Bible from a Gnostic perspective, specifically at the Hebrew Bible, or Old Testament, it is easy to find passages where it looks as if God is the source of evil. If evil is the result of sin, then, according to the Bible, evil entered the world with the temptation of Adam and Eve in the Garden of Eden. God places the tree of the knowledge of good and evil in the Garden of Eden and commands Adam and Eve, "Ye shall not eat of it, neither shall ye touch it, lest ye die" (Genesis 3:3, King James Version). But without having the knowledge of good and evil, of knowing what right and wrong are, how can human beings know that it is wrong to disobey? God must have known what they would do. Moreover, the serpent (not identified as the devil in the text), tells them what God said is not true, and, indeed, once they eat the fruit they do not die. Later, in the Flood, God kills everyone on earth except Noah and his family, an act of genocide. Moreover, he does this supposedly to correct his mistake and eliminate sin from the world, but immediately thereafter, humankind returns to sin and God has to intervene again to destroy the tower of Babel. How can these stories be reconciled with an all-knowing, all powerful, all-good God? The Gnostics answered the question in this way: Originally, undivided divinity existed. As the process of creation unfolded, individual divine beings emerged, until one being, Wisdom, or Sophia (Proverbs 8), became trapped in matter. This accident—the intermingling of spirit and matter—is the source of evil for the Gnostics. Ahab refers to this when he says, "Moby Dick...tore my soul and body until they bled into each other."

Because creation is an inherent quality of the divine, Sophia goes on creating new offspring, but they are more and more mixed with matter and so are unable to comprehend the divine world. One of them, Ialdabaoth, because he is ignorant of the greater divinity that exists above him, cries out, "I am father, and God, and above me there is no one." He goes on to produce seven lesser gods (who all bear names for God from the Hebrew Bible)—the planets of astrological mythology, whom he calls archons—and goes on with them to create the world as in the Genesis account. Ialdabaoth becomes the creator, or demiurge (from the Greek for "craftsman"). This explains the plural pronouns in the Hebrew text. Sophia tricks Ialdabaoth into creating the first man and infusing most of the divine light trapped in him into his new creation. Because the demiurge is ignorant, he wishes to keep humans ignorant and so denies them the fruit of the tree of the knowledge of good and evil. The serpent comes and tells the first humans to eat the fruit, but in this case, the serpent is Jesus in disguise. (It is for this reason that Ophites were called serpent worshippers, as Melville mentions.) He has been sent as a sort of secret agent from the world above to bring back the divine light by saving humankind. His act of salvation is to bring human beings knowledge (*gnosis*) of the true state of the world. The demiurge realizes he is losing control of humanity and tries to kill them all in the flood, but they are saved by Sophia. The goal of Jesus's incarnation and Crucifixion is the harvesting of the divine in human souls, sparks of divine light, and their connection to the divine world. This salvation will end the physical world created by the demiurge and allow the original process of creation without matter to continue as was intended.

Gnosticism attempted to answer the problem of evil by splitting the Christian God into two parts, the evil demiurge, responsible for the oppression of the divine souls of human beings, and Jesus the redeemer, whose mission is to redeem human souls from matter. Evil is an accident, and God's intervention in the world is to repair it. Moby Dick, the God that Ahab hates and wants to kill, is not Jesus the redeemer but the corrupt and fallen demiurge.

Gnostic themes are densely woven throughout the novel *Moby Dick*, and Huston could not translate all of them to the screen. One principle of Gnosticism is that the demiurge, or creator god, is ignorant of the true nature of the universe, and his creation, humankind, is equally ignorant. Jesus's purpose is to reveal the truth to humankind. The form that Gnostic salvation takes is frequently magical. Gnostics thought of the physical structure of the universe as a fortress or prison built to keep the divine light in human souls locked away from heaven. Each of the planets is a guardhouse that will turn the souls of the dead back to earth to be reincarnated by the demiurge's archons. In some Gnostic books, Jesus comes to tell his followers the magic words that will act as passwords after death to compel the archons to let them pass. Much of the background for this idea comes from the Greek philosopher Plato, who taught that human beings are ignorant of the true nature of the world. Just as fish live in the sea and must think that the surface of the sea is the upper limit of creation, human beings think that the upper limit of the air, or heaven, is the extent of the world. But Plato says that gods live "round the air, as we live around the sea. . . . In a word, as water and the sea are to us for our purposes, so is air to them" (*Phaedrus* 111A). It is obviously significant for Melville that whales are the only sea creatures that regularly breach the water's surface to come up into the air. However, Melville loosely paraphrases the passage of Plato:

> Methinks we have hugely mistaken this matter of Life and Death. Methinks that what they call my shadow here on earth is my true substance. Methinks that in looking at things spiritual, we are too much like oysters observing the sun through the water, and thinking that thick water the thinnest of air. Methinks my body is but the lees of my better being.

While human beings think life goes on here on earth, the true life begins once humans can escape through heaven into the world that is above the heaven of the demiurge.

It follows from the Gnostics' use of magical words that many of their rituals and texts would seem magical to outsiders. In the first place, Gnostic rituals were more often conceptual than actually performed. Gnostic writers delighted in piling complexity on top of complexity, but they did not have to worry about the performance of rituals that would, for instance, only be enacted by the dead on their way to heaven. Another consideration is that *magic* was a loaded term in antiquity. One group, such as the Roman state, would call their own rituals "religion," and those of their enemies, such as the Christians, they would call "magic." The fact that there was a logical consistency and similarity between them (with elements such as prayer and invocation) was irrelevant compared with the political power of the charge of magic (a capital crime). And Christians just as readily denounced Roman rituals as magic and demon worship. But some groups embraced the term magic precisely because it was seen as powerful and illicit. To judge from the generic and detailed similarities between works written by professional magicians and by Gnostics, some ancient Gnostics must have fallen into this category. At least in part because of the Gnostic interest in or similarity to magic, *Moby Dick* is filled with magical rituals. They begin with the many forms of divination (fortune-telling or foretelling the future) practiced through the book: the pagan Queequeg's throwing of pig's bones to foretell his own death, the prophecy of Elijah, and even Ahab's map of whale migration routes, which was probably closer to divination than to modern science (as Huston in particular tries to nuance it in the film).

The most important magic in Moby Dick is the oaths sworn by the crew to hunt down the whale, or, one might just as well say, the spells cast by Ahab. When Ahab first appears, he leads the crew in a series of rituals. He passes around a pitcher of grog that he has drunk from and that he requires every member of the crew to drink from, without it's being refilled. This shared drinking is meant to unify the group into a single entity, in the same way the ritual of the Eucharist is meant to bind the Church together. The same kind of thing happens again later in the novel, when Ahab binds Starbuck to himself through contagious magic: "Something shot from my dilated nostrils, he has inhaled it in his lungs. Starbuck now is mine; cannot oppose me now, without rebellion." Next in the ritual, Ahab commands the three mates to bring their spears (the instruments that are generally used to kill a whale after it has been harpooned) and cross them together. He grasps them where they overlap and says, "That same lightning which struck me I now strike to this iron!" Next he pours more of the grog into the hollows of the harpoons and has the harpooners drink from them. He then binds the whole crew by an oath to hunt Moby Dick to his death or die themselves. Although Ahab later orders the ship's smith to reforge the spears and harpoon, in this case, he merely says the thing that is to happen, and that is taken as equivalent to it actually happening. This performative power of language is one of the core principles of magic and logically underlies prayer and spells alike. Ahab's use of the word *lightning* is interesting. He means the divine power that struck him down in the form of Moby Dick. But it is also true that the saving gnosis that Gnostics believed they received from Jesus was commonly described in metaphor as lightning or thunder. While the crew—as much

as the reader—might be at a loss to understand the complexities of the gnosis involved in salvation, Ahab passes it on to the men through ritual.

In *Moby Dick*, Melville questions traditional Christian explanations of the origin of evil in the world, and he proposes an answer that was first given orthodox Christianity's ancient Gnostic rivals. It is a thought experiment in the basic pessimism about the world that he shared with his friend Nathaniel Hawthorne and their contemporary Edgar Allan Poe. Melville had been brought up in the Dutch Calvinist Church, which unhesitatingly gave as answer to the problem of evil the doctrine of predestination: before the foundations of the world were laid God knew and foreordained every tiny movement of Ahab's arm as well as the whole drama of sin and redemption. Melville left that faith for the Unitarian Church, which offers no set answers to such a question. It may be that one thing *Moby Dick* accomplishes is to narrate Melville's own loss of faith. For Huston, who considered the work an experiment in blasphemy, it did not have so personal a meaning.

Source: Rita M. Brown, Critical Essay on *Moby Dick*, in *Novels for Students*, Gale, Cengage Learning, 2013.

Walter C. Metz

In the following excerpt, Metz examines John Huston's Moby Dick *in light of a desire by critics to reinterpret it based on Cold War ideology.*

. . . Herman Melville's *Moby-Dick* offers another such testament to the power of ideas to guide us in our response to September 11. After all, what is *True Lies*' Harry if not a modern-day Ahab who defeats his whale, the vilified Arab terrorists who "task" him? Melville's bitter warning about Ahab as a Romantic hero who does not win is a textual template that we would do well to consider when constructing arguments about the United States' potential course of action over the coming years. For in truth, *George Bush* is also Captain Ahab, hell bent on avenging the loss of his buildings, New York City's legs, if you will.

If ever there was good evidence for a political unconscious in the novel, it would be the imagined headlines about Ishmael's life presented in the first chapter, "Loomings": "Grand Contested Election for the Presidency of the United States," "Whaling Voyage by one Ishmael," and "Bloody Battle in Afghanistan,"

> **THE IRONY OF COURSE IS THAT THE SCREENWRITER WAS RIGHT; BENCHLEY'S NOVEL IS A SORT OF POPULAR CULTURE VERSION OF MELVILLE'S NOVEL."**

indicating if nothing else, the long standing historical trauma that the Afghanis have had to endure. For the Afghanis suffering Bush's bombs, the distinctions between 1850 and 2001 that motivate my historical study do not pertain in the least.

The pertinence of this intertextual analysis of the Cold War's *Moby-Dick* as articulated in John Huston's film version can be seen most directly, perhaps, in the recent 1998 USA Network television production. This version, starring Patrick Stewart as Ahab, does not topple Huston's film's Cold War interpretation as we might hope a post-Cold War production would, but instead *perpetuates* it by replacing Orson Welles as Rev. Mapple with Gregory Peck, he who played 1956's Ahab. In *The Errant Art of Moby Dick*, William Spanos argues for what is at stake here: "Pease's enabling contribution to the struggle to free Melville—indeed, American literature at large—from the bondage of American Cold War discourse is precisely his decisive displacement of the question of its contemporary intelligibility from the domain of the sovereign subject to that of hegemony" (274).

For precisely this reason, I believe that to effectively discuss *Moby-Dick* in light of September 11, we must image the novel in ways that do not perpetuate, but instead transcend, its Cold War canonical reading. To do so, I want to focus on the identity political position from my earlier, now abandoned, project that I have not as yet breeched, namely questions of gender. I have chosen an extremely unlikely starting place, Chris Carter's sci-fi television show, *The X-Files*. There is a terrific moment in Season 3, in the episode, "Quagmire," first aired on 3 May 1996, when agents Mulder and Scully, having been on a case to catch a Loch Ness-style watery monster, have endured the sinking of their boat.

Stranded on a rock in the middle of a lake, Scully compares Mulder to Ahab, arguing that they both maniacally pursue some abstract and ultimately destructive paranoia that they label "Truth." If Mulder is Ahab, then who is Scully? There is a psychoanalytic possibility: Scully tells Mulder that her father used to call her Starbuck and she called him Ahab. Thus, Scully's dead father, much a source of trauma in the first season of the show, as he never approved of her becoming an FBI agent instead of a doctor, has been replaced by Mulder, her will-they-or-won't-they romantic foil, a position sealed by a season-ending episode in which Mulder and Scully kiss, having formed a "normal" family complete with new-born infant.

This line of reasoning would position Scully as Ahab's lover, a possibility that would seem all but ludicrous if not for the astonishing pre-Cold War film version of Melville's novel, made in 1930 by Warner Bros. as a star vehicle for John Barrymore. In this film, perhaps the most interesting adaptation I have ever seen, there is no Ishmael. Yes, that's right, the central character of the novel, Melville's grand solution to his crisis of how to justify the after-the-fact narration of an apocalyptic narrative, is left on the cutting room floor. Bacon's film does not give a whit for the canonical reading of Melville's novel, largely because such a reading, an artifact of the Cold War, had not yet been articulated. Instead, Bacon's film produces a conventional Hollywood love story between Ahab and Faith, the invented daughter of Rev. Mapple, whose moral purity reforms Ahab from a bawdy sailor into a marriageable man. Being a pre-Production Code affair, the film is fairly aggressive about representing this transformation from sexual scoundrel to family man.

Once she has reformed him, Faith agrees to wait to marry Ahab when he returns from his next three-year whaling voyage. However, when Ahab's leg is bitten off by Moby-Dick (in a very funny scene thanks to an equally rubbery special effects whale), Ahab's brother tricks him into thinking Faith no longer desires him because of his handicap. Bitter at Moby-Dick for ruining his sex life, Ahab relentlessly pursues the whale, seeking vengeance. However, this time, Ahab wins. The men carve up Moby-Dick, return to New Haven, and Ahab marries Faith.

My point here is to entertain the possibility that to seek out the contemporary significance of a classical novel, we must entertain the idea that the novel is extremely malleable. Given the confines of a canonical reading, there is no question that the 1930 version of *Moby-Dick* is horrendous. However, once we highlight the complex ideological terrain of the canonical reading that contains the text, in this case, that the novel's misogyny is to be found in its marginalization of female characters, we have a path to begin appreciating extremely, shall we say, aberrant film adaptations.

The 1930 version—not being beholden to the idea that *Moby-Dick* is a masterpiece that should not be tampered with—produces a series of radical transformations of the novel. Sometimes these transformations seem absurd—the film focuses on the back-story of Ahab, thus adding to what is already a 569-page novel. Thus, under no circumstances could a seventy-five-minute film hope to capture any significant thematic content of the novel. However, the introduction of Faith allows for an examination of gender that the Cold War reading pushes to the sidelines.

In her article, "Melville at the Movies: New Images of *Moby-Dick*," Susan Weiner pursues a similar gender studies agenda when she analyzes the references to *Moby-Dick* in Michael Lehmann's teen-pic, *Heathers* (1988). *Heathers* focuses on J. D., an aptly initialed juvenile delinquent who murders off the popular girls in the school, all of whom are named Heather. Weiner argues of J. D., "This young rebel with a cause is the dark side of Veronica, just as Ahab was a buried part of Ishmael" (87). In this way, the radical approach of the 1930 film, by combining Ishmael, Melville's narrator and central character, and Ahab into the one character of John Barrymore's Ahab, while not palatable to the canonical Cold War reading of Ishmael as freedom and Ahab as totalitarian, dovetails with the post-Cold War *Moby-Dick* as it is begun to be formulated by *Heathers*.

The 1930 film and *Heathers*, unified not by their historical contexts but instead by their insistence on *not* being Cold War texts, in fact make many of the same adaptational moves, including imposing a happy ending, about which Weiner argues:

> It is then that J. D. designs a plan for the annihilation of his society, an idea he finds in *Moby-Dick*. But *Heathers* rewrites the novel by offering a positive solution to the problem it poses. The good leader triumphs as Veronica kills J. D. and saves the school. Unlike

Melville, this director changed his ending to stress optimism rather than nihilism. (87–88)

Victor Salva's *Powder* (1995), about an impossibly white albino boy with Christ-like empathic powers, also extracts a happy ending out of *Moby-Dick*. As in Melville's novel, but not the 1930 film version, Powder, the sought-after white whale of Salva's film, defeats his pursuers and ascends to heaven (as Melville's whale descends triumphantly into his oceanic depths). Like *Heathers*, Salva's film directly invokes *Moby-Dick* as its primary literary intertext. When Jesse the social worker first goes down to the basement where Powder has been kept by his grandfather, she discovers that he has memorized Herman Melville's novel. Powder quotes a passage from near the end of the novel, from Chapter 114, titled "The Gilder":

> Where lies the final harbor, whence we unmoor no more? In what rapt ether sails the world, of which the weariest will never weary? Where is the foundling's father hidden? Our souls are like those orphans whose unwedded mothers die in bearing them: the secret of our paternity lies in their grave, and we must there to learn it. (492)

Obsessed with what he believes to be his impending death at the hands of the mad Romantic Ahab, Ishmael reflects upon all people's orphaned nature, curable only in death. Powder, Salva's film's white whale, reflects upon his own alienated position, as the representatives of "civilization" like the cruel neo-conservative deputy, Harley Duncan, his Ahab, penetrates his basement abode, his oceanic depths.

To conclude, and to return to the larger political implications of my intertextual argument, I would like to throw one more *Moby-Dick* film intertext into the tank, 1975's *Jaws*. In an interview with Steven Spielberg, the director relates that he and the producers had to fire one of the early screenwriters because he insisted on calling the shark from Peter Benchley's novel a whale. The irony of course is that the screenwriter was right; Benchley's novel is a sort of popular culture version of Melville's novel.

The political significance of this observation is best appreciated by turning our attention back to William Spanos. To conclude his book, Spanos compares Melville's novel to Michael Herr's Vietnam novel, *Dispatches*, suggesting that Melville's "errant art" lies in its ability to indict the American imperialist project in its infancy. Unfortunately, no one listened to Melville, and when they did, reconstructed his critique of imperialism into a Cold War defense of freedom. The legacy of this, Spanos argues, is the disastrous American experience in Vietnam.

I believe *Jaws* is a *Moby-Dick* film in this Cold War sense. It is a film that features a crazed sea captain, Quint, who relentlessly pursues his object to the point of apocalypse. Both his boat, the Orca, and he himself, like Ahab, are destroyed by the shark. Like Melville's novel as read by the Cold War critics, the representatives of normative American whiteness survive in the guise of Chief Brody and Hooper, Ishmaels in their own way.

In terms of gender, the marginalization of women in *Jaws* is deliberate and diabolical in a way never approached by *Moby-Dick*. For *Jaws* is a backlash film against the Women's Liberation Movement. A sexually active woman is the shark's first victim, predicting the narrative tradition of the slasher film for which *Jaws* is the prototype: one victim after the other dismembered by the monster. Chrissie's jog into the water is then answered at the end of the first act of the film, as Quint's sexist banter frightens Mrs. Brodie, the only other major female character in the film, away from the dock. Mrs. Brodie is literally banished from the film, forced to answer Chrissie's sexual advance into the water with a maternal retreat back to her children on shore. From this point onward, *Jaws* becomes a war film in which the grizzled sergeant, Quint, must train his recruits, the technologically inclined but green "lieutenant" Hooper and the equally green grunt "private," Chief Brodie.

A reading of *Jaws* as a war film is illuminated by Spanos's reading of *Moby-Dick* as a text that resonates with the Vietnam War. For *Jaws*, released the same year as the fall of Saigon, is a film that proposes how America should have won the Vietnam War. While drinking one night on the boat, Quint tells the story of why he will never put on a life jacket ever again: he was on the *USS Indianapolis*, the boat that delivered the atomic bomb at the end of World War II, but was then sunk by a Japanese submarine. Forced to fight off shark attacks day and night, Quint was one of the lucky survivors, as most of his buddies were eaten.

Like *Moby-Dick* before it, *Jaws* sets up a complex allegorical structure. When Chief Brody stuffs an oxygen tank down the shark's throat and uses his rifle to blow him up, *Jaws* is producing a multifaceted image. After Brodie blows up the

shark, it sinks to the bottom of the ocean, looking distinctly like a sinking submarine. Thus, Brodie is able to avenge the shark's murder of his friend Quint, which is polysemically also revenge against the Japanese who traumatized him via his experience on the *USS Indianapolis*.

This collapse has frightening allegorical consequences on the 1975 context of *Jaws*. For if the use of the nuclear bomb at Hiroshima is celebrated by Quint ("We delivered the bomb...August 1945"), then the film's positioning of Brodie's lesson as doing the same to the shark means allegorically that the way to win Vietnam would be the re-use of similar atomic weaponry. Throughout the film, the shark is positioned as a Vietcong-like entity: skulking around an underwater jungle, unseen, ready to spring out at any unexpected moment. And after all, the beach is the safe place for Americans, both in Vietnam and in *Jaws*.

On the last page of Spanos's book, he reflects on the significance of his study. He claims, "It is not, to extend a resonant motif in Michel Foucault, simply a genealogy, a 'history of Melville's present': it is also a history of the American future, of the present historical occasion that we precariously inhabit" (278). Unfortunately, this paper concludes that George Bush as Ahab, the son of the George Bush who really did re-win Vietnam in the guise of the Gulf War, affirms the bleak prediction that Spanos made in 1995.

Source: Walter C. Metz, "The Cold War's 'Undigested Apple-Dumpling': Imaging Moby-Dick in 1956 and 2001," in *Literature Film Quarterly*, Vol. 32, No. 3, 2004, pp. 222–28.

John Carman

In the following review, Carman compares the 1998 adaptation of Moby-Dick *with John Huston's 1956 adaptation.*

These are the voyages of the whaling ship *Pequod*, where an allegorical sea captain obsesses once again over a metaphorical white whale.

Bless cable's USA Network for bringing four hours of Herman Melville's *Moby Dick* to television (in two parts, at 8 p.m. Sunday and Monday) with Patrick Stewart, known most dearly as Jean-Luc Picard of *Star Trek: The Next Generation*, starring as Captain Ahab.

It's ambitious, it's high-minded, it's sometimes lovely to look at and, here and there, it's even exciting to watch. It also took nerve; John Huston couldn't quite sink his harpoon into

Melville in the 1956 screen version, so who's to think a TV remake could succeed?

Sadly, it doesn't. This *Moby Dick* drifts into the doldrums, where its sails sag, and the movie practically stops dead. It rallies mildly at the end and then, however nobly, it's gone.

Moby Dick is an Australian and British co-production, apparently with substantial American participation. Francis Ford Coppola is one of the executive producers. Franc Roddam (*Quadrophenia*), who is English, directed. Besides Stewart, the cast includes Henry Thomas (*E.T.*) as the story's sailor narrator, Ishmael; Ted Levine as the conflicted first mate, Starbuck; and Piripi Waretini as the tattooed Indian harpooner, Queequeg.

And there's a sharp little salute to the 1956 film, with Gregory Peck getting a single big scene as the bellowing Father Mapple, who preaches brimstone and Jonah from his ship's-bow pulpit in Nantucket.

All those years ago, Peck was accused of a plywood performance as Ahab, the peg-legged captain who regards the elusive white whale as evil incarnate.

If Peck had a certain Gothic quality as Ahab, with his deep voice and fierce eyebrows, Stewart gives the role his best Shakespearean shot—gruff but definitely declamatory.

But he too is beaten. There is a nice hint of self-awareness in his Ahab, as if he knows he's mad yet desperately wants to win his ship's crew over to his obsession. That's as interesting as it gets. We can see, finally, that this simply isn't a rangy part. Melville's captain is a great literary creation, but he is idea more than man. There isn't much flesh and blood for an actor to ply.

The rest of the cast doesn't pick up the slack. And once the *Pequod* is sailing hither and yon in search of Moby Dick, there is a great deal of slack in the action.

Thomas is a cipher as Ishmael, and Waretini, a Maori from New Zealand, soon ceases to startle with his bogeyman tricks as Queequeg. The liveliest presence on board the *Pequod* is Hugh Keays-Byrne, an Australian actor, as the robust second mate Stubb.

What this *Moby Dick* does best is to re-create the raucous life aboard a 19th century sailing ship—the hazing, the pest-infected food, the quick tempers and rough comradeship.

That pinch of veracity extends to the on-board processing of freshly harpooned whales. After one frenzied hunt in Monday's segment, the ship's deck is crowded with fleshy slabs and organs from the slain animal, and the men's clothes are soaked in blood.

I wondered how this *Moby Dick* would handle a change in audience perceptions about whaling. That was the deft answer. The ships were slaughterhouses; nothing more need be shown or said . . .

Source: John Carman, "*Moby Dick* Sinks under Its Weight," in *San Francisco Chronicle*, March 13, 1998, p. C1.

SOURCES

Brill, Lesley, *John Huston's Filmmaking*, Cambridge University Press, 1997, pp. 7–10, 67.

Huston, John, *An Open Book*, Alfred A. Knopf, 1980, pp. 252–60.

Jameson, Richard T., "John Huston," in *Perspectives on John Huston*, edited by Stephen Cooper, G. K. Hall, 1994, pp. 37–88.

Irenaeus, *Against Heresies*, in *The Ante-Nicene Christian Fathers*, Vol. 1, edited by Alexander Roberts and James Donaldson, Charles Scribner's Sons, 1913, pp. 354–58.

Laws, Page, "King Adapter: Huston's Famous and Infamous Adaptations of Literary Classics," in *John Huston: Essays on a Restless Director*, edited by Tony Tracy and Roddy Flynn, McFarland, 2010, pp. 123–35.

Melville, Herman, *Moby Dick, or the Whale*, in *Redburn, White-Jacket and Moby Dick*, Library of America, 1983, pp. 771–1408.

Moby Dick, DVD, MGM Vintage Classic, 2001.

Plato: The Collected Dialogues, Including the Letters, Bollingen Series LXXI, edited by Edith Hamilton and Huntington Cairns, Princeton University Press, 1961.

Sobchack, Vivian C., "Beyond Visual Aids: American Film as American Culture," in *American Quarterly*, Vol. 32, No. 3, 1980, pp. 280–300.

FURTHER READING

Bradbury, Ray, *Green Shadows, White Whale*, Alfred A, Knopf, 1992.
    Ray Bradbury wrote the screenplay for Huston's *Moby Dick*. Huston invited him to a manor house he was renting in Ireland for the purpose. This story uses a frame that is a fictionalized memoir of that experience, into

which are set several short stories based on Irish folktales. The title plays on *White Hunter, Black Heart*, Peter Viertel's 1953 novel, also based on Huston's life.

Forester, C. S., *Mr. Midshipman Hornblower*, Back Bay, 1998.

It is often observed that at the surface level *Moby-Dick* is a boy's sea adventure story, a genre that is well represented by the series of Horatio Hornblower novels. *Mr. Midshipman Hornblower* is part of the sixteen-volume series that concerns the adventures of a young British Navy officer during the Napoleonic Wars of the early nineteenth century.

Layton, Bentley, *The Gnostic Scriptures: A New Translation with Annotations and Introductions*, Yale University Press, 1995.

Gnosticism is one of the main themes of *Moby-Dick*. Thanks to archaeological discoveries as well as renewed attention to obscure Gnostic texts known since the seventeenth century, we now have a far broader knowledge of the Gnostic religion than Melville had at his disposal. Layton here translates the widest variety of texts available in any anthology, with extensive explanatory introductions and commentaries.

Philbrick, Nathaniel, *In the Heart of the Sea: The Tragedy of the Whaleship* Essex, W. W. Norton, 2001.

Philbrick presents a popular history of the sinking of the *Essex*, an event that served as one of the inspirations for *Moby-Dick*, with extensive examination of original documents.

SUGGESTED SEARCH TERMS

Herman Melville

John Huston

Moby Dick AND Huston

Moby Dick AND film adaptations

sperm whale

whaling

Gnosticism

Ophites

Divination

The Monkey Wrench Gang

EDWARD ABBEY

1975

The Monkey Wrench Gang is the most widely read and uproarious novel by Edward Abbey, an American writer whose unbounded appreciation for nature—and outspoken disdain for the bureaucratic and industrial interests that spoil it—earned him legendary status in environmental circles. Born in the Northeast, Abbey fell in love with the majestic rocky canyons, plateaus, buttes, and deserts of the Southwest. He moved there in the late 1940s to attend university and later spent numerous seasons serving in such jobs as fire lookout and park ranger. His earliest novels address the passing of the true and honorable cowboy mentality and lifestyle in a somewhat fatalistic way, as if conceding the eclipse of an era. By the 1970s, however, Abbey was goaded by civilization's affronts to his adopted homeland—especially the damming of the Colorado River at Glen Canyon in 1963—to write a more proactive, inspirational, and controversial tale, one that effectively introduced to literature a new breed of cowboy, the eco-vigilante.

First published in 1975, *The Monkey Wrench Gang* revolves around the activities of four individuals who band together for their common goal: to preserve the wilderness of their home region using any and all means deemed both necessary and morally justified. Not content to merely protest, sign petitions, or lobby the government, they start off by sabotaging a herd of construction vehicles being used to level and desecrate the landscape for the sake of a convenient

Edward Abbey (© Everett Collection Inc | Alamy)

byway. As time passes, the gang's methods, ethics, and circumstances evolve in riveting ways.

Readers should be aware that in this cult classic of the seventies, the author makes liberal use of off-color language and periodic reference to the various parts of the human body and their biological functions; this includes a few vaguely detailed scenes of a sexual nature. There is also very mellow drug use and a fair deal of gleefully unbridled violence against machines and other man-made things.

AUTHOR BIOGRAPHY

Edward Paul Abbey was born on January 29, 1927, in Indiana, Pennsylvania. His family lived in the Appalachian backwoods near the town of Home. His father, Paul Revere Abbey, was a logger, trapper, and farmer. He was an anarchist (someone who believes in rebellion against established authority), and although he was agnostic (believing that God is unknowable), he had a rigid sense of morality. The family lived the lives of self-sufficient pioneers. Abbey's mother,

Mildred, was an artistic and intelligent school-teacher and choir organist.

Abbey immersed himself in the woods around their home, where he and his four younger siblings imagined Indian spirits still lingered. He would avoid farm chores whenever possible but would listen with rapt attention when his father discussed with friends Soviet Communism, socialism, and radical labor organizers. His father also recited the poems of Walt Whitman. Abbey's own literary inclinations emerged early on; in the fifth grade, he created a newspaper for his siblings and friends to read and produced a comic book, *The Adventures of Lucky Stevens*.

In 1944, appalled by industrial advances into his beloved woods, Abbey hitchhiked through the West. Occasionally performing migrant work like fruit picking, he saw places ranging from Yosemite National Park to the southwestern rangelands and desert, which, in particular, captured his heart. He returned to Pennsylvania to finish high school as a top student and was drafted into the military just as World War II was winding down. From 1945 to 1947, he received basic training and then served police duty in Naples, Italy.

Upon returning home, he locally advocated draft evasion, bringing him to the attention of the FBI, which would monitor him for a number of years. Under the GI Bill, Abbey attended the University of New Mexico, where his singular personality as a literary environmental beatnik anarchist began to solidify. He best loved spending his time writing, exploring the desert, and chasing after women; between 1950 and his death, he would go through five marriages and father five children. He graduated in 1951 with a degree in English and philosophy and earned a Fulbright to study in Edinburgh, Scotland. When he returned, he gained work as a fire lookout in New Mexico's Carson National Forest.

Abbey published his first novel, *Jonathan Troy*, in 1954. Over the next two decades, while continuing with his writing, he worked in such wilderness refuges as the Gila Forest, Sunset Crater National Monument, Casa Grande National Monument, and Canyonlands National Park. His 1956 novel, *The Brave Cowboy*, a western with modern touches, would later be turned into the feature film *Lonely Are the Brave*; Abbey played a bit part as a cop. After writing another novel, Abbey gained a great deal of literary traction with *Desert Solitaire* (1968), which contained nonfiction essays about his season at Arches National Monument ten years earlier. In the book, he explains that nature is the ideal place for humankind to find fulfillment and that the wilderness must be preserved from the onslaughts of industrial development and pave-over-everything tourism.

Writing another novel and several more collections of nature essays through the early 1970s, Abbey became famous, especially among environmentalists. In 1975, he published *The Monkey Wrench Gang*, for which he did much undocumented field research. For the remainder of his life, he spent time writing, teaching, lecturing, and supporting the activist movement he inspired, Earth First! He was eventually afflicted with esophageal varices, which involves internal bleeding connected to the liver. He died on March 14, 1989, on the outskirts of Tucson, Arizona. According to his wishes, he was illegally buried by his friends beneath a pile of rocks in a secret spot out in the desert.

MEDIA ADAPTATIONS

- Though it was optioned by Hollywood during Abbey's lifetime, *The Monkey Wrench Gang* was yet to be adapted as a film as of 2012. A production is planned for release as early as 2013, directed by Henry Joost and Ariel Schulman.

- For a tenth-anniversary edition, *The Monkey Wrench Gang* was republished with illustrations by R. Crumb in 1985. While Abbey's text sketches out caricatures of the main characters, Crumb's cartoonish yet realistic drawings bring these caricatures to life, directly shifting the reader's visual conception of the novel onto a comical, even absurdist plane.

PLOT SUMMARY

Prologue

The Monkey Wrench Gang opens with a prologue, ironically titled "The Aftermath"; presumably, the bulk of the story will take place before the action described here. With long lines of automobiles waiting to cross the Glen Canyon bridge for its grand opening, while a group of Indians watch from a hillside, the official ribbon cutting is interrupted when the ribbon proves to be a fuse that sets off fireworks. After everyone flees, real explosives destroy the bridge. Authorities believe that those responsible are now targeting the Glen Canyon Dam.

Chapters 1–4

The first four chapters give the origins of the four major characters. Dr. A. K. Sarvis is driven around by Bonnie Abbzug, his nurse and romantic partner, to destroy billboards by dousing them with gasoline and torching them.

George Hayduke, a recently returned Vietnam War veteran, leaves home in Tucson, Arizona, to drive toward the Grand Canyon, drinking and pitching his beer cans along the roadside. Remembering a cop named Hall who once unjustly arrested him for public intoxication in Flagstaff, Hayduke stakes out Hall's house, steals his cop car, taunts the police over the radio, and leaves

the car in front of an oncoming train, which smashes it. Hayduke escapes on foot and proceeds in his jeep toward Lee's Ferry, stopping at a bridge just before to climb up a knoll and howl over the canyon.

After visiting a couple of his three wives in Utah, "Seldom Seen" Smith collects supplies and arranges for assistance for his next trip with the outdoor adventuring business he runs, Back of Beyond. Hiring a woman to drive, he heads toward Page, Arizona, and Lee's Ferry. Crossing the bridge over Glen Canyon, they stop in the middle, and Smith prays for an earthquake to destroy the dam. At Lee's Ferry, they hear a distant howl.

As for Bonnie, she fell in with Doc Sarvis after his wife died and he pathetically appealed to her for consolation. But she remains independent, living in a small geodesic dome elsewhere in Albuquerque, New Mexico. After she and Doc, on their rounds, happen upon a billboard with metal supports, they get an acetylene torch and return the next night to cut it down. At a celebratory dinner out, he asks her to marry him, but she refuses. He invites her on a trip down the Colorado River with Seldom's outfit.

Chapters 5–7

As the rafting trip is set to begin, the boatman Smith had arranged for is absent; for a replacement, he hires the disheveled Hayduke. The driver picks up Sarvis and Abbzug, and two secretaries from San Diego arrive separately. As they ride three rafts lashed together, Hayduke holds his own as oarsman until some rapids spill him out. The group stops to make camp, and Seldom ogles Bonnie. They drink and eat around the fire, and after the women retire for the night, the three men make a pact to start wreaking havoc with the destructive industry overrunning the region—with the Glen Canyon Dam their ultimate target.

Collecting needed items—explosives, gloves, peanut butter, etcetera, but no guns—they deposit hidden caches around the region. Just west of Blanding, Utah, they stop and scout out Comb Wash, where a new road is being paved, and construction vehicles seem to be left unattended at night. Camping up on Comb Ridge, they descend during the night for sabotage, pulling up survey stakes along the way. Sarvis takes the first lookout post, and the others proceed to the vehicles, where Smith and Hayduke clip wires, add sand to engine oil, and pour Karo into gas tanks. A night patrol drops by, but Doc warns the others with an owl call. They hide and then head back to camp.

Hayduke sticks around after the others leave, waking before dawn. He watches as the crews arrive and find their machines inoperable or breaking down. Heading north along the ridge toward the old road, Hayduke stops to nap, continues down to Comb Wash onto a plateau, and then sleeps for the night. At dawn, he wakes and follows the planned new road, pulling up all the survey stakes along some twenty miles, to find the rest of the group further on at Natural Bridges National Monument.

Chapters 8–10

Leaving the campground in Smith's truck, they meet a roadblock set by the San Juan County Search & Rescue Team, led by Bishop Love. Love describes the bootprints of the saboteur, but Smith plays dumb. Hayduke pretends to nap in the back of the truck. Sarvis and Abbzug fly out of Fry Canyon, and Smith and Hayduke proceed to scout out the three sequential bridges at White, Narrow, and Dirty Devil Canyons, with the Colorado River flooded below to form the squalid Lake Powell. At the last bridge, they

find an airstrip construction site near Hite Marina, where a workman abandons his bulldozer, apparently leaving the rotor arm in; knowing they can start the machine, they head down, and Smith gives Hayduke a crash course in driving it. Hayduke plows into a loader and sends both vehicles over the canyon wall. They flee.

Having pulled onto a side road to let the workman's truck fly past, Smith and Hayduke watch as the truck meets Love's rescue team over Narrow Canyon; the team heads back to the dirt road, and the two saboteurs race ahead. They set fire to a cattle guard, but Love drives his Blazer straight through the flames. The saboteurs head up an antique trail, and Hayduke gets out to lever rocks into the road; eventually he sets several loose down the slopes, with the biggest crushing Love's Blazer. Smith and Hayduke escape.

In Albuquerque, Doc and Bonnie go shopping for explosive materials. Bonnie expresses increasing antipathy to their romantic arrangement, and Doc suspects she likes one of the other guys. She drops him off at the medical center and goes back to her dome to meditate. She is ready for serious action.

Chapters 11–14

After a business trip in Utah's Henry Mountains, Smith and Hayduke proceed southwest. Along the highway, they sabotage and torch a bulldozer. Finding a string of geophones (seismic sensors) along the road, they tear them up. At a drilling rig, Hayduke drops whatever he can down the ultra-deep hole and ruins some engines. After they find George's jeep at Wahweap Marina, George tries to drunkenly incite everyone at a bar in Page. They head for Betatakin, on the Navajo Reservation, to meet the others.

Driving to Black Mesa, they scout out the Peabody Coal excavation setup on Navajo lands. Hayduke wants to blow everything up, but the others fear loss of life. The strip-mining site is like a desolate battlefield. They plan to blow up a bridge and derail the automated coal train.

Chatting in pairs, Doc and Seldom wonder if Hayduke can be trusted. Hayduke laments to Bonnie that Smith compromises his plans. Bonnie tells Doc that both the others are crazy; then she splits up with Doc. Bonnie invites Hayduke to kiss her, but Hayduke, deferring to Doc, blows his chance.

The gang wakes before dawn to head for the BM & LP railroad at the bridge. Hayduke plants the explosives, and Bonnie is assigned to push down the blaster at his signal. When the train comes, Hayduke signals—and only then sees a man in the train. Bonnie cannot bring herself to push the handle down; Doc helps her, after the engine is past the bridge. The charges work, and as the train starts plummeting into the canyon car by car, the man inside escapes. The gang flees.

Chapters 15–19

Back at Navajo National Monument, a ranger interrogates Doc and Bonnie, asking about the departed jeep and Smith's empty truck. Dissatisfied, he demands to search their car. Inside he finds dynamite boxes—filled with foodstuffs. Bonnie says that some Shoshone Indians left the boxes behind. The rangers roar off, and Hayduke and Smith emerge from the woods.

Doc flies out of Page back to Albuquerque, while Bonnie stays with the others; before leaving, Doc tells Hayduke to feel free to pursue Bonnie. Out for a drink, a cowboy rudely overrules Bonnie's choice of Janis Joplin on the jukebox. Hayduke slugs him, insults his friends, and then gets badly beaten. While he recovers at a hotel, he and Bonnie establish intimate relations.

Smith heads back to Utah to tend to his homes and wives, leaving Bonnie and Hayduke to scout and camp at Kaibab Plateau, defacing a Smokey the Bear sign along the way. At a Georgia-Pacific Corp. clear-cutting operation at dusk, they find the work-site office evidently empty.

In Albuquerque, Sarvis performs surgery, has a couple of drinks, and bikes home. He irks and incites a truck driver, whom he baits into smashing through a billboard. At home, after a nauseating Exxon commercial, he shatters his television.

At the logging site, Bonnie acts as lookout while Hayduke begins the sabotage. While he drains some oil under a bulldozer, a man with a shotgun accosts him—but tells him to finish his task. The masked, one-eyed stranger proves to be a friend; he has bound and gagged the night watchman and teaches Hayduke to run the newer push-button machines. Two other watchmen arrive, and the stranger flees on horseback. Hayduke and Bonnie drive off.

Chapters 20–25

The two head back to the railroad, where Hayduke uses a chain saw to down eleven power-line poles, hiding from a helicopter halfway through. After the poles crash down, the helicopter returns.

At his wife Susan's house in Green River, Utah, Smith dreams of being led through the inner workings of the Glen Canyon Dam facility to face the Director—a computer. The Director interrogates and threatens him; he wakes up not knowing where he is.

The helicopter lands, and two men chase after Bonnie. They catch her in a gulch, but as they return, Hayduke ambushes them. Taking the men's guns and getting them to lie down and partially disrobe, Hayduke proceeds to set the helicopter on fire. He and Bonnie flee in the jeep. After siphoning gas from tourists at the Betatakin campground, they pass a node in the coal conveyor belt at Black Mesa. Hayduke sends Bonnie on to the Holiday Inn at Kayenta with the jeep so he can stay behind and finish the job.

At the hotel five days later, Bonnie reads about the coal train being derailed again, while explosions rent the loading and storage towers. The suspect calls himself Rudolf the Red. The group plans for blowing the big dam and move on to wait for Hayduke at the Hidden Splendor Mine.

Reaching Kayenta at last, Hayduke finds his jeep and drives north into Utah. At a café in Mexican Hat, Bishop Love and his brother, Sam, confront Hayduke. After he eats, Hayduke throws coffee in Love's face, runs for his car, and drives off. Stopping in an auto yard to let them pass him, Hayduke follows, takes a right fork (where they went left), and goes up a dirt road. Soon realizing the authorities actually have him hemmed in, he stops atop a dead-end escarpment. They slowly close in at the peak—but Hayduke and his jeep have disappeared.

Back with the others, Hayduke explains how he used the jeep's winch and a lone juniper tree to lower his jeep over the hundred-foot cliff and hide it under an overhang. After the authorities left, he drove down. The gang stays hidden under trees while a plane canvases the area.

Chapters 26–30

Breaking camp the next evening, the gang heads back to White Canyon. On the way, they send two bulldozers into a side canyon, where they burn brightly. On the bridge, Hayduke sets up some thermite, but it fails to burn through the beams. Then three vehicles approach from the west, two from the east. Cutting down a side loop to the west and waiting, they see one vehicle head their way. They shine a spotlight in the driver's eyes and squeal past, shots ringing out from behind.

Flinging some caltrops (spikes) out the back of the truck, Doc flattens the rescue team's tires. After stopping to unlock their bumpers, they head along a decrepit dirt road toward a placed called the Maze, where they previously hid two caches. The two vehicles now in pursuit far back send up flares, signalling a helicopter. Hiding their vehicles in a canyon, the saboteurs shoulder their packs and continue on foot. After a long while, the chopper spots them, and they run, dropping their packs. George rappels the others down a canyon, then slides himself down the wall.

Fleeing up the canyon and extremely thirsty, they eventually spy a tree and oasis up ahead. A frog grows suddenly quiet, and Hayduke and Smith sense a trap; they head back and go up a side canyon, which runs into a dead end. Hayduke uses a crack to climb up the wall and then hauls the others up after him. Sam Love then comes running up the canyon with a white flag, calling for the doctor. Doc demands to be lowered back down, as does Bonnie, and they run back with Sam. Sarvis gives the delirious Bishop Love, who has likely had a heart attack, an injection.

Above the Maze, Hayduke and Smith find that the authorities have set up camp at Lizard's Rock, coincidentally the site of their nearest cache. As Smith naps, Hayduke leaves in the rain to circle around to the cache. When Smith wakes, he heads for the jeep trail leading up and out of the benchlands. Reaching an overlook, he steals raw meat from elderly tourists, continues, eats the meat, and falls asleep; he hears heavy distant gunfire. He wakes to a ranger accosting him, and he confesses and is hauled away. Rumor has it that Rudolf the Red is dead.

Waiting until the authorities quit the camp, Hayduke sneaks to the cache, a hundred yards from the camp, when a dog emerges barking from the tent, followed by two men. George heads for the rim of the Maze, stranding himself on a peninsula surrounded by five-hundred-foot drops. Wedging himself down in a crack, Hayduke exchanges gunfire and then removes his soiled clothes. Sam Love and a newspaper reporter consider Hayduke's hopeless situation. When the figure of Hayduke emerges from a bush, they watch through binoculars as his body appears to be torn up by bullets, to pitch into the Green River below. Finding a trail of blood, the authorities conclude that Rudolf has been killed; Sam wonders if he is still hiding unseen down the crack.

Epilogue

There is a drawn-out legal process. Because of a lack of hard evidence, Bonnie, Doc, and Smith are able to plea bargain for one-to-five-year sentences on a single felony charge each, spending only six months in jail before being released to four and a half years' probation. Doc and Bonnie get married and live in a houseboat near Smith's residence in Green River with his one remaining wife, Susan.

They are playing poker one night two years into their probation when a masked, one-eyed stranger appears at the door and asks Doc to come see a friend. Hayduke is alive. There is a probation officer inside, so Hayduke and his friend, the masked man called Kemosabe, stay outside. Doc tells George that Bonnie is pregnant. Hayduke—now known as Fred Goodsell—asks Doc if that was them that blew the Glen Canyon bridge, but Doc professes innocence. Hayduke has a special new night watchman job; Doc does not want to know where.

CHARACTERS

Edwin P. Abbott Jr.

The ranger who interrogates Bonnie and Doc at the Navajo National Monument campground happens to bear a name strikingly similar to his creator's (the author). He falls for the gang's ploy, convinced that Shoshone Indians must be responsible for the railroad destruction. Abbott is also the ranger who arrests Smith at the end.

Bonnie Abbzug

An attractive woman in her late twenties, Bonnie proves a motivational force within the gang; Seldom, especially, is willing to follow her every move. A Jewish hippie from the Bronx with hair down her back, Bonnie lives in a geodesic dome that she built herself, listens to Ravi Shankar, meditates, and smokes marijuana. As Doc Sarvis's office assistant, she becomes involved with him when he appeals to her after the death of his wife, but she repeatedly refuses marriage.

Once the gang begins operations, Bonnie is reluctant to accept the static lookout assignments, preferring active involvement. When the time comes for her to push the plunger and blow the train off its tracks, however, she cannot do so; this reluctance, apparently moral in nature, saves a man's life. She eventually falls for

Hayduke and, breaking up with Doc, boldly invites George's advances. She is clearly affected when she professes her love for Hayduke only to hear him respond by saying "Fine" and then, "You love me and I'm glad. Now get the hell out of here." When she realizes she is risking her life to be with a man with the mentality of a kamikaze pilot, she joins Doc in assisting, and surrendering to, the authorities. Bonnie seems to conclude that whatever Doc's faults may be, at least he truly loves her. In the end, they marry, and she gets pregnant.

Colonel Jim Crumbo

A military officer, Crumbo is among those who assist in the capture of the gang outside the Maze. The reader first meets him in the prologue, where, now assigned to investigate such sabotage, he counsels the Utah governor about the destruction of Glen Canyon bridge and the targeting of the dam.

J. Bracken Dingledine

Dingledine is Bishop Love's business associate and the prosecutor in the trial of the three captured Monkey Wrench Gang members.

Driver

For the expedition on the Colorado River, Smith hires a female driver to transport his truck to their destination downstream. She is reasonable and nice.

Judge Melvin Frost

The judge in the trial of Doc, Bonnie, and Smith proves sympathetic to the convicts, obliging them to spend only six months in jail.

J. Calvin Garn

The gas-pump attendant in Glen Canyon City is a wholehearted believer in the virtues of industry.

Greenspan

The saboteurs' probation officer is a young man named Greenspan. He plays poker with them.

Officer Hall

Hayduke takes revenge on the police officer named Hall, who unjustly arrested him once, by stealing and destroying his patrol car.

George Washington Hayduke

Time has proved George W. Hayduke to be the most memorable of the various colorful characters in *The Monkey Wrench Gang*. While the novel gives fairly even attention to the four saboteurs, Hayduke is the one who steals the show, with his unique combination of coarse attitude, slovenly habits, ethical outrage, childish delight, and willingness to put his life at risk for the sake of preserving the natural ecosystems of the Southwest.

Hayduke served as a Green Beret in the Vietnam War, and as a prisoner of war, he was obliged to serve as a medic for the North Vietnamese—and to consider from the Vietnamese perspective the US war effort, which entailed extensive environmental destruction through the use of such chemicals as napalm and which took the lives of not just soldiers but Vietnamese women and children as well. When he sees the same sort of senseless environmental destruction in his own backyard, thoughts of Vietnam rise to agitate him, and he cannot bear it. His military training, especially with regard to explosives, proves essential for the gang's activities.

Despite Hayduke's uncouth nature, Bonnie recognizes his virtuousness and cannot help falling for him. Hayduke, however, has become accustomed to a life of constant action and adversarial engagement; once he formulates a mission for himself—"My job is to save the . . . wilderness"—like a true warrior he will not allow anything, even love, to prevent him from devoting himself to that mission.

Thanks to the messages he leaves behind, the authorities come to know him as "Rudolf the Red." In the end, all his dubious gambles bring a huge payoff: with circumstances forcing him to fake his death, he becomes a true man of the wilderness, living off the land in and around the Maze in the years afterward, and gets a chance to forge a convenient new identity for himself, as Fred Goodsell. At the novel's close, in light of Hayduke's inside track to the workings of Glen Canyon Dam—presumably the site of his new post as night watchman—the reader likely imagines the Monkey Wrench Gang reuniting to accomplish their greatest goal.

Kemosabe

The masked man who befriends Hayduke at the clear-cutting site and then, after George's faked death, becomes his traveling companion refers to himself only as "Kemosabe"—suggesting that he is a version of the fictional vigilante known as the Lone Ranger, of American radio, TV, and film lore. The masked man has also been identified (though not originally by the author himself) as a reincarnation of the character Jack Burns, from an earlier novel of Abbey's, *The Brave Cowboy*.

Bishop J. Dudley Love

At fifty-five, Love has accomplished a great deal in life: he is the bishop of Blanding in the Mormon church, has numerous successful economic ventures, has eight children, and is captain of the San Juan County Search and Rescue Team. He now has state-level political aspirations. Smith irked Love before by helping block his attempt to lease state land around Lake Powell. Love's selfish desire to claim the credit for the capture of the Monkey Wrench Gang allows them leeway to escape at first, but eventually state and federal authorities are summoned. The bishop becomes a more honorable man after one of his foes, Doc Sarvis, prevents him from dying of a heart attack. He forgives the destruction of his Blazer, and he presides over Doc and Bonnie's wedding.

Sam Love

The bishop's younger brother, age forty-eight, is little more than a sidekick to the domineering Dudley. Sam is an engineer for a natural gas company. His humanity shines through when he bears a white flag and begs Sarvis to attend to the bishop after he has what seems to be a heart attack. Sam also cordially arrests Doc and Bonnie. After Hayduke seems to get shot to pieces, Sam evidently keeps to himself his suspicion that "Rudolf the Red" remains hiding unseen down the crack in the cliff, enabling Hayduke's ultimate survival.

Observer

When the gang sabotages the automated train on the Black Mesa & Lake Powell railroad, there happens to be a friendly observer on board. He escapes.

Pilot

The helicopter pilot is one of the two men who chases Bonnie down when Hayduke downs the power lines during their second visit to the coal railroad. The pilot advocates the decent treatment of their prisoner; he wears purple briefs.

Dr. Alexander K. Sarvis

Pushing fifty, Doc Sarvis still has a youthful spring in his step, as seen in his habitual jaunts around Albuquerque downing billboards. Being a doctor,

he tends to see things from a scientific, logical perspective, and at times he skirts more complicated matters by, for example, identifying botanical species. While the idea to blow up the dam originates with him, his most essential contributions to the group come from his bank account. He also makes sure to preserve the integrity of the group, insisting that they act only under full consensus among all four saboteurs. His dependence on Bonnie is likely part of what leads her to stray, but heartbroken as he is, he accepts the split gracefully and continues to contribute to the group. When he gets the chance to demonstrate his honorable dedication to giving medical aid whenever needed by helping even their enemy, the bishop, Bonnie realizes that Doc, not Hayduke, is the man to settle down with.

Security Guard

During the second excursion at the railroad, a security guard emerges from the helicopter to chase and capture Bonnie. He mistreats her, despite the pilot's objections, but Hayduke turns the tables and emasculates him, taking his gun and forcing him to strip to his stained undershorts.

Reporter

At the edge of the Maze, a newspaper reporter who has been monitoring the standoff with "Rudolf the Red" informs Sam Love about the situation.

Rudolf the Red

See George Washington Hayduke

Joseph Fielding "Seldom Seen" Smith

A thirty-five-year-old "jack Mormon," meaning a lapsed one, Smith nonetheless has three wives in three different towns in Utah, whom he sees so rarely that he has earned the nickname Seldom Seen. His absences are mostly due to the adventurous outings he leads through his barely profitable Back of Beyond business, officially based in Hite, Utah, which was flooded by the hated Glen Canyon Dam. Smith resents governmental and industrial intrusion into the Southwest because he depends on the region's natural beauty for his living. He is willing to pray for a destructive earthquake, but he is reluctant to break the law at first. He comes to serve as the gang's ethical barometer, eventually swayed by Hayduke's persuasive arguments to use greater force (though not violence to humans)—especially once Bonnie stands behind Hayduke and his wild ideas.

Smith has his eyes on Bonnie for much of the book, but he never acts dishonorably toward her. Smith remains with Hayduke till nearly the end, reflecting his sincere devotion to the Monkey Wrench Gang's cause, but he is finally willing to allow himself to be arrested rather than jeopardize his life.

Kathy Smith
Kathy is one of Seldom's wives and lives in Cedar City. She divorces him after his conviction.

Sheila Smith
Sheila is one of Seldom's wives and lives in Bountiful. She divorces him after his conviction.

Susan Smith
Susan is one of Seldom's wives and lives in Green River. She patiently endures his confusion over her identity when he wakes from his nightmare, and she stays married to him after his conviction.

Waitress
At the café in Mexican Hat, Utah, a beautiful young Ute woman kindly waits on Hayduke. After he splashes coffee in the bishop's face, she takes care to wish him well.

THEMES

Nature
At the heart of Abbey's novel is the immense appreciation for nature that unites the four protagonists. Each approaches the natural world from a slightly different perspective. Smith's appreciation may appear to be founded in commercial interests, because his business depends on the wilderness, but he makes clear that he holds the greatest reverence for undisturbed nature. He claims that Glen Canyon was "the most beautiful canyon in the world" before the hated dam flooded it. Any successful wilderness guide—and Smith is moderately successful—must instill such appreciation in one's clients.

Doc's natural interests, in turn, may seem overly scientific, fond as he is of reeling off the genus and species names of plants and animals, but he is also aware of the role nature plays as a "psychiatric refuge"—something that keeps men (like him) from going mad in the sensory pressure cooker of the modern urban environment. For Bonnie, nature is a place where, unlike behind a desk, she can exercise the full use of her body—she enjoys hiking, bicycling, and camping and feels perfectly at home in the midst of wild animals. As for Hayduke, returning from the horrors of war, nobody has a greater need for the overarching tranquility in engagement that the wilderness can bring.

The phrases of both the characters and the narrator establish the natural world as veritably sacred. In his thoughts, Hayduke considers the southwestern wilderness to be "the holy land" and, later, "holy country" that must be defended. Doc likewise calls the river in the canyon "a holy place." Meanwhile, the narrator pointedly refers to a canyon called Salvation and the Sangre de Cristo (Blood of Christ) Mountains—names that shift the concept of divinity away from Christianity and onto nature. In fact, the idea of a God up in heaven is casually or comically contested in scattered instances, such as when the young Bonnie, fasting in seek of a vision, finds that "God appeared incarnate on a platter as a roasted squab with white paper booties on His little drumsticks," or when the narrator refers to Smith's prayers as "useless Mormon mumbling."

In some traditions, like that of the transcendentalists, God is, in a sense, equated with nature, but Abbey seems intent on maintaining a distinction between the two. In an exchange with Doc, Smith remarks, "One crack in that dam and nature she'll take care of the rest. Nature and God." When Doc asks, "Whose side is God on?," Smith replies, "That's something I wanta find out." In other words, it is not clear that the Christian God can even be considered allied with nature, because in the worldviews of such representatives as Bishop Love, financial and political concerns—like his investments in uranium, oil, and gas and his intended tourist development on state land by Lake Powell—outweigh the preservation of natural resources and beauty. Thus the reader, instead of concluding that God is nature, may conclude that God is whatever God is, but nature is divine.

Industrialization
Diametrically opposed to the notion of the sacredness of nature is the Western industrial notion of the sacredness of machines. Abbey's over-the-top text may at times suggest that this motif of machines as sacred is invoked simply for comedic effect. For example, when the gang first destroys an earth-moving machine, "All were impressed by what they had done. The murder

TOPICS FOR FURTHER STUDY

- Create a map that includes all of the sites visited by the protagonists in *The Monkey Wrench Gang*, either using posterboard or on a computer. Trace out the routes that the gang members follow over the course of the story (with a different color for each character), labeling distances as appropriate. Include information boxes (using lines or links) that provide information about the gang's targets and destinations, such as the Peabody Coal Company operation, the bridges they seek to destroy, and the Maze.

- Read *Hoot* (2006), by Carl Hiaasen, a young-adult novel about the efforts of a group of adolescents to save a habitat for endangered owls from the construction of a restaurant. Write an essay analyzing the merits of this novel, drawing comparisons to *The Monkey Wrench Gang* where appropriate. Give consideration to the personality types of the characters and how they fit the circumstances; the use of comedy and action to usher the story along; the aptness of explanatory text regarding the real-life

problems the novel addresses; and other qualities worthy of comment.

- Write a research paper on the establishment, activities, and evolution of the environmental activism organization Earth First! Be sure to profile the founding personalities, relate major protests and accomplishments, and address the extent of Abbey's involvement, citing relevant speeches and writings and describing the impact of his participation.

- Use the Internet and local libraries to research the construction and operation of a hydroelectric dam in your state or region. Try to locate pictures of the stretch of river in question before it was dammed and flooded; if possible, interview someone who was familiar with the river in its original state. Also, conduct e-mail correspondence with current dam officials to help you compile information on the profits accrued by the dam and where that money goes. Produce a written report or a multimedia presentation to share the results of your research with your class and draw conclusions about the dam.

---

of a machine. Deicide. All of them, even Hayduke, a little awed by the enormity of their crime. By the sacrilege of it." Abbey's melodramatization of their awe serves to better illuminate the true feeling there.

In the code of American ethics, the right to private property plays a foundational role in shaping the character of both individuals and society. From the land people claim as "theirs" to the houses in which they can securely accumulate belongings (often unneeded), the entire American lifestyle is founded in the notion of private property. Many Native American groups had no such notions, especially not with regard to the land. Crops raised and game killed by a given community would surely be claimed by that community but not by individuals; rather,

everyone in the community would share in the proceeds, and no one within the community would profit at the others' expense. The land was not parceled up for persons but claimed by communities—a practice preserved in the establishment of American Indian reservations.

In the present day, the notion of private property is so ingrained in the American psyche that in *The Monkey Wrench Gang*, "even Hayduke," the biggest anarchist of them all, still has an internal sense of how wrong it is to disrespect another person's property. The narrator reinforces this by continuing to satirically refer to machines in divine terms, such as when a bulldozer looms over Hayduke and Smith "with the indifference of a god." The jamming of an engine's pistons is imagined to perhaps be "a

The team wants to protect the environment of the American west. (© *Konstantin Sutyagin / Shutterstock.com*)

crime against nature in the eyes of *deus ex machina*"; the Latin phrase ordinarily refers to a plot device introduced at the end of a novel to conveniently resolve the conflict but here is adapted by Abbey to more literally mean "the god from the machine"—the god of industry that inhabits and emanates from the machine.

In fact, machines and technology hold such sway over ordinary Americans that the gang's outlook on what they are up against gradually changes to reflect their realization of this. Early on Smith says to Hayduke of the authorities, "They're people too, like us. We got to remember that." However, by the time they are considering those responsible for the sprawling, monstrous coal-extraction setup, Smith remarks, "It ain't people. It's a mechanical animal." Doc affirms this thought: "We're not dealing with human beings. We're up against the megamachine. A megalomaniacal megamachine." Doc also later calls this foe "a *mad machine*...which mangles mountains and devours men." The idea of a mad machine representing modern culture is personified in Smith's nightmare as the Director, who effectively plugs Smith into the great system and threatens to dismember him.

The imagery may be extreme, but Abbey thus makes the metaphorical point that the man who cedes to the demands of machines and technology—the ease of travel for beloved cars, the ubiquity of electricity and telephone lines (and now cable and cellular service), the functionality of computerized devices—is in the end so beholden to those machines and devices that he can no longer function as a living, breathing human being. Rather, he has become little more than an assistant, a caretaker for the things that supposedly belong to him but, in reality, to which he belongs.

Environmentalism

Knowing that they are up against a larger American culture whose collective soul has been taken over by the megamachine formed by the coalition of capitalist industry and government—"its brain a bank of computer data centers, its blood the flow of money, its heart a radioactive dynamo, its language the technetronic [sic] monologue of number imprinted on magnetic tape"—the four eco-vigilantes go to great lengths to moralize and justify the approach to environmentalism that they adopt. At first, the reluctance of the three most rational members of the gang—Bonnie, Smith, and Doc—to engage in any sort of explosive violence rules the day. As Smith says, "We can't do it right if we do it wrong." Gradually, however, as Hayduke realizes how ultimately ineffective a moderate tack will be—the machines will just get fixed or replaced—he convinces the others that to make a real difference, they need to not just slow but destroy the enemy machines and infrastructure.

While the bulk of the novel is devoted to this destruction, the crimes against nature committed by industry are elaborated in scattered locations: barbed-wire fences kill wild animals by the thousands, America is said to account for "six percent of the world's population gulping down forty percent of the world's oil," industrial smog has come to blanket the entire Rio Grande valley, with lung cancer and leukemia on the rise. As the novel suggests, government cannot be trusted to alleviate these problems because industrial and state interests like US Steel and the Pentagon are "intertwined in incestuous embrace," too self-involved to care that they are profiting at the expense of the priceless natural world.

Although Abbey has his characters draw the conclusion that extremist action is needed to confront this "conglomerated cartel," he also throws into question the sanity of the lead saboteur, Hayduke, and the gang ceases to function once the other three get arrested and Hayduke disappears. Then again, Abbey does allude to a new generation of activists responsible for the destruction of Glen Canyon bridge, and the Monkey Wrench Gang is poised to reunite at the novel's close. Thus, while this extreme activism makes for a good adventure story, the reader must conclude for oneself whether or not any actual persons would be wise to engage in such activism.

STYLE

Entertainment

Regarding his nuanced intentions in writing *The Monkey Wrench Gang*, Abbey remarked in a *Publishers Weekly* interview (cited by Ann Ronald in *The New West of Edward Abbey*) soon after its publication,

> I think of it primarily as an adventure story with an environmental theme.... I guess you could say there is also a strong element of wish fulfillment. Everyone will read it in their

own way, but I intended it to be mock-heroic, or perhaps a little more than that. But above all I wanted it to be entertaining.

Indeed, the reader cannot fail to absorb the sense that Abbey must have had a great deal of fun writing this novel. To begin with, the characters straddle a fine line between complexity and caricature. Abbey has given them adequate backstories explaining the sources of their antagonism to industry and bureaucracy, and their outlooks evolve in sensible ways in the course of the novel. On the other hand, the physical descriptions verge on the cartoonish, such as where Smith is "lean as a rake" with large hands and feet, "a nose like a beak, a big Adam's apple, ears like the handle on a jug, sun-bleached hair like a rat's nest, and a wide and generous grin." These metaphors can only leave the reader with a comical image. As for Hayduke, his hairiness and apelike stature are frequently invoked. It is no wonder that the famed countercultural artist Robert Crumb was enlisted to provide illustrations for a 1985 reissue of *The Monkey Wrench Gang*, putting the comic aspects of the novel front and center.

With the sabotage and adventure, Abbey uses straightforward realism to bring the reader along for the ride, going into precise detail with regard to how the billboards are brought down, how the old construction vehicles are cranked into gear, and how the explosives are planted at the coal railroad. Some may find the abundance of fine details overwhelming, but in terms of the style, they effectively balance the comedic elements, leaving the reader engrossed in a world that is not so vague as to seem strictly fantastic, yet not so mundane as to seem strictly real. In other words, the reader is easily swept up in the entertaining adventure.

Postmodernism

Abbey's novel bears a few hallmarks of the postmodern era in which it was written, and his treatment of the material as such in this case proves especially apt. A postmodern outlook is laid out in the very first words, in the author's note that precedes everything else: "This book, though fictional in form, is based strictly on historical fact. Everything in it is real or actually happened. And it all began just one year from today." Quite the opposite of an ordinary disclaimer denying any connections between the fiction and reality, this note proclaims that everything in the book truly occurred—but in an indefinite future defined as a year from the unspecified day that Abbey wrote the note in Wolf Hole, Arizona—or perhaps a year from the day that the reader reads the note. This note can thus be seen to frame the novel as anything from prediction to prophecy to historical record. Then, where the prologue marks "The Aftermath" while the epilogue marks "The New Beginning," the sense of the novel's unique engagement with historical reality is reinforced. In a postmodern way, the reader's chronological expectations are thrown to the wind. At the end, the anticipation of the future destruction of Glen Canyon Dam is left intact; the potential energy signified by that possibility is sustained and thus left with the reader upon the novel's close.

Another postmodern aspect of the novel is the narrator's occasional direct engagement with the action, repeatedly drawing attention to the fictional nature of the work. For example, after Smith and Hayduke sabotage the geophones and the oil rig, a narrated paragraph that begins, "Into other parts" and ends by referring to "the wrinkled skin of the Utahn earth" leads directly to Hayduke's question, "We're still in Utah?" It is as if the narrator's comments elicit the character's question. Elsewhere, the narrator favors a certain phrasing, as Hayduke "slept the sleep of the just—the just plain tired" and then Smith and Hayduke "slept the sleep of the just. The just plain satisfied." Doc echoes this narrative quirk, as he tells Smith, "Our cause is just (just one damn thing after another)"—another conflation of narrator and character that may inspire a double take in the reader. Later, Hayduke is also cued by the narrator: "And come to think of it—'And come to think of it,' he adds . . . ."

Not content to provide an involved but anonymous narrator, Abbey specifically invokes himself more than once, such as in the conspicuous naming of one forest ranger as Edwin P. Abbott Jr. He also mentions a "personally autographed extremely valuable first-edition copy of *Desert Solipsism*"—a play on Abbey's critically acclaimed essay collection *Desert Solitaire* (originally named "Desert Solecism") that both exaggerates the value of the work and also belittles, through the pun, the self-centered author. In sum, this unorthodox involvement by the narrator can be seen to undercut the reader's engagement in the fictional reality the story presents. Abbey enjoyed riling the orthodox; if one is too uptight to appreciate these moments when

Abbey winks at the reader through the text, then perhaps one takes things too seriously to appreciate such an outlandish novel anyway.

Treatise

While Abbey professed his intent to entertain with this novel, suggesting that the portrayals are only "mock-heroic," and used a postmodern approach that may distance the reader from the text, he also confessed that he intended "perhaps a little more than" just mock heroism. In other words, while his characters may be caricatures on the surface, the environmentally conscious message of the novel remains and stands on its own merits. Whether or not the reader agrees with the tactics of the Monkey Wrench Gang, one has to appreciate that there are in reality expansive environmental tragedies being enacted in the Southwest and in fact pretty much everywhere, and something must be done to address them.

In this vein, Abbey presents the possibilities of both social activism—such as, but not restricted to, the sort engaged in by the gang— and the individual activism of an altered lifestyle: of living off the land and in touch with nature (as Hayduke does); or perhaps in a sustainable way in a small town, maintaining farm or ranch land for support (as Smith does); or making as small an imprint as possible on the environment, such as by riding bicycles instead of cars when possible (as Doc and Bonnie do). Thus in writing a book that has found its way into the hands of a great number of readers in large part because of its entertainment value, Abbey also exposed all these readers to a sort of freewheeling treatise on environmental ethics, advocating not despair but hope, not indifference but active involvement.

HISTORICAL CONTEXT

Eco-sabotage and the Environmental Movement

As a work of literature, *The Monkey Wrench Gang* has a singular relationship to historical reality. Some historical novels are based on precisely what is known about an event or time period, and some embellish the known details with invented characters and occasions. Abbey's novel is loosely based on some of his own experiences, but the precise nature of that relationship can only be vaguely sketched out, because he

COMPARE & CONTRAST

- **1970s:** With political attention over the preceding decades directed primarily toward the civil rights movement and the Vietnam War, environmental concerns have been left out of mainstream discussions. Legal environmental protections are few, with the Sierra Club (established in 1892) and the much-younger Greenpeace (established in 1971) being the major outlets for involvement and protest.

  Today: With global warming threatening to exacerbate droughts and extreme weather events—and even inundate entire island nations—the environment is a top concern among progressive governments. In America, a wide range of newer activist organizations, such as the Natural Resources Defense Council, the Pew Environment Group, and Earth First!, have joined the fight to protect the wilderness.

- **1970s:** Following the creation of Lake Powell, the Glen Canyon National Recreation Area is established in 1972. As a recreation area, rather than a national park or monument, the accommodation of human activities, rather than strict ecological preservation, is the priority.

  Today: For those tourists who would prefer not to leave the comfort of their homes, the Glen Canyon National Recreation Area can be "explored" via Facebook and YouTube pages, a blog, podcasts, and even e-hikes.

- **1970s:** In 1979, the Roadless Area Review and Evaluation (RARE) II project designates less than a quarter of existing roadless areas as protected wilderness, angering environmental advocates like Earth First! cofounder Dave Foreman.

  Today: Following a project initiated by the Bill Clinton administration, the Roadless Area Conservation Rule of 2001 protects the remaining 58.5 million acres of US roadless areas from logging, mining, and drilling. Timber and state interests litigate to block the rule, causing extended uncertainty, but in 2011 the 10th US Circuit Court of Appeals definitively upholds the rule.

---

could reveal few specifics of any actual sabotage undertaken as "research."

Still, a number of interesting details can be found in biographical sources such as *Adventures with Ed: A Portrait of Abbey*, written by Jack Loeffler, Abbey's closest male friend. Loeffler quotes another friend, John DePuy, who relates that around 1960 in Taos, New Mexico, where Abbey was then the editor of the weekly newspaper *El crepúscolo de la libertad*, the newspaper's staff made multiple excursions downing billboards with chain saws—and one time they even ran into the local pharmacist and a poet who were doing the same thing. DePuy related in an interview (cited by David Pozza in *Bedrock and Paradox: The Literary Landscape of Edward Abbey*) a classic anecdote about the aftermath

of their destruction of a dozen Melody Sign Company billboards:

> The next week, the owner of the company came to put an ad in the paper for the apprehension of these criminals, and Ed being the editor took the ad and burst out laughing, so Mr. Melody asked him what was so funny. He said, "nothing, I'm thinking of something else."

As Loeffler quotes, after advancing to pouring sand in the crankcases of construction equipment, Abbey once remarked, "We really ought to throw a monkey wrench in it."

It was around this time that plans for the damming of the Colorado River at Glen Canyon came to the fore. Although the Grand Canyon, farther down the same river, received the bulk of tourist attention in the Southwest for its sheer vastness and accessibility, the more remote Glen

Canyon rivaled its neighbor in terms of geologic beauty and intricacy. However, environmental protection laws were minimal in that era, leaving the government leeway to infiltrate the wilderness with little to no public notice. This is not to say there was no chance for the dam plan to be stopped, but ironically, even tragically, the plans were given a seal of approval by the Sierra Club, which allowed the project to continue in order to ensure that a different site, Echo Park in Dinosaur National Monument, would be preserved.

Bureaucrats imagined that the dam would prove a hydroelectric economic boon and would resolve interstate disputes over access to the waters of the Colorado River basin. Authorized in 1956, the concrete dam was finished in 1963, staunching the Colorado's flow and creating the artificial Lake Powell, with over 1,800 miles of sprawling shoreline marking out the flooded canyons. Abbey is said to have been one of the last people lucky enough to float through Glen Canyon, which he considered the very heart of the canyonlands, before it was inundated—and he was heartbroken. In Loeffler's words, "He was haunted by the Glen Canyon Dam, that symbol of the prevailing cultural paradigm of turning habitat into money."

By the early 1970s—shortly after the death of his third wife, Judy, of leukemia—Abbey was ready to direct his anarchist impulses toward the despised industrial development that surrounded him. (The thesis that earned him a master's degree from the University of New Mexico in 1956 was titled "Anarchy and the Morality of Violence.") Hand in hand with the Glen Canyon Dam, a coal strip-mining project was initiated on Navajo lands by the Peabody Coal Company, tearing up the sacred mountain of Black Mesa to transport coal to regional power plants (in a scheme represented in *The Monkey Wrench Gang*). Abbey had all kinds of ideas as to how to sabotage such operations, such as shooting an armor-piercing missile from a high-powered rifle at a key flywheel (he even tried to obtain a bazooka), placing split wedges on the tracks to derail the coal train (except there was always someone on board), or blowing away a portion of the conveyor belt. He also left nails and other sharp things on roads to damage tires and pulled up surveyors' stakes. With nods to his friends Doug Peacock and Ken Sleight—the inspirations for George Hayduke and Seldom Seen Smith, respectively—Abbey conceived and

wrote his seminal novel about the possibilities inherent in an eco-sabotage movement.

In addition to reflecting aspects of past and present reality in the Southwest, *The Monkey Wrench Gang* would play into future reality as well. In 1981, a group calling itself Earth First! and claiming Abbey as their patron saint staged a dramatic protest at Glen Canyon Dam. One of the group's founders, the former Washington lobbyist Dave Foreman, was convinced, like Abbey, that the failure of the Sierra Club to save Glen Canyon demonstrated that compromise and moderation in the defense of nature were no longer adequate; radical action had become necessary.

In their foundational act of guerrilla theater, the group unfurled a giant black banner down the face of Glen Canyon Dam, a fake but realistic-looking crack signifying the beginning of a new era in environmental activism. The event was filmed to produce the nine-minute videotape *The Cracking of the Damn* (1982), with Abbey himself being the first person introduced to the viewer, as he participated in the protest by giving a speech. Earth First! adopted the monkey wrench for its insignia and George Hayduke's words as slogans, and they advanced eco-sabotage and protest to inventive new levels: they discovered that putting spikes in the trunks of old-growth redwoods and firs could prevent them from being felled, while camping out in treetops could accomplish the same goal. Abbey would continue to contribute to the efforts of Earth First! through writings and appearances until his death.

As for Glen Canyon Dam, Abbey's thoughts on it proved prescient. Objecting not only to the sacrilegious destruction of Glen Canyon, Abbey believed the dam would prove a financial disaster. For years state and federal authorities ignored this possibility, operating the dam strictly for the sake of profits by sporadically reducing the Colorado to a trickle or letting it flood to produce the most electricity at times of peak use. This practice devastated the ecosystem downstream, including that through the Grand Canyon, flushing virtually all biological life out of the riverbanks; the banks also eroded at increased rates because over 99 percent of the silt that would ordinarily be deposited along the river was instead trapped in Lake Powell. Only in 1991 were destructive water-flow practices halted, thanks to the efforts of the Grand Canyon Trust.

Many now believe that only with the destruction of Glen Canyon Dam will the habitats of the

Glen Canyon Dam in Arizona bears the brunt of the wrath of the group. *(© vladoskan | Shutterstock.com)*

Colorado River be able to repair themselves. Abbey, in his essay "The Damnation of a Canyon" (cited by Bill McKibben in "The Desert Anarchist"), predicts that the dam's destruction "will no doubt expose a drear and hideous scene: immense mud flats and whole plateaus of sodden garbage strewn with dead trees, sunken boats," and other remains and debris. Abbey continues,

> To those who find the prospect too appalling, I say give nature a little time. In five years, at most in ten, the sun and wind and storms will cleanse and sterilize the repellent mess.... Within the lifetime of our children Glen Canyon and the living river, heart of the canyonlands, will be restored to us. The wilderness will again belong to God, the people, and the wild things that call it home.

As far as Glen Canyon goes, only time will tell how truly prescient Abbey will prove.

CRITICAL OVERVIEW

The Monkey Wrench Gang is nothing if not provocative, but at first the critical response was muted. Abbey's editor at McGraw-Hill was surprised, believing the book ought to have been an immediate sensation. Perhaps editors beholden to advertising and industry were reluctant to draw attention to it. Also, as Douglas Brinkley acknowledges in his introduction to the book, "No one claimed it a fictional masterwork—it isn't." Nonetheless, word of the novel's merits soon buzzed through counterculture magazines and activist and undergraduate circles, the realms of society Abbey was most interested in anyway, as well as broader literary culture.

In Brinkley's words, "Astute reviewers saw *The Monkey Wrench Gang* for what it was: a wildly satiric, clever, postmodern pulp Western that ... was a rousing wake-up call." A *National Observer* critic (cited by Ronald) called the novel "a sad, hilarious, exuberant, vulgar fairy tale— part adventure story, part melodrama, part tragedy." Jim Harrison, in a *New York Times* review, calls the novel "a long, extravagant, finely written tale," featuring characters that Abbey renders "as convincingly as he does the landscape with all the breathless intensity of a true desolation angel" (an allusion to a Jack Kerouac novel, speaking to Abbey's philosophical/stylistic Beat influence). Harrison finds that the book makes clear how "in the Southwest we have a torn a hole in creation."

Taking an in-depth look at the novel in *The New West of Edward Abbey*, Ann Ronald calls it "boisterous, witty, and full of life" and admires how it "charges past the bounds of western fiction and proposes a new doctrine of frontier behavior." In providing an ethically ambiguous portrayal of the law-breaking protagonists, "like all good novels, Abbey's fiction raises more questions than it answers." Still, Ronald acknowledges stylistic drawbacks, noting that some readers "may feel victimized by overkill on the part of both the ecoraiders and their creator. If *The Monkey Wrench Gang* has a flaw, it is one of excess." Specifically, the many scenes of sabotage are extensively detailed and often similar; Ronald suggests that "only the most devoted Abbeyphile would concur that the book itself benefits from the episodic stockpile." In addition, she cites one of his more complex ranting passages, replete with subclauses, parentheses, and loaded terminology, to point out,

> Unfortunately Abbey inadvertently loses part of his effectiveness when he writes like this, spitting propaganda staccato-style. When his inner rage overrides his control, his prose rhythm accelerates so quickly that the result . . . pounds cacophonously on the reader's ear.

In his essay "Aestheticism and Awareness: The Psychology of Edward Abbey's *The Monkey Wrench Gang*," Scott Slovic likewise notes the book's stylistic discrepancies, but instead of considering them flaws, he concludes that they attest to the author's mischievous nature, his acknowledgment of the contradictions inherent in the circumstances he portrays, and his desire to bring about the reader's full engagement. Slovic states,

> The playfulness and ornateness of the prose in such works as *The Monkey Wrench Gang*, qualities that often seem to detract from narrative coherence and ideological dissemination, are part of an attempt to create textual paradoxes or incongruities that force readers to intensify their own attentiveness.

As Slovic concludes, "The strain of trying to interiorize disparate elements . . . lifts us to higher levels of awareness." Focusing on the virtues of the book's revelation of tragic environmental truths, James Bishop Jr. states in *Epitaph for a Desert Anarchist: The Life and Legacy of Edward Abbey*,

Because of Abbey's madcap but deadly serious novel, people of all ages can never again look the same way at massive freeway systems where desert and farmland used to be, at blankets of smog over cities, at once-lush forests now clearcut into lunar landscapes—or at huge dams on once-free rivers.

Bishop observes that it was due to Abbey's groundbreaking portrayal of "environmental hooliganism that he was elevated from the rank of regional author to that of international recognition."

CRITICISM

Michael Allen Holmes

Holmes is a writer with existential interests. In the following essay, he considers how the stereotypical depictions of Native Americans in The Monkey Wrench Gang *detract from the novel and reflect on the author.*

There are so many aspects of Edward Abbey's phenomenal novel *The Monkey Wrench Gang* worth discussing that little attention has been paid to certain side issues, like his treatment of American Indians. Native characters do not appear often, but when they do, they elicit unfortunate commentary on the part of both the protagonists and the narrator. In a novel full of colorful caricatures, the reader may shrug off what can only be termed stereotypical depictions as being just another aspect of the comedy, if surely a more questionable one. On the other hand, the reader may be so offended by the parade of insulting depictions of Indians that it becomes difficult to appreciate the rest of the novel—like when a stand-up comic's one appalling racist joke makes an audience member unable to laugh at any of the others, however funny they might be. Indeed, in a novel that demonstrates the author's great pride in his ethical consciousness with regard to the wilderness, it is surprising that he provides such disparaging portrayals of Native Americans, the original inhabitants of that wilderness, as if racial consciousness is not even on his radar. The matter is worth exploring further, in the interest of understanding why these portrayals ended up the way they did.

Although most of the novel's mentions of American Indians are not worth propagating any further, it is worth considering them more closely in order to establish what is so problematic about

WHAT DO I READ NEXT?

- The reader of *The Monkey Wrench Gang* may be most interested in turning next to the sequel, *Hayduke Lives!* (1990). It was finished shortly before the author's death, was published posthumously, and continues the lives and adventures of the familiar characters.

- A collection of some of Abbey's best and favorite nonfiction essays, as well as sample chapters from his fiction, is *Slumgullion Stew: An Edward Abbey Reader* (1984), edited and illustrated by Abbey himself.

- *Edward Abbey: A Life* (2001) is a comprehensive biography of the author by James M. Cahalan, detailing the experiences that inspired his writings and how his career shaped his life.

- An envisioning of the actual destruction of Glen Canyon Dam is part of the action of Laguna Pueblo author Leslie Marmon Silko's novel *Almanac of the Dead* (1991). In presenting an array of activists of different races as well as sexual orientations, she takes some of the revolutionary notions posited in Abbey's novel a step further, expanding them to be relevant not only to white male society but, indeed, to all of society.

- Abbey professed admiration for the novels by his friend William Eastlake set in contemporary New Mexico. Collected in the volume *3 by Eastlake* (1970) are the titles *Go in Beauty*, *The Bronc People*, and *Portrait of an Artist with 26 Horses*.

- Abbey's taste for adventure is reflected in his considering the mysterious author B. Traven a literary hero. Traven showed socialist and anarchist leanings in his fiction, and almost nothing certain is known about him. Traven's most famous novel was *The Treasure of the Sierra Madre*, originally published in German in 1927 and first translated into English in 1935, about prospecting for gold in Mexico.

- The formula established by Abbey in *The Monkey Wrench Gang* is drawn on by Richard Melo in his novel *Jokerman 8* (2004), which follows a group of eco-saboteurs based in San Francisco as they wreak havoc with industrial interests, like whalers and loggers, that are threatening wildlife.

- Another novel that owes a debt to Abbey is Neal Stephenson's *Zodiac: An Eco-Thriller* (1995). Known for his futuristic cyberadventures, Stephenson here presents Zodiac, a sort of eco-superhero who chases down corporate evildoers in solving a contamination mystery.

- In T. A. Barron's young-adult environmental fantasy novel *The Ancient One* (1992), thirteen-year-old Kate Gordon's efforts with her aunt to stop loggers from felling redwoods in Oregon evolve, after a trip through a time warp, into a fight to stop an evil creature from destroying the same forest.

---

them. Abbey might be said to cast a negative, if humorous, light on practically all of his characters. Hayduke is vulgar, evidently an alcoholic, and has difficulty thinking hard about things. Smith is a shameless womanizer, racking up three wives while seeming to ogle, handle, and carouse with other women (Bonnie, his driver, and the San Diego secretaries, respectively) every chance he gets. Even worse, Doc is lecherous and pathetically fantasizes about any woman whose job involves serving him. Even Bonnie at times comes across as a self-centered whiner (though her role as a blatant sex object has sparked accusations of misogyny on Abbey's part). As for people of other races, in the absence of any African Americans or Hispanics, American Indians play a unique role in the book—the one window outside of an otherwise strictly white world. Thus, the depiction of Indians

ABBEY'S UNDERLYING WHITE

ETHNOCENTRISM IS ALL TOO EVIDENT."

would naturally stand out no matter how that depiction has been handled.

The novel does contain one crass figurative reference to African Americans: at the beginning of the rafting trip, Abbey has Seldom Seen Smith make the racist comment, "He's gonna be number-two nigger this trip," with the epithet here effectively meaning "slave to your (white) interests." In this case, with no black characters to provide perspective, the comment comes across primarily as reflecting poorly on the personality of Smith; it does not necessarily imply that Abbey himself would say or think such a thing. Nor is the reader encouraged to sympathize with Smith by the context.

References to American Indians tell a different story. The reader's first impression may actually be a positive one, because in the prologue Abbey refers to "the sandstone Navajo formation, fifty million years emplaced." Abbey's choice of words uses the Indian ethnic group as an adjective to describe the rocky earth itself. That is, the wording connotes the Navajos' status as the original inhabitants of the land; the land is, in effect, theirs. The word is used similarly elsewhere. Later in the prologue, Abbey presents a crowd of Ute, Paiute, Hopi, and Navajo, all in possession of "brand-new pickup trucks"—a detail that may make the reader suspicious, because these likely are not all successful businessmen. Indeed, we soon find that the adults are drinking alcohol, the "swarms of children" drink sugary cola, "all munching on mayonnaise and Kleenex sandwiches of Wonder, Rainbo, and Holsum Bread." In sum, the reader gets the impression that none of these Indians has the slightest sense of nutritional value. After this line, the narrator's characterization of the group as "our noble red brethren" can only be taken sarcastically; far from presenting the sort of idealization of the "noble savage" found in such works as James Fenimore Cooper's Natty Bumppo novels, Abbey would appear to be intentionally contradicting that idealization. These Indians' hearts, by the way, are said to lie not with the aforementioned

Navajo land but with the white country singers being broadcast over the radio.

Stereotypical depictions—presenting members of an ethnic or racial group with negative characteristics that are perhaps drawn from a sample from that population but assigned to all such persons or prominent token persons—continue throughout the novel. In chapter 2, the reader learns that Hayduke's company in jail the night of his arrest in Flagstaff consisted of "twenty puking Navajos"—a blatantly stereotypical image. When Hayduke thinks regarding that night, "Somehow it rankled," the text implies that the ethnic identity of his companions was a significant reason for this.

Hayduke later goes on to expressly state that Indians are "just as stupid and greedy and cowardly and dull as us white folks." By now the reader understands that Hayduke's impression of Indians cannot be considered unbiased; his comments must be taken with a grain of salt. Nonetheless, Abbey is making a broad sociological statement through his character here, one that the reader will duly consider. The author is once again defying the "noble savage" idealization, but now he is couching that assertion in a framework where this only reduces them to the level of white people—as if this might excuse the stereotypical depictions. This posited framework merits a response—one might argue that if Indians do share these qualities with whites, it is important to acknowledge that white culture essentially infected them with these qualities—but that would be another essay entirely.

Just before those comments in chapter 2, Hayduke passes through the slum villages of the Navajo, who are "spreading, fruitful as a culture bouillon: from 9500 in 1890 to 125,000 today. Fecundity! Prosperity! Sweet wine and suicide, of thee we sing." The implication, of course, is that Indians are blindly multiplying only to drink themselves to death. Of course, no mention is made of how Indian populations were decimated earlier in history by the disease and destruction brought by white America, or how the psychological effects of this process would have carried forward from generation to generation. As the novel continues, Indians are further enmeshed in poverty and drink. In chapter 5, the reader is told of "the traditional pastoral slums of Navajoland." When Bonnie, appalled by the sight of the slums, is told that Indians live there, she remarks, "It's too good for them." Thus another white character is expressing the opinion that Indians are a race beneath the level of ordinary society. Through a variety of comments later in the book not worth repeating, Doc, too, expresses a racist opinion of Indians.

To a certain extent an author, as Abbey once proclaimed in a *Bloomsbury Review* interview, is not responsible for the behavior of his characters; an author is obliged by his art to depict his characters truthfully as he has conceived them, such that what they say and do cannot be held to reflect the author's own opinions. However, when the reader is presented through a collection of characters with only a single perspective on a group, and it happens to be a racist outsider's perspective, the reader may absorb this perspective whether he wants to or not. Abbey as author may not be responsible for the words of each of his characters, but he is responsible for the sum of those words. In fact, Abbey himself, in a journal entry on *The Monkey Wrench Gang* quoted by biographer Jack Loeffler, directly linked his characters' thoughts and words with his own. In light of his stereotyping, his private comments reflect quite poorly on him:

> Having trouble as usual with people: character. How to create personality in the novel. Tough to do. All my characters—Doc, Bonnie, Hayduke, Capt. Smith—seem thin, superficial, one dimensional. Worse, they tend to get blurred, to sound alike. Worse yet, they all tend to talk like me. Or like I think.

In addition to the sum of his words, the author is also responsible for the sum of his portrayals, and drunk and inconsequential Indians are scattered throughout the book. In chapter 11, "drunk and abandoned Navajos" lie around in vacant lots. In chapter 12, "genuine nonworking Indians"—another sarcastic reference—crowd a parking lot. In chapter 16, lounging Indians are compared to animals, specifically "hungry rabbits" (watching Bonnie), and are said to be telling "Pleistocene jokes," that is, primitive ones. Chapter 24 presents "a few aborigines passed out against a cinderblock wall." None of these Indians is individuated, that is, depicted in a way that elevates them beyond the stereotypical collective characterization.

When Indians are finally given active roles, they are portrayed as inept, and they remain mostly silent. Hayduke and Bonnie watch as two Indian police officers get a van stuck in sand and yell at each other hopelessly. The fact that these officers' names are parenthetically given only

seems to heighten the condescension inherent in the portrayal—as if to show that even if the reader knows who these men are, they do not matter. When Hayduke needs to escape the clutches of the Love brothers in a café, two Navajo men sit near the entrance and do nothing more substantial than slide their briefcases in Hayduke's path, playing the role of mere stagehands or obstacles. The only Indian given a positive portrayal in the entire book is the Ute waitress, but this is palpably not due to ethnic open-mindedness but to Hayduke's and the narrator's/author's attraction to her.

By now the reader has to ask, what is Abbey's problem? Why has he produced a book full of stereotypes without a single honest portrayal of a decent Native American to balance the lot? One naturally wonders what interactions Abbey might have had with Indians, or the idea of Indians, in the course of his life. Indeed, it was only the idea of Indians that he was first exposed to—in the wilderness that his family inhabited in Pennsylvania. Although Native Americans had been driven from the area some hundred years earlier, he and his siblings, playing in the marvelous expanses of woods around them, imagined that Indian spirits still lingered and even influenced or inhabited their own souls. Abbey would later tell interviewers that he had some Shawnee Indian blood, but if so, in the words of biographer James Bishop Jr., "it wasn't much more than a few drops."

It would seem that Abbey did idealize Indian consciousness, at least, as a child, but this had little to no basis in interaction with actual Indians. For him to claim Shawnee ancestry without legitimate evidence would strike many as presumptuous—as trying to take advantage of the perceived virtues of another race through association. Such an approach to other races also surfaced during his time at the University of New Mexico. As Bishop relates,

> He often tried to date black women, because it was then a cool and rebellious thing to do, but when he asked them they would laugh at him, all except for one who went out with him—once.

The reader is perhaps glad to learn that these black women could see through Abbey's surface interest to realize that he was, as with the claim of Indian blood, simply trying to take advantage of their racial identity.

If Abbey failed to get chances to benefit from genuine friendship with people of other races as an undergraduate, it would not be long before he had opportunities to develop antagonism toward them. In his biography *Adventures with Ed*, Abbey's good friend Jack Loeffler cites a letter by another friend, John DePuy, revealing how Abbey's temporary employment as a welfare worker in Taos, New Mexico, as colored by a single incident, affected his outlook. The work, DePuy writes,

> was wretched and he was depressed about his job. Then one day he was walking back to his house in Cañon and a pachuco teenager took a shot at him with a .22. That was the end. After that he was very nervous about the Hispanics. He never got over it. He would go into a bar and he would put his hand on his wallet because there were Hispanics around.

This is a classic description of how a person can come to a stereotypical conclusion about another race: a single incident that sparks terror in a person's mind, enacted by an individual of a certain race, leads the person to fear everyone of that race, a fear that surfaces in physical behaviors (covering one's wallet) as well as ethnic opinions; the physical sense translates into an (unjustified) intellectual conclusion. While this incident involved a Mexican American, Abbey's experiences as a welfare worker in Albuquerque may have led him to conflate Mexicans and Indians in his mind. As Loeffler notes, "Most of his clients were Indians and Hispanos whose main source of income was the welfare check."

One can see, then, how Abbey might have come to negative conclusions about both Hispanics and Native Americans. This is not to say that he remained ignorant about Indian society and culture. In his nonfiction collection *Desert Solitaire: A Season in the Wilderness*, his essay "Cowboys and Indians, Part II" provides a substantial sociological discussion on the state of the Navajo. He begins by reflecting intelligently on the artwork Indians left behind on canyon walls in southern Utah, which is said to range in style "from the crude and simple to the elegant, sophisticated and subtle." He considers the Indian artwork to be a "poignant sign of their humanity." Yet he still makes clear that he is talking not about modern humans but about "primitive savages."

As he delves into modern-day Navajo society, he demonstrates that he is well informed about problems of overpopulation, poverty, inadequate education, and substance abuse (all of which he was undoubtedly exposed to as a

welfare worker). He declares that a majority of Navajo are settling "more deeply into the second-class way of life, American style, to which they are fairly accustomed," meaning steady welfare checks, dilapidated housing, and persistent drinking. He proceeds to astutely acknowledge that the Indian's present-day plight is founded in his being "caught in a no man's land between two worlds," which leaves him understandably "clinging to the liberty and dignity of his old way of life."

These comments are sensitive enough, but the remainder of the passage straddles a fine line between truthfulness and opinionated condescension. In discussing traditional Navajo notions of communal responsibility, he laments, "Shackled by such primitive attitudes, is it any wonder that the Navajos have not yet been able to get in step with the rest of us?" In proposing that industrial tourism would bring jobs that involve housework, pumping gas, washing dishes, cleaning bathrooms, and so forth, he states that these are "simple tasks for which the Navajos are available and qualified." He drily concludes that Navajos will simply have to abandon their traditional ways, "or at least learn to be ashamed of these old things and to bring them out for the amusement of tourists." Abbey's underlying white ethnocentrism is all too evident.

By now, Abbey's broader perspective on American Indians has become much clearer. He is not nearly as ignorant as *The Monkey Wrench Gang* suggests. His stereotypical depictions of Indians are founded not in simple racism but in actual life experiences that primarily exposed him to the less successful side of Indian society. In fact, it is not clear that he ever established a meaningful friendship with a "genuine" successful Indian. If he had, one might imagine that a depiction of such a person could have found its way into *The Monkey Wrench Gang*—indeed, that it *should* have found its way into the novel, because in the absence of such a depiction, the reader's impression of Native American culture is based strictly on the stereotypes.

This is no better than if an author were to litter a novel with images of black people strictly taken from the welfare rolls of the inner city or of white people strictly taken from the welfare rolls of the rural backwoods. No such novel could be considered ethically responsible from a racial point of view; poor people of every race exist in concentration

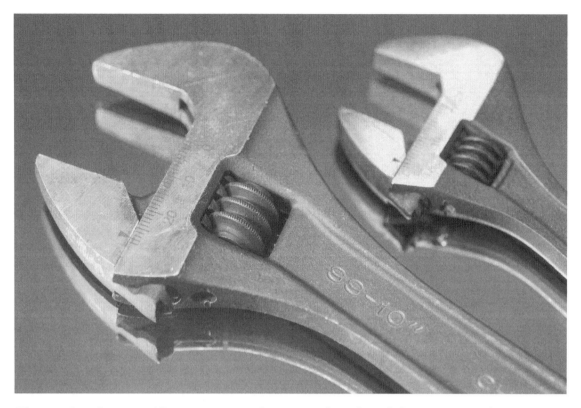

The term "monkey wrench" means to cause chaos or mayhem through destruction or other means.
(© blojfo | Shutterstock.com)

somewhere, and the reasons for their poverty are almost always more complex than their individual situations attest. To present in a novel only impoverished persons of a given race and to furthermore allow one's protagonists to freely criticize those persons is to provide an incomplete, and thus untruthful, picture of that race.

Abbey has had decent things to say about Native Americans. In *Desert Solitaire*, with reference to the stock solutions proposed for alleviating poverty among the Navajo, he laments that

> they fail to take into account what is unique and valuable in the Navajo's traditional way of life and ignore altogether the possibility that the Navajo may have as much to teach the white man as the white man has to teach the Navajo.

If Abbey had kept these thoughts in mind while writing *The Monkey Wrench Gang*, he might have seen fit to modify his depictions of Indians to produce a more palatable, and wiser, novel.

Source: Michael Allen Holmes, Critical Essay on *The Monkey Wrench Gang*, in *Novels for Students*, Gale, Cengage Learning, 2013.

James Holt McGavran

In the following essay, McGavran demonstrates that the two nature writers William Wordsworth and Edward Abbey, not known for openness in terms of gender actually "found and inhabited these salubrious textual spaces."

This paper starts with two premises. The first is that one's understanding of gender, like one's knowledge of the natural world, is never entirely determined by material conditions but is always at least partly constructed in the mind. The second premise, more difficult to internalize, is that these constructions, like the material conditions with which they interact, are mutable. After reviewing some relevant commentary from the fields of gender studies and ecocriticism, I argue that writers whose texts integrate these concerns can re-imagine themselves and their worlds in strange but life-affirming ways. The paper, then, will demonstrate that William Wordsworth and Edward Abbey, two nature writers not generally known for their openness in matters of gender, actually found and inhabited these salubrious textual spaces.

> CURIOUSLY ENOUGH, THIS FLUIDITY APPEARS IN THE WORK OF WILLIAM WORDSWORTH AND EDWARD ABBEY, TWO NATURE WRITERS OFTEN REGARDED AS ANYTHING BUT MUTABLE IN THEIR UNDERSTANDING OF GENDER, OR INDEED OF SOCIAL ISSUES GENERALLY."

Arguments for fluidity or mutability in one's experience of gender—though they date to antiquity—have not always had an easy time of it in twentieth-century critical discourse. Virginia Woolf's somewhat tentative exploration of androgyny in *A Room of One's Own* (1929)—she called it "two sexes in the mind corresponding to the two sexes in the body" (102)—was attacked, not at all tentatively, by Elaine Showalter in *A Literature of Their Own* (1977). Showalter insisted that instead of getting in touch with their inner man (293, 34), women should recognize and resist patriarchal oppression. Since then, though androgyny has had its defenders (Heilbrun; Weil), many feminists, including some prominent Romanticists, have denounced the idea as just another cultural tool that men use to colonize or even cannibalize women's lives and minds (Richardson 13–25; Hoeveler xv–xvi).

However, Adrienne Rich, in "Compulsory Heterosexuality and Lesbian Existence" (1980; rev 1983), implicitly attacked critics like Showalter for what she saw as a heterosexist and thus patriarchal bias. Rich also graphed women's sexual experience along the line she called a "lesbian continuum," whereby some might be located at either end as exclusively heterosexual or homosexual in their sexual feelings and practices, but many others, if they could free themselves of patriarchal preconceptions, might move in either direction over time and thus be more accurately considered bisexual (Rich 217, 220). In *Between Men* (1985) Eve Kosofsky Sedgwick argued that a parallel patriarchal force, which she named "homosexual panic," polices alternative sexuality in men (1–5). In the same year Toril Moi attempted to reclaim androgyny for feminists by suggesting that what Woolf had in mind when she used the

term was not to yoke women to their male oppressors but, rather like Rich with her sliding continuum, to destabilize traditional gender stereotypes (3–7).

In *Difference Troubles* (1997) Steven Seidman summarizes the history of gender criticism from the liberatory and utopian post-Stonewall hopes of the late 1960s and early 1970s, through the highly politicized recognition of difference that characterized the 1980s, to the emergence of queer theory in the 1990s. "Liberation theory posited humans as innately bisexual and polymorphous," Seidman writes; "homosexuality and heterosexuality were not seen as mutually exclusive desires, psychic conditions, or human types; they were described as universal aspects of humankind" (118). According to Seidman, the separationist, come-out-and-be-counted emphasis of gay and lesbian movements in the 1980s pushed aside the polymorphous perspective. But Seidman argues that it has been the mission of queer theory to resist these tendencies, to "view . . . identity as a relation rather than an essence" and to deconstruct an either-or "hetero/homosexual code that structures the 'social text' of daily life" (132). He believes that this destabilization can potentially reopen an awareness of gender that is less utopian or politicized and more directly experiential.

The empirical research work of Paula C. Rust with self-identified lesbian and bisexual women supports both Rich's continuum and Seidman's emphasis on gender fluidity as an experiential reality for many. Rust writes, "Bisexual women's frequent identity changes do not indicate a state of searching immaturity, but a mature state of mutability"; she warns that this "construction of a bisexual identity . . . is threatening to a monosexual identity" whether heterosexual or homosexual (Beemyn 66, 79). Seidman's title, *Difference Troubles*, deliberately echoes that of Judith Butler's influential *Gender Trouble* (1990), and Seidman draws strongly on Butler's post-Foucauldian arguments that not only gender but sex is socially constructed rather than biologically fixed, that all representations of gender are performances, and thus that all people, not just the transgendered or transsexual, are in drag all the time (Berger 3–5).

If Butler can claim that the mind constructs something as "natural" as biological sex, what about nature itself? Over a century ago Oscar Wilde anticipated the question, ungendering and de-naturalizing nature at one stroke: "Nature is no great mother who has borne us. She is our creation. It is in our brain that she quickens to life" (qtd. Kerridge 126). By insisting that nature, like gender, is always already a mental construct, Wilde does not deny the world's existence but doubts whether people can know it other than through their constructions of it and the interactions that may confirm or alter those constructions. Raymond Williams came to a similar conclusion from another direction when he wrote, "The idea of nature contains, though often unnoticed, an extraordinary amount of human history" (qtd. Cronon 25). Wilde anticipates not only Williams's materialist view of nature, but also Jacques Lacan's opposition of the Symbolic and the Real (Fink 24–26): whatever one can symbolize through language and thus articulate and attempt to control is no longer the Real, so the Real will always continue to change and to elude comprehension. Richard Kerridge has demonstrated how this desire for something beyond representation, the force behind much late twentieth-century nature exploration and nature writing, both drives and impedes recent attempts to grasp ecological issues thoroughly (1–3). But as Neil Sammells has evocatively suggested, "Wilde's mannered anti-naturalism, his apparent contempt for nature, paradoxically opens up a radical political space or landscape which contemporary ecocriticism might occupy" (Kerridge 124). This space between a changing Real and changing representations of that Real is, I believe, the same unstable space between the contraries where Woolf, Rich, Sedgwick, Moi, Seidman, Rust, and Butler locate their relational views of gender identity. Thus, the postmodern nostalgia for the Real might lead one to "Wilde nature" not as a place to rehearse predetermined gender roles but rather as a place where one might liberate the mind from any sort of pre/per/formed construction. In a remarkable essay, "'The Curious Peach': Nature and the Language of Desire," Charles Bergman brings gender trouble directly to bear on nature writing: "The body of nature and the human body intersect in the wild and even dangerous terrain of human desire" (Herndl 283). Bergman notes the strangely puritanical tendency of many contemporary nature writers, both male and female, to avoid direct discussion of the sexual in nature. As if to illustrate what Seidman et al. address, and what some nature writers miss, Bergman drolly asserts

that what makes his titular fruit an object of curiosity (the phrase is Andrew Marvell's, from "The Garden") is that while usually troped as female, the object could just as easily represent "a male ass" (293) while still retaining its identity as a peach.

Curiously enough, this fluidity appears in the work of William Wordsworth and Edward Abbey, two nature writers often regarded as anything but mutable in their understanding of gender, or indeed of social issues generally. Abbey has received much negative attention from proponents of political correctness, but he is not the only white-Anglo-male nature writer to come under attack for his alleged detachment from the social realities of his time and place and his apparent lack of diversity awareness. In spite of Jonathan Bate's eloquent efforts to rescue him from Jerome McGann, to substitute green environmental politics for McGann's red marxist politics (*Romantic* 8–9; "Green Romanticism"), the Lord of the Lakes William Wordsworth has not always fared well at the hands of the ecocritics—and for the same reasons as Abbey. Just as SueEllen Campbell attacks Abbey's lack of concern for the Native Americans living near his starkly beautiful desert monuments in Utah (Kerridge 21–22), so do Carl G. Herndl and Stuart C. Brown, in their classification of the rhetorical discourses of nature writing, reference Wordsworth's poetry as a cautionary tale to illustrate McGann's "romantic ideology of private, individual consciousness" which "emerged as a reaction against the urbanization brought on by the industrial revolution" (8), a reaction which, they claim, dodges the ongoing "public dilemma" (7) of past and present social and environmental concerns. Even Robert Pogue Harrison, while viewing Wordsworth's post-Rousseauvian return to the precivilized forest much more positively, emphasizes an ironic detachment implicit in the poet's reticent awareness of "what man has made of man" (164) and thus perhaps unwittingly contributes to the idea that Wordsworth has mounted a rear-guard effort designed to preserve a transhistorical "Merrie Olde Englande" that never existed anywhere outside Burke's Reflections.

Ecofeminist Campbell associates Abbey's lack of social field sensitivity with an accompanying sexism and latent homoeroticism apparent in both his life and writing styles (15–16). J. Gerard Dollar extends this name-calling to include misogyny. For Dollar, Abbey's evocation of the lost Glen Canyon, in the famous "Down the River" chapter of *Desert Solitaire*, becomes an Eden "for men only," since he unfairly associates women with all the corruption of the civilized world (Branch 98). Indeed, like many other male nature writers, Abbey prefers either solitude or the company of a male friend to female companionship in the wilderness. Similarly, Romantic feminist critics such as Anne Mellor, Susan Levin, and myself have found much to deplore in William Wordsworth, notably the subjugation of both feminine nature and feminine identity to his masculine Romantic ego and the exploitative relationship with his sister Dorothy (Mellor 148, 145–46; Levin 4, 26; McGavran "Dorothy" 232). And David Collings has gone so far as to speak of Wordsworth as "flaming," arguing "that he not only champions deviance and a nearly overt homoeroticism but links them intimately with his status as a poet" (14, 13).

Attempting to reclaim Abbey and Wordsworth for both gender studies and ecocriticism, including ecofeminism, without assigning labels based on alleged sexual practices, I suggest first that Wordsworth's turn to nature was determined not only by the tumultuous economic and political history of the late eighteenth century in France and England but also by changes in domestic history. As several critics have argued, the rise of the ideology of the nuclear bourgeois family—and of the accompanying gender roles of the powerful, protective father, the nurturing, caring mother, and their loved and loving children—conflicted with yet helped produce an accompanying ideology of wandering boyhood, that is, a boyhood literally if not figuratively aberrant, that was at once idealized/spiritualized and autoerotic/homoerotic (Richardson 121–30 and Myers 131–42 in Sadler; *McGavran Literature* 130–52). This ideology, newborn in the Wordsworths' time, was still alive and well for Abbey and has not yet disappeared.

Wordsworth often feminizes nature in *The Prelude*, usually as a caring mother: "Nature, oftentimes, when she would frame/a favored being" (1805 1:363–64); "Nature and her overflowing soul" (1805 2:416); and in the well-known passage in Book 2, the mother nursing her baby in her arms is simply reenacting "Along his infant veins . . . /The gravitation and the filial bond/Of Nature that connect him with the world" (1805 2:262–64). Over thirty years ago, Richard Onorato published an influential psychoanalytic study of Wordsworth which identified the poet's grief at the early loss of his mother (she died when he was only eight) as the driving force behind his search for the feminine in nature. But according to the contemporaneous and still-powerful argument of M. H. Abrams in *Natural Supernaturalism* (286–87), the godlike mind of the poet must eventually subjugate external nature. By the end of *The Prelude*, the speaker's masculine mind dominates feminized nature as the moon, shining above the clouds, dominates the mountainous Welsh landscape around Mount Snowdon (1805 13:66–90). For the more coercive side of the male poet's relationship with feminized nature, one can also look at the blank-verse fragment "Nutting," where the speaker, with considerable remorse and a warning for his female listener—"dearest Maiden" (l. 54, Stillinger 112)—recalls a boyhood incident when he figuratively raped a hazelnut bower.

In *Desert Solitaire* Abbey, by contrast, seems more overtly sexual when he feminizes the Utah desert scenery, but not without a degree of self-directed irony usually missing in his Romantic precursor that slips below the radar of the ecofeminists. On a drive through harsh desert land, he writes, "Everything is lovely and wild, with a virginal sweetness" (11); when he first sees the Arches National Monument, he says, "I feel a ridiculous greed and possessiveness come over me. I want to know it all, possess it all, embrace the entire scene intimately, deeply, totally, as a man desires a beautiful woman" (6). Of course, these are the very passages that bother SueEllen Campbell (15). But isn't Abbey simply trumpeting his own awareness that it's "ridiculous" to want to possess" all the "virginal sweetness" of the desert, or even to speak of the desert as having a virginal sweetness? Surely the recorder of neologisms as simultaneously bawdy and socially trenchant as "californicating" ("Great" 689) and "syphilization" (*Desert* 199) can be allowed to have some ironic awareness of the rigidities of stereotypical gender attitudes.

Collings (9, 16, 134–37, 139–41) and G. Kim Blank have noted the numerous images of the punishing, potent father which coexist with feminine images of mother and/or lover in *The Prelude*. Great, powerful, stalking presences and strange unearthly sounds and movements as of gods or monsters appear in descriptive passages of high emotional intensity: "Huge and mighty forms that do not live/Like living men moved slowly through my mind/By day, and were the trouble of my dreams" (1805 1:424–26). Male solitaries, most notably the discharged soldier, also lurk in the landscape of *The Prelude* with both menace and aberrant allure (McGavran "Defusing"). Moreover, frequent addresses to Wordsworth's best male friend and muse, Coleridge (and the nostalgic memories of his love for his childhood friend John Fleming and his French friend of the Revolution Michel Beaupuy), appear throughout the poem. Nature, for Wordsworth, in other words, is not always female, not "Mother nature," at these times; instead, it is "Daddy nature," and as Blank has convincingly argued, male presences, including that of his dead father, both inhabit and haunt it (55–65).

In "Down the River," Wordsworth himself appears as a looming forefather in Abbey's quotation of the opening line of a familiar sonnet, "It is a beauteous evening, calm and free" (197), in which, it is worth mentioning, the poet explores and attempts to dissolve the gendered differences separating himself, his unheeding French daughter, and an imagined nun "breathless with adoration" (l. 3, Stillinger 170). Stalking Wordsworthian male presences reappear in Abbey's consciousness of the exploits of his American precursor in wilderness exploration, Major John Wesley Powell, who led a harrowing trip down the Colorado River soon after the Civil War. Craving the wilderness as Powell did, Abbey also shares Powell's fear of the unknown, of what lies "around the next bend of the canyon" (210), projecting fear also into the minds of the pre-Columbian Anasazi Indians, whose ruins Abbey sees during his journey. Just as a male friend often accompanied Wordsworth in his travels, so too Abbey passes through Glen Canyon accompanied by the fatherly (but also motherly, as it turns out) presence of an older man, Ralph Newcomb. Abbey emphasizes Ralph's relatively weaker physical condition: "Ralph has only one good leg. He can walk but not hike; he can swim but not very far" (190). Yet after a nocturnal exploration to find fresh water, Abbey depends on Ralph's lack of mobility to get back to their camp safely:

> Dark when I return, with only the light of Ralph's fire to guide me. As I brush away sticks and stones on the ground, making a place for my sleeping bag, I see a scorpion scuttle off, tail up and stinger ready. Newcomb and I meditate on the red coals of the fire before turning in.

That unnerving phallic scorpion both threatens and enhances the close male bonding. As Wordsworth frankly acknowledges his feelings for John Fleming, "a friend/Then passionately loved" (*Prelude* 1805 2:352–53), Abbey openly avows the homoerotic aspect of his downriver trip with Ralph, their boats lashed together as if to secure their intimacy: "I am fulfilling at last a dream of childhood and one as powerful as the erotic dreams of adolescence—floating down the river" (191). Later he comments further: "We are merging, molecules getting mixed. Talk about intersubjectivity—we are both taking on the coloration of river and canyon, our skin as mahogany as the water on the shady side, our clothing coated with silt. . ." (232). Yet no serious reader of *The Prelude* or *Desert Solitaire* could conclude from this that Wordsworth or Abbey is to be labelled gay.

In addition to their parallel tensions regarding the troping of nature as feminine and their mutual troubled nostalgia for boyhood/adolescent male love and friendship, Wordsworth and Abbey's gendering of nature deliberately deconstructs both nature and gender stereotypes in moments of high intensity, effectively making both men explorers of what Sammells calls "Wilde nature." In a major climax in *The Prelude*, Wordsworth seems to anticipate Lacan's awareness of the limits of the Symbolic and the nostalgia for the Real when he attempts to express that he must search in nature, beyond form or image and their gendered implications, for something which paradoxically he has already had and lost:

> I deem not profitless those fleeting moods
> Of shadowy exultation; not for this,
> That they are kindred to our purer mind
> And intellectual life, but that the soul—
> Remembering how she felt, but what she felt
> Remembering not—retains an obscure sense
> Of possible sublimity, to which
> With growing faculties she doth aspire,
> With faculties still growing, feeling still
> That whatsoever point they gain they still
> Have something to pursue. (1805 2:321–41)

Wordsworth feminizes his supposedly sexist soul to reach for something beyond simple categorizations of either nature or gender. Later, in the 1850 revision, he does this again at the moment he recalls his frustration at having "crossed the Alps" unaware:

> Under such banners militant, the soul
> Seeks for no trophies, struggles for no spoils
> That may attest her prowess, blest in thoughts
> That are their own perfection and reward,
> Strong in herself and in beatitude
> That hides her . . . (1850 6:609–14)

And he yet again feminizes, or more accurately androgynizes or ungenders, his mind—not his soul this time—when he defines "spots of time" as a "spirit":

> [It] chiefly lurks
> Among those passages of life in which
> We have had deepest feeling that the mind
> Is lord and master, and that outward sense
> Is but the obedient servant of her will.
>   (1805 11:268–72)

That the mind is lord and master but possesses a female will seems not to have been a slip of the pen since the same language is repeated in the 1850 text.

In some of the passages in *Desert Solitaire* that Dollar reads as misogynistic, Abbey (as well as Wordsworth) could be yearning not for a world without women but a world without societally inscribed and sanctioned gender performances. In "Down the River" he speaks disturbingly, even violently, of "cutting the bloody cord" and then explodes in anger against the "incredible shit we put up with most of our lives—the domestic routine (same old wife every night)," proceeding to associate heterosexual marriage with arrogant politicians, greedy businessmen, wars, and ugly cities. I suggest that stereotyped maternal or other feminine roles, not women themselves, define what he wishes to escape. In the "Havasu" chapter in *Desert Solitaire*, where he recounts the stereotype-shattering experience of being trapped in a remote, rocky setting and believing there was no way out, Abbey, free of society's judgment, openly, even eagerly reports that he cried three times:

> I began to cry. It was easy. All alone, I didn't have to be brave. Across that narrow opening a small white cloud was passing, so lovely and precious and delicate and forever inaccessible that it broke the heart and made me weep like a woman, a child. In all my life I had never seen anything so beautiful. . . . I discovered myself bawling again for the third time in three hours, the hot delicious tears of victory.

"Weep[ing] like a woman, a child," Abbey finds in the tensions of these life-or-death moments not just relief but pleasure in escaping the socially imposed limits of his own macho masculinity. Much earlier in *Desert Solitaire*, Abbey uncannily unites both Wordsworthian and Lacanian insights as he looks at Delicate Arch and again thinks of the presexual child: "The shock of the real. For a little while we are again able to see, as the child sees, a world of marvels. For a few moments we discover that nothing can be taken for granted."

The indeterminate space one explores may be that of external nature or that of the body, or it may partake of both. However it occurs, ecocriticism and gender criticism, meeting textually in "Wilde nature," the desire-driven continuum between the contraries, have much to say to each other in current critical discourse. While risking marginalization or outright rejection, one may also live more intensely in this space. Perhaps the reason some people still feel discomfort about transgendered or transsexualized persons is not that they are unnatural, though they may be widely regarded as such, but because traditional constructions of nature and gender—those which try to pin either down—are finally unnatural. Perhaps, as the tragic love story of Army private Barry Winchell and drag queen Calpernia Addams implies (France), a preoperative transsexual—that is, a person in the process of changing sexes—is the most natural human being on earth.

Source: James Holt McGavran, "Gender Fluidity and Nature Writing: William Wordsworth and Edward Abbey," in *Wordsworth Circle*, Vol. 33, No. 1, Winter 2002, pp. 47–52.

Steve Norwick

In the following excerpt, Norwick explores Abbey's understanding of Friedrich Neitzsche's thought in The Monkey Wrench Gang.

Most readers find many of Edward Abbey's images and statements interesting but puzzling, troubling, challenging, and even nonsensical. I believe that most of these confusing, and bold, passages are Nietzschean. The influence is pervasive, evidenced by numerous quotes and several Nietzschean themes in his novels and essays. The purpose of this chapter is: (1) to shed light on the Nietzschean quality of Abbey's thought, and (2) to give a few examples of how understanding his brand of Nietzscheanism sheds light on his artistic and political motives.

...Nietzsche often attacked materialism and the gospel of progress (1964, 14:72–73). He hated unnecessary commercial activity. "One is now ashamed of repose.... Thinking is done with a stop watch as dining is done with the eyes fixed on the financial newspaper" (10:254). He warned that "in the lace of the monstrous machine, the individual despairs and surrenders" (14:29). This is the underlying political theme of all of Abbey's political nonfiction, especially *Desert Solitaire*, and his novels *The Brave Cowboy*, *Fire on the Mountain*, *The Monkey Wrench Gang*, and *Hayduke Lives!* Abbey especially attacked roads, dams, cities, and commerce, which all cause destruction of nature. His novels have become "the texts" of the Luddite elements in the United States today, especially the Earth First! movement.

Nietzsche was an advocate of social anarchy. He wrote that before civilization there was a "natural war of all against all," but the wars that created the modern nation-states were worse than that. To him, the state used violence to preserve itself: "The State [is] for the majority of men a continually flowing source of hardship" (1964, 2:10–11). He felt that we all live in "the state, where the slow suicide of all—is called life" (11:55). He literally demonized the government: "A state is called the coldest of all cold monsters. Coldly lieth it also; and this lie creepeth from its mouth: I, the state, am the people." He denied that the state should hold property, saying, "what ever [the state] hath it hath stolen" (54). Nietzsche attacked some of the German idealists who had provided philosophical support for the German national government, writing, "the doctrine ... that the state is the highest end of man and there is no higher duty than to serve it: I regard this not as a relapse into paganism, but into stupidity" (4:135). He also attacked the government's use of religion. He said that the state uses priests to subvert freedom and to make the state "something wholly sacred" (6:338). He felt that this collusion between church and state had created "the new idol!" which is served by the "preachers of death" (11:54–55).

Nietzsche believed that "There where the state cease—there only commenceth the man who is not superfluous ... there where the state ceaseth ... Do ye not see it, the rainbow and the bridges of the Superman?" (57). The image of the rainbow bridge is taken from Norse myth—the bridge connecting the pagans' heaven-on-Earth of the gods. At the end of the world, the giants will storm the bridge and set it afire (MacCulloch 1964, 23). Nietzsche was strongly opposed to the belief in gods or God. Perhaps this passage represents the end of the reign of ordinary humans by the evolution of Supermen, whom Nietzsche expected to symbolically destroy the bridge between the gods and humanity.

Even though he was an anarchist, Nietzsche did not offer specific plans to demolish the state, and he did not picture a Utopia. He did not approve of nineteenth-century working-class anarchists because they acted out of envy of the rich, not out of their own creative power: "The Christian and the Anarchist—both are decadents" (1964, 16:87). "The Anarchist and the Christian are offspring of the same womb" (220).

Edward Abbey considered himself an anarchist (1994a, 59, 257) and at the University of New Mexico he titled his master's thesis "Anarchism and the Morality of Violence." Abbey, like Nietzsche, thought of anarchism as a social movement. He wanted to ignore the state and the demands of polite society. Neither Nietzsche nor Abbey was the type of political anarchist who personally wanted to blow up state buildings or assassinate political leaders. Abbey wrote that "Anarchism is a secret yearning toward brotherhood. Anarchism is the demand for community" (1994a, 139). When he was near death, Abbey asked his friends to "Wrap my body in my anarch's flag" (276). Like Nietzsche, Abbey was not an advocate of any of the political forms of anarchism, even environmental anarchism such as Murray Bookchin's. Abbey did not have any specific plan to reach anarchy and did not design or advocate any particular utopian scheme. Abbey's and Nietzsche's anarchism is instead characterized by advocating extreme individualism. And for both writers, social anarchism was perhaps their most important issue.

To some readers who do not appreciate his irony, Nietzsche sounds like an anti-Semite, racist, and social Darwinist, but not to the late-nineteenth-century Nietzscheans who were liberals and who opposed overt racism. Here, too, Abbey resembles Nietzsche. Whereas most modern literary natural history writers in English also are liberals, antiracists, and opponents of anti-Semitism (Bridgman 1972), the persona of Abbey's essays is a mild, self-mocking racist (although he clearly disapproved of racism) (1971b, 97–98; 1994a, 220, 285, 305–7, 316, 333, 336, 352).

Nietzsche was an early advocate of population control, believing that overpopulation would lead to tyranny: "Many too many are born: for the superfluous ones was the state devised!" (1964, 11:55). Abbey believed that overpopulation leads not only to political tyranny but also to environmental damage. His mocking proposals for several politically unacceptable forms of birth control as well as U.S. immigration enforcement appeared in *Mother Jones* and several newspapers in 1983 (1994a, 307).

Abbey and Nietzsche also seem to have similar attitudes about women. Nietzsche, who seems to be a misogynist in some passages (1964, 11:75, 16:198), but many important modern feminists have found inspiration in his works (see Patton 1993). Abbey also seems sexist to some readers, and he actually mocked himself for it. His review of Susan Brownmiller's *Femininity* and Gloria Steinem's *Outrageous Acts* is a self-mocking, sexist essay in which he goes out of his way to insult both authors as well as Margaret Thatcher and Indira Gandhi, and to outrage feminists by quoting Doris Lessing, Joan Didion, and Margaret Mead out of context so that they appear to agree with his ironic, self-deprecating, comic sexism (1988, 199–205). *Black Sun* and *The Fool's Progress* both explore the problems that sexism created for Abbey and the women in his life.

Most of the English-speaking Nietzscheans were socialists or other leftists. Most American environmental or nature writers also tend to be anticapitalists, often dwelling on the ravages of industry on the natural environment. Nietzsche himself was very antisocialist. Abbey was not pro-industry, but he was primarily concerned with the destruction of the natural environment by federal agencies and other socialized segments of the American economy. "Industrial Tourism and the National Parks" (1971b) is primarily an attack on the U.S. Park Service for building too many roads and not promoting walking in the wilderness. *Fire on the Mountain* (1962) is an attack on the U.S. military. *The Monkey Wrench Gang* (1975) and *The Journey Home* (1977) are directed at federal agencies, the Bureau of Reclamation, the Corps of Engineers, the Forest Service, the Bureau of Land Management, and federally funded highway projects . . . .

> **THE MONKEY WRENCH GANG IS LESS A CLEAR-CUT CALL TO ACTION THAN A CALL TO FEELING."**

Source: Steve Norwick, "Nietzschean Themes in the Works of Edward Abbey," in *Coyote in the Maze: Tracking Edward Abbey in a World of Words*, edited by Peter Quigley, University of Utah Press, 1998, pp. 184–205.

Scott Slovic

In the following excerpt, Slovic examines the disorienting elusive world, depicted alternately as secure and deceptive, of The Monkey Wrench Gang.

. . . Is it also a goal of Abbey's fiction to evoke in us some sort of fundamental disorientation that will pass for awareness—awareness, at least, of the difficulty of knowing the world? I believe this is precisely the aim of Abbey's best-known novel, *The Monkey Wrench Gang* (and Paul T. Bryant has made a similar argument concerning the novel's posthumous sequel, *Hayduke Lives!*). In fact, the 1975 novel, far from being overtly ideological, calls into question the very notion of allowing a static ideology, whether pro-environment or pro-development, to govern our behavior in the wilderness. The world Abbey depicts in *The Monkey Wrench Gang* is a pliant, elusive one, alternately secure and deceptive. As we read, we find our attention shifting incessantly from the real-world issues of wilderness use to the conspicuously artificial realm of Abbey's adventure story, and further to the purely aesthetic level of lavish description and exuberant wordplay, then promptly back to the clashing ideologies. Abbey, it seems, delights in luring us to make a commitment to one ideology or another, to one mode of reading or another, only to pull the rug out from under our feet suddenly. Suckered into the novel by the fast-moving narrative of environmental sabotage, we find ourselves unable to halt the roller coaster until the ride comes to its scheduled end.

Reading *The Monkey Wrench Gang* is like attempting a controlled "friction descent" down a thirty-foot rock wall with George Washington Hayduke, the novel's Green-Beret-turned-ecoterrorist. Both the world and himself are deceptive to Hayduke, and he, it turns out at the conclusion of the novel, is the grandest deceiver of all. He commits himself to the firm, cool contours of the wall, only to realize too late that the cliff has no visible bottom and offers no real friction. He can't prevent his hands from releasing their grip; nor does he know whether he has uttered an audible cry. He is in a situation beyond his control, subject to the friction-lessness of the rock, the pull of gravity, and the solidity of the ground where he'll eventually land, where he'll experience the full "shock of the real." We don't actually see Hayduke hit the ground: Abbey cuts to a later scene as Hayduke and his three fellow saboteurs—Doc Sarvis, Bonnie Abbzug, and Seldom Seen Smith—continue their escape through the desert with Bishop Love's posse on their trail. But we do learn that he survives the fall, albeit with "bruised limbs and abraded hide [and] lacerated palms."

We, too, are never quite sure what is real as we free-fall through the narrative, expecting one thing and often (but not always) getting another. Just what is the ideological bedrock of the novel? Abbey, perhaps more than any other recent nature writer, has been cursed by some readers and exalted by others as a left-wing ideologue, as a cantankerous gadfly of the military-industrial complex. Edwin Way Teale calls *Desert Solitaire* "a voice crying in the wilderness, *for* the wilderness." And Grace Lichtenstein, reviewing *The Monkey Wrench Gang* for the *New York Times*, notes that Abbey "has been the most eloquent spokesman for angry nature-lovers"; "his message," she continues, "that only a radical change in the American life-style or even more radical action will preserve the land for future genera-tions—has become a watchword among the growing minority of those who call themselves 'eco-freaks.'" Indeed, *The Monkey Wrench Gang* inspired the formation of Earth First!, the coun-try's most visible and radical preservationist group. But what some readers have found to be the direct espousal of an extremist ideology has proven to be a more perplexing text for other readers—and rightly so. Ann Ronald points out in *The New West of Edward Abbey* that this work "has more ambition than an ordinary propa-ganda novel of eco-raiders and environmental protest and speaks more profoundly than a vul-gar little fairy tale." This novel, she continues, "broaden[s] the dimensions of romance" to "project Abbey's increasingly complex vision of

what man [sic] can do to stop the twentieth cen-tury from cannibalizing its land and its human-ity." In keeping with her assessment of *The Monkey Wrench Gang*, Ronald also observes that Abbey uses "his sense of humor to pro-nounce a sobering message." I suggest that the purely aesthetic element (including wordplay and other types of humor) in virtually all of Abbey's works is there not only to be entertain-ing, not only to make serious material more palatable, but chiefly to *conflict* with the moral strata of the texts. Rather than merging to "pro-nounce" Abbey's "sobering message" about the environment, the aesthetic and moral currents in *The Monkey Wrench Gang* strain to become sep-arate, like oil and water; they produce a tense disjunction that forces us, as readers, to stay on our toes.

After calling *The Monkey Wrench Gang* a "violently . . . revolutionary novel" and a "long, extravagant, finely written tale of ecological sab-otage in the American Southwest" in a 1976 *New York Times* review, Jim Harrison observes the "irony" that

> Edward Abbey wrote the book in an atmos-phere of political vacuum as a sort of soldier of the void when the only possible audience the book could truly resonate against, the New Left, had largely turned to more refined dope, natural foods, weird exercises, mail order con-sciousness programs, boutiques and Indians (jewelry). Surely a base of warhorses is left, a core of politically astute veterans who have changed their pace but not their intentions, but the sense of mass movement is deader than Janis Joplin. (59)

The Monkey Wrench Gang, however, is not really designed to launch a mass movement or to strike home merely with a base of stalwart "war-horses" such as the Earth First! activists who have come to bear out the author's mock dis-claimer on the copyright page of the novel: "This book, though fictional in form, is based strictly on historical fact. Everything in it is real and actually happened. And it all happened just one year from today." I think the goal of this novel is far more universal than Harrison and Lichten-stein suggest in their early reviews. That is, instead of merely presenting an environmental ideology or even a group of fictional role models for would-be activists, Abbey is trying to prompt a more base kind of consciousness among his readers, to provoke not a singleminded political movement but rather an awareness on the indi-vidual level of the need to question moral and aesthetic assumptions. *The Monkey Wrench Gang* is less a clear-cut call to action than a call to feeling.

To the extent that the novel *does* bear a political message, it does so in the manner of Raymond Barrio's postmodern protest novel *The Plum Plum Pickers*, which first appeared in 1969. Rather than engaging us in individual migrant workers' frustrated quests for self-realization or for mere day-to-day security, Barrio presents a series of disjunctive vignettes, skipping from scene to scene with scant narrative continuity, describing even the foulest situations with incongruously lush prose, as if to emphasize tacitly the gap between the characters' dreams and their actual predicaments. In one scene, a group of rowdy farm workers, after leaving a bar, winds up in a garbage dump to enjoy "a good long heartfelt piss":

> They were floating in the midst of a sea of garbage, all lit up by the light of the romantic moon, lovingly delineating every scrap, every crump of used paper, every bent straw, every spent can of lucky, every piece of string, every spawn of stinking, decaying, moldy, barnacled banana peel. Mounds and mounds of pure useless garbage gently degenerating in the warm moonlight.

Abbey, too—beginning in the initial scene of his novel, the ceremonial opening of a bridge over the Colorado River between Utah and Arizona that becomes an opportunity for flamboyant monkey-wrenchery—makes a point of depicting morally charged situations in lovingly amoral language. After several tedious speeches, fireworks are exploded and the crowd at the bridge cheers, "thinking this the high point of the ceremonies." "But it was not," Abbey writes:

> Not the highest high point. Suddenly the center of the bridge rose up, as if punched from beneath, and broke in two along a jagged zigzag line. Through this absurd fissure, crooked as lightning, a sheet of red flame streamed skyward, followed at once by the sound of a great cough, a thunderous shuddering high-explosive cough that shook the monolithic sandstone of the canyon walls. The bridge parted like a flower, its separate divisions no longer joined by any physical bond. Fragments and sections began to fold, sag, sink and fall, relaxing into the abyss. Loose objects—gilded scissors, a monkey wrench, a couple of empty Cadillacs—slid down the appalling gradient of the depressed roadway and launched themselves, turning slowly, into space. They took a long time going down and when they finally smashed on the rock and river far below, the sound of the impact, arriving much later, was barely heard by even the most attentive.

> The bridge was gone. The wrinkled fragments at either end still clinging to their foundations in the bedrock dangled toward each other like pendant fingers, suggesting the thought but lacking the will to touch. As the compact plume of dust resulting from the catastrophe expanded upward over the rimrock, slabs of asphalt and cement and shreds and shards of steel and rebar continued to fall, in contrary motion from the sky, splashing seven hundred feet below into the stained but unhurried river.

The description of this event defines it as neither heroic nor criminal. The morally neutral language beguiles us into forgetting what this final explosion means to the human observers, those who want the new bridge and those who don't. Despite the use of the word "catastrophe" in the midst of this descriptive passage, we are not made to feel that we are witnessing a genuine catastrophe. In fact, after reading these exquisitely violent and seemingly inhuman paragraphs, it shocks us when the narrative perspective returns suddenly to the petty human level and we overhear various public officials plotting to catch the saboteurs once and for all; the effect is more comical than moving. Then, in the next breath, we return to the cosmic perspective, to the "ultimate farthest eye" of the vulture high above in the sky, "so far beyond all consequence of dust and blue [of land and water]," who "contemplat[es] the peaceful scene below" and derives no meaning from it. But this shifting perspective does not instill the narrative with a discernible moral imperative, either in this first scene or elsewhere. We feel a constant tension between the passions of the human characters and the passionless gaze of the cosmos, represented intermittently by a circling vulture.

The focus of *The Plum Plum Pickers* is ultimately more restricted than that of *The Monkey Wrench Gang*, stimulating, if we can bear with its plotlessness, our awareness of the farm workers' lot, but nothing broader or deeper. On the other hand, Abbey's novel, though it doesn't attach us firmly to a single perspective on the environment, helps us to become aware of the interplay (and frequently the *opposition*) between morality (a sense of right and wrong) and the amoral perception of phenomena (including the perception of beautiful objects and beautiful language). In this respect, *The Monkey Wrench Gang* reminds me of Vladimir Nabokov's *Lolita* (1955); as a graduate student at Brown University, I occasionally taught them together in undergraduate courses to demonstrate this connection. In his 1980 interview with the *Bloomsbury Review*, Abbey mentioned his respect for Nabokov, "chiefly as a stylist, a master of the language" (Solheim and Levin 83). But I think *The Monkey Wrench Gang* betrays Abbey's deeper affinity with Nabokov's Rousseauvian novel about the wayward passion resulting from the narrator's obsessive yearning to recapture the innocence and beauty of childhood, particularly with the disjunctive use of lavish, punning language to tell such a violent and, to most readers, perverse story. In an early scene, the middle-aged Humbert Humbert recalls the "nymphet" Lolita sprawling innocently across his lap:

> She was musical and apple-sweet. Her legs twitched a little as they lay across my live lap; I stroked them; there she lolled in the right-hand corner, almost asprawl, Lola the bobby-soxer, devouring her immemorial fruit, singing through its juice, losing her slipper, rubbing the heel of her slipperless foot in its sloppy anklet, against the pile of old magazines heaped on my left on the sofa—and every movement she made, every shuffle and ripple, helped me to conceal and to improve the secret system of tactile correspondence between beast and beauty—between my gagged, bursting beast and the beauty of her dimpled body in its innocent cotton frock.

When *Lolita* first appeared in the mid-1950s, American readers recoiled from it, crying "pornography!" In response, the author attached a few notes to the end of the book, explaining that he was "neither a reader nor a writer of didactic fiction," that "*Lolita* has no moral in tow," and that for him "a work of fiction exists only insofar as it affords...aesthetic bliss" (286). But do most readers believe this? I've found that it requires considerable coaching to get student readers beyond the sexual surface of *Lolita*, to help them appreciate the tension between the playful language and the narrative of desire and remorse. Abbey himself refers similarly to "the sheer ecstasy of the creative moment" in his introduction to *Abbey's Road*: "It is this transient moment of bliss," he writes, "which is for the artist, as it is for other lovers, the one ultimate, indescribable, perfectly sufficient justification for the sweat and pain and misery and humiliation and doubt that lead, if lucky, to the consummation we desire" (xxiii). It may seem out of character for Edward Abbey, whom many

readers came to view as a rather traditional storyteller and environmental advocate in the wake of *Desert Solitaire*, to voice this postmodern devotion to rarefied "aesthetic bliss." A few years ago, at a conference on postmodernism, I heard John Hawkes state that *his* goal as a writer is to enjoy the eroticism of language, to seek the never-quite-attainable aesthetic bliss of crafting the perfect sentence. But Abbey claimed in a 1977 interview at the University of Arizona Poetry Center and again in the *Abbey's Road* introduction (note the explicit Beatles' pun in the title) that he "never wanted to be an environmental crusader, an environmental journalist." "I wanted to be a fiction writer," he explained, "a novelist" (Hepworth 39).

Indeed, in *The Monkey Wrench Gang* Abbey creates a highly aestheticized fictional world, but it's a world in constant tension with the real American Southwest that his readers know, or at least know about. Ronald calls the novel "simply another Edward Abbey romance," a book that "projects a fictive version of Edward Abbey's wildest nonfiction dreams. The Western formula circumscribes his exuberant imagination, inducing him to impose a nineteenth-century brand of frontier justice on the modern atrocities he sees everywhere." But beyond the evocation of anachronistic "frontier justice" in response to twentieth-century environmental problems, *The Monkey Wrench Gang* never lets us forget, at least not for long, that it is an artifact, a work of the imagination. Abbey seems to take advantage of his readers' perception of him as "an environmental crusader" to defy facile wish fulfilment. His artifice is evident at nearly every level of the novel, and the seams are intentionally left showing. Similarly, Bryant remarks in his study of *Hayduke Lives!* (1990), after listing the novel's precise echoes of such disparate works as *The Grapes of Wrath* and Kipling's poem "The Betrothed," that "[t]his is text calling attention to the literary nature of its own textuality" (317).

The first four chapters mechanically sketch the characters who will soon become the infamous gang of marauders, and although the characterizations are lively and, as Jim Harrison said, "convincing," they are nonetheless caricatures, exaggerated character *types*. "A. K. Sarvis, M.D.," the pollution-hating Albuquerque surgeon who underwrites the group's adventures, is immediately ascribed grotesque physical characteristics and a whimsical scholarly interest in the environment; Sarvis's "bald mottled dome and savage visage, grim and noble as Sibelius," and his "tall and ponderous [frame], shaggy as a bear," contrast strangely with his playful intellect and his actual inexperience in wild places. The first thing we learn about George Washington Hayduke is that he is an ex-Green Beret with a "grudge," for he returned after three years in Vietnam "to the American Southwest he had been remembering only to find it no longer what he remembered, no longer the clear and classical desert, the pellucid sky he roamed in dreams." Hayduke, "a short, broad, burly fellow, well-muscled, built like a wrestler," whose "face is hairy, very hairy, with a wide mouth and good teeth, big cheekbones and a thick shock of blue-black hair," represents the brawn of the Monkey Wrench Gang, his animal aspects emerging through ceaseless swearing, beer swilling, "pissing," sexual impulses, and love of guns and violence (later in the novel, he is called an "anthropoid ape"). Seldom Seen Smith, a maverick Mormon who makes his living as a river runner, is the gang's closest thing to a traditional environmentalist, but his earnest love of the Utah landscape is generally concealed beneath his eccentricities, which include his physical appearance; Abbey tells us early on that "Smith was a lanky man, lean as a rake, awkward to handle. His arms were long and wiry, his hands large, his feet big, flat and solid. He had a nose like a beak, a big Adam's apple, ears like the handles on a jug, sunbleached hair like a rat's nest, and a wide and generous grin." The fourth caricature is that of the New Age secretary and lover of Doc Sarvis (and later of Hayduke), "Ms. B. Abbzug," whose witty feminism and splendid sexuality become her trademarks. The physical, verbal, and philosophical traits of these four characters become prominent motifs in the novel; the four are at once convincingly consistent and exaggeratedly stylized.

The structure of the work is neatly symmetrical, framing the bulk of the narrative within a prologue subtitled "The Aftermath" (the bridge scene already discussed) and an epilogue called "The New Beginning." This conspicuously clever framing contributes to the reader's awareness of the work's fictionality. So, too, do the narrative's many premonitory moments—scenes such as Hayduke's previously discussed "friction descent" and his escape from Bishop Love's

WHEN THEIR FREEDOM IS PITTED AGAINST THEIR SOCIAL OBLIGATION TO RENDER MEDICAL AID, THEY CHOOSE TO HONOR THEIR SOCIAL OBLIGATION."

Search & Rescue Team early in the book by winching himself and his jeep down a cliff, scenes that foreshadow Hayduke's mysterious disappearance and presumed death at the edge of yet another cliff in the penultimate chapter of the book. The epilogue, of course, reveals semimysteriously that Hayduke has survived once again; indeed, as mentioned above, the title of the sequel to *The Monkey Wrench Gang* is *Hayduke Lives!* . . . .

Source: Scott Slovic, "Aestheticism and Awareness: The Psychology of Edward Abbey's *The Monkeywrench Gang*," in *CEA Critic*, Vol. 55, No. 3, Spring/Summer 1993, pp. 54–68.

Paul T. Bryant
In the following essay, Bryant argues that Abbey was a "balanced, eminently rational environmental moderate" despite the emphasis placed on his extreme characters.

When Edward Abbey visited my campus some years ago, I was curious to know what he was like. His public lecture was in the tone one might expect from his writing—a mixture of Jack Burns and George Washington Hayduke. But I was interested in the person behind the public image. At a reception at a colleague's house, after the lecture, I hoped to meet that person.

Before many people had arrived, Abbey was quiet, affable, relaxed. As the number of people increased to a loud, milling mob, he became visibly less comfortable. Finally, he retreated as unobtrusively as possible to the kitchen. I was already there, having made a similar retreat a few minutes earlier. We had a quiet conversation that ended only when others found where he had fled.

From that brief acquaintance, I got the strong sense that Edward Abbey was not the sharp-tongued, outrageous anarchist so many believe him to have been . . ., but rather a quiet, shy, thoughtful man who created a far different persona for public consumption. Confirmation has since come from others. Barry Lopez, for example, writes of Abbey's "ingenuous shyness, so at odds with the public image of a bold iconoclast."

My thesis here is that such a personality, and such a vision, lie at the bottom of the aggregate of Edward Abbey's writing. This idea is hardly new, of course. Other critics, such as Garth McCann, Ann Ronald, and Jerry Herndon, have found a balanced, eminently rational environmental moderate in Abbey's non-fiction nature writing, despite his more extreme statements, and despite popular emphasis on some of his more extreme fictional characters. I would like to demonstrate the soundness of that thesis, and to explore the complex ways this moderation beneath the surface of extremism has been stated outright in Abbey's non-fiction and has evolved as a definitive counterpoint to the more colorful extremism in his fiction.

[Abbey's] position is clearly stated in *Desert Solitaire*. Early in that book Abbey observes not, as readers of his fiction might expect, that wilderness is the desirable alternative to civilization, but rather that "wilderness is a necessary part of civilization." No Luddite, he can make use of the genuine benefits of civilization. The refrigerator, for example, is a useful machine for producing ice for his drinks: "Once the drink is mixed, however, I always go *outside*, out in the light and the air and the space and the breeze, to enjoy it. Making the best of both worlds, that's the thing." (*Desert Solitaire*). Despite his often stated enjoyment of solitude, Abbey in *Desert Solitaire* also denies that he is misanthropic. The one thing better than solitude, he says, is society, not of crowds but of friends. What he objects to, he insists, is what he calls anthropocentricity, not science, but science and technology misapplied. "Balance," he concludes, "that's the secret. Moderate extremism. The best of both worlds . . . ."

The same theme arises in *The Journey Home*. There Abbey denies that technology and industry are inherently evil, but insists that they must be kept under control, "to prevent them from ever again becoming the self-perpetuating, ever-expanding monsters we have allowed them to become." "Optimum industrialism, neither too much nor too little," a moderate level of technology, is what he urges.

Consistent with this Hellenic moderation is Abbey's praise of objective realism and rationality. Again in *The Journey Home* he says that the poet of our age must begin with the scientific view of the world. There is, he says, "more charm in one 'mere' fact, confirmed by test and observation, linked to other facts through coherent theory into a rational system, than in a whole brainful of fancy and fantasy." In short, Abbey does not display the romanticism or the sentimentality so often associated with extreme environmentalism. His vision is that of the moderate realist. As he says in *Abbey's Road*, he wishes "to stand apart, alone if need be, and hold up the ragged flag of reason. Reason with a capital R—sweet Reason, the newest and rarest thing in human life, the most delicate child of human history."

Thus the Abbey of his non-fiction takes moderate views, yet the colorful extremists of his fiction continue to attract the attention and usually the sympathy of Abbey's readers. Are they the true representative of Abbey's environmentalism? Once his imagination has left the realistic constraints of non-fiction, does it give us Abbey's deepest beliefs? And do these creations of Abbey's imagination contradict or somehow give the lie to his more restrained and rational essays? No, they do not. Examined with care, and as part of the larger pattern of Abbey's work, these characters fit his vision of realistic rationality, not contradicting it but only keeping it open-ended and still available to the idealistic imagination.

To consider this pattern, perhaps it will be useful first to distinguish between two closely related but not identical themes in these works: human freedom, on the one hand, and nature undominated by human activity, on the other. The extreme of human freedom is anarchy, and the extreme of nature without human domination is wilderness. The two are intertwined in Abbey's work because wilderness is the one possible site for anarchic freedom. Wilderness, Abbey says in *Desert Solitaire*, is an assurance of freedom. Urban masses in a technological landscape are more easily controlled.

The anarchists in Abbey's writing begin with Jonathan Troy's father, the one-eyed Wobbly in Abbey's first novel. An ineffectual figure, the father is killed in a bar, shocking the protagonist into fleeing the bonds of his childhood. Thus the pattern for the anarchists in Abbey's fiction begins with monocular vision—seeing things from only one side—and with defeat.

In *The Brave Cowboy*, on the other hand, resistance to the established order takes two forms: the active, atavistic resistance of Jack Burns, the brave cowboy, and the passive, somewhat self-centered resistance of Paul Bondi. Both, within that novel, fail, but in Jack Burns, Abbey has begun to develop a figure that will finally suggest the necessary unquenchability of the spirit of freedom.

In his reversion to nineteenth-century ways of living, and the idealism of the romanticized old West (the solitary stranger fighting always for justice and the underdog), Burns is a quixotic figure in modern Duke City (Albuquerque). To emphasize this quixotic quality, Abbey makes Burns tall, thin, a college man turned cowboy, a clear parallel with Don Quixote, who is tall, very thin, and comes to knight errantry after its time has passed, through reading books. Burns is addressed by the Chicano children as "don charro," another indicator of the parallel. The final quixotic comparison, of course, is that Burns's mission to free Paul Bondi is mistaken because Burns misunderstands Bondi's reasons for draft resistance. And Jack Burns fails.

John Vogelin, in *Fire on the Mountain*, again stands quixotically against all odds—in his case the U.S. Government—and again fails. Abbey does not even allow him a moral victory. Vogelin has to acknowledge that the land he is trying to keep the government from "stealing" from him had come to him through a long line of theft and chicanery back to the time it was taken from the Indians, and perhaps even before that. Again, the anarchist is at least partially in the wrong, and he fails.

At this point in the development of the anarchic idea in Abbey's work, the fiction and the non-fiction cross in an interesting detail. In *Desert Solitaire*, Abbey devotes an entire chapter to the moon-eyed horse, who has broken free from working for humans and fled to a hard and lonely life in an arid Utah canyon. It is a tall, gaunt animal, seventeen hands high, gelded, blind in one eye (monocular vision), and totally alone in a harsh life of the barest subsistence. Abbey pursues it and tries to bring it back to society by talking to it of grain, lush grass, easy living, and the companionship of its own kind, but the horse will have none of it.

The monocular vision of the lonely horse suggests the monocular vision of Nat Troy. Thus having one eye begins to suggest a single, extreme way of seeing the world, the way of completely untrammeled freedom. The fact that the horse is gelded suggests that the anarchic drive for complete freedom, a traditional western theme, is essentially sterile.

This set of images—the anarchist disposition associated with the single good eye, the tall, gaunt, quixotic figures of horse and man, continue in *The Monkey Wrench Gang* in the one-eyed "lone ranger" who befriends Hayduke. By the time Hayduke is resurrected at the end of the novel, he, rather than the one-eyed man, is riding the tall (as before, seventeen hands high) horse. By this time, too, the tall horse is named Rosie, clearly suggesting Don Quixote's tall, thin horse Rozinante.

Offsetting these figures, Abbey provides a suitable set of villains, but the most interesting of these are the sympathetic villains, the men who oppose Don Quixote, but do so with sympathy, and not totally to the death. In *The Brave Cowboy*, there is Sheriff Morlin Johnson, a complex, educated, balanced man who appreciates the wilderness, and understands Jack Burns's desire for freedom well enough to know how to pursue him successfully. In *Fire on the Mountain*, Lee Mackie is not a villain, but he presents again the balanced man who can understand both sides of the dispute.

In *The Monkey Wrench Gang*, the novel in which all the threads of Abbey's interest in wilderness and freedom come together most completely, there is a whole spectrum of figures ranging from George Washington Hayduke, the total anarchist, to Bishop Love, the arch-representative of the Establishment. Seldom Seen Smith loves the wilderness, freedom, and women, but lacks the preoccupation with violence that Hayduke has. Bonnie Abbzug and Dr. Sarvis are environmentalists but not anarchists *per se*. Anarchy merely becomes their hope for saving the habitability of the Southwest. When their freedom is pitted against their social obligation to render medical aid, they choose to honor their social obligation.

Perhaps the most interesting on the villains' side of this spectrum is Bishop Love's younger brother Sam. Again we have the sympathetic, less-than-total villain. He even appears to have guessed Hayduke's final trick on the rocky point, calling into the cleft in the rock, to "Rudolf," that he cannot always fool everyone.

Finally, even the Bishop softens his position, forgiving Seldom Seen Smith the cost of his vehicle. So at last only Hayduke and the one-eyed stranger remain unyielding extremists, defeated but still alive to fight another day. Even Hayduke has an unspoken debt to Sam for not revealing his trick on the rocky point: it is the moderate who allows the anarchist to survive.

Yet another sympathetic Villain appears in *Good News*, in the figure of Colonel Charles Barnes. Barnes is made the alienated but partially understanding son of the anarchist. By creating this connection Abbey seems again to be emphasizing the essential relationship, the shared humanity, of the extremists of both camps. Barnes finally conceals from authority the fact that Jack Burns, with his singular vision of freedom, may yet live. Again the moderate allows the anarchist to survive.

What has evolved, then, is an image of a quixotic searcher for freedom and wilderness undisturbed, a figure that is extreme, ironic, always doomed to failure, but nevertheless immortal. The immortality has been added as Abbey's themes have developed. With it, Abbey suggests that extremism cannot succeed, but that perhaps the extreme of anarchy and wilderness is necessary to counterbalance the repressive and environmentally destructive forces of unbridled technology and exploitation. For this reason, it should be allowed to survive.

Source: Paul T. Bryant, "Edward Abbey and Environmental Quixoticism," in *Western American Literature*, Vol. 24, No. 1, May 1989, pp. 37–43.

SOURCES

Abbey, Edward, "Cowboys and Indians, Part II," in *Desert Solitaire: A Season in the Wilderness*, McGraw-Hill, 1968, pp. 95–111.

———, *The Monkey Wrench Gang*, Harper Perennial, 2006.

Barber, Katrine E., "Wisecracking Glen Canyon Dam: Revisioning Environmentalist Mythology," in *Change in the American West: Exploring the Human Dimension*, University of Nevada Press, 1996, pp. 127–43.

Bishop, James, Jr., *Epitaph for a Desert Anarchist: The Life and Legacy of Edward Abbey*, Atheneum, 1994, pp. 54–140.

Brinkley, Douglas, Introduction to *The Monkey Wrench Gang*, Harper Perennial, 2006, pp. xv–xxiv.

Bryant, Paul T., "Edward Abbey and Environmental Quixoticism," in *Western American Literature*, Vol. 24, No. 1, May 1989, pp. 37–43.

———, "Edward Abbey and Gender," in *Coyote in the Maze: Tracking Edward Abbey in a World of Words*, edited by Peter Quigley, University of Utah Press, 1998, pp. 231–33.

"Glen Canyon National Recreation Area," National Park Service website, http://www.nps.gov/glca/index.htm (accessed September 9, 2012).

Harrison, Jim, Review of *The Monkey Wrench Gang*, in *New York Times*, November 14, 1976; reprinted in *The Monkey Wrench Gang*, Harper Perennial, 2006, pp. PS10–PS11.

Loeffler, Jack, *Adventures with Ed: A Portrait of Abbey*, University of New Mexico Press, 2002, pp. 53, 80–82, 94–96, 105–108, 125–26, 172–73.

McKibben, Bill, "The Desert Anarchist," in *New York Review of Books*, August 18, 1988; reprinted in *The Monkey Wrench Gang*, Harper Perennial, 2006, pp. PS12–PS25.

Pozza, David M., *Bedrock and Paradox: The Literary Landscape of Edward Abbey*, Peter Lang, 2006, pp. 75–81.

Raglon, Rebecca, "Surviving Doom and Gloom: Edward Abbey's Desert Comedies," in *Coyote in the Maze: Tracking Edward Abbey in a World of Words*, edited by Peter Quigley, University of Utah Press, 1998, pp. 168–83.

Ronald, Ann, *The New West of Edward Abbey*, 2nd ed., University of Nevada Press, 2000, pp. 181–209.

Rosen, Elyssa, "The Roadless Area Conservation Rule," Pew Environment Group website, November 28, 2011, http://www.pewenvironment.org/news-room/other-resources/the-roadless-area-conservation-rule-85899363802 (accessed September 9, 2012).

Slovic, Scott, "Aestheticism and Awareness: The Psychology of Edward Abbey's *The Monkey Wrench Gang*," in *CEA Critic*, Vol. 55, No. 3, Spring–Summer 1993, pp. 54–68.

Solheim, Dave, and Rob Levin, "The *Bloomsbury Review* Interview," in *Resist Much, Obey Little: Some Notes on Edward Abbey*, Dream Garden Press, 1985, pp. 79–91; originally published in *Bloomsbury Review*, November/December 1980.

Tudge, Colin, "Back in Print: The Good Fight," in *New Statesman*, Vol. 133, No. 4701, August 16, 2004, p. 40.

FURTHER READING

Foreman, Dave, and Bill Haywood, *Ecodefense: A Field Guide to Monkeywrenching*, 3rd ed., Abbzug Press, 1993.
    Earth First! cofounder Foreman presents here a technical manual offering advice as to how to follow in the footsteps of Abbey's novel's

characters and wreak havoc with industry. Abbey provides a "Forward!"

Gaskill, David L., and Gudy Gaskill, *Peaceful Canyon, Golden River: A Photographic Journey through Fabled Glen Canyon*, Colorado Mountain Club Press, 2002.

This book, one of several recent such publications, contains an archive of photographs that reveal the incomparable original beauty of Glen Canyon, many taken by the Gaskills themselves.

Lee, Katie, *Glen Canyon Betrayed: A Sensuous Elegy*, Fretwater Press, 2006.

Like Abbey, Lee had the privilege of seeing a great deal of the beauty of Glen Canyon before it was flooded, making some sixteen river trips through the area. Her memoir (originally published in 1998 as *All My Rivers Are Gone*) revolves around the delight and enchantment of her bygone experiences exploring the canyons.

Shay, Jonathan, *Achilles in Vietnam: Combat Trauma and the Undoing of Character*, Simon and Schuster, 1995.

This literary-historical work considers the psychological experiences of returning Vietnam War soldiers in light of insights from Homer's *Iliad*. Shay's volume may thus illuminate the unique position against American government and industry that Hayduke adopts in *The Monkey Wrench Gang*.

SUGGESTED SEARCH TERMS

Edward Abbey

The Monkey Wrench Gang

Abbey AND environment

Abbey AND Southwest

Abbey AND national parks

The Monkey Wrench Gang AND sabotage

Earth First!

Abbey AND Dave Foreman

Abbey AND Glen Canyon Dam

Mother to Mother

SINDIWE MAGONA

1998

Published in South Africa in 1998 and in the United States in 1999, Sindiwe Magona's fictional work, *Mother to Mother*, is based on the 1993 murder of Amy Biehl, an American student who was helping organize democratic elections in South Africa. The story is told from the perspective of Mandisa, a mother whose son participated in the murder. She writes a letter both to encourage Amy's mother, Mrs. Biehl, and to explain the culture that killed her daughter. This epistolary novel explores the effects of apartheid in South Africa. The themes of racism and hatred blend with the love and sorrow of motherhood in this story of loss and attempted reconciliation.

AUTHOR BIOGRAPHY

Magona was born on August 27, 1943, in Gungululu in Transkei, which is near Tsolo. Magona's family moved to Cape Town when she was four so her father could find work. She describes a nomadic childhood in her autobiography, *Forced to Grow*. "And there we had lived, moving from one segregated residential area to another until, in 1960, we were moved." The family was finally settled in the township of Guguletu. Despite the social injustice of apartheid, she was able to complete her secondary education and undergraduate studies from the University of South Africa by correspondence.

Magona worked as a teacher when she was nineteen, but she was forced to leave when she became pregnant. She married Luthando and worked in service jobs for wealthy white families until Luthando told her employer that he would no longer allow it. Her husband abandoned his family when Magona was twenty-three and pregnant with their third child. Magona again worked in domestic service to provide for her family while taking night courses, and she eventually returned to teaching. In 1981, she moved to New York City, where she attended Columbia University on a scholarship to earn a master's degree in social work.

After completing her education in 1983, Magona returned to her family in South Africa. She took a job at the United Nations in New York in 1984, where she worked toward ending apartheid by hosting radio programs until the rise of democracy in South Africa in 1994. In 1990, she published her first autobiography, *To My Children's Children*. *Forced to Grow*, another autobiography, soon followed in 1992. In 1993, she was granted an honorary doctorate by Hartwick College. *Mother to Mother* was published in 1998 on the five-year anniversary of Amy Biehl's murder, at the request of the Biehl family.

Magona retired from the United Nations and returned to South Africa in 2003. She continues to write while she works to promote a safe and just society in South Africa. Her other works include poetry, essays, plays, translations, and children's books. Magona has earned numerous awards, such as the Molteno Gold Medal for Lifetime Achievement and the Xhosa Heroes Award. In 2011, South African president Jacob G. Zuma presented her with the Order of Ikhamanga in Bronze.

PLOT SUMMARY

Chapter 1: Mandisa's Lament

Mother to Mother is an epistolary novel—taking the form of letters from one character to another—based on the 1993 murder of American Fulbright scholar Amy Biehl in South Africa. It is a letter to Biehl's mother from the mother of the teenage boy convicted of killing her. Magona includes words and phrases in the Xhosa language throughout the book, but they are either translated or clear from their context.

The first chapter is printed in italics because it directly addresses Mrs. Biehl. Mandisa introduces herself with the words: "My son killed your daughter." She goes on to explain that people blame her for the murder, assuming that she could control his actions. Mandisa, however, could not restrain her son. Even his conception was beyond her control; it was an event that she believes ruined her life.

Mandisa does say that she is not surprised her son committed murder because he is one of "these monsters our children have become." She is surprised, however, that Amy, a white woman, chose to come to Guguletu, an all-black reservation, or homeland, where she would be in danger. Here Mandisa contrasts the difference between her son and Amy. Amy did not realize her danger because her own experiences and good nature led her to believe that other people are good. Mandisa's son, on the other hand, knew only injustice, poverty, and violence. Now the government does more to protect his life than it did before he became a murderer. Mandisa ends the chapter by expressing her shame at her son's actions, confessing her love for him and asking God to forgive him.

Chapter 2: Mowbray—Wednesday 25 August 1993

The second chapter does not use italics because Mandisa shares what she imagines and experienced instead of addressing Mrs. Biehl directly. She begins by imagining Amy eating breakfast in a comfortable apartment before driving to the university. At the same time, Mandisa is waking her teenage children. Her daughter, Siziwe, has a room, but the boys, Mxolisi and Lunga, sleep in a tin hut, or *hokkie*, behind the house because the government-issued houses are too small for a family. She suppresses guilt at leaving her children alone while she works all day in the home of a white woman. She comes home too late and tired to keep her children in line. Mandisa knows that her family cannot survive without her job, but she also realizes that her absence creates another problem.

Mandisa shifts to a scene in which Amy says goodbye to her friends at the university. Amy is torn between happiness at the thought of going home and the sadness of leaving her friends. The rest of the chapter transitions quickly between the victim and her killer. Mxolisi, Mandisa's older son, does not go to school because of boycotts to protest the government. Instead he meets his friends in the street. At the university, Amy offers to drive her friends home to Guguletu. Meanwhile, Mxolisi and his friends vandalize a truck and chant political slogans as Amy's car approaches. They stone the car and kill the driver when they see that she is white.

Chapter 3: 5:15 p.m.—Wednesday 25 August 1993

Mandisa is working when her employer returns early and tells her that she has to go home because there is trouble in Guguletu. The employer drives Mandisa to the station because white people are not allowed in the district of Guguletu. The people on the bus speculate about what happened in their district. Mandisa considers the fact that there has been violence in the districts since the 1976 Soweto riots and the rise of student protests against apartheid.

She has a flashback to the time she came to Guguletu as a child. The district was already overcrowded and filled with broken families looking for their relatives. When Mandisa gets off the bus, she is nearly trampled by the police and other travelers. She loses a shoe and cuts her foot, but her primary concern is for her children, particularly Siziwe, as she makes her way home.

Chapter 4: 7:30 p.m.

Siziwe meets Mandisa when she arrives at the house. Lunga is home, but Mxolisi is not there. Mandisa is annoyed because she knows that Siziwe is hiding something from her. Her husband, Dwadwa, is not home either, but her main concern is for Mxolisi.

7:45 P.M.

Skonana, Mandisa's neighbor, comes over. She informs Mandisa that a white woman was stabbed on their street. Mandisa knows that the police, who do nothing to stop violence in Guguletu, will investigate this murder because the victim was white. The police are known to torture and kill innocent people in Guguletu, and she is afraid.

Chapter 5

Mandisa asks herself why anyone would come to Guguletu. She recalls how, as a girl, she came to the township in a "dispersal of the government's making.... More than three decades later, my people are still reeling from it." She has another flashback to the time when she was nine years

old. People in her village, Blouvlei, hear rumors that the government will remove all black people from their land, but no one believes it is possible. She remembers a happy home with her brother and parents, where her mother greets them every day after school. *Mama* is a term used for all older women, and *tata* means "father."

The next year, flyers are dropped from planes, informing the people that they have one month to relocate. Three months later, they are forcibly moved in the middle of the night as their homes are demolished. When the family comes to Guguletu, both parents have to work full-time for them to survive. She believes that "everything and everybody changed."

10:05 P.M.—WEDNESDAY 25 AUGUST 1993

Mxolisi and Dwadwa are still not home. Mandisa is concerned about her son and wonders why he stopped confiding in her. Dwadwa returns, and Mandisa cooks the spleen he brings home for the family supper. She considers how fortunate they are to have meat more than once a week.

Mandisa thinks about other times the help of white people was rejected; she recalls when three white nurses were attacked in 1960. After arguing with Dwadwa about Mxolisi's choice to abandon school and wander the streets, Mandisa reveals her belief that the education system failed and her children now suffer because of this failure.

In a section of the text that is in italics, she asks Mrs. Biehl whether her daughter went to school, and why she came to Guguletu if she was educated. She returns to describe the change that came over the children after school was rejected. At first, they burned down schools and stoned the cars of white people. This led to violence against members of their own community who were seen as traitors. The children became more difficult to control, but they were praised for their actions.

Chapter 6: 4:00 a.m.—Thursday 26 August 1993

Mandisa is awake in her bedroom when the police storm in to search for Mxolisi. The family is terrified, particularly Siziwe. Mandisa is questioned and slapped, and the *hokkie* is torn apart. Unable to find Mxolisi, the white police officers beat Lunga before leaving.

Chapter 7

The chapter begins by repeating an italicized statement from the first chapter, saying that Mxolisi was always trouble. Mandisa describes his conception as an event "totally destroying the me I was. The me I would have become." The chapter transitions from italics to a flashback of the circumstances surrounding Mxolisi's birth in 1973, when Mandisa was fifteen.

At the age of thirteen, Mandisa's mother panics that the teenager will "get a stomach," or become pregnant. Mandisa is not allowed to spend time with boys, but she meets China in school and becomes his girlfriend. Her mother becomes even more protective of her daughter's virginity when she learns that her son, Khaya, is dating Mandisa's now-pregnant friend Nono. She sends Mandisa away to live with her grandmother in Gungululu.

GUNGULULU—SEPTEMBER 1972

In Gungululu, Mandisa finishes primary school and is ranked second in her class. When Mandisa learns that her aunt is coming from the South African city of East London to have her baby, she plans on asking to accompany her home to East London so she can continue her education. Mandisa's dreams are shattered, however, when her aunt and grandmother notice that she is pregnant. Mandisa is confused because she is still technically a virgin. She cannot believe that she is three months pregnant. Her mother is contacted and brings Mandisa home in disgrace.

Chapter 8

In italics, Mandisa expresses the shame that Mxolisi brought her. His birth was a shame to her family.

During the ride home, the driver rants against the wealthy settlers who stole their land. When she arrives in Guguletu, Mandisa is not allowed to leave the house. She manages to contact China, but he refuses to take responsibility for the baby. Her family brings the case before China's clan, but they are slow to respond. A priest insists that they marry, and the clans begin negotiating.

Mandisa is still unmarried when her son is born, and she names him Hlumelo. Mandisa no longer wishes to marry China after the birth of her son; she wants to continue her education. Her clan, however, demands that her father make Mandisa go through with the marriage to China once the details are arranged. A few

months after her son is born, Mandisa is married when the families exchange a dowry and bride price, or *lobola*. She becomes part of a new clan. According to tradition, she is renamed, and the grandparents name her son. She is given a mocking name, and her son is renamed Mxolisi, meaning "he who would bring peace."

Her marriage is unhappy. As the newest wife, Mandisa must serve the rest of the family while caring for her son. She begins losing weight, and China's family refuses to fulfill their promise to allow her to go to school. Shortly after Mxolisi turns two, China disappears. Mandisa, who is left without any financial support, goes to work as a domestic servant. Soon she has the money to rent a *hokkie* and live on her own. Unfortunately, the changes affect her son, who misses his other relatives.

Mxolisi enjoys playing with the teenage boys of the family who rent Mandisa her *hokkie*. Zuzi and Mzamo treat Mxolisi like a brother. One day, the police chase Zuzi and Mzamo home, where they hide in a closet. Mxolisi tells the police where his friends are hiding, and he is traumatized when the boys are shot in front of him. Mxolisi does not speak after this incident. China's father intervenes and takes them to a healer, or *sangomo*. She tells Mandisa to free Mxolisi from her resentment of him. Mandisa knows that the *sangomo* is correct, and she tries to stop resenting her son for the life his birth took away from her.

Shortly after this meeting, Mandisa goes to her brother's wedding, where she meets Lungile. She refuses to marry him, but she allows him to stay with her as long as he wants. Lunga is born within a year. Mxolisi begins to wet his bed after the birth of his brother. After being punished, he asks, "Where is my own father?" These are the first words he has spoken in two years, and Mandisa has no answer.

Mxolisi is a bright student when he begins school. He starts to hate school, however, when teachers beat him for not having the money for fees. Meanwhile, Lungile leaves to become a freedom fighter. Mandisa persuades Mxolisi to stay in school, but he chooses to boycott classes in high school after becoming involved in politics. By this time, Mandisa has married Dwadwa, and Siziwe has been born.

Instead of going to school, Mxolisi roams the streets with his friends protesting and chanting slogans such as "One settler! One bullet!"

Mandisa's neighbors, however, tell her she should be proud of Mxolisi. He has a good reputation in the community. In fact, he saved a girl from being raped when no one else would intervene. Now the same people who praised Mxolisi scorn Mandisa.

Chapter 9

6 A.M.—THURSDAY 26 AUGUST

Mandisa returns the narrative to the morning after the murder. After the police leave, her neighbors come over, but Dwadwa chases them away. Lunga is beaten, but the wounds are superficial. Siziwe is traumatized, and she tells her mother that Mxolisi came home and left quickly before Mandisa arrived. Mandisa wonders why the police want Mxolisi, and Dwadwa tells her, "How long have I told you that this child will bring us heavy trouble one day?" He leaves for work, and Mandisa falls asleep.

Chapter 10

Mandisa has another flashback to her childhood. She remembers when her grandfather Tatomkhulu came to live with her family. From him, she learns the history of South Africa from the perspective of the native people. He begins, "For, let me tell you something, deep run the roots of hatred here." He explains that the white settlers came and took their land. To be rid of the settlers, the Xhosa people sacrificed all of their cattle and crops because the prophet Nongqawause promised that the land would be restored and the settlers driven away. The prophecy is printed in italics, emphasizing the importance of this oral history. The sacrifice was unsuccessful, and the people were forced to work in the mines or starve. The same hatred that motivated the sacrifice motivates Mxolisi's actions.

1 P.M.—THURSDAY 26 AUGUST

Siziwe wakes Mandisa and tells her that Lunga has gone with some boys. Siziwe also tells her that she believes Mxolisi had something to do with the murder. Mandisa does not have time to process this information before Reverend Mananga comes to the house. He leaves a message that Mxolisi's group may use the church to meet, and he gives Mandisa a note with instructions to take a taxi to the last stop. There, she is given instructions to go to a location where a car takes her to Mxolisi's hiding place.

Mandisa asks Mxolisi if he killed the girl, and he swears that he was not the only one to attack the car and was not the only one to stab her. Mandisa is both angry and terrified. She lashes out at the stupidity of killing a white woman and sees the fear in her son's eyes. They cling to each other and cry, and she finds herself unable to release his hand.

Chapter 11

Returning to italics, Mandisa questions her "Sister-Mother," asking what she should do with her son. She wonders if they are enemies and if caring for her son means that she does not mourn the death of the girl he murdered. She also wishes that Amy had known fear and stayed away from Guguletu.

Leaving italics, she says that the same people who praised her son now treat her family with derision. Although Mandisa is ashamed of what Mxolisi has done, she places some of the blame on the leaders who encouraged his behavior, saying, "They, as surely as my son, are your daughter's murderers." Mandisa sees no changes from the children in her community or the leaders who encourage them. She asks why her son was the only one punished for a mob attack, and she ends the chapter mourning the actions of her son and asking for God's help.

GUGULETU, MUCH LATER

Mandisa's friends and neighbors come to help her grieve. With their help, she is able to find strength and hope for the future. The knowledge that people are helping children in Guguletu gives her hope that violence will end. She also allows herself to hope that Mxolisi will find a better life. She ends the chapter in italics, attempting to console her Sister-Mother, telling her that she has nothing to be ashamed of in the way that she raised her child.

Chapter 12

In italics, Mandisa restates a question from the first chapter. "What had he to live for?" He saw his future in the lives of the men around him, who worked labor-intensive jobs with little pay. There are no chances for anyone to advance who is born outside the "white world." Mandisa believes his generation is lost because they see only despair for the future.

GUGULETU—LATE AFTERNOON, WEDNESDAY 25 AUGUST

The final chapter of the books plays out the events of the murder from the moment Amy's car enters Guguletu. Mandisa calls her son the "sharpened arrow of the wrath of his race" while Amy was "the sacrifice of hers." She ends by wishing that circumstances had been different and her son would not yet be a murderer, which implies that the hatred necessary to kill would always be with him.

CHARACTERS

Amy Biehl

Mandisa does not use Amy Biehl's name, but the character is clearly Amy from the introduction. A Fulbright scholar, Amy was assisting with the first democratic election in South Africa. Mandisa imagines her last day in detail. In Mandisa's mind, she spends the day saying goodbye to her friends because she will soon return to the United States. She drives her friends home to Guguletu, where she is murdered. In the real history, a group of boys in Guguletu were convicted of her murder. In the fictionalized version in this book, Mxolisi is the only one convicted of murdering Amy.

Mrs. Biehl

Mandisa does not call her "Sister-Mother" by name, but the letter is obviously addressed to Amy's mother. She is Mandisa's audience, and the reader must speculate on her reaction to the letter.

China

China is Mandisa's first boyfriend and, later, her husband. He resents Mandisa for not having an abortion. Bitter about being forced to marry Mandisa, he abandons his family after Mxolisi's second birthday.

Dwadwa

Dwadwa is Mandisa's second husband and Siziwe's father. He warns Mandisa that Mxolisi will cause them trouble.

Funiwe

Funiwe is Mandisa's aunt. She lives in East London, but she travels to Gungululu to be with her mother when she is pregnant.

Hlumelo

See Mxolisi

Khaya

Khaya is Mandisa's brother. He dates Mandisa's best friend, Nono, when they are teenagers. Nono becomes pregnant, which causes Mandisa's mother to grow even stricter with Mandisa. Khaya marries Nono when she is pregnant with their second child.

Kukwana

Kukwana is the childhood name of Mandisa and Khaya's mother. She works a service job to provide for her family after moving to Guguletu. She is overprotective of Mandisa and sends her away after she learns Nono is pregnant. She is humiliated when she discovers that Mandisa is pregnant.

Lunga

Lunga is the son of Mandisa and Lungile. His parents are never married, and his father leaves to become a freedom fighter. The police beat him because he is Mxolisi's brother.

Lungile

Lungile meets Mandisa at Nono and Khaya's wedding. He is the father of Lunga, but he leaves Mandisa to become a freedom fighter.

Makhulu

Makhulu is Mandisa's grandmother. Mandisa discovers that she is pregnant while staying with Makhulu in Gungululu.

Reverend Mananga

Reverend Mananga is a friend of Mxolisi's who come to Mandisa's home the day after the murder. Pretending to leave a message for Mxolisi, he secretly slips a note to Mandisa. The note provides instructions that take her to Mxolisi's hiding place.

Mandisa

Mandisa is Mxolisi's mother and the narrator of *Mother to Mother*. She feels conflicted between feelings of love for her son and shame that he murdered Amy Biehl. In an effort to comfort Mrs. Biehl, she writes a letter sharing details about her feelings, her life, and society under apartheid. Her private confessions explore the history of race relations in South Africa as well as the changes that apartheid brought to society.

Mandisa uses flashbacks to her own childhood and Mxolisi's childhood to explain life in Guguletu. As a child, she is relocated from her home to Guguletu. She finds herself pregnant with Mxolisi as a teenager, and she is both a wife and mother at the age of fifteen. Mandisa works in service jobs to provide for her family after her husband abandons her. She has a relationship with Lungile and gives birth to her second son, Lunga. After Lungile leaves, she marries Dwadwa and has her daughter, Siziwe.

Mandisa feels guilty that work prevents her from spending more time with her children, but she must work for her family to survive. After the murder, she suffers the rejection of her peers. After her neighbors reach out to her, she becomes hopeful that the future will be better.

Mxolisi

Mxolisi is the son of Mandisa and China. Mandisa names him Hlumelo, but his father's family renames him Mxolisi, meaning "he who would bring peace." China abandons him when he is two, and Mandisa raises him on her own. Shortly after his father leaves, Mxolisi innocently informs the police where two of his friends are hiding. He is traumatized when they are killed in front him, and he does not speak for two years.

As a teenager, Mxolisi boycotts school as a political protest. He saves a girl from being raped when no one else will help her. This noble act brings him respect in Guguletu, but the respect is short-lived. Filled with rage at white oppression, he participates in the murder of Amy Biehl simply because she is a white person in Guguletu. He hides, but he is discovered by the police and convicted of murder.

Mzamo

Mzamo is the teenage son of Mandisa's landlord. He and his brother, Zuzi, play with Mxolisi when he is a young child. The police kill him when Mxolisi innocently tells them where he and Zuzi are hiding.

Nongqawause

Nongqawause is the prophet who advised the Xhosa people to sacrifice all of their crops and cattle. She promised that the sacrifice would drive the settlers away and save their land. The prophecy is unfulfilled, and the people suffer starvation because of their sacrifice.

Nono

Nono is Mandisa's best friend. She dates Khaya, Mandisa's brother and becomes pregnant as a teenager. She marries Khaya when she is pregnant with their second child.

Sister-Mother

See Mrs. Biehl

Siziwe

Siziwe is Mandisa's youngest child and her only daughter. Siziwe's father is Dwadwa. She initially hides information about Mxolisi from Mandisa. After the police leave their house, she is traumatized and tells her mother that Mxolisi came home after the murder but left the house before Mandisa arrived.

Skonana

Skonana is Mandisa's neighbor. She comes over the night of the murder and tells Mandisa that a white girl was stabbed on their street that day. Long after the murder, she comes to help Mandisa grieve.

Tatomkhulu

Tatomkhulu is Mandisa's grandfather. He teaches her history from the perspective of the Xhosa people. He explains that hatred is part of South African history and culture. He tells her hatred for white settlers was the reason why the Xhosa people were willing to accept Nongqawause's prophecy and sacrifice their crops and cattle.

Zuzi

Zuzi is the teenage son of Mandisa's landlord. He and his brother, Mzamo, play with Mxolisi when he is a young child. The police kill him when Mxolisi innocently tells them where he and Mzamo are hiding.

THEMES

Hatred

The theme of hatred appears throughout *Mother to Mother*. As a child, Mandisa learns that "deep run the roots of hatred here." The hostility that arises when settlers first come to South Africa only grows with each injustice. Over time, this turns into a legacy of hatred. Mandisa's grandfather tells her about the time when the Xhosa

TOPICS FOR FURTHER STUDY

- Research Amy Biehl's parents and their reaction to their daughter's murder. Write a letter in the voice of Mrs. Biehl responding to Mandisa's letter in *Mother to Mother*. Knowing what you do about the family, how do you think she would react to Mandisa? Would she be able to forgive Mxolisi and Mandisa? Share your letter in front of the class and discuss the reasons for your response.

- Read *Climbing the Stairs*, by Padma Venkatraman. This young-adult book tells the story of Vidya, a teenage girl who lives in India under British occupation. She hopes to go to college, but her life is forever altered after her father is injured in a riot and suffers brain damage. Create mockups of social network pages (such as Twitter, Facebook, Myspace, Google+) for Mandisa and Vidya. What experiences do they share? How could Mandisa encourage Vidya?

- Research the history of apartheid in South Africa. Create a web page that includes links to influential laws, events, and individuals over the decades. Be sure to include a link to a biographical time line of Sindiwe Magona. You may also include links to personal stories of people affected by apartheid.

- Read *Forced to Grow*, by Sindiwe Magona. This autobiography shares her struggle to provide for her family under apartheid. Write a paper that compares and contrasts her experiences with Mandisa's. In what ways are their lives similar, and in what ways are they different? Why do you think Magona was finally able to continue her education and Mandisa was not?

- Research the life of Amy Biehl, beginning with the Amy Biehl Foundation. Write a one-act play in which Amy's spirit visits Mxolisi in prison. What do you think she would say to him? How do you think he would react to her? Perform the play with a friend and record it. Upload the performance to a blog or website.

---

people were willing to risk everything to remove the hated settlers from their land. After their sacrifice fails, the settlers continue to take more and more from the native peoples. The Xhosa people and other natives are left with poverty and little hope. All they have is their hatred.

As a community, people in Guguletu refer to white people as "white dogs." Their children grow up hearing this anger and are encouraged to take back power from the people who stole their land. The chant "One settler! One bullet!" shows the depth of their rage. Unfortunately, the result of the children's hatred is violence that tears apart their own community. Mandisa describes the social decline as children move from destroying the property of white individuals to attacking and killing people in Guguletu accused of collaboration.

The murder of a white American student is fueled by blind rage at a perceived oppressor. Mxolisi has no idea that she is a foreigner attempting to help his cause. Mxolisi does not act rationally. He embodies generations of hatred born from injustice that goes back centuries. As Mandisa explains, "My son was only an agent, executing the long-simmering dark desires of his race."

Racism

The Anti-Defamation League defines *racism* as the "hatred of one person by another—or the belief that another person is less than human—because of skin color, language, customs, [or] place of birth." Racism motivates the injustice and hatred that are described in *Mother to Mother*. The belief that the native peoples of South African people are inferior is used to

Mother to Mother *is told in the form of an epistle to Linda Biehl, the mother of Amy Biehl, whose story is fictionalized in the novel.* (© *AP Photo | Denis Farrell*)

justify taking their land and, eventually, to impose apartheid, the official policy of racial segregation. The racism that Mandisa and her family experience on a daily basis is exposed when the police, who are mainly white, come searching for Mxolisi and harass his family. The police do not take action to protect the inhabitants of Guguletu, and the people live with constant violence. In fact, the police are often the cause of violence. For example, the police beat Lunga for no reason and one officer says, "We are tired of this . . . of you people."

Racism takes away the hope of people outside white society, creating a festering resentment against the "white dogs" who took their land. Mxolisi attacks a girl simply because she is white. When he looks at her, all he sees is another white oppressor. Political leaders encourage racism and hatred, and Mandisa places some of the blame for her son's actions on them. As she tells her "Sister-Mother": "They knew, or should have known, better. They were adults. They were learned. They had key to reason."

Motherhood

Mandisa is able to sympathize with the loss and pain that Amy's mother feels because she suffers a similar loss. Motherhood and tragedy bind the two women together. Mandisa knows that, as a mother, Mrs. Biehl can understand the complex emotions that she feels. Mandisa grieves for her own loss and for Mrs. Biehl's; both of them have lost their children. Mandisa shifts between her own sense of anger, shame, love, and grief throughout the book.

Mandisa is ashamed of her son for killing another person. She is ashamed of herself because she leaves her children alone in Guguletu to work in a white household. She feels anger at the society that forces her to work away from her children in order for her family to survive. She grieves that other children live the same life as her son, and she is concerned about their futures. She feels that they are becoming monsters. "Does anyone see this? Do their mothers see this? Did I see it?"

Mandisa is quick to admit her shortcomings as a mother, particularly in her treatment of Mxolisi. Her feelings for Mxolisi have always been complicated. While pregnant, she feels only bitterness toward him, but this becomes love once he is born. Subconsciously, however, she still resents him for, as she puts it, "destroying the me I was." Still, she defends Mxolisi against her husband's assertions that he will bring trouble, loving him with the unconditional love of a mother.

Mandisa contrasts her perceived failure as a mother with what she assumes are the successes of Mrs. Biehl, who was able to give her daughter the opportunities and attention that Mandisa never could. They both mourn the loss of children, but that is through no fault of Mrs. Biehl'. Mandisa attempts to encourage Mrs. Biehl by pointing out that she was a good mother. "But you, remember this, let it console you some, you never have to ask yourself: What did I not do for this child?"

STYLE

Epistolary Novel
Mother to Mother is an epistolary novel. According to William Harmon in *A Handbook to Literature*, an epistolary novel is "a novel in which the narrative is carried forward by letters written by one or more of the characters." By creating a fictional letter from the mother of a murderer to the mother of the girl he killed, Magona allows the readers to glimpse Mandisa's conflicted feelings regarding her son. *Mother to Mother* does not use a traditional epistle style. It does not include a salutation or signature. She introduces the letter with the words "My son killed your daughter." Over the course of the book, Mandisa addresses Mrs. Biehl as "Sister-Mother." The book is a single letter, written to

connect with and console Amy Biehl's mother. It also sheds light on the history of the South Africa and the legacy of apartheid. Magona allows the readers to imagine how the letter is received.

Confession
Magona weaves elements of a confession into her epistle. According to Harmon, a confession is "a form of autobiography that deals with customarily hidden or highly private matters." In the letter, Mandisa tells her life story and Mxolisi's life story in the context of apartheid. Her personal feelings and reactions to deeply personal situations are exposed for Mrs. Biehl to read. For example, she confesses her feelings of resentment toward Mxolisi for taking away the life she could have had. She also admits that her shame for Mxolisi's crime is mixed with overwhelming love for her child.

Flashback
The story of *Mother to Mother* is not told in linear order but instead relies on flashbacks, which show events that occurred before the time frame of the novel. The book opens after the murder of Amy Biehl, and the narrative primarily occurs over two days, the day of the murder and the next day. Mandisa uses flashbacks, however, to share stories from her past throughout her letter, such as when, as a child, she was forced to move from her village to Guguletu. She also describes falling in love with China, giving birth to Mxolisi, and her unhappy marriage. These past events shed light on the present.

HISTORICAL CONTEXT

European Settlement of South Africa
The history of European settlers in South Africa plays an important role in race relations and Mandisa's story in *Mother to Mother*. The Dutch first arrived in South Africa in 1652, when Jan van Riebeeck landed at the Cape of Good Hope. They bartered with the native Khoekhoe people, but tension developed when the European settlers were seen as a threat. In 1657, slaves were imported to work farmland given to Jan van Riebeeck's men for their service. By 1662, there were two hundred fifty Europeans living in South Africa.

COMPARE & CONTRAST

- **1990s:** Apartheid laws, which oppress a majority of the population of South Africa, are in effect when Frederik Willem de Klerk becomes president in 1990. He begins loosening restrictions and repealing apartheid laws. The election of Nelson Mandela in 1994 is the result of the nation's first democratic election.

  Today: Apartheid laws have been abolished. South Africa is a republic with universal suffrage, and everyone, regardless of race, has the right to elect government officials. While it is true that racism still exists, the government no longer protects it.

- **1990s:** Limitations on education and unequal pay keep citizens who are not white from improving economically. Because of decades of apartheid laws, most people in South Africa live in poverty.

  Today: The country has improved economically, but it is still struggling to fix the damage created by apartheid. As the *CIA: World Fact Book* points out, "Daunting economic problems remain from the apartheid era—especially poverty, lack of economic empowerment among the disadvantaged groups, and a shortage of public transportation." Half of the nation lives below the poverty line.

- **1990s:** As the nation begins to shift away from apartheid, violence dominates South Africa. Political protests grow violent, and the government reacts brutally. Additionally, there is a high crime rate within the black community.

  Today: Crime rates within South Africa remain high. Racially motivated violence still occurs. Recent reports from the South African Police Service, however, show an overall decline in crime.

In the 1700s, European settlers, called *trekboers*, were encouraged to travel to South Africa. Once there, the settlers began to claim land that belonged to the native people. These settlers included people from Holland, France, and Germany. In 1792, the Cape of Good Hope came under British rule. It changed hands between the Dutch, British, and French several times over the years because of the Napoleonic Wars. By the second half of the century, the settlers had traveled to land occupied by the Xhosa people.

The British began the Cape Frontier Wars against the Xhosa people in 1820. The Xhosa people resisted the influx of settlers coming to take their land. This struggle ended in 1857 "with the mass starvation" of the people, as South-Africa.info notes. The people starved because of a failed prophecy. The Xhosa people were willing to slaughter their cattle and destroy their crops based on a prophecy that promised the sacrifice would drive the European settlers back to the ocean. This moment in history is important to the plot of *Mother to Mother*.

Apartheid

Apartheid officially began in 1948, when the Nationalist Party took control of the government. In 1950, the Population Registration Act divided the population into three different races: white, black/African, and colored/mixed. The colored category included people of mixed ancestry or individuals who were neither white nor African. The law also made interracial marriage illegal.

The following year, the Bantu Homelands Act allotted specific land to Africans. The homelands, similar to reservations, operated as separate nations, meaning that the inhabitants were no longer considered citizens of South Africa. Leaving the homelands required passports, and many people worked service jobs for white households, which forced them to travel beyond

Amy Biehl was murdered helping to ensure democratic elections in South Africa in 1993.
(© Vepar5 / Shutterstock.com)

their homelands. Over the years, people were forcibly moved from their land and homes to four homelands, which were too small to support all of the inhabitants. These relocations were traumatic. As Bradley Skelcher points out in an article in the *Journal of Black Studies*, the people "who were not at their homesteads when the trucks came, were left behind, forcing them to wander by foot in search of their families."

In 1953, nonwhites were prohibited from attending universities, and all education came under white government control. The Public Safety Act and the Criminal Law Amendment Act enacted the same year allowed the government to declare a state of emergency for any protest against apartheid laws. People could be beaten, whipped, or jailed without trial. Protests were met with violent opposition, such as the Sharpeville protest in 1960, where sixty-nine people were killed after refusing to carry their passes. Resistance increased in 1970s, spurred by the South African Students Organization.

International pressure and internal protest brought changes in the 1990s. In 1990, President de Klerk lifted restrictions on opposition groups

and began dismantling apartheid laws. Violence, however, continued to dominate the nation despite political negotiation. The first democratic elections were seen as a sign that apartheid was finally being ended. The elections were held from April 26 to April 28, 1994, and Nelson Mandela was sworn in as president on May 10, 1994.

CRITICAL OVERVIEW

Criticism of Magona's writing has been positive. Her first two books, *To My Children's Children* and *Forced to Grow*, are autobiographies, and critics praised her honesty, insight, and explanation of Xhosa culture. For example, the *Publisher's Weekly* review of *To My Children's Children* notes, "Her vivid descriptions of Xhosa customs unfold not as an anthropologist's field study but as a memory etched from experience." Likewise, Ann Burns praised Magona's writing style in her review of *Forced to Grow* for the *Library Journal*. She does say, however, that "a pronunciation guide would have been helpful for African languages."

Mother to Mother, Magona's first novel, which was published on the five-year anniversary of Amy Biehl's death, was embraced by critics. For example, Jennifer Hunt comments in *American Visions*, "Eloquence is deepened by pathos as Mandisa describes the legacy that the apartheid system has bestowed upon her family and upon all black South Africans." Kai Easton was equally complimentary, claiming in the *World Literature Today*, that this novel is "Magona writing at her best."

Critics continued to praise Magona for her brave and honest work addressing social issues in South Africa. Along with critical acclaim, her writing has been honored with awards in America and South Africa. For example, her novel *Beauty's Gift*, which addressed the issue of AIDS, was on the short list for the 2009 Commonwealth Writers' Prize.

CRITICISM

April Paris

Paris is a freelance writer with an extensive background in writing literary and educational materials. In the following essay, she examines how the oppression of apartheid influences behavior in Mother to Mother.

Mother to Mother explores the social consequences of apartheid. The oppression of apartheid leads to the loss of culture, hope, childhood, and potential. As Magona explains in an interview published in *English in Africa*, Mandisa is the "perfect example of the success of apartheid—she is the perfect product of that system—her talent is stillborn; so is that of her children." Oppression, anger, and rebellion drive the actions of Mandisa and Mxolisi, leading to circumstances that forever define them and their family. Soon, the legacy of apartheid devastates the Biehl family along with Mandisa's. Despite all that has been lost, however, Mandisa believes there is hope for the future.

The cruelty of apartheid first enters Mandisa's life when she is nine and hears about the plan to relocate all black people to separate reservations, or homelands. A year later, her world is torn apart by a forced relocation in the middle of the night. Born in the village of Blouvei, she has a happy childhood in a close-knit community

> REBELLING AGAINST OPPRESSION WITH BLIND ANGER AND RAGE DESTROYS TWO FAMILIES IN *MOTHER TO MOTHER*. DESPITE THE TRAGEDY SHE SUFFERS, MANDISA HAS HOPE FOR THE FUTURE."

before relocation. At home, her mother works half-days and welcomes Mandisa when she comes home from school. Her secure world is ripped away when the government demolishes the village and forces her family to the urban homeland, Guguletu. Her world is shattered further when the people of Blouvei do not all travel to Guguletu together. They are scattered to different communities. Mandisa notices, "We got here, and everything and everybody changed." With the community divided, culture and tradition suffer as people focus on survival.

Surviving in the homelands requires people to find new ways of providing for their families. For example, mothers are no longer able to be home when their children are out of school. In fact, the parents are not even in Guguletu; they are working for white families in what is essentially another country. Mandisa soon notices that her parents are always angry when they come home from work. She watches as her parents suffer under an unjust system. Changes in the way people live cause the culture to unravel. Magona states: "I consciously set out to *reveal* rather than conceal the communal and cultural destruction" that was the result of such relocations. This cultural loss alters the way that Mandisa and everyone in Guguletu view the world. Children are forced to raise themselves in their parents' absence. As a result, they grow up too quickly, essentially losing their childhoods, but not their hope.

Mandisa's hope for a better life is destroyed when she is a young teenager. This occurs as she rebels against her overly strict mother while still attempting to hold on to the traditions passed down to her. By the time Mandisa is thirteen, her mother is consumed by fear that she will become pregnant like so many girls her age. With parents working to provide for their families, teenagers are left to their own devices, but Mandisa's mother guards her closely, forbidding all contact

WHAT DO I READ NEXT?

- Written in 2010, *The Other Half of Life* explores anti-Semitism—that is, prejudice against Jewish people. Based on the history of the MS *St. Louis*, a ship attempting to transport Jewish refugees from Nazi Germany, Kim Ablon Whitney's young-adult novel is a story of racism, loss, and hope.

- Walter Dean Meyers's *Shooter* is a young-adult novel that examines the circumstances surrounding a school shooting. Published in 2005, the story focuses on the impact that racism and bullying have on the shooter and the community.

- The second edition of Nancy L. Clark and William H. Worger's *South Africa: The Rise and Fall of Apartheid* details apartheid from 1948 to the 1990s. Published in 2011, the text includes information on South African politics in the twenty-first century.

- Nadine Gordimer's novel *July's People* was published in 1989, before the end of apartheid. In this fictional account, the apartheid government is overthrown and racial roles are reversed in South Africa, exposing the racial tension entering the 1990s.

- *To My Children's Children*, Sindiwe Magona's first book, was published in 1994. This autobiographical account of her life in South Africa showcases her personal struggles and provides a glimpse into what it was like to live under apartheid.

- *A Long Walk to Freedom* is Nelson Mandela's autobiography. Published in 2000, the book is a careful self-examination of a life spent fighting against the injustice of apartheid.

- Martin Merideth's *Diamonds, Gold, and War: The British, the Boers, and the Making of South Africa* is a nonfiction account of British colonialism and mining in South Africa. Published in 2008, the book reveals the relationship between European settlers and the native peoples.

- *A History of South Africa*, by Leonard Thompson, is a history book that begins with the country's original inhabitants and ends with Nelson Mandela and Thabo Mbeki. Published in 2001, this book is a useful overview for students interested in researching the complex history of South Africa.

with boys, dressing her conservatively, and questioning her every move. This oppression irritates Mandisa, who eventually rebels. Breaking away from her mother's domineering rules, Mandisa chooses to be China's girlfriend, which she keeps a secret. Both Mandisa and China rebel, but they have too much respect for their families and traditions to have sex outside of marriage. Additionally, both of them are hopeful about the future, and they do not want to risk pregnancy.

Mandisa plans on continuing her education after completing primary school, but her hope does not last long. Although Mandisa is still technically a virgin, she discovers that she is pregnant shortly after finishing school. When

she is fifteen, Mandisa's childhood officially ends as she is forced into the role of wife and mother. Now, Mandisa faces another type of oppression: she is trapped in a loveless marriage with a man who resents her and a new clan that overworks her. It is only through China's abandonment of her that Mandisa finds the strength to take control of her own life and make adult decisions. She takes a service job and moves into a home of her own. She believes that she will never live up to her potential, but she hopes that her son will have a better life.

In her letter, Mandisa asks, "And my son? What had he to live for?" According to an article by Pearl Amelia McHaney in the *Southern*

Literary Journal, Mandisa's direct statements and questions to Mrs. Biehl are "an overt act both of reaching out for Amy's mother and of forcing her to listen." Mandisa does not condone her son's actions, but she understands his feelings. She understands what was lost to him before he was ever born. She attempts to show Mrs. Biehl how a culture produced by oppression and injustice contributed to the death of her innocent child.

Mxolisi is a true child of apartheid. As a young girl, Mandisa experienced a safe and loving community. Although she suffers most of her life in Guguletu, she knows a better life is possible. Mxolisi, on the other hand, knows injustice and violence from an early age. He is traumatized as a young boy when the police kill his friends in front of him. This culture of racism, hatred, and violence defines his life. With the legal limitations placed on him and the substandard education he boycotted, he has no hope for a better world. As Mandisa explains, "He had already seen his tomorrows; in the defeated stoop of his father's shoulders."

Mxolisi rebels against the oppression of a white-dominated society in the only way that he knows how. He becomes involved in political movements that encourage violence against perceived enemies. In fact, he becomes a leader who organizes youth protests. Mxolisi participates in acts of vandalism. This criminal activity is done with the belief that he is helping people. In his mind, he is fighting back against the government. Many of these violent acts, however, occur within his own township, and they negatively affect the people who live in Guguletu.

Despite her disapproval of Mxolisi's actions, Mandisa attempts to show Mrs. Biehl that Mxolisi had the potential for goodness in him. Unlike other young protesters, Mxolisi never participates in the violent attacks on the people from Guguletu who are accused of conspiracy. Mandisa explains that the community respected him. People would say, "Mother of Mxolisi, your child is really a child to be proud of. In this day and age, when children do everything but what is decent." His actions are not always motivated by anger and rebellion. He saves a girl from being raped when no one else would intervene. One act of rebellious rage, however, forever changes his life, ending his potential to help his community. The result of

his behavior brings loss and grief to the Biehl family as well as his own.

Mandisa never names Amy Biehl in *Mother to Mother*, but there is no mistaking her identity. Mandisa must imagine details about the girl she considers as much a victim of apartheid as herself and Mxolisi. In many ways, Amy represents what the children of Guguletu could have been. She is the embodiment of their potential. As a white American, she has the benefits of a safe community. She is not the product of violence or injustice. She is already well educated and accomplished. She has the opportunity to become successful. As Mandisa says, "She had a tomorrow. Much to look forward to. Much yet to do, even though she had already accomplished much in her young days."

Unfortunately, Amy's life never prepared her to understand the violent society that apartheid created. In a cruel twist of fate, she is killed by the very people she came to help. Mandisa describes this lack of understanding as a weakness of Amy's and other people like her: "They so believe in their goodness, know they have hurt no one, are, indeed, helping, they never think anyone would want to hurt them." Unable to fathom the depth of racial hatred in South Africa, she drives into Guguletu to take her friends home.

Mxolisi and the other boys who attack Amy do not see an individual. Through the lens of hatred, he sees her only as part of the "white world" responsible for his suffering. Like the police who murdered his friends in front of him, she is white, and she is the enemy. In Guguletu, Amy pays the price for centuries of hatred and oppression for a system that shattered the hopes of a generation. As Mandisa says: "Now, your daughter has paid for the sins of the fathers and mothers who did not do their share of seeing that my son had a life worth living."

Although the Biehl family never lived under apartheid, it transforms their lives forever. The hatred no longer flows only among the people of South Africa. It spills over to an American family. Mandisa knows that she and Mrs. Biehl are both victims of apartheid, bound together in sorrow. Each mother suffering with loss also carries the knowledge that her child's potential for greatness is gone. Mandisa faces her loss with shame and anguish. She hopes that sharing their experiences "might ease the other mother's pain."

The novel tells the story of apartheid and the implications of the murder in Cape Town, South Africa. (© Oxlock | Shutterstock.com)

The violent society that came from apartheid is not surprising. As Kai Easton points out in a review for *World Literature Today*, its victims "tried to answer the government's brutality with a force of their own." Rebelling against oppression with blind anger and rage destroys two families in *Mother to Mother*. Despite the tragedy she suffers, Mandisa has hope for the future. She hears of people working with the young and hopes this can bring change. "Helping. So that violence may stop.... We need to help each other ... all of us, but especially the children."

Source: April Paris, Critical Essay on *Mother to Mother*, in *Novels for Students*, Gale, Cengage Learning, 2013.

Kai Easton

In the following review, Easton describes the novel as a "haunting elegy" of rage and bitterness.

After ten months at the Western Cape Law Centre, where, in the year before South Africa's first democratic elections, she had volunteered to help with voter registration, American Fulbright scholar Amy Biehl was preparing to leave Cape Town and return to the United States. Tragically, however, in August 1993, the very week of her scheduled flight home, she was stoned and stabbed to death by a mob of militant black youths in the South African township of Guguletu. Sindiwe Magona's fifth book and debut

novel *Mother to Mother* is a beautifully imagined letter and memoir narrated to Biehl's mother.

Like her other works (two autobiographies and two collections of short stories), Magona's *Mother to Mother* has an autobiographical element: eight months after Biehl's murder, Magona learned that her childhood friend was the mother of one of the four young men implicated in her death. What was this killer's world? What circumstances could have led to such a tragedy?

Magona frames her story over the course of two days, but a series of flash backs provides the historical and personal backdrop of the mother/narrator Mandisa. This is Magona writing at her best: in the intercutting of memories from Mandisa's own childhood, particularly before the family's forced removal in 1968 from the happiness and hardship in the sprawling tin-shack community of Blouvlei to the rows of identical houses of this township in the desolate, sandcovered Cape Flats: "& I came to Guguletu borne by a whirlwind & perched on a precarious leaf balking a tornado ... a violent scattering of black people, a dispersal of the government's making. So great was the upheaval, more than three decades later my people are still reeling from it."

Mandisa is only a child herself when she unexpectedly falls pregnant at the age of fifteen. The birth of her son Mxolisi dashes her hopes and dreams for an education. Patriarchy, apartheid, gender relations, and expectations are all themes in this memorable book, which is as much about a mother's own journey as it is about her son's downfall: "Understand the people among whom he has lived all his life. Nothing my son does surprises me any more. Not after that first unbelievable shock, his implanting himself inside me; unreasonably and totally destroying the me I was. The me I would have become."

Sindiwe Magona captures the world in which women like Mandisa and her children had to grow up, witnessing the difficulties of childhood and motherhood during the turbulent years of apartheid. For some of the sons of these mothers, "Humaneness, ubuntu, took flight" as they tried to answer the government's brutality with a force of their own. Like Nongqawuse's prophecy which led to the tragic Xhosa cattle-killing in 1857—a history which Magona weaves (somewhat schematically) into her story as a tale told to Mandisa by her grandfather—they rather hoped to drive the abelungu (whites) into the sea. *Mother to Mother* is a haunting elegy of the

> WRITTEN IN THE LAST DECADE IN BOTH
> ENGLISH AND XHOSA, MAGONA'S OEUVRE EMBRACES
> PRACTICALLY THE ENTIRE RANGE OF LITERARY
> GENRES: AUTOBIOGRAPHY, BIOGRAPHY, NOVEL,
> SHORT STORY, POETRY AND DRAMA."

seething rage and bitterness which led to Amy Biehl's murder while South Africa was yet on the brink of transformation.

Source: Kai Easton, Review of *Mother to Mother*, in *World Literature Today*, Vol. 76, No. 1, Winter 2002, pp. 124–25.

Siphokazi Koyana, Rosemary Gray, and Sindiwe Magona

In the following interview, Magona discusses her career, writing process, and works, including Mother to Mother.

Sindiwe Magona is the author of a two-volume autobiography, *To My Children's Children* (1990) and *Forced to Grow* (1992). She has also published two collections of short stories: *Living, Loving and Lying Awake at Night* (1991) and *Push-Push! & Other Stories* (1996). Her first novel, *Mother to Mother*, inspired by the politically motivated murder of Amy Biehl, an American Fulbright scholar conducting research in South Africa in 1993, was published in 1998. Magona was born in August 1943 in Gungululu, a village in the former Transkei. She grew up in the squatter camps and townships of Cape Town. She holds degrees from the University of South Africa and Columbia University. She is presently working for the United Nations in New York, where she has held a full-time position since 1983. In 1992 she was awarded an honorary doctorate in Humane Letters from Hartwick College, New York.

The following interview was conducted through e-mail correspondences in November 2000 between the author and Siphokazi Koyana, a PostDoctoral Research Fellow, and Professor Rosemary Gray, both of the English Department at the University of Pretoria.

Koyana: A whole year has gone by since I last saw you in New York. I see you have co-authored a book called Teach Yourself Xhosa. *Knowing how busy you keep, one can't help but ask what else you have been up to recently.*

In the Xhosa book you refer to I was involved more as a consultant, really. I'm the mother-tongue 'expert,' if you will. The authors are Beverley Kirsch and Silvia Skorge, excellent linguists and scholars.

I do have an unpublished book of Xhosa essays, *Imida*. A university professor has long wanted to use it for course work and a reputable publisher accepted the manuscript and had it edited—only to come back, three years later, to tell me there is no market for books in indigenous languages!

I have just completed a play, *Vukani/Wake Up!* in English. Set in South Africa, the play explores post-apartheid themes, including violence against women and the HIV/AIDS epidemic.

I am in the process of writing a biography of my parents, in poetry. A third of the book is done; my American publisher has seen it and likes it, but, as I've mentioned, I am in the throes of completing my second novel, on relationships.

Koyana: When I interviewed you in November 1997, when I was beginning research for my doctoral thesis, you mentioned that you were writing a novel called The Last School Year *and had outlined a Xhosa one called* Alitshoni Lingenandaba. *What happened to those two books?*

As regards the Xhosa book, I got discouraged by the lack of progress vis-a-vis Imida. Perhaps, one day, I will revisit the novel. The same applies to *The Last School Year*. For different reasons, I began to see the book as 'not urgent' and started and completed my first novel: From *Mother to Mother* (published in 1998 in South Africa; in hardcover in 1999 in the US, 2000 in paperback). Other projects, meanwhile, took over in demanding attention.

This past Sunday, 19 November 2000, my play: *Vukani/Wake Up!* was read, for the first time, at a church in Harlem. The discussion that followed was quite stimulating. We are hoping to tour South Africa next year. I co-wrote the play with an American woman, Laura Symons, a teacher at Sweet Briar College in Virginia, where the play will be read in January 2001. And, as I've already mentioned, I am also working on "Penrose and Lilian," the biography of my parents, in verse

I poetry. That has come to a halt because of the novel on relationships—"Anatomy of a Second Marriage." I hope to finish it by end November / first week of December 2000.

Koyana: Are you exploring romantic relationships or other kinds as well in the novel you're completing?

This novel is on relationships among older / more mature adults—i.e. people who are trying the love thing / marriage for the second time. Hopefully, the novel explores questions such as: what possesses someone who has already failed (at least once) in a relationship s/he believed would last 'for ever and ever' to do the same thing again, when personal experience should point out that there are no 'for ever and evers'... only disappointment and heartache? Are such couples stronger for the experience they bring to the new union?

Are they changed by the previous ones? If so, is the change positive—i.e. for better—or is it negative—for worse? Who helps and abets the older adult falling in love? The children? The parents? Friends? On both sides? Colleagues at work? Fellow worshippers? Who hinders them? Why and how?

Of course, all this is seen through the prism of a couple 'no longer in the first flush of youth'—both divorced, both unattached for years, both having been burnt in their first marriages and decided 'never again!'

Gray: Does your novel, Mother to Mother, *engage in a dialectical way with the autobiographies? Or how do you see the novel as revising or reflecting on what you'd written about motherhood in the autobiographies?*

If there is a link between *Mother to Mother* and the two books of autobiography, it is that the first-person mother is about the same age as I am and, therefore, has undergone some of the same experiences I have undergone. However, her plight is much more desperate than mine ever was. She does not finish primary school. She is a teen mother and never recovers from this—highlighting the enormous loss of human potential that comes through children getting children: the young mother's potential is lost to the world, which will never benefit from whatever talent she was to have brought it. Also lost to the world is the potential of her child. It is a well-known fact that children of children are at high risk of not finishing school. Mandisa is a

perfect example of the success of apartheid—she is the perfect product of that system—her talent is stillborn; so is that of her children. Society will never benefit from the gifts they brought to the world. I firmly believe no child is born without potential. Thus, by neglecting the young, we deny ourselves great blessings and rewards.

Gray: What makes you so versatile as a writer? Autobiographies, short stories, novels, and now poetry!

Coming to writing with no formal training, perhaps I am still exploring, trying out the various / different modes of expression. I might yet emerge as excelling or better or best at only one of these, I don't know. You left out drama... I would really love to do children's books. What makes me so versatile? I want to tell stories. More and more stories. Different stories that will appeal to different tastes. The more I tell, the more I want to tell. My appetite for telling is insatiable. I pray someone out there is listening!

Koyana: What is your next writing project after all the ones you're currently working on?

I'm thinking of essays / short stories after I finish "Penrose and Lilian."

Gray: What function do you see the short story collections as playing in the body of your literary work? Do they allow you a space in which to explore the issues that did not fit easily in the narrative of your own life (the autobiographies)? Issues that perhaps are important to you but not large enough to warrant an entire novel?

The short story, although not as exacting as the novel as regards length, is actually more taxing in that it demands more rigorous attention to detail. Thus, it gives greater pleasure, by allowing itself to be completed in less time while providing invaluable training for the longer fiction. To the contrary, there are issues in some of the stories I feel could have been better dealt with in the novel / longer fiction... I may still explore some of these, who knows?

Koyana: If the two-part autobiography was first written as one book, as you say in the Attwell interview, why did you break and publish a short story collection, Living, Loving and Lying Awake at Night, *in between?*

Living, Loving and Lying Awake at Night was published before *Forced to Grow* to give part one of the autobiography a full life.

Koyana: Mothering three children as a single parent who was also trying to reconstruct her own life was no easy task, as you so clearly record in your autobiographies. Given that background, what would you say has been the most stressful aspect of your mothering experience?

The most stressful experience, in my own life, was when black education ground to a halt, because of the schools boycotts. As a single parent, I had pinned my hopes of effective parenting on giving my children an education. No one was going to die and leave them an inheritance; how were they ever going to be responsible, upright, contributing members of society without an education?

The year 1976 was a point of rupture vis-a-vis the motherhood experience. For the first time I stood up against the popular voice when I disagreed with the idea of not sending children to school. What is more, I voiced my disagreement aloud, despite the danger this posed to me. Very, very, very stressful.

Gray: Have your perspectives or your ideas on motherhood changed since you wrote your autobiographies? In other words, would your representation of motherhood be different now, almost ten years later? If yes, how so exactly?

In terms of scope, perhaps, a little. It has expanded. I now see that the African Village of Old was wise, indeed. It is not enough for me to mother only my biological offspring. The interconnectedness inherent in community living is inescapable. One does well, of course, by minding one's own children. However, neither the children nor the parents live / will live / can live / will ever live in isolation. If not all the children are being responsibly raised, the child being raised responsibly will suffer: her very life and lifestyle will be jeopardised by the children who have not been prepared for responsible, respectful, productive living. Thus, good mothering entails ensuring it of others—i.e. working to see that it is possible and available to all mothers: that nurturing is available to all children; that children are being raised toward the fulfilment of their God-given talents and the promise that is the meaning of their lives. Does that mean my ideas on motherhood have changed? Expanded, perhaps.

Koyana: When you were using the maternal voice in the autobiographies, were you conscious of adhering to the notion of the African mother as espoused by the Black Consciousness Movement? I know you always insist that you were just recording your life for an unidentified audience, your

great grandchildren or perhaps some future archaeologists, who will be conducting research on what it was like to live in South Africa between the 1940s and 1980s. But, while you were writing, were you conscious of positioning your narrative voice in a manner that reflects the political ideals of any one organisation or movement?

I do not have the BCM notion you refer to, and I was not really conscious of reflecting the ideals of any one organisation or movement. However, the ideas / ideals of the BCM were pervasive and I dare say that although I was not an active member I can hardly have escaped what the movement espoused, much of which I admired—albeit, of necessity, from afar.

Koyana: Does your autobiographical account of your childhood and experiences as a mother attempt to conceal or to reveal the communal and cultural disintegration / destabilisation?

I consciously set out to reveal rather than conceal the communal and cultural destruction which was the direct result of the political dispensation of the time.

Koyana: Was it difficult to write about your experiences as an individual in a culture that puts so much emphasis on the collective?

It was not difficult to write about my experiences as an individual precisely because I perceived even those individual experiences as being more communal rather than personal (strictly speaking)...where the collective, effectively silenced, made the personal all the more important and pertinent. It was also that the collective was something I profoundly loved and appreciated that I write. My writing is, therefore, an attempt to put on record some of that collective consciousness...or, at least, a slice thereof.

Koyana: I find it interesting that after publishing two acclaimed autobiographies, collections of short stories and a novel, you still take creative writing classes, as you mentioned in the October 1999 interview with David Attwell et al. in Ohio. Is that because you still consider yourself a new writer?

Relatively speaking, I am still a new writer. I first published in 1990. That's ten years ago. There are writers around who have been writing for almost as long as I have been alive...certainly, most of my adult life. I do not attend classes; what I do is take the occasional workshop. I also give workshops for writers even less experienced than I am.

Koyana: How do these workshops benefit you at this point?

Creative-writing workshops: whether I give them or get them from acclaimed writers from whom I have a lot to learn are a great help. The association with my peers (or betters!) is not only stimulating and invigorating but an unrelenting yardstick against which one can hope to, perhaps, one day, measure one's own progress (or lack thereof).

Koyana: Do you ever read the analysis that literary academics / critics write about your work? If so, how does that affect your work? If not, why not?

Show me a writer who doesn't and I'll show you a liar! I get tremendously encouraged. I suppose this is because, so far, everyone has been so complimentary; it would be hard not to be happy about such comments. The effect is positive. Critics sometimes see things I didn't even know I had put there. That makes me, more and more, trust my gut feelings. So, I suppose one can say the effect has been positive. Critics have made me believe more and more that I can write—something about which I was very tentative, not so long ago. I've only been writing for a decade!

Gray: What kind of research goes into writing the books?

The only research I do as regards the fiction is to get accuracy about specifics. For example, if it's raining in the book, then this had better be the rainy season wherever the story is set. Or, if my characters travel by bus, there'd better be a bus route near their house.

Gray: Who are your favourite authors and why? To what extent does your own reading colour your writing?

I have no favourite authors—this too, changes. I am eclectic in what I read. For any number of reasons, I will pick up a book and read it—sometimes to the very end. Black women, all black writers, then all women writers—not necessarily in that order. I see these groups as the outsiders, shifting and changing as the groups are, at one or another time, I see myself as belonging to them.

I admire all good writing and I daresay, to a large extent, the reading I do does affect my writing. We do by emulation. I don't mean I will actively, consciously, copy another writer's style, but, because of my admiration for that writer's work, I may find myself writing in similar ways ... or trying to be as funny (if she were) or whatever.

Koyana: In our 1997 interview you mentioned that you were starting 'Baleka,' an organisation which addresses the concern you have for South Africa's youth. What has been the progress in that project?

The idea is still there. I shared it with a few people in South Africa, got very excited responses from all. The trouble is, one cannot start an organisation / movement from afar. I have had to recognise this fact, accept that I have to wait till retirement before I embark on the project. I have 32 months to go. Meanwhile, to keep it from dying out on me, I talk about 'Baleka' and, even here in the States, people think it's a great idea—one whose time has come! We did start in Gala ... a small group. However, how that is doing, I don't really know. I have lost touch, a little, with the couple who were spearheading the movement there. *Vukani!*, I believe, is part of my work on youth. Were I not committed to seeing improvement in the lives of the young, perhaps, I would not have written the play.

Gray: Having started this project, what can you say about the responsibility of a writer as an agent for change, about the movement from defining and interpreting the problem to helping solve it?

A writer is, first and foremost, a writer. Her responsibility, as I see it, is to tell the story she has set about telling. She may, while doing that, define and interpret a problem—after all, she is not divorced from the society in which she lives. Therefore, her concerns will tend to mirror the concerns of the wider society. It is by bringing these up to the notice of the society (she doesn't invent them, they were always there!) that, if very, very lucky, a writer might find herself provoking dialogue among the people. Through that dialogue, the community might arrive at a solution. She did not set out to be an agent of change. . . she set out to tell a story. That is her responsibility, to tell a story. What society does with her work is another thing altogether. But then, a writer is also a citizen, perhaps a mother or even a grandmother. In that capacity, she may demand of herself that she be active in social change. Is that the writer, or the mother? The writer or the member of a certain congregation? . . . It is a complex question; the answer is not simple. Perhaps she writes because she would like to see change. She writes to be an agent of change. But even then, all a writer can do is state her truth, her hopes and her fears. Alone she can change nothing. It is in joining others in the community that she can be an agent of change.

Gray: As the above interview, so graciously fitted into an extraordinarily busy schedule at the United Nations, testifies, Sindiwe Magona is a multitalented writer of catholic interests and singular productivity. Written in the last decade in both English and Xhosa, Magona's oeuvre embraces practically the entire range of literary genres: autobiography, biography, novel, short story, poetry and drama.

In spite of her success—her first novel (1998) has already enjoyed three imprints—this South African-born author remains endearingly modest and committed—attending and presenting creative-writing workshops as integral to her philosophy of lifelong learning. Although Magona is adamant that the writer's first responsibility is that of 'telling' (honestly and authentically), she is also unequivocal on the subject of the author's role as an agent for change. Adhering to her credo that 'telling is sharing,' she writes in a realist mode. Often, she is responding to the nostalgic imperative or engaging in hegemonic discourse as she explores the multifaceted themes of motherhood, labour, interpersonal relationships (including the dilemmas of failed relationships), and, not unnaturally, the burning post-apartheid issues of violence against women, unwanted pregnancies and the HIV/AIDS epidemic.

Her concern for the disadvantages as well as the far-reaching impact of lack of education on economic and social life catapulted Magona into activism early in life. Aware of working against the grain of popular thinking, her innate integrity forced her to speak up for the centrality of education as the only valid insurance policy for the underprivileged, the only protection against 'still-born talent' or wasted potential.

Koyana: Since the interview was conducted in November 2000, Magona has kept very busy. She is currently revising the play Vukani! *and hopes to complete it mid-May. She has also decided to submit the biography of her parents that she was writing in verse in three volumes: "Penrose"; Penrose and Lillian"; "Lillian"; since "Penrose," the section about her father, alone has turned out to be 60 manuscript pages.* Anatomy of a Second Marriage, *the novel she was writing about romantic*

relationships among more mature adults, is undergoing its final revision and will be submitted at the end of May. Without Bootstraps, *a novel based on the first story in* Living, Loving and Lying Awake at Night, *is also undergoing its final revision and will be completed at the end of May as well. Magona is also busy collaborating on a one-woman play in which she will be acting. It is called "I Promised Myself a Fabulous Middle Age." She hopes to start rehearsals in June.*

Source: Siphokazi Koyana, Rosemary Gray, and Sindiwe Magona, "An Electronic Interview with Sindiwe Magona," in *English in Africa*, Vol. 29, No. 1, May 2002, pp. 99–108.

Ellen Flexman

In the following review, Flexman notes that this novelization tells the story of apartheid with "depth, honesty, and compassion."

Based on the death of Amy Biehl, a white American student killed by black youths in South Africa in 1993, this novel looks at the murder through the eyes of the killer's mother (in the novel, only one youth committed the crime). In a letter to the murdered woman's mother, Mandisa tells the story of her oldest son, Mxolisi, born when she was 14. Growing up under apartheid, with little education, crashing poverty, and no hope for the future, Mxolisi becomes one of the lost ones, so full of rage that every white face becomes the enemy and freedom is won only through blood. Yet as Magona shows, each character must share some responsibility for the tragedy that destroys two families, making this more than simply a novelization of a headline. Magona's portrayal of one mother's suffering is written with depth, honesty, and compassion for all of apartheid's victims. First published in South Africa in 1998, this is recommended for large public libraries and libraries with collections of modern African literature.

Source: Ellen Flexman, Review of *Mother to Mother*, in *Library Journal*, Vol. 124, No. 7, October 15, 1999, p. 107.

Hazel Rochman

In the following review, Rochman determines that this novel is a "gripping story of suspense and heartbreak."

"My son killed your daughter." The young white American Fullbright scholar Amy Biehl was murdered by a mob of black teenagers in 1993 on the eve of South Africa's first democratic elections. In this groundbreaking novel, the mother of one of the killers speaks to the mother of the victim in sorrow and anguish for them both. The story is set in the township Guguletu, near Cape Town, immediately after the murder. Mandisa is sent home early from her job as a domestic worker in a white suburb because there is trouble in the township streets. The children are rioting. They killed a white girl. The police vans are near Mandisa's home. Where is her son? Why hasn't he come home? Where is he? Why are the police smashing down her home? As the present tension rises unbearably, she remembers the past: her son's bitter childhood, her own youth and smashed hopes, her family's forced removal from their home to the Guguletu slum, the apartheid cruelty that made her son a monster who could kill. With other children, he heard the call to boycott school, to make the country ungovernable, and he heard the slogan, "One settler, one bullet." His mother's eloquent voice fuses her own terror about her son with her compassion for the bereaved mother and her fury at what the apartheid monster has wrought. This is a gripping story of suspense and heartbreak. This great novel, rooted in South African history, dramatizes what life is like for one woman and her child in the worst of times.

Source: Hazel Rochman, Review of *Mother to Mother*, in *Booklist*, Vol. 96, No. 2, September 15, 1999, p. 197.

Publishers Weekly

In the following review, a contributor praises what is termed "a noteworthy American debut."

The senseless killing of Amy Biehl, a young Fulbright scholar who had gone to South Africa to help residents prepare for the first democratic elections in the history of that country, is the basis for this novel. On the day before she was scheduled to return home to America in August 1993, Amy gave a ride to several co-workers who lived in the poverty-ravaged all-black township of Guguletu. Rioting students pulled her from her car and stabbed her. South African novelist and short story writer Sindiwe Magona eschews a tabloid recreation of the crime, envisioning instead the world of Amy's killers, and creating in Mandisa, the mother of one of those young men, a martyr whose heart and life reflect the tragedy of apartheid. As her son Mxolisi's guilt is revealed, Mandisa mourns him, equating her loss with Amy's mother's. Determined to strike a common chord of grief with the woman she views

as her Sister-Mother, Mandisa laments the circumstances of her own life, thereby hoping to explain her son's actions. She recalls with affecting clarity her coming of age in a stern but loving community whose reliance on established customs are a refuge from the relentless and brutal change instigated by the government's apartheid policy. Happy until the age of nine, when her family is forced to relocate to a desolate patch of land, Mandisa becomes a mother at 15 and a housemaid shortly thereafter. Mxolisi's introduction to racial violence occurs as a child, when he witnesses the shooting deaths of two older boys whom he idolizes; by age 20, he's become a respected leader of the student revolutionary movement. Although Magona's pacing seems irritatingly slow at times, the mood becomes taut as Mxolisi and Amy approach their moment of destiny in this chilling and ingenious docudrama, a noteworthy American debut for a writer whose work has received well-deserved praise in her own country. 3-city author tour.

Source: Review of *Mother to Mother*, in *Publishers Weekly*, Vol. 246, No. 37, September 13, 1999, p. 62.

SOURCES

"Apartheid Legislation 1850s–1970s," in *South African History Online*, http://www.sahistory.org.za/politics-and-society/apartheid-legislation-1850s-1970s (accessed August 10, 2012).

Burns, Ann, Review of *Forced to Grow*, in *Library Journal*, Vol. 123, No. 5, March 15, 1998, p. 78.

"Crime Report 2010/2011," in *South Africa Government Online*, http://www.info.gov.za/view/DownloadFileAction?id=150105 (accessed August 10, 2012).

Easton, Kai, Review of *Mother to Mother*, in *World Literature Today*, Vol. 76, No. 1, Winter 2002, pp. 124–25.

Harmon, William, *A Handbook to Literature*, 9th ed., Prentice Hall, 2003, pp. 113, 188, 210.

Hunt, Jennifer, Review of *Mother to Mother*, in *American Visions*, Vol. 15, No. 1, February–March 2000, pp. 36–37.

Magona, Sindiwe, *Mother to Mother*, Beacon Press, 1999.

———, *Forced to Grow*, Interlink Books, 1992, p. 13.

Magona, Sindiwe, Siphokazi Koyana, and Rosemary Gray, "An Electronic Interview with Sindiwe Magona," in *English in Africa*, Vol. 29, No. 1, May 2002, pp. 99–107.

McHaney, Pearl Amelia, "History and Intertextuality: A Transnational Reading of Eudora Welty's *Losing Battles* and Sindiwe Magona's *Mother to Mother*," in *Southern Literary Journal*, Vol. 40, No. 2, Spring 2008, pp. 166–81.

"Racism," Anti-Defamation League website, http://www.adl.org/hate-patrol/racism.asp (accessed August 10, 2012).

Review of *To My Children's Children*, in *Publisher's Weekly*, May 1994, http://www.publishersweekly.com/978-1-56656-152-5 (accessed August 1, 2012).

"Sindiwe Magona," in *South African History Online*, http://www.sahistory.org.za/people/sindiwe-magona (accessed August 10, 2012).

Skelcher, Bradley, "Apartheid and the Removal of Black Spots from Lake Bhangazi in Kwazulu-Natal, South Africa," in *Journal of Black Studies*, Vol. 33, No. 6, July 2003, pp. 761–83.

"South Africa," in *CIA: The World Fact Book*, https://www.cia.gov/library/publications/the-world-factbook/geos/sf.html (accessed August 10, 2012).

"South African History: Colonial Expansion," SouthAfrica.info, http://www.southafrica.info/about/history/521102.htm#.UEhOkUKBHd8 (accessed August 10, 2012).

"South African History: The Death of Apartheid," SouthAfrica.info, http://www.southafrica.info/about/history/521109.htm#.UEhPJkKBHd8 (accessed August 10, 2012).

FURTHER READING

Allen, John, *Apartheid South Africa: An Insider's Overview of the Origin and Effects of Separate Development*, iUniverse, 2005.
> Born in England and raised in South Africa, Allen includes personal experiences and South African history to bring an understanding of apartheid. He examines the motives behind apartheid and how it ultimately affected the country.

Magona, Sindiwe, *Beauty's Gift*, NB Publishers, 2011.
> This novel is a touching story that addresses AIDS in South Africa. Here, Magona shows that social action needs to continue in South Africa after the end of apartheid.

Mathabane, Mark, *Kaffir Boy: The True Story of a Black Youth's Coming of Age in Apartheid South Africa*, Scribner, 1986.
> Recommended for young-adult readers, this autobiography is an honest account of childhood in a ghetto during apartheid. Mathabane's story shows how difficult it was to escape government oppression in South Africa.

Ngcobo, Lauretta, *And They Didn't Die*, Feminist Press, 1999.
> Ngcobo's novel exposes the effect of apartheid on rural families and communities. She was a contemporary of Magona, and anyone interested in South African literature will appreciate her work.

Welsh, David, *The Rise and Fall of Apartheid*, University of Virginia Press, 2010.
> This insightful history book focuses on the beginning of apartheid and the subsequent struggles for liberation. It is a useful tool for anyone interested in the political landscape of South Africa.

Worden, Nigel, *The Making of Modern South Africa: Conquest, Apartheid, Democracy*, 5th ed., Wiley-Blackwell, 2012.
> Worden provides a comprehensive history of South Africa beginning with European settlement. The text includes updated information on the struggles the nation faced after apartheid.

SUGGESTED SEARCH TERMS

Sindiwe Magona

Sindiwe Magona AND biography

Mother to Mother AND Sindiwe Magona

Sindiwe Magona AND criticism

Mother to Mother AND Amy Biehl

apartheid

South Africa AND history

South Africa AND settlement

Mother to Mother AND review

My Jim

NANCY RAWLES
2005

Nancy Rawles's *My Jim* (2005) is about a woman, Sadie, who was born into slavery in Missouri. Throughout the book she relates the story of her life to a granddaughter who was born after the Civil War and has no idea of the kind of life that her people were forced to live so recently in the past. Speaking in the voice of an uneducated but passionate woman of her time, Sadie recounts the beatings and maiming, the separation of families as some members were sold away and never heard from again, and the forced pregnancies that gave the slave owners a fresh supply of human beings to sell. As she tells her story, Sadie and her granddaughter work on sewing a memory quilt, incorporating into it what few items she was able to keep as her own in a system that forbade slaves to own anything, as well as patterns of fabric that serve as symbolic reminders of people Sadie has known.

The most significant of these people, the Jim of the novel's title, was already familiar to generations of readers before this book was published: he is the slave who runs away from Hannibal, Missouri, with Huckleberry Finn in Mark Twain's famous 1884 novel, which is often considered one of the greatest works of American literature. Sadie is present at Jim's birth, and he is her one true love, her first husband, and the father of her first children. Characters and events from Twain's book weave through *My Jim*, though the focus of the story is always on Sadie and her struggle to survive. Readers

should be aware that this book describes, though not graphically, the atrocities inflicted upon slaves during that period, including numerous instances of rape. There is frequent use of a derogatory label used against blacks, a precedented stylistic choice that has sometimes gotten *Adventures of Huckleberry Finn* placed on lists of unacceptable books, though Rawles explains in Sadie's own voice the context in which such racial epithets are used.

AUTHOR BIOGRAPHY

Rawles was born in 1958 and grew up in Los Angeles. She majored in history at Northwestern University, where she received her bachelor of science degree from the Medill School of Journalism. Remaining in Chicago after graduation, she worked as a journalist for various publications, including the *Chicago Reporter*, and also studied playwriting, having several plays produced. In 2000, her play *Keeper at the Gate*, about the assassination of Seattle Urban League director Edwin T. Pratt, won the King County Arts Commission Publication Award.

Rawles's first novel, *Love Like Gumbo*, published in 1997, is about Grace Broussard, a woman whose family is loving and complex. It is set in South Central Los Angeles in the 1970s, an area Rawles was familiar with, and it won her the Before Columbus Foundation American Book Award and a Washington State Governor's Writers Award. Her second novel, *Crawfish Dreams*, published in 2003, is about Grace's mother, Camille, and her history in Los Angeles as the town changes over the decades. *Crawfish Dreams* was included in the Barnes & Noble Discover Great New Writers Program. *My Jim*, published in 2005, won Rawles an American Library Association Alex Award, honoring books written for adults but having special appeal for teens, and was the 2009 selection for the Seattle Reads program.

PLOT SUMMARY

Part One: Marianne Libre

JAR

The novel begins decades after most of the events it describes took place. It is the year 1884,

MEDIA ADAPTATIONS

- An unabridged audio version of *My Jim* was released on compact disc in 2008 by Recorded Books, read by Lizzie Cooper Davis and Brenda Pressley.
- In 2005, Realtime Audio of Seattle, Washington, released a compact disc recording of songs and poems related to this book, under the title *My Jim: A Companion Piece to the Novel by Nancy Rawles*.

and Marianne Libre, a young woman living in the South, has been given a proposal of marriage by her boyfriend, Chas Freeman, who is being called up for military service in the army at Fort Robinson, Nebraska. She is uncertain about whether or not to accept. Being only sixteen years old, she does not know if her feelings for Chas are true love or if she will regret tying herself down to him.

Marianne consults with her grandmother, Sadie Watson, to ask what she should do. Marianne makes the case that she is young and that life might have more to offer, but Sadie, who lived most of her life in slavery, thinks that a girl who has a chance at a stable life with a good provider should take it.

During their discussion, it comes up that Sadie might soon be evicted from her cabin. She once wanted to leave Louisiana, but now she is accustomed to it. Even in her old age, though, there is no stability in the life of a black woman. She recalls Marianne's mother, who left the eight-year-old with Sadie when she ran away to the West after the Civil War.

The chapter ends with Marianne and Sadie sewing a quilt together, which Sadie insists the young woman will need for her new, married life. Marianne looks over artifacts that her grandmother keeps in a jar by her stove, such as a knife, a piece of her Congo bowl, and a brass button, and the objects frame Sadie's recollection about her own young life.

Part Two: Sadie Watson

KNIFE

Sadie's story begins with her considering the knife that her mother smuggled from Virginia to Missouri in a hidden pocket in her skirt. That stolen knife and a bowl from her ancestral home in the Congo were the most prized possessions of Sadie's mother, Liza, who passed them on to Sadie. Sadie kept the knife and a shard of the bowl when she was sold and moved from Missouri to Louisiana.

After briefly remembering when she was sold off of the Watson farm and shipped downstream to Louisiana while Jim, who by that time was a free man, stood watching, Sadie recalls being present at Jim's birth. She was a little girl, too young to work in the fields, and Aunt Cora called her to help. Jim's mother did not want to have the baby, and she did what she could to cause a miscarriage. After the birth, she took Sadie's knife and tried to kill herself. But the baby and the mother both survived. Jim's mother named the baby after his father, who had run away from the farm. Feeling that she was inviting trouble by naming her child for a runaway slave, Mas (Master) Watson sold Jim's mother to another plantation downriver a few months later, leaving Jim to be raised by Cora and young Sadie.

Sadie's mother, Liza, is the first to recognize that Jim has supernatural ability. When he is sick one day and cannot work in the field, Tailor, the overseer, sends for him, but Liza (or Mama) stands up to the black overseer, Tailor, and she is subsequently whipped. Sadie is sent to bring Jim out to the field, but she finds him too sick to move and returns without him, so Tailor burns her with the ashes from his pipe.

Later, Jim shows his ability to predict things. He foresees the coming of a great flood and of a meteor shower. His ability to anticipate natural cataclysms frightens the other workers on the Watson farm. At the same time, Sadie is cultivating her ability to cure ailments by learning from her mother about the healing properties of indigenous plants.

Sadie accompanies her mother into Hannibal to visit a sick friend of Miss Watson's. There she helps her mother make a natural cure for the woman. In return, Mas Watson rewards them with fabric from the dry goods store. As they return to town, Mama tells Sadie that a slave girl she saw being beaten on the street of Hannibal was Sadie's sister, Jenny, who was sold to a family in town at an early age. Soon after that, Sadie spends a peaceful Sunday morning with her mother, walking through the woods. Her mother dies of malaria the following week.

Sadie narrates how her mother came to live at the Watsons' farm on Clear Creek. She worked for the Watson family in Virginia. At the time, Mas Watson was a headstrong son, leaving his family's established plantation to set out for the undiscovered territory out west. They traveled to Louisville, Kentucky, where Mas Watson's brother lived, but soon after their arrival, there was an argument between the brothers, so Mas and his slaves moved on, riding down the Ohio River to Cairo, Illinois, where he hired a man with a big dog to threaten the slaves so they would not run away. Sadie describes a shaking of the ground that her mother experienced—probably a reference to the 1812 earthquake centered in New Madrid, Missouri, which shook the entire Midwest. They settled in Cape Giradeau, Missouri.

After her mother's death, Sadie becomes valuable to Mas Watson for her ability to heal the sick. A plague passes through the area. She is in a state of constant nervousness when her owner has her treat white people, fearing that she will be beaten if she fails, but Jim comforts her. Because of her usefulness as a healer, Sadie spends little time out in the fields, which causes resentment in the other slaves.

One day, she is called on to go to the home of Mas Stevens, the most feared, loathsome slave master in the area. He has a knife wound in his stomach. He calls Sadie close to his bedside, then spits in her ear. While he is cursing her, she gives the slave who works for him orders about making a healing poultice. When the other slave is out of the room, Stevens grabs for Sadie; she throws whiskey on his wound and reaches for the knife her mother handed down to her, but the other woman returns before she can kill him.

After that, Sadie becomes sick herself. Mas Watson calls a white doctor for her, as a sign of how valuable she is to him, but the doctor can find nothing wrong. Her encounter with Mas Stevens has left her so bitter that she thinks constantly of murder.

She sees patrollers in the woods arrest one of the slaves from the Stevens farm; she assumes that the reason he called for her instead of a white doctor was that he did not want people to know that a slave had stabbed him. The slave was hung from a tree at the side of the road, in full view of the other slaves, as a warning. The chapter ends with Sadie explaining to Marianne that this is why she keeps that knife close to herself, ready for trouble.

HAT

As Sadie's narrative goes on, she describes the day Jim returned to the plantation from the docks where he had been working. He had used his wages to buy a fancy bowler hat, though Sadie thinks he should be saving to buy his freedom. She does not really believe him when he says that he wants to be her man. He comes to live with her and Cora and the children Cora cares for.

In Jim's absence, Sadie has become pregnant three times, working in the field with men who raped her with the consent of the overseer, since her owner always welcomed new slave babies to be sold. Each time, though, she knew which plants to combine to terminate her pregnancy. After Sadie becomes jealous of Jim for staying out all night, he explains that he was not with another woman and that the other slaves come to him to ask him to prophesy about their fates. Miss Watson's sister marries a man named Douglas (she is the Widow Douglas in Twain's *Huckleberry Finn*) and moves into Hannibal.

Soon Sadie has Jim's daughter, Lizbeth. Almost immediately after that, Mas Watson announces that he has plans to marry Jim off to another woman. Jim and Sadie perform a private marriage ceremony for themselves, even though it is not legally official. Jim becomes obsessed with running away but promises that he will not escape to freedom without taking Sadie and Lizbeth with him.

Jim and Sadie plan to take Lizbeth and escape to freedom with the help of some abolitionist whites who will hide them at the Stone School. The night that they are to leave, though, Miss Watson takes them to her Baptist church at Bear Creek. A storm makes them stay at Bear Creek overnight, and Sadie overhears some white people talking about the Supreme Court's 1857 *Dred Scott* decision. They devise another plan to escape, but as they are crossing a deep pond, Jim finds out that Sadie is pregnant again, and this escape attempt is called off, too. The baby is a son, Jonnie.

A scarlet fever epidemic comes through the area. The family survives, but Lizbeth loses her hearing. As time goes by, Jim becomes increasingly depressed, planning his escape. When Mas Watson beats Cora for being so weak with yellow fever that she drops a child, who then dies, Jim tells his owner that he will kill him if he hurts Cora again, wresting the whip from Mas Watson's hand.

After Mas Watson dies, his daughter, Miss Watson, plans to move to town and live with her sister. She arranges to sell the farm, its furnishings, and the slaves. Cruel Mas Stevens, from the next farm over, upsets the proceedings by coming in and offering one large sum for everything. Miss Watson moves into Hannibal with Jim, who was given to her as a present when she was born, and Sadie and the children move to the Stevens farm, where the slaves are all mistreated by Stevens's overseer, Banes. Sadie is put in a cabin on the Stevens farm with a woman named Fortune. Mas Stevens officially refers to Fortune as his cook, although she cannot cook. Her main function is to have sex with Mas Stevens and become pregnant often, so that he can sell babies off as slaves.

Jim sneaks onto the Stevens farm to see Sadie a few times. Once she cuts a small piece out of his treasured felt hat and keeps it with her. When Jim is caught in the yard before reaching Sadie, he is whipped.

Soon they hear that Jim has run away from Miss Watson's house. Authorities come to Sadie and beat her, though she has no information to give them. She is chained up in the tobacco-packing house for days.

News eventually comes that Jim's hat was found floating in the Mississippi River. Sadie, knowing how much he loved that hat, assumes that he would not leave it unless he was dead. Readers of *Huckleberry Finn* know that it was lost while he and Huck were rafting down the river.

BOWL

Jim is suspected by the white people of having killed "a white boy" (Huck Finn), so Mas Stevens has Sadie punished for his crime. The black people fear Sadie for being a witch. She is an outcast.

After briefly being married to an Indian woman he names "Flesh," Mas Stevens brings Sadie into his house as his cook, to replace

Fortune, who has died. She insists that he provide decent food for the slaves; he threatens her but then brings in a small pig from the yard and cuts its throat, letting her cook the pig. The slaves are too afraid to eat the meat that Sadie has gotten for them.

At a big fire celebrating the harvest, Sadie is approached by a free black man who was hired to help with the harvest, a man named Nate. He says he met Jim in Arkansas, at a place where there was a fight among the white people. He and Jim worked together there, and Jim told Nate about Sadie and Lizbeth and Jonnie. Jim, he explains, is working to raise money to come back and buy their freedom.

Mas Stevens, drunk, comes to Sadie's cabin and tries to force himself on her, but she successfully resists. He tries to rape her several times, but she always resists. Soon, she realizes that he has been having sex with Lizbeth, who has not resisted him because he feeds her well. After threatening him if he will not leave her daughter alone, Sadie begins putting poison in Stevens's food. He asks if she is poisoning him, but she tells him that there is a bug going around and that all of the slaves are sick. Eventually she is too desperate to wait for the poison to take effect, so she comes to his room while he is sleeping and draws her knife. He takes her bowl, which she uses for mixing healing herbs, and smashes it on the floor. Sadie is able to save only one shard, which she keeps into old age and shows to Marianne.

TOOTH

Sadie explains the button in the jar that Marianne is looking at as something that the Widow Douglas gave to Sadie's daughter Lizbeth. It was on the coat of the widow's old coachman, and she told him to tear it off and give it to the child. Young Lizbeth held on to the button as a magic charm.

Since Lizbeth is sleeping in Mas Stevens's house, Sadie is alone in her cabin. Jonnie is allowed to go and live with her, but he is suspicious of her: he does not know her well, and the other black people call her a witch. He does not want to show her when he has a bad tooth.

She removes one tooth, which becomes another of the mementos she saves into old age, but Jonnie still has a few bad teeth. She needs clove to help him. Knowing that there is some in the spice jars at Mas Stevens's house, she has

Lizbeth sneak her into the kitchen, but she is caught. In punishment, Jonnie is sold, and she never sees him again.

PIPE

With little to live for, Sadie tries to exact her revenge against Mas Stevens by setting his tobacco harvest on fire, but only a small portion of the drying shed burns. Mas Stevens comes to her and puts her eye out with his cane.

She is to be sold. While in the pen at the auction house, she is visited by Jim. He has been to see Lizbeth and has brought Sadie her belongings: her knife, the piece of brown hat, her piece of the Congo bowl, and Jonnie's tooth. He also gives her a pipe that Huck Finn gave him. He makes a patch with tobacco to soothe her damaged eye.

As the ship taking Sadie down to Louisiana moves down the river, she sees Jim, standing on the levee, tipping his hat to her.

TOBACCO

In Louisiana, Sadie is forced to work on a sugarcane plantation owned by a man named Cyprien. It is there that Sadie becomes pregnant with Elise, after being raped by the unnamed man who runs the plantation store. Unlike earlier pregnancies, she is not able to terminate this one; she does not have access to the roots that would cause a miscarriage, and she is told that Old Man Cyprien severely punishes slaves who interfere with the production of new slaves. The baby, Elise, is eventually going to be Marianne Libre's mother. She is taken away from Sadie soon after the birth, and they seldom see each other around the plantation.

Sadie is then forced to have four more children with a man named Andrew, whose function on the plantation is impregnating women. After their last child together, Andrew becomes impotent. Old Man Cyprien has no more use for him, so Andrew moves in with Sadie.

During the Civil War, all of the slaves on the Cyprien plantation are given their freedom. They travel north by foot: Sadie, Andrew, Elise, and two of the boys she had with Andrew who were not sold off before Emancipation. They come to a stop at a collective for black farmers at Smithfield Quarter, where Elise meets a man named Joseph, who is educated, and they become a couple.

Life is good for them in Smithfield until bands of white men with guns begin attacking the farmers. For protection, they move into the town of Colfax. Then the town is attacked. What is described is the historic Colfax Massacre of 1873. Joseph and Andrew die in the attack.

After escaping the massacre, Sadie and her children live in the woods. She meets Papa Duban there and cares for him, and he becomes the family's father figure. Elise leaves with a wagon full of religious people who are traveling west, leaving her eight-year-old daughter, Marianne, with the child's grandmother.

Part Three: My Nana

CROSS
Marianne is the narrator of this section. It takes place just after the first section, after she and Sadie have made the quilt together.

QUILT
Marianne describes the pieces that went into making her memory quilt and their significance. It includes a piece of Papa Duban's overalls, a white line to represent Elise's travels, a piece of Sadie's yellow dress, and Lizbeth's gold button. In the center of the quilt they plan to put a cross, representing a window, a symbol of the time Marianne has spent looking for her mother. She explains that she has traveled far, north and west, looking for her in her dreams.

BUTTON
Sadie tells Marianne about the last time she saw Jim. He came to her cabin after twenty years. He told her that he had seen Lizbeth right after the slaves were freed, in a refugee camp outside of Hannibal, but she died the very next day. He was not able to find any clue about Jonnie. He asked Sadie to leave with him, going west, but she refused because Papa Duban was her man. He promised to write to her, but she never heard from him again.

CHARACTERS

Andrew
Andrew is a slave on the Cyprien sugarcane plantation. His sole function is to get women pregnant, providing more slaves for his owner. Sadie has four children with him: Jake, Theo, Roy, and Guy. After he is not able to sire more

children, Andrew loses his status on the plantation, and Sadie lets him move in with her. He confesses to her that the one real love of his life was a young man named Lemuel.

Banes
The overseer of the Stevens farm, Banes is valued by Mas Stevens because he is cruel and sadistic toward the other slaves.

Cora
Cora is frequently referred to as "Aunt Cora." She is childless, but she is put in charge of nursing the newborn children on the Watson farm. As such, she is a mother figure to Sadie after the loss of her real mother. Sadie assists Cora in midwifing Jim's birth, and later Sadie and Jim and their children live in Cora's shack. Before they are separated, Sadie and Jim marry themselves in an unofficial ceremony, at which Cora officiates.

Old Man Cyprien
Cyprien owns a large sugarcane plantation in Louisiana, where Sadie is sent after burning Mas Stevens's tobacco barn.

Papa Duban
Duban is the man Sadie becomes involved with while living in the woods of Louisiana. She nurses him to health, and he becomes a part of the family. Later, when Jim returns to her as an old man, she says that she cannot leave with him because she is involved with Papa Duban now. In the novel's first chapter, Sadie mentions that Papa Duban died the year before.

Elise
Elise is the mother of Marianne Libre. She is born after Sadie is raped by a shopkeeper on the Cyprien sugarcane plantation. After the slaves are freed, Elise travels with her mother and her mother's other children for a while. She has Marianne with Joseph, an educated man who is killed by marauding white men. Elise leaves her eight-year-old daughter and travels out west with a group of church people. Marianne often wonders what happened to her mother and waits with diminishing hope for her return.

Emma
Emma is the crew leader among the women on the Watson farm. She is often noted controlling the mood of the workers through the songs she leads them in singing.

Huckleberry Finn

Huck Finn, the protagonist of Mark Twain's 1884 novel, does not appear directly in this book, but he is talked about. Incidents from that book, such as when Jim was accused of Huck's murder because they both disappeared at the same time, are referred to here. Jim wears around his neck a coin on a string that he acquired in that novel, and he gives Sadie a corncob pipe that was given to him by Huck.

Flesh

The Indian woman who is married briefly to Mas Stevens is called Flesh. She wants to use Sadie's bowl for grinding and mixing her own type of medicine, but Sadie tells her it will not work with Indian medicines.

Fortune

Fortune is officially the cook at the farm of Mas Stevens, though Sadie is quick to point out that she does not know how to cook. Unofficially, her function on the farm is to become pregnant by Mas Stevens, producing babies that can be sold into slavery. Sadie suggests that she can take certain herbs to curtail her pregnancies, but Fortune laughs at her. She feels that she has an easy life and is taking advantage of Mas Stevens. Later, during a difficult pregnancy, Sadie offers her some herbs that will help ease her pain, and she defiantly refuses. She dies giving birth.

Chas Freeman

Chas is mentioned in the first line of the book: he has set the plot in motion by asking sixteen-year-old Marianne Libre to marry him. He has proposed because he is being called up for military service in the army, to serve at Fort Robinson, Nebraska, to fight against the Plains Indians and the whites who work with them, and he wants Marianne to leave Louisiana and go with him. Although the book is nominally about her potential marriage to him, Chas is not mentioned again.

Gwen

Gwen was Sadie's friend on the Watson farm, but she was sold off one day to a mean slave owner named Judge Durman, who is assumed to want her because Gwen is so pretty. Sadie meets Gwen again on the Cyprien plantation in Louisiana.

Jenny

Jenny is the sister of Sadie. There are unconfirmed rumors that Mas Watson is Jenny's real father and that is why he chose to sell her to a family in Hannibal at an early age, because his wife wanted her off the Watson farm.

Jim

Jim is the character that readers know from *The Adventures of Huckleberry Finn*. In that novel, he is a somewhat naive figure, superstitious and fearful. He idly mentions that he has a wife and children that he left behind and wants to go back and buy out of slavery, but they are only mentioned once in that novel.

Jim was born to a slave who ran away and a mother who does not want to bring a baby into the world. She tries to kill herself, but she and Jim survive. As he grows, Jim is strong and handsome. He is popular with the women, but his one true love is Sadie, who was a young girl when she assisted at his birth. Jim is assumed by the other slaves to have the power to read the future: he predicts a flood and a meteor shower. The other slaves on the Watson farm go to him to hear his predictions about their lives. At the same time, however, they fear Sadie as a witch because she is able to heal illnesses with herbs. When all of the slaves on the Watson farm are sold, Jim is kept by Miss Watson, who was born at about the same time as he was and was "given" Jim as a child. Soon after that, he escapes and travels downriver with Huck Finn, having the adventures outlined in that book.

Jim comes back into Sadie's story sporadically. First, she hears word from another slave, Nate, that he did not drown in the river, as previously thought. Later, he returns as a free man; *Huckleberry Finn* explains that Miss Watson left him her freedom in her will when she died. He has money to buy Sadie and his children, but Mas Stevens orders that they are not to be sold to him. Jim returns to Sadie when she is old and her family with him has been disbursed, bringing news that their daughter, Lizbeth, is dead and that he can find no trace of their son, Jonnie. He tries to persuade her to leave for the West with him, which is the plan that Huckleberry Finn has when he is adopted by Tom Sawyer's aunt at the end of his book, but Sadie says that she has to remain faithful to her new man, Papa Duban.

Jonnie

Jonnie is the second child of Sadie and Jim. When the Watson farm is sold to Mas Stevens, Jonnie, a young boy, is separated from his parents. His father goes to live with Miss Watson, and he is taken from Sadie as a punishment. He is placed in a cabin with other slaves and hears them talk fearfully about Sadie, calling her evil because of her ability to create healing potions. When they throw him out of their cabin he moves in with Sadie, but he distrusts her. She tends to his toothache by pulling his bad tooth, but when she sneaks into Mas Stevens's house for some clove to help his pain, she is caught. To punish her, Mas Stevens sells Jonnie and she never sees or hears from him again.

Joseph

The father of Marianne, Joseph met her mother, Elise, after her family was freed. He is killed by white men in Louisiana in the Colfax Massacre.

Marianne Libre

Marianne is the sixteen-year-old girl who starts the novel faced with a quandary: her boyfriend has proposed marriage. By the standards of the time, she is not that young for marriage, but Marianne feels that she is too young. She is not certain that she loves Chas, and she wonders if life might hold many forthcoming adventures for her. She discusses her uncertainty with her grandmother, Sadie, and that forms the core of the novel: Sadie tells her story, so that Marianne can compare her expectations with the kind of real-life difficulties a person of an older generation has gone through. Sadie is so sure that Marianne will marry Chas that she immediately begins work on a memory quilt, citing the reason that Marianne will need a quilt to keep her warm when she moves to Nebraska to be with him.

By the end of Sadie's narrative, Marianne sees the world differently. In the beginning, she viewed her grandmother as a stranger, but she comes to look at the story Sadie has told as a gift. Marianne has some education, and the implication is that she has written Sadie's story down, which is something the older woman could not do herself, as her way of preserving the family history as she prepares to move away and start a new chapter of it.

Liza

See Mama

Lizbeth

Lizbeth is the first child of Jim and Sadie. She is born healthy but loses her hearing at an early age as the result of scarlet fever. When she is still but a child, she becomes the sexual partner of her owner, Mas Stevens. Sadie is angry and disappointed, but Lizbeth looks at the situation as a chance to eat better food and live a better life while she is under Stevens's control. When Sadie is sold downriver, she loses track of Lizbeth. Later, Sadie learns that Jim went to see Lizbeth after the slaves were freed and that Lizbeth died in a refugee camp soon after being emancipated, never having a chance to enjoy her freedom.

Mama

Sadie's mother, Liza—referred to throughout the book as "Mama"—was born in 1803, the year of the Louisiana Purchase. She was born into slavery in Virginia and moved with the youngest member of the Watson family across the country on a perilous journey, eventually settling in Missouri. Sadie learned from her mother how to heal with herbs. Her mother was sent off from Virginia with a bowl for crushing and mixing herbs that her family had brought from the Congo, which Mama gave to Sadie when she was young.

Nate

Nate brings Sadie news that Jim is alive. He met Jim in Arkansas, in a place where there was a big fight among the white people, presumably referring to the angry mob that ran the duke and the dauphin out of town in *Huckleberry Finn*.

Doc Renard

Sadie is rented out to the town doctor, who refuses to give any credibility to her knowledge of healing medicines. He orders her to warm a corpse overnight, so that he can work on it in the morning, an experience she finds so revolting that she insists to her owner, Mas Watson, that she will not go back to the doctor's office.

Mas Stevens

Stevens is the cruel tobacco farm owner who owns the land adjacent to the Watson farm. Early in the story, Sadie is called in to heal him from a knife wound inflicted, she assumes, by one of his slaves. After he purchases her, Stevens tries to have sex with Sadie, but she resists. To punish her, he enters into a sexual relationship with her daughter Lizbeth. After he sells her son

Jonnie downriver, Sadie is so angry that she tries to burn down his tobacco-drying shed. She is unsuccessful, and he comes to her and puts her eye out with his cane and then sells her downriver, refusing to allow Jim, who has returned with money, to buy her.

Stowe

Stowe is the preacher for the slave community around Hannibal.

Tailor

Tailor is the black overseer on the Watson plantation. He was hired out to a tailor shop, but he worked well, and Mas Watson brought him back to work the farm when he needed a foreman. Tailor is a cruel man who punishes the slaves ruthlessly. After he sends Sadie to bring Jim to the fields when Jim is sick and she returns alone, he tortures her with the cinders from his pipe. Sadie's mother promises to put a spell on him; soon after that the Mississippi River rises, and the bodies buried in the graveyard float up around Tailor. This quiets him for a while, but he eventually starts being cruel to Sadie again, angry because she does not have to work in the fields as much as he does.

Mas Watson

Mas Watson left his family in Virginia and went west with a group of slaves that included Sadie's mother. He is not the cruelest slaveholder in the area, but he is not very kind either.

Miss Watson

The daughter that Mas Watson, Sadie's owner, had at about the same time that Sadie was born is referred to as Miss Watson. At an early age, Jim foretells that Miss Watson will never marry, which upsets her greatly. Miss Watson appears in Twain's novel *Huckleberry Finn* as a spinster woman who tries to adopt Huck. Her sister, who in this novel marries a man named Douglas, lives with her in Twain's novel as "the widow Douglas." After their father dies, Miss Watson has no idea how to run the farm. She has the land, its implements, and all of the slaves held by her father sold at auction, forcing Sadie to go to the farm of the sadistic Mas Stevens.

Sadie Watson

The narrator of the main part of this novel, Sadie was born on the Watson farm near Hannibal, Missouri. She lives through the end of slavery and into the period of Reconstruction that followed.

Early in her life, Sadie becomes an outcast among other slaves. Initially, her ability to heal people with common herbs is valued by both the slaves and the white people, to such an extent that she is called in to work her cures on people whom the white doctor cannot cure. Later, when her husband Jim has run away, the slaves turn on her and look at her skill with herbs as a kind of witchcraft. She is isolated.

Throughout her story, Sadie is constantly protecting herself. She becomes pregnant several times by field hands who attack her, but she terminates the pregnancies with herbs. Later, at the Cyprien sugar plantation, she does not have access to those herbs and has four sons by a man sent by her owner to impregnate her. She does not create much of a bond with those sons. The children she focuses on are the two, Lizbeth and Jonnie, that she has had with the love of her life, Jim.

Sadie knows Jim all of his life, having been present for his birth. She watches him grow up to be a handsome man, and she is jealous, and then skeptical, when he professes his own love for her. When they are separated by the death of their owner, Sadie does what she can to protect Lizbeth and Jonnie, but they are taken away from her too. When she strikes out and tries to burn the crop of Mas Stevens, her owner, he blinds her in one eye.

Sadie tells all of the twisted events of her life as a slave to her granddaughter, Marianne, who was born after Emancipation and does not know the kinds of difficulties life during slavery could offer. Marianne has received a proposal of marriage but is not sure that she is ready for such a bold step at sixteen, so Sadie tells about her own life, how she tried to stay alive and to reunite with Jim, to give Marianne some perspective on love and life.

Widow Douglas

Widow Douglas is a character familiar to readers of Twain's *Huckleberry Finn*. She is the sister of Miss Watson, raised on the Watson farm and leaving briefly to marry a man named Douglas.

When Jim is believed dead, Widow Douglas takes an interest in Sadie and her two children. She gets permission from Mas Stevens to take them to church. Seeing that Lizbeth is interested in the gold buttons on her coachman's jacket, an old Revolutionary War uniform coat, she has the coachman remove the button and give it to Lizbeth as an act of sympathy.

TOPICS FOR FURTHER STUDY

- Choose a minor character from another novel you have read and write a short story from that character's point of view. In your story, include events that were recounted in the original.

- Sadie's ability to heal illnesses with plants is admired originally, but after bad circumstances befall her, it becomes the basis for viewing her as a witch. Research herbal medicines that were once rejected, and write a report on at least three that are recognized by doctors and chemists today, explaining the medical theory behind how they work.

- Read a historical slave narrative, such as Lucy Delaney's 1891 book *From the Darkness Cometh the Light; or, Struggles for Freedom*, about her mother's lawsuit to free herself from slavery, or Harriet Ann Jacobs's *Incidents in the Life of a Slave Girl*, published in 1861. Compare the language that Rawles gives Sadie in this book with the language used in these books. Rewrite a section of *My Jim* as you think either Delaney or Jacobs would have written, and explain the word choices you have made.

- Throughout the telling of her story, Sadie frequently refers to the songs that the slaves sang in the fields, often led by Cora. Review some slave songs at the website for PBS's

"Slavery and the Making of America" at http://www.pbs.org/wnet/slavery/experience/education/feature.html. Then write a song describing Sadie and Marianne Libre making a quilt together, using the same kinds of chords and rhythms. Explain which aspects of your slave song resemble the traditional music.

- Patricia McCormick's 2006 book *Sold*, a National Book Award finalist, tells the contemporary story of a thirteen-year-old girl in Nepal who is dragged from the life she is leading and forced into slavery. Read it, and compare modern-day slavery with the way slavery is described in this novel: which aspects are similar, and how has this practice changed with time?

- Write a paper that maps where Confederate slaves would have gone when they were released from slavery. Try to concentrate on slaves released in Louisiana, which is where Sadie is living when she is emancipated.

- President Abraham Lincoln signed the Emancipation Proclamation in 1863, declaring an end to slavery. At the time, though, it applied only to slaves held in Confederate states that did not acknowledge Lincoln as their president. Form sides and debate the two theories of whether the Emancipation Proclamation was a significant move for slaves or an empty gesture.

THEMES

African American History

Rawles's novel concerns an era in the history of African Americans that has not been documented as much as other historical epochs, if only because the people most affected by the times were largely forbidden access to education, to reading and writing. The novel was intensely researched to present an accurate view of life during slavery, but that research is partly obscured by the limitations put on the first-person narrator. Through the voice that Rawles gives Sadie, readers can see the way that facts were kept from slaves: Sadie's knowledge of geographical locations and historical events, in particular, is sketchy.

Still, in having Sadie tell her tale to her granddaughter, Rawles shows how history about this period has been passed down to the present time through oral tradition, with many slaves and former slaves dictating their stories to people fortunate enough to have an education. Far fewer slaves and former slaves had adequate education to write down their own stories—with notable exceptions, including the famed abolitionist orator Frederick Douglass. Otherwise, if not for personal connections and the willingness of people like Marianne Libre to transcribe tales that were told to them, many details of slave life in America might have been lost.

Memory

The structure of this novel helps readers see how objects can help a person like Sadie, who does not know how to read or write, remember the details of her life. Throughout the course of the book, she is making a memory quilt with Marianne, which drives her to reconsider the seemingly random objects that she has kept in a jar for years. Rawles draws attention to the significance of these objects by naming chapters after them: "Hat," "Bowl," "Button," "Pipe," etcetera.

The memory quilt is a method used for generations to commemorate important people and events in a family. In *My Jim*, it helps take Sadie through her personal history, reminding her of events from her long life. With these specific items to jog her memory, she is able to fill in the details from within her mind.

Family

Sadie never has an official, legal family, but it is the love that she has for Jim and her children by him that keeps her alive. She marries Jim in a ceremony of their own making when she learns that she is pregnant with their daughter, Lizbeth. Yet as a slave she has no rights to her own children, and she must restrain herself from striking out against her captors in order to protect those she considers her family. Despite all that Mas Stevens and his overseer, Bane, inflict on her, Sadie is quietly accepting, until she discovers that Lizbeth has agreed to be Stevens's sexual partner and Jonnie is sold downriver. After that, she has no one to protect, and she strikes out by burning Stevens's tobacco crop.

Sadie never truly forms an emotional bond with the children that she has later, the ones that are not a part of her marriage with Jim: Elise, Jake, Theo, Roy, and Guy. After being freed of slavery, however, she accepts Papa Duban as her spouse, and she takes her commitment to

him so seriously that she considers herself unavailable to her one true love, Jim, when he returns to her.

Rape

Rawles uses this novel to show how the oppressors made rape a tool to their advantage during slavery. The most obvious way was as a means of demoralizing women, making them feel powerless when raped by their white owners or other slaves. Slave owners also benefited by allowing rape to occur among slaves, using the female slaves to keep the male slaves somewhat content. Sadie describes her constant rape and impregnation by workers in the field as a way of life for a slave. When slave women did become pregnant, either by slaves or by owners, the slave owners stood to benefit financially, since the children that they bore automatically became the property of their owners and could be sold for a good price.

Abandonment

Sadie and Jim's relationship is complicated because he is betting that he will be able to free her if he leaves her; he tries to escape to a place where he can be free so that he can earn enough money to buy Sadie and their two children from their owner, Stevens. While he is gone, Sadie can only wonder where he is and whether he will return.

He is often gone from her life. For years, he works in town while she is on the Watson farm, and she thinks he will be involved with other women. Then he is moved to Miss Watson's house while Sadie and the children are moved to the Stevens farm. When he leaves Miss Watson, Sadie thinks he is dead, drowned in the Mississippi before he even got away from Hannibal, until she runs into a free black man who says that he saw Jim alive in Arkansas. After that, he comes into her life a few times but always is forced to leave to avoid being enslaved again. The last time she sees him, they are both legally free, but she is bound by her honor to Papa Duban. Jim leaves her once more, promising to write to her, but he never does.

This relationship is mirrored in the relationship Marianne has with her mother. Marianne's mother, Elise, leaves her when the child is eight years old, promising to come back when she has her fortune. But she never returns. In the chapter "Cross," Marianne describes how much she

Sadie Watson narrates the tale of her love for Jim to her granddaughter. *(© Daleen Loest | Shutterstock.com)*

misses her mother, having traveled the country in her dreams, looking for her without any luck.

STYLE

First-Person Narrator

This novel has two narrators. Most of it is told from the point of view of Sadie Watson, while the first chapter and the later chapter called "Cross" are narrated by Marianne Libre.

Using a first-person narrator limits the amount of information that a writer can give to the reader. In the beginning, for instance, readers do not know who is being talked about or what their relationships are to one another: Marianne is talking, but her monologue is more to herself than to the reader, so she does not bother explaining the details. Throughout most of the book, information is given by someone who has purposely been kept in the dark about slaveholders.

Even while using a voice that does not feel the need to explain every last detail, Rawles

manages to drop historical signposts into the book, so that readers can relate things Sadie is talking about to matters of historical record. One specific example of this is when Sadie overhears white people talking about their fear of an uprising among the slaves and Rawles has her note that Jim "say they talking bout Dred and Harriet," a reference to the historical figures Dred Scott, who sued to free his family but ultimately lost, and his wife, Harriet. For the most part, Rawles can only refer to historical facts carefully, in order to maintain the authenticity of Sadie's voice.

Dialect

Some readers might have trouble reading this novel because it is written in dialect, using the pronunciations of words that Marianne and Sadie would have used instead of standard English. For years, black American dialect in literature was considered an embarrassment, mainly because it was written by white people who were trying to render how the voices of black people sounded to them. The result was that stereotypes born during the days of minstrel shows, when white actors in blackface did comic imitations of black people, were carried along in print. In *My Jim*, the dialect the narrators use is more authentic. It uses established words, for the most part, instead of trying to chop them up with apostrophes or mixing together letters to make new words. Readers are reminded of the sound of African American dialect, but it does not cross the line into parody of a sound that has not often been effectively captured in print.

Existing Characters

In telling this story, Rawles includes and refers to Jim, the major character in Mark Twain's *Adventures of Huckleberry Finn*, as well as several other characters from Twain, such as the Widow Douglas and Miss Watson. She also refers to some events from the Twain novel, such as Jim's reported death and the coin that Huck gave him, which he wears on a string around his neck. Still, the references to Twain's novel are few and incidental. Most of Twain's characters who are mentioned in *My Jim* are mentioned only in passing and do not appear at all. Even Jim, who this book is named after, shows up only infrequently. Keeping Twain's characters in the background frees Rawles to present the characters as she wants to imagine them, from her own perspective as a black writer of the twenty-first century, instead of being locked into the artistic vision of a white man from the nineteenth century.

HISTORICAL CONTEXT

Slavery in America

Slavery was not an American invention: it had been established in Western culture for two centuries before reaching North America. Europeans were taking people from Africa as far back as the fifteenth century. In 1493, the year after Christopher Columbus's voyage to the American continent, the Catholic Church granted exclusive rights to the African slave trade to Portugal, because Portuguese explorers were the first Europeans to establish bases on the African continent. This exclusivity did not last long, however. By the middle of the 1500s, there were Dutch, French, English, Swedish, Danish, and Prussian companies involved in the slave trade.

The first Africans to be brought to America came as indentured servants who were able to work off the cost of their passage over the course of decades. Twenty such workers arrived at the early colony of Jamestown, Virginia, in 1619. For years, farmers were able to get along hiring Africans as they hired Europeans, but as immigration from Europe slowed down, more and more Africans were brought as slaves. A lucrative slave industry sprang up in the early eighteenth century. About five thousand black soldiers fought in the Revolutionary War, but at the same time the US cotton industry was growing. The original draft of the Declaration of Independence called the king of England to task for promoting slavery in the colonies, but the states that needed slaves voted that language out. In the Constitution's enumeration clause, which measures out how many representatives are to be elected from each state, each slave is given the value of three-fifths of a white citizen. To placate the colonists who found the slave trade a barbaric practice, the Constitution also outlawed the importation of any new slaves after January 1, 1808.

After that date, slavery continued, of course, with the slave population being constantly replenished by the children of people already enslaved. Throughout the first half of the nineteenth century, opposition to slavery grew, mostly in the industrial North, while farmers in the agricultural areas of the South, who relied on slave labor, fought for their right to own people. As the abolitionists (those who wanted to abolish slavery) gained in political power, slave owners fought for constitutional rights to continue as they had been.

Soon after Abraham Lincoln, who opposed slavery, was inaugurated to the presidency in 1861, seven states seceded from the Union to form the Confederate States of America. Four more states followed soon after that, and two territories aligned themselves with the Confederacy. The Civil War, fought from 1861 until the South surrendered at Appomattox on April 9, 1865, was about several differences that separated the industrial North and the agrarian South, but the key difference was slavery. Though President Lincoln declared an end to slavery in the United States with his Emancipation Proclamation in 1863, slavery was not universally outlawed until the former Confederate states were readmitted into the Union at the end of the war.

COMPARE & CONTRAST

- **1840s–1860s:** Future novelist Samuel Clemens grows up in Hannibal, Missouri, a town on the Mississippi River that is the setting of his most celebrated novels and later provides the setting for *My Jim*.

  1880s: Mark Twain revisits characters from *The Adventures of Tom Sawyer*, a novel published a decade earlier, in his new book *Adventures of Huckleberry Finn*.

  Today: *Adventures of Huckleberry Finn* is considered one of the greatest novels in American literature and is certainly the crown jewel in Twain's long and illustrious career.

- **1840s–1860s:** Slaves have no power to keep their families together. Slave owners will often sell slaves without any regard for their family relations or sometimes to purposely break up families and punish slaves considered disobedient.

  1880s: Families that have been separated by slave traders stand little chance of being reunited, as news of missing relatives travels primarily by word of mouth.

  Today: Social media help reconnect people who have lost track of one another.

- **1840s–1860s:** To stop slaves from gaining their freedom by moving north out of slave states, Congress passes the Fugitive Slave Act of 1850, which makes it a crime to help an escaped slave. Many freed black people are pulled back into slavery by the vague wording of this law.

  1880s: Nearly twenty years after the end of the Civil War, former slaves are free but find that, in many states, the conventions that restricted where they can live and work are written into segregationist law.

  Today: The turbulent civil rights era of the 1950s and 1960s and the legislation enacted in its wake have made much racial inequality punishable by federal law.

- **1840s–1860s:** The end of the Mexican American War in 1848 opens the area between the Mississippi River and the Pacific Ocean for expansion by the United States.

  1880s: The western area of the continent is still considered "wild." There are only thirty-eight states in the Union, and people can escape to "the territories" to start a new life.

  Today: The territories have all become states, with no part of the continental United States not under the jurisdiction of local, state, and/or federal governments.

Reconstruction

Even as the war was going on, Lincoln was concerned with how the defeated Confederate states could pick themselves up financially after the destruction wrought on their fields and with how the citizens of the Confederacy could be made to feel themselves to be citizens again with the people they had fought against so recently. Lincoln's assassination just a week after the South's surrender complicated the matter. Four million former slaves suddenly had their freedom, half of the country had been economically destroyed by the other half, and instead of having Lincoln to guide them, the country was under the control of Lincoln's vice president, Andrew Johnson, a man who historians generally agree was never prepared for the position.

Johnson sought to calm the southern states by giving powers to the state legislatures of the former Confederacy. Under the presidential Reconstruction of 1865–1867, southern states enacted a series of "black codes" that limited the rights of former slaves. These codes ranged widely throughout the states, from proclamations that made the refusal of black humanity

Jim runs away with Huck Finn down the Mississippi River because he believes he is about to be sold.
(© sue120502 / Shutterstock.com)

the official state policy to laws that required blacks to work only if they contracted to stay at a job for a year or more, under threat of penalties, to stringent rules segregating the races and limiting education of blacks. Overall, the new laws created conditions that resembled the conditions of slavery.

Politicians in the North were appalled by the way Johnson allowed southern legislatures to ease back into these dehumanizing practices, which many felt the war was fought to obliterate. Johnson became the first US president to be impeached by the House, though he was acquitted by the Senate. Congress took over control of Reconstruction, passing laws over Johnson's veto that constituted what came to be called Radical Reconstruction. Established politicians were forced out of office, and blacks and northerners were encouraged to become involved in southern politics. Laws were passed to finance public schools in the South and to relieve blacks of oppressive taxation. Although Radical Reconstruction was a victory for the millions of

former slaves, it came with a price. Whites lashed out violently, as they did in the Colfax Massacre (mentioned in the novel as the place where Andrew and Joseph die) and in the ascent of the Ku Klux Klan.

CRITICAL OVERVIEW

My Jim was a critical success upon its publication, lauded by a range of reviewers. On a national level, two of the most widely read publications in the country, *People* magazine and *Entertainment Weekly*, took the time to give it attention that most novelists would relish. Jennifer Reese, writing in *Entertainment Weekly*, gave the novel an "A-" rating, explaining that "Rawles has produced a gritty, imaginative companion piece to *Huckleberry Finn*." Similarly, the Picks and Pans column of *People* gave *My Jim* a three-and-a-half star review, calling it a "harsh, powerfully personal portrait of slavery."

Reviewing the book for the *New York Times Book Review*, often considered one of the most influential book review forums in the country, Helen Schulman called *My Jim* "as heart-wrenching a personal history as any recorded in American literature." Schulman also wondered, though, whether the novel would be as successful or popular if it were a narrative titled after some other slave. As Schulman puts it, "It's hard not to wonder if it is the brush with Twain and Finn that give Sadie's story its jolt of vitality."

Overall, most reviewers found this book to be a tour de force for Rawles. Ron Charles, writing in the *Christian Science Monitor*, captures the general consensus when he notes that "there's just no escaping" the voice of the book's narrator. "In her perfectly artless manner," Charles remarks, "Sadie moves through a love story that's horrible and harrowing, but somehow she arrives at an affirmation earned with her own blood."

My Jim also received favorable reviews in local presses. John Marshall of the *Seattle Post-Intelligencer*, for instance, starts his review with the understated observation that it is "a powerhouse little book." Acknowledging that Rawles is a Seattle writer, Marshall is particularly appreciative of the care she gave to crafting the voice of Sadie: "Rawles' use of simple dialect, often with little or no punctuation, rings so true, page after page, that the reader indeed feels transported into the room with Sadie." Marshall concludes his review by noting that Rawles "succeeds in such a convincing way that it is not a stretch to imagine her novel being taught in countless schools as a supplementary text to Twain's classic," even though it does contain controversial racial language and violent imagery.

CRITICISM

David Kelly

Kelly is a professor of creative writing and literature. In the following essay, he examines how the structure of framing Sadie's story with Marianne's story is integral to the success of My Jim.

Nancy Rawles's novel *My Jim* tells the story of Sadie, a slave in the American South for most of her life. Rawles surrounds the events of Sadie's life with a number of storytelling techniques that serve to help modern readers relate to her.

The flashiest of *My Jim*'s techniques is the Jim of the title—an old familiar face in the world of literature. The significance of referencing *Adventures of Huckleberry Finn*'s Jim is questionable. There are a few specifics about Twain's Jim woven into Rawles's story, but they occur at a distance from the central action. If Sadie's one true love had been some other person, would this story have been different? Probably not, but if that had been the case, then the novel would not have garnered the critical attention that it did. Just about every review of the book starts out by mentioning the connection to a book that has been taught to generations of students, a book that has become more and more controversial as time has passed, with the controversy specifically centering on its depiction of Jim. In a modern world where the best-selling films are sequels, remakes, or adaptations from such broad sources as television, comic books, and video games, the idea of having a recognizable character on the cover of a novel can be significant, whether he appears often in the book or not.

The dialect Rawles has written in, too, is a technique that catches readers' attention. Rawles has Sadie narrating the book in a slave dialect, and the chapters of the book narrated by her granddaughter, Marianne, are written in a variation of that dialect. Both are readable to twenty-first-century readers, if only after a bit of acclimation. And both are relevant to the story Rawles tells. There have been centuries of well-meaning white authors, Twain included, whose idea of "Negro dialect" comes off the page as the grossest of parodies, no more true to nineteenth-century southern blacks than any minstrel in blackface ever was. Rawles, of course, has never heard the voice of a person who lived before sound recording was invented, but she renders Sadie's voice with respect and precision, using real words, not awkward phonetic contractions, to show that Sadie is not speaking a foreign language but is in fact using English as she knows it. Some books written in dialect seem to be struggling to establish how well the author knows his or her characters, but Sadie's voice blends smoothly with her circumstances without ever straining beyond the author's skill set.

Rawles could easily have done without either of these techniques. If Jim had been an anonymous slave named, say, Tim or Jack, Sadie's story would have been just as compelling, and if the dialect had been a bit less pronounced, Sadie would still have come off as a credible character.

WHAT DO I READ NEXT?

- It is not necessary to read Mark Twain's novel *Adventures of Huckleberry Finn* in order to understand and enjoy Rawles's novel, but being familiar with Twain's novel will give readers a deeper appreciation of *My Jim*. Of the Twain novel, Ernest Hemingway famously once wrote, "All modern American literature comes from one book by Mark Twain called *Huckleberry Finn*." Twain merges a scathing social critique of the time with an adventure story and a fantasy about freedom. Published in 1884, it is available in dozens of editions, most notably in W. W. Norton's *Adventures of Huckleberry Finn: An Authoritative Text, Contexts and Sources, Criticism* (1999).

- In modern times, Twain's novel has been subject to criticism for the way that it depicts Jim, generally presenting him as a foolish, superstitious man who cannot survive without the guidance of two white boys. One of the clearest and most convincing of these criticisms was written in an essay in *Harper's* magazine by noted novelist Jane Smiley. Her essay, found in the January 1996 issue, is called "Say It Ain't So, Huck: Second Thoughts on Mark Twain's 'Masterpiece.'"

- *My Jim* is Rawles's third novel. Her second, *Crawfish Dreams*, takes place in the 1980s. It concerns a woman who moved from Louisiana to Los Angeles decades earlier and watched her neighborhood sink deeper and deeper into poverty and violence and relates her success in opening a Creole food business in her sixties. It was published in 2003.

- Dred Scott is referred to in this novel: the moment he lost his lawsuit to free his family was one of the darkest moments for slaves, who saw their hopes in the legal world tumble. In *Dred and Harriett Scott: A Family's Struggle for Freedom*, published in 2004, noted young-adult author Gwenyth Swain does something similar to what Rawles does in *My Jim*: she uses historical facts as a basis for a novel about one family's perseverance.

- During the Great Depression, the government sent workers out to interview 124 former slaves, as part of the Federal Writers' Project. Their memories about life on plantations are recorded in *Remembering Slavery: African Americans Talk about Their Personal Experiences of Slavery and Emancipation*. First published in 1998, the book was edited by Ira Berlin, Steven F. Miller, and Marc Favreau.

- Alex Haley's 1976 novel *Roots: The Saga of an American Family*, based on his own family history, follows several generations from Africa, where young Kunta Kinte is captured and sold to slave traders, through generations living in slavery and freedom, right up to the author's time. It is considered one of the most admirably written and researched novels about African American life. A special thirtieth-anniversary edition was released in 2007.

- Among the number of books written by former slaves while slavery was occurring, one of the most famous is *Narrative of the Life of Frederick Douglass, an American Slave*, published in 1845. Marked by Douglass's massive intellect and eloquent explanation of his childhood in slavery, the book was a powerful tool for helping the abolitionists make their case against slavery. It is considered one of the greatest autobiographies in American history and offers a clear reading for students of high-school age.

> SADIE IS A VICTIM WHO FEELS GUILTY, AND
> SHE WOULD TAKE ALL THAT SHE HAS SEEN TO HER
> GRAVE, EXCEPT UNDER THESE VERY SPECIFIC CIR-
> CUMSTANCES. MARIANNE IS THE ONLY PERSON
> SADIE CAN TELL HER STORY TO."

One stylistic technique that turns out to be indispensable, though, is the way Rawles frames this story. Instead of simply having Sadie speak to the reader, as first-person narratives often do, she establishes an external situation: sixteen-year-old Marianne is weighing a marriage proposal from Chas Freeman, who wants to take her from Louisiana to Nebraska, where he is to serve in the army. Wrapping Marianne's story—of which readers are given very little—around Sadie's story of a long life of degradation and triumph turns out to be the very thing that allows Rawles to transcend her story's roots. It is no longer *a* "slave narrative," one of many. Instead it becomes the story of an individual, in a way that simply including Twain's Jim or replicating authentic dialect never allows it to be.

A problem that arises with first-person narratives is that readers tend to wonder why the narrator is speaking. Often, the narrator's motive is just left as a given—they talk about what happened, but in no particular context. Sometimes there is a vague purpose implied, as when the narrator of Charles Dickens's *David Copperfield* begins with "Whether I shall turn out to be the hero of my own life, or whether that station will be held by anybody else, these pages must show." Sometimes the first-person narrator is addressing someone who is not part of the story, such as with the protagonist of *The Catcher in the Rye*, who reveals at the end that he has told his story because a psychiatrist suggested its telling for his therapy.

It says a lot about slave culture, about the shame and fear that made millions of people watch their lives drip away for the pleasure of others, that Marianne has been kept in the dark about her grandmother's life. Rawles is true to Sadie's character by making her guard her slave life like a terrible, guilty secret. Readers find out

from her interaction with Marianne that Sadie has never mentioned the man she loved and married or the two children she had with him. Sadie is a victim who feels guilty, and she would take all that she has seen to her grave, except under these very specific circumstances. Marianne is the only person Sadie can tell her story to.

For one thing, she is family. Rawles makes clear that there was little emotional bond between Sadie and her daughter Elise, Marianne's mother, and one can see that the relationship between grandmother and granddaughter is marked by aloofness. Still, Sadie raised Marianne and has been responsible for her. Talking about her life as a slave is not something Sadie would do for her own self-satisfaction, but she would sacrifice her privacy for her granddaughter's sake, because she knows the responsibility of children.

Also, though the child has been shielded from the horrors of slave life, Marianne has known a kind of suffering that puts her in a unique position to understand what Sadie tells her. She is no stranger to racial violence, having lost her father in an attack by white marauders during Reconstruction. The school she attended briefly was closed down by whites, giving her a taste of what it was like to be at the mercy of people who, like Sadie's slaveholders, feel it is in their interest to keep black people suffering.

Perhaps most significantly, grandmother and granddaughter share the bond of waiting. Sadie's life is defined throughout the novel by her intermittent reunions with Jim. As a slave he is sent to work at different locations, and then after he is freed by the death of Miss Watson, he is refused the chance to buy Sadie. When both of them are eventually free, Sadie sends Jim away because she is loyal to Papa Duban, even though it is Jim that she really loves. At the time of the novel, Papa Duban is dead, and Sadie is free for a final reunion with Jim, but she has no idea where to reach him. She can only wait for him to return to her again. Marianne can share her sense of anticipation: she has spent half her life holding out hope that her mother might come back to her, unlikely though that seems. The fact that they mirror each other's deepest sorrow gives Sadie an emotional bond with Marianne that no other interviewer would share.

What really brings Sadie out of her shell, though, is Marianne's reticence about love. She appears to love Chas Freeman at the time of his

Slave quarters much like those where Sadie and Jim would have lived (The Library of Congress)

proposal, but she questions whether she can count on that love to last. From Sadie's perspective, this is a fear that only someone who has lived a sheltered life can entertain. She sees no reason why Marianne and Chas cannot live a happy life together: after all, they are emancipated. Sadie knows that terrible things can arise, but she also knows that nothing is going to arise that will be worse than the horrors her love for Jim endured. A slave may have spent her entire long life keeping her thoughts hidden, but love is one subject that Sadie feels herself qualified to lecture her granddaughter about—subtly, though, teaching her by example.

In having Sadie struggle against her own secretive nature, so that she can help her granddaughter make a sound decision, Rawles makes the character transcend her function. Sadie becomes more than a representative of the many slave stories Rawles has read, as she becomes a human being in her own right. The other techniques, like using Twain's characters or writing in dialect, might help readers find a place for Sadie Watkins in her literary and historical contexts, but framing the story within Marianne's story shows her in a different light. Throughout the book, Sadie suffers unimaginable humiliation without raising her voice, but she cannot sit by and watch quietly as the free woman she raised lets love go by.

Source: David Kelly, Critical Essay on *My Jim*, in *Novels for Students*, Gale, Cengage Learning, 2013.

Patricia Bangs, Jackie Gropman, and Susan Woodcock

In the following review, Bangs, Gropman, and Woodcock find Rawles's book to be "moving and real."

Rawles turns an American classic on its head with this story of Sadie Watson, the wife Jim left behind when he joined Huck Finn on his adventure down the Mississippi. As a child, Sadie helps deliver Jim in a tobacco field. Her mother, the midwife, comforts his mother, "This baby might buy you freedom, one day." As an adult, Jim is obsessed with that freedom, but his schemes are continually thwarted. Once he and Sadie "jump the broom," he refuses to leave without his family. Circumstances change when their master, Watson, dies and Sadie and her children are sold. When Jim tries to visit her, he is caught and beaten, and finally runs away. His hat is found floating on the Mississippi, and he is feared drowned. Sadie, however, never gives up hoping for his return. *My Jim* is a love story. But it is also a vivid portrayal of Jim's other life—harsh at times, poignant at others. Even young adults unfamiliar with Huckleberry Finn's companion will find Rawles's tale moving and real. The author creates a heartbreaking world where farewells to husbands, wives, and children are common.

Source: Patricia Bangs, Jackie Gropman, and Susan Woodcock, Review of *My Jim*, in *School Library Journal*, Vol. 51, No. 5, May 2005.

Vanessa Bush

In the following review, Bush contends that My Jim *will find a place as a "fixture on high-school reading lists."*

This novel, evocative of slave narratives, explores what life must have been like for Jim, the slave who escapes down the Mississippi River with Huck Finn. But Jim's flight to freedom is only a backdrop to a story that is more about his wife, Sadie, and her fierce determination to survive the cruelties of slavery and to pass on the hopefulness of love to the next generation. When her granddaughter Marianne is frightened of leaving Louisiana in 1884 to make a new life with a buffalo soldier in the West, Sadie recalls the family's history as she makes a quilt for the young woman to take with her. Speaking in first-person dialect, Sadie recalls the loss of mother, children, and husband but also recalls the struggle to hold on to bits and pieces of family that she weaves into her story and the quilt. She recalls her talent for healing, her defiance of the master that eventually provoked her sale, and her abiding love for Jim, a slave she saw birthed into the world, This is a moving novel of American slavery and enduring love.

Source: Vanessa Bush, Review of *My Jim*, in *Booklist*, Vol. 101, No. 6, November 15, 2004, p. 563.

Publishers Weekly

In the following review, a contributor concludes that Rawles provides a "skillful addition to a small sub-canon."

In her spare, moving retelling of the story of escaped slave Jim from Mark Twain's *The Adventures of Huckleberry Finn*, Rawles shifts the focus to Jim's wife, Sadie, whose unspeakable losses set the tone for Jim's flight. Trained as a healer, Sadie helps bring Jim into the world when she herself is "no higher than a barrel." As they grow up together on Mas Watson's Missouri plantation, Jim only has eyes for Sadie, and after an informal marriage following their daughter Lizbeth's birth, they consider fleeing together. Their plans change when Mas Watson dies, and Sadie is taken by a hateful neighbor while Jim is kept on by Mas Watsons daughter. Jim finally escapes on his own, but is presumed dead when his hat is found floating in the Mississippi. After countless tribulations, Sadie meets up again with Jim, who has ventured down the Mississippi with Huck Finn in the meantime, but the pair are not reunited. Further disappointment comes after emancipation, when Sadie learns that freedom looks an awful lot like slavery. Writing in sonorous slave dialect, Rawles creates a memorable protagonist in Sadie and builds on Twain's portrayal of Jim while remaining true to the original.

Source: Review of *My Jim*, in *Publishers Weekly*, Vol. 251, No. 48, November 29, 2004, pp. 22–23.

Rebecca Stuhr

In the following review, Stuhr notes the immediacy and intimacy of the narrative in the novel.

Told entirely in dialect, this first-person narrative features Sadie, a third-generation slave emancipated during the Civil War. Sadie is making a quilt with her granddaughter, Marianne Libre, who was born free and must decide whether to marry and move away or remain with the grandmother who raised her. This inspires Sadie to tell the story of her own separation and loss. It is Sadie's story, but it is an archetypal story likely shared in some form by most slaves. In particular, Sadie recalls her husband, Jim, and their two children. Jim was sold away and later escaped to freedom with none other than Huckleberry Finn (a surprising detail that is not further developed). Sadie was later sold away from her children, neither of whom survived to freedom. As Sadie tells this story she clearly depicts both her inner life and the details of her daily existence. The intimate and immediate nature of the narrative draws the reader quickly into Sadie's story of physical and emotional pain. Rawles won the American Book Award for her first novel, *Loire Like Gumbo*; this new work is highly recommended for all YA and academic fiction collections.

Source: Rebecca Stuhr, Review of *My Jim*, in *Library Journal*, Vol. 129, No. 20, December 1, 2004, p. 102.

SOURCES

Charles, Ron, Review of *My Jim*, in *Christian Science Monitor*, January 18, 2005, http://www.csmonitor.com/2005/0118/p15s01-bogn.html (accessed August 29, 2012).

"Constitutional Topic: Slavery," U.S. Constitution Online, http://www.usconstitution.net/consttop_slav.html (accessed August 31, 2012).

Dickens, Charles, *The Personal History of David Copperfield*, Oxford University Press, 1998, p. 1.

Hemingway, Ernest, *Green Hills of Africa*, Simon and Schuster, 1998, p. 23.

Marshall, John, " 'My Jim' Pulls No Punches in Its Depiction of American Slavery,' in *Seattle Post-Intelligencer*, February 25, 2005, p. WH21.

"Teachers Guide: About This Author," Random House for High School Teachers website, http://www.randomhouse.com/highschool/catalog/display.pperl?isbn = 9781400054015&view = tg (accessed August 29, 2012).

Nancy Rawles website, http://www.nancyrawles.com/ (accessed August 29, 2012).

"Picks and Pans Review: *My Jim*," in *People*, Vol. 63, No. 7, February 21, 2005, http://www.people.com/people/article/0,,20146884,00.html (accessed August 24, 2012).

"Reconstruction," History.com, http://www.history.com/topics/reconstruction (accessed August 31, 2012).

Reese, Jennifer, Review of *My Jim*, in *Entertainment Weekly*, January 21, 2005, p. 93.

Schulman, Helen, "*My Jim*: Never the Twain," in *New York Times Book Review*, January 30, 2005, p. 26.

Stewart, Jeffrey C., *1001 Things Everyone Should Know about African American History*, Main Street Books/Doubleday, 1996, pp. 4–23.

FURTHER READING

Davis, David Brion, *Inhuman Bondage: The Rise and Fall of Slavery in the New World*, Oxford University Press, 2006.

> Many students choose to study slavery from slave narratives, the stories of individuals. Here Davis gives a compelling, concise overview of this complex issue, a situation that endured for centuries.

Du Bois, W. E. B., *Black Reconstruction in America, 1860–1880*, Free Press, 1999.

> Du Bois was one of the most important intellectual figures in American history, a participant in the Harlem Renaissance and the longtime editor of the *Crisis* magazine. This book, written in the 1930s, took the controversial view that Reconstruction was not the disaster for civil rights that it is generally thought to be but that it laid the groundwork for later gains in racial equality.

Johnson, Sarah Anne, "Nancy Rawles: I Try to Write Rhythmically," in *The Very Telling: Conversations with American Writers*, University Press of New England, 2006, pp. 169–80.

> In this 2005 interview with Rawles, the author talks about her influences and her theories of writing and describes an average day in her writing life.

Lane, Charles, *The Day Freedom Died: The Colfax Massacre, the Supreme Court, and the Betrayal of Reconstruction*, Henry Holt, 2008.

> The Colfax Massacre plays an important part in Rawles's novel, as related from the perspective of a person who lived through it. In this book, Lane looks at the larger social context—how this one moment in time exemplified and also crystallized what was wrong with postbellum America.

SUGGESTED SEARCH TERMS

Twain AND Rawles

Nancy Rawles AND character

Adventures of Huckleberry Finn AND controversy

Nancy Rawles AND My Jim

Jim AND wife AND Huckleberry Finn

Nancy Rawles AND slavery

Mark Twain AND Reconstruction

Reconstruction AND black education

Hannibal, Missouri AND slavery

Louisiana sugarcane AND slavery

The Rise of Silas Lapham

WILLIAM DEAN HOWELLS

1885

William Dean Howells, a prolific writer in a variety of genres, published one of his best-known works, *The Rise of Silas Lapham*, in 1885. A work of realistic fiction, the novel explores Bostonian society and the figure of the American businessman. Howells features two prominent Boston families in the novel, the Laphams, originally hailing from Vermont, and the Coreys, an upper-class, well-established Bostonian family. While contrasting the characters of Silas Lapham, who has earned his wealth by building his mineral paint business from the ground up, and Bromfield Corey, who has inherited his wealth and his high social standing, Howells crafts a romantic tale that centers on the young-adult children of the two men. Business ethics and the pangs of young love are intertwined in a story that simultaneously investigates the intricacies of social class in late-nineteenth-century Bostonian society.

The Rise of Silas Lapham was originally published in 1885. It is available in several modern editions, including the 1982 edition published by the Library of America.

AUTHOR BIOGRAPHY

Howells, the second of eight children, was born on March 1, 1837, in Martins Ferry, Ohio, to Mary Dean Howells and William Cooper

William Dean Howells (© *Interim Archives | Getty Images*)

Howells. During his childhood, Howells worked as an assistant typesetter on his father's paper, the *Hamilton Intelligencer*, after the family moved to Hamilton, Ohio. That paper failed, as did a second one Howells's father began. Howells's father also sought to establish a utopian commune, but the endeavor was abandoned in 1850 because of lack of financial support. For the next several years, the Howells family moved around the state, as the elder Howells followed employment leads in the publishing world. In 1853, with his father settled, sixteen-year-old Howells worked as a printer for the *Ashtabula Sentinel* and began to teach himself several languages.

In the years that followed, Howells began to write and publish as a journalist and essayist and embarked on a career as a novelist and poet as well. After writing a campaign biography for Abraham Lincoln in 1860, Howells was appointed to the US consulate in Venice by President Lincoln in 1861. Howells served in Venice until 1865. He married Elinor Mead in Paris in 1862.

After his return to the United States, Howells settled in Cambridge in 1866, where he became an assistant editor of the *Atlantic*,

publishing fiction and literary criticism, including his first novel, *Their Wedding Journey* (1872). He resigned the editorship in 1881. Howells continued to write works of realist fiction, including *The Rise of Silas Lapham* in 1885, *Indian Summer* in 1886, *The Minister's Charge* in 1886, *Annie Kilburn* in 1888, and *A Hazard of New Fortunes* in 1890. In the early 1900s, Howells traveled extensively. His wife died in 1910, after which Howells continued to travel and to publish fiction and nonfiction, including travel literature, such as the 1913 *Familiar Spanish Travels*. Howells died of pneumonia on May 11, 1920, in New York.

PLOT SUMMARY

Chapter I
Howells introduces the protagonist of *The Rise of Silas Lapham* as Silas is being interviewed by a journalist, Bartley Hubbard. The reader is provided with the details about how Silas built his mineral paint business, following the discovery of a mineral mine on his family's Vermont property. Silas highlights the integral role his wife, Persis Lapham, has played in his success as a businessman. The wealth Silas has gained through his business endeavors is a focus of Hubbard's article, but the journalist also mocks Silas's bragging and uncouth nature.

Chapter II
As the narrator describes the family life of Silas and Persis and their two daughters, Penelope and Irene, the social awkwardness the family experiences is explored. The family does not invite people to dinner or attend the parties that are so fashionable among high-society Boston families, for example. Penelope and Irene have gone to public rather than private schools, and Persis is disappointed that her daughters have not attended a private "finishing" school, where they would have learned about matters related to the social decorum and manners expected of upper-class young women.

In addition to introducing the Lapham women, the narrator also briefly describes an incident in which Mrs. Lapham and her daughters come to the aid of another mother and her two daughters when they all find themselves in a small town in Canada. The Laphams learn that the other family is also from Boston, and when

MEDIA ADAPTATIONS

- *The Rise of Silas Lapham* is available in an unabridged 2012 audio version, in MP3 or CD format, published by Blackstone Audio and read by Grover Gardner.

the mother becomes ill, Mrs. Lapham tends to her until a doctor arrives. After the son of the second family arrives, he expresses his gratefulness to the Laphams. It is later revealed that the individuals involved in this incident are members of the Corey family.

Chapter III

The narrator describes Silas's former involvement with a business partner, Mr. Rogers. Rogers assisted Silas when he was short on the capital necessary to develop the business. When the business was once again on track, Lapham decided to end his partnership with Rogers. Lapham's treatment of Rogers is one of the few business decisions Persis has disagreed with. The narrative then shifts to Silas's discussion with his family about the prospect of building a new home in a more fashionable part of town, where Penelope and Irene will be better positioned to participate in social events and be able to eventually find husbands.

Chapter IV

When Lapham and his daughters are reviewing the progress on the new home as it is being built, a young man appears and notices the Laphams on the property. He approaches and Irene recognizes him. She introduces him to her father as Mr. Corey. Mr. Lapham and his daughters converse with Tom Corey as they review the progress of the building with him.

Chapter V

Tom Corey, it is now revealed, is the son of the woman Mrs. Lapham assisted while in Canada. He and his father, Bromfield Corey, discuss Tom's future. Tom expresses an interest in approaching

Lapham to ask him for a position in his company. His father conveys his disapproval, feeling that Silas is not of the same educated, firmly upper-class social circle as the Coreys' own family, despite the wealth Lapham has accumulated.

Chapter VI

Tom approaches Lapham about a job in the paint business and proposes to Lapham that he handle foreign sales and distribution. Secretly delighted to have someone of Tom's social standing approach him in such a manner and also believing Tom to be interested in his daughter Irene, Lapham invites Tom to accompany him to his summer cottage, in nearby Nantasket, where his wife and daughters are currently staying.

Chapter VII

To his family's surprise, Lapham arrives at the cottage with Tom Corey. Tom discusses business with Lapham and also spends time with Irene and Penelope. Irene wonders if he might be interested in her and presses Penelope regarding her opinion of Tom. Mrs. Lapham and her husband discuss Tom's possible role in the business, with Mrs. Lapham urging Silas to be cautious where Tom was concerned, in terms of both Tom's employment and his interest in Irene.

Chapter VIII

Mr. Bromfield Corey and his wife, Anna, discuss with each other their worries about Tom and his affiliation with the Laphams. They do not approve of Tom's either working with Silas Lapham or socializing with Lapham's daughters. The Coreys regard the Laphams as beneath them socially and fear the censure of their upper-class friends. Tom Corey, however, is pleased with his business venture with Lapham and settles into the firm with enthusiasm. Lapham's chatty bookkeeper, Mr. Walker, keeps Tom up to speed on all work-related gossip, while Tom notices the pretty but quiet typist, Miss Dewey.

Chapter IX

Tom and Irene spend a few moments together, leading Irene to wonder about his feelings for her. The brief encounter deepens her feelings for him. With his father, Tom rehashes the subject of the Coreys' perception that the Laphams are somehow inferior to them. Tom defends the family. Mrs. Lapham and Penelope ponder Irene's infatuation with Tom and speculate about his interest in her.

Chapter X

Silas is approached by Mr. Rogers, who asks him for a business loan. Although Silas has long convinced himself that he treated Mr. Rogers fairly in the past, he is aware that his wife views the matter differently, and this troubles him. Silas, feeling financially comfortable, agrees to lend Mr. Rogers a large sum of money. Tom visits with Irene and Penelope, and he leaves the Lapham home in Nantasket feeling elated.

Chapter XI

Tom's father decides to visit Silas at his office. Mr. Corey is doing so in order to cultivate the social appearance of the family's approval of Tom's activities, but Silas regards the visit as validation of his own social standing. Tom again visits the family, and Mrs. Lapham questions Penelope about her opinion regarding Tom and Irene. Penelope tells her mother that Tom has said nothing to her about Irene. Silas and Persis both seem eager for a relationship between Tom and Irene, but Persis is wary as well and more concerned about the social differences between the two families than Silas seems to be.

Chapter XII

Mrs. Corey and her daughters, Lily and Nanny, return to Boston from their summer in Maine. As a group, they disapprove of Tom's association with the Laphams, yet Mrs. Corey feels it is her duty to call on the Laphams. She does so, but only Penelope and Mrs. Lapham are in. The visit is awkward. Penelope is in tears afterward and feels that Mrs. Corey is intensely judgmental and disapproving. Afterward, Mrs. Corey feels as though she must invite the Laphams to dinner in order to keep up the appearance that they are not trying to hide Tom's business and personal associations.

Chapter XIII

Mrs. Corey plans her guest list for the dinner party. The Laphams receive their invitation, and all feel the social pressures of the event. Penelope insists she will not go.

Chapter XIV

The dinner party begins in an awkward but polite manner. Penelope's absence is noted. Not normally a wine drinker, Silas finds that this is all that is offered after he has finished his water. Wanting to do what is expected of him as a guest in the Corey home, Silas drinks the wine. By the time the men retire with their cigars and drinks, Silas begins to feel intoxicated. He grows loud and boastful, but in his drunken state, he is pleased with himself for being able to hold his own in the company of the upper-class family. The next morning, he begins to realize that perhaps he has not behaved as well as he thought.

Chapter XV

Fearful of what he may have said or done, Silas talks to Tom Corey about his behavior the night before at the party. Silas is enormously embarrassed. Tom tries to reassure him that everyone understood that Silas did not normally drink wine and that they attributed any unmannerly behavior to this fact. Silas's candor about his shame is extremely off-putting to Tom, more so than Silas's drunkenness at the dinner party. Later, however, Tom feels that he has judged Lapham too harshly. He makes his way to Lapham's home.

Chapter XVI

At the Laphams', Tom finds that Penelope is the only one home. Gathering his courage, he confesses his love to a shocked Penelope. She reveals haltingly that her feelings are similar to his, but she nevertheless begs him to not approach her in this way again. Penelope does not tell Tom that all the Laphams assumed that Tom was interested in Irene, nor does she confess that Irene is in love with him.

Chapter XVII

Distraught, Penelope tells her mother about her visit from Tom. Persis is shocked and dismayed. Penelope berates her mother for never considering the fact that Tom might be in love with her instead of Irene.

Chapter XVIII

Persis reveals to Silas all that has happened between Penelope and Tom. Silas and Persis agree that Penelope is more compatible with Tom intellectually than Irene ever could hope to be, yet they sympathize with Irene, for they know her heart will be broken when she learns the truth about Tom's affections. Silas and Persis decide to call on the minister, Mr. Sewell, and ask him for advice. They do not reveal Tom's name, but Mr. Sewell, being a friend of the Corey family, is nevertheless aware of whom they are speaking. Mr. Sewell advises them to give their blessing to Penelope and the young man and to be sympathetic to Irene but know that she will recover.

Chapter XIX

Silas and Persis decide to take Mr. Sewell's advice. When they arrive home, Persis tells Irene what has happened. Irene takes the news unflinchingly. She is polite to Penelope and thereafter throws herself into housework and generally avoids talking to anyone. Soon she escapes to the family's property in Vermont with her mother. Silas invites Tom over and encourages Penelope to speak with him. Once Penelope has explained about Irene, Tom is flabbergasted, insisting he never had any feelings for Irene and that it was always Penelope he cared for. Still, Penelope believes it is her duty to sacrifice her own happiness, as she feels as though she has somehow stolen Irene's chance at happiness. Tom promises that he will not give up on her.

Chapter XX

Persis returns to Boston after settling Irene in Vermont. Meanwhile, Tom tells his parents about his feelings for Penelope and his desire to marry her. Mr. and Mrs. Corey believed that Tom was interested in Irene. Mrs. Corey, who finds Penelope unlikable, is particularly shocked.

Chapter XXI

Silas begins to realize his financial situation is increasingly dire. He lost money on various investments in the stock market, and Mr. Rogers has been unable to pay him back any of the money he has borrowed.

Chapter XXII

The Laphams receive a note from Irene. She appears to be having a pleasant time in Vermont with her uncle's family. Silas seems to experience fluctuations in his financial fortunes. At times, he believes he will make it through and retain some of his wealth, yet he also expresses to Persis his fears that he might lose everything he has worked so hard for.

Chapter XXIII

The past comes back to haunt Silas in increasingly powerful ways. In addition to the trouble with his former business partner, Mr. Rogers, Silas is also once again faced with his sense of duty to the family of a soldier, Jim Millon, who gave his life to save Silas during the Civil War. Millon's widow and her daughter, Zerilla, have been the recipients of Silas's financial assistance since Jim's death. The daughter, now grown, is married to Henry Dewey, an unemployed, usually intoxicated sailor. Silas employs Zerilla Dewey as the typist in his office. His payments to Zerilla and her mother have dwindled because of his own financial troubles, and Mrs. Millon is beginning to resent the reduction in funds.

Chapter XXIV

Tom begins to suspect that Silas's financial woes are quite serious, and he offers to put money into the business, but Silas rejects this offer. Penelope still refuses to marry Tom, particularly when her father is in such dire circumstances. As Silas is trying to decide what to do with the new, as-yet-unfinished house, he decides to try out one of the fireplaces while having a cigar. Later that evening, he discovers that the house has burnt down. The insurance policy has already expired, and Silas realizes he can never recover the losses.

Chapter XXV

Silas decides to travel to New York to meet with two of the three West Virginian brothers who own a new, rival paint company. The men agree to merge if Silas can raise the necessary capital. He returns to Boston and considers the ways in which he might raise the money. That same evening, Rogers informs Silas that there are several English investors interested in purchasing the mills Rogers previously put up as collateral on the loan he took from Silas. The land on which the mills sit is without value. A railroad company wishes to buy the land at a bargain price, which it feels it can dictate, because it can choose not to service the area by rail if anyone but the railroad company purchases the land. The English investors are aware of the valueless nature of the land but are unconcerned, because they are interested in purchasing the land for a group of extremely wealthy Englishmen who know nothing of the risk and can afford to lose the money. Silas is uneasy with the idea of cheating them and begins to realize that Rogers and the English investors are in on the swindle together. He decides not to sell, knowing that this decision will be the death of his own business.

Chapter XXVI

Silas thinks he might still be able to come to a deal with the West Virginians, and he travels to New York to try to stall them. Meanwhile, Persis learns that, despite her insistence years ago that Silas does not owe Jim Millon's widow anything, her husband has still been giving Mrs. Millon and Zerilla money. As Irene is returning from Vermont, Penelope and Persis learn that Silas has come back from New York and left quickly to go to Vermont himself. Penelope has had to ascertain from Tom her father's whereabouts. Encouraged by Penelope's affection after this meeting, Tom discusses her once again with his parents, who decide to pay the Laphams a visit.

Chapter XXVII
Silas returns to Boston, realizing there is nothing he can do to save his home in Boston or his business. He meets with his creditors and sells everything, except the land and home in Vermont, in order to pay his debts. He has retained the ability to continue to manufacture and distribute one line of his paint, the one named after his wife, and does so on a small scale. Penelope finally agrees to marry Tom, who, upon Silas's urging, has taken a position with the West Virginians. Tom is to see to their foreign distribution and is about to embark on a lengthy stay in Mexico. Penelope will accompany him as his new bride. The reader is informed that Tom and Penelope remain in Mexico for three years. At the time of their return, Irene remains unmarried. Silas, having sold to the West Virginians, now has a stake in their company.

CHARACTERS

Charles Bellingham
Charles Bellingham is the son of Mrs. Corey's deceased cousin. Charles attends the dinner party the Coreys give and joins in on the discussion of contemporary fiction.

James Bellingham
James Bellingham is Mrs. Corey's brother. He meets the Laphams at the Corey's dinner party, and Silas later seeks out Bellingham's financial advice.

Anna Corey
Anna Corey is the wife of Mr. Bromfield Corey and the mother of Tom, Lily, and Nanny. Mrs. Corey is quite vocal and adamant in her disapproval of the Laphams as social acquaintances and as business associates, and she repeatedly

expresses her dislike of Tom's seeking employment with Silas and courting either of Silas's daughters. Through condescending comments, she makes Penelope feel judged. Nevertheless, Mrs. Corey seeks to maintain the appearance that Tom is doing nothing of which the rest of the Coreys should be ashamed. She consequently invites the Laphams to dinner. Through the course of the novel, Mrs. Corey's views regarding the Laphams change very little.

Bromfield Corey
Bromfield Corey is the husband of Anna Corey and the father of Tom, Lily, and Nanny. With his wife, Mr. Corey is lighthearted, joking, and good-natured. He has inherited his now dwindling wealth from his own father and is frustrated with Tom's need to build his own wealth, rather than try to live a little more frugally on what his family is able to provide for him. He attempts to show approval of Tom's choices by meeting with Silas and by agreeing with his wife's plan to invite the Laphams to dinner. Although Mr. Corey's role in the novel is not large, he serves as a symbol of upper-class society in Boston and of the notion of "old money," or inherited wealth, which Howells contrasts with Silas's self-made fortune. To a large degree, Mr. Corey shares his wife's misgivings about Tom's personal and business relationships with the Lapham family, agreeing with Mrs. Corey that the Laphams are socially inferior to them.

Lily Corey
Lily Corey is the older of the two daughters of Anna and Bromfield Corey. She is influenced by her mother's disapproval of the Laphams.

Nanny Corey
Nanny Corey is the younger of the two daughters of Anna and Bromfield Corey. Although she initially shares in her mother's disapproval of the Laphams, Nanny is the most open to getting to know Penelope after Tom announces his plan to marry her.

Tom Corey
Tom Corey is the son of Anna and Bromfield Corey, and he plays a central role in the novel as he links the main plot of Silas Lapham's crisis as a businessman to the subplot of the love triangle between him, Irene, and Penelope. While exhibiting some of his family's social prejudices, Tom

nevertheless staunchly defends Silas and the rest of the Laphams to his own family. His desire to earn an honest living rather than to simply live on his inheritance appears earnest, but his love for Penelope also guides his actions and influences his attitude toward Silas and the paint business.

Being polite and reserved by nature, Corey is undemonstrative of his love for Penelope and friendly toward Irene. Given the fact that Irene is regarded as prettier and thought by her family to be the most sought after, all the Laphams believe that Tom's social visits and romantic intentions are directed toward Irene rather than Penelope. When the veil of confusion is lifted, Tom vows to continue to woo Penelope, despite her own guilt regarding her sister's unrequited love for Tom. In the end, Tom succeeds as a businessman, because Silas has assisted him in securing a position with the West Virginians' company. He is finally able to persuade Penelope to marry him.

Henry Dewey

Henry Dewey (called "Hen" is the husband of Zerilla Millon Dewey. He benefits from Silas's guilt-laden payments to Jim Millon's widow and daughter. Portrayed as an alcoholic, Dewey repeatedly refuses to grant the divorce Zerilla seeks.

Zerilla Dewey

Zerilla Dewey, formerly Zerilla Millon, is the daughter of Mrs. Millon and the deceased Jim Millon. She is married to Hen Dewey. Like her mother and husband, she has relied on Silas's generosity, but Zerilla works in Silas's office in return for the assistance Silas bestows upon her family. She is attempting to divorce Dewey but has been unsuccessful.

The Englishmen

The Englishmen are investors brought forth by Rogers. They express interest in purchasing the mills Rogers has put up as collateral for the money Lapham has loaned Rogers. Rogers and the Englishmen are out to swindle the buyers the Englishmen represent.

Bartley Hubbard

Hubbard is a journalist who interviews Silas about his upbringing and business as the story opens. Although Silas is initially flattered to be the subject of the article, he gets the sense as the interview proceeds that Hubbard will not paint him in the best light. His fears are confirmed when Hubbard's article is published.

Miss Kingsbury

Miss Kingsbury is a friend of the Corey family. She is present at the dinner party the Coreys give. There, she discusses the novel *Tears, Idle Tears*, sparking a conversation about the theme of self-sacrifice in contemporary sentimental novels.

Bill Lapham

Bill Lapham is Silas's brother; he lives with his family on land in Vermont. Irene spends time with her uncle and her cousin, Will, when she travels to Vermont after Tom reveals his feelings for Penelope. Bill does not directly appear in the story.

Irene Lapham

Irene Lapham is the younger daughter of Persis and Silas and is often referred to as the prettier of the two young women. Irene develops feelings for Tom Corey early in the novel. The narrator informs the reader of an incident that occurs before the action of the novel commences, in which Persis and her daughters, while traveling through Canada, come to the aid of Mrs. Corey, who has taken ill. Tom arrives later and thanks them. It is during this encounter that Irene first becomes enamored of Tom. Back in Boston, when Tom passes the new home the Laphams are building, Tom spies the Lapham girls through the window and stops to speak to them and Silas. Having renewed his acquaintance with the family, Tom finds other opportunities to visit the Laphams, and he additionally propositions Silas about employing him. Irene convinces herself that Tom is interested in her, and the whole family, in fact, labors under this delusion. Irene is crushed to find out that Tom is really in love with Penelope. When she returns from her seclusion in Vermont, she is a more serious and practical young woman who informs herself about her father's financial troubles. She remains unmarried by the story's conclusion.

Penelope Lapham

Penelope Lapham is the older daughter of Silas and Persis Lapham, frequently described as the plainer but smarter of the two young women. Seemingly more at ease when Tom Corey visits the Laphams than her sister is, Penelope converses easily with him and displays the sense of humor for which she is known among family members. The family, Penelope included, is shocked to discover that Tom has been interested in Penelope, rather than Irene, from the beginning. Penelope is hurt that no one thought Tom could fall in love with her, but her mother does concede that Irene was never Tom's intellectual equal the way that Penelope is. Penelope clings to the notion that she must sacrifice her own happiness, and consequently Tom's, because she feels that she has somehow stolen Tom from Irene. She isolates herself from her family and repeatedly rebuffs Tom's efforts to change her mind about marrying him. Eventually, Penelope agrees to marry Tom.

Persis Lapham

Persis Lapham is Silas's devoted wife. Silas relies on Persis at times as his moral compass. She judges him harshly for allowing Rogers to help save the paint business when it struggled in the early years only to cast him off as the business's success was imminent. Aside from this one area of disapproval, Persis repeatedly demonstrates her pride in and devotion to Silas. She feels free to speak her mind with him, and Silas typically considers everything she says, even if he does not always agree with her. Persis is protective of her daughters and nurtures a close relationship with them both, although she judges Penelope very harshly when Tom reveals his love for Penelope instead of Irene. When Persis becomes aware of Rogers's duplicity with Silas after he has borrowed money from him, her former sympathy with Rogers is challenged, and she finds that for once she is unable to counsel her husband. Persis admits to regretting her failing in this regard.

Silas Lapham

Silas Lapham, a former colonel in the army during the Civil War, is the novel's protagonist. Through his ingenuity and hard work, he has built a mineral paint business after a mineral mine was found on his family's property. Silas is at the height of his success as the novel opens. Having accrued great wealth through his business and investments, Silas now sets his sights on a new goal. He seeks to gain acceptance into Boston's upper-class society. He and his wife Persis decide on this course of action in order to secure their daughters' futures. Silas and Persis hope that by building a new home in the more fashionable section of Boston and by welcoming further contact with Tom Corey, they will

be able to marry their daughters off to well-respected and financially secure members of the community.

Silas is depicted as a loving husband and a caring father. He is proud of having earned, rather than inherited, his wealth, and he makes no apologies for who he is. Spurred by his wife's negative judgment regarding his decision to cast off his former business partner, Mr. Rogers, Silas agrees to lend Rogers a large sum, after which Silas's other investments begin to lose money. Unable to collect from Rogers, Silas begins to lose his fortune. Unwilling to make a business deal that he would later regret as unethical but would save his business, Silas loses his home and business. His conscience, however, is now untroubled. Despite his losses, Silas seems content at the conclusion of the novel.

Will Lapham

Will is the son of Bill Lapham and the nephew of Silas. For a short time, Persis wonders if a romance is blossoming between Will and Irene, and she decides that she does not object to a union between cousins. Irene, however, later reveals that she has no romantic interest in her cousin Will.

Jim Millon

Jim Millon was a soldier in the Civil War serving under Silas, who was his commanding officer. Millon stepped in front of a bullet intended for Silas.

Mrs. Millon

Mrs. Millon is the widow of Jim Millon. She readily accepts Silas's guilty offer of financial assistance after her husband sacrifices his own life to save Silas's during a Civil War battle years before the novel's opening. Like her son-in-law, Hen Dewey, Mrs. Millon is a heavy drinker and is only too happy to rely on Silas for an income.

Milton K. Rogers

Milton Rogers is Silas's former business partner. Silas took on Rogers when he needed capital to keep the business afloat, and he bought Rogers out just as the paint business was about to take off. Persis feels that because Rogers was bought out just before the business boomed, Silas treated him unfairly. This doubt about his past business decisions weighs on Silas, and when Rogers returns seeking money, Silas readily lends Rogers a large sum. Having taken advantage of Silas's generosity and possible guilt, Rogers involves Silas in a scheme of his own, one that is designed to make Rogers wealthy and becomes one of several factors in Silas's financial ruin.

Mr. Sewell

Mr. Sewell is a minister and friend of the Corey family. He is invited to the Coreys' dinner party, and later Silas seeks his advice on the relationship between Tom Corey and his daughters. Mr. Sewell is the novel's most vocal opponent of the notion of self-sacrifice found in sentimental novels, and his practical approach to the situation involving Tom, Irene, and Penelope is rooted in his disdain for Penelope's view that she must sacrifice her own happiness because her sister has been unintentionally wounded.

Mrs. Sewell

Along with her husband, Mrs. Sewell is invited to the Coreys' dinner party. After Silas consults Mr. Sewell about the awkward situation that has arisen between his daughters and Tom Corey, Mr. Sewell discusses the matter with his wife, wondering if his advice to Silas is sound.

Mr. Seymour

Mr. Seymour is Lapham's architect. He skillfully guides Lapham toward agreeing with him about the design for the house Lapham is having built.

Mr. Walker

Mr. Walker is Silas Lapham's gossipy bookkeeper.

The West Virginians

The West Virginians are three brothers from West Virginia who have developed a paint to rival Lapham's. Silas is steadily losing business to the West Virginians, while simultaneously his other investments fail. Attempting to recover, he proposes a joint venture to the West Virginians, but he cannot raise enough capital to close the deal. Eventually, after losing nearly all of his assets to pay his debts, Silas sells what is left of the paint-manufacturing business to the West Virginians but retains a share in the company.

THEMES

Ethics

Howells examines the notion of business ethics in *The Rise of Silas Lapham*. Silas begins his paint business with the assistance and support of his wife, Persis. In the early years of the business, however, hard work takes Silas only so far, and he knows that an influx of capital is needed to develop his business. When Mr. Rogers enters into a partnership with Silas, he brings with him this vital capital. Silas is able to build the business and instinctively senses when it is about to become wildly profitable. Just before this point in the business's development, he buys out Rogers's interest in the company and dissolves the partnership and is thereby able to enjoy the profit alone. At the time, Silas felt entitled to this success, and he considers his decision to cut Rogers loose to be a wise business decision. Persis has always felt that Silas treated Rogers unfairly and that the business would never have thrived without Rogers's assistance.

Although Silas has attempted to justify his actions both in his own mind and to his wife over the years, the return of Rogers into his life offers Silas a chance to redeem himself, at least in Persis's eyes if not his own. After lending Rogers a large sum of money, Silas feels as though his debt has been paid, and Persis's high regard for this decision buoys Silas. Rogers now has business schemes of his own, and he continues to borrow from Silas in order to pursue his own endeavors. He hatches a scheme involving the sale of land made worthless by the railroad company's promise to leave it undeveloped if it is sold to anyone but them. Silas finds he cannot, in good conscience, dupe the buyers that the English investors represent, even though it would mean that his own business would be saved. Although Silas's refusal to participate in the scheme precipitates his financial fall, the "rise" that the title of the novel refers to now takes place, as Silas chooses an ethical path. Although he has lost so much in terms of material wealth, Silas realizes he has "come out with clean hands."

Sacrifice

In *The Rise of Silas Lapham*, Howells repeatedly returns to the idea of sacrifice, specifically self-sacrifice. This theme is examined through Silas and his experiences. When forced to choose between making a dishonest business

TOPICS FOR FURTHER STUDY

- The subplot of *The Rise of Silas Lapham* focuses on the Lapham daughters and their mutual romantic interest in Tom Corey. Irene and Penelope are both aware of their social inadequacies and of the way they do not fit in with their upper-class counterparts. Similarly, the protagonist in Madeline L'Engle's young-adult novel *And Both Were Young* feels out of place and socially awkward, yet she finds herself at ease with the French boy she meets, just as Penelope discovers that she is able to be herself in Tom's company. With a small group, read L'Engle's novel and compare the way the relationships develop in Howells's nineteenth-century novel with the development of the romance in L'Engle's 2011 work. In what ways do Howells's young-adult characters seem similar to L'Engle's? What types of social conflicts do the characters face? How do the authors treat the themes of isolation and young love? Discuss these issues in an online blog you have created with your group.

- Howells's novel focuses on Bostonian society in the late nineteenth century. Native Americans at this time had been forced off of their own land and relocated onto reservations. Diane Glancy, a Cherokee author, explores the challenges faced by a recently relocated Cherokee community in the 2009 historical novel *Pushing the Bear: After the Trail of Tears*. Read Glancy's novel and consider the way American expansion in the nineteenth century changed the lives of Native American communities. How does Glancy treat this issue? How do the Cherokees in her book interact with or feel about white Americans and the US government? Write an essay about Glancy's novel, summarizing the plot and characters and focusing specifically on the author's treatment of American expansion and its effect on Native American communities.

- The American economy in the late nineteenth century is a central concern of Howells's novel. Research the economic history of the United States in the 1880s, detailing the causes and effects of the recessions, depressions, and economic recoveries. Investigate the role of government legislation and its impact on the economy during this time. Prepare your research paper either in print or electronic form, creating a website, for example, which can be accessed by your classmates. Be sure to cite all of your sources.

- In *The Rise of Silas Lapham*, Persis Lapham gives up her career as a teacher when she marries Silas. She subsequently becomes instrumental in assisting Silas to build his business but gradually becomes relegated to the domestic sphere, where she functions exclusively as a mother and homemaker. Research the roles of women in late-nineteenth-century American society. What rights were denied women during this time? What access did they have to education and employment? How greatly did such opportunities vary based on social class? Also describe the achievements of prominent women's rights activists during these years. Create a written report or a visual presentation, such as a time line or a PowerPoint presentation, in which you explore these issues.

arrangement and his own sense of ethical behavior, Silas sacrifices his wealth, his business, and all that he has worked for in order to adhere to his principles. The financial and material loss is enormous. Throughout the novel, Howells depicts Silas as intensely proud of the success he has created for himself and the wealth that has come along with it. To sacrifice all that he has gained is incredibly difficult for Silas, but his desire to act ethically in the end triumphs over his desire for financial well-being.

The narrator describes the way Mr. Sewell discusses Silas's choice with his wife, stating that Sewell "could see that the loss of his fortune had been a terrible trial to Lapham, just because his prosperity had been so gross and palpable." After Sewell asks Silas if he has any regrets about choosing an ethical business decision over an unethical one that would have left him financially stable, Silas responds that it sometimes seems "as if it was a hole opened for me, and I crept out of it." His attitude appears to be one of relief rather than regret, and he comprehends that his sacrifice was a meaningful one that left him with a genuine sense of pride in the way he conducts his affairs.

Howells likewise tackles a different type of sacrifice in the romance subplot. Not long after guests at Mrs. Corey's dinner party mock the way sentimental novels idealize and romanticize the notion of self-sacrifice, Penelope embraces self-sacrifice as if it is the highest virtue one could strive toward. She is convinced she must sacrifice her own happiness by refusing to marry Tom Corey, because Irene, too, loves him and because Irene believed that he had feelings for her. Corey asserts that he never thought of Irene in that way and believes he never did anything to lead her on. He cannot fathom why Penelope would adhere so eagerly to the notion of self-sacrifice.

Tom inquires of Penelope, "We have done no wrong. Why should we suffer from another's mistake as if it were our sin?" Penelope replies that she does not know, "But we must suffer." Growing increasingly frustrated with her stubbornness, Tom points out that not long ago Penelope criticized the character in a sentimental novel for acting much the same way that Penelope is now, stating, "Don't you remember that night ... you were talking of that book; and you said it was foolish and wicked to do as that girl did. Why is it different with you?" Penelope's reply suggests that it is her loyalty to her sister that prevents her from accepting Tom's love.

Mr. Sewell is similarly frustrated with Penelope's behavior when Silas and Persis bring the matter to him for advice. Sewell exclaims, "I lose all patience! ... This poor child of yours has somehow been brought to believe that it would kill her sister if her sister does not have what does

Silas Lapham was a rags-to-riches paint business owner in the late 1800s. (© lynea | Shutterstock.com)

not belong to her." Despite the fact that everyone, even Irene, urges Penelope to accept Tom's proposal, she clings to the idea of self-sacrifice, of denying herself the love she has admitted she deserves, out of a sense of duty to Irene. Only at the close of the novel, when Tom is prepared to leave for Mexico for several years, does Penelope relinquish her insistence upon her guilty self-sacrifice and agree to marry Tom.

STYLE

Realism

During the late nineteenth century, some American novelists, following the lead of their European counterparts, began to explore a more realistic approach to fiction than the romantic or sentimental novels that prevailed at the time. Fiction written in the romantic mode was focused on idealistic conceptions of the world and centered on an individual's personal experience within that world. Realism, on the other hand, sought to capture the details of everyday life in a relatively objective manner and often served as commentary on contemporary society in general rather than focusing solely on the experiences of an individual.

In *The Rise of Silas Lapham*, Howells uses the Lapham and Corey families to explore the notions of American business ethics and the social class conflict inherent in American society during the late nineteenth century. Although Howells's novel includes a romantic subplot—the love triangle between Irene, Penelope, and Tom—*The Rise of Silas Lapham* focuses more heavily on the business dealings of Silas Lapham and the ethical dilemmas he faces as a businessman, in addition to the social challenges the whole family confronts. In order to explore these varied themes and story lines, Howells uses an omniscient third-person narrator to relate the events of the story. An omniscient third-person narrator is an all-knowing storyteller who describes the events in the story from a viewpoint outside the narrative.

Howells, through his narrator, is able to convey the thoughts and feelings of any character he chooses. The reader is therefore able to assess the discrepancies between characters' thoughts, words, and actions. Additionally, the voice Howells gives Silas is that of a relatively uneducated man. His grammatical errors, casual speech, and colloquial manners do not go unnoticed by the Coreys and serve as the primary clues to the social class differences between the Laphams and the Coreys. Through dialogue and detailed descriptions of Bostonian society, Howells realistically captures the conflicts that exist for Silas as a self-made businessman in a city built on "old money," or the wealth of an established upper class.

Sentimentalism

Despite Howells's focus on realism in *The Rise of Silas Lapham*, the novel nevertheless includes a sentimentalized romantic love triangle between the Lapham daughters and Tom Corey. At several points in the novel, the characters deride the sentimentalism in contemporary novels. Miss Kingsbury refers to a romantic novel that she and others at the dinner party have read. The fictional novel, *Tears, Idle Tears*, is described by Miss Kingsbury as "perfectly heart-breaking." Nanny Corey comments that the book should be called "Slop, Silly Slop," while Charles Bellingham observes, "How we do like books that go for our heart-strings. And I really suppose that you can't put a more popular thing than self-sacrifice into a novel. We do like to see people suffering sublimely."

The characters seem to agree that this type of fiction is as silly and frivolous as it is entertaining and appealing, and the romantic triangle between Irene, Penelope, and Tom appears to fit this mold. Penelope and Tom, in fact, directly compare Penelope's behavior to the melodramatic self-sacrifice found in *Tears, Idle Tears*, as Penelope insists on sacrificing her own happiness in order to make herself—and Tom—as miserable as Penelope's rejected sister, Irene. The minister, Mr. Sewell, also makes this point when he compares Penelope's notion of sacrifice with that found in novels. Howells's characters express their disdain for sentimentalized romance in novels, and Mr. Sewell condemns their unrealistic nature.

At the same time, however, Howells includes the same type of unrealistic romance in his own otherwise realistic work. Tom confesses a passionate love for Penelope, when the whole Lapham family assumed he sought Irene. Penelope, who has demonstrated both her intelligence and practicality elsewhere in the novel, suddenly clings to the romantic conventions of sentimental fiction and vows to sacrifice her own love in order to atone for errors she did not commit and assuage her guilt over her sister's suffering. Howells's inclusion of a romantic subplot of this nature stands in sharp contrast to the realism of the main plot and has been regarded as either a criticism of such sentimentality or as a means of appealing to a broad audience.

HISTORICAL CONTEXT

The US Economy in the 1880s

In the years following the Civil War, which ended in 1865, the United States underwent a period of economic depression. As Frederick A. Bradford observes in *The Dictionary of American History*, "Extended wars always breed depression and the Civil War was no exception." This depression was relatively short-lived, and by 1867 a period of recovery and increasing prosperity ensued, lasting until roughly 1873, when depression once again took hold of the nation for several years. Recovery began again during the first few years of the 1880s but was halted by another period of economic depression, beginning in 1883, according to analysts such as Bradford, or 1884, according to Warren M. Persons in *Forecasting Business Cycles*.

Persons describes a number of factors leading to the depression of the mid-1880s, including the drastic decline in commodity prices. Commodities, or raw materials and agricultural products, include such items as iron, copper, corn, hogs, and oats. Persons also cites a decline in imports to the United States, as well as the slowing of growth in new railroad construction, which had increased rapidly in the years leading up to the depression. Such shrinkage in the economy led to rapid declines in stock prices and to subsequent bank failures. By late 1885, the economy began to stabilize once again, and a new recovery was under way by 1886.

In works of realistic fiction such as Howells's *The Rise of Silas Lapham*, such economic cycles and their effects on individuals are explored. Howells realistically depicts the effects of the depression on businessmen such as Silas Lapham, whose financial failure is attributed in part to falling stock prices and business failures. Susan L. Mizruchi, in *The Rise of Multicultural America: Economy and Print Culture, 1865–1915*, asserts that "the making of large fortunes, through manufacturing, developing land, creating commodities, and locating markets had become a distinctly American activity," and novelists such as Howells, as well as Henry James and Theodore Dreiser, focused their works on such economic and social developments in America. Mizruchi notes that, in particular, *The Rise of Silas Lapham* "foregrounds costs, consequences, and compensations: the price paid by individuals and by society as a whole for the nation's unequivocal embrace of capitalism."

Late-Nineteenth-Century American Realism

During the years following the Civil War, through the beginning of the twentieth century, realism became a prominent feature in American literature. American society was evolving quickly, as advances in industrial manufacturing and railroad expansions fueled a growing economy and made businessmen into a class as wealthy as established New England and southern families with enormous accumulated and inherited wealth. The social and economic implications of such developments became the focus of a number of realist authors.

As Robert Shulman observes in *The Columbia History of the American Novel*, in their explorations of "moral and ideological conflicts" and of "moral, epistemological, and sociopolitical implications," American realist novelists focused on "the intimate connection between houses and selves, between possessions and character in the new America." In terms of style, realists attempted to capture accurately the nuances of character and speech of individuals and the subtle characteristics of society as a whole. Gregg Crane, in *The Cambridge Introduction to the Nineteenth-Century American Novel* asserts that American realists of this period possessed "a general conception of fiction as a detailed and accurate representation of historically specific characters and settings—their manners, ways of dress, speech patterns, social habits, main concerns, and topics of conversation."

Some writers, such as Mark Twain, Sarah Orne Jewett, and Kate Chopin, sought to accurately depict the specifics of particular regions in the United States and came to be known as local colorists, or regional writers. Their work moved toward portrayals of individuals and society that were rooted in the specifics of everyday life. Other writers, such as William Dean Howells, Henry James, and John DeForest, brought to their fiction a relatively objective exploration of contemporary society. The protagonists in these novels were not typical sentimental, larger-than-life heroes but men and women who struggled with the challenges faced by real people. As a literary critic, Howells was instrumental in

COMPARE
&
CONTRAST

- **1880s:** The US economy undergoes a cycle of depressions and recoveries. From 1883 to 1885, such factors as decreasing commodity prices, a slowing of growth in the railroad industry, and a decline in stock prices contribute to a period of economic depression. Recovery begins near the end of 1885, as stock and commodity prices begin to rise.

  Today: A global financial crisis occurs in 2008 and 2009, leading to long-term economic recession in the United States and around the world. Inflated oil prices, along with risky lending practices by financial institutions, are often cited as factors contributing to the crisis and subsequent recession. Legislation is enacted to prevent the types of financial abuses by banks that contributed to the crisis. Reports describe the economic recovery in 2012 as tentative but note that unemployment, which remains high at just under 8 percent, has declined since 2009.

- **1880s:** Fiction written during this time is increasingly realistic in tone, as authors attempt to capture the nuances of American culture and society. Through objective presentation of detail and accurate representation of speech patterns, realist writers comment on issues pertinent to their readers, such as the cultural and social effects of an increasingly capitalistic and industrialist society.

  Today: For decades, realism has prevailed as a highly popular mode, and it remains so in the twenty-first century. At the same time, writers have experimented with incorporating supernatural or magical elements into otherwise realistic works. Trends in young-adult fiction in the first decade of the twenty-first century include dystopian (describing an imaginary setting where the characters are dehumanized, restricted, and often fearful) fiction and fiction in which magic or supernatural creatures, including zombies and vampires, play an integral role in the plot.

- **1880s:** Women in the 1880s continue to fight for suffrage, or the right to vote, along with other liberties still denied them, including property rights, the right to equal wages, and the right to divorce. Although some women's rights activists, including Elizabeth Cady Stanton and Susan B. Anthony, fight for political and economic equality, other suffragists, such as Frances Willard, while still fighting for women's right to vote and other social reforms, also regard women as possessing moral qualities that distinguish them from men and that position them uniquely as defenders of domesticity and traditional notions of morality.

  Today: Advocates for women's rights still fight for economic equality, for an end to sexual discrimination, and for reproductive rights, among other issues. Lilly Ledbetter takes a stand for equal pay in a pay discrimination lawsuit against Goodyear Tire and Rubber Company but loses her Supreme Court battle. In 2009, President Barack Obama nullifies this decision and signs the Lilly Ledbetter Fair Pay Act, but the law has never been enacted because it failed to garner enough votes in the Senate. The act would remove legal hurdles for individuals fighting wage discrimination. The National Women's Law Center states that American women with full-time employment receive seventy-seven cents for every dollar earned by male full-time employees.

introducing Americans to the work of European realist authors, such as Leo Tolstoy and George Eliot. In his own fiction, Howells explored the nuances and possibilities of the realist approach to fiction and aided in popularizing realist fiction in America.

Howells also tells the story of the rise of business in America in the late 1800s and the moral conflicts that accompanied it. (© Matthew Jacques / Shutterstock.com)

CRITICAL OVERVIEW

Howells is counted among the forerunners of American literary realism, and his novel, *The Rise of Silas Lapham*, is regarded as exemplifying the burgeoning trend toward realist fiction. James Woodress, in an essay for *Dictionary of Literary Biography*, states that *Silas Lapham* and a number of other novels by Howells "exemplify his principles and achieve remarkable verisimilitude in their depiction of character and setting." Woodress goes on to note that "his effects are achieved by a careful attention to ample, accurate detail and reasonable motivations." The work's contemporary reception was not completely positive; Woodress notes that its reviewers "were not very happy with the novel." Howells's realism is faulted, Woodress states, because reviewers found Lapham to be an ordinary and uninspirational protagonist.

The function of the subplot in relation to the main plot is the subject of some critical debate. Woodress asserts that the main business plot and

the social, romantic subplot of *Silas Lapham* do not always blend well and that "the reader is left with the feeling that it all did not quite come off at the end." Donald Pizer, in *Realism and Naturalism in Nineteenth-Century American Literature*, contends that although some critics have regarded the romantic plot either as a gesture to appease readers seeking romance or as an attack on sentimental themes, the subplot actually functions as a thematic complement to the main plot. Pizer maintains, "The thematic similarity in the two plots is that both involve a principle of morality which requires that the individual determine correct action by reference to the common good rather than to an individual need." In his study of nineteenth-century American realism for *The Columbia History of the American Novel*, Robert Shulman examines Howell's realism as exemplified in *The Rise of Silas Lapham*, arguing, "Far from being literal and artless, Howells's practice of realism is full of revealing contradictions, nuances and a suggestive interplay between surface and depth."

CRITICISM

Catherine Dominic

Dominic is a novelist and a freelance writer and editor. In the following essay, she examines Howells's treatment of gender issues in The Rise of Silas Lapham *and demonstrates the way Howells contributes to the stereotype of women as frivolous and sentimental creatures by depicting the Lapham women as impaired by emotions that distort their ability to behave reasonably.*

Howells offers a treatment of women and gender issues in *The Rise of Silas Lapham* in which women are allowed to occasionally break out of the stereotypical roles allotted to them by nineteenth-century conventions. In many ways, however, Howells characters reflect the stereotypes of Howells's society. The women in the novel remain largely consigned to the domestic sphere, and they are portrayed as frivolous creatures impaired by their emotions rather than as reasonable, thinking adults.

The reader sees early in the novel that Silas relies on his wife, Persis, in a substantial way. He repeatedly seeks out and considers her opinion; she is presented in many ways by Howells as Silas's moral compass. In *Gender and the Writer's Imagination*, Mary Suzanne Schriber describes the way Silas's financial success serves as a means of stripping the Lapham women of the dignity associated elsewhere in the novel with work. Money shifts Silas's attitude toward the women in his life, and his pride in the wealth he has accumulated shapes his view about what the focus of the women's lives should be. They should not worry about work or his business but should turn their mind toward social endeavors. Schriber explains, "Persis has been elevated to idleness and that is exactly where Silas wants her to stay."

Schriber demonstrates the way wealth changes the Lapham women, yet they are also shown by Howells to be easily transformed by emotion as well. As he depicts the evolution of the romantic relationships of the Lapham daughters, as well as Persis's feelings of sympathy for Mr. Rogers, Howells seems to assert that sentiment destroys rather than informs or complements a woman's intellect. By following the trajectory of the women's relationships and emotions, the reader witnesses the way Howells allows the Lapham women to dissolve into the stereotypical, sentimental figures of the novels the characters themselves mock. From the opening of the

> AS HE DEPICTS THE EVOLUTION OF THE ROMANTIC RELATIONSHIPS OF THE LAPHAM DAUGHTERS, AS WELL AS PERSIS'S FEELINGS OF SYMPATHY FOR MR. ROGERS, HOWELLS SEEMS TO ASSERT THAT SENTIMENT DESTROYS RATHER THAN INFORMS OR COMPLEMENTS A WOMAN'S INTELLECT."

novel, Howells puts forth a notion of women that was prevalent during the time the novel was written, when women were seeking greater independence and the right to vote in the face of great opposition to these goals. After Silas tearfully praises his mother's self-sacrificing and hard-working nature, he laments angrily, "When I hear women complaining nowadays that their lives are stunted and empty, I want to tell 'em about my *mother's* life." Silas respects that his mother worked to the point of exhaustion taking care of her home and her children. "She cooked, swept, washed, ironed, made and mended from daylight till dark—and from dark till daylight."

In addition to all of these tasks, Silas's mother also washed the dirty feet of her six boys. This image, which Silas goes on to describe in great detail, is imbued with religious significance, because it recalls the biblical story of a woman, described as a sinner, who washes Jesus' feet. Silas feels both worshiped and cared for by his devoted mother, and he expresses his disgust with women "nowadays" who complain about lives that are "stunted and empty." Silas seems shocked that a woman could possibly feel unfulfilled by a life of sacrifice and service to her family.

At the same, Silas acknowledges how much of his financial success he owes to his wife, Persis. He describes the way he sold everything he had in order to sink capital into the paint business and the way his wife supported him, giving up her job as a schoolteacher when she married him. "No hang back about *her*. I tell you she was a *woman*," Silas tells the reporter who is interviewing him. The reporter laughs and states that that is the type of women "most of us marry," but Silas disagrees, saying, "Most of us marry

WHAT DO I READ NEXT?

- Howells's *Indian Summer*, published in 1886, has been highly praised and is regarded as a romantic comedy or a comedy of manners. Set in Italy, the work features a love triangle between a forty-year-old American businessmen, a former acquaintance, and her much-younger friend.

- Henry James's *The Bostonians* was published in serial form in 1885 and 1886 and like *The Rise of Silas Lapham* explores Bostonian society at this time. *The Bostonians* focuses heavily on political issues, specifically feminism and gender roles.

- Kate Chopin published numerous short stories in which she realistically portrayed American women and their personal struggles against the confines of domesticity. A number of her short stories, most published in the 1890s, have been collected in the 2011 *Lilacs and Other Stories*.

- In *The Sea of Regret* and *Stones in the Sea*, Chinese author Fu Lin explores the political events of late-nineteenth-century and early-twentieth-century China, as well as the contemporary debate over marriage freedom in the two novels, which were published together in 1995 under the title *The Sea of Regret: Two Turn-of-the-Century Chinese Romantic Novels*. The books were translated into English for this edition by Patrick Hanan.

- The 2012 young-adult novel *My Life as the Ugly Stepsister*, by Juli Alexander, features issues similar to those in the subplot in Howells's novel, as two stepsisters struggle with their insecurities and the sense that they are competing for the same young man.

- *William Dean Howells: A Writer's Life*, by Susan Goodman and Carl Dawson, is a 2005 critical biography that examines, in particular, the political and economic culture of Howells's society. The authors additionally trace Howells's influence on the realist tradition in American fiction.

silly little girls grown up to *look* like women." He further praises Persis and her business acumen, observing that if had not been for Persis, "the paint wouldn't have come to anything."

However, in the present of the narrative, this Persis, the one intricately involved in Silas's business affairs, has been transformed by Silas's success into one of the "silly" women. She has retreated from the business world to raise her daughters and is now invested in helping them succeed rather than helping the business succeed. Irene, the younger daughter, is pretty and enjoys shopping and "housekeeping," whereas Penelope, "did not care for society" but does enjoy reading; she is regarded as smart but plain. When Tom Corey enters the Laphams' lives, Irene fantasizes about a romance with him, and when he begins to visit the family, all the Laphams assume that it is as much because of Irene as it is his interest in seeking employment from Silas.

As this story line involving the social aspect of the Laphams' lives unfolds, Howells's portrayal of the Lapham women begins to take shape. Persis, once energized about and engaged in the paint business, is now focused on the need to insert Irene and Penelope into Bostonian society. Irene is eager for this development, already half in love with Tom. Penelope seems to find the need for greater socializing distasteful and frivolous. As the story progresses, Howells demonstrates the way the women's emotions transform them. Persis falls ever farther from her former self, and once Penelope becomes aware of Tom's love for her, she too devolves into a figure negatively associated with a character from a sentimental novel. Irene, who begins the story as a silly girl in love with Tom, experiences a trajectory that is the reverse of Penelope's. Having been rejected by Tom, Irene detaches herself from social affairs and any possibility of romantic involvement and becomes practical and astute about her father's business matters.

Early in the story, Persis expresses her long-held opinion regarding her disapproval of Silas's treatment of his former business partner, Mr. Rogers. She accuses Silas of becoming too greedy and of behaving unfairly to the "man that had saved you." Silas regards this move as a smart business decision, and he tells Persis, "If you'll 'tend to the house, I'll manage my business without your help." Persis points out, "You were very glad of my help once." When Rogers reenters Silas's life, looking for money, Silas loans it to him. He repeatedly asserts, when he tells Persis about the meeting with Rogers, that he never felt that he did any wrong. He does not characterize his actions as being motivated by a desire to set things straight with Rogers or to ease a guilty conscience, but he does contend that what he has done, "I done for you, Persis." Persis is grateful that Silas has at least heeded her words and made things right with Rogers for *her*, even if he refuses to admit wrongdoing.

Persis's sense of ethics guides Silas to make a business decision he does not find strictly necessary and one that ends up costing him his fortune. Rogers continues to borrow from Silas and places Silas in a position where he must decide to either swindle investors in a deal that would benefit both him and Rogers or lose his own business. While Silas is attempting to find his way through this ethical maze, he turns to his wife and sees that

> her head had fallen; he could see that she was so rooted in her old remorse for that questionable act of his, amply and more fully atoned for since, that she was helpless, now in the crucial moment, when he had the utmost need of her insight.

Howells depicts Persis as hobbled by her sympathy for Rogers, sympathy rooted in her perception that Silas treated Rogers unfairly in the past. She is now unable to see clearly, and Silas realizes that the intuition and insight he has previously relied on is no longer dependable. When she does offer to help Silas think things through, Silas tells her, "You couldn't do any good."

Persis's emotions—in particular her sympathy for Rogers, which is characterized as unwarranted—have rendered her useless to Silas in terms of his business decisions. Persis is out of touch with Silas's business because he engineered her life to be so structured, having built up his business and having directed Persis increasingly into a domestic world of child rearing. Once ensconced in that world, Persis occasionally peeks out, attempting to remain in some way involved with the business, if only to speak as an advisor to Silas on issues related to business ethics. However, Howells depicts her ability to serve even in this capacity as increasingly distorted by and eventually permanently damaged by her emotions.

Howells depicts the Laphams' daughters as similarly crippled by sentiment. The Laphams have created for their daughters a world in which the only possible future is marriage. Irene is eager to pursue this goal, and she falls for Tom Corey early in the novel. Persis, Silas, and even Penelope, who develops her own feelings for Tom, all encourage Irene in the belief that there is a possible future for her and Tom. After every conversation with Tom, Irene turns to her mother or her sister to dissect the dialogue she repeats to them, seeking in Tom's polite words some sign of affection. Yet it is Penelope in whom Tom is romantically interested.

The contrast between the sisters is plain, as when Howells states,

> Irene liked being talked to better than talking, and when her sister was by she was always, tacitly or explicitly, referring to her for confirmation of what she said. She was content to sit and look pretty as she looked at the young man and listened to her sister's drolling.

Tom and Penelope converse intelligently, Penelope makes Tom laugh, and Irene listens and looks pretty while she looks on. When Tom reveals his feelings, Irene is crushed and Penelope is shocked. Irene flees to Vermont as soon as possible. When she returns to Boston, she is a soberer person than before, less frivolous. Howells demonstrates that once the distraction of love has been removed from Irene's thoughts, she grows more sensible: "She required from her mother a strict and accurate account of her father's affairs, so far as Mrs. Lapham knew them; and she showed a business-like quickness in comprehending them that Penelope had never pretended to."

In contrast to Irene, now that Penelope is in love with Tom, she has suddenly become insensible, shutting herself away in her room, punishing herself for a betrayal she never committed. She acknowledges that neither she nor Tom can rightly be accused of any transgression, but she nevertheless feels that she has stolen Tom from Irene. She refuses to allow herself the happiness of accepting Tom's proposal. Even after Irene has returned and exhibited no animosity toward her sister, Penelope seems to wallow in remorse and sadness, seemingly against her true nature and in contrast to her previously exhibited sensibility and intelligence. Love has transformed Penelope into a foolish girl remarkably like the self-sacrificing sentimental character in *Tears, Idle Tears*, the novel she, Tom, and others have mocked.

Howells creates female characters with exaggerated emotional responses that impair their judgment and inspire behavior inconsistent with the characters' more practical, intelligent natures. The Lapham women are limited to constrictive domestic roles by Silas and by the world he has created for them. Forced into a sphere where their intelligence is not valued or encouraged, their emotions are consequently amplified and distorted.

Source: Catherine Dominic, Critical Essay on *The Rise of Silas Lapham*, in *Novels for Students*, Gale, Cengage Learning, 2013.

Atlantic Monthly

In the following excerpt, a contributor maintains that Silas Lapham *is flawed by over-attention to character development at the expense of plot.*

While a novelist is living and at work, his growth in power is more interesting to critics than the expressions of that power in any one piece of work. *The Rise of Silas Lapham* would probably affect a reader who should make Mr. Howells's acquaintance through it, in a different manner from what it does one who has followed Mr. Howells, as so many have, step by step, ever since he put forth his tentative sketches in fiction. We do not think that Mr. Howells has kept back the exercise of certain functions until he should have perfected his faculty of art by means of lighter essays, but that, in the process of his art, he has partly discovered, at any rate has convinced himself of the higher value to be found in a creation which discloses morals as well as manners. An art which busies itself with the trivial or the spectacular may be ever so charming and attractive, but it falls short of the art which builds upon foundations of a more enduring sort. A pasteboard triumphal-arch that serves the end of a merry masque is scarcely more ephemeral than the masque itself in literature.

The novel before us offers a capital example of the difference between the permanent and the transient in art. Had Mr. Howells amused himself and us with a light study of the rise of Silas Lapham in Boston society, what a clever book he might have made of it! We should have chuckled to ourselves over the dismay of the hero at the failure of the etiquette man to solve his problems, and have enjoyed a series of such interior views as we get in the glimpse of Irene "trailing

> IN BRIEF, SILAS LAPHAM, A MAN OF COARSE GRAIN AND EXCESSIVE EGOTISM, IS, IN THE CRUCIAL SCENES, TREATED AS A MAN OF SUBTLETY OF THOUGHT AND FEELING."

up and down before the long mirror in *her* new dress [Mr. Howells never seems quite sure that we shall put the emphasis where it belongs without his gentle assistance], followed by the seamstress on her knees; the woman had her mouth full of pins, and from time to time she made Irene stop till she could put one of the pins into her train;" we should have followed the fluctuations of pride and affection and fastidiousness in the Corey family, and have sent a final shuddering thought down the vista of endless dinner parties which should await the union of the two houses. All this and much more offered materials for the handling of which we could have trusted Mr. Howells's sense of humor without fear that he would disappoint us.

But all this is in the story; only it occupies the subordinate, not the primary place, and by and by the reader, who has followed the story with delight in the playful art, discovers that Mr. Howells never intended to waste his art on so shallow a scheme, that he was using all this realism of Boston society as a relief to the heavier mass contained in the war which was waged within the conscience of the hero. When in the final sentence he reads: "I don't know as I should always say it paid; but if I done it, and the thing was to do over again, right in the same way, I guess I should have to do it," he recognizes, in this verdict of the faithfully illiterate Colonel, the triumphant because unconscious attainment of a victory which justifies the title of the story. No mere vulgar rise in society through the marriage of a daughter to a son of a social prince, or the possession of a house on the water side of Beacon Street, would serve as a real conclusion to the history of a character like that of Silas Lapham; as if to flout such an idea, the marriage when it comes is stripped of all possible social consequences, and the house is burned to the ground. In place of so trivial an end there is a fine subjection of the mean and ignoble, and as in Balzac's *César Birotteau*, a man of accidental vulgarity discloses his essential nobility; it is with this added virtue in the case of Mr. Howells's hero, that we see the achievement of moral solvency unglorified by any material prosperity, and the whole history of the rise unadorned by any decoration of sentiment.

We have intimated that this bottoming of art on ethical foundations is a late development in Mr. Howells's work. In truth, this is but the second important example. *An Undiscovered Country* hinted at the possibility of there being other things than were dreamt of in the philosophy of light-minded young women, but it has always seemed to us that the book suffered from its use of an essentially ignoble parody of human far-sightedness. The real break which Mr. Howells made in his continuity of fiction was in *A Modern Instance*. That book suffered from too violent an effort at change of base. With all our respect for the underlying thought..., we think that the author's habit of fine discrimination misled him into giving too much value in his art to the moral intention and too little I to the overt act.

[Though] there can be no mistaking Mr. Howells's intention in this novel, and though he uses his material with a firmer hand, we confess, now that we are out of the immediate circle of its charm, that *The Rise of Silas Lapham* suffers the same defect as *A Modern Instance*. The defect is not so obvious, but it arises from the same super-refinement of art. In brief, Silas Lapham, a man of coarse grain and excessive egotism, is, in the crucial scenes, treated as a man of subtlety of thought and feeling. We do not say that the turnings and windings of his conscience, and his sudden encounters with that delicious Mephistopheles, Milton K. Rogers, are not possible and even reasonable; but we complain that the author of his being, instead of preserving him as a rustic piece of Vermont limestone with the soil clinging to it, has insisted upon our seeing into the possibilities of a fine marble statue which reside in the bulk. Moreover, when one comes to think of it, how little the rise of this hero is really connected with the circumstances which make up the main incidents of the story. The relations with Rogers, out of which the moral struggle springs, are scarcely complicated at all by the personal relations with the Corey family arising from the love of young Corey for Penelope Lapham. The Colonel goes through the valley of tribulation almost independently of the fact that he and his are sojourning meanwhile in another half grotesque vale of tears.

This same over-refinement of motive, as supposed in natures which are not presumably subtle, impresses us in the whole history of Penelope's love affair. We feel, rather than are able to say why we feel it, that there is something abnormal in the desolation which falls upon the entire Lapham family in consequence of Irene's blindness and Penelope's over-acuteness. We frankly confess that when reading the scenes, it seemed all right, and we gave ourselves up to the luxury of woe without a doubt as to its reality. But when *thinking* about them (forgive the italics), it seems an exaggeration, a pressing of the relations between these interesting people beyond the bounds of a charitable nature.

But when all is said, we come back with satisfaction to the recollection that Mr. Howells hits distinctly set before himself in this book a problem worth solving, and if his statement and solution are presented with an art which has heretofore been so cunning as quite to reconcile one to the fragility of the object under the artist's hand, and this art still seems sometimes to imply the former baselessness, we can at least thank our stars that when we criticise such a book as *The Rise of Silas Lapham*, we are dealing with a real piece of literature, which surely will not lose its charm when the distinctions of Nankeen Square and Beacon Street have become merely antiquarian nonsense.

Source: "A Review of *The Rise of Silas Lapham*," in *Atlantic Monthly*, Vol. 56, No. 336, October 1885, pp.554–56.

Hamilton Wright Mabie

In the following excerpt, Mabie evaluates the emotional power of Howell's novel and the aesthetic value of realistic fiction in general.

In *The Rise of Silas Lapham* Mr. Howells has given us his best and his most characteristic work; none of his earlier stories discloses so clearly the quality and resources of his gift or his conception of the novelist's art. As an expression of personal power and as a type of the dominant school of contemporary fiction in this country and in France, whence the special impulse of recent realism has come, this latest work of a very accomplished and conscientious writer deserves the most careful and dispassionate

> MR. HOWELLS HAS SAID, IN SUBSTANCE, THAT REALISM IS THE ONLY LITERARY MOVEMENT OF THE DAY WHICH HAS ANY VITALITY IN IT, AND CERTAINLY NO ONE REPRESENTS THIS TENDENCY ON ITS FINER SIDE MORE PERFECTLY THAN HIMSELF."

study. If Mr. Howells's work possessed no higher claim upon attention, its evident fidelity to a constantly advancing ideal of workmanship would command genuine respect and admiration; whatever else one misses in it, there is no lack of the earnestness which concentrates a man's full power on the thing in hand, nor of the sensitive literary conscience which permits no relaxation of strength on subordinate parts, but exacts in every detail the skill and care which are lavished on the most critical unfoldings of plot or disclosures of character. Mr. Howells evidently leaves nothing to the chance suggestion of an inspired moment, and takes nothing for granted; he verifies every insight by observation, fortifies every general statement by careful study of facts, and puts his whole force into every detail of his work. . . . It is this quality which discovers itself more and more distinctly in Mr. Howells's novels in a constant development of native gifts, a stronger grasp of facts, and a more comprehensive dealing with the problems of character and social life to which he has given attention. In fact, this popular novelist is giving thoughtful readers of his books a kind of inspiration in the quiet but resolute progress of his gift and his art; a progress stimulated, no doubt, by success, but made possible and constant by fidelity to a high and disinterested ideal.

Nor has Mr. Howells spent his whole force on mere workmanship; he has made a no less strenuous endeavor to enlarge his knowledge of life, his grasp of its complicated problems, his insight into the forces and impulses which are the sources of action and character. If he has failed to touch the deepest issues, and to lay bare the more obscure and subtle movements of passion and purpose, it has been through no intellectual willfulness or lassitude; he has patiently and unweariedly followed such clews as he has been able to discover, and he has resolutely held

himself open to the claims of new themes and the revelations of fresh contacts with life. The limitations of his work are also the limitations of his insight and his imagination, and this fact, fully understood in all its bearings, makes any effort to point out those limitations ungracious in appearance and distasteful in performance; if personal feeling were to control in such matters, one would content himself with an expression of hearty admiration for work so full of character, and of sincere gratitude for a delicate intellectual pleasure so varied and so sustained. The evidence of a deepened movement of thought is obvious to the most hasty backward glance from *The Rise of Silas Lapham* and *A Modern Instance* to *Their Wedding Journey* and *A Chance Acquaintance*. In the early stories there is the lightness of touch, the diffused and delicate humor, which have never yet failed Mr. Howells; but there is little depth of sentiment, and almost no attempt to strike below the surface. These slight but very delightful tales discover the easy and graceful play of a force which deals with trifles as seriously as if it were handling the deepest and most significant problems of life. Seriousness is, indeed, the habitual mood of this novelist, and in his early stories it was the one prophetic element which they contained. There is a progressive evolution of power through *The Lady of the Aroostook*, *The Undiscovered Country*, *Dr. Breen's Practice* and *A Modern Instance*; each story in turn shows the novelist more intent upon his work, more resolute to hold his gift to its largest uses, more determined to see widely and deeply. His purpose grows steadily more serious, and his work gains correspondingly in substance and solidity. The problems of character which he sets before himself for solution become more complex and difficult, and, while there is nowhere a really decisive closing with life in a determined struggle to wring from it its secret, there is an evident purpose to grapple with realities and to keep in sympathy and touch with vital experiences.

In *The Rise of Silas Lapham* Mr. Howells has made a study of social conditions and contrasts everywhere present in society in this country; not, perhaps, so sharply defined elsewhere as in Boston, but to be discovered with more or less definiteness of outline in all our older communities. His quick instinct has fastened upon a stage of social evolution with which every body is familiar and in which everybody is interested. The aspect of social life presented in this story is well-nigh universal; it is real, it is vital, and it is not without deep significance; in dealing with it Mr. Howells has approached actual life more nearly, touched it more deeply, and expressed it more strongly than in any of his previous stories. The skill of his earliest work loses nothing in his latest; it is less evident because it is more unconscious and, therefore, more genuine and effective. There is the same humor, restrained and held in check by the major interests of the story, but touching here and there an idiosyncrasy, an inconsistency, a weakness, with all the old pungency and charm; a humor which is, in fact, the most real and the most distinctive of all Mr. Howells's gifts. There is, also, stronger grasp of situations, bolder portraiture of character, more rapid and dramatic movement of narrative. Still more important is the fact that in this novel life is presented with more of dramatic dignity and completeness than in any of Mr. Howells's other stories; there is a truer and nobler movement of human nature in it; and the characters are far less superficial, inconsequential, and unimportant than their predecessors; if not the highest types, they, have a certain force and dignity which make us respect them, and make it worth while to write about them. Add to these characterizations of *The Rise of Silas Lapham* the statement that Mr. Howells has never shown more complete mastery of his art in dealing with his material; that his style has never had more simplicity and directness, more solidity and substance, and it will be conceded that the sum total of excellence which even a reader who dissents from its underlying conception and method discovers in this story is by no means inconsiderable; is, indeed, such as to entitle it to very high praise, and to give added permanence and expansion to a literary reputation which, from the standpoint of popularity at least, stood in small need of these things.

And yet, when all this has been said, and said heartily, it must be added that *The Rise of Silas Lapham* is an unsatisfactory story; defective in power, in reality, and in the vitalizing atmosphere of imagination. No one is absorbed by it, nor moved by it; one takes it up with pleasure, reads it with interest, and lays it down without regret. It throws no spell over us; creates no illusion for us, leaves us indifferent spectators of an entertaining drama of social life. The novelist wrote it in a cool, deliberate mood, and it leaves the reader cold when he has finished it. The appearance and action of life are in it, but not the warmth; the frame, the organism, are admirable, but the divine inbreathing which would have given the body a soul has been withheld. Everything that art could do has been done, but the vital spark has not been transmitted. Mr. Howells never identifies himself with his characters; never becomes one with them in the vital fellowship and communion of the imagination; he constructs them with infinite patience and skill, but he never, for a moment, loses consciousness of his own individuality. He is cool and collected in all the emotional crises of his stories; indeed, it is often at such moments that one feels the presence of a diffused satire, as if the weakness of the men and women whom he is describing excited a little scorn in the critical mind of the novelist. The severest penalty of the persistent analytic mood is borne by the writer in the slight paralysis of feeling which comes upon him at the very moment when the pulse should beat a little faster of its own motion; in the subtle skepticism which pervades his work, unconsciously to himself, and like a slight frost takes the bloom off all fine emotions and actions. There are passages in Mr. Howells's stories in reading which one cannot repress a feeling of honest indignation at what is nothing more nor less than a refined parody of genuine feeling, sometimes of the most pathetic experience. Is Mr. Howells ashamed of life in its outcries of pain and regret? Does he shrink from these unpremeditated and unconventional revelations of character as vulgar, provincial, inartistic; or does he fail to comprehend them? Certainly the cool skillful hand which lifts the curtain upon Silas Lapham's weakness and sorrows does not tremble for an instant with any contagious emotion; and whenever the reader begins to warm a little, a slight turn of satire, a cool phrase or two of analysis, a faint suggestion that the writer doubts whether it is worth while, clears the air again. Perhaps nothing more decisive on this point could be said of Mr. Howells's stories than that one can read them aloud without faltering at the most pathetic passages; the latent distrust of all strong feeling in them makes one a little shy of his own emotion.

This failure to close with the facts of life, to press one's heart against them as well as to pursue and penetrate them with one's thought; this lack of unforced and triumphant faith in the worth, the dignity, and the significance for art of human experience in its whole range; this failure of the imagination to bridge the chasm between the real and the fictitious reproduction of it, are simply fatal to all great and abiding work. Without faith, which is the very ground upon which the true artist stands; without love, which is both inspiration and revelation to him, a true art is impossible. Without faith there would never have come out of the world of the imagination such figures as Jeanie Deans, Colonel Newcome, Eugénie Grandet, Père Goriot, and Hester Prynne; without love—large, warm, generous sympathy with all that life is and means—the secret of these noble creations would never have been disclosed. Mr. Howells and Daudet practice alike the art of a refined realism, but what a distance separates the Nabob from Silas Lapham! Daudet is false to his theory and true to his art; life touches him deeply, fills him with reverence, and he can no more rid himself of the imagination than he can part the light from the flower upon which it falls. The Nabob might have suggested a similar treatment of Silas Lapham. How tenderly, how reverently, with what a sense of pathos, through what a mist of tears, Daudet uncovers to us the weakness and sorrows of Jansoulet! The Nabob is always touched by a soft light from the novelist's heart; poor Silas Lapham shivers in a perpetual east wind. Imagine the "Vicar of Wakefield" treated in the same spirit, and the fatal defect of Mr. Howells's attitude towards life is apparent at a glance.

The disposition to treat life lightly and skeptically, to doubt its capacity for real and lasting achievement, to stand apart from it and study it coolly and in detail with dispassionate and scientific impartiality, is at bottom decisive evidence of lack of power; that is, of the dramatic power which alone is able to reproduce life in noble dramatic forms. A refined realism strives to make up in patience what it lacks in genius; to make observation do the work of insight; to make analysis take the place of synthesis of character, and "a more analytic consideration of the appearance of things"—to quote Mr. James—the place of a resolute and masterly grasp of characters and situations. The method of the realism illustrated in *The Rise of Silas Lapham* is external, and, so far as any strong grasp of life is concerned, necessarily superficial. It is an endeavor to enter into the recesses of character, and learn its secret, not by insight, the method of the imagination, but by observation, the method of science; and it is an endeavor to reproduce that character under the forms of art, not by identification with it, and the genuine and

almost unconscious evolution which follows, but by skillful adjustment of traits, emotions, passions, and activities which are the result of studies more or less conscientiously carried on. The patience and work involved in the making of some novels constructed on this method are beyond praise; but they must not make us blind to the fact that no method can take the place of original power, and that genius in some form—faith, sympathy, insight, imagination—is absolutely essential in all true art. The hesitation, the repression of emotion, the absence of color, are significant, not of a noble restraint of power, a wise husbanding of resources for the critical moment and situation, but of a lack of the spontaneity and overflow of a great force. Ruskin finely says that when we stand before a true work of art we feel ourselves in the presence, not of a great effort, but of a great force. In most of the novels of realism it is the effort which impresses us, and not the power. In Turgénieff and Björnson, masters of the art of realism, and yet always superior to it, the repression and restraint are charged with power; one feels behind them an intensity of thought and feeling that is at times absolutely painful. No such sensation overtakes one in reading *The Rise of Silas Lapham* or *The Bostonians*; there is no throb of life here; the pulse of feeling, if it beats at all, is imperceptible; and of the free and joyous play of that supreme force which we call genius there is absolutely not one gleam. If either novelist possessed it, no method, however rigidly practiced, could wholly confine it; it would flame like lightning, as in Björnson, or suffuse and penetrate all things with latent heat, as in Turgénieff, or touch all life with a soft, poetic radiance, as in Daudet.

Mr. Howells has said, in substance, that realism is the only literary movement of the day which has any vitality in it, and certainly no one represents this tendency on its finer side more perfectly than himself. Its virtues and its defects are very clearly brought out in his work: its clearness of sight, its fixed adherence to fact, its reliance upon honest work; and, on the other hand, its hardness, its lack of vitality, its paralysis of the finer feelings and higher aspirations, its fundamental defect on the side of the imagination. Realism is crowding the world of fiction with commonplace people; people whom one would positively avoid coming in contact with in real life; people without native sweetness or strength, without acquired culture or accomplishment, without that touch of the ideal which makes the commonplace significant and worthy of study. To the large, typical characters of the older novels has succeeded a generation of feeble, irresolute, unimportant men and women whose careers are of no moment to themselves, and wholly destitute of interest to us. The analysis of motives that were never worth an hour's serious study, the grave portraiture of frivolous, superficial, and often vulgar conceptions of life, the careful scrutiny of characters without force, beauty, aspiration, or any of the elements which touch and teach men, has become wearisome, and will sooner or later set in motion a powerful reaction. One cannot but regret such a comparative waste of delicate, and often genuine, art; it is as if Michael Angelo had given us the meaningless faces of the Roman fops of his time instead of the heads of Moses and Hercules.

Source: Hamilton Wright Mabie, "A Typical Novel," in *Andover Review*, Vol. 4, No. 23, November 1885, pp. 417–29.

Catholic World

In the following excerpt, a contributor characterizes the novel as morally bankrupt.

[In *The Rise of Silas Lapham*] Mr. Howells has produced the most scientifically realistic novel that has yet been written. M. Zola's books are as the awkward gropings of an amateur compared with this finished treatise. The field that Mr. Howells takes for his investigation is, he tells us, "the commonplace." By studying "the common feelings of common people" he believes he "solves the riddle of the painful earth."

Silas Lapham is a type of the self-made American. He has grown rich through the instrumentality of a mineral paint of which he is the proprietor. He lives in Boston and entertains social ambitions for his wife and two daughters. Bromfield Corey is a Boston aristocrat with a wife, two daughters, and a son. The Laphams and the Coreys are thrown together in consequence of a contemplated misalliance between young Corey and one of the Lapham daughters; and in the contrasts and developments that appear among all these "types" is supposed to consist the main interest of the story. There are no incidents that are not sternly commonplace, but everything connected with these incidents and their psychological effect on the actors is analyzed and detailed with microscopic accuracy.

[Howells] studies men and women as a naturalist does insects. We read his book on the manners, habits, sensations, nerves of a certain set of people as we might a treatise on the coleoptera. And he investigates, and expounds his theme with the same soullessness and absence of all emotion. Even Mr. Henry James, beside this chilly *savant*, appears quite a child of sentiment. He is capable of receiving "impressions"—which, in Mr. Howells' eyes, would be a most unscientific weakness—and he manages to retain some smack of art about the work he does.

Is this kind of novel-writing an elevating pursuit? and is the reading of it beneficial? To these two queries the answer must be emphatically, No.

Novels like *Silas Lapham* mark a descent, a degradation. Of course art is debased when it has fallen so low into realism. Art is ever pointing upward, and the influence of true art upon man is to make him look upward, too, to that vast where his Ideal sits,

—pinnacled in the lofty ether dim,

where all is beautiful, but where all is immeasurable by him until he beholds it with his glorified intelligence. Science points downward, and when science is unguided by religion it leads its followers lower and lower into the mud beneath their feet. And even as we see some scientists making a distinct "progress" downward from the study of the higher to that of the lower forms of animal life, so in the novel-writing of Mr. Howells we can already mark this scientific decadence. He began with people who were not quite commonplace, whose motives and acts and ideas were a little bit above the common. He now declares that nothing is worthy to be studied but the common feelings of common people; and having begun *Silas Lapham* with people who were inoffensively commonplace, he was unable to finish the book without falling a stage tower. Towards the end he introduces a young woman who speaks thus of her husband: "If I could get rid of Hen I could manage well enough with mother. Mr. Wemmel would marry me if I could get the divorce. He said so over and over again." He introduces a scene in which this young woman, her tipsy sailor-husband, her drunken mother, and Silas Lapham as the family benefactor, figure—a scene that, for hopeless depravity both in the author and subject, out-Zolas Zola. The old woman, who has a bottle in her hand, complains of her son-in-law not giving the daughter an opportunity to obtain a divorce. "'Why don't you go off on some them long v'y'ges?' s'd I. It's pretty hard when Mr. Wemmel stands really to marry Z'rilla and provide a comfortable home for us both—I han't got a great many years more to live, and I *should* like to get more satisfaction out of 'em and not be beholden and dependent all my days—to have Hen, here, blockin' the way. I tell him there'd be more money for him in the end; but he can't seem to make up his mind to it." Again says this old harridan: "Say, Colonel, what should you advise Z'rilla do about Mr. Wemmel? I tell her there an't any use goin' to the trouble to git a divorce without she's sure about him. Don't you think we'd ought to git him to sign a paper, or something, that he'll marry her if she gits it? I don't like to have things goin' at loose ends the way they are. It an't sense. It an't right." Before Mr. Howells reaches the end of the book he makes even the worthy Mrs. Lapham suspect her husband of infidelity and make a scene, accusing him, in the hearing of her children. It has seldom been our duty to read a book whose moral tone was so unpleasantly, so hopelessly bad; it is a book without heart or soul, neither illuminated by religion nor warned by human sympathy. This is all the more astonishing that Mr. Howells seems convinced that he is fulfilling a high moral purpose in writing it. It might be explicable on the theory that it was the legitimate outcome of the doctrine of total depravity; but it is more probably the logic of the downward progress of godless science. We shall not be surprised if the next books of Mr. Howells deal with characters and feelings that shall be so far below the commonplace from which he has already fallen that even M. de Goncourt will not enjoy reading about them. It is the progress from man to the apes, from the apes to the worms, from the worms to bacteria, from bacteria to—mud. It is the descent to dirt.

Source: "Novel-Writing as a Science," in *Catholic World*, Vol. 42, No. 248, November 1885, pp. 274–80.

"Equal Pay," National Women's Law Center website, http://www.nwlc.org/our-issues/employment/equal-pay (accessed September 6, 2012).

Howells, William Dean, *The Rise of Silas Lapham*, in *William Dean Howells: Novels 1875–1886*, Library of America, 1982.

Isenberg, Nancy, "Women's Rights Movements," in *American National Biography Online*, http://www.anb.org/cush_rights.html (accessed September 6, 2012).

"Jesus Anointed by a Sinful Woman," Biblegateway.com, http://www.biblegateway.com/passage/?search=Luke+7%3A36-50&version=NIV (accessed September 6, 2012).

"The Lilly Ledbetter Fair Pay Act," Lilly Ledbetter website, http://www.lillyledbetter.com/ (accessed September 6, 2012).

MacAskill, Ewen, and Dominic Rushe, "OECD Says U.S. Economy Is Recovering but Income Inequality Problematic," in *Guardian*, http://www.guardian.co.uk/business/2012/jun/26/oecd-us-economy-income-inequality (accessed September 6, 2012).

Mizruchi, Susan L., "Corporate America," in *The Rise of Multicultural America: Economy and Print Culture, 1865–1915*, University of North Carolina Press, 2008, pp. 213–55.

Persons, Warren M., "The Future Indicated by the Past," in *Forecasting Business Cycles*, J. Wiley & Sons, 1931, pp. 7–19.

Pizer, Donald, "The Ethical Unity of *The Rise of Silas Lapham*," in *Realism and Naturalism in Nineteenth-Century American Literature*, Southern Illinois University Press, 1984, pp. 121–26.

Schriber, Mary Suzanne, "William Dean Howells: The Male Imagination at the Crossroads," in *Gender and the Writer's Imagination: From Cooper to Wharton*, University Press of Kentucky, 1987, pp. 86–116.

Shulman, Robert, "Realism," in *The Columbia History of the American Novel*, Columbia University Press, 1991, pp. 160–88.

"United States," in *CIA: World Factbook*, Central Intelligence Agency, https://www.cia.gov/library/publications/the-world-factbook/geos/us.html (accessed September 6, 2012).

Woodress, James, "William Dean Howells," in *Dictionary of Literary Biography*, Vol. 12, *American Realists and Naturalists*, edited by Donald Pizer, Gale Research, 1982, pp. 270–97.

SOURCES

Bradford, Frederick A., "Business Cycles," in *The Dictionary of American History*, Vol. 1, 2nd ed., revised, Charles Scribner's Sons, pp. 261–62.

Crane, Gregg, "The Realist Novel," in *The Cambridge Introduction to the Nineteenth-Century American Novel*, Cambridge University Press, 2007, pp. 156–207.

FURTHER READING

Baker, Jean H., *Sisters: The Lives of America's Suffragists*, Hill and Wang, 2005.
  Baker traces the personal lives and political achievements of five women who are counted among the leaders of the American suffrage movement.

Kearns, Catherine, *Nineteenth-Century Literary Realism: Through the Looking Glass*, Cambridge University Press, 1996.

> Kearns examines the ways in which nineteenth-century realists, including Howells, employed realism as a means of exposing the need for political and economic reforms and, in doing so, linked realism with reformism. Kearns further explores the way the boundaries of realism have been explored by a number of British and American authors whose works are not typically associated with realism.

Licht, Walter, *Industrializing America: The Nineteenth Century*, Johns Hopkins University Press, 1995.

> Licht traces the evolution of the U.S. economy in the nineteenth century and examines the sociopolitical impact of industrialization in America.

Petrie, Paul R., *Conscience and Purpose: Fiction and Social Consciousness in Howells, Jewett, Chestnutt, and Cather*, University of Alabama Press, 2005.

> Petrie uses Howells and his focus on the social mission of literary realism to explore the way

several writers adapted Howells's philosophy and promoted their own ethical and aesthetic agendas.

SUGGESTED SEARCH TERMS

William Dean Howells AND The Rise of Silas Lapham

William Dean Howells AND American realism

William Dean Howells AND Boston

William Dean Howells AND social class

William Dean Howells AND American economy

William Dean Howells AND gender issues

William Dean Howells AND literary critic

William Dean Howells AND social reform

William Dean Howells AND industrialization

William Dean Howells AND American business

The Samurai's Garden

GAIL TSUKIYAMA

1995

The Samurai's Garden (1995), by Gail Tsukiyama, tells the story of Stephen Chan, a Chinese college student recovering from tuberculosis. The novel consists of Stephen's journal entries starting in September of 1937, when he arrives at his family's vacation house in a small seaside town in Japan, and continuing into autumn of the following year, when he leaves, having healed physically and matured emotionally.

While Stephen is there, he is befriended by Matsu, who has been caretaker of the house and garden since he was a young man. Stephen also has his first brush with romance, all the while worrying about the Japanese soldiers fighting their way through China toward his family in Hong Kong. As Stephen learns to find his place in the world, Tsukiyama explores themes of personal and cultural identity, isolation, and family over the threatening background of the war. *The Samurai's Garden* also reflects Tsukiyama's own heritage as an Asian American with both Chinese and Japanese cultural influences.

AUTHOR BIOGRAPHY

Tsukiyama was born in San Francisco on September 13, 1957. Her father was a Japanese American who was raised in Hawaii, and her mother was of Chinese descent, having immigrated

Yukio Mishima *(© AP Photo | Nobuyuki Masaki)*

to the United States from Hong Kong. Thus Tsukiyama's life was rich with both of her parents' cultural backgrounds, and it clearly had a great influence on her work.

Tsukiyama began writing as a teenager. She mostly created poetry, but when she started college at San Francisco State University, she first studied film. After deciding that writing allowed her to express herself creatively better than film, she changed her major to creative writing. She earned her bachelor's degree and then continued on at San Francisco State to earn her master's. Her master's thesis was a collection of poetry, but soon after finishing school, Tsukiyama switched to prose. She began to write short stories and soon started work on a novel.

Her first published book, *Women of the Silk* (1991), became a best seller. *The Samurai's Garden* (1994) was her second book; her most recent work is *A Hundred Flowers* (2012). Many of Tsukiyama's novels take place in the past or in very specific communities. For example, *Women*

of the Silk and its sequel, *The Language of Threads* (1999), recount the lives of Chinese silk workers in the first half of the twentieth century. The characters in *The Street of a Thousand Blossoms* (2007) provide glimpses into the Japanese traditions of sumo wrestling and Noh theater. In *The Samurai's Garden*, which takes place in the late 1930s, readers see the citizens of Yamaguchi, all of whom have been afflicted with leprosy. To add to the realism of her stories and their historical settings, Tsukiyama researches her topics extensively.

In addition to being a fiction author, Tsukiyama has taught creative writing at her alma mater, San Francisco State University. She also writes book reviews and has worked as a judge and then the chairperson for the Kiriyama Pacific Rim book award panel. In addition to popular success, she has received several critical awards, including the Academy of American Poets Award and the PEN Oakland/Josephine Miles Literary Award.

Tsukiyama still lives and works in her home state of California. As quoted in *A to Z of American Women Writers*, by Carol Kort, Tsukiyama calls herself "as American as apple pie." However, like many Americans, she is a mix of cultures: "All the Chinese traditions from my mother's side of the family are within me, and have somehow found expression through my books."

PLOT SUMMARY

The novel is told in the form of Stephen's diary. The first entry is dated September 15, 1937, and the setting is indicated: Tarumi, Japan. The book is also divided into sections by seasons of the year.

Autumn

The reader meets the narrator Stephen Chan, who has just arrived at his family's vacation home in Japan. He describes how he became ill at school in Canton, went home to Hong Kong, and now has been sent to recover in the cooler, drier climate of the seaside town of Tarumi. Stephen is still suffering from some of the effects of tuberculosis: coughing, fevers, and weakness, and his parents are worried about him. There is a brief mention of Stephen's brother and sisters: Anne, Henry, and Penelope, who is nicknamed

MEDIA ADAPTATIONS

- *The Samurai's Garden* was produced in 2004 as an audiobook on CD from Recording for the Blind and Dyslexic.

Pie. The children were given Christian names because Stephen's "father believes it an asset in the business world to be addressed with ease by Westerners."

Stephen describes his journey. He stopped briefly in Kobe to see his father, who spends much of his time in Japan on business, and then continued by train to Tarumi, where he was met by Matsu, the "caretaker of the beach house." Matsu is quiet but polite, and he tries to make Stephen feel at home. His work includes everything from tending the garden, which he loves, to cooking and drawing Stephen's baths. The next day Stephen finds his way around, describing the house in his journal and walking to the beach. While he is there, he sees two girls running and laughing on the sand. Stephen's father comes to visit after a few days, and they discuss Japan's attacks on China. Stephen is curious about Matsu because he does not talk about himself, but Mr. Chan does not know much about him.

Stephen is sad when his father leaves, so Matsu invites him to come on a visit to a friend in another village, Yamaguchi. Stephen is concerned when he learns that it is a "Village of Lepers," but Matsu assures him that leprosy cannot be spread by casual contact. The houses in the village are shabby and "mismatched." Stephen sees the sores and bandages of the people who live there and tries not to be afraid or stare rudely.

Matsu introduces Stephen to Sachi, who lives in a nice house set a little bit outside the rest of the village. Stephen sees that Sachi is beautiful in spite of the places where her skin is damaged by leprosy. On the walk home, Matsu explains that he lost his younger sister to the

disease and that he has taken care of Sachi ever since she moved to Yamaguchi.

Matsu works in his garden while Stephen paints and goes to the beach. He meets Keiko and Mika, the sisters he saw there earlier. Another visit to Yamaguchi cements Stephen's fascination with Sachi, and Matsu tells Stephen a little more of her story: she left her family when she contracted leprosy and never saw them again. Matsu introduces Stephen to his friend Kenzo, who runs the tea house in Tarumi. He was also friends with Sachi, but she would not see him once she got sick.

Stephen receives a letter from his mother in which she tells him of her suspicion that his father has been having an affair. Stephen is very upset and does not completely believe her. A storm hits Tarumi, and Stephen is injured while trying to help Matsu prepare the house to withstand the bad weather. Concerned for Stephen, Sachi ventures out of Yamaguchi for the first time since she moved there to visit him. The storm has ruined Matsu's garden, and Sachi and Stephen both work to help him repair the damage.

Stephen sees Keiko again, and they plan to meet in secret on the beach. They take a walk together, and Keiko tells him that her brother is with the Japanese army in China. It makes them both quiet. Keiko will not let Stephen walk her home because she does not want her parents to know she has met him.

When Stephen returns to the beach house, Kenzo is there. He has seen Sachi and is very angry. He shoves Matsu and calls Sachi a "monster" when he sees her face without the scarf she usually wears. Matsu throws Kenzo out of the garden, and Sachi goes home to Yamaguchi. Matsu explains to Stephen that Kenzo and Sachi were once engaged. When she became ill, Kenzo "didn't have the courage to face" her, so Matsu became their go-between. Kenzo was angry because Matsu had led him to believe Sachi would never leave Yamaguchi and then Kenzo found her visiting Matsu.

Winter

Stephen visits Sachi on his own. He tries to convince Sachi that she has done nothing wrong by visiting Matsu, but she insists that she has dishonored herself, Stephen, and Matsu. Stephen touches the scars on her face in an effort to convince her that they make no difference to him. Sachi shows Stephen her garden, which Matsu helped her create. It is a rock garden rather than one of plants and trees. She encourages him to try raking patterns into the pebbles, and it does indeed help soothe him.

Sachi tells him about the death of Tomoko, Matsu's sister. She was one of the first to show the symptoms of leprosy, and she committed *seppuku*, a traditional suicide ritual, because she could not live with the feeling that she had shamed her family. Sachi and Tomoko had been good friends, but Sachi largely ignored Matsu until after his sister died. Knowing how close the girls were, Matsu brought Tomoko's "lucky stone," which matches one that Sachi has. Sachi explains how she and Tomoko "found them when we were young girls and always associated them with good luck and all the other dreams of youth."

When Stephen returns home, Matsu tells him that his father has arrived for a visit. Stephen is nervous, not wanting to confront him with his mother's accusations that he is having an affair. Mr. Chan compliments Stephen's painting, which surprises and embarrasses Stephen, because his father usually thinks little of Stephen's art. Mr. Chan brings up the issue of the affair, admits that there is another woman, and says that Stephen's mother "was never to have known." Mr. Chan says that nothing will change, that he will continue to spend time both with his family in Hong Kong and with his mistress, Yoshiko, in Kobe. In the evening, they discuss the war, but before Stephen wakes in the morning, his father has left.

Matsu and Stephen visit the Shinto shrine in another village. Matsu prays and encourages Stephen to do so as well. On the walk home, Stephen discovers that Matsu knew about his father's mistress and becomes angry. The Christmas and New Year's holidays pass quietly, and Stephen receives a letter from his friend King. It is full of news about the fighting in China and a terrible massacre in Nanking, and Stephen is shocked by it—he has heard only the Japanese news broadcasts, which did not mention the massacre.

Stephen and Matsu attend a village celebration of the beginning of spring, but the festivities are interrupted by the news that Kenzo has killed himself. Matsu, even through his shock and grief, cares for Stephen, who felt ill after hearing of Kenzo's death. Matsu tells Stephen that he went to Yamaguchi to bring the terrible news to Sachi. She was saddened but will not come to the funeral. Matsu finds some comfort in his garden. The entire village attends Kenzo's funeral. Stephen sees Keiko there but does speak with her because she is with her parents. Stephen spies Sachi—she comes to pay her respects to Kenzo after all, but no one else sees her. Keiko comes to visit Stephen briefly later and promises to see him again soon.

Spring

Stephen and Matsu go to visit Sachi and find Yamaguchi in the middle of a crisis, a fire. Stephen helps one of the village men, Hiro, to carry buckets of water, and the fire is put out, but not before several houses are destroyed. Matsu and Stephen spend the night at Hiro's house. Stephen goes to see Sachi and promises her that he will never tell Matsu that she attended Kenzo's funeral. Sachi tells him the story of her life: when she first met Matsu, how her friendship grew with his sister Tomoko, how she began to fall in love with Kenzo, and what happened when she noticed the first signs of leprosy.

Sachi kept the disease a secret from everyone except Matsu, who tried to help her as much as he could. When Sachi finally decided to tell Kenzo, it was too much for him. She tried to commit suicide with some other people from the village who were also afflicted. Many held the belief that those with leprosy were somehow shaming their families. Sachi and four others walked into the sea; the others drowned, but she could not do it. "The greatest honor I could have given my family was that of my death, and I ran from it," she tells Stephen.

Sachi ran away and hid in the woods. Matsu found her and took her to Yamaguchi. At first Sachi was frightened and disgusted by the wounds of the villagers, but she lived with Michiko, a patient and kind elder, who took care of Sachi but was also honest with her, telling her, "There aren't many choices for us." Sachi, with the help of Michiko and Matsu, learned to rebuild her life. After Michiko died, Matsu helped Sachi build her rock garden.

Matsu and Stephen provide supplies and help the villagers of Yamaguchi rebuild after the fire. Stephen receives a letter from his mother explaining that she and Pie will not visit for the summer as planned because Mr. and Mrs. Chan are "still sorting everything out." When the homes in Yamaguchi are rebuilt, there is a big celebration that Stephen calls "one of the best nights of my life."

Summer

The weather gets warmer. Stephen and Matsu walk into Tarumi, and Stephen sees Keiko. They make plans to meet at the Shinto shrine. When Stephen and Matsu return home, Sachi is there to tell them that Hiro has died. Matsu insists that Stephen does not need to attend the funeral. Matsu has still not returned from Yamaguchi when Stephen has to leave to meet Keiko. Keiko brings refreshments. She and Stephen have a romantic picnic.

Stephen's father visits. They make small talk until Stephen asks about the war. He is concerned about his mother and sister alone in Hong Kong. Mr. Chan says that he and Mrs. Chan have agreed that Stephen should stay at the beach house through the summer. He believes there is no danger of the fighting reaching their home.

Stephen plans to take part in Tarumi's O-bon festival, during which people return to their hometown to visit the graves of their ancestors and have a big celebration. Matsu's sister Fumiko comes for the festival. Fumiko is much more talkative than her brother. She insists on preparing lunch when she arrives and talks to Stephen about Matsu as she cooks.

Early the next morning, they go to the cemetery, where the townspeople clean their families' grave sites and leave tea, sake, and food. Then everyone returns to the village, which is decorated with paper lanterns. There is laughter and dancing and food, but Stephen seems melancholy. He sees Kenzo's dark tea house and thinks of the people in Yamaguchi and the people being killed in the war in China.

Autumn

The weather begins to turn, and the summer visitors begin to leave Tarumi. Stephen meets Keiko on the beach, and she tells him that they cannot be together. Her brother was killed while fighting in China, and she knows that her family would not accept her falling in love with a Chinese boy.

Stephen and Matsu go to Yamaguchi to visit Sachi. Stephen watches Matsu check Sachi's home for problems, like the heavy fall rain leaking through the roof, and realizes that Matsu is

"the master of the house" even though he would say he does not even live there.

Stephen receives a letter from King, who describes the fighting as "awfully hot." He tells Stephen that some items are being rationed because of shortages caused by the war and that a girl they knew in school was killed. The letter disturbs Stephen—he cannot remember the girl from school, but hearing details of life at home brings the war to life for him. There is also a letter from his father, who invites Stephen on a business trip to Tokyo.

Tokyo seems huge to Stephen after over a year in Tarumi and Yamaguchi. Stephen walks around the city streets, sees the Imperial Palace, and feels he has to keep his voice down when speaking to his father in Chinese. Mr. Chan suggests that Stephen should probably return to Hong Kong before Christmas. While they are at their hotel, Stephen and his father hear on the radio that the Chinese city of Canton has fallen to the Japanese army. After such news, they feel they had better leave Tokyo.

Knowing that he will soon be going home, Stephen goes to Yamaguchi to say goodbye to Sachi. They go to the garden, and Stephen moves the pebbles with a rake. He asks Sachi, "Who will take care of you if something happens to Matsu?" She reassures him. Sachi tells Stephen that he has given her and Matsu something very important: he has become like their child, the one they "lost so many years ago." Stephen feels sadness for his friends for the grief they must have felt for their stillborn child.

Stephen gives Sachi a beautiful vase as a gift. In return, she gives him the two lucky stones that she and Tomoko had found when they were young. Stephen spends one last day on the beach. He cannot imagine how it will be when he returns to Hong Kong. Sachi comes down to the beach house for one last goodbye, which makes Stephen very happy.

On Stephen's last afternoon in Tarumi, he and Matsu go to the Shinto shrine in Tama and have dinner together. The next morning, Stephen takes a few minutes to appreciate Matsu's garden, remembering the comfort it brought him when he first arrived at the house. Stephen finds a white flower on the garden gate and knows that it is Keiko's way of saying goodbye.

Matsu walks Stephen to the train station. It is difficult for them to say goodbye. Once the train pulls away, Stephen finds a gift Matsu has tucked in among his other belongings, two leather-bound journals. As the train carries him on the first leg of his journey home, Stephen begins writing, starting the new chapter of his life as his time in Tarumi comes to an end.

CHARACTERS

Anne Chan

Anne is Stephen's older sister. She does not appear in the story directly, but Stephen thinks of her at her school in Macao.

Henry Chan

Henry is Stephen's younger brother. Like Anne, he is at school in Macao and does not appear in the story.

Mr. Chan

Mr. Chan is Stephen's father. He travels back and forth between the family home in Hong Kong and Kobe, Japan, for his work. Stephen sometimes thinks his father seems "more Japanese than Chinese." Mr. Chan is a businessman and very practical. He does not seem interested in things he finds frivolous, such as Stephen's painting, which he considers a "time-consuming hobby." Stephen and his father seem to have a difficult time talking to one another. Their relationship is made more strained when Stephen learns that his father has kept a mistress in Kobe for twelve years. Mr. Chan insists that nothing about their lives will change, even though Stephen and his mother know about the affair, but it changes the way Stephen views his father.

Mrs. Chan

Mrs. Chan is Stephen's mother. She is a nervous woman who does not seem close to her children. When Stephen thinks of family vacations at the beach house when he was young, he remembers his mother on her own in the garden, suffering from the heat. When Mrs. Chan suspects her husband of having an affair, she writes Stephen and asks him to confront Mr. Chan. In fact, her letters seem to be full of her own complaints and worries rather than interest in and concern for her son.

Penelope Chan

Penelope, known as Pie, is Stephen's little sister. She is a bright, cheerful girl, and Stephen is close to her. Part of the reason Stephen is sent away to recover from tuberculosis is to protect Pie from contagion, because she cannot resist coming into his room to talk to him. She writes him a letter telling him that she is doing work for the Red Cross because of the war in China. When Stephen is preparing to leave Tarumi, he tries to find a gift to bring home to her.

Stephen Chan

Stephen is the narrator of the story. Most of the book is Stephen's diary, so it is from his point of view. He is a young man who has been ill with tuberculosis, an infection of the lungs that causes fevers and persistent coughing. Stephen's family sends him to their vacation home in Japan to recover. While Stephen is there, he swims in the ocean, sketches and paints, and falls in love for the first time.

The most significant relationship in the book is Stephen's friendship with Matsu, the caretaker of the beach house. Stephen learns a lot from Matsu and through him is introduced to Sachi and all of the villagers who live in Yamaguchi. Meeting the people whose lives have been changed by leprosy and especially having Matsu as an example highlight for Stephen the important things in life: inner strength, loyalty, and kindness rather than physical appearance or social position.

The novel is the story of Stephen's coming of age. Although he becomes disillusioned with his father, who has been secretly keeping a mistress for twelve years, Stephen tries to handle the situation in a mature manner. From his first romance, he learns about love, and when the young woman breaks up with him, he learns a little about heartbreak. In the year that Stephen spends in Japan, he becomes an adult.

Ching

Ching is the Chan family's servant. Although she is an employee, she has been with the Chans so long she is like a member of the family. Stephen explains that "my mother told Ching secrets, then listened to her like a wise older sister."

Fumiko

Fumiko is Matsu's sister. She comes to Yamaguchi near the end of the novel for the O-bon festival. She is more talkative than her brother, and it makes Stephen happy to see Matsu with someone who knows him so well and loves him.

Keiko Hagashi

Keiko is the older of the two sisters that Stephen meets on the beach. She is beautiful and shy, but she likes Stephen and agrees to meet him on several occasions. She keeps her meetings with Stephen secret from her parents. Near the end of the novel, Keiko tells Stephen she cannot see him anymore, but before he departs from Tarumi, she leaves a flower for him on the garden gate to say goodbye. Through his romance with Keiko, Stephen learns about both love and loss.

Mika Hagashi

Mika is Keiko's younger sister. When Stephen first sees them on the beach, they seem to enjoy each other's company, but later, when Keiko wants to meet Stephen alone, she thinks of Mika as a nosy pest. Keiko tricks Mika so that she can go out without her.

Toshiro Hagashi

Toshiro is Keiko and Mika's brother. Stephen learns fairly early on in his relationship with Keiko that Toshiro is fighting with the Japanese army in China. He does not appear in the story, but he is significant because his death in the war makes Keiko conclude that she and Stephen cannot be together.

Hiro

Hiro is one of the villagers in Yamaguchi. Although he has lost one of his hands to leprosy, he is strong, and Stephen is impressed when he helps Hiro while fighting the fire. When Hiro dies, Matsu thinks Stephen would be too tired to come to the funeral. Sachi tells Stephen not to think of Hiro's death but to remember his life: "Hold on to your last memory of Hiro-*san*, the night of the celebration when he was happiest and most alive."

Kenzo

Kenzo has known Matsu and Sachi since they were very young. He owns the teahouse in Tarumi. Kenzo and Sachi were engaged to be married when she contracted leprosy. Kenzo could not face her disease, and Matsu took over as her caretaker and protector, but Kenzo stayed loyal to her in his own way, never marrying. Matsu always led Kenzo to believe that Sachi would never leave Yamaguchi, but Kenzo comes to the beach house and sees Sachi in the garden there. He is angry and pushes Matsu, feeling betrayed and likely feeling ashamed of his own disgust at Sachi's disfigurement. He calls her a "monster." After the confrontation in the garden, Kenzo will not speak to Matsu. He hangs himself in the teahouse because of his anger and confusion.

King

King is Stephen's friend from college. Unlike Stephen's father, King seems to understand why painting is important to Stephen. King does not appear in the story, but he sends Stephen letters that make him miss his old life. The letters also tell Stephen what is going on with the war in China, giving a personal perspective to the announcements Stephen hears on Matsu's radio.

Matsu

After Stephen, Matsu is the most important character in the novel. He is a quiet man, and when Stephen first meets him, he thinks that Matsu "seems the type of man who's more comfortable alone, and it's not hard to figure out that he must be annoyed at my disturbing his tranquil world." However, Matsu's reserved exterior hides a huge heart. Sachi says, "With Matsu, everything is in what he does not say." In Matsu's actions, we can see the sort of person he is.

Matsu spends his life helping other people and tending the plants in his garden. When he was a very young man, he fell in love with Sachi, but he stood aside when she chose Kenzo. When Sachi realized that she had leprosy, it was Matsu who helped her, speaking with the doctor and then taking her to Yamaguchi and helping her to make a life there.

The samurai were a warrior class of nobility in Japan. Although Matsu is a servant, usually thought of as a lower social position, he proves himself to be noble and admirable, like a samurai.

Michiko

Michiko was the old woman who took care of Sachi when she first came to Yamaguchi. She appears in the novel only in Sachi's stories of the past. Michiko was so disfigured by leprosy that at first Sachi was afraid of her, but then Sachi was able to look past her appearance and came to see her wisdom and kind heart. Sachi believes that Matsu and Michiko saved her from her thoughts of suicide when she first contracted leprosy.

Pie

See Penelope Chan

Sachi

Sachi was a beautiful young woman who was engaged to be married when leprosy struck her. From that point on, she lived on the outskirts of an isolated village. Her fiancé could not stand by her, and her family would have preferred for her to commit suicide rather than have to live with the shame she is made to feel about her illness. Matsu helped her build a life for herself, including a lovely rock garden where she found some peace and happiness.

Her strength and her deep relationship with Matsu are inspiring to Stephen, but he also helps her. Before Stephen came, Sachi had never left Yamaguchi, but when he is injured in a storm, her concern for him brings her back into Tarumi. She continues to visit the beach house and comes to Kenzo's funeral, although he had hurt her and said hateful things to her. Her leaving Yamaguchi is important because it shows that she is opening her heart a bit more to the world after hiding away for almost forty years. By the end of the novel, she tells Stephen that he has become like a son to her and Matsu.

Tomoko

Tomoko is Matsu's younger sister. She died many years before the story takes place. She was very close friends with Sachi. Tomoko was one of the first people in Tarumi to show symptoms of leprosy. She killed herself because she felt that the disease had dishonored her family. Her death brought Matsu and Sachi together. Matsu brought Sachi Tomoko's lucky rock after her death, so when Sachi first suspected she herself had leprosy, she felt she could trust him.

Yoshiko

Yoshiko is Mr. Chan's mistress. She does not appear in the story, but she has an impact on Stephen's relationship with his father. After Stephen learns of the affair, he cannot see his father in the same way. Stephen's discovery of his father's infidelity is a loss of innocence for him.

THEMES

Isolation

Throughout *The Samurai's Garden*, there are ways that the characters are isolated. Perhaps the most obvious example is Stephen. At the start of the novel, he must leave his home and travel to Japan to recover from an illness. He feels lonely in Tarumi, where he is both physically isolated from his family and socially out of place: he is an outsider, a young Chinese man in a Japanese town where many of the young men have gone to join the army.

There are also examples of the divisions of social classes that isolate people from one another. Stephen's father admits that when he was young, he thought that Matsu's sister was pretty, but they were "kept apart by class and custom." The distinction between employer and servant is a blurry line. Both Matsu and Ching have worked for the Chan family so long that they are like members of the family, but there is a certain reserve and respect that the servants must always maintain for their masters. For example, Stephen remembers Ching waiting for Mr. Chan "to taste the food and give his approval." She "appeared as anxious as a small child." Stephen describes how he "always felt uncomfortable being waited on." He does not like to be reminded of the differences in their social positions.

The village of Yamaguchi is also an important symbol of isolation in the novel. The people there have been cast out by their families and their communities and forced to live apart from the rest of the world. Many people afflicted with leprosy feel so rejected and isolated because of their disease that they, like Matsu's sister Tomoko, commit suicide. Tsukiyama does, however, offer a hopeful note: the people living in Yamaguchi have banded together to create their own strong community, helping each other in bad times and celebrating the happy times.

Family Relationships

In *The Samurai's Garden*, Tsukiyama explores different types of family relationships. At first, Stephen's family does not seem to be at all close. When Stephen remembers a summer at the beach house in Tarumi years before, it certainly does not sound like the ideal family vacation: "My father had remained in Kobe that time because of business, while my mother spent

TOPICS FOR FURTHER STUDY

- Rather than a garden with lots of plants and trees, Matsu creates a rock garden for Sachi. She uses a rake to trace patterns in the pebbles. With print and online sources, research Japanese rock gardens and how they relate to Zen Buddhism. Find images of gardens that you find beautiful and, using a program like PowerPoint, create a presentation to demonstrate the importance and beauty of these gardens to your class.

- Although the main story in *The Samurai's Garden* takes place in a peaceful seaside town, the war in China is often a worry in the back of Stephen's mind as the Japanese army makes its way closer to his home in Hong Kong. Research Japan's attacks on China in 1937 and 1938. Make a time line that compares historical events with the events of the novel. Note the differences in what Stephen hears on the radio in Japan versus what he learns in letters from his friend King.

- In *Why Does the Coquí Sing?*, by Barbara Garland Polikoff, teenager Luz Sorrento moves from Chicago to Puerto Rico. Just as Stephen feels out of place when he first comes to Tarumi, sure that he will be bored and lonely, Luz is certain that she will not like living in Puerto Rico, but both Stephen and Luz find a place in their new homes. Read *Why Does the Coquí Sing?* and write an essay comparing Luz's coming-of-age journey with Stephen's, noting what people and events help them along the way.

- *The Samurai's Garden* is made up of Stephen's journal entries during his time in Tarumi. Think about the story from the other characters' points of view. For example, what does Kenzo feel when he comes to Matsu's garden and finds Sachi there? What goes through Matsu's mind when he learns that his friend Kenzo has committed suicide? Why does Keiko tell Stephen that she cannot see him any longer? Choose an important scene in the novel and write a journal entry as if you are that character, describing in detail what happened and how you would feel in that situation.

---

most of each day alone in the garden, shaded from the sun by a large, red-paper parasol." We also learn that the children do not live at home: Stephen is in school in Canton, while Anne and Henry are studying in Macao. The family situation seems even more hopeless when Stephen learns that his father has been having an affair for twelve years.

However, Stephen and Pie are close, and in spite of Mr. Chan's mistress, Stephen's parents seem to want to try to stay married. Stephen's relationship with his father is strained, but in some ways they know each other better by the end of the story than they did at the beginning. Stephen might not approve of his father's affair, but it helps him understand why his father has always divided his time between Hong Kong and

Kobe. For the first time, Mr. Chan shows some slight interest in Stephen's painting rather than dismissing it as unimportant.

Perhaps the strongest, most positive model for the importance of family in the novel is Matsu. Although when Matsu is first introduced, Stephen writes that "Matsu has lived alone ... for the past thirty years," the reader gradually discovers that Matsu is far from alone. He has an extended network of family and friends. He and his sister Fumiko still seem close, although she no longer lives in Tarumi; he often sees his friend Kenzo; and he has extended his affection and protection throughout the entire village of Yamaguchi.

It seems that Tsukiyama does not believe that one's family must include only blood

Stephen is sent to a Japanese seaside village to recover from tuberculosis. *(© Sam Dcruz | Shutterstock.com)*

relatives. There are several examples of people being cared for by someone other than their parents. Michiko adopts Sachi when she comes to Yamaguchi, afraid. Matsu takes Stephen under his wing, and it seems impossible to disagree with the fact that Sachi and Matsu have become a family, although they are not related and are never married in the legal sense. Sachi welcomes Stephen into their family, as she explains to him near the end of the novel: he has become like their child, giving them "the one thing we've lacked."

STYLE

Symbolism

The title of *The Samurai's Garden* is an important cue to the reader: gardens are a central symbol in the story, and by examining the role the gardens play, the reader can understand more about the characters. Throughout the novel, comparisons and connections Tsukiyama makes between the characters and the garden or

the earth symbolize something that is grounded, restorative, and good. Sometimes the references are fleeting, as when kind and patient Michiko is described as being "as silent as the earth." In other places, the relationship is more extensive, such as Stephen's interaction with Matsu's garden at the beach house.

At first, Stephen sees the garden's "quiet beauty," but his first response is to try to capture that beauty in a painting. Stephen calls the garden "seductive," and it is, but not in a negative sense: the garden draws Stephen out into life instead of letting him hide himself away. In several places, Tsukiyama shows how tending the garden leads to healing. For example, after Stephen is injured in the big storm, he and Sachi work to help Matsu repair the damage in the garden. Stephen writes in his journal, "Each day I work in the garden with Sachi, I feel stronger. The headaches lose their urgency once my hands dig deep into the cool, dark soil and I smell the damp dirt and pine."

Sachi's garden also helped her to heal. She explains to Stephen how she rebuilt her life with

Matsu's help: "As if I were a child learning to walk again, Matsu enticed me to take one step at a time: Bringing me first to Yamaguchi, then building me a house, and finally, creating this garden for me to tend." Sachi does not want flowers and plants in her garden. The fact that her garden is made of rocks and pebbles echoes the fact that her life may not be quite as full and rich as it would have been without her disease and isolation, but still the rocks are from the earth, and the garden helps her heal.

Epistolary Novel

An epistolary novel is one written as a series of documents. Often epistolary novels are in the form of letters, but they can also include diary entries, as in *The Samurai's Garden*; newspaper articles; and other documents. Because *The Samurai's Garden* consists almost completely of Stephen's journal entries, the reader gains an in-depth perspective on his thoughts, feelings, and motivations. Tsukiyama includes a few letters, which, along with the dialogue and some flashback stories that Stephen transcribes in his diary, provide hints of what other characters are thinking. When the story is largely limited to only one character's thoughts and feelings and told in the first person (where the narrator refers to himself as "I"), however, the reader must be careful not to assume that the words are unbiased truth. The story is not told by an impartial narrator, so everything has the slant of Stephen's own prejudices and possible misunderstanding.

HISTORICAL CONTEXT

Sino-Japanese War

In the mid-nineteenth century, Japan was an isolated country. Its leaders refused to allow trade with other nations, and for the most part, people maintained their traditional culture and way of life. Things began to change in July of 1853, when Commodore Matthew Perry of the US Navy demanded that Japan open its ports to trade with the West. Almost a year of negotiations followed, with Commodore Perry returning to Japan several times, but at last, on March 31, 1854, the Japanese signed the Treaty of Kanagawa, in which they promised to provide provisions for American ships and help shipwrecked American sailors. When the treaty was signed, Japan still did not want to allow trade but eventually gave in on this matter as well. The country underwent a rapid change from a largely agricultural economy to a modern industrialized nation. Japan is a relatively small island nation, however, and began to look to its neighbor, China, when it required more resources and a bigger economic market.

China was also a country that maintained its traditional society and politics. It was ruled by emperors until 1911, when revolutionaries proclaimed the first Chinese republic. Sun Yat-sen was elected president, but the new republic was not strong. It lacked military force, and for a decade, warlords squabbled over control of Beijing, the capital city. A group called the Guomindang became powerful, and a man named Chiang Kai-shek became their leader.

With the help of the Soviet Union and the Chinese Communist Party, which was also gaining in strength at the time, Chiang and the Guomindang managed to take control of China from the warlords. Then the Guomindang turned their attention to reducing the power and influence of the Communists. Some things improved under the republican government, but the day-to-day lives of most Chinese citizens did not change, so people increasingly looked to the Communists to make substantial changes.

In addition to the political turmoil inside China, diplomatic relations with Japan were worsening. In 1931, Japan attacked Manchuria, in the northeastern part of China, beginning years of armed conflict between the two countries. The League of Nations condemned the attack, but Japan refused to yield. Chiang chose not to confront Japan, however, and instead continued to direct his military power against the Communists.

The Japanese marched through China, taking control of much of the coast and many of the major cities. The Japanese army was notoriously brutal, killing and torturing civilians. Looting and arson were also common. The Chinese government estimates that as many as three hundred thousand people were killed in the Nanjing Massacre in 1937. Japan disputes this figure, claiming that number to be closer to forty thousand. Japan's attacks on China and the acts committed by the Japanese military have created a lasting rift between Japan and China that still sours relations between the two countries. Japan's aggression also angered more established Western world powers, contributing to the global conflicts that sparked World War II.

COMPARE & CONTRAST

- **1937–1938:** Japan attacks China in the hope of gaining control of the vast country, its economy, and its resources.

  Today: There is still political tension between China and Japan. In the summer of 2012, a dispute between the two countries regarding a chain of uninhabited islands (which provide access to huge deposits of oil and natural gas) in the East China Sea flares up. The conflict is believed to be fueled by Japan's past treatment of China.

- **1937–1938:** The Japanese army is merciless, killing not just Chinese soldiers but also civilians. Japan also uses germ warfare and brings some Chinese citizens back to Japan as forced labor.

  Today: Many Chinese citizens are still furious about Japan's actions in the war. In Beijing, there is a Museum of the War of Resistance against Japanese Aggression,

  and in 2005 the London *Independent* quoted a young schoolteacher visiting the museum: "I feel angry about the Japanese and their extremely cruel behavior towards the Chinese people." Some survivors of mistreatment continue to fight for compensation from the Japanese government.

- **1937–1938:** When left untreated, leprosy causes sores on the skin, muscle weakness, and nerve damage. Doctors understand that the disease does not spread easily, but many people fear catching leprosy and force those afflicted to less-populated areas. The available treatments are fairly ineffective.

  Today: Leprosy is sometimes called Hansen's disease. Modern antibiotics can kill the bacteria that cause the illness, and those with the disease are no longer isolated in "leper colonies."

CRITICAL OVERVIEW

Reviews of *The Samurai's Garden* vary widely. All of the reviewers claim to find the story interesting, but several complain of Tsukiyama's writing style. Writing for *Library Journal*, for example, one reviewer says the novel has "the potential to be a winner" but "is sunk by a flat, dull prose style, one-dimensional characters who fail to engage the reader's interest, and the author's tendency to tell rather than show." Similarly, the writer for *Kirkus Reviews* describes the story as "slow and detached" and criticizes Stephen's journal entries as "lacking emotion and passion." Even his romance with Keiko "does nothing to bring out his oblique personality." The reviewer concludes that *The Samurai's Garden* is an "engaging story ... dulled by the dim voice of its narrator" and seems to include both Tsukiyama and her character Stephen in this critique.

The Samurai's Garden is not the only one of Tsukiyama's novels to receive such harsh reviews. Her next novel, *The Street of a Thousand Blossoms*, is also criticized for its style. This novel is about two brothers, one who wants to become a sumo wrestler and one who hopes to make masks in a traditional Japanese Noh theater. Louisa Thomas, in a *New York Times* review, says that

> Tsukiyama's prose is simple and slow, at times seeming to strive for the kind of eloquence found in a Noh play, whose centuries-old art depends on stylized action to create tension and drama.... But the evident care that Tsukiyama takes in her language is sometimes undermined by the hard task of communicating a wealth of technical and historical information. It is also weakened by trite phrasing.

Other reviewers disagree, approving of Tsukiyama's style. A review in *Publisher's Weekly* describes the novel as "beautifully crafted" and asserts that "Tsukiyama's writing is crystalline

Matsu was Stephen's mentor. *(© Jane September /*
Shutterstock.com)

and delicate, notably in her evocation of time and place." Donna Seaman in *Booklist* agrees, calling *The Samurai's Garden* "an extraordinarily graceful and moving novel about goodness and beauty" and naming Tsukiyama "a wise and spellbinding storyteller."

In *A to Z of American Women Writers*, Kort also calls Tsukiyama a "gifted storyteller." Kort believes that Tsukiyama's writing is "controlled and straightforward but also richly descriptive" and praises in particular Tsukiyama's ability to portray "the challenging lives of Asian women realistically but with dignity and sensitivity."

CRITICISM

Kristen Sarlin Greenberg

Greenberg is a freelance writer and editor with a background in literature and philosophy. In the following essay, she examines how the characters' identities vary with the setting in The Samurai's Garden.

Early in *The Samurai's Garden*, very soon after Stephen first arrives in Tarumi, he senses the changes that being in a new place can bring about. He writes in his diary, "Here in Tarumi it's different. Even the light is revealing; you can't miss the smallest nuance, the slightest sound. It's as if the world were concentrated into just these small rooms." With this, Tsukiyama makes it clear that Stephen's time will be spent not only healing his body after his bout of tuberculosis but also learning and maturing.

At the beach house, Stephen is more introspective, but it is more than just having spare time that leads him to grow more thoughtful. The fact that he is away from home means that he is more aware of his surroundings and more open to new experiences. Where he is influences how he sees the world, how he interacts with other people, and how he sees himself. Throughout the novel, Tsukiyama explores the issue of identity, and there are many instances in which characters' sense of their own identity or how they are seen by others changes based on where they are.

The first clues the reader has of this association between identity and location come when Stephen first writes in his journal about his father. Mr. Chan often travels to Kobe for his work, and Stephen explains that "it seems the apartment he keeps in Japan is more his home than our family house in Hong Kong. He makes his life in both places." Mr. Chan's behavior "seems at times more Japanese than Chinese," bowing with his "eyes averted."

Mr. Chan visits Stephen after he has been at the beach house for a little while, and the thoughtfulness that comes over Stephen when he arrives in Tarumi is already evident. Stephen and his father do not spend much time together at home—Stephen was studying in Canton, and Mr. Chan frequently travels for business. In Tarumi, however, there is nothing to distract them. Stephen studies his father and realizes "it had been a long time since I had so closely felt his presence." Because Stephen is in Tarumi, in his more thoughtful mood, he is open to seeing his father more clearly.

Mr. Chan surprises Stephen: rather than his usual business suit, he is "wearing white slacks, a white shirt and hat," and to Stephen, "he appeared more like an acquaintance of our family, someone I hadn't seen in a long time." When Stephen walks Mr. Chan to the train station for

WHAT DO I READ NEXT?

- In *Women of the Silk* (1991), Tsukiyama brings to life the world of silk workers in a Chinese village in the 1920s. The young women become friends and go on strike to improve their working conditions.

- Looking for his place in the world, a Mexican American teenager struggles with his family and neighborhood gangs in *Parrot in the Oven: Mi Vida* (2004) by Victor Martinez. This coming-of-age novel is a string of vignettes rather than a single continuous narrative.

- The Sino-Japanese War does not often receive much attention in itself because it contributed to the start of the larger conflict of World War II. *When Tigers Fight: The Story of the Sino-Japanese War, 1937–1945* (1983), by Dick Wilson, is one of the few histories of the war written in English. Wilson uses first-hand accounts to bring the events of the war to life.

- Amy Tan's *The Joy Luck Club* (1989) tells the story of four Chinese American women and their daughters. Jing-Mei, one of the younger generation, learns that her mother abandoned twin babies while fleeing a Japanese attack during World War II. Like *The Samurai's Garden*, *The Joy Luck Club* explores themes of cultural identity and portrays strained relationships between parents and children.

- *Snow Country* (1956), by Nobel Prize–winning author Yasunari Kawabata, is considered a classic of Japanese literature. Set in a hot-spring resort in Japan's coldest region, the novel portrays the melancholy love affair between Shimamura, a wealthy, self-centered gentleman from Tokyo, and Komako, a local girl struggling to become a successful geisha.

- *The Good Earth* (1931), by Pearl S. Buck, tells of life in a rural Chinese village. It was influential in creating public sympathy for China and animosity toward Japan on the eve of World War II.

his trip back to Kobe, he becomes "again the father I recognized in a business suit."

It is also important that, as the reader later learns, the time that Mr. Chan spends in Kobe is spent with his mistress of twelve years. It is as if Mr. Chan is several different people: the husband and father in Hong Kong, the man in casual white clothes at the beach house in Tarumi who treats Stephen more as an equal, and the businessman, "more Japanese than Chinese," who lives in Kobe with his mistress.

Setting is also important for the people of Yamaguchi. When Matsu first takes Stephen to meet Sachi, he says, "Yes ... she's a leper," as if it defines who she is, but it is because she lives in Yamaguchi that she is not restricted by her illness. In Tarumi, she could never feel that she was anything other than a "leper" because of the prejudice and fear of her neighbors. Even Kenzo, the man she had intended to marry, calls her a "monster." She is not a monster, of course, but if she had stayed in Tarumi, she might have always felt that she was. Instead, she lives in Yamaguchi, where people respond to her based on who she is rather than on how she looks because of her disease.

This is true for all of the people living in Yamaguchi: their isolation allows them to live without fear and to be who they are rather than being identified solely by their disease. When Stephen first arrives in the town, he cannot take his eyes off the wounds of the villagers. To him, "it looked as if they were all wearing monstrous masks that I kept waiting for them to remove." However, once Stephen learns to see past the effects of the illness, he befriends Sachi and her neighbors. He helps them during the fire and shares their joy once the damaged homes are repaired, a celebration that he calls "one of the best nights of my life." Yamaguchi is the one place where those afflicted with leprosy have no need to wear a mask and hide themselves, making setting central to their sense of identity and how they are seen by the world.

There are exceptions to the overall pattern in the novel of characters' identities changing with the setting. The Chan family servant, Ching, is a steady, never-changing presence. Stephen describes her as "set in her ways." When Stephen was a boy and his family traveled, Ching

> would only eat Chinese food, so she brought her own white rice, long beans, lotus roots, and soy sauce chicken in jars and clay pots. Pretty soon the rich aroma filled our room so that if

> **PERHAPS STEPHEN COULD FIND NO BETTER ROLE MODEL THAN MATSU, FOR IN YAMAGUCHI, MATSU BECOMES THE SAMURAI OF THE NOVEL'S TITLE: NOBLE AND LOYAL, LIVING TO SERVE, PROTECTOR OF THE VILLAGE."**

we closed our eyes, we couldn't tell if we were in Tokyo or at home.

Ching seems to alter her setting to suit her preference rather than allowing herself to be changed. Because Ching is a secondary character and not as important as the central characters of the story, she does not need to be as fully developed. We do not need to see her grow and change like Stephen and Sachi. The implication remains, however, that for good or ill, some people, like the character Ching, stay the same regardless of where they are or whom they are with.

Perhaps Matsu is Tsukiyama's most interesting example of a character changing with his location. When Stephen first meets Matsu, he is identified clearly as a servant. Stephen explains that Matsu "has worked for our family since he was a boy." When they arrive at the beach house, Matsu opens the gate and gestures for Stephen to pass through first. Matsu is quiet and gruff by turns, but he is a respectful and capable servant, cooking for Stephen and drawing his bath.

In Yamaguchi, however, Matsu is no longer subservient. Almost as soon as they enter the village, Stephen seems to sense the change in Matsu. Stephen is overwhelmed by seeing the villagers' wounds, which would indeed be shocking, and Matsu takes charge. He leads Stephen toward Sachi's house, and Stephen "follow[s] Matsu as if he were the master." Once they are inside Sachi's house, Stephen finds it "strange to be standing in a different house with Matsu, seeing him for the first time in a new light. He seemed gentler, less in command."

The fact that Stephen sees Matsu as "less in command" seems to contradict the trend of Matsu's behaving less as a servant and more as a leader in Yamaguchi, but Matsu's gruffness in the beach house in Tarumi might very well result

from his discomfort at being in an awkward position: Matsu is supposed to be a respectful servant. It may be difficult for him to maintain his role as caretaker, always polite and deferential, even when interacting with someone as young and inexperienced as Stephen. Matsu is much more at home in Yamaguchi, where he is "the master of the house." Because he feels more sure of himself in Sachi's home, Matsu is more at ease and seems "gentler" to Stephen. It is in Yamaguchi that Matsu appears to his best advantage: showing his affection for and devotion to Sachi, doing everything he can to help all of the villagers, and teaching Stephen by example.

The Samurai's Garden is a coming-of-age novel. The reader watches as Stephen learns more about himself and the kind of man he wants to be. He disapproves of his father's affair, but as he writes in his diary, "Every time I see him, it's with new eyes." Stephen is beginning to realize that he himself, not his father, is the one going through changes, and it is not an easy process. By the end of the story, Stephen feels that he is "a stranger, like I no longer belonged anywhere." However, he will return to his family and try to live according to what he has learned during his year in Tarumi. Perhaps Stephen could find no better role model than Matsu, for in Yamaguchi, Matsu becomes the samurai of the novel's title: noble and loyal, living to serve, protector of the village.

Source: Kristen Sarlin Greenberg, Critical Essay on "The Samurai's Garden," in *Novels for Students*, Gale, Cengage Learning, 2013.

Gail Tsukiyama

In the following essay, Tsukiyama presents details about why she writes, her work habits, her choice of settings, and the importance of being truthful in writing.

Gail Tsukiyama's novels are finely woven tapestries in which the threads of her impeccable workmanship are invisible. The reader is transported seamlessly into the multicultural worlds of Chinese silk workers (*Women of the Silk*), a humble Samurai (*The Samurai's Garden*) or the intimate landscape of a mother dealing with her daughter's illness (*Dreaming Water*). Tsukiyama's language is lyrical and her use of detail precise and telling, always serving the characters. With beauty and ease, she makes the characters real and their stories powerful and moving.

The samurai's garden (© SipaPhoto / Shutterstock.com)

Raised in San Francisco by a Chinese mother and Japanese father, Tsukiyama often explores multicultural themes. The author of five bestselling novels, she taught creative writing at San Francisco State University and the University of California-Berkeley. She will speak June 24 at the Santa Barbara Writers Conference.

Credits: Her novels also include *Night of Many Dreams* and *The Language of Threads*.

On writing: Writing gave me my voice—both literally and figuratively. When I was young I was very quiet, someone who preferred to stand in the shadows, and it wasn't until I began writing in high school and college that I really began speaking. Since then, my primary motivation has been the gift of discovery, of crossing new borders into worlds a reader may not know about and yet can identify with. In the end, the more I write about other cultures, the more that I see how much we're all alike as a humanity. One constant theme that seems to reoccur in all my novels has been that of social groups living apart from the general society—the subcultures within a culture. I'm interested in how we as a humanity persevere. In a way, it has become a starting point for almost all my books.

Work habits: I try to write every day, even if I get very little down on the page. It's the thought process and the discipline that's important to me. I have two very different places in which I do most of my writing, in two different locations, one closer to the city and the other in a more rural setting. But, if need be, I can acclimate to new places without many problems. I'm not one of those writers who works well writing in public places such as cafés, bookstores or parks. I'd end up people-watching and getting nothing written.

Setting: In all my novels, most of which have been set in China or Japan, setting has always been another character to me. It's just as much a voyage of discovery for me, the writer, as it is for the reader. I'm constantly trying to incorporate everything into the flow of the story without appearing intrusive. I've always believed that if I could make the reader feel comfortable in a completely different culture, they would understand the characters moving within that world.

"

WAR AND LEPROSY ARE CAREFULLY PARALLELED IN TSUKIYAMA'S NOVEL. BOTH START SMALL, ESCALATE, GROW IN SECRET, AND LEAVE VICTIMS AND CARNAGE, BUT AS TSUKIYAMA PRESENTS THE TWO CONDITIONS THERE ARE CLEAR DISTINCTIONS."

It's so important to keep in mind all the influences that go into developing a character and how it affects the direction in which he or she will move through the plot. Where a character lives and grows up defines so much of who she is and how she thinks; race, language, religion, education, profession, how she looks and what she wears all stem from where and how she lives. These telling details not only create a sense of place, but a sense of character.

Finding the heart of the story: Sometimes it takes writing half of the book before I get to know my characters and realize the direction they're going in. Writing is often rewriting, learning as you go along. There have been times when I didn't realize the heart of the story until it was finished.

Biggest challenge: The sheer amount of time and energy it takes to create a beginning, middle and end that sings.

Advice: Always tell the truth. Or the truth of the story you're writing. Be passionate about the story and write it without the concerns of being published. Always remember that the act of writing, of creating a story, is the real gift.

Source: Gail Tsukiyama, "How I Write," in *Writer*, Vol. 120, No. 7, July 2007, pp. 66.

Claire Manes

In the following essay, Manes analyzes the treatment of leprosy and war as they develop in the novel and suggests "that despite centuries of prejudice against leprosy the book valorizes the woman Sachi and decries the war as the new leprosy."

In 1937, Japan invaded China. In that same year Sachi, a resident of the fictional leper village of Yamaguchi, Japan, returned to her hometown of Tarumi for the first time in forty years

and told her story to Stephen Chan, an outsider from China. The two seemingly unrelated events, one historical and one fictional, are skillfully woven together in Gail Tsukiyama's book *The Samurai's Garden* written and published some forty years after the episodes at a time when Japan was making some reparation for its actions in the Sino-Japanese war and for the unnecessary incarceration of leprosy patients in Japan.

The novel written by Gail Tsukiyama, herself an American of Chinese Japanese ancestry, relates the coming of age of young Stephen Chan, a Chinese youth who is in Japan recuperating from tuberculosis. The story, according to correspondence with the author, "explores themes of illness, courage, beauty and isolation against the reality of war" (email March 31, 2001). Lonely in his new surroundings, Stephen admits to "thinking [of] my time in Tarumi [like] a quiet resembling death" (Tsukiyama). That loneliness and emptiness open him to the invitation offered by Matsu, the caretaker of Stephen's ancestral beach home, to "visit a friend who lives in a small mountain village near here." Matsu explains that "Yamaguchi was a small village in the mountains also called the Village of Lepers." Once in Yamaguchi, Stephen initially recalls stories of China "where lepers had always been feared and shunned [. . . forced to live on the streets, left to beg or eat rats, while they simply rotted away." He soon becomes curious rather than fearful, however, and is rapidly captivated by Matsu's friend Sachi whose face on the left side not only showed the ravages of the disease but also revealed a right side which was "the single most beautiful face I'd ever seen." Stephen's enchantment with the woman "who had instilled a sense of richness and mystery in Tarumi" leads him during his time in Tarumi to discover the woman behind the veil.

In his ensuing pilgrimages to Yamaguchi and in Sachi's brave returns to Tarumi, Stephen discovers not the disabled resident of a leper village, but a woman with a story. This story recorded by Stephen, himself an outsider, subverts the notion of leprosy as a stigmatizing condition which leaves its supposedly unclean sufferers as outcasts. Tsukiyama through Stephen's journal does not shirk from harsh descriptions of the disease, but she manages to reveal a woman who though physically scarred by her condition and lost to her family and fiancé has made a life for herself and her soul mate husband Matsu, a resident of Tarumi and a man free of leprosy and leprophobia. The author depicts a woman who "let[s] go of the past [by] facing it again" and ultimately appears in Tarumi "in the bright light of day." Not only does Tsukiyama subvert the prejudice against leprosy in her story of Sachi, she further undermines it by paralleling Sachi's story with the gradual revelation/deception about the Sino-Japanese war which figures in her novel as a discordant chord. Tsukiyama in her book develops both horrors, leprosy and war, as she presents the story of Sachi spiraling into light and the story of war barreling into darkness. This paper proposes to analyze the treatment of both tropes as they develop in the novel *The Samurai's Garden* and to suggest that despite centuries of prejudice against leprosy the book valorizes the woman Sachi and decries the war as the new leprosy.

The analogy works. Leprosy and war share some common elements: secrecy; small eruptions that ravage bodies, families, villages, and countries leaving people disabled, isolated, and alienated. However, there are differences as well. Leprosy in its effects on others is neither more nor less than a slightly contagious disease. It preys mysteriously on a small minority of people whose genetic makeup lacks immunity to the condition. Contrary to prejudice and erroneous notions about the disease, it is not caused by sin or dissolute living; sufferers of the disease do not choose or cause their condition. In Sachi's words, it is the disease that does the choosing. War, however, represents a more complex contagion that is on some level chosen. Ironically, leprosy for much of human history has been the more feared condition. "Leper" is a term of opprobrium; "warrior" is a designation of valor. Tsukiyama by setting the story of Sachi at the brink of the Sino-Japanese war juxtaposes these two eruptions, subverts long held attitudes toward leprosy, and offers readers the opportunity to draw their own conclusions about the condition.

Tsukiyama uses as her narrator Stephen Chan, an outsider himself who experienced alienation in China both because of his good looks and his tuberculosis which engenders isolation and looks of shock at his appearance. In Japan as the war with his country progresses, he also experiences the position of the reviled outsider, a position familiar to those with leprosy. Stephen's journal recorded from September 15, 1937,

through October 29, 1938, gives him the "opportunity to find [his] own way," but the time also enables him to record Sachi's story which she tells for the first time in more than forty years. It is that story and Stephen's fascination with it that subvert the prejudices about leprosy that folklorist Alan Dundes would characterize as "folk ideas [. . .] the unstated premises/which underlie the thoughts and actions of a given group of people" (Dundes, *Folk Ideas* 95–96).

Folk ideas about leprosy include fears about its contagion, notions about victims losing limbs, and tasteless jokes about the dissolution of the victims' bodies. Such unsubstantiated and erroneous ideas about the condition have led to the isolation and stigmatization of Hansen's disease patients and have made the term "leper" representative of a reviled outsider. However, the Yamaguchi residents that Stephen meets and their community that he writes about reflect a far different image and represent more closely Dundes's notion of a folk as, "any group of people whatsoever who share at least one common/factor [. . . and who] have some traditions which it calls its own" (*Who*, 6–7). Marcia Gaudet in her writing about Hansen's disease residents in Carville, Louisiana, shows them to be a "true folk community [. . .] isolated from the rest of the world with their own traditions, celebrations, stories, and views of the outside world." Gail Tsukiyama's novel depicts a similar community, a village created in the late 1800s, "[w]hen some of those who had the disease [and] were no longer wanted by others in town, [. . .] took what few belongings they had and went up into the mountains, hoping to die peacefully. Away from the cruelty of the healthy."

As Tsukiyama's story progresses it reveals the village of Yamaguchi as a community with its own old timers, narrative traditions, and festal celebrations. Although Yamaguchi is a fictional village, such communities did exist in Japan in the early 1930s. Susan L. Burns in her essay "From Leper Village to Leprosarium: Public Health, Nationalism and the Culture of Exclusion in Japan" describes one such village, Yu no Zawa, which began in the late 19th century near, but isolated from, the hot springs town of Kusatsu. In 1902, "Yu no Zawa had a population of 126 people, which included thirty-two married couples. Five children had been born there in the preceding year. The residents worked at a variety of professions." This village could be Carville, Louisiana or Tsukiyama's Yamaguchi, Japan where "[M]en were gathered in small groups sipping tea and talking while others worked in small gardens, and women sat mending clothes." All three villages exhibited characteristics similar to any other small village, but all are different in that their residents were forced there because of leprosy that left them stigmatized in their home communities.

This condition, leprosy, happened gradually appearing first as a "rash . . . no larger than a yen coin," a "rash . . . that wouldn't go away," but eventually spread. So insignificant was its initial appearance that the early victims of the disease "thought it was nothing." It was a condition that had "been incubating for years before it showed its face." Once it became visible, however, the unaffected "wanted the affected ones sent away from them." Many chose suicide "to end [their] misery and restore honor to [their] families"; others fled to the village of Yamaguchi. Although the condition was slow moving and subtle, it was virulent in the physical and emotional devastation that it caused its victims.

War, too, in Tsukiyama's novel has small beginnings before it erupts into the conflict and violence that lasted through the end of World War II. As Stephen first describes it, it seems small and relatively innocuous. His initial account simply notes "the news came over the radio that the Japanese had captured Tientsin and surrounded Peking." The journal entry seems as insubstantial as the small rash that first appeared on Sachi's arm or the rumors of Yamaguchi village seen as "a place for our kind in the mountains." Both Hansen's disease and the Sino-Japanese war in *The Samurai's Garden* begin with minor eruptions and stories told through rumors and third parties. Neither condition initially presages the horrors that ensue, but both rapidly develop into full-scale devastation as the seemingly innocent rash of leprosy "won't go away" and the Japanese begin "swarming all over China."

The rash on Sachi's arm grows and spreads to her face finally leaving her severely scarred and veiled. The rash that is war also grows from seemingly innocuous reports on the radio to descriptions that scream for attention. It "escalates" and becomes "insane." The Japanese war efforts are "fierce" and leave the "carnage of death and destruction." Implicit in the term carnage is the sense of physical destruction, a casualty of both leprosy and war. Tsukiyama's description

of Yamaguchi residents with "stumps of [. . .] arms" and "heads and hands bandaged" parallels the devastation of war. There are "Chinese losses, whose numbers were so large, so unreal, that it would take the shrill voiced woman on the radio days to count them all." The numbers of war dead far surpass the victims of leprosy in Yamaguchi, but both images testify to the physical destruction of the nameless victims created by both contagions.

The contagion of leprosy and war is rapid, physically debilitating, and noisy. Sachi recalls that at her diagnosis "a terrible scream [. . .] filled my head, drowning all the rest of [the doctor's] words" and again a "scream [. . .] brought the entire village to the door of the shack" when she first saw Michiko, a woman badly defaced by leprosy. The war, too, is announced with raucous, grating noise that fills the airwaves in Matsu's home and assaults Stephen's ears. The news of war "blared" on the radio; was announced in a "high, scratchy voice"; and "interrupted" the "music from Matsu's radio."

Noisy eruptions in the case of both leprosy and war leave the victims not only disfigured but displaced and homeless. The war leaves its victims as refugees with "gaunt, desolate faces begging for money and understanding" and "starving in the streets." They appear like those people suffering from leprosy who "were forced to live on the streets" as outcasts, victims of the insidious eruptions they did not control. Likewise both groups are forced to seek makeshift shelters of their own devising. Those with leprosy in Tsukiyama's novel find a place in the village of Yamaguchi where they built homes "painstakingly pieced together with mismatched scraps of wood." The Chinese refugees also "built their makeshift homes in the crowded streets of Hong Kong." They are "makeshift houses made of whatever they can find, like wood scraps or cardboard."

Not only are victims of both leprosy and war isolated by injury and dislocation, they are victims of a public secret as defined by Michael Taussig in his book *Defacement: Public Secret and the Labor of the Negative*. Their stories are public secrets "which [are] generally known but cannot be articulated." Historically, the full truth about both Hansen's disease patients in Japan in the 1930s and the Japanese atrocities in the Sino-Japanese war is only now gradually being revealed. Fictionally in *The Samurai's*

Garden in 1937–1938 both are secrets. Sachi's family assumes she has died; she and Matsu hide their relationship from Kenzo, her fiancé who disowned her after her diagnosis; and the village of Tarumi does not reveal the leprosy in its midst. Matsu explains, "It was kept quiet among the local villagers. After all, Tarumi was a place for outsiders to come on holiday. If they'd heard about the disease, no one would return. We didn't want to frighten anyone away." Likewise the brutality of the war was kept secret. Iris Chang's book *The Rape of Nanking: the Forgotten Holocaust* records the "deliberate attempt [even until today] by certain Japanese to distort history." Tsukiyama's novel also testifies to the secrecy surrounding the Nanking invasion. Although Stephen learns about much of the war through raucous radio commentary that interrupts Matsu's classical music, "there had been nothing on Matsu's radio about the massacre." It is a secret that Stephen learns a month later in a letter from his college friend King who writes, "I'm sure you've heard of the Nanking massacre [. . .] thousands of innocent Chinese men, women, and children have been killed and raped needlessly by the Japanese bastards."

Secrecy and dissimulation also figure into the way some Hansen's disease patients negotiate their stories. They recognize that those with war injuries are often valorized or viewed with sympathy, while leprosy patients may find themselves feared, reviled, or curiously objectified. They, too, are tainted by the notion that war images are perhaps a more acceptable presentation of their condition. Marcia Gaudet in her article, "Telling It Slant: Personal Narrative, Tall Tales, and the Reality of Leprosy," recounts the experiences of those with Hansen's disease who cover or explain their injuries with "responses [such as] 'I was in an accident,' or 'I was burned' or 'War injury.'" One man's story which "may be on its way to becoming a local legend in the extended Carville community" illustrates one approach to explaining the injuries from Hansen's disease. It is an approach that seems particularly relevant to this study.

As Gaudet relates it, Billy, whose hands were badly deformed from untreated Hansen's disease, responds to those who question him with two stories, one the truth, the other a lie. He offers his listeners the option of choosing for themselves the real story. In relating his tale he

notes that he clearly states at the beginning that the first story is a lie and the second is the truth. After he spins his lie regaling his listeners with his heroics in the Korean War, he tells them again, "'Now that's the lie. The true story is I got leprosy.'" Invariably the listeners choose to or appear to believe the lie. Leprosy as an explanation for a disfigured body is perhaps too remote or too uncomfortable a reality to contemplate. War injuries seem to be more understandable and acceptable.

Tsukiyama uses a rather different tact [sic] in representing the carnage of leprosy and war. She graphically describes the injuries from leprosy without hiding their cause. She is clear sighted and unflinching in describing the devastation of untreated leprosy, but she also ameliorates her images. Sachi's face is seen in its devastation, but according to Stephen, its "unblemished right side [is] the single most beautiful face I'd ever seen." By contrast the injuries from war in *The Samurai's Garden* are not personalized and they clearly depict carnage. Letters from home and accounts on the radio recount "Chinese . . . being slaughtered" and "thousands of innocent Chinese men, women and children . . . killed and raped needlessly." The injuries from war and leprosy coalesce in Stephen's "saki-induced sleep that had me dreaming of Yamaguchi. Only instead of being in Japan, the village was in the midst of a bustling Hong Kong, the cars and crowds going about their daily business. And in the center of it all, I could see Pie passing out warm clothes and wrapping white bandages around Sachi and Hiro's eaten away limbs."

War and leprosy are carefully paralleled in Tsukiyama's novel. Both start small, escalate, grow in secret, and leave victims and carnage, but as Tsukiyama presents the two conditions there are clear distinctions. The direction she takes in the development of her story clearly valorizes Sachi and leaves one reading war as the new leprosy with Stephen as its latest named victim.

Sachi, from the first, is seen not as a victim of leprosy but as a woman scarred by a disfiguring disease. She is a gentle, soft spoken woman, a gracious hostess and a good friend, sensitive to the discomfort and needs of others. She is the one who for Stephen "instilled a sense of richness and mystery in Tarumi." She takes charge of her life, caring for her garden, serving Matsu and Stephen during their visits to her, and courageously returning to

Tarumi forty years after she was exiled because of her condition. She tells her own story at Stephen's behest, but she tells it in her own way and in her own time. While she clearly acknowledges the pain that her condition has caused her, she is not identified by the disease. She has the "ulcers" and "white scaly scabs" of untreated leprosy, but these are accidents of her appearance, not the essence of her person. As Stephen sees her, she is a woman of beauty and grace who captivates him and whose "damaged side of her face seemed to glow in the sunlight." As Stephen portrays her, Sachi is more rhapsodized than reviled. Her luminosity seems to link her to the "kami [or life force of . . .] the sun known as the goddess Amaterasu" (French 200) and to a Buddhist legend related by Burns. In the "eighth-century empress Kimyo [. . .] offered to bathe personally one thousand people. [When confronted with the one thousandth person] a leper [. . . T]he empress hesitated for a moment, but then proceeded to wash him with care. When she was finished the afflicted one emanated a bright light and revealed himself to be a boddhisatva [a representation of the Buddha]" (Burns 106).

Sachi, a woman of beauty and grace has as her soul mate the warrior Matsu, her "savior" and the "true kami of Yamaguchi." As Stephen sees him he is a man who has "a strong face [. . . L]ike a samurai." Tsukiyama describes this gentle man as one who is out of the fray of the Sino-Japanese war, but who possesses not only the face but the duty, devotion and steadfast loyalty of a samurai as aptly described in Thomas Cleary's text, *Code of the Samurai: A Modern Translation of the Bushido Shoshinshu of Taira Shigesuke.* Like "the bridge [that] represented the samurai's difficult path from this world to the afterlife," Matsu mediates leprosy to Sachi and the war to Stephen. He has lived with the reality of leprosy at least as long as Sachi but possesses no fear or revulsion of it. When the rash chose Sachi, Matsu promised to "take care of everything," a promise he kept throughout Sachi's forty years in Yamaguchi. He knew before Sachi did about the existence of Yamaguchi, and from leprosy's initial appearance in Tarumi he accepted a young doctor's enlightened reassurance "that the disease couldn't be spread by simple touch."

Matsu interprets the war to Stephen in the same patient, diligent way telling him early in the conflict that "Japan is like a young woman who thinks too much of herself. She is bound to get herself into trouble." Although he cannot stop the spread of the war any more than he could control the spread of leprosy, Matsu does remain sensitive to Stephen's position as a young Chinese man in Japan learning about the invasion of his country through reports on a Japanese radio. When the "high scratchy voice coming from his radio had just declared another Japanese advancement in their struggle against Shanghai Matsu leaned over and played with the dial until a Bach concerto filled the room." His is the wisdom and strength that carry both Sachi and Stephen. He plants a garden for Sachi when she is still "filled with anger and rage." It is this garden that enables her "to relish the fact that its beauty was one that no disease or person could ever take away from me. [. . .] I was no longer myself at all, but part of the garden." Stephen too learns important lessons from Matsu who "moved slowly, meticulously to cut back the branch in just the right place."

"'Isn't it interesting, Stephen-san,' he said 'how sometimes you must cut away something in order to make it grow back stronger? . . .

It may seem lonely and barren at first, only to flower again in the spring.'"

The terse, stoical, reticent warrior Matsu continues in what may be his longest conversation in the book. Shaking his head at "the stupidity" of war, he continues "'[W]e aren't so different, humans [. . .] and plants. We are all a part of one nature and from each other we learn how to live . . . .

'I won't say we humans don't still have much to learn. Sometimes we love and hate without thought. . . . But in the end, Stephen-san, you can only look back, hoping everything that happens in your life is for a purpose.'"

Although Matsu remains philosophical about both leprosy and war, Tsukiyama's portrayal of the war represents it as an essentially virulent condition. By the novel's end Sachi's position as a reviled and condemned outsider has been subverted as she and Matsu have been linked with the Japanese belief in kami and with numinous revelations. Now a new villain, the "Japanese devils," has appeared, and war's virulent contagion has created a new victim. Stephen's face now bears the mark of an outsider. The novel moves toward the light for Sachi who by story's end has come again to visit in Tarumi, "daring all in the bright light of day" and for Matsu who would "maybe eventually move to Yamaguchi." Leprosy remains a reality for Sachi, but it is not her defining characteristic. Her face reveals her suffering, but it is also testimony to her courage and endurance. The stigma of leprosy has been subverted in Tsukiyama's portrayal of Sachi not as its victim but as a courageous woman who happens to have a debilitating condition.

The face of Stephen, however, has been marked because of the war which barrels rapidly toward new destruction. This Chinese youth who had earlier attested to a charmed life and a face that was "too good looking" is now "trapped behind the bamboo fence." War has begun to separate him from loved ones as surely as leprosy ever did. Initially he experiences "stares . . . not only because I was a Chinese face in their village, but . . . also [because] there were very few young men in Tarumi." Earlier in China, he had experienced only the subtleties of the encroaching war as "small group of soldiers loitering in public places, rifles slung on their shoulders . . . appeared harmless." By story's end, however, Stephen has become a victim of the leprosy of war. More and more he realizes he is the hated outsider and despite the refuge of Tarumi, he recognizes "it would just be a matter of time" before he would have to leave. The "glare [that] cut right through [with . . .] a look so full of hate," indicated to him that he was "amidst some kind of enemy here in Tarumi." It was an enemy that no longer appeared "harmless" but "menacing." Tarumi has once again ceased to be a place of refuge for those with marked faces. It forces Stephen out just as surely as it forced Sachi out forty years earlier. No longer can he "be like everyone else." Ironically now, however, he is very much like his beloved Sachi, for he too now bears a mark that is reviled and his awareness of his condition causes "an unexpected blow to my stomach" every bit as visceral as Sachi's "scream" when she first learned of her diagnosis. Stephen has become the new victim, an outcast and refugee, a Chinese enemy in the midst of the Japanese people in their own homeland and he now experiences "what it meant to be a . . . disgraced one."

Source: Claire Manes, "The Representation of Leprosy and War in *The Samurai's Garden*," in *Atenea*, Vol. 25, No. 2, December 2005, pp. 49–59.

Publishers Weekly

In the following review, a contributor calls The Samurai's Garden *"a quiet tale of affection that transcends geopolitics."*

In this beautifully crafted second novel by Tsukiyama (*Women of the Silk*), the world outside the small Japanese village of Tarumi is a world of polarities: East vs. West, Japanese vs. Chinese, etc. Within Tarumi, however, a person can exist as simply as a polished stone in a garden. When Chinese university student Stephen Chan's tuberculosis pushes him to the thin border of death, his father sends him from their home in Hong Kong to the family's beach house in Tarumi. The year is 1937, and the Japanese Imperial Army is on a steamrolling conquest through China. In idyllic Tarumi, however, Stephen swims, paints and grows healthier, meanwhile befriending Matsu, the caretaker of the house. Strong, silent Matsu is the epitome of the samurai, displaying his aristocratic heritage in the tender way that he cares for his exquisite garden. The storm that demolishes years of work is a counterpart to the grief that washes over Matsu when he thinks of his beloved, Sachi, who is a leper. Becoming engrossed in the lovers' tragic story, Stephen stays on in Tarumi, aware that by doing so he is avoiding a confrontation with his own father, who has confessed to an affair that will break up the family. Tsukiyama's writing is crystalline and delicate, notably in her evocation of time and place. This quiet tale of affection between people whose countries are at war speaks of a humanity that transcends geopolitics.

Source: Review of *The Samurai's Garden*, in *Publishers Weekly*, Vol. 242, No. 5, January 30, 1995, pp. 85–86.

Donna Seaman

In the following review, Seaman applauds Tsukiyama as a storyteller and notes that she has extended herself in this latest novel.

Praised for her lovely first novel, *Women of the Silk* (1991), Tsukiyama has extended herself even further and written an extraordinarily graceful and moving novel about goodness and beauty. The daughter of a Chinese mother and a Japanese father, Tsukiyama used the Japanese invasion of China during the late 1930s as a somber backdrop for her unusual story about a 20-year-old Chinese painter named Stephen who is sent to his family's summer home in a Japanese coastal village to recover from a bout with tuberculosis. Here he is cared for by Matsu, a reticent housekeeper and a master gardener. Over the course of a remarkable year, Stephen learns Matsu's secret and gains not only physical strength, but also profound spiritual insight. Matsu is a samurai of the soul, a man devoted to doing good and finding beauty in a cruel and arbitrary world, and Stephen is a noble student, learning to appreciate Matsu's generous and nurturing way of life and to love

Matsu's soul mate, gentle Sachi, a woman afflicted with leprosy. Tsukiyama is a wise and spellbinding storyteller.

Source: Donna Seaman, Review of *The Samurai's Garden*, in *Booklist*, Vol. 91, No. 13, March 1, 1995, p. 180.

SOURCES

Andressen, Curtis, "Japan–Profile," in *Encyclopedia of Modern Asia*, Vol. 3, edited by Karen Christensen and David Levinson, Charles Scribner's Sons, 2002, pp. 204–10.

"Conversations: Acclaimed Novelist Gail Tsukiyama," in *Water Bridge Review*, http://www.waterbridgereview. org/122007/cnv_tsukiyama.php (accessed August 30, 2012).

Eimer, David, "Chinese Look Back in Anger at Japan's Wartime Atrocities," in *Independent*, August 15, 2005, http://www.ezilon.com/information/printer_7957.shtml (accessed September 13, 2012).

"Gail Tsukiyama's Biography" Red Room website, http://redroom.com/member/gail-tsukiyama/bio (accessed August 30, 2012).

Kenley, David L., "Republican China," in *Encyclopedia of Modern Asia*, edited by Karen Christensen and David Levinson, Vol. 5, Charles Scribner's Sons, 2002, pp. 78–80.

Kich, Martin, "Tsukiyama, Gail," in *Encyclopedia of Asian-American Literature*, edited by Seiwoong Oh, Facts on File, 2007, p. 291.

Kort, Carol, "Tsukiyama, Gail," in *A to Z of American Women Writers*, Facts on File, 2007.

"Leprosy: Hansen's Disease," National Center for Biotechnology Information website, http://www.ncbi.nlm. nih.gov/pubmedhealth/PMH0002323/ (accessed September, 2, 2012).

Meyers, Chris, "Japan Nationalists Land on Isle at Heart of Row with China," in *Reuters*, http://www.reuters.com/ article/2012/08/19/japan-china-idUSL4E8JH37C20120 819 (accessed September, 2, 2012).

"Nanjing Massacre," in *Encyclopedia of Modern China*, edited by David Pong, Vol. 3, Charles Scribner's Sons, 2009, p. 282.

Review of *The Samurai's Garden*, in *Kirkus Reviews*, January 1, 1995, https://www.kirkusreviews.com/book-reviews/gail-tsukiyama/the-samurais-garden/#review (accessed September 3, 2012).

Review of *The Samurai's Garden*, in *Library Journal*, Vol. 120, No. 3, February 1995, p. 184.

Review of *The Samurai's Garden*, in *Publishers Weekly*, Vol. 242, No. 5, January 30, 2005, p. 85.

Seaman, Donna, Review of *The Samurai's Garden*, in *Booklist*, Vol. 91, No. 13, March 1, 2005, p. 1180.

Thomas, Louisa, "Orphans of War," in *New York Times*, October 14, 2007, http://www.nytimes.com/2007/10/14/ books/review/Thomas-t.html (accessed September 3, 2012).

Tsukiyama, Gail, *The Samurai's Garden*, St. Martin's Griffin, 1994.

FURTHER READING

Mehta, Geeta K., Kimie Tada, and Noboru Murata, *Japanese Gardens: Tranquility, Simplicity, Harmony*, Tuttle Publishing, 2008.

> The text and striking photographs in this book illustrate the techniques and elements that make Japanese gardens unique.

Tsukiyama, Gail, *The Street of a Thousand Blossoms*, St. Martin's Press, 2007.

> Tsukiyama is fascinated by specialized communities, for example the town of Yamaguchi in *The Samurai's Garden*. This interest is reflected in her novel *The Street of a Thousand Blossoms*. Tsukiyama writes of two orphaned brothers, each of whom looks forward to a career in Japanese tradition. Kenji hopes to make masks for Noh theater productions, and his older brother, Hiroshi, wants to be a sumo wrestler.

Yamamoto, Tsunetomo, *Bushido: The Way of the Samurai*, edited by Justin F. Stone, translated by Minoru Tanaka, Square One Publishers, 2001.

> Yamamoto was a samurai of the late seventeenth and early eighteenth centuries. This book translates his writings, which describe the principles of the samurai class, including the central traditions of service and loyalty.

Yang, Gene Luen, *American Born Chinese*, Square Fish, 2008.

> In this graphic novel, which is popular with young-adult readers, Yang introduces Jin Wang, a Chinese American student who longs to fit in. Using humor and fantasy, the book tackles issues of cultural stereotypes and identity.

SUGGESTED SEARCH TERMS

Gail Tsukiyama

Gail Tsukiyama AND heritage

Gail Tsukiyama AND social groups

The Samurai's Garden

Japanese rock gardens

Sino-Japanese War

seppuku

leprosy

The Sound of Waves

YUKIO MISHIMA

1954

Yukio Mishima, a Japanese author, actor, director, model, and socialite, stunned the world when, in 1970, at the age of forty-five, he committed ritual suicide in the manner of a samurai warrior after attempting a coup at the headquarters of the Japanese Self-Defense Forces in Tokyo. For this shocking act of seppuku (known in the West by the informal title *hara-kiri*) he became internationally known, but before 1970 he was already an enormous celebrity at home as one of Japan's most talented and prolific writers, admired for his deeply passionate and often violent prose. *The Sound of Waves*, published in 1954, tells a beautiful love story between two island teenagers. Atypical of Mishima's work, the novel is an innocent and subdued retelling of the ancient Greek story of Daphnis and Chloe. Written in Mishima's characteristically sensual style, *The Sound of Waves* was an instant best seller in Japan and received excellent reviews in the United States as the first of his work to be translated into English. Mishima himself was surprised to have produced such an appealing story, calling it, according to John Nathan in *Mishima: A Biography*, "that joke on the public." Despite his affectation of nonchalance, *The Sound of Waves* reflects Mishima's love of Greek culture and history after first visiting the country in 1952. In Greece, the always troubled Mishima learned, as quoted by Nathan, that "creating a beautiful work of art and becoming beautiful oneself were ethically

identical." *The Sound of Waves* is the result of this revelation, a glittering outlier in the otherwise dark world of Mishima's fiction. Meredith Weatherby's 1956 translation was republished by Vintage International in 1994.

AUTHOR BIOGRAPHY

Mishima, born in Tokyo, Japan, on January 14, 1925, as Kimitake Hiraoka, was taken to live with his ailing grandmother until he turned twelve. Victims of his grandmother's possessiveness, his father and mother, who lived separately in the same house, were powerless to interfere with her wishes owing to the strict family dynamics of respect. Mishima's two younger siblings lived relatively normal childhoods with their parents, but Mishima, confined to the dark of the apartment downstairs and rarely allowed outside, could only entertain himself quietly with origami, reading, and writing or playing with his female cousins. Released from his grandmother's grasp in 1937, Mishima excelled as a student. He was awarded a silver watch from the emperor as the best student in his high school when he graduated in 1944. During World War II, he escaped the draft as the result of his unhealthy appearance (mistakenly ascribed to tuberculosis). But witnessing the war's devastation on the home front had a profound effect on Mishima, and afterward he never grew accustomed to peace.

Completing law school at Tokyo Imperial University in 1947, Mishima took a high-ranking bureaucratic position in the Finance Ministry, as was expected of him by his demanding father, who raided his bedroom weekly and destroyed any writing he found. But Kimitake Hiraoka, who had published work under his pseudonym, Yukio Mishima, since high school, could not continue as a bureaucrat. He quit his job in 1948 to become a novelist. With the publication of his novel *Confessions of a Mask* in 1949, Mishima began his rise to fame. He traveled the world in 1951, stopping in the United States, Brazil, France, and, finally, Greece. His obsession with Greece led to his emulation of Greek classicism in *The Sound of Waves* as well as his adoption of Greek style in dress and decor. When he published *The Sound of Waves* in 1954, the novel broke postwar sales records. By 1956, Mishima was at the height of his fame.

In the mid-1950s, Mishima began bodybuilding, modeling, and acting in films—in an effort to erase his weak appearance, brought on by a childhood spent indoors. He wrote with exceptional self-discipline, usually through the night. In 1958, he married Yoko Sugiyama, and the couple later had two children. In the 1960s, amid antigovernment protests, Mishima turned to radicalism. He gathered a personal army composed mainly of students, called the Shield Society, who were pledged to defend the emperor against the democracy of postwar Japan. He published political essays denouncing outside influence and modernization. His lifelong obsession with death—a product of his disturbing childhood and coming of age in the midst of the destruction of World War II—culminated in a failed coup. Mishima and select men from the Shield Society invaded the headquarters of the Japan Self-Defense Forces in November of 1970, taking the commandant hostage and assembling the soldiers for a speech. Mishima's speech could not be heard over the dissenting crowd. He then knelt in the office of his hostage and drove a sword through his stomach. One of his men then completed the ritual by beheading him. Nathan writes, "In two months, Mishima would have been forty-six. He had written forty novels, eighteen plays (all lavishly performed), twenty volumes of short stories, and as many of literary essays."

PLOT SUMMARY

Chapter 1

The Sound of Waves begins with a description of Uta-jima, or "Song Island"—a small island with magnificent views of the sea. The best views are from the Yashiro Shrine, dedicated to the sea god that the islanders worship, and from the lighthouse, which stands high on a cliff.

After sunset, an eighteen-year-old boy walks the steep path to the lighthouse carrying a fish. He thinks of earlier in the day, as he and the other fishermen were pulling ashore. On the beach he saw a mysterious girl, though she was dressed like a local. The boy passed by close to her, staring into her face. The girl did not shift her gaze from the sea. At first he was happy to have looked but now realizes how rude he was to have stared so openly.

MEDIA ADAPTATIONS

- A five-hour audiobook edition of *The Sound of Waves* was released in 2010, with Brian Nishii narrating.

The lighthouse keeper and his wife helped the boy graduate despite flunking his final exams. In gratitude, the boy brings them part of his catch. The wife greets the boy as Shinji and invites him in for dinner.

Chapter 2

At sea, Shinji remembers the night before. He returned from the lighthouse to his home, where his twelve-year-old brother, Hiroshi, and widowed mother live. After dinner, the brothers went to the public bath. Shinji strained to hear gossip of the girl but heard nothing.

On the boat with his master, Jukichi, and his master's apprentice, Ryuji, Shinji distracts himself fishing for octopus. When the men break for lunch, Jukichi mentions the girl—she is the daughter of the wealthy Uncle Teru, who recently lost his wife and only son. Lonely, Uncle Teru brought her back from her adopted family to be married on the island. Shinji realizes with disappointment that he is too poor to be chosen as a husband for the girl, Hatsue. Uncle Teru owns two freighters and is an intimidating man of great esteem on Uta-jima, while Shinji's only wish is to own a single engine-powered boat one day.

Chapter 3

At a meeting of the Young Men's Association, Shinji hears talk of Hatsue. The leader, Yasuo, arrives, son of an important family in the village. He hurries through the meeting, then leaves to attend a party thrown by Uncle Teru for Hatsue's return. Upset, Shinji walks the beach alone, making his way to the Yashiro Shrine, where he tosses two coins in offering. He prays for the safety of his family, success in fishing, and to marry a girl like Hatsue. As he finishes his prayer, the wind picks up. Shinji hopes the sea god accepts his prayer and does not punish him for selfishness.

Chapter 4

In stormy weather, Shinji's mother asks him to collect the firewood she has gathered and stored near an abandoned military tower—the highest point on the island. Inside the tower he finds his mother's firewood but hears someone sobbing. He climbs onto the roof to find Hatsue. She got lost on her way to the lighthouse for etiquette lessons from the lighthouse keeper's wife. Shinji offers to guide her back. As they walk down the slope, Shinji asks Hatsue not to tell anyone they have met: "Thus their well-founded fear of the village's love of gossip changed what was an innocent meeting into a thing of secrecy."

Chapter 5

Shinji overhears gossip that Hatsue is to marry Yasuo. His spirits drop, but he distracts himself fishing. When the fishermen dock, Shinji receives his split of the profit for the week. Shinji stays on the beach to help other boats land. Hatsue is pushing a boat in, but they do not speak. He returns home to give his money to his mother but finds that he has lost his envelope. He runs out of the house to search for it.

Hatsue arrives at the house, returning the envelope she has found to Shinji's mother. She goes out to find Shinji and ease his panic, discovering him on the beach. He asks about the rumor he heard about Yasuo. She denies it. Laughing, she falls to the ground, and Shinji follows her, "Their dry, chapped lips touched. There was a slight taste of salt." They agree to meet at the lighthouse the next day.

Chapter 6

Shinji returns to the Yashiro Shrine to offer a prayer of thanks. The lighthouse couple have grown fond of Hatsue. Their daughter attends college in Tokyo, but they think of the island girls as their own. Shinji arrives for dinner. When the lighthouse keeper's wife sees Shinji and Hatsue smiling shyly at each other, she brings up her daughter Chiyoko's crush on Shinji, who leaves the house abruptly.

Shinji waits outside, but Hatsue walks right past him. Shinji catches up with her after she trips, dropping her flashlight. She asks about

Chiyoko, but Shinji reassures her. They make plans to meet at the abandoned military observation tower the next time a storm hits.

Chapter 7

Hiroshi embarks on a school trip to mainland Japan. The schoolboys travel by ferry and are seen off by their worried mothers. Raised in island isolation, many of the boys are seeing city life for the first time on this trip. After dropping off the children, the ferry returns with Chiyoko, home for spring break, and Yasuo, coming home after a business meeting. Yasuo engages the gloomy Chiyoko in conversation, showing off to the college-educated girl. Chiyoko dislikes Yasuo's arrogance. He helps her onto the boat, but she imagines it is Shinji's hand holding her own. Yasuo mentions Hatsue, her beauty, and his expectation to become her fiancé. Chiyoko is jealous of any mention of beauty, as if it condemns her own plain looks. The boat pulls into harbor at Uta-jima, tilting in the choppy water.

Chapter 8

A storm hits the island. Shinji cannot wait to meet Hatsue. His mother watches in wonder as he sings and jumps around the house, finally going out into the storm. At the beach, Shinji finds a beautiful pink shell before returning home.

After lunch, Shinji takes the path past the lighthouse to the tower. He arrives soaked. Building a fire, he falls asleep in the warm shelter. He wakes to find Hatsue, naked, drying her clothes by the fire. She catches him looking, ordering him to close his eyes. The women of the island dive naked for pearls, so Shinji cannot understand why Hatsue would be uncomfortable. He asks her what would make her comfortable, and she responds that she would be more comfortable if Shinji were naked too. He complies. Just then the storm grows fierce outside, and Shinji leaps over the fire to calm Hatsue. They embrace and lay down on the floor, but Hatsue objects. She wants to marry Shinji but cannot go any further until then. Shinji does not share her views but respects her wishes. He gives her the pink shell. On the way home, they do not separate before the lighthouse as usual but continue on together as the storm whips the island.

Chiyoko has been bored at the lighthouse, the only excitement coming from a meeting of the etiquette class in which she saw and confirmed Hatsue's beauty. Studying at home during the storm, Chiyoko gazes out the lighthouse window, longing for her big-city life in Tokyo. She spots Hatsue and Shinji walking in the rain, holding each other.

Chapter 9

Chiyoko visits Yasuo to tell him what she saw during the storm. Yasuo's sense of entitlement is deeply injured: "The most unbearable thought of all—was that Shinji had had his way with the girl fairly and squarely, with complete honesty." He studies the schedule of water drawing from the village well to find the time of Hatsue's turn and ambushes her that night. He tells her she has slept with Shinji. She denies it. He attempts to rape her, but an angry hornet stings him. She escapes. Yasuo begs her not to tell her father, finally securing her promise by offering to carry her water jugs back for her. She follows him at a distance.

Chapter 10

Hiroshi returns from his trip excited beyond words. But when he and his friends explore an island cave, he learns of a nasty rumor that his brother and Hatsue had *omeko*, or slept together. He asks his mother about it, enraging her. His mother, embarrassed, asks Shinji if the rumor is true. Shinji says no, and his mother believes him. Still, the rumor spreads quickly through the village until Hatsue's father overhears it in the bathhouse. He erupts in a rage.

Chapter 11

On the fishing boat, Jukichi hands Shinji a message from Hatsue. She has been forbidden by her father to see Shinji, but she will hide notes for him beneath a water jar outside her house. Jukichi reads the letter out loud. He and Ryuji feel sympathetic. Ryuji agrees to retrieve the messages. The men read the letters daily on the boat. Hatsue writes of Yasuo's attempt to rape her and her father's ambivalence at this news. Meanwhile, Chiyoko learns through gossip that Shinji and Hatsue are forbidden contact. She is overcome with guilt. She goes to Shinji to confess but instead asks him if she is ugly. Shinji answers simply that she is pretty. Delighted, Chiyoko returns to Tokyo for school without confessing.

Chapter 12

Shinji's mother dreams of solving her son's sadness. She goes to Uncle Teru's house, but he will not see her—forcing Hatsue to send her away. Shinji's mother does not tell her son about her failure, but Shinji finds out from Hatsue's letters. They attempt to meet again the night of a party at Uncle Teru's house, but he catches them and calls Hatsue away.

Chapter 13

With the arrival of summer, the women of the island begin pearl-diving season. During a moment of relaxation after a dive, an old peddler interrupts them to show his wares. After a few women make purchases, he suggests an abalone-diving contest, with one of his fashionable purses as a prize. Shinji's mother places second in the contest to gather the most abalone, and Hatsue places first. She gives the prize to Shinji's mother, winning her favor and her forgiveness for turning her away from Uncle Teru's house.

Chapter 14

One of Uncle Teru's freighters docks at Uta-jima. Yasuo and Shinji are asked to join the crew. Hatsue sneaks Shinji a package with her portrait the day he sets sail. Shinji works hard as a deckhand while Yasuo acts lazy and privileged, quickly falling out of favor with the captain. A strong typhoon approaches, endangering the freighter at its port in Okinawa. A cable anchoring the ship snaps suddenly in the powerful wind. Shinji volunteers to swim out to the buoy to reattach the broken cable. He barely survives the dangerous waves and harsh wind but completes his task, saving freighter and crew.

Chapter 15

Returning to Uta-jima, Shinji gives thanks at Yashiro Shrine and celebrates his homecoming at Jukichi's house. Chiyoko admits her guilt to her mother in a letter, refusing to return to the island until her mother persuades Uncle Teru to allow Shinji and Hatsue to be together. The lighthouse keeper's wife respects her daughter's wish, enlisting other women of the village to help her convince Uncle Teru that Shinji is worthy. They crowd into his house, only to discover that Uncle Teru has changed his mind after hearing of Shinji's heroic actions during the typhoon.

Chapter 16

Shinji and Hatsue walk up the many steps to Yashiro Shrine to announce their engagement and give thanks to the sea god. Next, they go to the lighthouse to have dinner with the couple. Shinji has no idea of Chiyoko's role in the drama that has just unfolded. The lighthouse keeper takes them up the stairs to the lighthouse itself, tactfully leaving them alone. They gaze out at the beautiful view of the ocean. Hatsue shows Shinji the pink shell he gave her, and Shinji takes out the picture Hatsue gave him. Shinji realizes it was not the picture of Hatsue but "his own strength that had tided him through that perilous night."

CHARACTERS

Chiyoko

Chiyoko is the serious-minded daughter of the lighthouse keepers. She has an unrequited crush on Shinji. Yasuo tries to impress her as she takes the ferry back to Uta-jima for spring break from her college in Tokyo. But Chiyoko is not impressed: "She was always wishing that she could have a man look at her at least once with eyes saying 'I love you' instead of 'You love me.'" At home, she catches Shinji and Hatsue walking to the village together in the storm and, jealous, tells Yasuo—starting the rumor that Shinji and Hatsue slept together. When she finds out that this has caused the two to be separated, she feels guilty and regretful. After Shinji tells her that she is pretty during a confrontation on the beach, she returns to Tokyo for school. She refuses to come back to Uta-jima until Shinji and Hatsue are together, asking her mother in a letter to act as the go-between in their engagement. Although she likes Shinji, he is in the dark about Chiyoko's deep feelings and rash actions in the novel.

Hatsue

Hatsue is the daughter of Uncle Teru. She was adopted away at an early age, but after the deaths of his wife and only son, Uncle Teru brings Hatsue back to the island to live with him. She has a rustic beauty, attracting both Shinji and Yasuo. However, she loves Shinji and detests Yasuo after he attempts to rape her. Hatsue is well mannered, earning the admiration of the lighthouse couple. She is intelligent and respectful of island morals, except when her father bans her from seeing Shinji. After Uncle Teru makes Hatsue ask Shinji's mother to leave the house, she apologizes by winning a purse for his mother in the abalone-diving contest: "The mother's simple, straightforward heart had immediately understood the modesty and respect behind the girl's gesture." She gives Shinji a portrait of herself to take with him on the freighter. When he returns safely, they are engaged to be married.

Hiroshi

Hiroshi is Shinji's twelve-year-old brother. Shinji and his mother support his education through fishing and pearl diving, respectively. Hiroshi is beside himself with excitement for his first trip by ferry to the mainland. He sends home a postcard about seeing his first movie that reduces his mother to proud tears. When he returns to Uta-jima, he cannot put his feelings into words. Instead, he remembers a prank he once pulled: polishing a spot on the floor at school so thoroughly that a teacher slipped and fell. That is all he can think of when he remembers the flashing streetcars and tangle of lights and metal that was the mainland. He returns to his normal island life, playing with his friends from school. He learns from them the rumor that Shinji and Hatsue slept together and repeats this rumor to his mother.

Jukichi

Jukichi is a master fisherman with two apprentices on his fishing boat, Shinji and Ryuji. When Shinji's luck in love runs out, Jukichi is moved by sympathy. He reads Hatsue's letters aloud on the boat each day during lunch and gives excellent advice to the unfortunate Shinji, such as to not physically attack Yasuo after he learns of the attempted rape. Jukichi is asked to release Shinji from his boat temporarily to work on Uncle Teru's freighter. He realizes Shinji is being tested for Hatsue's hand in marriage. He is very proud of Shinji's actions during the typhoon, and the two get drunk on sake, celebrating his safe return to Uta-jima.

Lighthouse Keeper

The lighthouse keeper is a former serviceman who now works in the lighthouse, charting the paths of ships and telegraphing locations to ports. He is a kindly man who cares for Shinji and Hatsue. When the two are finally engaged, he takes them on a tour of the lighthouse, leaving them alone at the very top.

Lighthouse Keeper's Wife

The lighthouse keeper's wife, or mistress of the lighthouse, conducts etiquette lessons with the village girls. She is an avid reader of celebrity magazines and has a love for learning. Her only daughter, Chiyoko, goes to college in Tokyo, but she and her husband care for all of the children in the village. They adore Shinji, who is indebted to them for helping him finish high school. However, the lighthouse keeper's wife upsets Shinji, Hatsue, and her husband when she mentions Chiyoko's feelings for Shinji at an inappropriate moment. However, her intentions are usually good. After her daughter refuses to come home out of guilt, the lighthouse keeper's wife marches right into Uncle Teru's house to argue on Shinji and Hatsue's behalf.

Old Peddler

The old peddler comes to Uta-jima to sell his wares to the women of the island. He finds them recovering their strength by a fire after diving for pearls. He organizes a playful contest in which the woman who collects the most abalone will win one of three purses. One purse is for a younger woman, one is fashionable for a middle-aged woman, and one purse suits a distinguished older woman. When Hatsue wins the contest, she picks the purse most appealing for a middle-aged woman and presents it to Shinji's mother.

Ryuji

Ryuji is an apprentice of Jukichi's on the fishing boat. He is younger than Shinji but sympathetic to his troubles with Hatsue. He volunteers to act as messenger for the couple, hiding and retrieving messages hidden under a water jar on Uncle Teru's property.

Shinji

Shinji is the hero of *The Sound of Waves*: level-headed, strong, and pure of heart. He works as a fisherman on Jukichi's boat to help support his family. He brings fish to the lighthouse couple to show his appreciation for their help in his graduation from school. He prays to the sea god at Yashiro Shrine, giving yen (Japanese currency) in offering despite his poverty. He and Hatsue share a deep love for each other that they are too young to fully express. However, Shinji does all he can to be with Hatsue and never lets hope die in his heart. He joins the crew of Uncle Teru's ship, saving it from destruction in a typhoon and proving himself worthy of Hatsue. Shinji is associated with natural and spiritual forces in the island throughout the novel: "He heard the sound of waves striking the shore, and it was as though the surging of his young blood was keeping time with the movement of the sea's great tides." But Shinji comes to realize at the end that it was his strength alone that carried him through the storm safely.

Shinji's Mother

Shinji's mother is widowed, with two sons: Shinji and Hiroshi. She supports her family by diving for pearls. Her husband died during the war, when a plane bombed his rescue boat. She cries at the thought that her sons will leave the island one day, though she feels that it is inevitable. When Hiroshi is on his school trip and Shinji leaves the house during the storm, she sits alone in the house admiring her own body, which is smooth and fit from pearl-diving. She boasts to herself that she could have five more children with such an attractive body and then, ashamed, prays before her husband's shrine. When Uncle Teru turns her away from his house, she does not tell Shinji because of her embarrassment. After Hatsue apologizes for this incident by giving Shinji's mother a purse, Shinji's mother approves of Hatsue and hopes for the couple to be together.

Uncle Teru

Uncle Teru is a wealthy islander who owns two freighters. His daughter, Hatsue, is his youngest, unmarried child. He lost his wife and only son, causing him great loneliness. He then brought Hatsue home from her adopted family to cure this loneliness. He wants to find a worthy husband for his daughter. At first, it seems that this will be Yasuo. Shinji is too poor to even be considered at first, and after the rumor that Hatsue and Shinji have slept together reaches Uncle Teru, he bans them from seeing each other. But when Shinji proves himself after Uncle Teru tests his character (through working on the freighter), Uncle Teru gives in to his daughter's wishes and allows them to be engaged. He also plans to support Shinji's struggling family by taking them in.

Yasuo

Yasuo is the leader of the Young Men's Association. A wealthy teen from a prominent family on the island, he feels that he is perfect to be chosen as Hatsue's husband. When Chiyoko tells him what she saw the day of the storm, he becomes enraged and hides in the bushes by the well, waiting for Hatsue. He attacks Hatsue and tries to rape her. A hornet, disturbed by his movement in the bushes, stings him all over his body, preventing the rape: "Yasuo would have liked to run away without more ceremony, but his fear that she would tell her father kept him wheedling." He begs her not to tell Teru, promising to carry her water home for her. Hatsue allows him to carry the water but tells her father about the attempt anyway. He and Shinji are chosen to join the crew of Uncle Teru's freighter, where Yasuo proves himself to be lazy. The captain grows to dislike him. Yasuo loses favor with Uncle Teru as a result of his selfish, privileged behavior on the freighter.

THEMES

Love

At the heart of *The Sound of Waves* is the love story between Hatsue and Shinji, reminiscent of a fairy-tale romance in its structure. The two young lovers are at odds with the world because Shinji's poverty makes him ineligible as a suitor for the daughter of the wealthiest islander. But fate intervenes, and the two meet on the roof of the observation tower, unobserved. Their actions together are harmonious, yet secretive. Although they respect the moral code of the island, their private meetings stir vicious rumors. Still, the couple remains independent of others' wishes, passing notes and pursuing their love under the radar of Uncle Teru. Chiyoko's jealousy and Yasuo's fiendish plan are trumped. First Shinji's mother, then the lighthouse keepers, and finally stubborn Uncle Teru are won to the lovers' side. They stay loyal to their own wishes and are rewarded for this strength of will, but they pay tribute to those who helped them come together: a purse for Shinji's mother, a prayer at Yashiro Shrine, and dinner at the lighthouse each announce the couple as a legitimate and respectful new addition to the insular culture of Uta-jima.

TOPICS FOR FURTHER STUDY

- Form groups of two or three and scan the novel for instances of symbolism. Using your memory of the book, as well as the help of flipping through the text, try as a group to discover a few symbols as well as what you think each symbol represents. Write down what you find as a group to prepare for class discussion.

- Mishima is one of the most translated Japanese authors of his time. Read another work by Mishima and then write a comparative essay in which you discuss the opinion that *The Sound of Waves* represents an exception to Mishima's usual style. How do the two works compare in language, content, setting, protagonists, or any other aspect you find important? Which work do you prefer?

- Write a short story or poem based on your favorite myth or fairy tale. Be creative as you reimagine the story. Your work can be any length, but be sure to note which story you chose to retell. For a guide to common myths, reference *Aesop's Fables: A Classic Illustrated Edition*, published by Chronicle

Books in 1990 or *D'Aulaires' Book of Greek Myths*, published by Delacorte Books for Young Readers in 1992.

- Read a work by another Japanese author of your choice. What conclusions can you draw about Japanese fiction using Mishima and your chosen author as examples? Consider aspects of style, form, and content. Write an essay with quotes from the books to support your examples. Some Japanese authors to consider are Haruki Murakami, Yasunari Kawabata, Junichiro Tanizaki, Akira Yoshimura, Kenzaburo Oe, Kobo Abe, and Yoko Ogawa.

- Mishima based Uta-jima on a real island. Using your online search skills, discover the name of the island. Compile information about that island, which could include its population, a map or picture of the island, its nearby neighbors, or anything else that you found interesting during your search. Hint: Although there is a real island named Uta-jima, this is not the correct answer.

Rites of Passage

Shinji faces many tests on Uta-jima. He must brave storms, rough seas, temptation, and deceitful gossip. However, his strong, honest actions in the end prove his worth. When Chiyoko tests him on the beach, asking suddenly if she is pretty, Shinji's affirmative response is a pure one: "As everyone well knew, Shinji was incapable of flattery." Because his honest answer delights Chiyoko, she eventually asks her mother to help him find happiness with Hatsue. But the greatest challenge comes on Uncle Teru's freighter, when a cable snaps in the winds of the typhoon. Shinji's feat of courage and strength in the water saves Uncle Teru's property and crew: "The boy swam with all his might. And, inch by inch, step by step, the huge mass of the enemy fell back, opening the way for him."

By surviving this trial at sea, Shinji becomes a man worthy of Hatsue.

Although Shinji is the hero of this tale, he is not the only character who must complete a rite of passage in the novel. Hatsue must prove her worth to Shinji's mother after a disastrous meeting between the two at Uncle Teru's house. Both women work in the dangerous depths of the sea as pearl divers and compete against each other in the old peddler's abalone-diving contest. Yet when Hatsue wins, she gives the prize to Shinji's mother, apologizing respectfully for her earlier actions at her father's house: "Hatsue smiled, and Shinji's mother told herself how wise her son had been in his choice of a bride.... And it was in this same fashion that the politics of the island were always conducted." Typical of Hatsue's demure personality, she works within the

Shinji is content to work on a fishing vessel.
(© Hiroshi Ichikawa | Shutterstock.com)

moral code of the island to accomplish her goal of a life with Shinji.

Although he is younger than the hero and heroine, Hiroshi experiences a rite of passage as well. He is of age to journey to the mainland for the first time. Stunned by the contrast between Uta-jima and the modern metropolis, he can find no words to describe it when he returns home: "Those towering buildings and neon lights that had so amazed him—where were they now?" By nightfall on the day of his return Hiroshi has, like those who made the trip before him, resettled into his rural life: "At the end of long lives spent on the island they would no longer even so much as remember the … streetcars clanging back and forth along the streets of a city."

Self-reliance

Shinji and the other villagers of Uta-jima are characterized as strong, healthy, and independent. The islanders may not have wealth, but they can support themselves. Self-reliant people such as Jukichi, Shinji's fishing master; the lighthouse couple; and Shinji's mother, whose skin is unwrinkled by age, populate the book as positive

forces. Meanwhile, Yasuo, a product of his parents' money, acts lazy and entitled throughout the novel, serving as the villain. Self-reliance, as opposed to Yasuo's selfishness, means helping others, as well as oneself, succeed, and many characters are seen at the aid of their fellow villagers—culminating in the gang of women who storm Uncle Teru's house to demand Shinji and Hatsue be allowed to love each other. Although the sea god is placated with prayers and Hatsue's love comes at the end with the support of the villagers, who abandon their gossiping in favor of approval, Shinji realizes in the surprising final line that he is singularly responsible for surviving the typhoon and thus in control of his own destiny.

STYLE

Pastoral

In retelling Longus's *Daphnis and Chloe*, an ancient Greek pastoral, Richard F. Hardin writes in *Love in a Green Shade*: "Mishima removes the setting from the world of shepherds to that of rural types more familiar to his readers, fishermen." The setting, or the outside world surrounding and influencing the characters, plays a significant role in *The Sound of Waves*. Uta-jima, a small, self-reliant, and picturesque island, provides the fantasy-like backdrop to the romance of Hatsue and Shinji. Pastoral works, so called for their pasture setting describing the pleasant, simple rural life, have existed as long as storytelling, but Mishima reengineers this common genre in Japanese terms. Gwenn Boardman Petersen writes in *The Moon in the Water*, "The sea and sky, the scents and sounds of the enchanted island, are beautifully evoked in language reminiscent of the harmony of old Japan." The Yashiro Shrine is the spiritual center of the book and one of the highest physical points on the island, where prayers to the sea god are earnestly whispered and hard-earned money given up in offering. The village generator is broken, bathing the island in darkness, and the pearl-diving women work unself-consciously in the nude. These aspects of life cannot be found in the big city, and Hardin points out how Hiroshi's school trip "allows the usual country-city contrast." Returning home to Uta-jima after his surreal trip to the mainland, "his became again an existence in which everything was understood without the need for words." By surrounding Hatsue and Shinji's drama with such a setting, in which life is tranquil and complications are few, Mishima's love story is made more powerful as trouble comes to the little island.

Folklore

Mishima uses folklore to lend his love story on Uta-jima a deeper history and significance. Folklore—the stories and beliefs of a culture passed down orally through generations—unites the island characters as members of the same culture with shared cultural knowledge. Their superstitions, legends, and stories illustrate their specific outlook on life. For example, when a woman who dives too deeply off the shore falls ill and dies, the other pearl divers say that it is because she saw something in the depths that humans were not supposed to see. This story—that humans will be punished by the divine for reaching too far into the unknown—illustrates the conservative nature of the islanders, a conservatism Shinji and Hatsue must defeat when their love for each other is not accepted as appropriate. On their side is Shinji's mother, who dived even deeper after the woman died, clearly a more daring woman than the other divers and willing to break the rules.

In another tale from the island's folklore, a wealthy royal named Prince Deki floated to the island on a golden ship, took a local girl as his wife, and lived out his years on Uta-jima peacefully. The legend of Prince Deki inspires both Shinji and Hatsue (who each have a dream about the prince) to persevere against their troubles. Like Prince Deki, Shinji feels that he is destined to live peacefully on Uta-jima with Hatsue by his side. As the tragic story of the diver teaches a lesson in conservatism, Prince Deki, a mythical figure on the island, illustrates the islanders' feelings about their small home. Uta-jima is fit for a prince—even a prince who sails in a golden ship. The legend of Prince Deki idealizes the islanders' lives of peaceful isolation. Uta-jima's folklore adds an additional layer of meaning to Shinji and Hatsue's story as deep-rooted cultural beliefs both aid and hinder the lovers.

HISTORICAL CONTEXT

Postwar Japan

Mishima was a member of Japan's war generation. Jan Walsh Hokenson writes in *Japan,*

France, and East-West Aesthetics: "He had survived the war, as a boy in Tokyo, under American bombings then occupation. He saw the profound Westernization of the country during 1950 to 1965." The war never left him. Coming of age in the midst of destruction and terror, Mishima could not reconcile the later peaceful years with what he had seen as a young man. Even in isolated Uta-jima, the war has made its mark. Hatsue and Shinji meet in an abandoned military observation tower, now used by the villagers to store their firewood. In the otherwise tranquil novel's most graphic scene, Mishima reveals how Shinji's father died: "The plane dropped a bomb on the boat and then strafed it with machine-gun fire.... Both the deck and the bilge became a lake of blood."

After surrendering, Japan came under the occupation of American forces under General Douglas MacArthur, and for the first time the country was exposed to outside influence. Hiroshi, on a trip to the mainland of Japan, sends home a telling postcard of Westernization's hypnotizing effect: "Hiroshi's closely written card was all about seeing his first motion picture, with not so much as a word about the famous scenic spots and historic places he was seeing." Uta-jima suffered in the war, but the effects of Westernization have not spread to the island. This is Mishima's ideal, for he grew more extreme with time toward the loss of Japanese tradition as the result of the popularization of Western ways. One exception Mishima allowed was for Greece, as Gwen Boardmaan Petersen explains: "Mishima worshipped at the Greek temple while urging, right up to the moment of his *seppuku*, a revival of the Japanese spirit."

Greek Influence

In 1952, when he was already a celebrity in Japan, Mishima traveled to Greece on the last leg of a vacation around the globe. A friend had given Mishima press credentials from his magazine so that he could leave the country for the first time. As Nathan notes, in postwar Japan "there were still no passports, only travel permits signed by MacArthur himself, and these were next to impossible to get." Mishima went to San Francisco, New York, Rio de Janeiro, and Paris, but Greece was his ultimate destination.

In Athens, the beauty and history of the ruins of ancient Greek civilization affected Mishima deeply. He wrote, as Nathan quotes,

COMPARE
&
CONTRAST

- **1954:** After the end of World War II, modernization and Westernization begin to spread across the defeated country, rapidly overtaking older traditions of Japanese society.

  Today: Emerging from loss as a world power, Japan has become respected for great modernizing achievements across many fields, including technology, entertainment, and business.

- **1954:** Pearl diving is a traditional occupation for the rural women of fishing villages, a physically challenging and dangerous job performed in cold water with no protective gear.

  Today: Japan has modernized the collection of pearls through the growing of pearl cultures, making pearls easier to harvest. No longer strictly a job for rural women, pearl collection is a Japanese industry.

- **1954:** Shrines such as the Yashiro Shrine on Uta-jima island are important religious sites to the Japanese people, where offerings of money can be made to the gods in the hope that the supplicant's prayers will be answered.

  Today: Shrines are still prominent throughout the country, attracting visitors from around the world to view these beautifully preserved landmarks. Money given in offering is used to protect and repair the shrines for future visitors.

"Greece cured my self-hatred and my loneliness and awoke in me a *will to health*." Back home in Tokyo he enrolled in a Greek language course and began to mimic Greek fashion. But the most sophisticated expression of Mishima's love of Greece and the happiness he found pursuing this love is *The Sound of Waves*, written in 1954 at the peak of his passion. The novel's ideal setting and heroic characters follow the original *Daphnis and Chloe* closely. Petersen writes, "Mishima's island ... blend[s] elements of universal fairy tale, of the Greek hero-against-the-sea, and of a Japanese past of gods."

Shinji and Hatsue's trials to prove their love, the chorus of gossiping villagers, and the ageless physical fitness of the pearl divers and fishermen reflect Greek traditions as Mishima saw them with an innocence not found in his other work. Shinji stands "like some piece of heroic sculpture," and with his body "shining in the flames" he leaps over a fire to comfort Hatsue. A year after *The Sound of Waves* was published. Mishima began weight lifting in order to achieve the same heroic physique. Petersen writes, "Physical perfection is in his view linked to Greek wisdom." He had observed this perfection in Greek statues, and he had written about it in the character of Shinji—the simple but valiant hero who combines the best of Greek and Japanese virtues.

CRITICAL OVERVIEW

The Sound of Waves broke postwar sales records in Japan. In America, Meredith Weatherby's translation of the novel received widespread praise. This was Mishima's first novel to appear in English, chosen to be released before earlier work by Mishima for its more subdued treatment of sexuality. While unanimously acknowledging it as a great novel, literary critics often focus on the mood of *The Sound of Waves* compared with the majority of Mishima's work. Nathan describes *The Sound of Waves* as a "sun-lit book" and believes that "the book is unremittingly normal in the most conventional sense; in fact, it is Mishima's most assiduously healthy work." Hokenson states that Mishima "had been known in the West as a novelist of brilliantly

Shinji's bravery and courage are evident during the big storm. *(© Willyam Bradberry | Shutterstock.com)*

character psychology coexist with sympathizing nature." Patrick M. O'Neil, in *Great World Writers: Twentieth Century*, argues that although the book tells a tranquil story, Mishima's dark tone lives on beneath the surface: "Even in the earliest idyllic fairy-tale romance, *The Sound of Waves*, characters seem happiest when a happy ending is not certain." As examples, he points to the drawn-out process of secret letter writing and the slow walk Shinji takes up the steps of the temple "to meet his beloved Hatsue." These moments of savoring the anticipation, not the actual goal, are capped by the final line of the novel: Shinji realizes—with Hatsue at last by his side—that it was his own power alone that allowed him to survive the storm. This surprising jab at the otherwise mystically unified nature of their love is more the Mishima aesthetic, as it is known in Japan, than the coming together of two happy lovers in a peaceful place.

somber themes, descriptive skill, lyric power, and an extraordinary breadth of knowledge." That he produced such a compelling love story, free of the shock implicit in his other work, most critics link to his Greece-induced high spirits. Nathan writes of Mishima's determination "to demonstrate to himself not only that he was capable of creating a world so different from his own but even that he had a place in it." Petersen writes of Mishima's reception in his own country, "It is not surprising that Japanese critics—including his mentor Kawabata—use such terms as 'ornate' and 'gorgeous' in describing Mishima's language." Some impressive and untranslatable elements of Mishima's syntax, such as puns and other plays on words, are lost in the conversion to English. However, his work with color translates perfectly: "Dark whirlpools and stormy waters hint at mystic depths of the past, while foaming water, white freighter and brilliant beams of lighthouse and beacon suggest the hero's conquest ... of a threatening universe." In *Love in a Green Shade*, Hardin states that the novel "offers an affecting and human story reviving the possibility of an authentic idyllicism or joyous unity in love and nature." This is very much in line with the classic Greek text that Mishima is emulating in *The Sound of Waves*. Hardin continues, "Mishima finds a way to put novelistic realism in the service of Greek romance material: scrupulous description and

CRITICISM

Amy Lynn Miller

Miller is a graduate of the University of Cincinnati and currently resides in New Orleans, Louisiana. In the following essay, she discusses Mishima's use of setting in The Sound of Waves, *the spiritual and natural worlds of Uta-jima that combine in the protagonist Shinji.*

Mishima's island love story is remarkable not for the romance itself, which follows the beaten path of many hero's tales, but for its remarkable setting. Uta-jima blends the natural and spiritual worlds, while Shinji would seem to personify all three: island, nature, and spirits come together in the soul of the fisher-boy. This harmony, observable throughout the novel, is suddenly disrupted in the final line when Shinji declares his independence of all others in his trial by sea in favor of his own strength.

Uta-jima, with a small, peaceful population of villagers, is an ideal world free from modernity: "Unlike the environment of city youths, always exploding with thrills, Uta-jima had not a single pin-ball parlor, not a single bar, not a single waitress." Additionally, there are no strangers on the island—one of the reasons gossip spreads so quickly, yet also a reason why the villagers are generally seen helping one another. Although the novel is set after World War II,

WHAT DO I READ NEXT?

- In *The Sailor Who Fell from Grace with the Sea* (1963), Yukio Mishima writes again of life on the water. A sailor falls in love with a woman, but her son—a member of a violent gang of boys—seeks terrible revenge on this man as an unworthy suitor. The fairy-tale world of *The Sound of Waves* is replaced in *The Sailor Who Fell from Grace with the Sea* by the carnality and violence typical of Mishima's later works, following his path as an artist from classicism to extremism. The English translation of the novel, by John Nathan, was published in 1965.

- *Waiting* (1999), by the Chinese American author Ha Jin, won the National Book Award the year it was published. The frustrated love triangle of a nurse, an army doctor, and his wife leads to year upon year of waiting for a resolution as Chinese culture shifts around the three main characters. A study of life in China and a touching tale of love based on true events, *Waiting* impressed critics with its depiction of the effects of Communist rule on an individual within its culture.

- Henry Scott Stokes's biography *Life and Death of Yukio Mishima* (1974) describes Mishima's short but successful rise to fame and prominence, ending suddenly with the act of seppuku. Beginning with his strange and isolated home life, Stokes follows Mishima through the years of his youth during World War II, his introduction to the literary world, his first trip to the West, and his emergence as an author, actor, director, and cultural icon. His survey of Mishima's life concludes with the spectacle of his death: his careful plans, the reality of his failed coup, and his final act of suicide.

- *Real World* (2008), by Natsuo Kirino, is a young-adult novel that poses questions concerning stress and criminality among Tokyo teens immersed in big-city life. Unlike Mishima's *Sound of Waves*, with its gentle island characters, Kirino's *Real World* is populated by modern teenagers confronted with murder, scandal, and mystery.

- *Snow Country* (1947), written by Mishima's lifelong mentor, the Nobel Prize–winner Yasunari Kawabata, tells the story of Shimamura, a wealthy layabout who begins an affair with a geisha named Komako on a visit to the hot spring resorts in Japan's coldest region. Considered one of Kawabata's best works, *Snow Country* is a desolate love story between two people who cannot come together, victims of the cold that dominates the atmosphere of the novel. The novel was translated into English in 1956 by Edward Seidensticker.

- In Haruki Murakami's *Sputnik Sweetheart* (1999), love in the life of the protagonist, Sumire, is divided between her writing mentor "K" and an older Korean woman named Miu. Sumire navigates between the pressures of an older man and her growing love for Miu as they travel to Greece together, all while trying to establish herself as an author. Like all of Murakami's work, the nebulous plot and beautiful characterizations combine to create a haunting and memorable style with a story as original as it is fleeting. The novel was translated into English by Philip Gabriel and published in 2001.

- *Daphnis and Chloe*, by the ancient Greek author Longus (translated by Ronald McCail, 2009), is the love story on which Mishima based *The Sound of Waves* during his enthusiastic period of emulating Greek literature. Two teens fall in love but lack any sophisticated knowledge of how to come together in this much-adapted and widely praised story written sometime in the second century.

> UTA-JIMA BLENDS THE NATURAL AND
> SPIRITUAL WORLDS, WHILE SHINJI WOULD SEEM TO
> PERSONIFY ALL THREE: ISLAND, NATURE, AND SPIRITS
> COME TOGETHER IN THE SOUL OF THE FISHER-BOY."

Petersen writes, "Setting is deliberately evocative of the legendary past." Into this steps Shinji—or more appropriately—Shinji is shown already immersed emerged in the legendary past as he walks the darkened hill toward the lighthouse with the fresh catch of the day in his hands. His skin is tanned as deeply as the sun could possibly tan a man—immediate evidence that he and nature are closely linked. A simple boy without pretenses or affectations, Shinji is the strong, silent type: "It was doubtless because nature itself satisfied his need that Shinji felt no particular lack of music in his everyday life." Until Hatsue—a mystical romantic match—appears he does not think of girls, music, friends, or vices. He simply loves to fish, to hand his mother his envelope on payday, and to relax at the lighthouse keeper's house. His life is pure and untroubled.

At Yashiro Shrine, where communication with the sea god is possible, Shinji is at his most peaceful: "The boy felt a consummate accord between himself and this opulence of nature that surrounded him." Although he has spent days tossing and turning over the pretty new face he saw on the beach, at the shrine he feels the waves keeping time with his heartbeat. The sea god whom the islanders worship is, logically, ruler of the one element on which Uta-jima's residents most depend. At the heart of the matter, it is not a god they worship but the sea itself. In the sea god, Mishima sets the tone for the fusion of the natural and spiritual in Shinji. After he prays and tosses in his offering at the shrine,

> the wind came blowing, and the pine branches set up a clamor. It was a gust of wind that raised solemn echoes even in the dark interior of the shrine. Perhaps it was the sea-god, accepting the boy's prayer.

Shinji's humility, above all, makes him worthy of the sea god's blessing; even walking away from the shrine, he hopes he has not been too selfish to ask for a happy marriage one day. Although he is worthy of the natural and spiritual world from the start of the novel, it is in the world of economics where he falls short. His poverty makes him ineligible to court Uncle Teru's daughter, though they fall in love at first sight. But the natural balance of the island and sea will eventually fix this discrepancy, just as waves on the shore smooth the sand.

As human complications intervene and obstruct the two lovers, nature provides them with openings and opportunities. In the midst of a storm, Shinji finds the remarkably pink, shining, shell-washed inland: the perfect present for a beloved girl, provided free of charge to the peasant boy. Hardin writes, "The cooperation between inner and outer nature frequently speaks in Mishima's images of the sea." The shell, beautiful in the midst of violent waves, answers Shinji's unspoken call to the sea for guidance as he paces the shore ahead of his secret meeting with Hatsue. In the abandoned military tower, it is again nature's power that brings the lovers closer. Naked on opposite sides of a warming fire, the two have a stand-off. Shinji moves to the right to get closer to Hatsue, but she steps to the right as well. Perhaps they would move like this forever, circling, except that the storm outside grows so violent that Hatsue, terrified, calls for Shinji. He leaps over the fire—a true heroic deed—to hold her in his arms. Nature has brought them together physically. Then Shinji presents the shell. Nature and Shinji's connection to nature have brought them together emotionally as well. In the tradition of stories about first love, Hardin observes, "The novel . . . follows the seasons, from love's beginning in the early spring to the couple's engagement in late August."

Some characters, like Shinji, show an unspoken connection to nature as well. Shinji's mother, an excellent pearl diver, has been treated kindly by her work in the water. Although she is middle-aged, her skin is lustrous and firm; when troubled, she stands on the shore to gaze out at the waves. Jukichi, the master fisherman, has an inherent understanding of the sea as well as a sympathetic heart and wise counsel for Shinji. Other characters, however, are obviously unenlightened. In the fairy-tale world of Uta-jima, Petersen writes, "there is of course a wicked-prince figure: the crafty Yasuo. . . . There is even an ugly sister—a part given to the lighthouse keeper's jealous daughter." Chiyoko and Yasuo, who arrive on the island ominously in unison after separate trips to the mainland, are not representatives of Uta-jima but of the modern, outside world. Although Yasuo is head of the Young Men's Association, he travels away from the island frequently on his father's business errands. The scoundrel Yasuo's rape attempt is interrupted, but it is not Shinji who comes to the struggling girl's aid: "Hatsue had not known what god it was who had come to her rescue. But now . . . she realized it was all the doing of a clever hornet." The moment is silly, cutting through the potential violence in a gentle way not typical of Mishima's style. Yet it is also another example of the fusion of the natural and spiritual as the question, What god? is answered with an inexplicable act of nature—the sting of a hornet.

The final test arrives. Uncle Teru, anonymously hiring Shinji and Yasuo to work on his freighter, seeks to judge their character. Even before the storm, Yasuo's lazy attitude has caught the attention of the captain, while Shinji's silent work ethic is praised once the others notice. But a trial by sea is the true divider. Petersen writes, "The hero must go out in a Herculean test of strength. . . . The challenge is met with appropriately heroic physical endurance." Maybe so, but Shinji is spiritually and naturally one with the waves. When he dives into the water to retie the ship's cable, he cannot be defeated. In fact, running out of energy, he succeeds only when a wave simply scoops him up: "By good luck a wave swept him forward again . . . lifted him up with a single sweep and deposited him on the buoy." With the helpful flick of a wave, Shinji returns to the island a hero at last worthy of Hatsue in Uncle Teru's eyes. Teru, who understands only money and ownership, appreciates the rescue of one of his expensive freighters as well as his crew. This makes Shinji finally worth something in his eyes, where before he saw only a poor fisher-boy.

With the most stubborn obstacle now smoothed over and made placid, Shinji and Hatsue can be together. They have already been together, spiritually, through nature, from the beginning. Only human elements conspired to interrupt their mystic love. As one cannot stop the waves, none can stop spiritual law. Shinji lives by that law, surrendering himself to the sea in a typhoon, and thus personifies the natural

and spiritual world. At the novel's conclusion, he comes to the realization "that, in short, it was this little island, enfolded in darkness, that had protected their happiness and brought their love to this fulfillment." But then, unexpectedly, he has a second epiphany: "It had been his own strength that had tided him through that perilous night." This switch toward independence has troubled many critics. On the implications of Shinji's final thought, Petersen writes: "There would seem to be no myths and no gods in this world: only the self-reliant and ultimately commonplace boy." Not so. As the embodiment of sea and island, nature and spirit, Shinji alone represented them all in the chaotic water. Helped along because of his own pure connection to the land and sea, Shinji is worthy of their influence and capable of navigating their power. He is more than commonplace: he is the place itself. Petersen writes, "Mishima Yukio fits no categories, follows no single tradition, writes in dizzying profusion." And only Mishima could weave such a tapestry of spiritual wisdom and natural power into the unassuming mind of a poor boy from an island fishing village.

Source: Amy Lynn Miller, Critical Essay on *The Sound of Waves*, in *Novels for Students*, Gale, Cengage Learning, 2013.

Rodica Frentiu

In the following excerpt, Frentiu analyzes the autobiographical elements of the desire for recognition evident in Mishima's works.

. . . Art, more precisely the art of writing, may turn its unconditional energy towards itself, but words have lost their power and the Japanese writer felt that the road to follow lay elsewhere. Politics, with all its ambitions, compromise, lies, indignities or crimes, more or less camouflaged into state reasons, certainly seemed to be the road to avoid. Still, Yukio Mishima's last gestures and his death would be intensely political in his attempt to save the Japanese soul.

Although Yukio Mishima always denied possible influences on his personal biography, the events that took place before, during or after Japan's defeat had all been traumatic experiences that the twenty-year-old man had denied or not understood. Among these were the mass suicides of soldiers and civilians on the conquered islands, Hiroshima only mentioned in passing, the bombing raids described in *Kamen no kokuhaku* (*The Confessions of a Mask*, 1949)

The Sound of Waves *is a romantic coming-of-age novel.* *(© Stuart Jenner / Shutterstock.com)*

as effects of natural catastrophes such as a typhoon or earthquake, or the political processes in which only the "winner's justice" was upheld. The sacrifice of *kamikaze* pilots, the radio broadcast discourse of the Emperor who reneged his status as the representative of a solar dynasty did not seem to have troubled him much at the time. The memories would resurge, however, like a merciless boomerang, twenty years later. In *Voices of the Heroic Dead* (1966), he deals with the pointless sacrifice of the *kamikaze* heroes:

> "Brave soldiers died because a god has commanded them to go to war; and not six months after so fierce a battle had stopped instantly because a god declared the fighting at an end, His Majesty announced: 'Verily, we are a mortal man.' Scarcely a year after we had fired ourselves like bullets at an enemy ship for our Emperor, who was a god! Why did the Emperor become a man?"

These heroes' voice had become the voice of another world, which clamored the decay of the age at a time when the old Nippon ideal seemed betrayed. In the novel *Kinkajuki* (*The Temple of the Golden Pavilion*, 1956) he mentions the

American occupation, even if apparently only in passing, through the scene in which the uniformed American giant, almost drunk, asks the seminary student to walk on the stomach of the young Japanese woman accompanying him, and then rewards Mizoguchi with two packs of cigarettes.

The characters are created like a new I, a double of the writer, similar to him in his egocentric manipulation of the world, in his erotic and narcissistic fascination with death and in his obsession for the period that ended in August 1945. What Plato in his *Republic* called *thymos*, "courage" or "desire for recognition" is manifest here in desire and resentment.

History does not seem to be a coherent or intelligible process at all. An example to this effect is the Japan of the Meiji period (1868–1912), in which a technologically advanced capitalism coexisted with political authoritarianism.

In the historic process, human beings, like animals, strive for food, shelter and, first and foremost, physical self-preservation. Unlike animals, however, man also desires other people's desire, that is he wants to be "recognized" in circumstances where he can ignore the basic instinct of self-preservation and risk his life for ideals or noble purposes. The bloody fight at the beginning of history is not about food, but about prestige, and as the purpose of fighting is not biologically determined, we could see here the first manifestation of human freedom.

The desire for recognition is first mentioned by Plato in *The Republic*, where he notes that there are three sides to the soul: a desiring one, a reasoning one and one that he called "thymos" or "courage." One may generally explain human behavior through the combination of the first two, as desire makes people always yearn for new things and reason shows them the best way to attain them. But human beings also yearn for the recognition of their own value or the value of those they trust. *Thymos* is an innate human sense, as each person believes he/she has a certain value. When this value is not recognized he becomes angry, and when he feels he is not worthy of his own perception of value he is ashamed, just as the correct evaluation of value leads to pride. The desire for recognition and the feelings of anger, shame or pride derived from it are essential elements of human personality, decisive for political life, and they accompany the entire historical process of humanity:

> "*Thymos* or the desire for recognition is thus the seat of what social scientists call 'values.' It was the struggle for recognition, as we have seen, that produced the relationship of lordship and bondage in all of its various manifestations, and the moral codes that arose out of it—the deference of a subject to his monarch, the peasant to his landlord, the haughty superiority of the aristocrat, and so forth."

Perhaps what truly satisfies man is not necessarily given by material wealth, but by the recognition of personal value. By recognizing the role of the desire for recognition as the motor of history, one can see essential phenomena for the destiny of humanity, such as religion, work, war or nationalism, in a new light. If a believer asks for the recognition of the gods or practices he cultivates, a nationalist will ask for the same recognition for his linguistic, cultural or ethnic group, just like a Japanese after the Meiji period will ask that his work be recognized. *Thymos* is thus a state of consciousness and, in order to have the subjective certainty of the perception of one's own value, this must be recognized by another conscience. Thus, typically but not inevitably, *thymos* makes people look for recognition.

The desire for recognition seems to be the psychological source of two passions: religion and nationalism. The believer values everything his religion considers sacred: moral laws, way of life or objects of worship, just as the nationalist does for his national or ethnic group. Older or newer forms of recognition, not entirely rational, religion and nationalism have most often been the propagators, hidden behind something higher called ideology, of the fight for recognition and the source of strong conflict. In Yukio Mishima's case, his religion was called *bushidō*, the ethics of the samurai class, an aristocratic warrior ideology that focused on risking one's life and did not encourage the rich and leisurely life of the master but asceticism, restraint and study. And the ultranationalism that he wanted recognized determined the Japanese writer to prepare the fight to save the traditional Japanese values, among them that of the Emperor's image. Compromise no longer had a place among these thymotic passions. In the search for "justice," *thymos* had turned into pure fanaticism, obsession and hatred, as strong thymotic pride becomes irrational in what concerns the political system and the way of life. The most important problem of politics in the course of human history seems to have been precisely the attempt to solve this issue of recognition.

Due to a particularly strong *thymos*, Yukio Mishima managed to defeat one of the strongest natural instincts, self-preservation, in the name of an ideal: the salvation of the Japanese soul.

For Nietzsche, the typical citizen of liberal democracy was a "last man" who renounced his own superiority in favor of self-preservation. His contemporaries thus became only desire and reason, lacking *thymos* entirely, which makes them find various little ways to fulfill their various desires, calculating only long-term personal interest. The philosopher (Nietzsche) believes that if a man loses his *thymos*, he loses his very human essence. Content with his fate and incapable to feel shame for his inability to be superior to others, man slowly ceases to be human. Without ambitions and aspirations, man avoids fight, danger and risk, thus threatening his own survival. Even if men were indeed born equal, they would not try to overcome their own limitations if their only interest were being equal to the others. Any human creation is due to this desire to be recognized as superior to the others. Self-contentment leads to passivity and only *thymos* deliberately searches [for] fight and sacrifice. And those who have this *thymos* also have a thirst for knowledge that cannot be satisfied by being recognized as equals to others.

The novel considered to crown Yukio Mishima's work, *The Temple of the Golden Pavilion* (*Kinkakuji*, 1956), has a not unusual plot, centered on the present and immediate reality: in 1950, a novice at the Golden Zen Temple in Kyoto, sets fire to the temple, a five-hundred-year-old building famous for its architectural beauty, testimony to the glorious age of Yoshimitsu. The Japanese writer attempts to reconstruct the actions and the motivation behind them based on court evidence. He notes, along with frustrated ambition and rancor, the novice's hatred for the beauty of the temple, "steadfast in its secular perfection." The protagonist, Mizoguchi, an ugly stuttering man, escapes existential monotony through his contradictory feelings for the temple. On the one hand, under the threat of bombing raids, a danger they both share, he comes to love the temple. On the other hand the stone thrown into the lake that reflects the perfect object, breaking and spreading in moving waves the Buddhist image of a world in which nothing is permanent makes him want to destroy the masterpiece. This is probably why beauty becomes so difficult to grasp for Mizoguchi:

> "It occurred to me that the Golden Temple might have adopted some disguise to hide its true beauty. Was it not possible that, in order to protect itself from people, the beauty deceived those who observed it? I had to approach the Golden Temple closer; I had to remove the obstacles that seemed ugly to my eyes; I had to examine it all, detail by detail, and with these eyes of mine perceive the essence of its beauty. Inasmuch as I believed only in the

beauty that one can see with one's own eyes, my attitude at the time was quite natural."

"When ye meet the Buddha, kill the Buddha; when ye meet your ancestor, kill your ancestor; when ye meet your father and mother, kill your father and mother! Only thus will ye attain deliverance!"—Mizoguchi remembers a Zen principle from Rinzai-roku when he first thinks of setting the temple on fire. Freedom, it seems, can only be earned by extreme gestures; through a criminal act, it awakens from its slumber and turns into life:

> "I was there alone and the Golden Temple— the absolute, positive Golden Temple—had enveloped me. Did I possess the temple, or was I possessed by it? Or would it not be more correct to say that a strange balance had come into being at that moment, a balance which would allow me to be the Golden Temple and the Golden Temple to be me?"

Indeed, at first, after Mizoguchi sets the temple on fire, he lets the flames engulf him, but then he changes his mind. He is caught on the neighboring hill, after he also gives up his plan to commit suicide after the arson, for which he had bought a dagger. He eventually wanted to live without being tormented by the obsession of absolute beauty. . .

For Yukio Mishima, the age of contemporary Japan, pragmatic and materialistic, seemed to become extremely pessimistic. History brought along an increase in consumption, altering the harmony of traditional Japan. The technological ability to improve human existence seemed to inevitably alter the Japanese people's moral evolution. The resulting product of the Japanese consumerist society was the bourgeois man, first and foremost concerned with his own material welfare, without civic spirit and without ideals. And the economic man, who lives his life only between "costs" and "benefits" will never desire to get out of the system. Only the thymotic man, the "man of anger," is the one who, in order to have his value system recognized, a system which consists of more than an accumulation of desires that make up his physical existence, is ready to stand before a death squad. The act of ritual suicide, although it seems only an act of defiance, is the way in which Yukio Mishima tried to fight for the recognition of the Japanese soul in a world that seemed to bury it deeper every day.

If, according to Hegel, an individual cannot become self-aware, that is aware of himself as an individual, without being recognized as such by other human beings, the most deeply human feature in this fight for recognition seems to be that of risking one's own life against the strongest natural instinct, creating a *new self for oneself*. However, in a world of thymotic selves for whom the content of moral values is never the same, most often will the result inevitably be disaccord, as *thymos*, even in its most humble form, can be a source of conflict. Moreover, people generally do not see themselves as equal to others, but will try to be recognized as superiors in the family, in the work place, nationally or universally. *Thymos* can create, just as well as it can destroy.

After the shogun Hideyoshi seized power at the end of the 15th century, Japan enjoyed a period of internal and external peace that looked very much like the end of history postulated by Hegel. But instead of succumbing to the pleasures of the senses and returning to animality against this rich economic backdrop, the Japanese proved that one can be human by coming up with arts for art's sake, such as *noh* theatre, the tea ceremony, the art of flower arrangements, etc. A tea ceremony does not serve any economic or political purpose, but it is a proof of superiority: there are several schools for the tea ceremony and *ikebana*, each with its own traditions and canons, which create codes and rules lacking all utilitarian purpose.

To the contrary, however, the process of modernization described by contemporary social sciences may be understood as a gradual triumph of the desiring part of the soul, led by reason, over the thymotic one. Renouncing thymotic pride ensures, in exchange, a quiet life with increasing material prosperity:

> "In some countries like Japan, this trade was made overtly: the modernizing state set up members of the former samurai or warrior class as businessmen, whose enterprises grew into the twentieth-century *zaibatsus*."

Yukio Mishima's point of view categorically rejected this tendency for Japan. The writer who described in the tetralogy *Sea of Fertility* a Japan that had probably reached "the point of no return," believed now that only a violent gesture could change things. He saw the moment of action from the perspective of the Nietzschean conclusion according to which the decisive issue will always be whether one is ready to sacrifice, not what one wants to sacrifice for. Opting for an absolute moral value through which one can demonstrate inner strength and superiority to material issues and natural determination, Yukio Mishima

understood that this was the only possible beginning for freedom and creativity.

Man's opinions and passions are interconditioned, however, as the former becomes the object of the latter. The desire for recognition is the most specifically political part of human personality and Yukio Mishima stated his own by exacerbating it to fanaticism, which made him want to assert himself in front of the others, Japanese and foreigners alike. Contemporary Japanese society thus became the scene for the manifestation of his own thymos, as the writer fought for the recognition of his personal view of the contemporary world.

The reaction of his contemporaries to his gesture was one imposed by the historic moment. Taking him seriously would have meant that the Japanese society denied not only its adaptation to defeat, but also its comfortable settling into a world considered problem-free, governed by the progress of modernization and prosperity. Thus, it was better to see in the violent act merely an absurd mixture of literature, ideology and theatricality: the writer's *thymos* was called "love of fame" and interpreted as the thirst for glory of a strong ambitious man.

Yukio Mishima was, ultimately, a sociologist and a social philosopher who tried to predict and draw the attention to the subsequent historical development of the archipelago, resonating to the tensions of civilization and the personal responsibilities this requires in a society that strived for humanism and rationality, equality and freedom. Platonic to a certain extent, the world proposed by Yukio Mishima seemed to be the intellectual intuition of the world of pure beauty, and politics became to him the "royal Art." Similar to Plato's political man, the Japanese writer had imagined citadels meant to embody the beautiful, hence the aestheticist rejection of any compromise:

> "The moment I set the wordless body, full of physical beauty, in opposition to beautiful words that imitated physical beauty, thereby equating them as two things springing from one and the same conceptual source, I had in effect, without realizing it, already released myself from the spell of words. For it meant that I was recognizing the identical origin in the formal beauty in the wordless.... body and the formal beauty in words, and was beginning to seek a kind of platonic idea that would make it possible to put the flesh and words on the same footing. At that stage, the attempt to project

words onto the body was already a stone's throw away."

Yukio Mishima proposed, however, a world in which those who had expressed the wish to cooperate and the institutions that would make their dreams and projects for a better world possible manifested standards of decency and morality that belonged to a social system that would disappear. This inevitably implied not only the destruction of his utopic plan, but also self-destruction. The political artist demanded a point outside of the social world from where he could lever the world out of its joints, and found it in the notion of death promoted by *bushidō*, the way of the samurai. Naturally, however, the social world must go on during any reconstruction.

Aestheticism and radicalism lead the Japanese man of letters to abandon reason and replace it with a desperate belief in political miracles. But the irrational attitude rooted in the belief in a beautiful world speaks ultimately to the emotions, not to reason:

> "At one time, I had been the type of boy who leaned at the window, forever watching out for unexpected events to come crowding in towards him. Though I might be unable to change the world myself, I could not but hope that the world would change of its own accord. As that kind of boy, with all the accompanying anxieties, the transformation of the world was an urgent necessity for me; it nourished me from day to day; it was something without which I could not have lived. The idea of the changing of the world was as much a necessity as sleep and three meals a day. It was the womb that nourished my imagination. What followed in practice was in one sense a transformation of the world, in another it was not. Even though the world might change into the kind I hoped for, it lost its rich charm at the very instant of change. The thing that lay at the far end of my dreams was extreme danger and destruction; never once had I envisaged happiness. The most appropriate type of daily life for me was a day-by-day world destruction; peace was the most difficult and abnormal state to live in."

Yukio Mishima fought for the recognition of spiritual values, then of physical ones and ultimately for the affirmation of total freedom, that is becoming free from any physical constraints and conquering the metaphysical, completely undetermined by nature. For him, it was not the calculation of economic profit that made human life noble, but precisely this freedom of moral option, which values man himself in the

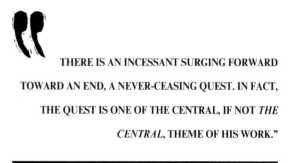

THERE IS AN INCESSANT SURGING FORWARD TOWARD AN END, A NEVER-CEASING QUEST. IN FACT, THE QUEST IS ONE OF THE CENTRAL, IF NOT *THE CENTRAL*, THEME OF HIS WORK."

first place, but also the people, events and objects that surround him . . . .

Source: Rodica Frentiu, "Yukio Mishima: Thymos between Aesthetics and Ideological Fanaticism," in *Journal for the Study of Religions and Ideologies*, Vol. 9, No. 25, April 2010, pp. 69–90.

Sascha Talmor

In the following excerpt, Talmor discusses Mishima's view of mortality.

Yukio Mishima (the pseudonym of Kimitake Hiraoka) was born in Tokyo in 1925. He belonged to an old Samurai family and was brought up on its traditional values. When he graduated from the exclusive Peers' School in 1944, he received a citation from the Emperor as the highest honour student. He graduated from the Tokyo Imperial School of Jurisprudence, making good use later in his fiction of his knowledge of the law, the ways of life and thought of lawyers, judges, of judicial proceedings and technicalities, as well as of his knowledge of everything connected to the prison-world.

He published his first story at the age of thirteen and, encouraged by his teacher, continued writing. His vast literary work comprises all genres—short stories, novels, novellas, essays, plays, and travel books. In addition, he also wrote the script of, played in, and produced a number of films. Like Dickens, Balzac, and other famous writers before him, he also wrote for the popular press (in order to make a living), but, since these writings have not been translated, we do not know their worth.

Most of his other work has been translated into the major European languages, especially into English and French: *The Sound of Waves* (1956), *Five Modern No Plays* (1957), *Confessions of a Mask* (1958; 1967), *The Temple of the Golden Pavilion* (1959), *After the Banquet* (1963),

The Sailor Who Fell From Grace With the Sea (1965), *Forbidden Colours* (1968), *Thirst for Love* (1950; 1969), and *The Sea of Fertility*, a cycle of four novels—*Spring Snow* (1972), *Runaway Horses* (1973), *The Temple of Dawn* (1975), and *The Decay of the Angel* (1974). One of his films deserves special mention—*Patriotism*—since it prefigured his own death.

In 1970, on the morning when he wrote the last page of his novel, he committed ritual suicide—*seppuku*—in a spectacular way, in the sight of his group of followers, after a desperate political attempt to reinstate a traditional military regime. His life, his work, his death, have caught the imagination of millions in the whole world.

It is difficult to discuss a writer of Mishima's stature within the limits of a short article. I shall, nevertheless, try to give an overview of his major novels and attempt to outline his view of life and death.

… In his very short life, Mishima has produced a great *oeuvre*. It comprises 257 books, of which 15 novels in Japan and 77 translations into English and other European languages, countless short stories and plays. Ten of his books have been filmed, but I want to mention only one of them because it depicts his own death some years later.

Based on his novella *Patriotism*, Mishima wrote the script, acted in it and directed it. It possesses all the purity and simplicity of a great work, and portrays, with reticence and economy, the double suicide of a young couple. (Such double suicides of a couple were not unusual in Japan). The central motive of this suicide is loyalty and, as a critic has rightly noted, this would have been a better title for the film. The story is simple: after an unsuccessful revolt by a group of right-wing officers, they are all to be executed—all, except their lieutenant who has been spared because he has recently married. But both husband and wife refuse this dishonour: he will die out of loyalty to his brother officers and the Emperor, she out of loyalty to her husband. (It is worth noting that the story is based on an actual political event, the abortive military coup of 1936) . . . .

It is very difficult, if not impossible, to evaluate the greatness of Mishima in a short space, and by trying to do so much will necessarily be left out. He has been compared to Proust, Gide

and Sartre, to Thomas Mann and Dostoevsky, in one word, to some of the greatest writers of our time. But what is so unique about him is the fusion of Western and Japanese culture which pervades all his work. He could do it because he himself was a product of both these cultures, so much so that some of his novels appear to many to be more Western than Japanese. He had mastered not only English and French literature and art, but also Greek and Latin, in addition to his mastery of classical Japanese.

The fictional world he has created is peopled with innumerable characters, and all of them, from the major characters in the centre to the minor ones in the background, are all with a personality of their own, distinct from the others by their ways, words, thoughts, feelings and gestures—just like in life. Like in Thomas Mann, the centre is occupied by the family (Japan being, like Mann's nineteenth[-century] Germany a family-centred society), with their dependents, servants, near and distant relatives. A series of brilliant figures occupy the stage (e.g. Kiyoaki, Honda, Isao), all related by ties of blood or marriage; we follow them from early childhood, through youth, maturity, to old age and death. And in the description of their lives, experiences, friendships, loves, successes and failures, ambitions, hopes, played out against the background to which they belong and the social and political fabric of the whole country, we get a life-like picture of Japan in its new form. And all this panorama throbs with the energy of life and a sense of great intensity—the same that pervaded Mishima's own life. There is an incessant surging forward toward an end, a never-ceasing quest. In fact, the quest is one of the central, if not *the* central, theme of his work. It is of course also the central theme of the ancient Greek, English and French epics.

The intensity of life is there from the beginning of his work, as well as the passion, the violence, the conflicts, and the quest. For all Mishima's characters are on the quest for something above and beyond the life of every day, for beauty, love, honour, for the spiritual or religious. This quest is symbolized by an ascent—be it of a hill, a tower, the stone-stairs of a temple or religious shrine. (We recall Kiyoaki's repeated ascents of the hill leading to the convent of Gensshi, an ascent repeated after his death for the last time by his aged friend Honda). That this quest always ends in failure is perhaps to be expected: for Mishima was a Buddhist and believed in Shinto Buddhism as do many Japanese. (It was, in fact, till 1945 Japan's official religion). And for such believers this world is all appearance, transitoriness, ephemera. If one is to seek something of value one can find it only in detachment, contemplation, and serenity. Perhaps one of the most memorable scenes in all of Mishima's work is that last scene of his last book when the Abbess reveals to Honda the great secret of the Buddhist faith—the Void.

But there is not only the world of men with their vain pursuit of pleasure and possessions, there is also the world of Nature. Its presence informs every one of Mishima's works, and his love of nature in all its aspects is skillfully imparted to his readers. We see the country in its changing seasons and colours, with its trees, flowers, shrubs, its rivers, waterfalls, seashore and finally the wide, wide sea. The sun, moon and stars, the sky, clouds, rain, storms, and typhoons are described in all their changing phases and forms. The sun naturally occupies a central place since it represents the Emperor in all his power and glory. The land is seen in all its changing features, colours and sounds, but is, for the most part stark and bare, giving a feeling of great space. When his heroes are about to take their life they are seen in a lonely, beautiful spot where they can, for the last time, look at the land, at a tree, a flower, the sea. Since it is with Isao that Mishima most identifies himself and has endowed him with those qualities which, following his family traditions, he valued most, it is appropriate to end with a passage describing Isao's death:

> The orchard gate opened easily. At the bottom of the steps, he saw the white spray leaping high as the waves worried the rocks. For the first time he became conscious of the echo of the sea . . .
>
> Finally he came to a place where the cliff was gouged out to form something like a cavern. A greenish, twisted mass of rock had been partly eroded away, and from its top the branches of a great evergreen tree hung low over this ledge. A slender stream of water, sheltered by ferns, meandered over the rock surface, flowed through the grass, and apparently fell into the sea below.
>
> Here Isao hid himself. He quieted his throbbing pulse. There was nothing to be heard but the sea and the wind . . . Though there was no moon, the sea reflected the faint glow of the sky, and the waters gleamed back.
>
> "The sun will not rise for some time", Isao said to himself, "and I can't afford to wait. There is

no shining disk climbing upward. There is no noble pine to shelter me. Nor is there a sparkling sea."

And then the final moment has come and he commits what he had sworn to do from the very beginning: "Then, with a powerful thrust of his arm, he plunged the knife into his stomach. The instant that the blade tore open his flesh, the bright disk of the sun soared up and exploded behind his eyelids."

(*Runaway Horses*, the end)

On his last day, beside the completed manuscript of his last novel, there was found on Mishima's desk a slip of paper with a single sentence: "Human life is short, but I would like to live for ever."

His passion for life had been intense—and so had his passion for death.

Source: Sascha Talmor, "Mishima—A Passion for Life and Death," in *Durham University Journal*, July 1991, pp. 269–76.

SOURCES

Hardin, Richard F., *Love in a Green Shade: Idyllic Romances Ancient to Modern*, University of Nebraska Press, 2000, pp. 223–24.

Hokenson, Jan Walsh, *Japan, France, and East-West Aesthetics: French Literature, 1867–2000*, Farleigh Dickenson University Press, 2004, p. 316.

Mishima, Yukio, *The Sound of Waves*, translated by Meredith Weatherby, Vintage International, 1994.

Nathan, John, *Mishima: A Biography*, Da Capo Press, 2000, pp. xiv, 110, 115, 120–21.

O'Neil, Patrick M., *Great World Writers: Twentieth Century*, Vol. 7, Marshall Cavendish, 2004, p. 913.

Petersen, Gwenn Boardman, *The Moon in the Water: Understanding Tanizaki, Kawabata, and Mishima*, University of Hawaii Press, 1979, pp. 201, 204–205, 217–19, 221, 252–53, 255.

Spencer, J. E., "Marine Life and Animals in Oriental Economy," in *Asia, East by South: A Cultural Geography*, John Wiley & Sons, 1954, pp. 90–105.

FURTHER READING

Keene, Donald, *Five Modern Japanese Novelists*, Columbia University Press, 2005.
    Keene introduces Western readers to the lives and works of Mishima, Junichiro Tanizaki, Yasunari Kawabata, Kobo Abe, and Ryotaro Shiba in this

book of essays that includes reflections on personal encounters with each of these important novelists. Keene is a well-respected scholar of Japanese literature and has a unique perspective on Mishima as one of his closest friends.

Napier, Susan, *Escape from the Wasteland: Romanticism and Realism in the Fiction of Mishima Yukio and Oe Kenzaburo*, Harvard University Asia Center, 1996.
    In *Escape from the Wasteland*, Napier compares the work of Mishima and Oe in the context of postwar Japan. After the war left Japan in ruins, the country was opened to outside influence for the first time in its very long history. Both Mishima's and Oe's works are rife with the effects of this sudden cultural shift, despite their opposing political and social beliefs.

Ross, Christopher, *Mishima's Sword: Travels in Search of a Samurai Legend*, Da Capo Press, 2006.
    Ross traveled to Japan in search of the antique sword that Mishima had used in his ritual suicide. In *Mishima's Sword*, he tells the story of this journey off the beaten path, exploring unfamiliar cultural territory while discovering more about Mishima's biography and aesthetic.

Yourcenar, Marguerite, *Mishima: A Vision of the Void*, translated by Alberto Manquel, University of Chicago Press, 2001.
    Mishima: A Vision of the Void details Mishima's life from birth to death, with a specific focus on Mishima's challenging family life as a child, the enormous effect of Western influence on his behavior and writing style, and his final act of seppuku. Mishima's life is as complex as it is impressive, but a great darkness followed and eventually consumed him. Any biography of Mishima is not for the faint of heart.

SUGGESTED SEARCH TERMS

Yukio Mishima

The Sound of Waves

Daphnis and Chloe

Pastoral novel

Postwar Japan

Japanese shrines

Pearl diving

Greek classicism

Japanese folklore

The Wizard of Oz

1939

In the years since Victor Fleming's film *The Wizard of Oz*, based on the novel by L. Frank Baum, was released in 1939, it has become one of the foundations of American, indeed world, popular culture. Baum's novel, *The Wonderful Wizard of Oz*, had been a children's classic ever since its publication in 1900 and had already been filmed several times—once with Baum himself as the director—as well as adapted into musical stage plays. But the 1939 film became an American classic, as beloved as any film ever made in Hollywood, familiar to practically everyone and the source of such universally remembered lines as "There's no place like home," "I have a feeling we're not in Kansas anymore," and "Pay no attention to that man behind the curtain." The film turned a beloved children's book into an enduring secular myth that is a touchstone of the American imagination.

PLOT SUMMARY

The Wizard of Oz begins in Kansas. On screen it is a gray dustbowl world that might come from John Steinbeck's *The Grapes of Wrath*, an America wracked by the Great Depression, an image that comes from Baum's sojourn on the plains of South Dakota during the depression of the 1890s. Baum makes a point of noting that Dorothy "could see nothing but the great gray prairie

FILM
TECHNIQUE

- The use of color is almost as old as film itself. In many films of the silent era, the director would attempt to create visual themes by tinting groups of scenes a certain color—for example, showing night scenes in a monochrome blue or scenes of battle in red—and some of the earliest films (for instance, those of Georges Méliès) would have entire sequences where color was hand-painted onto the prints to highlight their vividness. The Technicolor process, which was invented in 1922, was used sparingly in Hollywood films through the 1950s. But the startling effect of seeing the first shot of Oz open up in full color after the gray-toned world of Kansas has rarely been equaled in modern films. This simple device creates a wholly new world for the viewer. However, the original impetus to use color came from commercial considerations, to compete with Disney's Technicolor *Snow White and the Seven Dwarfs* (1937).

- During the scene in which Dorothy's house is uplifted into the tornado, the viewer easily becomes distracted by the effects shots of the other citizens of Kansas also flying in the storm that Dorothy sees through the window. It is worth noting that this window is very oddly shaped for a Kansas farmhouse (and, indeed, there is no such window visible on the Kansas farmyard set that shows the outside of the house) but is of precisely the same dimensions as a movie screen from 1939. What the film viewer sees in these scenes is effectively an image of Dorothy, reclining on her bed and viewing a film—a film within a film.

- The set design and dressing of *The Wizard of Oz* were innovative in many ways. Sets for black-and-white films usually used different shades of brown to stand in for colors, but the Technicolor scenes in Oz required an entirely different approach to color. The sets could not be dressed in true colors either, since the Technicolor process introduced distortions. For example, to make the ruby slippers appear bright red on film, they had to be a dark wine color. The set designers purposefully avoided modeling the set after the Baum book's illustrations, since they felt they had to create something modern in feel, no matter how fantastic. One prominent element of the set dressing is the flowers and plants in Munchkinland. A modern-day viewer will immediately see that they are all made of plastic. But in 1939, hardly anyone in the general public had even seen plastic, so they seemed fantastic and mysterious. Musicals were usually filmed on soundstages so that the choreography could be tightly controlled. But this meant they generally could not show outdoor, or exterior, scenes. To achieve this, *The Wizard of Oz* was filmed on stages dressed to look like exteriors, pioneering a device that would be used in many later Hollywood musicals.

on every side." Even her Uncle Henry "was gray also." But Baum says as little else as possible about Kansas, and the long segments of the film set in Kansas are largely new inventions. Dorothy, just back from school, plays around her aunt and uncle's farmyard, where she is rescued from the pigpen by their three farmhands, Hank, Zeke, and Hickory. Almira Gulch, an unpleasant but wealthy woman, soon arrives on her bicycle with an order from the sheriff that Dorothy's dog, Toto, be destroyed because he nipped at her once. She leaves with the dog, but Toto escapes from her clutches and runs home, and Dorothy decides that she has no choice but to escape also. When she runs away from home she gets as far as the wagon of Professor Marvel, a traveling stage magician. Pretending to use his magic powers to see the

future and what is happening far off, he persuades her to go back home, but a tornado is coming, and her aunt and uncle and the farmhands have taken shelter in the storm cellar. Dorothy, however, looks for them in the house and is inside it when the cyclone arrives. She is immediately hit on the head by flying debris and knocked unconscious. In the film, everything that happens from this point on, until she wakes up back in Kansas, seems to be some sort of fevered dream of Dorothy's. This is perhaps the film's greatest departure from the book, where there is no question that Dorothy's adventure in Oz is meant to be read as real experience, calling on the reader's willing suspension of disbelief.

The cyclone picks up Dorothy's house and sends it flying through the air. Looking through the window, she sees that it has picked up Miss Gulch also, whom Dorothy sees transform into a witch flying on a broomstick. When the house lands, Dorothy and Toto go outside, into a world that is now in full color. She is in a village of Munchkins (played by dwarf actors) who more typically sing and dance rather than speak. Glinda the Good Witch of the North flies onto the scene in a sphere of pink light and explains to Dorothy that the Munchkins are grateful to her for killing their oppressive ruler, the Wicked Witch of the East, who was crushed under her house. After a long legalistic procedure to declare the witch dead, the Munchkins put on a parade in Dorothy's honor. But the dead witch's sister, the Wicked Witch of the West, appears in a puff of smoke. She tries to strip the magical ruby slippers off of her sister's corpse, but Glinda casts a spell to put them onto Dorothy's feet, where their power protects her from the witch's magic. The witch disappears, vowing to somehow get the slippers. Glenda tells Dorothy that the Wizard of Oz is the only person in Oz who might be able to get her back to

Kansas. So Dorothy sets out on the Yellow Brick Road toward the Wizard's Emerald City.

Along the way, Dorothy encounters a living Scarecrow who wants a brain, a Tin Man who wants a heart, and a Cowardly Lion who wants courage. They accompany Dorothy, hoping that the Wizard can give each one what he lacks. They soon sight the Emerald City, a mass of tall green art deco towers (in the book, the city was not green, but the Wizard required everyone who entered it to wear green-tinted glasses so it would appear green to them). The Wicked Witch of the West casts a spell to put a field of poppies in their path, which makes the Cowardly Lion and Dorothy and Toto pass out. Glinda counters this by sending a snowstorm to kill the flowers, which revives Dorothy and her breathing companions. This device was borrowed from Baum's Oz stage play. In *The Wonderful Wizard of Oz*, they are rescued by an army of mice whose queen the Tin Man has saved from a wild cat.

Once they are in the Emerald City, the Wizard dashes their hopes and refuses even to see Dorothy and her companions. But then the Wicked Witch flies on her broomstick and writes "Surrender Dorothy!" above the city, like a skywriting airplane writing an ad. The Wizard now agrees to see them. He is manifest as a giant floating head surrounded by fire. He promises he will send Dorothy back to Kansas and give her companions the attributes they desire, but only if they first get the Wicked Witch's broomstick. Dorothy points out they could get that only if they were to kill her, which is what the Wizard ultimately wants.

Dorothy and her companions journey westward toward the witch's castle, but she sends out her army of flying monkeys to kidnap Dorothy and her dog; the witch is unconcerned about the others. The witch tries to take the ruby slippers off of Dorothy but is prevented by their magic charm. She determines that she must kill Dorothy first, before she can get the shoes. While Dorothy waits for execution, the witch leaves her locked in a tower room with her crystal ball, in which Dorothy sees a vision of Aunt Em frantic over the disappearance of her niece, which transforms into a mocking image of the witch.

Meanwhile, the Scarecrow, Tin Man, and Cowardly Lion have reached a hill overlooking the drawbridge of the witch's castle. They fight with and overpower a group of Winkie guards who have been patrolling the hill. When the guard at the drawbridge is changed, they sneak into the castle disguised as Winkie soldiers. They soon break Dorothy out of the tower but are chased around the castle by the witch and her soldiers. When they are cornered, the witch announces she will carry out her intention to kill Dorothy, but will make her watch the deaths of her friends and dog first. In the days before running water was common in buildings, many workshops and other structures that were especially prone to burning down had buckets filled with water or sand deployed throughout them as a fire-prevention measure. There is such a bucket on the wall near where Dorothy is standing. She seizes it and splashes water on the witch's broomstick when she lights it on fire to ignite the Scarecrow. The water splashes onto the witch too and melts her. Once the witch is dead, the Winkies seem to be released from a spell, or perhaps just from the fear of their mistress, and they hail Dorothy as their savior, just as the Munchkins have done. They gladly give her the broomstick to take back to the Wizard.

Dorothy and her companions walk back to the Emerald City. In Baum's book, Dorothy has inherited control of the flying monkeys, and they carry her and the others there. Oz grants them another audience, but as the giant head is attempting to renege on his promises, Toto pulls aside a curtain toward the rear of the throne room and reveals the Wizard (identical to Professor Marvel from Kansas) operating the controls of machinery. This is the true Wizard, and everything else was just his trickery. He is no wizard but is a balloonist who has been blown from Omaha to Oz in much the same way as Dorothy. He proceeds to give the Scarecrow a diploma, the Tin Man a testimonial, and the Cowardly Lion a medal, which leave each of them satisfied that he finally got the thing he wanted. Dorothy he proposes to take back to Kansas in his balloon. But owing to a mishap, he and the balloon go off without her. At this point in the book, Dorothy and her companions set off on another arduous journey, past fighting trees and a village inhabited by living china dolls, to reach Glinda, who might be able to help her. But in the film, Glinda again flies into the scene and tells Dorothy that the ruby slippers have the power to send her back. They have all along, but Dorothy only had to come to realize that home meant her heart's desire. She clicks the shoe's heels together saying, "There's no place like home," and the magic shoes send her back to Kansas.

In *The Wonderful Wizard of Oz*, Dorothy says just once, "There is no place like home," in answer to the Scarecrow's question of why she should want to go back to a gray place like Kansas when she might stay in Oz; but Mervyn LeRoy, the producer of *The Wizard of Oz*, decided to make this phrase the mantra of the film, with Dorothy's overt desire to return home as the driving force of the film, hence Dorothy's incantation of it almost as a spell. Perhaps during the hard times that still prevailed during the film's release, the phrase was intended to comfort audiences that might have had little to value except home in its larger sense, regarding family and America's traditions and values. Once Dorothy wakes up back in Kansas to find that the whole experience in Oz has been a dream induced by a concussion she suffered during the tornado, she indeed swears never to leave the family farm again, an already old-fashioned virtue in 1939.

CHARACTERS

Auntie Em

Auntie Em, played by Clara Blandick, is one of the few Kansas characters who lacks an Oz counterpart. Blandick began her career playing romantic leads on the stage, but as she aged, she became a character actress. She has taken the place of the orphaned Dorothy's mother, and though she might seem harsh to Dorothy, because of her no-nonsense attitude to the farmwork, the bond between the aunt and niece seems to be the most important thing in Dorothy's life and what draws her back to Kansas from Oz.

Cowardly Lion

The same actors played the three farmhands in Kansas and Dorothy's three companions in Oz, with Zeke and the lion played by Bert Lahr. This conceit is entirely lacking from Baum's book, in which the Kansas framing story is far less developed than in the film. This double casting was done because the studio feared that the audience would not accept the fantastic idea of a talking lion or scarecrow, such that the characters needed to be firmly drawn from the real world. The three farmhands were borrowed from the 1925 *Wizard of Oz* film, where the fantastic Oz personae are

merely disguises worn by the farmhands who accompanied Dorothy to Oz. In a thematic device used with all three of her companions, the character of the Cowardly Lion is someone who is brave but does not know it; this already begins to be developed in Zeke, who saves Dorothy when she falls into a pen full of hogs, which are remarkably aggressive and dangerous compared with other farm animals. As for the Cowardly Lion, he acts the bully to make up for his anxieties over cowardice and terrorizes the Scarecrow and Tin Man when they and Dorothy first encounter him. When he goes after Toto, Dorothy smacks him on the nose, and he slinks away, mistaking his shame for cowardice. But with all the courage of a predatory animal, he takes the leading part in overcoming the guards and infiltrating the Wicked Witch's castle, complaining all the while that he is too afraid to do what he is doing. He only becomes convinced of his courage when the Wizard gives him the talisman of a medal.

Dorothy Gale

In *The Wonderful Wizard of Oz*, Dorothy is only about six or seven years old. For this reason, the child star Shirley Temple was seriously considered for the film role. However, in Baum's stage version as well as in earlier film adaptations, Dorothy is played by a slightly older actress as an ingenue, a seductive young woman. Although Judy Garland, who was sixteen during production of the 1939 film, could have played the role that way, the filmmakers resisted the temptation and stressed Dorothy's innocent and childlike qualities. Garland was chosen especially for her singing ability.

Dorothy is named Gale in connection with the cyclone that carriers her to Oz and her tempestuous adventures there. Although the name was invented by the filmmakers, it is true to the spirit of Baum, who had a love of punning. Dorothy is the main character, with the story telling of her journey across Oz in an attempt to find a way to get back home to Kansas. In the book, she is clever and cynical beyond her years, but in the film she is an innocent. Aside from her ruling impulse to go home, Dorothy is primarily motivated by her sense of justice. She is not afraid of the Cowardly Lion when he threatens her and her companions but is outraged that he is acting as a bully, and she slaps him on the nose as the proper way to humiliate a bully, exposing his cowardice. She complains about many of the

Wizard's pronouncements because she considers them unjust, and her arguments with him provide Toto with the opportunity to expose him as a fraud. Her adventure provides her with the opportunity to understand her true character and the true importance of home to her.

Glinda, the Good Witch of the North

Glinda is one of the most prominent characters in the later Oz books, but in *The Wonderful Wizard of Oz*, her role is less pronounced: Dorothy is assisted by an unnamed Witch of the North when she first arrives in Oz, while Glinda is the Witch of the South and the ruler of the Quadling country there; Dorothy goes to her for help only at the end of the story. There is similar confusion about the West and East. In the book and film alike, the Winkie country is in the West and the land of the Munchkins in the East, but in many later Oz books this order is reversed. Glinda was played by Billie Burke, a prominent musical comedy actress who was the ex-wife of the Broadway impresario Flo Ziegfeld. Glinda acts as Dorothy's guru, protecting her and advising her but mainly teaching her by guiding her own self-realization. Thus she does not simply tell Dorothy that the ruby slippers have the power to take her back to Kansas when they first meet in Munchkinland, but allows her to have emotionally building experiences that let her more clearly understand why she wants to go home and realize the shoes' power on her own.

Almira Gulch

See Wicked Witch of the East *and* Wicked Witch of the West

Hank

See Scarecrow

Uncle Henry

Uncle Henry, played by Charley Grapewin, is another Kansas character without an Oz counterpart. Grapewin was a character actor, portraying the same old codger in each of his nearly one hundred film roles. Henry appears unpresupposing, but he constantly manages to get the upper hand over Almira Gulch in their verbal sparring by pretending to be as stupid as she thinks he is and then wheeling on her with biting sarcasm, although he eventually has to yield to the difference in their social status.

Hickory

See Tin Man

Professor Marvel

See Wizard of Oz

Nikko

The King of the Flying Monkeys is a well-developed character in *The Wonderful Wizard of Oz* who narrates the history of his species to Dorothy, but in the film he does not appear to have the power of speech. Pat Walshe, the dwarf actor who played him, had worked only on the fringes of Broadway and vaudeville, but he parlayed the fame from his film role (gained despite having worn a suit that completely obscured his features) into a successful vaudeville career.

Scarecrow

The Scarecrow is the first and most important of Dorothy's companions, as he succeeds the Wizard as the ruler of the Emerald City. He corresponds to the Kansas farmhand Hank and was played by the prominent Broadway dancer Ray Bolger. The Scarecrow believes he has no brains because his "head is full of straw." But like the other companions, he has more of what he wants than he believes, and he wisely develops the plan to rescue Dorothy from the witch's castle. He was made by a Munchkin farmer as a simple scarecrow (a task he was not very good at), and although he is animated by the magic of Oz, it is unclear in both the book and film versions exactly how and why he came to life.

Tin Man

The Tin Man, played by vaudevillian Jack Haley, is, like the Scarecrow and Cowardly Lion, a new persona of one of the Kansas farmhands (his Hickory incarnation was originally shown as an amateur inventor, but these scenes were cut from the film). The Tin Man, or Tin Woodsman, believes that, lacking a heart, he also lacks feeling, though he is repeatedly moved by pity for Dorothy ("If I had a heart it would be breaking"). He began as an ordinary person but was cursed by a witch so that he would cut off pieces of his own body when he swung his ax. He had each part replaced by the village tinsmith with a metal prosthesis, until his whole body was made of tin. Although in the film he is at first terrified of the Cowardly Lion's bluster, in the book he repeatedly kills wild animals with his ax to protect Dorothy.

Toto

Only in later Oz books do animals, including Toto, automatically gain the power of speech in Oz, so in the film he remains an ordinary dog. Nevertheless, Toto is the most important character in driving the plot. It is to save him from being killed that Dorothy decides to run away from home; later, it is Toto who pulls back the curtain revealing the fraud of the Wizard of Oz; and it is for Toto's sake that Dorothy misses the balloon ride with the Wizard. The Latin phrase *in toto* (meaning "in all") was an important concept in Baum's religion of Theosophy, expressing among other things the inherence of divinity in each part of the universe, and that was probably the source of the dog's name. Toto was played by a female cairn terrier named Terry who was owned by the animal trainer Carl Spitz. She appeared in many Hollywood films.

Wicked Witch of the East

It is easy to forget that the Wicked Witch of the East is even a character, since she has such a small role. She was played by Margaret Hamilton, who also played her sister, the Witch of the West. But when Almira Gulch is swept up into the tornado, it is into the Witch of the East that she transforms, flying on her broomstick past the house. However, Dorothy's house immediately falls upon and kills her, the ruby slippers she is wearing being no help to her. In his essay on *The Wizard of Oz*, Salman Rushdie perceptively suggests that the only thing we can know about her character comes from the state of the Munchkinland over which she ruled, which is seemingly a place of a far happier character than the gloomy and oppressed country of the Winkies. Rushdie claims, for instance, that she seems to have had no army to correspond to the Winkie guards who chase Dorothy and her friends through the western castle. In fact, she did have an army of Munchkins, and they are armed far more terribly than the Winkies with their huge halberds. When the Munchkin soldiers march in the parade in honor of Dorothy, they are carrying muskets. Also, the mayor and other Munchkin officials are presumably her appointees, and they are all officious and bureaucratic past any bound of reason, which would produce a tyranny of its own kind.

Wicked Witch of the West

The Wicked Witch of the West is even worse than her sister. She is nevertheless also played by Margaret Hamilton. The Witch of the West is principally driven by the desire for power. This is what makes her wicked, since in Oz witches are neither intrinsically good nor evil. She wants magical power and so covets the ruby slippers. But this is only a means to an end for her, since she ultimately wants political power. She used her army of flying monkeys to conquer and enslave the Winkies and, in an episode that is only alluded to in the book, once tried to conquer the Emerald City, although the Wizard managed to foil her. (It is his fear that the witch will make another attack that leads him to send Dorothy and her companions on their quest to assassinate her.) Salman Rushdie, in his *Wizard of Oz* essay, rightly sees her as a film image of the fascist dictators of the 1930s. The witch is also personally sadistic, taking pleasure in threatening to burn up the Scarecrow, since fire is the only thing he fears, and, when she thinks she has Dorothy and her companions at her mercy, terrorizing the girl by saying, "And the last to go will see the first three go before her! And your mangy little dog, too!"

Wizard of Oz

Professor Marvel is an aerialist and stage magician who works in the traveling shows and circuses common at the turn of the last century. Part of his act is a spiritualist show in which he has private consultations with show-goers. He is skillful at manipulating people to part with money, but he uses his skills to help Dorothy, on whom he takes pity and whom he convinces to go home. His character as the Wizard of Oz is essentially unchanged. When he found his balloon carried off to the Emerald City, he used his talents to overawe the people there into believing in his magical powers and making him their ruler. Although he makes his living from deceiving and manipulating people, he can do this because he understands human nature. He is essentially good-hearted toward the innocent, when it does not interfere with his own interest. His reward for the Scarecrow, Tin Man, and Cowardly Lion is simply to convince them of the truth about themselves that they have refused to accept, that they are, respectively, wise, compassionate, and brave. But he is just as quick to send Dorothy and her friends to what must seem like almost certain death on their quest to the witch's castle when it serves his purpose. He says of himself, "I'm a very good man—I'm just a very bad wizard."

The Wizard is portrayed by Frank Morgan, who also plays three other roles in the film: the doorman of the Emerald City, the cabby who drives Dorothy and her companions through the city, and the guard of the Wizard's palace. It is far from clear if the producers of the film simply used Morgan's comic talents to create these other personae, or if the audience is to understand that the Wizard is disguised as these other characters. If the latter is the case, he must use disguises such as these to go out into the Emerald City and gain information about his subjects that he uses to manipulate and subjugate them, just as Professor Marvel secretly found out information about Dorothy to control her (albeit for her own good) back in Kansas.

Zeke

See Cowardly Lion

THEMES

Magic

Having determined to film a fairy tale to compete with Disney's 1937 *Snow White and the Seven Dwarfs*, the MGM studio decreed that magic and the fantastic in its Oz film must be kept to a minimum. But the creators of the film were not hindered by this seeming paradox. Magic receives an exceptionally subtle and sensitive treatment for a Hollywood film. Baum's handling of magic reflects a Theosophical understanding: once a person realizes one's own potential, one need only wish for something and the wish will come true. This is reflected in the film in Oz itself, and especially in the ruby slippers, which allow Dorothy to wish herself back home. But the filmmakers present an entirely different take on the subject in the scenes set in Kansas, adopting a skeptical attitude toward magic that is paradoxically more in keeping with the generally hardheaded nature of Baum's modern American fairy tale and in harmony with Baum's own views about religion.

When Dorothy encounters Professor Marvel, she finds a very different and a very real, even commonplace, sort of magic. Marvel interrogates her and finds out she is running away from home. But he does not seem to ask her questions; rather, he makes statements, and she agrees that they are true, becoming increasingly impressed that he seems to know things that he ought not to know. He begins by telling her,

"Professor Marvel never guesses—he *knows*!" He tells her that she is running away from home—but what else could she be doing walking along the road with her luggage? He tells her things that are true of almost any teenager and so are true of Dorothy: "They don't understand you at home. They don't appreciate you. You want to see other lands." Dorothy is suitably impressed. She says, "Why, it's just like you could read what is inside of me!" "Just like" is the operative phrase here. Professor Marvel is using a technique of stage magicians called "cold reading," which has also been used by professional fortune-tellers since ancient times. In a cold reading, the fortune-teller or mentalist rapidly makes a number of statements that are very likely to be true and lets his client pick out the ones that she recognizes as true about herself. Unless the client is very sophisticated, she will think that the fortune-teller has some uncanny power to know hidden truths. Once he has her hooked, Professor Marvel invites Dorothy into his wagon, where he gives her a reading in his crystal ball. He tells the girl to close her eyes, so she may get "better in tune with the infinite." But while she has her eyes closed, he searches her bag and finds a picture of Aunt Em standing in front of the family farmhouse. He then describes what he saw in the photo, telling her he is seeing it in the crystal ball. Dorothy recognizes the details of her home and her aunt's appearance and believes in Marvel even more. Dorothy herself interprets the alarming detail that her aunt is sick as meaning that she is sick with worry over her niece disappearing without a word, exactly as Marvel intended. He uses the authority he has gained with her to shape her beliefs. In contrast to the earlier cold reading, this is a "hot reading," in which the fortune-teller finds out personal information about his client without her knowing it and then feeds it back to her as if he had found it out from divination. Whether performed by a stage magician in a mentalist act in front of a paying audience, or by a fortune-teller to bilk money from his client, cold and hot readings are usually done for gain. But Marvel has taken pity on Dorothy, and he uses the authority of the "infinite" and the "spirits" he builds up in her to persuade her to take the good advice to go home, which she might have been too stubborn to accept from a mere mortal. Perhaps no other scene has ever been filmed that so clearly shows how fortune-tellers, mediums, and psychics who claim to have magical powers actually operate.

READ, WATCH, WRITE

- Much effort has been, still is, and no doubt will continue to be applied to creating another *Oz* film that might rival 1939's *The Wizard of Oz* in appeal, although a fully satisfactory result has yet to be achieved. Try your own hand and write a scenario for a new *Oz* film, based either on one of the many Oz books written by Baum or your own imagination.

- Amateur musical adaptations of *The Wizard of Oz* are frequently performed as high-school plays or in community theaters. Watch one of them live or from among the large number posted on the Internet and write a critical essay comparing it with the film. Various clips of plays can be found online at the following links: http://www.youtube.com/watch?v = ub9lzSAMl0k&feature = related, http:// vimeo.com/43033372, and http://vimeo. com/19510914.

- New *Oz* films, as well as new *Oz* stage plays, such as Andrew Lloyd Weber's *Wizard of Oz* musical, the film version of *Wicked*, *Dorothy and the Witches of Oz*, and *Oz: The Great and Powerful*, are going to be continuously released or staged throughout the 2010s. Review one of these you have seen, especially considering the new work in comparison to the 1939 film. This can be done either as a paper or as a class presentation with clips from the film(s).

- The Chronicles of Narnia series of fantasy books for young people is nearly as popular as the Oz books. The first book in the series to be published, *The Lion, the Witch and the Wardrobe*, involves a group of schoolchildren who are magically transported to a fantastic land filled with magical creatures and ruled over by a wicked witch who has usurped the rightful ruler. It has also been adapted for film or television several times. Give a talk to your class discussing the similarities and differences between the two stories, illustrated by a PowerPoint presentation with clips from the films.

Religion

Although it is populated by witches and the Wizard, and all kinds of marvelous beings such as the living Scarecrow and Tin Man and talking animals, Oz is a country without religion, in the book as well as the film. Rushdie observes this fact in his *Wizard of Oz* essay:

> The film is breezily godless. There's not a trace of religion in Oz itself; bad witches are feared, good ones liked, but none are sanctified; and while the Wizard of Oz is thought to be something very close to all-powerful, nobody thinks to worship him.

This may seem hard to comport with the story's reputation as an American myth, given the deeply religious American character. But it speaks rather to another, and just as essential, part of the American character. Founded on the principles of the Enlightenment, America has set out a public space from which religion is excluded, allowing all of the many religions of Americans to coexist. This makes America a secular as well as a religious country, and as Rushdie also observes, *The Wizard of Oz* speaks to the very best traditions of Americans' secular nature in that Oz is "a world in which nothing is deemed more important than the loves, cares and needs of human beings."

Not because of America's secularism but along with its secular and religious natures, many Americans also developed a distrust not of religion but of the men and women who make their living from religion as clergy. Baum deeply embraced this native anticlericalism. It perhaps impelled him more strongly than anything else toward Theosophy, which holds that all

© *Pictorial Press Ltd | Alamy*

religions are true in the sense of their revelations coming from God, but also that all religions as institutions are false and manipulative, managed for the benefit of their professional practitioners. (For all that, one could make such a charge against Madame Blavatsky, the founder of Theosophy, and her successors.) Baum had already expressed his anticlericalism, alongside his respect for religion, before his discovery of Theosophy. In an editorial in his South Dakota newspaper, the *Saturday Pioneer*, on October 18, 1890 (quoted by Michael Patrick Hearn in his *Annotated Wizard of Oz*), Baum said,

> When the priests acknowledge their fallibility ... when they are able to reconcile reason and religion and fear not to let the people think for themselves, then, and then only will the Church regain its old power and be able to draw to its pulpits the whole people.

The Wizard as a character is commonly understood as an expression of Baum's mistrust of the clergy. He puts on an elaborate and seemingly miraculous show to overawe his subjects and petitioners, but it is a deception that he uses to keep power. The childish simplicity of Dorothy, and even of her dog, Toto, is able to expose him as a fraud. Baum and, even more so, the filmmakers are suggesting that masses and revival meetings are just as much a stage show as Professor Marvel's carnival act.

STYLE

Musical

The producers of *The Wizard of Oz* decided to film Baum's story as a musical, one of the most popular genres of film in America in the 1930s. Baum had already produced his novel as a stage musical that ran for eight years on Broadway, up until 1912, although none of that music was used for the 1939 film. The film was scored by Harold Arlen with lyrics by E. Y. "Yip" Harburg. The musical style, developed over the previous generation on Broadway as well as over the previous decade of movie musicals, employed music similar to popular dance tunes that rose toward the conventions of operetta when it had to. For its genre, many of the lyrics are delightfully inventive. For example, Dorothy describes in song the flight of her house that killed the witch: "The wind began to switch, / The house to pitch, / And suddenly the hinges start to unhitch. / Just then the witch / To satisfy an itch / Went flying on her broomstick thumbing for a hitch." When the Munchkin chorus take up the narrative, it comes out as: "It landed on the Wicked Witch in the middle of a ditch / Which / Was not a healthy sich- / Uation for / The Wicked Witch."

The lyrics are entirely conversational but at the same time perfectly metrical—the gross irregularities are calculated for effect—while playing with convention nearly like contemporary free verse. Of a wholly different character is "Somewhere over the Rainbow," which in the technical jargon of the musical is a *ballad*, meaning a song calculated for emotional evocation and intended to stand alone for radio play and single disc sales. As often in film, the truly dramatic music in the score is borrowed from the classical repertoire. Snatches of Igor Stravinsky's ballet *Rite of Spring* can be heard during the actual fall of Dorothy's house, while the chase through the witch's castle is accompanied by music from Modest Mussorgsky's tone poem *Night on Bald Mountain*.

It Was All a Dream

The narrative of *The Wizard of Oz*, unlike Baum's novel, presents all of the Oz action as a dream or hallucination that Dorothy had while she was unconscious after being knocked out during the cyclone. All of the major characters she meets in Oz are distortions of people she knows in her waking life: the farmhands, Almira Gulch, and Professor Marvel. The studio executives decided that this device was necessary because they feared audiences would reject such a fantastic story presented to them as real even in the context of the film. But the device is very common, especially in Hollywood films and television shows. It had been used in the 1925 *Wizard of Oz* film and may also have been inspired by the 1920 expressionist classic *The Cabinet of Dr. Caligari*. The device was parodied brilliantly, with direct reference to *The Wizard of Oz*, in *The Kentucky Fried Movie* in 1977.

CULTURAL CONTEXT

The Great Depression

The Wonderful Wizard of Oz was written at the end of a period of economic depression that began in 1893, while the film *The Wizard of Oz* was released during the Great Depression, which began in 1929. Baum's gray land of Kansas derived from his one visit to Kansas during his time as a traveling actor and from the time he lived in the similar area of South Dakota up until 1891. But the Kansas of the film would have been recognized by viewers as an American heartland wracked by the Great Depression. The crisis that is disturbing the Gale farm on the day of the cyclone, with the incubators for the newly hatched chicks failing, is a symbol of the failure of the entire economy. Kansas and much of the rest of middle America was wracked at the same time by dust-bowl conditions, as a prolonged drought made farming in the area nearly impossible, causing many farmers to move away from their homes forever, seeking new opportunities in places like California. Viewers would inevitably have recognized Oz as a place of escape, or rather a fantasy of escapism, from the economic and ecological disasters that were plaguing America in the 1930s.

Populism

In the early 1960s, a high-school history teacher named Henry M. Littlefield had trouble interesting his students in the history of Populism, an American political movement of the 1890s spearheaded by the People's Party, whose members were called Populists. The 1960s were also the period of *The Wizard of Oz*'s greatest popularity, with its annual showings on television garnering the highest ratings of any program. Littlefield worked with his students to develop a new curriculum that used Oz to solve the problem of interesting his students in Populism. In 1964, he published his results in an article in the *American Quarterly*: "*The Wizard of Oz*: Parable on Populism." In this article, Littlefield argues that "Baum created a children's story with a symbolic allegory implicit within its story line and characterizations." The allegorical interpretation reads *The Wonderful Wizard of Oz* as propaganda supporting the Populist movement. Populism appealed, it is argued, to the three classes of Americans most affected by the 1893 depression: farmers, laborers, and members of the military, symbolized by the Scarecrow, the Tin Woodman, and the Cowardly Lion. Littlefield compares, for instance, the Tin Woodman's slowly cutting off pieces of his anatomy under the Wicked Witch of the East's spell, only to replace them with tin, to the eastern industrialists opposed to Populism who "dehumanized a simple laborer so that the faster and better he worked the more quickly he became a kind of machine." Populism hoped to help the working classes through bimetalism, the expansion of the money supply by printing paper money backed by silver as well as gold, a policy immortalized in the famous "Cross of Gold" speech given by the populist Democratic leader William Jennings Bryan. This is seen to relate to the silver shoes (changed to ruby slippers for the film) and the road of yellow brick of the novel. Bryan, often caricatured as a lion, is seen as the Cowardly Lion of the novel, cowardly perhaps because he had lost the presidential election of 1896, though he was about to run again in 1900 (never mind that the Cowardly Lion was already used in the allegory). The false Wizard is the Republican president William McKinley. This allegorical framework has become immensely popular at both the high-school and college levels and is used in countless history and political science courses every year; it has become the subject of numerous books and articles, and there is even a comic book refining the allegory.

The only problem is that Baum had no such intention. Although he generally voted Democrat because he favored women's suffrage, he was far from being a Populist, and there is very little in the novel to suggest he had a Populist purpose, and nothing in his other writings or his life. The

idea also seems incompatible with the better-established and evidenced Theosophical reading of *The Wonderful Wizard of Oz*. Littlefield has been debunked just as often as he has been supported, most definitively by David B. Parker in his 1994 article "The Rise and Fall of *The Wonderful Wizard of Oz* as a 'Parable on Populism.'" But there seems no way to get the djinn back into the bottle. The allegory's supporters no longer care if it is true to Baum's intention or not, so long as they find it useful, as Ranjit S. Dighe argues in his 2002 political commentary on the novel, *The Historian's "Wizard of Oz": Reading L. Frank Baum's Classic as a Political and Monetary Allegory.*

CRITICAL OVERVIEW

Because it is a fairy tale and a work of popular literature, for most of its history *The Wonderful Wizard of Oz* was not taken seriously, and it was only in the last quarter of the twentieth century and beyond that serious critical work has been undertaken on either the book or the film. Michael Patrick Hearn is the leading scholar writing on L. Frank Baum and his creation, Oz. Hearn has published many important reference works, including his annotated edition of *The Wonderful Wizard of Oz* and an edition of the screenplay of the 1939 film. In his introduction to the screenplay, Hearn gives an especially useful history of earlier film and stage versions as well as an overview of the evolution of the 1939 shooting script. Although he insists that the success of the film is ultimately derived from the success of Baum's books rather than the reverse, as popular commentators often assume, Hearn is sensible that in the 1950s, when the Oz books had been banned from public libraries as Communistic and rejected as poorly written trash by many critics of children's literature, the revival of the film *The Wizard of Oz* on television kept Baum's legacy alive. Hearn chronicles how the annual screening of the film in the 1950s and 1960s, especially after color television sets became common, garnered the highest ratings of any show and truly made Oz a common touchstone of American life.

Salman Rushdie, one of the greatest living novelists, was commissioned by the British Film Institute to write an essay on the film, called by the same title, "*The Wizard of Oz*," which was published in 1992. Rushdie produced one of the most insightful works of criticism on the film. He begins with his personal interest in the film as a boy watching it in India. He recognized it as so superior to the Bollywood musicals he was used to seeing that he counts it as his chief inspiration to become a writer. For him, *The Wizard of Oz* is "a film whose driving force is the inadequacy of adults, even of good adults, and how the weakness of grown-ups forces children to take control of their own destinies, and so, ironically, grow up themselves." His only objection to the film is that Dorothy, after her adventure in Oz, should profess to think that there is no place like home and want to return to the gray world of Kansas. He considers this idea a reactionary fable that privileges community over the individual, and he observes that Baum himself did not believe it in those terms, since after a few more Oz books, Dorothy moves to Oz permanently, where, after all, she is a princess and a mighty sorceress. He also points out that the song "Somewhere over the Rainbow" expresses the longing to leave home for somewhere better, which he sees as the more powerful, and the more genuinely American, longing. Rushdie decides, finally, that

> the real secret of the ruby slippers is not that "there's no place like home," but rather that there is no longer any such place *as* home: except, of course, for the home we make, or the homes that are made for us, in Oz: which is anywhere, and everywhere, except the place from which we began.

That is, he decides that home, from this perspective, is the world one creates through one's own accomplishments, a conclusion entirely in line with the story's Theosophical origins, though Rushdie betrays no knowledge of Baum's involvement with that philosophy.

The popular film critic Roger Ebert ranks *The Wizard of Oz* among the hundred greatest films ever made. In his *The Great Movies*, Ebert provides a conspectus of the famous, almost folkloristic, stories about the production of the

film: Buddy Ebsen being cast as the Tin Man but succumbing to an allergic reaction to the silver make-up, Margaret Hamilton's costume catching on fire when she disappears in a puff of smoke from the Munchkin village, et cetera. He sees *The Wizard of Oz* as an expression of

> the key lesson of childhood, which is that someday the child will not be a child, that home will no longer exist, that adults will be no help because now the child is an adult and must face the challenges of life alone.

CRITICISM

Bradley A. Skeen

Skeen is a classicist. In the following essay, he discusses the character of the Wizard of Oz, from the film version of The Wizard of Oz, *as an American myth.*

One of L. Frank Baum's ambitions as a writer was to create a specifically American form of the fairy tale. He did not consider his Oz series as the final word in this endeavor, compared with other works like *The Magical Monarch of Mo*. But no other books that he wrote ever approached the popularity of his Oz series, and today his work is almost entirely forgotten except for Oz. So Oz is Baum's mythical legacy, one that was strengthened by the 1939 film *The Wizard of Oz*, whose universal popularity has sustained the reputation of his writings. In the 1950s, for instance, the Oz books went out of print and were banned from most libraries because of their supposedly Communist character during the hysteria of McCarthyism, but the film was untouched by such modern American fantasies, and its annual screening on television was always among the highest-rated shows of that era.

The Wizard of Oz, the film more than the book, is often called by critics an American myth, or a secular myth, signaling that Baum succeeded in his ambition. According to Evan I. Schwartz in his *Finding Oz*, Baum "rooted his vision in American images that were so vivid and concrete that they could capture the attention of children." The myth is indeed both American and secular on many levels. The most American thing about it is that simple folksy characters constantly deflate the pretensions of characters who try to puff themselves up into something better than other people. At the very beginning

WHAT DO I SEE NEXT?

- Baum produced a stage musical of *The Wonderful Wizard of Oz* that premiered on Broadway in 1902 and made several films based on various of his Oz books: *The Wizard of Oz* (1910), *The Magic Cloak of Oz* (1914), and *His Majesty, the Scarecrow of Oz* (1914). His son Frank Baum Jr., supervised two films, the 1925 *The Wizard of Oz*, which stared Oliver Hardy as the Tin Man, and a 1933 cartoon short, *The Wizard of Oz*. These short films are often included in video releases of the 1939 film. These films were produced by the Baum family, through short-lived production companies.

- *The Cabinet of Dr. Caligari*, a German film directed in 1920 by Robert Wiene and produced through Decla-Bioscop AG, deals with the same kind of fantastic subject matter as *The Wizard of Oz* but takes a diametrically opposed approach, presenting its supposedly real world as a terrifying, unreal place constructed with jarring editing, bizarre camera angles, and expressionist set design.

- *The Wiz* was originally a Broadway musical adapted from *The Wizard of Oz* film in the 1970s, with music of that period and an all-black cast. It was filmed in 1978 by Sidney Lumet and produced by Universal and Motown, starring Diana Ross and Michael Jackson.

- Walter Murch's long-awaited Disney Oz film, the 1985 film *Return to Oz*, adapts *The Marvelous Land of Oz* and *Ozma of Oz* but derives many of its elements from the 1939 film, including the ruby slippers. Murch treats his subject matter as serious drama without a musical-comedy element.

- Shirley Temple was seriously considered for the part of Dorothy in 1939's *The Wizard of Oz*. In her 1950s live-performance NBC drama series, Temple stared as Ozma in an adaptation of *The Land of Oz*. The kinescope of the show is now widely available on DVD and other formats.

- *Dorothy and the Witches of Oz*, directed by Leigh Scott for Palace/Imaginarium, had its theatrical release in 2012, as edited down from a larger television miniseries called *The Witches of Oz* (2011). The plot concerns Baum's fictional granddaughter, who has been writing new Oz books based on repressed memories of a childhood trip to Oz, and her return there again in the present day.

- Prana Studio's *Dorothy of Oz* is a computer-animated 3-D film being directed by Will Finn and Dan St. Pierre and scheduled for release in 2013. It is based on the 1989 novel of the same name by Roger S. Baum, L. Frank Baum's great-grandson.

---

of the film, Uncle Henry and Auntie Em waste no time in exposing Almira Gulch as a mean-spirited fool, for all that she lords it over everyone just because she owns half the county. When Gulch first appears, she tells Henry, "I want to see you and your wife right away about Dorothy.... I'm all but lame from the bite on my leg!" To which Henry replies, "You mean she bit ya?" pointing out her foolishness by pretending to foolishly misunderstand her himself. Equally American, however, is the fact that, although Dorothy's guardians see through Gulch, they are still unable to resist her because the law favors the wealthy and powerful, and if they don't agree to destroy Toto, they risk losing their farm in a lawsuit. Auntie Em personifies the true American spirit in that she grew up in the same town as Gulch and attended the same school and so considers her an equal, whereas Gulch puts on airs of superiority and privilege simply because she is rich. The same theme is played out again in the Emerald City, where the lowly Toto exposes Oz the great and powerful as a fraud by pulling the curtain back.

"

BAUM'S BOOK AND THE FILM BASED ON
IT HAVE HELPED TO ACTUALIZE HIS WISH FOR
NEW AGE SPIRITUAL RENEWAL."

The myth of Oz is American too in its secularism. Baum himself was not a Christian, and there is no mention of Christianity in the book and likewise none in the film, except when Auntie Em cannot bring herself to tell Gulch at last what she thinks of her, because she is "a Christian woman" and so cannot utter a curse. America is one of the most religious countries on earth, but part of the American experiment was to make religion an entirely private matter, creating for the first time a secular public space that is all-inclusive. While Oz is filled with magic, there is no open religious observance in the public square there either.

The intersection of the secular with the world of magic that is on display in *The Wizard of Oz* is of special interest because it gives rise to a peculiarly American kind of myth that is commonly called the New Age. The name *New Age* is given to a host of belief systems that, for the most part, are descended by historical links from Theosophy and Spiritualism. Theosophy used the term "New Age" to indicate its doctrine that the world was about to undergo a transformation of spiritual consciousness, but in recent years this original usage has receded into the background, and the term now refers to more general beliefs that the world operates according to spirituality and magic rather than the physical laws known to science. New Age believers generally consider that divinatory practices like astrology are able to reveal the future and spiritual truths and that the lives of individuals can be shaped by rituals and spiritual practices that often boil down to simply wishing. Most importantly, the New Age emphasizes a personal quest of spiritual self-discovery far removed from institutionalized religion.

Baum was a Theosophist. During his years in Chicago in the late 1890s, including the time he was writing *The Wonderful Wizard of Oz*, he was a member of the Ramayana Theosophical chapter. Chicago had become a springboard for Theosophy to become a worldwide religion thanks to its presence at the World Congress of Religions, which was held in conjunction with the 1893 World's Columbian Exposition in Chicago. Theosophy was founded by Helena Blavatsky, a Russian émigré who claimed to constantly produce new religious revelation by channeling a group of secret masters in Tibet, beings somewhere between Buddhist monks and gods. By *channeling*, of which Blavatsky was one of the earliest practitioners, she meant that she claimed these entities took possession of her body and spoke through her, using her voice as a channel. Blavatsky built support for Theosophy by associating it with progressive, even radical, political causes, such as women's suffrage, antivivisection, and the independence of India. Baum may have come to Theosophy in this way since, in the early 1890s when he was a newspaper editor in South Dakota, he was a powerful advocate of women's suffrage—although his mother-in-law converted first and exercised a powerful influence on him. Baum's deep concern for women's rights is reflected in the abundance of powerful female characters in the Oz series.

The Wonderful Wizard of Oz contains many elements of Theosophy. The new religion embraced the old idea of the great chain of being, which held that there was a continuity, even a spiritual continuity, between everything in the universe. This doctrine holds that all matter is alive and that life is a reflection of divinity in a material fashion. Rocks progress to fungus, to plants, to animals, and to human beings—which are the middle term of the universe, being both composed of animate matter and in possession of a divine soul—then through angels and other spiritual entities up to God. This is why things like trees and china dolls are alive and able to speak in Oz: even objects we think of as inanimate share in the universal soul and godhead. It also explains the baffling nature of the Tin Woodman and Scarecrow. All matter is essentially the same, and if it possess a divine soul, it will have intelligence and the ability to move, even if it is just a sack of straw. The Tin Woodman is a finer demonstration, since he was originally human but gradually had all of his physical parts replaced by metal ones, yet he remained the same person because at each step he continued to possess his spark of divinity.

Another element of Theosophy inspired the whole idea of the Land of Oz. Theosophists teach that there is somewhere in the solar system a place called the *astral plane* (later a widely used buzzword of the New Age). It is not material, but it is a real place, and the spirit of the Theosophist adept can journey there and create any reality and have any experience that one wishes. Because this experience is less physical and more divine, it is more real to the Theosophist than everyday reality. Oz likewise is a place with an unclearly defined relationship to the physical world (it is "over the rainbow"), where Dorothy can come and go, which is governed by fantasy rather than the physical laws of earth, and where, eventually, she is able to make her wishes become reality through the agency of the ruby slippers. The name Oz, despite the widely circulated story that it came from the O-Z drawer of Baum's file cabinet, may derive from the Vedanta guru Swami Vivekananda, Vedanta being a form of Hinduism he imported to America, with many filiations to Theosophy. Vivekananda's crest showed a cobra encircling a swan in a design very suggestive of the O-Z monogram common in the illustrations Baum commissioned for his book. Vivekananda was also an enthusiastic hot-air balloonist, just like the Wizard. Baum probably knew him personally.

An incidental use of a Theosophical idea is the Wicked Witch's army of flying monkeys. Theosophy preferred Hindu scripture to the Bible, and privileged texts like the Indian epic poem Ramayana. This work was enshrined in the name of Baum's own chapter of the Theosophical brotherhood. It will not be a surprise to readers of Baum's work to learn that the Ramayana concerns the adventures of the god Rama incarnated in human form while he wanders in exile from his home through a fantastic land ruled by the evil wizard Ravana. In his struggles against Ravana, Rama is aided by an army of flying monkeys. Once he defeats Ravana, Rama needs to return to his home to reclaim the throne that is rightfully his. He is flown there by the monkeys, just as Dorothy is flown to the Emerald City after overcoming the witch (although this was left out of the film). Rama's return to his home city provides one possible model for the somewhat puzzling desire of Dorothy to return to Kansas.

According to Theosophy, each person is a god but is unaware of it because he is imprisoned in a material body. Once he realizes it, he has only to will something, and it will come to pass. This is a core belief of the New Age movement,

often known as the power of positive thinking. It is reflected in several ways in Baum's novel. It is clear throughout the book and, even more so, in the film, to everyone but themselves, that the Scarecrow, Tin Man, and Cowardly Lion already possess the wisdom, compassion, and courage that they desire. They do not so much have to realize it as come to believe it. The Wizard has only to convince them of it by giving them tokens of the desired qualities—the diploma, testimonial, and medal in the film version. Significantly, even after the Wizard is exposed as a fraud, the three never lose faith in his abilities to grant their desires. Even more plain is the case of the ruby slippers (silver in the book). Once Dorothy comes to believe it, the magic slippers have the power to make any wish of hers come true. This seemingly fantastic idea is the centerpiece not only of Theosophy but also of the entire spectrum of New Age religions. They believe that everything that happens to a person is entirely caused by one's own wishes and that if a person can only come to know oneself and control what one actually desires, only the good things that one wants to happen will come to pass. This is an oversimplified version of the Indian idea of karma, which teaches that suffering in this life is atonement for evil committed during a past life and was chosen by the soul to purify itself prior to reincarnation.

Dorothy's adventure in Oz is a quest. Everything she does is in the service of her goal of returning home. The New Age, famously in Joseph Campbell's *Hero with a Thousand Faces*, tends to reduce all of religion and mythology to the quest motif, which it reads as a metaphor for self-discovery, inevitably the recognition of the supposed divinity within oneself. It is easy to see *The Wizard of Oz* as an exemplar of this idea. The physical journey acts as a metaphor for the spiritual journey that the New Age follower pursues through superficial versions of the world's religions.

The presence of these esoteric ideas in Baum's works have been a tremendous, though largely unrecognized force in helping them spread through the community of New Age believers at large. Even if no overt reference is made to Oz by New Age gurus, the content of their teaching is made more familiar and therefore acceptable to potential followers who have fond memories of *The Wizard of Oz*, consciously or not. The studio executives at MGM were

afraid that the fantastic elements in *The Wizard of Oz* would make it unacceptable to a naturally skeptical American audience. But paradoxically, the film itself, with its tremendous popularity, has helped to spread the fantastic beliefs of the New Age insofar as it faithfully reflects Baum's novel. If the Theosophical idea of creating a new world through wishing is literally cultish nonsense, it can be read as a symbol of a profound truth, that human beings create themselves through their own efforts. Baum's book and the film based on it have helped to actualize his wish for New Age spiritual renewal.

Source: Bradley A. Skeen, Critical Essay on *The Wizard of Oz*, in *Novels for Students*, Gale, Cengage Learning, 2013.

Linda Rohrer Paige

In the following essay, Paige opines on the importance of the change in Dorothy's slippers from silver to ruby red in the film adaptation as a feminist symbol.

> What hardships our ancestors suffered seem
> unreal
> and gray, like stones in the forest.
> Yet many beautiful children sit in frescoes,
> awaiting the red slippers of their inheritance.
> —Barbara Jordan, "To Those who Think
> about History"

We all know the film version of L. Frank Baum's classic story. Living on a farm on the dusty Kansas plains with her hardworking Uncle Henry and Auntie Em, Dorothy finds farm life harsh, and her friendly companions, the farmhands, will have to be let go. Worst of all, because of the dictates of the vindictive Elvira Gulch, Dorothy is about to lose her faithful dog Toto. When the cyclone hits, our heroine whirls into the electrifying world of the imagination, Oz. Wearing the ruby red slippers, she

> BECAUSE SHE INHERITED WOMAN'S SYMBOL—
> THE RED SLIPPERS—DOROTHY UNKNOWINGLY
> REVEALS HER KINSHIP TO THE WITCHES."

ventures down the yellow brick road seeking the fabulous Wizard of Oz, despite the perils lurking at the edges of the paint.

Baum's *The Wonderful Wizard of Oz* was first adapted into a 1902 musical, *The Wonderful Wizard of Oz*, then remade into the film *The Wizard of Oz* in 1939. Though the musical never became a success, the film has become a classic, presented yearly on television to the delight of millions. The screen adaptation returns to the original text; importantly, however, the silver shoes of Baum's classic are repainted and sequined a bright ruby red. Crucial to our understanding of Dorothy and her insistence on returning home are those slippers.

Even though Baum's story has been in circulation for almost a hundred years—the original having been published in 1900—few feminists have commented on the book or the film. This essay proposes a new reading of the 1939 film's central symbols, one at variance with the messages that MGM originally expected its audiences to receive. It follows Dorothy, as archetype, on her journey through Oz—metaphorically, on her quest for self-realization. Further, it examines her relationship (woman's) to patriarchy and unravels the clues inherent in the red shoes themselves, finding them to be a sign of the female imagination—capable of signaling life (imagination) or death (repressed imagination) for those who walk in them. Moreover, I hypothesize, contrary to popular belief, that Dorothy chooses poorly when she elects to return home; she succumbs to the patriarchal voices of her subconscious, and thereby represses her imagination and wastes her powers. Before Dorothy, other females have traveled this path—they, too, have "danced" in the red shoes.

More than any other image associated with women in literature and film, the ruby slippers represent woman's "inheritance" from members of her own sex. Before leaving the Land of the Munchkins, Dorothy inherits the shoes, which previously belonged to the recently "deflated" Wicked Witch of the East. Though critics have ascribed differing, often paradoxical, values to both the slippers and Dorothy's quest, they commonly agree on one indisputable fact: the red shoes are exclusively woman's symbol.

Finding their original counterpart in Hans Christian Andersen's classic fairy tale, *The Red Shoes*, these shoes surface repeatedly in poems and novels of the nineteenth and twentieth centuries. In the tale, they are the dancing shoes of little Karen, who, when forbidden to wear them, compulsively slips them on anyway. To her astonishment, she cannot kick them off—try as she might. Dancing her feet across meadows and forests, the shoes take a relentless toll on the child. Wretched and exhausted, poor Karen finally begs an executioner to chop off her feet: "Don't chop my head off," said Karen, "for then I can never repent of my sins. But pray, pray chop off my feet with the red shoes!"

He complies, and the red shoes, in macabre fashion, dance away with Karen's little feet still in them. These are the shoes of power, which signal anxiety or death for those who dance in them; they are Dorothy's slippers in *The Wizard of Oz*.

In *The Madwoman in the Attic*, Sandra Gilbert and Susan Gubar introduce the notion of women's "inheritance" of the red shoes in such popular fairy tales as *Snow White*. They maintain that the shoes, "passed furtively down from woman to woman," are the "shoes of art, the Queen's dancing shoes": the "red-hot iron shoes" with which the Wicked Queen of Snow White dances herself to death. Referring to the "feverish dread of the suicidal tarantella of female creativity," Gilbert and Gubar intimate that the red shoes promise both creativity and "death." They quote, from Ann Sexton's poem:

All those girls
who wore red shoes,
each boarded a train that would not stop.
. . .
They could not listen.
They could not stop.
What they did was the death dance.
What they did would do them in.

Though wearing the red shoes hints of rebellion, it simultaneously presents a visible reminder of the penalty for woman's insurrection (the color red, symbolic of passion, also suggests spilled blood).

Not only are the red slippers critical to our understanding of *The Wizard of Oz*, but so, too, is the house, the home from which Dorothy wishes to escape. The reality of home for Dorothy appears dismal: a life of drudgery, of pig sties, of broken incubators. Even the people of home somehow seem broken, withered, similar to the gray-tipped grass of their surroundings. Over the past several decades, feminists have speculated about the significance of home as an expression of patriarchy's oppression of women. Josephine Donovan defines home as both a restricted and a restricting area ("the domestic sphere, inside enclosures"), and Susan Brownmiller submits that women were men's "first acquisition," the original "building block" of the "house of the father." Home in *The Wizard of Oz* represents "woman's place" and seems emblematic of patriarchy's prescription for all females: "Stay at home." Critics have considered females who adhere to traditional roles of women in the home as "angels" (the "angel in the house"), whereas those who have defied patriarchal dictates often have been categorized as "monsters."

Auntie Em—Dorothy's graying, careworn aunt, whose heart can take no excitement—embodies the angel in the house. She has fulfilled patriarchy's prescription for her: nurturing and loving, but powerless, she seems particularly fearful of defying the law (patriarchy). Though the farm appears to be under Auntie Em's matriarchal control—she appears to run things, working both inside and outside the house—she nonetheless seems fettered to a life of domesticity, symbolically accentuated by the apron she always wears. Ultimately, Auntie Em has no real power and is easily silenced by a "higher" authority, patriarchal law. When Elvira Gulch insists that the sheriff (patriarchal law) has signed the orders for Toto to be turned over to her, a defeated Auntie Em merely hangs her head in silence as the "wicked witch" has Toto placed in her basket. Indeed, Auntie Em is effectively silenced, admitting that her Christian upbringing (the ultimate patriarchal law) prohibits her from telling Elvira Gulch what she thinks of her. In *The Wizard of Oz*, Dorothy's loving aunt appears to be but a slight variation of the typical angel in the house.

At first glance, audiences may likely overlook Dorothy's important psychological connection to her house (an important symbol in the film). In fact, Dorothy's house literally accompanies her to Oz. Sent careening on Dorothy's whirlwind journey through the imagination, with all the dizziness of a wild carousel, the house drops into Munchkin fairyland. Miraculous events abruptly occur: Dorothy kills the Wicked Witch of the East with the symbolic house, and the Good Witch of the North kisses Dorothy and presents her with the ruby red slippers. An instant celebrity, our heroine becomes a symbol of adoration, even though she has killed the Wicked Witch of the East accidentally. Besides Auntie Em, Glinda (the Good Witch), represents yet another variation of the "angel," her puffy gossamer sleeves even suggest wings. Though she has powers, she has chosen to direct them toward ensuring patriarchal dominance. Advising Dorothy to seek the aid of the Wizard, whom she intimates has more power than she to help the Kansas girl, the Good Witch conceals the fact that the power to return home lies within Dorothy. As an agent of patriarchy, she uses her magical powers subtly, guiding Dorothy in the direction of patriarchy—and, ultimately, toward home. Further, though her link to the other "witches" remains ambiguous, most certainly, she is pitted against them. Ironically, too, she shares the epithet, witch, which suggests, metaphorically, that all women, even the ones patriarchy deems "good," have a bit of "witch" (traditionally, a negative appellation) in them.

Before dancing away from the Munchkins, however, the Kansas farm girl receives honors for having rid the territory of the evil witch. To the heights of their tiny voices, the Munchkins praise Dorothy in song: she will "go down in history," a bust cast in her likeness to be erected in the Munchkin Hall of Fame. Thus, Dorothy's fate is to be memorialized as a statue, immobile—metaphorically, she will be "frozen into art" by her worshipers.

Ostensibly, the fabulous Wizard seems the object of Dorothy's quest; however, on another level, our heroine's true search is for the power within herself, the power of the female imagination—that which patriarchy, the Wizard, denies women. *The Wizard of Oz* represents the voice of patriarchy—the authority behind the curtain—hidden, but loudly demanding that women fulfill its prescriptions. Indeed, Dorothy (woman) must please this voice if she hopes to find her "reward" of home.

The Wizard's alter-ego appears initially in the person of Professor Marvel, the seemingly good-natured and fatherly traveling magician, whom Dorothy meets when she runs away from home, just before the tornado touches down. Himself a sort of patriarch, interested in returning Dorothy to her home, Professor Marvel, like the Wizard, appears magical. Scrawled across his wagon, his credentials boast that he has been "Acclaimed by the Crowned Heads of Europe" ... (symbols of authority, in perpetuity). His is a life, unlike Dorothy's, filled with travel, adventure, and experience. Traditionally, women have not been privy to the professor's world (patriarchy's uncircumscribed world).

Like the Wicked Witch of the West, Professor Marvel has a crystal ball that bears a peculiar resemblance to the great Oz's monstrous globe-like head. With it, he pretends to see into other dimensions. While Dorothy's eyes are closed, he takes her picture of Auntie Em and safely describes the old woman's furrowed brow and wrinkled face as "careworn," withered by time and hardship. Though he appears to be well intentioned, the professor remains, nonetheless, a fraud, his "magical" powers mere chicanery.

The message inherent in the patriarch's voice—the voice that seemingly can read the crystal ball and peer into woman's present—dictates immobility for women. By toying with her mind, Professor Marvel tricks Dorothy into returning home. Thus, being homebound is patriarchy's prescription for Dorothy (woman). The world of experience, open only to men who may travel across continents, symbolized by the wagon (wheeled), remains closed to women.

When he first meets Dorothy, Professor Marvel needs no magic to identify her as a runaway. Accurately, he surmises that she feels misunderstood at home and that she longs for adventure. Symbolically, Dorothy, who dreams of lands beyond the rainbow, "where troubles melt like lemon drops," inadvertently divulges that hers is a rebellious spirit. In her desire for adventure—to soar beyond the ordinary and the mundane—and in her attempt to escape the boring, drab, and painful existence of home, this normal, Kansas farm girl threatens the patriarchal order. Dorothy's plan to experience the world is foiled when the professor supposedly sees through his magic crystal that Dorothy's aunt is having a heart attack. Sacrificing her own needs for those of Auntie Em, Dorothy temporarily aborts her journey, and she and her dog scurry back to the farm.

Unlike Professor Marvel's crystal ball or the Wizard's huge globe-head, the Wicked Witch of the West's crystal is genuine. With it, she can peer into other dimensions, transcending time and space (apparent in the scene in which she transforms the image of a grief-stricken Auntie Em into a reflection of herself), unlike the Wizard, who only pretends to use magic.

More complex than the "wizards" (the professor and the Great and Powerful Oz), Dorothy's nature is truly dichotomous: on one level, she appears almost angelic in her innocence, beauty, and willingness to sacrifice for others; yet, on the other hand, she appears self-assertive, determined, desirous of experience. She has a marvelous imagination—if she chooses to use it. Not just a dreamer, Dorothy is willing to act—which makes her somehow "monstrous." In her desire to leave home, to soar beyond the ordinary and mundane, Dorothy becomes a potential rebel to patriarchy. Patriarchy would wish women to be content with staying at home, happy with their lot.

Like Dorothy, the "bad" witches of *The Wizard of Oz* share a common bond of rebellion, a kind of subversive sisterhood. Self-absorbed, self-centered, and powerful, the witches subvert societal order. Significantly, a house—symbol of women's prescribed "place"—is the instrument of the Wicked Witch of the East's death. We only get a glimpse of her red-and-white striped (and colorful) socks from underneath the fallen house. Further, the Wicked Witch of the West subverts the traditional symbol of woman's domesticity in the house—the broom—by transforming it into a flying machine that defies space and gravity.

The Wicked Witch of the West's "other self," of course, is Elvira Gulch, who also eschews patriarchal restraints. Flying down the road on her bicycle, the monstrous Miss Gulch, who "owns half the county," seems to intimidate the very highway which she rides. In addition to threatening Dorothy's aunt and uncle with legal prosecution, Miss Gulch further reveals herself to be a rebel by claiming ownership in the town—ownership of property, traditionally a male prerogative.

Whether traversing the skies or the country plains, the wicked witches intimidate the good "little people" beneath them. The Wicked Witch of the West even subjugates her cossack-like battalions (the military), who silently detest her. The witches, like Dorothy, represent the power of the female imagination. The wicked witches reject prescribed roles for women and are neither wives, mothers, nurturers, nor inspirers; nor do they become instruments in patriarchy's hands, as does their "sister," the Good Witch. Embodying what patriarchy and its angels in the house fear most—aggressive and powerful women—the wicked witches are detested: Everyone wants them dead, including the seemingly innocuous Wizard, who lamely proclaims himself a "very good man"—though a "poor wizard." Even the cute little Munchkins rejoice jubilantly about the death of the Wicked Witch of the East, whom they feared. To assure the Munchkin community's apprehensions, a coroner must examine the corpse of the Wicked Witch of the East to "verify legally" that she is "morally, ethically, spiritually, physically, positively, absolutely, undeniably, and reliably dead!"

The ruby slippers constitute evidence of Dorothy's symbolic kinship to the wicked witches. Although they belonged to the first witch, they fit Dorothy's feet perfectly. They are Dorothy's inheritance of the female imagination and thus function as a semiotic marker of her sisterhood to the two wicked witches. Because she inherited woman's symbol—the red slippers—Dorothy unknowingly reveals her kinship to the witches.

When the Wicked Witch of the West arrives in a cloud of smoke, demanding to know who has "killed [her] sister," she fails to recognize Dorothy as kin, as one of her "sisters." Nor does Dorothy recognize her—even though the Munchkins readily identify both of them as "witches," a title that Dorothy denies. On a symbolic level, women traditionally have been blinded, divided by patriarchy and unable to recognize their "sisters," viewing one another as adversaries.

Not only have many women failed to recognize their sisterhood, but they also have sought to destroy other women as seeming enemies. After Dorothy and her friends arrive at the Emerald City and introduce themselves to the "great and powerful Oz"—the enormous head, the voice of patriarchy—they are ordered to bring back the broomstick of the Witch of the West in order to have their wishes granted. This implies, of course, destroying the wicked witch. Thus, patriarchy pits woman against woman. Only in killing her seeming rival can Dorothy win Oz's favor. Chastised early on by the trees, whose patriarchal voices castigate her for stealing apples (reminiscent, perhaps, of Eve's reproach in the Garden of Eden and Original Sin), and later, besieged by the Wicked Witch of the West and her flying monkeys, Dorothy,

quite by accident, melts the wicked witch, thus completing the task patriarchy has assigned her.

Upon returning to Oz's throne room for the second time and approaching the enormous head with no body, the weary pilgrims find that the powerful Wizard is but a hoax from Omaha. He awards substitute prizes in place of those that the pilgrims really wanted: to the Scarecrow who wants a brain, he awards a "Th.D." (a doctorate of "thinkology"); to the Tin Woodman who longs for a heart, he presents a heart-shaped watch that ticks; and to the Cowardly Lion who yearns for courage, he offers a medal that only reads "Courage."

Left amid the chaotic aftermath of the Wizard's bungled balloon lift, Dorothy faces the most critical decision of her life—to remain in the Land of Oz or to return home. Not only has she demonstrated that she already has what her companions lack—a heart, a brain, and courage—but she has also shown herself to be imaginative and powerful. Sadly, however, Dorothy has swallowed patriarchy's prescription for woman. No longer does she dream of a life away from home. Though wearing the ruby slippers has been exhilarating and imaginatively intoxicating, it also has frightened her. Just as little Karen of *The Red Shoes* would rid herself of the shoes and repent her sins, so, too, would Dorothy discard her ruby slippers and regret her insurrection, thus ending her rebellion.

Suddenly, the Good Witch of the North materializes in a pink bubble and reveals that Dorothy, all along, has had the power (the female imagination) to return home—just by clicking together the heels of her ruby slippers. Dorothy then exercises her powers, not to explore uncharted worlds, but to return to the familiar, worn path of home and security. Promising never to look any further for her "heart's desire" than in her own "backyard," the heroine of *The Wizard of Oz* chooses home, thus fulfilling patriarchy's prescription for her. By repeating the "lesson" she has learned, "There's no place like home; there's no place like home; there's no place like home"— a symbolic patriarchal catechism for woman— the once rebellious Kansas farm girl becomes initiated as yet another angel in the house. In the click of her heels, Dorothy departs the magical world of Oz to return to a land of black and white—and to an undetermined fate for Toto.

Source: Linda Rohrer Paige, "Wearing the Red Shoes: Dorothy and the Power of the Female Imagination in *The*

> **DOROTHY NEVER VOLUNTEERS TO INHERIT THE RUBY SLIPPERS AND THE PROBLEMS THEY CAUSE, BUT FORTUNATELY FOR OZ, SHE IS A BORN LIBERATOR, AND CANNOT CONTAIN HER IMPULSES TO FREE THE CAPTIVE AND CHAMPION THE MEEK AND DEFENSELESS."**

Wizard of Oz," in *Journal of Popular Film and Television*, Vol. 23, No. 4, Winter 1996, pp. 146–53.

Lynette Carpenter

In the following essay, Carpenter argues that the cinematic version of The Wizard of Oz *reflects the influence of world political events at the time of the filming.*

In one of the most memorable scenes in American cinema, a tearful Dorothy, who has just missed her balloon back to Kansas, discovers that she could have left Oz the day she arrived by invoking the power of the ruby slippers. But, the good witch Glinda tells her, she needed to learn something first, and her friends crowd around to hear what Dorothy has learned: "It's that if ever I go looking for my heart's desire again, I won't look any further than my own back yard." The discovery itself is magic: with three taps of her heels, Dorothy returns to Kansas (Toto too), chanting, "There's no place like home. There's no place like home. There's no place like home."

This is not *The Wizard of Oz* as written by L. Frank Baum in 1900, but *The Wizard of Oz* as rewritten by Metro-Goldwyn-Mayer in the late 1930s. Since Dorothy does not run away from home in the original version, she is not required to learn any particular lesson through her adventures and misadventures in Oz. Like the film, the original book advances subtle arguments about the nature of wisdom, love, and courage; unlike the film, the book does not develop an overt moral. Henry M. Littlefield has argued persuasively that the book carries a covert moral as a "parable on populism," pointing to leftist political leanings which, had they been recognized, might well have disqualified the book for

production at politically conservative MGM. In contrast, according to film historian Aljean Harmetz, MGM executives saw the film as pure fantasy in the tradition of the enormously successful 1938 Walt Disney film, *Snow White and the Seven Dwarves* (Harmetz, p. 3). Yet the film version of *The Wizard of Oz* released in the summer of 1939 does reflect the influence of world political events in its revision of the original Baum story. Specifically, when set in this larger political context, its sentimental message reflects the spirit of isolationism prevalent in Hollywood and in the country as a whole: "There's no place like home."

By the time MGM writers began work on the script in February of 1938, Italy was occupying Ethiopia, Japan was occupying parts of China, and the Spanish Civil War was well under way. Congress had registered the national mood by repeated declarations of neutrality. During the nearly twelve months of script writing which followed, Hitler took the Rhineland, Austria, and the Sudetenland; Japan repudiated the Open Door Policy in China. Throughout 1938, President Roosevelt continued to insist that the United States would remain neutral in any international conflict, writing during the Czech crisis in September that the U.S. had "no political entanglements" in Europe. That those involved in the re-shaping of *The Wizard of Oz* should imagine Dorothy's sojourn in Oz as reluctant participation in foreign military struggles is not surprising.

The major creative influences on the *Oz* project, in addition to the credited scriptwriters, were predominantly Republican and conservative, in line with the political views of studio head Louis B. Mayer: sentimentalist Mervyn LeRoy, ultraconservative Arthur Freed, and Victor Fleming, who would later form an anti-Communist organization with John Wayne after the war. Odd man out was socialist E. Y. Harburg, whom Harmetz identifies as the final script editor, and whose political opinions generated more than one confrontation with Freed (Harmetz, p. 73). At the same time, though, fed by strong popular sentiment, the stance of neutrality drew overwhelming support from all parties. Isolationism ran high among Republicans as well as Democrats, making it a respectable stance at MGM. And despite the company in which they found themselves, both communists and socialists agreed in opposing American involvement, fearing what they believed would be another imperialist war fought to defend American business interests. As Colin H. Schindler points out in his book, *Hollywood Goes to War*:

> the mood of the film industry throughout the 1930s, like the mood of the country in general and that of Congress in particular, was overwhelmingly isolationist. The division between 'isolationists' and 'internationalists' cut across traditional political groupings, although the internationalists were normally Democrats who lived in the larger cities. The centre of isolationism was, as ever, in the rural Mid-west.

MGM, a studio which had done more than most to mythologize America's heartland, was well qualified to transmit its politics. And who better to convey its spirit than a new American sweetheart, a girl-next-door from the home state of the 1936 Republican Presidential candidate, Governor Alfred M. Landon? Enter Dorothy from Kansas.

Baum's Kansas, which Littlefield traces to his experiences in the South Dakota dust bowl of the 1880s, would have sounded familiar to readers of another dust bowl era:

> Not a tree nor a house broke the broad sweep of flat country that reached the edge of the sky in all directions. The sun had baked the plowed land into a gray mass, with little cracks running through it. Even the grass was not green, for the sun had burned the tops of the long blades until they were the same gray color to be seen elsewhere. Once the house had been painted, but the sun blistered the paint and the rains washed it away, and now the house was as dull and gray as everything else.

Concerning the metamorphosis of Baum's Kansas into MGM's, Harmetz observes:

> Baum had wasted less than one thousand words of his book on Kansas . . . . But all of the scriptwriters . . . focused almost as much of their attention on Kansas as they did on Oz. They felt it necessary to have an audience relate to Dorothy in a real world before transporting her to a magic one. (Harmetz, pp. 26–27)

Yet the transformation of Baum's Kansas also served another purpose: it set the stage for the film's idealization of home. The film retains something of the effect of Baum's prose through its contrast of black and white photography in the Kansas sequences with Technicolor photography in the Oz sequence. But MGM's version of Kansas poverty is idealized. A separate bedroom would have been an unthinkable luxury to the residents of Baum's one-room farmhouse. Nor does Baum make any mention of farmhands. The rows in the fields of MGM's Kansas and the water in the creek over which Dorothy and Toto cross belie the drought that Baum portrays. If audiences are reminded of the unspoken half of the adage which provides the film's theme statement, "Be it ever so humble," they are reminded with a version of humility that exceeded the material capabilities of most rural Kansas residents in the 1930s. The characters here are more fully developed and benignly drawn than Baum's: the caring and concern of Uncle Henry and Aunt Em, the kindliness of the farmhands, and the sympathy of Professor Marvel help motivate Dorothy's later obsession with going home. The film suggests that even small Kansas farmhouses are not to be carelessly abandoned, for they will survive, literally and figuratively, at the heart of the cyclone, an apt if unintentional image for the advancing threat of world war.

Dorothy's cyclone propels her into the midst of a civil war, touched off when her house drops from the sky and effectively assassinates the dictator of Munchkinland, the Wicked Witch of the East. Audiences in the late thirties remembered only too well the part played by political assassination in causing the Great War. In the original book as in the film, the bewildered Dorothy is hailed as a liberator; the Witch of the North explains the significance of the Wicked Witch's death: "'She has held all the Munchkins in bondage for many years, making them slave for her night and day. Now they are all set free, and are grateful to you for the favor'" (Baum). The film expands on this scene with an elaborate production number involving scores of little people singing a tribute to their "national heroine," as Glinda calls her. Munchkin soldiers perform impromptu drills. The mayor of the Munchkin city proclaims it "a day of Independence," and E. Y. Harburg's lyrics underscore the momentousness of the occasion: "From now on you'll be history, / and we will glorify your name. / You'll be a bust in the Hall of Fame." The attention must surely be flattering to a little girl from Kansas, but Dorothy resists her role as heroine, a resistance which characterizes her throughout. What she really wants is a ticket back to Kansas.

In Glinda the film collapses the roles assigned to two witches in the original book, the Good Witch of the North and the Good Witch of the South. This economy simplifies what is by now becoming a complicated cast of characters, but it also simplifies the politics of Oz. Dorothy is caught between two enemy factions, good as represented by the Good Witch of the North and the Wizard, and evil as represented by the Wicked Witch of the West, or put another way, between the forces of democracy and benevolent monarchy and those of totalitarianism. The exclusion of the south in this scheme may also suggest associations with North America's potential relationship to aggressors in the East (Japan) and West (Germany and Italy). The scene in Munchkinland serves to clarify this state of affairs in the confrontation between the two witches. The Wicked Witch of the West, who does not appear at this point in the book, promises to avenge her sister's "murder" and acquire the ruby slippers, which Glinda says must be "very powerful." Glinda also observes that Dorothy has made "rather a bad enemy," and admits, "The sooner you get out of Oz altogether, the better you'll sleep nights"—an ironic comment in light of the film's final revelation that Oz is all part of a dream.

Dorothy never volunteers to inherit the ruby slippers and the problems they cause, but fortunately for Oz, she is a born liberator, and cannot contain her impulses to free the captive and champion the meek and defenseless. She first frees the Scarecrow, whose language reiterates the theme of liberation: "My, but it's good to be free!" Baum's Scarecrow, in contrast, only remarks: "Thank you very much. I feel like a new man." In her song with the Scarecrow, "If I Only Had a Brain," Dorothy refers to another great liberator, the man for whom America's volunteer brigade in Spain was named, a man whom both Republicans and socialists could admire: "With the thoughts you'd be thinkin' / You could be another Lincoln." Next Dorothy frees the Tin Man from his imprisonment in rust. Finally, she confronts the Cowardly Lion, delivering a lecture on the cowardice of tyranny along with a slap on the lion's nose: "Naturally, when you go about picking on things weaker than you are—! Why, you're nothing but a great big coward!" By the time Dorothy introduces herself to Oz as "Dorothy, the Small and Meek," the epithet hardly seems an accurate one. Nor does she hesitate to chastise the great wizard himself for bullying the Cowardly Lion. A democrat at heart, she is willing to offer this national leader respect and courtesy, not abject awe.

The language and imagery of the film become increasingly militaristic as it progresses, and the periodic reappearance of the witches reminds the audience of the power struggle in which Dorothy is entangled. The Wicked Witch tells her commander, "When I gain those ruby slippers, my power will be the greatest in Oz!" This emphasis on the Wicked Witch's appetite for power is not so strong in Baum's version, since his witch does not threaten Dorothy or attempt to acquire the magic slippers (silver in this case) until Dorothy is inside the castle. Thus MGM's Wicked Witch is a more active aggressor than her fictional counterpart. Whereas the deadly poppy field is presented as a natural danger in the original, the film implicates the Wicked Witch in its appearance. As Harmetz points out, since even MGM could not stage the original rescue by a multitude of field mice, the filmmakers relied on Baum's own solution in his 1902 *Wizard of Oz* play—snow—and tied its appearance to the Wicked Witch's arch rival, Glinda.

When Dorothy arrives in the Emerald City, the Wicked Witch takes to the air, exhorting her to "surrender" with an impressive display of sky writing. The frightened response of the citizens of Emerald City might have had special meaning to contemporary audiences who had witnessed struggles for air supremacy in Europe and the Far East. Air supremacy is, in fact, crucial to the Wicked Witch's initial success, since she is supported by an army/air force of winged monkeys. Once the four comrades reach the Haunted Forest, the Witch directs her commander to take his "army" there and capture Dorothy. Although the Winged Monkeys appear in the original book, they are characterized differently. In Baum's version, the monkeys are victims of a spell and are forced to obey the possessor of a Golden Cap. Their leader is the King of the Winged Monkeys, and they are never portrayed as an army. Most importantly, they serve evil or good, depending upon the owner of the Cap. Their transformation into an evil army whose commander is the Witch's confidant simplifies the plot for the purpose of condensation, but it also produces a situation more familiar to the filmmakers and their audiences. The image of the winged battalions in flight must have had a particularly eerie effect on viewers in the late thirties.

The castle guards are Winkies, who, as the script directs, "goose-step" outside the castle. It turns out, of course, that they, too, are in need of liberation, and when the Witch is melted, exclaim, "Hail, Dorothy!" This time Dorothy does not linger for the victory celebration, but takes the broomstick as proof of her conquest.

The scene which follows Toto's exposure of the Wizard's humbuggery marks an interesting departure from Baum's original. In the book, the Wizard attempts a more literal translation of the requests made of him: he stuffs the Scarecrow's head with pins and needles, inserts a heart-shaped watch in the Tin Man's chest, and has the Lion drink a bottle of "courage." The film version, added by E. Y. Harburg, reveals Harburg's politics as well as his ironic wit. A supporter of the Chinese and Loyalist causes, Harburg seems to have taken the common view among socialists concerning American involvement. In 1937, he had co-authored with Harold Arlen, his partner on *Oz*, a popular anti-war musical comedy, *Hooray for What!* In a previous *Oz* musical number, Harburg tempers the Cowardly Lion's lust for power with plans for benevolence: "I'd command each thing / As I'd click my heel / I'd show compash / For every underling." In fact, MGM's Cowardly Lion is less obsessed by power than Baum's, who once proposes to the other forest animals: "If I put an end to your enemy will you bow down to me and obey me as King of the Forest?" (Baum). Although this scene may merely have fallen victim to condensation, any serious tendency on the Lion's part to exact obeisance and obedience in the film might well have lost him sympathy in an age troubled by expanding totalitarianism. Moreover Harburg is careful to clarify his position toward the Lion's desire for courage in the Wizard's presentation speech:

> "You are under the unfortunate delusion that you have no courage merely because you run from danger. You are confusing courage with wisdom. Back where I come from we have men who are called heroes. Once a yeaqr they take their fortitude out of mothballs and parade it down the main street of the city. They have no more courage than you!"

This speech is remarkable for its implied insult to veterans of World War I, and, one suspects, could only have appeared in an MGM film during that relatively brief period of time when left and right agreed on the folly of the past war and future involvement. The Wizard suggests that avoiding danger when possible is the best course, wisdom the better part of valor.

The final scenes emphasize the film's moral, using the platitude, "There's no place like home," to transport Dorothy back to Kansas. In Baum's

version, Dorothy says only, "Take me home to Aunt Em!" (Baum). Once "home," Dorothy expands on the lesson she has learned, and ends the film with the by now predictable last line. Even if Dorothy's adventures in Oz were part of a dream, they were sufficiently unpleasant to make her repent of running away and promise never to leave home again. The liberator has returned home triumphant, but is sorry she ever left home in the first place.

Nevertheless, Dorothy remains a hero; the suggestion that she has been dreaming cannot undercut her heroism. She is not afraid to fight, only too intelligent and too attached to her Kansas home to want to be involved in other people's battles. Once she undertakes the fight, she succeeds, as any plucky American would do, even a little girl from Kansas. As the war in Europe spread, so did Dorothy's fame. Her love of home combined with her courage made Dorothy an idol of the British people, who were called upon to defend their homeland in the fall of 1939. As Harmetz reports: "RAF pilots used 'We're Off to See the Wizard' as theme music for their defense of London against the German Luftwaffe" (Harmetz). Later in the war, the Australians adopted the same song as their marching music in the Libyan desert (*Lion's Share*). But in 1939, Americans, for the most part, took Dorothy's message to heart and stayed home, perhaps forgetting that an aerial invasion of her own backyard was the event which had precipitated Dorothy's engagement in the first place.

Source: Lynette Carpenter, "'There's No Place like Home': *The Wizard of Oz* and American Isolationism," in *Film and History*, Vol. 15, No. 2, May 1985, pp. 37–45.

SOURCES

Abbott, David P., *Behind the Scenes with the Mediums*, 4th ed., Open Court, 1912, pp. 266–80.

Baum, L. Frank, *The Annotated Wizard of Oz: "The Wonderful Wizard of Oz,"* Centennial Edition, edited by Michael Patrick Hearn, W. W. Norton, 2000.

Campbell, Joseph, *The Hero with a Thousand Faces*, 3rd ed., New World Library, 2008, pp. 1–18.

Dighe, Ranjit S., *The Historian's "Wizard of Oz": Reading L. Frank Baum's Classic as a Political and Monetary Allegory*, Praeger, 2002, pp. 1–40.

Ebert, Roger, "*The Wizard of Oz*," in *The Great Movies*, Broadway Books, 2002, pp. 492–96.

Hammer, Olav, "New Age Movement," in *Dictionary of Gnosis & Western Esotericism*, edited by Wouter J. Hanegraaff, Brill, 2006, pp. 855–61.

Kreskin [George Kresge], *Secrets of the Amazing Kreskin: The World's Foremost Mentalist Reveals How You Can Expand Your Powers*, 2nd ed., Prometheus, 1991, pp. 105–20.

Langley, Noel, Florence Ryerson, and Edgar Allan Woolf, *The Wizard of Oz: The Screenplay*, edited by Michael Patrick Hearn, Delta, 1989.

Littlefield, Henry M., "*The Wizard of Oz*: Parable on Populism," in *American Quarterly*, Vol. 16, No. 1, Spring 1964, pp. 47–58.

Loncraine, Rebecca, *The Real Wizard of Oz: The Life and Times of L. Frank Baum*, Gotham Books, 2009, pp. 177–78.

Nathanson, Paul, *Over the Rainbow: "The Wizard of Oz" as a Secular Myth of America*, State University of New York Press, 1991, pp. 7–14.

Parker, David B., "The Rise and Fall of *The Wonderful Wizard of Oz* as a 'Parable on Populism,'" in *Journal of the Georgia Association of Historians*, Vol. 15, 1994, pp. 49–63.

Rogers, Katharine M., *L. Frank Baum: Creator of Oz*, St. Martin's Press, 2002, pp. 33–34.

Rushdie, Salman, *The Wizard of Oz*, British Film Institute, 1992, pp. 9–57.

Santucci, James A., "Theosophical Society," in *Dictionary of Gnosis & Western Esotericism*, edited by Wouter J. Hanegraaff, Brill, 2006, pp. 1114–23.

Scarfone, Jay, and William Stillman, *The Wizardry of Oz: The Artistry and Magic of the 1939 MGM Classic*, Applause Theatre & Cinema Books, 2004, pp. 103–45.

Schwartz, Evan I., *Finding Oz: How L. Frank Baum Discovered the Great American Story*, Houghton Mifflin Harcourt, 2009, pp. 261–82.

The Wizard of Oz, DVD: Three-Disc Collector's Edition, Turner Entertainment, 2005.

FURTHER READING

Baum, Roger S., *The Lion of Oz and the Badge of Courage*, Yellow Brick Road, 1995.

> The fictional world of Oz and its characters are long out of copyright and so have been used by a large number of writers of various degrees of professionalism. One of the best regarded of such series of novels, in this case aimed at children, as the original books were, is by Baum's great-grandson Roger S. Baum. This

volume concerns the adventures of the Cowardly Lion in the time before Dorothy's arrival in Oz.

Farmer, Philip José, *A Barnstormer in Oz; or, A Rationalization and Extrapolation of the Split-Level Continuum*, Phantasia Press, 1982.

> Farmer was one of the most prominent science-fiction writers of the twentieth century. In this work, he revisits Oz by sending Dorothy's son there in 1923. Farmer's goal is to reinvent the world of Oz as a logically coherent, realistic fantasy world, dominated by realpolitik and consistent laws of magic that operate like the laws of physics in the real universe.

Maguire, Gregory, *Wicked: The Life and Times of the Wicked Witch of the West*, HarperCollins, 1995.

> This retelling of the Oz story (based on the film at least as much as the book) from the viewpoint of an alternate title character, and with considerable newly invented backstory, became the basis of a popular Broadway musical that premiered in 2003 and is currently being produced as a film.

Sragow, Michael, *Victor Fleming: An American Movie Master*, Pantheon Books, 2008.

> While 1939's *The Wizard of Oz* had at least three different directors, and others who worked on the film had unusual amounts of creative control (the lyricist Yip Harburg, for instance, had final approval of the script), Fleming was the main artistic force behind the realization of the film. He did not finish it because he was called away to work on *Gone with the Wind*. Sragow's book is now the standard biography of Fleming and devotes considerable attention to *The Wizard of Oz*.

SUGGESTED SEARCH TERMS

L. Frank Baum

Victor Fleming

The Wizard of Oz AND film

The Wonderful Wizard of Oz

American fairy tales

Theosophy

astral plane

New Age

The Baum Bugle

Ramayana

Glossary of Literary Terms

A

Abstract: As an adjective applied to writing or literary works, abstract refers to words or phrases that name things not knowable through the five senses.

Aestheticism: A literary and artistic movement of the nineteenth century. Followers of the movement believed that art should not be mixed with social, political, or moral teaching. The statement "art for art's sake" is a good summary of aestheticism. The movement had its roots in France, but it gained widespread importance in England in the last half of the nineteenth century, where it helped change the Victorian practice of including moral lessons in literature.

Allegory: A narrative technique in which characters representing things or abstract ideas are used to convey a message or teach a lesson. Allegory is typically used to teach moral, ethical, or religious lessons but is sometimes used for satiric or political purposes.

Allusion: A reference to a familiar literary or historical person or event, used to make an idea more easily understood.

Analogy: A comparison of two things made to explain something unfamiliar through its similarities to something familiar, or to prove one point based on the acceptedness of another. Similes and metaphors are types of analogies.

Antagonist: The major character in a narrative or drama who works against the hero or protagonist.

Anthropomorphism: The presentation of animals or objects in human shape or with human characteristics. The term is derived from the Greek word for "human form."

Anti-hero: A central character in a work of literature who lacks traditional heroic qualities such as courage, physical prowess, and fortitude. Anti-heroes typically distrust conventional values and are unable to commit themselves to any ideals. They generally feel helpless in a world over which they have no control. Anti-heroes usually accept, and often celebrate, their positions as social outcasts.

Apprenticeship Novel: See *Bildungsroman*

Archetype: The word archetype is commonly used to describe an original pattern or model from which all other things of the same kind are made. This term was introduced to literary criticism from the psychology of Carl Jung. It expresses Jung's theory that behind every person's "unconscious," or repressed memories of the past, lies the "collective unconscious" of the human race: memories of the countless typical experiences of our ancestors. These memories are said to prompt illogical associations that trigger powerful emotions in the reader. Often, the emotional process is primitive, even primordial. Archetypes are the literary images that grow out of the "collective unconscious." They appear in literature as incidents and plots that repeat basic patterns of life. They may also appear as stereotyped characters.

Avant-garde: French term meaning "vanguard." It is used in literary criticism to describe new writing that rejects traditional approaches to literature in favor of innovations in style or content.

B

Beat Movement: A period featuring a group of American poets and novelists of the 1950s and 1960s—including Jack Kerouac, Allen Ginsberg, Gregory Corso, William S. Burroughs, and Lawrence Ferlinghetti—who rejected established social and literary values. Using such techniques as stream of consciousness writing and jazz-influenced free verse and focusing on unusual or abnormal states of mind—generated by religious ecstasy or the use of drugs—the Beat writers aimed to create works that were unconventional in both form and subject matter.

Bildungsroman: A German word meaning "novel of development." The *bildungsroman* is a study of the maturation of a youthful character, typically brought about through a series of social or sexual encounters that lead to self-awareness. *Bildungsroman* is used interchangeably with *erziehungsroman,* a novel of initiation and education. When a *bildungsroman* is concerned with the development of an artist (as in James Joyce's *A Portrait of the Artist as a Young Man*), it is often termed a *kunstlerroman.*

Black Aesthetic Movement: A period of artistic and literary development among African Americans in the 1960s and early 1970s. This was the first major African-American artistic movement since the Harlem Renaissance and was closely paralleled by the civil rights and black power movements. The black aesthetic writers attempted to produce works of art that would be meaningful to the black masses. Key figures in black aesthetics included one of its founders, poet and playwright Amiri Baraka, formerly known as LeRoi Jones; poet and essayist Haki R. Madhubuti, formerly Don L. Lee; poet and

playwright Sonia Sanchez; and dramatist Ed Bullins.

Black Humor: Writing that places grotesque elements side by side with humorous ones in an attempt to shock the reader, forcing him or her to laugh at the horrifying reality of a disordered world.

Burlesque: Any literary work that uses exaggeration to make its subject appear ridiculous, either by treating a trivial subject with profound seriousness or by treating a dignified subject frivolously. The word "burlesque" may also be used as an adjective, as in "burlesque show," to mean "striptease act."

C

Character: Broadly speaking, a person in a literary work. The actions of characters are what constitute the plot of a story, novel, or poem. There are numerous types of characters, ranging from simple, stereotypical figures to intricate, multifaceted ones. In the techniques of anthropomorphism and personification, animals—and even places or things—can assume aspects of character. "Characterization" is the process by which an author creates vivid, believable characters in a work of art. This may be done in a variety of ways, including (1) direct description of the character by the narrator; (2) the direct presentation of the speech, thoughts, or actions of the character; and (3) the responses of other characters to the character. The term "character" also refers to a form originated by the ancient Greek writer Theophrastus that later became popular in the seventeenth and eighteenth centuries. It is a short essay or sketch of a person who prominently displays a specific attribute or quality, such as miserliness or ambition.

Climax: The turning point in a narrative, the moment when the conflict is at its most intense. Typically, the structure of stories, novels, and plays is one of rising action, in which tension builds to the climax, followed by falling action, in which tension lessens as the story moves to its conclusion.

Colloquialism: A word, phrase, or form of pronunciation that is acceptable in casual conversation but not in formal, written communication. It is considered more acceptable than slang.

Coming of Age Novel: See *Bildungsroman*

Concrete: Concrete is the opposite of abstract, and refers to a thing that actually exists or a description that allows the reader to experience an object or concept with the senses.

Connotation: The impression that a word gives beyond its defined meaning. Connotations may be universally understood or may be significant only to a certain group.

Convention: Any widely accepted literary device, style, or form.

D

Denotation: The definition of a word, apart from the impressions or feelings it creates (connotations) in the reader.

Denouement: A French word meaning "the unknotting." In literary criticism, it denotes the resolution of conflict in fiction or drama. The *denouement* follows the climax and provides an outcome to the primary plot situation as well as an explanation of secondary plot complications. The *denouement* often involves a character's recognition of his or her state of mind or moral condition.

Description: Descriptive writing is intended to allow a reader to picture the scene or setting in which the action of a story takes place. The form this description takes often evokes an intended emotional response—a dark, spooky graveyard will evoke fear, and a peaceful, sunny meadow will evoke calmness.

Dialogue: In its widest sense, dialogue is simply conversation between people in a literary work; in its most restricted sense, it refers specifically to the speech of characters in a drama. As a specific literary genre, a "dialogue" is a composition in which characters debate an issue or idea.

Diction: The selection and arrangement of words in a literary work. Either or both may vary depending on the desired effect. There are four general types of diction: "formal," used in scholarly or lofty writing; "informal," used in relaxed but educated conversation; "colloquial," used in everyday speech; and "slang," containing newly coined words and other terms not accepted in formal usage.

Didactic: A term used to describe works of literature that aim to teach some moral, religious, political, or practical lesson. Although didactic elements are often found in artistically pleasing works, the term "didactic" usually refers to literature in which the message is more important than the form. The term may also be used to criticize a work that the critic finds "overly didactic," that is, heavy-handed in its delivery of a lesson.

Doppelganger: A literary technique by which a character is duplicated (usually in the form of an alter ego, though sometimes as a ghostly counterpart) or divided into two distinct, usually opposite personalities. The use of this character device is widespread in nineteenth- and twentieth-century literature, and indicates a growing awareness among authors that the "self" is really a composite of many "selves."

Double Entendre: A corruption of a French phrase meaning "double meaning." The term is used to indicate a word or phrase that is deliberately ambiguous, especially when one of the meanings is risqué or improper.

Dramatic Irony: Occurs when the audience of a play or the reader of a work of literature knows something that a character in the work itself does not know. The irony is in the contrast between the intended meaning of the statements or actions of a character and the additional information understood by the audience.

Dystopia: An imaginary place in a work of fiction where the characters lead dehumanized, fearful lives.

E

Edwardian: Describes cultural conventions identified with the period of the reign of Edward VII of England (1901-1910). Writers of the Edwardian Age typically displayed a strong reaction against the propriety and conservatism of the Victorian Age. Their work often exhibits distrust of authority in religion, politics, and art and expresses strong doubts about the soundness of conventional values.

Empathy: A sense of shared experience, including emotional and physical feelings, with someone or something other than oneself. Empathy is often used to describe the response of a reader to a literary character.

Enlightenment, The: An eighteenth-century philosophical movement. It began in France but had a wide impact throughout Europe and America. Thinkers of the Enlightenment valued reason and believed that both the individual and society could achieve a state of perfection. Corresponding to this essentially humanist vision was a resistance to religious authority.

Epigram: A saying that makes the speaker's point quickly and concisely. Often used to preface a novel.

Epilogue: A concluding statement or section of a literary work. In dramas, particularly those of the seventeenth and eighteenth centuries, the epilogue is a closing speech, often in verse, delivered by an actor at the end of a play and spoken directly to the audience.

Epiphany: A sudden revelation of truth inspired by a seemingly trivial incident.

Episode: An incident that forms part of a story and is significantly related to it. Episodes may be either self-contained narratives or events that depend on a larger context for their sense and importance.

Epistolary Novel: A novel in the form of letters. The form was particularly popular in the eighteenth century.

Epithet: A word or phrase, often disparaging or abusive, that expresses a character trait of someone or something.

Existentialism: A predominantly twentieth-century philosophy concerned with the nature and perception of human existence. There are two major strains of existentialist thought: atheistic and Christian. Followers of atheistic existentialism believe that the individual is alone in a godless universe and that the basic human condition is one of suffering and loneliness. Nevertheless, because there are no fixed values, individuals can create their own characters—indeed, they can shape themselves—through the exercise of free will. The atheistic strain culminates in and is popularly associated with the works of Jean-Paul Sartre. The Christian existentialists, on the other hand, believe that only in God may people find freedom from life's anguish. The two strains hold certain beliefs in common: that existence cannot be fully understood or described through empirical effort; that anguish is a universal element of life; that individuals must bear responsibility for their actions; and that there is no common standard of behavior or perception for religious and ethical matters.

Expatriates: See *Expatriatism*

Expatriatism: The practice of leaving one's country to live for an extended period in another country.

Exposition: Writing intended to explain the nature of an idea, thing, or theme. Expository writing is often combined with description, narration, or argument. In dramatic writing, the exposition is the introductory material which presents the characters, setting, and tone of the play.

Expressionism: An indistinct literary term, originally used to describe an early twentieth-century school of German painting. The term applies to almost any mode of unconventional, highly subjective writing that distorts reality in some way.

F

Fable: A prose or verse narrative intended to convey a moral. Animals or inanimate objects with human characteristics often serve as characters in fables.

Falling Action: See *Denouement*

Fantasy: A literary form related to mythology and folklore. Fantasy literature is typically set in non-existent realms and features supernatural beings.

Farce: A type of comedy characterized by broad humor, outlandish incidents, and often vulgar subject matter.

Femme fatale: A French phrase with the literal translation "fatal woman." A *femme fatale* is a sensuous, alluring woman who often leads men into danger or trouble.

Fiction: Any story that is the product of imagination rather than a documentation of fact. Characters and events in such narratives may be based in real life but their ultimate form and configuration is a creation of the author.

Figurative Language: A technique in writing in which the author temporarily interrupts the order, construction, or meaning of the writing for a particular effect. This interruption takes the form of one or more figures of speech such as hyperbole, irony, or simile. Figurative language is the opposite of literal language, in which every word is truthful, accurate, and free of exaggeration or embellishment.

Figures of Speech: Writing that differs from customary conventions for construction, meaning, order, or significance for the purpose of a special meaning or effect. There are two major types of figures of speech: rhetorical figures, which do not make changes in the meaning of the words, and tropes, which do.

Fin de siecle: A French term meaning "end of the century." The term is used to denote the last decade of the nineteenth century, a transition period when writers and other artists abandoned old conventions and looked for new techniques and objectives.

First Person: See *Point of View*

Flashback: A device used in literature to present action that occurred before the beginning of the story. Flashbacks are often introduced as the dreams or recollections of one or more characters.

Foil: A character in a work of literature whose physical or psychological qualities contrast strongly with, and therefore highlight, the corresponding qualities of another character.

Folklore: Traditions and myths preserved in a culture or group of people. Typically, these are passed on by word of mouth in various forms—such as legends, songs, and proverbs—or preserved in customs and ceremonies. This term was first used by W. J. Thoms in 1846.

Folktale: A story originating in oral tradition. Folktales fall into a variety of categories, including legends, ghost stories, fairy tales, fables, and anecdotes based on historical figures and events.

Foreshadowing: A device used in literature to create expectation or to set up an explanation of later developments.

Form: The pattern or construction of a work which identifies its genre and distinguishes it from other genres.

G

Genre: A category of literary work. In critical theory, genre may refer to both the content of a given work—tragedy, comedy, pastoral—and to its form, such as poetry, novel, or drama.

Gilded Age: A period in American history during the 1870s characterized by political corruption and materialism. A number of important novels of social and political criticism were written during this time.

Gothicism: In literary criticism, works characterized by a taste for the medieval or morbidly attractive. A gothic novel prominently features elements of horror, the supernatural, gloom, and violence: clanking chains, terror, charnel houses, ghosts, medieval castles, and mysteriously slamming doors. The term "gothic novel" is also applied to novels that lack elements of the traditional Gothic setting but that create a similar atmosphere of terror or dread.

Grotesque: In literary criticism, the subject matter of a work or a style of expression characterized by exaggeration, deformity, freakishness, and disorder. The grotesque often includes an element of comic absurdity.

H

Harlem Renaissance: The Harlem Renaissance of the 1920s is generally considered the first significant movement of black writers and artists in the United States. During this period, new and established black writers published more fiction and poetry than ever before, the first influential black literary journals were established, and black authors and artists received their first widespread recognition and serious critical appraisal. Among the major writers associated with this period are Claude McKay, Jean Toomer, Countee Cullen, Langston Hughes, Arna Bontemps, Nella Larsen, and Zora Neale Hurston.

Hero/Heroine: The principal sympathetic character (male or female) in a literary work. Heroes and heroines typically exhibit admirable traits: idealism, courage, and integrity, for example.

Holocaust Literature: Literature influenced by or written about the Holocaust of World War II. Such literature includes true stories of survival in concentration camps, escape, and life after the war, as well as fictional works and poetry.

Humanism: A philosophy that places faith in the dignity of humankind and rejects the medieval perception of the individual as a weak, fallen creature. "Humanists" typically believe in the perfectibility of human nature and view reason and education as the means to that end.

Hyperbole: In literary criticism, deliberate exaggeration used to achieve an effect.

I

Idiom: A word construction or verbal expression closely associated with a given language.

Image: A concrete representation of an object or sensory experience. Typically, such a representation helps evoke the feelings associated with the object or experience itself. Images are either "literal" or "figurative." Literal images are especially concrete and involve little or no extension of the obvious meaning of the words used to express them. Figurative images do not follow the literal meaning of the words exactly. Images in literature are usually visual, but the term "image" can also refer to the representation of any sensory experience.

Imagery: The array of images in a literary work. Also, figurative language.

In medias res: A Latin term meaning "in the middle of things." It refers to the technique of beginning a story at its midpoint and then using various flashback devices to reveal previous action.

Interior Monologue: A narrative technique in which characters' thoughts are revealed in a way that appears to be uncontrolled by the author. The interior monologue typically aims to reveal the inner self of a character. It portrays emotional experiences as they occur at both a conscious and unconscious level. images are often used to represent sensations or emotions.

Irony: In literary criticism, the effect of language in which the intended meaning is the opposite of what is stated.

J

Jargon: Language that is used or understood only by a select group of people. Jargon may refer to terminology used in a certain profession, such as computer jargon, or it may refer to any nonsensical language that is not understood by most people.

L

Leitmotiv: See *Motif*

Literal Language: An author uses literal language when he or she writes without exaggerating or embellishing the subject matter and without any tools of figurative language.

Lost Generation: A term first used by Gertrude Stein to describe the post–World War I generation of American writers: men and women haunted by a sense of betrayal and emptiness brought about by the destructiveness of the war.

M

Mannerism: Exaggerated, artificial adherence to a literary manner or style. Also, a popular style of the visual arts of late sixteenth-century Europe that was marked by elongation of the human form and by intentional spatial distortion. Literary works that are self-consciously high-toned and artistic are often said to be "mannered."

Metaphor: A figure of speech that expresses an idea through the image of another object. Metaphors suggest the essence of the first object by identifying it with certain qualities of the second object.

Modernism: Modern literary practices. Also, the principles of a literary school that lasted from roughly the beginning of the twentieth century until the end of World War II. Modernism is defined by its rejection of the literary conventions of the nineteenth century and by its opposition to conventional morality, taste, traditions, and economic values.

Mood: The prevailing emotions of a work or of the author in his or her creation of the work. The mood of a work is not always what might be expected based on its subject matter.

Motif: A theme, character type, image, metaphor, or other verbal element that recurs throughout a single work of literature or occurs in a number of different works over a period of time.

Myth: An anonymous tale emerging from the traditional beliefs of a culture or social unit. Myths use supernatural explanations for natural phenomena. They may also explain cosmic issues like creation and death. Collections of myths, known as mythologies, are common to all cultures and nations, but the best-known myths belong to the Norse, Roman, and Greek mythologies.

N

Narration: The telling of a series of events, real or invented. A narration may be either a simple narrative, in which the events are recounted chronologically, or a narrative with a plot, in which the account is given in a style reflecting the author's artistic concept of the story. Narration is sometimes used as a synonym for "storyline."

Narrative: A verse or prose accounting of an event or sequence of events, real or invented. The term is also used as an adjective in the sense "method of narration." For example, in literary criticism, the expression "narrative technique" usually refers to the way the author structures and presents his or her story.

Narrator: The teller of a story. The narrator may be the author or a character in the story through whom the author speaks.

Naturalism: A literary movement of the late nineteenth and early twentieth centuries. The movement's major theorist, French novelist Emile Zola, envisioned a type of fiction that would examine human life with the objectivity of scientific inquiry. The Naturalists typically viewed human beings as either the products of "biological determinism," ruled by hereditary instincts and engaged in an endless struggle for survival, or as the products of "socioeconomic determinism," ruled by social and economic forces beyond their control. In their works, the Naturalists generally ignored the highest levels of society and focused on degradation: poverty, alcoholism, prostitution, insanity, and disease.

Noble Savage: The idea that primitive man is noble and good but becomes evil and corrupted as he becomes civilized. The concept of the noble savage originated in the Renaissance period but is more closely identified with such later writers as Jean-Jacques Rousseau and Aphra Behn.

Novel: A long fictional narrative written in prose, which developed from the novella and other early forms of narrative. A novel is usually organized under a plot or theme with a focus on character development and action.

Novel of Ideas: A novel in which the examination of intellectual issues and concepts takes precedence over characterization or a traditional storyline.

Novel of Manners: A novel that examines the customs and mores of a cultural group.

Novella: An Italian term meaning "story." This term has been especially used to describe fourteenth-century Italian tales, but it also refers to modern short novels.

O

Objective Correlative: An outward set of objects, a situation, or a chain of events corresponding to an inward experience and evoking this experience in the reader. The term frequently appears in modern criticism in discussions of authors' intended effects on the emotional responses of readers.

Objectivity: A quality in writing characterized by the absence of the author's opinion or feeling about the subject matter. Objectivity is an important factor in criticism.

Oedipus Complex: A son's amorous obsession with his mother. The phrase is derived from the story of the ancient Theban hero Oedipus, who unknowingly killed his father and married his mother.

Omniscience: See *Point of View*

Onomatopoeia: The use of words whose sounds express or suggest their meaning. In its simplest sense, onomatopoeia may be represented by words that mimic the sounds they denote such as "hiss" or "meow." At a more subtle level, the pattern and rhythm of sounds and rhymes of a line or poem may be onomatopoeic.

Oxymoron: A phrase combining two contradictory terms. Oxymorons may be intentional or unintentional.

P

Parable: A story intended to teach a moral lesson or answer an ethical question.

Paradox: A statement that appears illogical or contradictory at first, but may actually point to an underlying truth.

Parallelism: A method of comparison of two ideas in which each is developed in the same grammatical structure.

Parody: In literary criticism, this term refers to an imitation of a serious literary work or the signature style of a particular author in a ridiculous manner. A typical parody adopts the style of the original and applies it to an inappropriate subject for humorous effect. Parody is a form of satire and could be considered the literary equivalent of a caricature or cartoon.

Pastoral: A term derived from the Latin word "pastor," meaning shepherd. A pastoral is a literary composition on a rural theme. The conventions of the pastoral were originated by the third-century Greek poet Theocritus, who wrote about the experiences, love affairs, and pastimes of Sicilian shepherds. In a pastoral, characters and language of a courtly nature are often placed in a simple setting. The term pastoral is also used to classify dramas, elegies, and lyrics that exhibit the use of country settings and shepherd characters.

Pen Name: See *Pseudonym*

Persona: A Latin term meaning "mask." *Personae* are the characters in a fictional work of literature. The *persona* generally functions as a mask through which the author tells a story in a voice other than his or her own. A *persona* is usually either a character in a story who acts as a narrator or an "implied author," a voice created by the author to act as the narrator for himself or herself.

Personification: A figure of speech that gives human qualities to abstract ideas, animals, and inanimate objects.

Picaresque Novel: Episodic fiction depicting the adventures of a roguish central character ("picaro" is Spanish for "rogue"). The picaresque hero is commonly a low-born but clever individual who wanders into and out of various affairs of love, danger, and farcical intrigue. These involvements may take place at all social levels and typically present a humorous and wide-ranging satire of a given society.

Plagiarism: Claiming another person's written material as one's own. Plagiarism can take the form of direct, word-for-word copying or the theft of the substance or idea of the work.

Plot: In literary criticism, this term refers to the pattern of events in a narrative or drama. In its simplest sense, the plot guides the author in composing the work and helps the reader follow the work. Typically, plots exhibit causality and unity and have a beginning, a middle, and an end. Sometimes, however, a plot may consist of a series of disconnected events, in which case it is known as an "episodic plot."

Poetic Justice: An outcome in a literary work, not necessarily a poem, in which the good are rewarded and the evil are punished, especially in ways that particularly fit their virtues or crimes.

Poetic License: Distortions of fact and literary convention made by a writer—not always a poet—for the sake of the effect gained. Poetic license is closely related to the concept of "artistic freedom."

Poetics: This term has two closely related meanings. It denotes (1) an aesthetic theory in literary criticism about the essence of poetry or (2) rules prescribing the proper methods, content, style, or diction of poetry. The term poetics may also refer to theories about literature in general, not just poetry.

Point of View: The narrative perspective from which a literary work is presented to the reader. There are four traditional points of view. The "third person omniscient" gives the reader a "godlike" perspective, unrestricted by time or place, from which to see actions and look into the minds of characters. This allows the author to comment openly on characters and events in the work. The "third person" point of view presents the events of the story from outside of any single character's perception, much like the omniscient point of view, but the reader must understand the action as it takes place and without any special insight into characters' minds or motivations. The "first person" or "personal" point of view relates events as they are perceived by a single character. The main character "tells" the story and may offer opinions about the action and characters which differ from those of the author. Much less common than omniscient, third person, and first person is the "second person" point of view, wherein the author tells the story as if it is happening to the reader.

Polemic: A work in which the author takes a stand on a controversial subject, such as abortion or religion. Such works are often extremely argumentative or provocative.

Pornography: Writing intended to provoke feelings of lust in the reader. Such works are often condemned by critics and teachers, but those which can be shown to have literary value are viewed less harshly.

Post-Aesthetic Movement: An artistic response made by African Americans to the black aesthetic movement of the 1960s and early '70s. Writers since that time have adopted a somewhat different tone in their work, with less emphasis placed on the disparity between black and white in the United States. In the words of post-aesthetic authors such as Toni Morrison, John Edgar Wideman, and Kristin Hunter, African Americans are portrayed as looking inward for answers to their own questions, rather than always looking to the outside world.

Postmodernism: Writing from the 1960s forward characterized by experimentation and continuing to apply some of the fundamentals of modernism, which included existentialism and alienation. Postmodernists have gone a step further in the rejection of tradition begun with the modernists by also rejecting traditional forms, preferring the anti-novel over the novel and the anti-hero over the hero.

Primitivism: The belief that primitive peoples were nobler and less flawed than civilized peoples because they had not been subjected to the tainting influence of society.

Prologue: An introductory section of a literary work. It often contains information establishing the situation of the characters or presents information about the setting, time period, or action. In drama, the prologue is spoken by a chorus or by one of the principal characters.

Prose: A literary medium that attempts to mirror the language of everyday speech. It is distinguished from poetry by its use of unmetered, unrhymed language consisting of logically related sentences. Prose is usually grouped into paragraphs that form a cohesive whole such as an essay or a novel.

Prosopopoeia: See *Personification*

Protagonist: The central character of a story who serves as a focus for its themes and incidents and as the principal rationale for its development. The protagonist is sometimes referred to in discussions of modern literature as the hero or anti-hero.

Protest Fiction: Protest fiction has as its primary purpose the protesting of some social injustice, such as racism or discrimination.

Proverb: A brief, sage saying that expresses a truth about life in a striking manner.

Pseudonym: A name assumed by a writer, most often intended to prevent his or her identification as the author of a work. Two or more authors may work together under one pseudonym, or an author may use a different name for each genre he or she publishes in. Some publishing companies maintain "house pseudonyms," under which any number of authors may write installments in a series. Some authors also choose a pseudonym over their real names the way an actor may use a stage name.

Pun: A play on words that have similar sounds but different meanings.

R

Realism: A nineteenth-century European literary movement that sought to portray familiar characters, situations, and settings in a realistic manner. This was done primarily by using an objective narrative point of view and through the buildup of accurate detail. The standard for success of any realistic work depends on how faithfully it transfers common experience into fictional forms. The realistic method may be altered or extended, as in stream of consciousness writing, to record highly subjective experience.

Repartee: Conversation featuring snappy retorts and witticisms.

Resolution: The portion of a story following the climax, in which the conflict is resolved.

Rhetoric: In literary criticism, this term denotes the art of ethical persuasion. In its strictest sense, rhetoric adheres to various principles developed since classical times for arranging facts and ideas in a clear, persuasive, appealing manner. The term is also used to refer to effective prose in general and theories of or methods for composing effective prose.

Rhetorical Question: A question intended to provoke thought, but not an expressed answer, in the reader. It is most commonly used in oratory and other persuasive genres.

Rising Action: The part of a drama where the plot becomes increasingly complicated. Rising action leads up to the climax, or turning point, of a drama.

Roman à clef: A French phrase meaning "novel with a key." It refers to a narrative in which real persons are portrayed under fictitious names.

Romance: A broad term, usually denoting a narrative with exotic, exaggerated, often idealized characters, scenes, and themes.

Romanticism: This term has two widely accepted meanings. In historical criticism, it refers to a European intellectual and artistic movement of the late eighteenth and early nineteenth centuries that sought greater freedom of personal expression than that allowed by the strict rules of literary form and logic of the eighteenth-century neoclassicists. The Romantics preferred emotional and imaginative expression to rational analysis. They considered the individual to be at the center of all experience and so placed him or her at the center of their art. The Romantics believed that the creative imagination reveals nobler truths—unique feelings and attitudes—than those that could be discovered by logic or by scientific examination. Both the natural world and the state of childhood were important sources for revelations of "eternal truths." "Romanticism" is also used as a general term to refer to a type of sensibility found in all periods of literary history and usually considered to be in opposition to the principles of classicism. In this sense, Romanticism signifies any work or philosophy in which the exotic or dreamlike figure strongly, or that is devoted to individualistic expression, self-analysis, or a pursuit of a higher realm of knowledge than can be discovered by human reason.

Romantics: See *Romanticism*

S

Satire: A work that uses ridicule, humor, and wit to criticize and provoke change in human nature and institutions. There are two major types of satire: "formal" or "direct" satire speaks directly to the reader or to a character in the work; "indirect" satire relies upon the ridiculous behavior of its characters to make its point. Formal satire is further divided into two manners: the "Horatian," which ridicules gently, and the "Juvenalian," which derides its subjects harshly and bitterly.

Science Fiction: A type of narrative about or based upon real or imagined scientific theories and technology. Science fiction is often peopled with alien creatures and set on other planets or in different dimensions.

Second Person: See *Point of View*

Setting: The time, place, and culture in which the action of a narrative takes place. The elements of setting may include geographic location, characters' physical and mental environments, prevailing cultural attitudes, or the historical time in which the action takes place.

Simile: A comparison, usually using "like" or "as," of two essentially dissimilar things, as in "coffee as cold as ice" or "He sounded like a broken record."

Slang: A type of informal verbal communication that is generally unacceptable for formal writing. Slang words and phrases are often colorful exaggerations used to emphasize the speaker's point; they may also be shortened versions of an often-used word or phrase.

Slave Narrative: Autobiographical accounts of American slave life as told by escaped slaves. These works first appeared during the abolition movement of the 1830s through the 1850s.

Socialist Realism: The Socialist Realism school of literary theory was proposed by Maxim Gorky and established as a dogma by the first Soviet Congress of Writers. It demanded adherence to a communist worldview in works of literature. Its doctrines required an objective viewpoint comprehensible to the working classes and themes of social struggle featuring strong proletarian heroes.

Stereotype: A stereotype was originally the name for a duplication made during the printing process; this led to its modern definition as a person or thing that is (or is assumed to be) the same as all others of its type.

Stream of Consciousness: A narrative technique for rendering the inward experience of a character. This technique is designed to give the impression of an ever-changing series of thoughts, emotions, images, and memories in the spontaneous and seemingly illogical order that they occur in life.

Structure: The form taken by a piece of literature. The structure may be made obvious for ease of understanding, as in nonfiction works, or may obscured for artistic purposes, as in some poetry or seemingly "unstructured" prose.

Sturm und Drang: A German term meaning "storm and stress." It refers to a German literary movement of the 1770s and 1780s that reacted against the order and rationalism of the enlightenment, focusing instead on the intense experience of extraordinary individuals.

Style: A writer's distinctive manner of arranging words to suit his or her ideas and purpose in writing. The unique imprint of the author's personality upon his or her writing, style is the product of an author's way of arranging ideas and his or her use of diction, different sentence structures, rhythm, figures of speech, rhetorical principles, and other elements of composition.

Subjectivity: Writing that expresses the author's personal feelings about his subject, and which may or may not include factual information about the subject.

Subplot: A secondary story in a narrative. A subplot may serve as a motivating or complicating force for the main plot of the work, or it may provide emphasis for, or relief from, the main plot.

Surrealism: A term introduced to criticism by Guillaume Apollinaire and later adopted by Andre Breton. It refers to a French literary and artistic movement founded in the 1920s. The Surrealists sought to express unconscious thoughts and feelings in their works. The best-known technique used for achieving this aim was automatic writing—transcriptions of spontaneous outpourings from the unconscious. The Surrealists proposed to unify the contrary levels of conscious and unconscious, dream and reality, objectivity and subjectivity into a new level of "super-realism."

Suspense: A literary device in which the author maintains the audience's attention through the buildup of events, the outcome of which will soon be revealed.

Symbol: Something that suggests or stands for something else without losing its original identity. In literature, symbols combine their literal meaning with the suggestion of an abstract concept. Literary symbols are of two types: those that carry complex associations of meaning no matter what their contexts, and those that derive their suggestive meaning from their functions in specific literary works.

Symbolism: This term has two widely accepted meanings. In historical criticism, it denotes an early modernist literary movement initiated in France during the nineteenth century that reacted against the prevailing standards of realism. Writers in this movement aimed to evoke, indirectly and symbolically, an order of being beyond the material world of the five senses. Poetic expression of personal emotion figured strongly in the movement, typically by means of a private set of symbols uniquely identifiable with the individual poet. The principal aim of the Symbolists was to express in words the highly complex feelings that grew out of everyday contact with the world. In a broader sense, the term "symbolism" refers to the use of one object to represent another.

T

Tall Tale: A humorous tale told in a straightforward, credible tone but relating absolutely impossible events or feats of the characters. Such tales were commonly told of frontier adventures during the settlement of the west in the United States.

Theme: The main point of a work of literature. The term is used interchangeably with thesis.

Thesis: A thesis is both an essay and the point argued in the essay. Thesis novels and thesis plays share the quality of containing a thesis which is supported through the action of the story.

Third Person: See *Point of View*

Tone: The author's attitude toward his or her audience may be deduced from the tone of the work. A formal tone may create distance or convey politeness, while an informal tone may encourage a friendly, intimate, or intrusive feeling in the reader. The author's attitude toward his or her subject matter may also be deduced from the tone of the words he or she uses in discussing it.

Transcendentalism: An American philosophical and religious movement, based in New England from around 1835 until the Civil War. Transcendentalism was a form of American romanticism that had its roots abroad in the works of Thomas Carlyle, Samuel Coleridge, and Johann Wolfgang von Goethe. The Transcendentalists stressed the importance of intuition and subjective experience in communication with God. They rejected religious dogma and texts in favor of mysticism and scientific naturalism. They pursued truths that lie beyond the "colorless" realms perceived by reason and the senses and were active social reformers in public education, women's rights, and the abolition of slavery.

U

Urban Realism: A branch of realist writing that attempts to accurately reflect the often harsh facts of modern urban existence.

Utopia: A fictional perfect place, such as "paradise" or "heaven."

V

Verisimilitude: Literally, the appearance of truth. In literary criticism, the term refers to aspects of a work of literature that seem true to the reader.

Victorian: Refers broadly to the reign of Queen Victoria of England (1837-1901) and to anything with qualities typical of that era. For example, the qualities of smug narrowmindedness, bourgeois materialism, faith in social progress, and priggish morality are often considered Victorian. This stereotype is contradicted by such dramatic intellectual developments as the theories of Charles Darwin, Karl Marx, and Sigmund Freud (which stirred strong debates in England) and the critical attitudes of serious Victorian writers like Charles Dickens and George Eliot. In literature, the Victorian Period was the great age of the English novel, and the latter part of the era saw the rise of movements such as decadence and symbolism.

W

Weltanschauung: A German term referring to a person's worldview or philosophy.

Weltschmerz: A German term meaning "world pain." It describes a sense of anguish about the nature of existence, usually associated with a melancholy, pessimistic attitude.

Z

Zeitgeist: A German term meaning "spirit of the time." It refers to the moral and intellectual trends of a given era.

Cumulative Author/Title Index

Cumulative
Nationality/Ethnicity Index

Subject/Theme Index

Class conflict
  A Fine Balance: 34
Classicism
  The Sound of Waves: 296–297
Cold War
  Moby Dick: 145–146, 151–154
Coming of age
  The House of the Scorpion: 84, 90, 91
  The Samurai's Garden: 269, 278
Communications
  Anything but Typical: 4, 5, 7, 9, 13, 18
Community
  A Fine Balance: 40, 42
Compassion
  The Guernsey Literary and Potato Peel Society: 51
  Mother to Mother: 215
Comradeship
  Moby Dick: 142–144, 155
Condescension
  The Rise of Silas Lapham: 243
Confession
  Mother to Mother: 199, 203
Conflict
  Anything but Typical: 1, 9
  A Fine Balance: 37
  Moby Dick: 142
Conformity
  Anything but Typical: 7
Confusion
  Anything but Typical: 9, 13
  The Samurai's Garden: 270
Connectedness
  Anything but Typical: 16
Consciousness
  The Monkey Wrench Gang: 186
Conservatism
  A Fine Balance: 39–42
Contradiction
  The Rise of Silas Lapham: 252
Contrast
  The Light in the Forest: 107
  The Samurai's Garden: 285
Corruption
  A Fine Balance: 30, 33, 41
Courage
  The Guernsey Literary and Potato Peel Society: 44, 50, 53
  The House of the Scorpion: 85
  The Samurai's Garden: 283–284
  The Sound of Waves: 294
  The Wizard of Oz: 331, 334
Cowardice
  The Wizard of Oz: 314
Crime
  The House of the Scorpion: 79–80
  Mother to Mother: 208
Cruelty
  A Fine Balance: 31
  The House of the Scorpion: 67, 71, 72, 74, 77, 91
  Mother to Mother: 206
  My Jim: 221, 224–225, 235

Cultural conflict
  The Light in the Forest: 94, 102, 107
Cultural identity
  The Samurai's Garden: 264
Cynicism
  The Wizard of Oz: 314

D

Death
  A Fine Balance: 35
  The Guernsey Literary and Potato Peel Society: 49
  The House of the Scorpion: 70
  The Light in the Forest: 103, 109
  Middle Passage: 117
  Moby Dick: 140, 153
  The Samurai's Garden: 270
Decay
  A Fine Balance: 29–30
Deception
  The Monkey Wrench Gang: 185
  The Samurai's Garden: 281
Dedication. *See* Devotion
Defeat
  A Fine Balance: 35
Defiance
  My Jim: 236
Denial
  Anything but Typical: 14, 15
Dependence
  The Monkey Wrench Gang: 164
Depression (Psychology)
  A Fine Balance: 25
Despair
  A Fine Balance: 25, 27, 35
Destruction
  The Monkey Wrench Gang: 168, 171–172
  The Samurai's Garden: 285
Determination
  The Wizard of Oz: 329
Devastation
  The House of the Scorpion: 83
Devotion
  The Monkey Wrench Gang: 164
  The Rise of Silas Lapham: 245
Difference
  Anything but Typical: 2, 19
Disability
  Anything but Typical: 1, 4, 10–13, 19
Disappointment
  My Jim: 236
Disapproval
  The Rise of Silas Lapham: 241, 243
Disdain
  The Light in the Forest: 99
Diseases
  The Samurai's Garden: 267, 280–285
Dishonor. *See* Shame

Disillusionment
  The Samurai's Garden: 269
Disorientation
  The Monkey Wrench Gang: 185
Divine judgment
  Moby Dick: 139–140
Domesticity
  The Rise of Silas Lapham: 256
  The Wizard of Oz: 327–330
Dreams
  The Wizard of Oz: 320
Drug trafficking
  The House of the Scorpion: 79, 86
Dualism (Philosophy)
  Middle Passage: 133

E

Economics
  A Fine Balance: 37
  The Rise of Silas Lapham: 250–251
Education
  Mother to Mother: 212
Embarrassment
  The Sound of Waves: 293
Emotions
  Anything but Typical: 4, 12, 16
  The Guernsey Literary and Potato Peel Society: 61
  The Rise of Silas Lapham: 254–256, 259, 260
  The Wizard of Oz: 315
Empathy
  Middle Passage: 121
Endurance
  The Light in the Forest: 109
  The Sound of Waves: 301
English history
  The Guernsey Literary and Potato Peel Society: 55–57
Environmentalism
  The House of the Scorpion: 85, 86–87
  The Monkey Wrench Gang: 157, 167–173, 181–183, 186
Epistolary novels
  The Guernsey Literary and Potato Peel Society: 55
  Mother to Mother: 194, 195, 203
  The Samurai's Garden: 274
Escape
  The House of the Scorpion: 84, 91
  The Light in the Forest: 109–110
Ethics
  A Fine Balance: 37
  The House of the Scorpion: 87–88
  The Monkey Wrench Gang: 166, 173
  The Rise of Silas Lapham: 238, 246, 257–261
Ethnic identity
  The Light in the Forest: 100
  Middle Passage: 129

Subject/Theme Index